The Hornbook

Dr. Johnson described the hornbook as "the first book of children, covered with horn to keep it unsoiled." Pardon's New General English Dictionary (1758) defined it as "A leaf of written or printed paper pasted on a board, and covered with horn, for children to learn their letters by, and to prevent their being torn and daubed."

It was used throughout Europe and America between the late 1400s and the middle 1700s.

Shaped like an old-fashioned butter paddle, the first hornbooks were made of wood. The paper lesson the child was to learn was fastened to the wooden paddle and covered with a piece of horn. The transparent strip of horn was made by soaking a cow's horn in hot water and peeling it away at the thickness of a piece of celluloid. The horn was necessary to protect the lesson from the damp and perhaps grubby hands of the child. Hornbooks commonly contained the alphabet, the vowels, and the Lord's Prayer. Later hornbooks were made of various materials: brass, copper, silver, ivory, bronze, leather, and stone.

As the art of printing advanced, the hornbook was supplanted by the primer in the book form we know today. Subsequently West Publishing Company developed its "Hornbook Series", a series of scholarly and well-respected one volume treatises on particular areas of law. Today they are widely used by law students, lawyers and judges.

EVIDENCE LAW

A Student's Guide to the Law of Evidence as Applied in American Trials

By

Roger C. Park

James Edgar Hervey Chair of Litigation
University of California—Hastings College of the Law

David P. Leonard

Professor of Law, William M. Rains Fellow
Loyola Law School, Los Angeles

Steven H. Goldberg

Professor of Law
Pace University School of Law

HORNBOOK SERIES®

WEST GROUP

ST. PAUL, MINN., 1998

COPYRIGHT © 1998 By WEST GROUP
                              610 Opperman Drive
                              P.O. Box 64526
                              St. Paul, MN 55164–0526
                              1–800–328–9352

Library of Congress Cataloging-in-Publication Data

Park, Roger.
    Evidence law : a student's guide to the law of evidence as applied
to American trials / by Roger C. Park, David P. Leonard, Steven H.
Goldberg.
        p.   cm. — (Hornbook series)
    Includes index.
    ISBN 0–314–21475–5 (pbk.)
    1. Evidence (Law)—United States.   I. Leonard, David P.
II. Goldberg, Steven H., 1941–   . III. Title. IV. Series.
KF8935.P368   1998
347.73'6—dc21   98–26831
                                                        CIP

ISBN 0–314–21475–5

TEXT IS PRINTED ON 10% POST
CONSUMER RECYCLED PAPER

To Suzanne
R.C.P.

To Susan, Matthew, and Adam
D.P.L.

For Julia
and
In memory of Barbara
S.H.G.

*

Preface

This is a lawyer's treatise designed specifically for law students. It is an adaptation of the TRIAL OBJECTIONS HANDBOOK, a work for practitioners that provided a concise description of the law of evidence from the perspective of the advocate who had to offer and oppose it, rather than from the perspective of the judge who had to rule on it. Where possible, the HANDBOOK discussed evidence issues in the language of the courtroom—full of examples and arguments in context as spoken by trial lawyers. In preparing this version for students, we have kept the advocate's perspective and have tried to be true to the notion that lawyers must employ evidence rules quickly and concisely in the courtroom.

We have been mindful that law students do not have the courtroom experience of practicing lawyers. The first four chapters on the operation of the courtroom have been added to give law students a sense of the context and environment that has so much influence on individual evidence rulings. In addition, we have expanded discussions of major cases and doctrines beyond that presented in the Handbook.

We hope this approach will enhance the student's understanding of the law of evidence in action. Wherever possible, we have employed examples to give the student a feel for the context in which the particular evidence problem might arise and for the language used by lawyers and judges in resolving it. We have also discussed the rationales and purposes of particular rules, believing that effective advocacy often means persuading the decision-maker that the result sought is beneficial as a matter of policy.

If law students come away from this hornbook with a sense of how to speak the language of evidence in the courtroom, as well as with an understanding of the law of evidence, we will have fulfilled our desire to help beginning trial lawyers on their way.

For able research on the practitioner's edition, we wish to thank Mark Dunn, Julia Erickson, Tom Holm, and Brendan Randall, graduates of the University of Minnesota law school. Julia Erickson deserves special recognition for editorial contributions. Only her untimely death prevented us from inviting her to participate in this edition. Two trial lawyers, John Sands and Peter Wold, gave selflessly of their time and made perceptive comments on the practitioner's edition.

Students in the Trial Objections courses at Minnesota and Hastings and in Evidence classes at Pace offered helpful suggestions and spotted errors in earlier versions. Christine Cupino, Loyola Law School class of 1999, Gene Sitnitsky, Loyola Law School class of 2000, Melanie Slaughter, Pace University Law School Class of 1998, and Russell Stein, UC Hastings Class of 1999, provided helpful research assistance on the student edition. We also owe thanks to Stephen Lothrop, head of Faculty Support at UC Hastings, for his diligent and careful work.

Roger Park owes his largest debt to his wife and best friend, Suzanne Park—not only for her love and support and her large if not endless patience, but also for her tireless proofreading, editing, and counseling on both editions. Her organizational abilities alone made it possible to miss deadlines by much smaller margins than would otherwise have been the case.

ROGER C. PARK
San Francisco, California

DAVID P. LEONARD
Los Angeles, California

STEVEN H. GOLDBERG
White Plains, New York

June, 1998

Westlaw® Overview

Evidence Law, A Student's Guide to the Law of Evidence as Applied in American Trials, by Roger C. Park, David P. Leonard and Steven H. Goldberg, offers a detailed and comprehensive treatment of basic rules, principles and issues relating to evidence. To supplement the information contained in this book, you can access Westlaw, a computer-assisted legal research service of West Group. Westlaw contains a broad array of legal research resources, including case law, statutes, expert commentary, current developments and various other types of information.

Learning how to use these materials effectively will enhance your legal research. To help you coordinate the information in the book with your Westlaw research, this volume contains an appendix listing Westlaw databases, search techniques and sample problems.

THE PUBLISHER

*

Summary of Contents

*

Table of Contents

The Subsequent Remedial Measures Rule [FRE 407]

Exceptions That Apply Only if the Declarant Is Unavailable [FRE 804]

Other Hearsay Issues

EVIDENCE LAW

A Student's Guide to the Law of Evidence as Applied in American Trials

*

Chapter 1

PRESENTING EVIDENCE AT TRIAL: AN OVERVIEW

Table of Sections

§ 1.01 Adversary Justice Through the Common Law Trial

The justice system in the United States is based upon the common law trial—a contest waged by at least two opposing parties before a neutral decision-maker in a court of law. Inherited from the English common law tradition, the trial is the theoretical centerpiece of adversary justice—a system of dispute resolution in which the parties control the gathering, preparation, and presentation of information for decision by a relatively passive neutral. Of course, trial itself is only the tip of a very large iceberg. Barely half of our societal grievances ripen into disputes and an infinitesimal percentage of those disputes end up in court filings.[1] Less than 10 percent of those court filings ever end up in trial.[2] Adversary justice, nevertheless, pervades our dispute resolution culture, influencing even some of the forms of what is popularly described as Alternative Dispute Resolution. Trial results cast a long

---

1. Richard E. Miller & Austin Sarat, *Grievances, Claims, and Disputes: Assessing the Adversary Culture*, 15 Law & Soc'y Rev. 525 (1980–81).

2. David M. Trubek, et al., *The Costs of Ordinary Litigation*, 31 UCLA L. Rev. 72 (1983).

shadow over other stages of litigation and methods of dispute resolution, because actors use them as guides to settlement.

In common parlance, "justice" means a fair, equitable, or morally correct result, no matter the forum in which it occurs. We say, "justice was done" when a situation resolves in a manner of which we approve, irrespective of the process, as for example, when the villain of the piece is dispatched by the hero.

The "adversary justice" that we achieve in the common law trial, however, is something a little different. A particular common law trial might not produce a result of which we approve. It might not produce a result that we believe accurately mirrors what happened. We employ the adversary system because we have faith that most of the results from trials will be fair, equitable, morally correct, and reflective of the events that actually occurred. We understand, however, that no after-the-fact determination can produce "the real and verifiable truth." We call the result of the common law trial "justice" as much from our belief that the adversary process is the fairest way to resolve disputes, as from our conviction that every case will be resolved with equity and accuracy.

In criminal trials, for example, justice does not depend upon the decision-maker's best estimate of what happened, but rather, upon the decision-maker's extraordinary certainty—proof beyond a reasonable doubt—that the defendant did what the prosecution claims. If the decision-maker believes it is more likely than not that the defendant did the crime, but it has "reasonable" doubts, the defendant is found not guilty and is not punished. In civil trials, if the opposing presentations are equally persuasive, leaving the decision-maker unable to determine what probably happened, justice is done even though one of the two equal sides wins and the other equal side loses.

We accept these individual results that may be a less-than-perfect reflection of what actually happened, or that seem less than "fair," not only because we know that perfect re-creation is impossible, but because our dispute resolution incorporates other values of importance. Our interest in determining what really happened in a criminal matter, for example, must co-exist with our judgment that it is better to mistakenly leave at liberty someone who ought to be incarcerated than it is to mistakenly incarcerate someone who ought to be left at liberty. In civil disputes, equity must co-exist with society's interest in stability, so we affirm the status quo (the possession of the property, the cost of repairing an injury, etc.) even though the case for change in a particular dispute is equally as strong as the case for the status quo. Our interest in "the truth" co-exists with privileges such as those that encourage privacy (communication between spouses) and confidential relations (lawyer/client, physician/patient, priest/penitent, etc.); with our desire to make sure that parties have their say and with our desire to reach peaceful settlements.

Adversary justice is at once more complex and simpler than finding the "truth," determining what "really happened", or achieving results that seem equitable to everyone. It is a system of dispute resolution that is sufficient to order a society—good enough to keep us from resolving our differences by other less systematic, less predictable, less reliable, and ultimately less peaceful methods. Although the validity of the system depends, at one level, upon our belief that the common law trial will help us discover what really happened, it depends equally upon our belief that our less-than-perfect process is the best available in light of a myriad of societal values.

The idea that justice will emerge when people with opposing interests gather, shape, and present information to a neutral decision-maker has not been accepted universally. Predecessors to modern rational systems–the ordeal, trial by battle–depended at least in theory upon divine intervention. Today, other societies seek justice in systems other than the adversary system. Active-judge or "inquisitorial" systems are distrustful of a process in which interested parties control the generation and presentation of information. Continental systems, for example, often depend more upon neutrals than upon adversaries for development of evidence and questioning of witnesses, especially in criminal cases. (Civil cases on the continent are often party-controlled.) There is a lively dispute about whether tendentious presentations by partisans are preferable to a more active fact-finder–one who, though officially neutral, might be subject to prejudgment and less satisfactory to parties eager to have their "day in court."[3]

§ 1.02   Stages of a Common Law Trial

Lawyers dominate the American trial process. They interview witnesses and gather information; they shape the client's legal posture; they prepare the pleadings; they conduct the formal discovery; they prepare the witnesses; and they oversee the production of exhibits that will convey information to the fact-finder. At trial, they have a role in choosing the fact-finder; they speak to the fact-finder about the case before the evidence is presented; and they sum it up afterwards. During presentation of evidence to the fact-finder, it is the lawyer who examines the witnesses and limits the information that the opponent can present. Lawyers even assist the judge in determining the law that will be applied to the evidence presented to the fact-finder.

Rules and statutes about the conduct of a common law trial vary from jurisdiction to jurisdiction, but the general structure is the same. The Federal Rules of Civil Procedure and the Federal Rules of Evidence provide a general outline for the conduct of trials in the federal courts and in most states, although there are differences in the various jurisdictions, some of which remain dear to a jurisdiction's lawyers and judges.

3. *See, e.g.,* Mirjan Današka, Evidence Law Adrift, 74–124 (1997); Samuel R. Gross, *The American Advantage: The Value of Inefficient Litigation*, 85 Mich. L. Rev. 734 (1987); John H. Langbein, *The German Advantage in Civil Procedure*, 52 U. Chi. L. Rev. 823 (1985).

Today, many trials involve multiple parties on one or both sides. Any of the parties may bear the burden of persuasion on one or another of the issues to be decided by the fact-finder. The common law trial reduced to a minimum, however, assumes that there are two parties who disagree about an issue the law is competent to decide. Usually, the party who wants to change the status quo brings the lawsuit, is called the plaintiff or prosecution, and bears the burden of persuasion on the issue about which the parties disagree. The party who wants to maintain the status quo must answer the suit and bears no burden of persuasion in order to maintain the status quo.[4]

We employ this minimum model—two opposing parties, one issue for which the plaintiff, or prosecution in criminal cases, bears the burden of persuasion—in examining the conduct of the common law trial.

Pre-trial

Pre-trial discovery, motions, and hearings have come to dominate our adversary system. There is often more adversarial activity before trial than during. Many more disputes are resolved in the pre-trial period than following a full trial. Although most of the substantial number of rules, procedures, and activities of pre-trial litigation are beyond the scope of this book, many important evidentiary issues are raised, considered, and sometimes decided during pre-trial hearings.[5]

Jury Selection

When one of the parties demands a jury trial, jury selection is the first trial activity. Much of the law about the conduct of a trial, particularly the law of evidence, is based upon assumptions about how jurors think and act as fact-finders, even though many trials are conducted with the judge as fact-finder.

The group of prospective jurors first brought to the courtroom is called the venire. Members of the venire are questioned in court to determine their qualifications to sit as jurors on the case at hand. The process is called *voir dire*. In most federal courtrooms, the questioning is done by the judge, with the lawyers having the right to submit questions for the judge to ask. In many state courts, the lawyers are allowed to question the prospective jurors, either as a group or individually. The right of parties to question prospective jurors through their lawyers, rather than through the judge, is one of those differences between the federal system and the states that many lawyers hold dear.

The venire is reduced to the proper number of jurors and alternates through a series of challenges made by the lawyers for the parties. (A judge may remove a prospective juror *sua sponte*, but judges rarely do so.) A challenge for cause may be asserted against any prospective juror. A cause challenge will be sustained if the judge finds that the juror either does not meet the statutory qualifications for jury service or

---

4. See **Ch. 4** for a full discussion of burdens and presumptions.

5. See §§ **2.02, 2.06.**

because responses made during *voir dire* demonstrate that the person will not hear the matter impartially. A party may exercise a peremptory challenge for any reason and to any prospective juror. The right to exercise peremptory challenges is limited, as to reason, only by the United States Constitution[6] and, as to number, only by the statutes or rules of the various jurisdictions. Generally, more peremptory challenges are permitted in criminal cases than in civil. The number in criminal cases often varies with the seriousness of the charge.

Opening Statements

Once the jurors and alternates have been sworn in, the lawyers have an opportunity to make opening statements. Often mischaracterized in the media as opening arguments, opening statements are limited to a description of the evidence the lawyer expects to present to the jury in support of the client's theory of the case. The lawyer may describe the evidence in a persuasive manner, but is prohibited from drawing inferences or asking the jury to reach conclusions about the described evidence. Although argument is supposed to be restricted to summation, many courts are less than strict in enforcing the prohibition against argument in an opening statement.[7]

The party with the burden of persuasion—the plaintiff or prosecutor in our model—has the opportunity to make the first opening statement. In many jurisdictions, the defendant may reserve making an opening statement until after the plaintiff's case-in-chief. As a matter of practice, this is now rare, most defendants seizing the opportunity to address the jurors immediately following the plaintiff.

Plaintiff's Case-in-Chief

The plaintiff calls witnesses to testify (subject to cross-examination) and produces tangible evidence in support of the plaintiff's cause of action. Witnesses are first examined by the plaintiff and then cross-examined by the defendant. When the plaintiff has produced all the evidence in support of the plaintiff's case, the plaintiff rests. The testimony from the witnesses and the exhibits offered in the plaintiff's case-in-chief must be sufficient to support a jury finding in favor of the plaintiff for every proposition for which the plaintiff bears the burden of persuasion. If it is not, the judge will grant a defense motion for judgment as a matter of law. The plaintiff's obligation to produce evidence sufficient to avoid a judgment as a matter of law at the end of the plaintiff's case (sometimes referred to as a *prima facie* case) is called the burden of production. It is sometimes also described as the burden of going forward or the burden of producing evidence.[8]

---

6. *See, e.g.,* Batson v. Kentucky, 476 U.S. 79 (1986)(restricting exercise of peremptory challenges based solely upon race).

7. For the various objections to Opening Statements, see Roger C. Park, Trial Objections Handbook, ch. 10 (1991).

8. See § **4.06.**

Defendant's Case-in-Chief

If the judge has denied a defense motion for judgment as a matter of law (because the plaintiff produced sufficient evidence to support a finding for plaintiff) it is the defendant's turn to proceed.

Despite the judge's determination that the plaintiff has presented a *prima facie* case, the defendant might choose not to present any evidence, believing that while the evidence is sufficient to support a finding for the plaintiff, it is not sufficient to obtain that finding. If the defendant believes it will prevail with the jury without presenting evidence of its own, the defendant rests and argues to the jury based upon the evidence in the plaintiff's case-in-chief, including evidence elicited on cross-examination of plaintiff's witnesses. This tactic–admittedly rare in civil cases–is possible because of the important difference between the burden of producing evidence and the burden of persuasion. The burden of producing evidence is satisfied if the plaintiff's evidence meets the bare minimum needed to support a jury verdict for the plaintiff, while the burden of persuasion is carried only when the evidence is powerful enough actually to persuade the jury to find for the plaintiff.

In the usual case, the defendant presents the testimony of witnesses and offers exhibits in roughly the same fashion as was done in the plaintiff's case-in-chief. The defendant's evidence may be offered to establish the defendant's positive contentions (the defendant was somewhere else, the defendant has legal title to the property, etc.) or may be offered to discredit the plaintiff's witnesses or counter the plaintiff's evidence. When the defendant has presented all of the evidence relating to the plaintiff's claim, or any affirmative defenses the defendant may have to that claim, the defendant rests.

Plaintiff's Rebuttal and Defendant's Surrebuttal

The plaintiff has an opportunity, after the defendant has rested, to offer witnesses and exhibits to rebut matters or discredit witnesses put forth during the defendant's case-in-chief. The plaintiff may not, however, present evidence that does not in some way qualify or otherwise relate to the evidence or witnesses produced in the defendant's case-in-chief. For example, if the defendant presents testimony that tends to discredit the testimony of the plaintiff's second witness, the plaintiff may present rebuttal testimony that credits the plaintiff's second witness or that witness' testimony. The plaintiff may not present rebuttal testimony, however, that credits testimony given by plaintiff's third witness, because that witness or that witness' testimony was not attacked in the defendant's case-in-chief.[9]

When the plaintiff's rebuttal case is concluded, the defendant has an opportunity for surrebuttal (or rejoinder). The defendant's surrebuttal

---

9. Our model does not assume a counter-claim by the defendant. If the defendant asserts a counter-claim, the defendant presents that claim in the defendant's case-in-chief and the plaintiff presents evidence on that claim during the plaintiff's rebuttal case.

case is limited to qualifying or otherwise responding to the evidence produced in the plaintiff's rebuttal case.

The trial judge may allow a departure from the ordinary practice of keeping rebuttal within the scope of the defendant's case and surrebuttal within the scope of rebuttal if circumstances and fairness warrant.

Motions for Judgment as a Matter of Law or Judgment of Acquittal

When there is no more rebuttal testimony from either side, and both sides have rested, one or both parties in a civil action may move for a judgment as a matter of law. The motion asks the judge to rule that on all of the evidence presented in the trial, no reasonable jury could find in favor of the other party. The motion is often different from the defendant's motion for judgment as a matter of law at the end of the plaintiff's case-in-chief for failure to make a *prima facie* case. Even if the plaintiff has met the burden of production, the judge may enter judgment for the defendant as a matter of law, if a reasonable jury could not conclude, based on all of the evidence from both sides, that the plaintiff has met the burden of persuasion. The judge will not grant the motion merely because the judge, if sitting without a jury, might find in favor or the moving party. The judge must be willing to say that no reasonable jury could reach any other conclusion. In a criminal case, only the defense may move the judge to take the decision away from the jurors and enter a judgment of acquittal.

Closing Arguments (Summation)

After all of the evidence has been presented to the jury, the lawyers have an opportunity to address the jurors. Closing argument is the lawyer's opportunity to sum up the case, to explain why the evidence presented to the jurors, combined with the law they will hear from the judge, mandates conclusions that lead inexorably to a verdict for the lawyer's client.

In the federal system and in many state jurisdictions, the party with the burden of persuasion is given the first and last word to the jury. The plaintiff makes the first closing argument, the defendant makes the second, and the plaintiff is then allowed a rebuttal to respond to arguments made by the defendant. Various jurisdictions employ different rules concerning the order of summation.

Jury Instructions

After the lawyers have made their closing arguments, the judge instructs the jurors on the law that is applicable to the case before them. These instructions are usually worked out with the lawyers in an instruction conference held sometime before the closing arguments, so that the lawyers may use the legal principles as a framework for arguing their cases to the jurors. In a few jurisdictions, judges instruct juries on the law before the lawyers make their closing arguments, but the predominant method is to the contrary.[10]

Jury Deliberations, Verdict Forms, and Verdicts

When the judge finishes instructing on the law, the jurors retire to the jury room to deliberate alone, separated from contact with all outside influences. They take with them into the jury room the verdict form agreed to by the lawyers and the judge and, usually, all of the tangible evidence introduced at trial.

In most jurisdictions, the jurors' first task is to select one of their members as a foreperson to lead the discussion and communicate, if necessary, with the court. (In a few jurisdictions, the court appoints the jury foreperson before the beginning of testimony.)

In most criminal cases, in most jurisdictions, a jury verdict must be unanimous. Jurisdictions differ as to whether civil verdicts require unanimity or might be reached by some kind of a majority—often three quarters or five sixths of the jurors are required to join in the verdict.

Verdict forms in criminal cases are general, giving the jurors options of "guilty" or "not guilty" on the various charges being considered. Verdict forms in civil cases vary. Many jurisdictions provide options of a general verdict form, a special verdict form, or a verdict form that requires the jurors to answer specific interrogatories.

If the jury reaches a verdict, the foreperson completes the verdict form, signs it, and delivers it to the judge.

After the verdict has been read, a party may request that the judge poll the jurors, asking each juror individually and in open court whether the verdict read is that juror's verdict. If the number of jurors needed to return a verdict affirm that the verdict read is their verdict, the judge enters judgment accordingly, unless the judge is asked to consider post-trial motions for judgment notwithstanding the verdict or for a new trial.[11]

§ 1.03   Evidence in a Common Law Trial–Overview

Evidence has many meanings in common parlance and more than one meaning as lawyers use the term. We commonly say, in response to someone's assertion of some proposition, "show me the evidence." It is a way of saying, "prove it." The great evidence teacher, Irving Younger, was fond of using the various meanings lawyers employ for "evidence" in describing the process of bringing information about a disputed event

---

10. Our model does not include the situation in which the defendant asserts affirmative defenses for which the defendant carries the burden of production–insanity in a criminal case, for example. If there is an affirmative defense for which the defendant has the burden of producing evidence, the judge will include the law about the affirmative defense in the instructions only if the defendant has produced sufficient evidence to raise the issue with the jury.

11. These motions are not available to the government in a criminal case.

to the attention of jurors: "Evidence is admissible in evidence in accordance with the law of evidence."

The first "evidence" is the entire collection of perceptions and objects available about and from the event at issue—the totality of the information the lawyer might gather during the process of interviewing witnesses and engaging in formal discovery. It is the representation, by word or object, of all the information about what happened, whether it is legally important or not. It is the starting point for the lawyer, the haystack of information in which the lawyer may find the needle(s) of information that will support the client's cause of action. The process of finding out everything that happened, without any prejudgment about its importance at trial, is a critical step for the lawyer. If the lawyer prejudges too severely which pieces of information about the event will be important, something crucial almost always goes undiscovered.

The second "evidence" is that portion of the perceptions about and objects from the event that support the client's position at trial and that the lawyers present to the jury through witnesses and exhibits. These are the needles of trial evidence that the lawyer found in the haystack of initial information. It is what the jurors consider in deciding what happened.[12] Most of this is *viva voce* evidence–from the mouths of witnesses–but tangible evidence also plays a significant role in jury decision making. Tangible evidence includes both "real" and demonstrative evidence. "Real" evidence is an object that played a role in the events at issue, for example, the knife found at a crime scene, a written contract, or nurses' notes about the progress of a hospital patient. Demonstrative evidence is an object that although it played no role in the events at issue, illustrates something about those events–a map, diagram, model, photograph, or the like.

The third "evidence" is the body of rules that determines which parts of the first kind of "evidence"–all of the perceptions about and objects from the event–may become the second kind of "evidence"–what is presented to the trier of fact for consideration in deciding what happened. This third kind of "evidence"–the Law of Evidence–is a subset of the law of procedure. Unlike the law of property, or torts, or contracts, evidence law does not define relationships and determine substantive rights between people. Evidence law, in the words of the drafters of the Federal Rules of Evidence, exists "to secure fairness in administration, elimination of unjustifiable expense and delay ... to the end that truth may be ascertained and proceedings justly determined."[13]

The common law of evidence evolved over the centuries, as did most other law, appellate case by appellate case. But, it grew, also, through constant usage by lawyers and trial rulings about evidence by judges. Although there was no shortage of evidence cases in the appellate courts, the evidence questions raised on appeal represented an infinitesimal

12. *See* Scott W. Howe, *Untangling Competing Conceptions of "Evidence,"* 30 Loy. L.A. L. Rev 1199 (1997) (stating that jurors consider substantially more than what judges instruct is "evidence").

13. Fed. R. Evid. 102.

percentage of the evidence issues decided by trial judges and an even smaller percentage of the evidence issues considered by trial lawyers in the heat of trial.

Evidence law in the United States was relatively homogeneous, despite the plethora of jurisdictions and the lack of opportunity for appellate courts to decide the great variety of evidence issues that arose hundreds of thousand times a day in tens of thousand courtrooms around the country. The law of evidence evolved in the fashion of a language, influenced as much by the usage of lawyers and the on-the-spot rulings of judges in courtrooms as by appellate opinions.[14] As a result, the words that lawyers used in talking about evidence in the various jurisdictions were remarkably similar, even though the accents were different. A trial lawyer, familiar with one jurisdiction's law of evidence, might try a case in a different jurisdiction, confident that a general familiarity with the language of the courtroom would be sufficient to deal with most of the evidence questions that might arise during an average trial day. That is not to say that evidence law did not vary significantly among the jurisdictions, but those major areas of difference were often statutory or the subject of an important appellate decision in the jurisdiction, relatively easy to find and assimilate.

Although the language of the courtroom was more similar than different throughout the United States, the differences were strongly held. Various attempts to codify evidence law were defeated by apathy and procedural conservatism,[15] until the enactment of the Federal Rules of Evidence in 1975.

The Federal Rules of Evidence reduce the way lawyers and judges talk about evidence to about sixty relatively short rules. Though they constitute the law of evidence only in the federal system, their influence has been much wider. Most jurisdictions have now codified their common law of evidence, and most of the codifications are similar in organization and substance to the Federal Rules of Evidence. Even in New York, the largest remaining common law evidence jurisdiction, the evidence spoken in state courtrooms is almost identical to that spoken in federal courtrooms.

The common law system of adversary justice depends upon the lawyers to find, produce, and refine the evidence. Judges have the power to call witnesses and to exclude evidence on their own motion, but they rarely do so.

To be an effective evidence advocate in court, the lawyer must have a firm grasp of the legal theory of the case, an ear for the nature of

14. See Ronald J. Allen, *The Simpson Affair, Reform of the Criminal Justice Process, and Magic Bullets*, 67 U. Colo. L. Rev. 989, 995 (the common law, like natural languages, is a grown order rather than a made order).

15. *See* Roger C. Park, *A Subject Matter Approach to Hearsay Reform*, 86 Mich. L. Rev. 52, 53 at n.11–13 (1987)(concerning the failure of the 1942 Model Code of Evidence and the 1953 Uniform Rules of Evidence to achieve significant support). The 1966 California Evidence Code was the first major enactment of an evidence code within the United States. *Id.*

evidence being offered, and an almost automatic understanding of the law of evidence–a speaking facility for the language of the courtroom.

Relevance is the first consideration for any evidence and is often important in arguing other rules of exclusion, particularly hearsay. Without a clear understanding of the elements of the claim and defense, the trial lawyer is not equipped to handle questions of relevancy.

Knowing the law of evidence, or where to find it, is not enough to be an effective evidence advocate in the courtroom. Evidence at trial comes as fast as every question and answer. The lawyer's primary task is to pay attention to the substance of the testimony, not its admissibility. To deal effectively with admissibility, the lawyer must learn the language of the courtroom—must be able to anticipate when a question is objectionable or an answer should be struck and make an instant fact based legal argument for why evidence law does not allow the evidence. There is a rhythm to the admission and exclusion of evidence that the evidence advocate must master in order to make the law of evidence work for the lawyer's client.

§ 1.04 Admission and Exclusion of Evidence; Preliminary Questions of Fact [FRE 104]

A trial judge's most frequent, if not most important, role in jury trials is to rule on evidence questions. For every question of substantive law a judge must decide in a trial, there are hundreds of evidence questions presented. Some evidence issues are sufficiently foreseeable and important for lawyers to present by motion and to brief. Many of the most important evidence issues, issues that are often outcome determinative, are handled at pre-trial hearings. The great volume of evidence questions, however, are raised unexpectedly during the heat of trial. One lawyer asks a question. The other lawyer stands and says, "objection," followed by a one or two word label for the evidence issue–leading, hearsay, best evidence, or some similar reference to a rule of exclusion. The judge says "sustained" or "overruled." The question of evidence law was raised, discussed, and decided in about twenty seconds. Occasionally one of the lawyers will ask permission to argue the matter to the judge. It might take a minute or two before that question of evidence law has been handled. It is not surprising, therefore, that the common law of evidence placed an uncommon amount of discretion in the trial judge, and that appellate courts afforded substantial deference to the trial judge's evidence rulings. There was too much happening, too fast, for any other result. More importantly, it was happening in the midst of an intellectual contest in which context was of critical importance to the decision–a context apparent to the trial judge, but unlikely to be apparent in the cold transcript available to the appellate bench.

The extraordinary discretion that the common law lodged with the trial judge found its way into the Federal Rules. The Federal Rules of Evidence codified more than they changed the common law, so most evidentiary objections under the Rules still involve questions that depend for resolution on an understanding of the context. In addition, some of the Rules place explicit discretion with the trial judge to determine specific issues.[16]

Rule 608(b), for example, makes it discretionary with the trial judge whether a lawyer may attack the credibility of a witness, by asking that witness, on cross-examination, about specific instances of the witness' conduct that demonstrate untruthfulness. Rule 102 charges the trial judge with the duty to exercise discretion to ensure that "the truth may be ascertained and the proceedings justly determined." Rule 403 invokes the judge's discretion to exclude admittedly relevant testimony if it carries "the danger of unfair prejudice, confusion of the issues, or misleading the jury." Rule 611 gives the judge discretion to modify the order and the mode of interrogation and presentation. It allows the judge to change the normal conduct of the trial, if the judge believes it will aid in ascertaining the truth, save time, or protect witnesses. Rule 614 gives the judge the power to examine witnesses called by the parties or to call and examine the judge's own witnesses.

What does the judge do when a lawyer raises an issue of admissibility by lodging an objection to a question put to a witness or an exhibit that is being offered?

Rule 104(a) places the obligation on the judge to decide whether evidence that is objected to by one of the lawyers is admissible. The judge is not bound by the rules of evidence, except for privileges, in making the decision.[17] The standard the judge employs to determine whether the evidence objected to is admissible is the civil standard–more probably true than not true. If, for example, the question is whether a witness is qualified to testify as an expert, the judge hears the qualifications of the witness, any discrediting or qualifying information from the opponent, and then decides whether the witness is more likely an expert than not. Besides the qualification of witnesses, the existence of a privilege, the voluntariness of a confession, and the applicability of a hearsay exception are indicative of the kinds of questions that usually are decided by the trial judge under Rule 104(a).

Example

Plaintiff sues defendant for speeding, running a red light, and smashing his blue Miata sports car into plaintiff's car. Defendant admits being involved in the accident, but denies speeding and running the red light. Plaintiff calls a witness who was a back seat passenger in another car driving along the same road the defendant

16. *See generally,* David P. Leonard, *Appellate Review of Evidentiary Rulings,* 70 N.C. L. Rev. 1155 (1992) (discussing the use of discretion in Rules 608 and 611); David P. Leonard, *Power and Responsibility in Evidence Law,* 63 S. Cal. L. Rev. 937 (1990) (discussing the extent to which the Federal Rules of Evidence grant discretion to the trial court); Jon R. Waltz, *Judicial Discretion in the Admission of Evidence Under the Federal Rules of Evidence,* 79 Nw. U. L. Rev. 1097 (1985) (discussing discretion in evidence law).

17. See **Ch. 8** for a discussion of evidentiary privileges.

was traveling. At what is established as being about two minutes before the accident, the passenger in the front seat of the car said something.

Plaintiff's lawyer: What did he say?

Defense lawyer: Objection, hearsay.

Plaintiff's lawyer: Your honor, may we approach?

> [At sidebar] The witness will say that the passenger in the front seat said: "That blue Miata sports car just passed us going about 90. That big guy driving it is going to hit someone." It is either within the present sense impression exception or the excited utterance exception to the rule against hearsay.

The passenger's statement is hearsay–an out of court statement offered to prove the truth of what is asserted in the statement–and is inadmissible unless it qualifies under one of the two exceptions to the rule against hearsay for which the plaintiff's lawyer has argued. Rule 104(a) designates the judge as the one to determine whether the statement qualifies under either the present sense impression exception or the excited utterance exception to the rule against hearsay.

In order to admit the passenger's statement as a present sense impression, the judge must find the preliminary fact that it was "a statement describing . . . an event . . . while the declarant was perceiving the event . . . or immediately thereafter."[18] In order to admit the passenger's statement as an excited utterance, the judge must find the preliminary fact that the statement related to a "startling event" made while the passenger was "under the stress of excitement caused by the event."[19] The judge will admit the statement upon finding either the preliminary facts required for a present sense impression or the preliminary facts required for an excited utterance to exist more likely than not. The judge will exclude the statement upon finding it more likely than not that neither preliminary fact existed. It is the judge, rather than the jury, who decides these "facts," even though the jury is normally the fact finder in a trial.

The judge's responsibility to apply the civil standard and to be the fact finder of the preliminary facts under Rule 104(a) exists even in those cases in which the jurors will consider the same question. Moreover, the judge applies the civil standard even in those cases in which the jurors will decide the same question by applying a more rigorous standard. In a criminal conspiracy prosecution, for example, the jury must decide beyond a reasonable doubt whether the defendant was a conspirator. The judge must admit the statement of another claiming the defendant was a conspirator, however, if the judge finds it barely more

---

18.   Fed. R. Evid. 803(1).   **19.**   Fed. R. Evid. 803(2).

likely than not that the person making the statement was a co-conspirator.[20] The judge, of course, may not contaminate the jury's deliberation on the conspiracy issue by telling the jurors that the judge has already decided the question, albeit using a different standard.

Why have the judge involved in this preliminary fact finding under Rule 104(a)? Why not have the judge admit the statement and then instruct the jurors: If you find either that the passenger was excited when making the statement or was describing an event as it was happening you may consider the statement in deciding the case. If you do not find one of those two preliminary facts to exist; you must decide the case without considering the passenger's statement?

Rule 104(a) takes this fact finding from the jury and gives it to the judge in order to safeguard operation of the rules of evidence–many of which exist because we are fearful that jurors will not process certain information in the way the law deems appropriate. If the jurors had to determine whether the witness was either describing an event as it took place or was sufficiently excited to allow the hearsay statement into evidence, they would be in an untenable position. If they found neither of the preliminary facts to exist, they would have to ignore relevant evidence they had already heard. Asking people who typically are not lawyers and who serve for only one case to uphold technical rules of evidence, rather than consider relevant evidence in the one case that they have to decide, asks too much. Human nature dictates that the jurors will not follow the court's instruction to ignore the passenger's important out-of-court statement, even if they do not believe the passenger was describing an ongoing event or was excited when speaking.

It is particularly important for the judge to make this kind of fact finding because Rule 104(a) contemplates that the decision maker should be able to consider inadmissible evidence in making the determination of whether the preliminary facts needed for admissibility exist.

Example

Same sports car accident as described in the above example, except that the front seat passenger does not say anything about the speeding car as it passes, but rather, says something as their car comes upon the scene of the accident. The witness is the back seat passenger in the car.

Plaintiff's lawyer: What did he say?

Defense lawyer: Objection, hearsay.

[At sidebar]
Plaintiff's lawyer: The witness will say that the passenger in the front seat said: "When I saw that blue Miata sports car speed past us, at 90, I thought to myself, the big guy driving that car is going to

---

20.   Fed. R. Evid. 801(d)(1)(E); Bourjaily v. United States, 483 U.S. 171 (1987).

hit someone." It is either within the present sense impression exception or the excited utterance exception to the rule against hearsay.

Defense lawyer: Your honor, that statement is not a present sense impression, because it neither describes nor explains the event of the speeding sports car. That it relates to that event of seeing the speeding sports car would be all right if this was an excited utterance, but there is no evidence that the declarant was under the stress of excitement when making the statement.[21]

Judge: Well, it is not a present sense impression, so let's find out whether the witness was excited.

Defense lawyer: This witness testified at a deposition in this matter that the front seat passenger made the statement in a calm voice and with no sign of excitement.

Judge: [To plaintiff's lawyer.] That doesn't sound like excitement to me. Is that what happened?

Plaintiff's lawyer: I have an affidavit from the person who talked to the front seat passenger when he was dropped off. Here's what the passenger said: "I'm calm now, but when I saw the accident, the sight of that speeding car came into my head. The accident scene made my heart race. I was so excited, I don't know how I got out any words. I told the guys in the car about the premonition I had when I saw the speeding car. I don't know how I kept my voice so calm when I told them. I've never been so upset." That sounds like excitement to me.

Defense lawyer: Judge, that affidavit is not admissible evidence. And even if the person making the affidavit were here, the conversation about being upset would be inadmissible hearsay.

Judge: When I am deciding something preliminary to the admission of evidence under 104(a), I don't have to follow the rules of evidence. I am going to consider the affidavit. Based on what it says, I find that what the front seat passenger said to the others in the car when they passed the accident was an excited utterance and admissible as an exception to the rule against hearsay.

---

21. The statement relates to the event of the sports car speeding. Although an excited utterance may be a statement "relating to" a startling event, a present sense impression may only "describe or explain" an event while or immediately after perceiving it. See §§ 7.11, 7.12

The judge not only may consider inadmissible evidence in finding Rule 104(a) preliminary facts; the judge may also assess the credibility of witnesses in making the determination. The judge, normally, has no role in determining the credibility of witnesses. Once evidence has been admitted, the jurors alone determine whether the witnesses are credible and, therefore, whether they ought to give weight to the witness' testimony. But Rule 104(a) recognizes that a judge often will be unable to determine the existence of a preliminary fact without believing one witness and disbelieving another. In the example above, what if, rather than a single affidavit, there had been two witnesses with opposite versions of the passenger's statement about being excited by the accident? In order to determine the preliminary fact of whether the passenger was excited, the judge would have to hear the two witnesses outside the presence of the jury, believe one, and disbelieve the other.

Although Rule 104(a) makes the judge the primary keeper of the evidence rules, there is one evidence rule for which there is often no risk of jury non-enforcement–the rule that "evidence which is not relevant is not admissible."[22] Rule 104(b) creates an exception, albeit in unfortunately complex terms, to the 104(a) rule that the judge decides questions preliminary to the admissibility of evidence:

> When the relevancy of evidence depends upon the fulfillment of a condition of fact, the court shall admit it upon, or subject to, the introduction of evidence sufficient to support a finding of the fulfillment of the condition.

This is often described as "conditional relevancy."[23] When the relevance of the evidence depends upon the existence of some other fact, the judge alone does not determine the existence of that other fact. The judge involves the jury, because the preliminary fact finding needed to determine relevance will not put the jurors in the untenable position of choosing between an evidence rule for which they have little understanding and almost no stake, and reaching a decision using all of the relevant information. This is apparent if we look at the prior example, assuming that the front seat passenger had not included the color and make of the sports car in the statement.

---

22. Fed. R. Evid. 402.

23. Some commentators have questioned the logic of the concept of "conditional relevancy." In a case in which defendant's negligence depends upon proof that the defendant was driving over the speed limit, they would contend that evidence a car was speeding is relevant, without any evidence that the defendant was driving the car. They would argue that evidence a car was speeding increases to some degree the probability that the defendant was driving a speeding car and is, therefore, relevant in the Rule 401 sense–i.e., its relevance is not "conditioned" on proof that the defendant was driving. *See, e.g.,* 1 John H. Wigmore, Evidence in Trials at Common Law § 14.1 (Peter Tillers rev. 1983); Ronald J. Allen, *The Myth of Conditional Relevancy,* 25 Loy. L.A.L. Rev 871 (1992); Vaughan C. Ball, *The Myth of Conditional Relevancy,* 14 Ga. L. Rev. 435 (1980); Richard D. Friedman, Conditional Probative Value: Neoclassicism Without Myth, 93 Mich. L. Rev. 439 (1994). Though the scholarship in the area is intriguing and clever, it has yet to have much impact on the way courts view the subject. We, therefore, will use the traditional concept of conditional relevancy as set forth in the Rules and the Advisory Committee Note.

Example

Plaintiff's lawyer: What did he say?

Defense lawyer: Objection, hearsay.

[At sidebar]
Plaintiff's lawyer: The witness will say that the passenger in the front seat said: "That sports car just passed us going about 90." It is admissible either as a present sense impression or as an excited utterance.

Judge: [Having decided that the circumstances establish the preliminary fact that it is more likely than not that the passenger was describing an event as it was being perceived.] Present sense impression. The hearsay objection is overruled.

Defense lawyer: It may be a present sense impression, your honor, but it isn't relevant. There is no evidence that the sports car the declarant saw was the defendant's.

The defense lawyer's relevance objection raises a question of "conditional relevancy" that the judge will handle under 104(b), rather than under 104(a).

That the speeding sports car belonged to the defendant is the "condition of fact" upon which the relevance of the passenger's statement depends. The jurors can decide that question without being put in the untenable position of ignoring important information, in the event that they find the preliminary fact that it was the defendant's sports car does not exist. If the jurors do not find that the speeding sports car was the defendant's, they will naturally ignore the passenger's statement. Rule 104(b) requires the judge to overrule the relevance objection and to let the jury decide the existence of the preliminary fact, unless no reasonable jury could reach such a conclusion. If there is not enough evidence to support a jury finding that it was the defendant's sports car that the passenger saw, the judge will sustain the objection and exclude the statement.

Example

Defense lawyer: Judge, there is not enough evidence "to support a finding"[24] that the car the passenger saw belonged to the defendant.

Judge: I agree. The only evidence the sports car belonged to the defendant is the coincidence that the accident and the sighting were on the same road. Need more to support a jury finding that it is more likely than not it was the defendant's car the passenger saw.

---

24. Fed. R. Evid. 104(b).

Plaintiff's lawyer: Your honor, I have another witness who saw the sports car. He was sitting right next to the declarant. Unfortunately, he cannot be here to testify for two days. When he testifies, he will say that the sports car was a blue Miata, driven by a big man with long black hair, both characteristics of the defendant. I ask that you allow the back seat passenger to testify to what the front seat passenger said and allow me to show the relevance–to "connect it up"–when the driver testifies.

Judge: Rules 104(b) and 611(a) give me discretion to allow this testimony now and to withdraw it from the jurors' consideration, if you do not connect it up. Given the flow of the case, I think it is important for this evidence to come out at this time.

[Two days later the driver testifies.]

Plaintiff's lawyer: Did you see the sports car that the passenger said was "going about 90?"

Witness: Yes.

Plaintiff's lawyer: Please describe it.

Witness: It was a blue Miata with a big guy behind the wheel.

Plaintiff's lawyer: Could you see the driver's face?

Witness: No, all I could see was that he was big man with long black hair.

Defense lawyer: Sidebar, your honor?

[At the sidebar]
Defense lawyer: Your honor, I renew my objection that the passenger's statement is not relevant because the fact has not been established that the car was the defendant's. I am prepared to bring in a witness who will testify that he was speeding in his blue Miata on the same road at the same time that the passenger saw the speeding sports car. My client will testify that he was not speeding.

Judge: Let me stop you, counsel. Even if you produce those witnesses, and even if I believe it is more likely than not that the speeding sports car the passenger saw belonged to the other witness, I have to admit the passenger's statement and leave it to the jury to decide whose sports car the passenger saw. There is plenty of evidence to support a jury finding that the passenger saw the defendant's car. It was on the same road as the accident. The car was the same color and make as the defendant's and it was driven by someone the same size and with the same hair color and style as the defendant.

Defense lawyer: But your honor, what about my evidence that there was another car there and my client's testimony that he was not speeding?

Judge: Whether those witnesses–or any witnesses, for that matter–are to be believed is the sole province of the jurors. There is enough evidence here if the jurors believe it, and if they reject any evidence that might lead to a contrary judgment, for the jurors to conclude that it is more likely than not that the car the passenger saw belonged to the defendant. Your relevance objection is overruled. Argue it to the jury.

But what happens if the information suggesting that the car the passenger saw speeding was not admissible evidence from the driver, but rather, inadmissible evidence? Suppose the only connection between the car the passenger saw speeding and the car at the accident is the front seat passenger's statement, made after passing the scene of the accident and in an unexcited state. The witness, the passenger in the back seat, could tell the judge that the front seat passenger said, "That car back there was the same one we saw speeding earlier." The statement is inadmissible hearsay. When the judge was making a 104(a) determination about whether the declarant was excited, the judge could use inadmissible information to make the determination. When the judge is making a 104(b) judgment, the judge is not deciding whether the judge believes, based on whatever information the judge has, that the preliminary fact more likely than not exists. Under 104 (b) the judge is deciding whether there will be "introduction of evidence *sufficient to support a finding*"[25] *by the jury*.

Both logic and authority[26] suggest that the judge may not use inadmissible evidence in deciding whether there is sufficient evidence to support a jury finding. The judge could not possibly use inadmissible

25. Fed. R. Evid. 104(b)(emphasis added).

26. *In re* Japanese Elec. Prod. Antitrust Litig., 723 F.2d 238, 285 (3d Cir. 1983), *rev'd on other grounds*, 475 U.S. 574 (1986) (" [T]he evidence required to establish a prima facie case that the evidence is what the proponent claims it to be must itself be admissible.")

information to make a decision that there is information to "support a jury finding" and then tell the plaintiff's lawyer, who must establish the preliminary fact that the car was the defendant's, to "argue it to the jury." There would be no evidence from which to argue.

Authentication of documents and other tangible items is a common exception to the general proposition that the judge alone decides questions of evidence admissibility. Authentication generally is treated as a matter of "conditional relevance" under Rule 901(a). Rule 1008, delineating the fact-finding functions of judge and jury for the authentication of documents is to the same effect.[27]

Example

Plaintiff sues defendant to enforce a written contract. Defendant claims there was no contract. To prevail, plaintiff must prove the existence of the contract and its terms. During its case-in-chief, plaintiff offers a copy of the contract, claiming that the original is in the possession of the defendant. The defendant, claiming there never was an original, objects to the copy, because it is not the original document required by Rule 1005. If the judge admits the copy under Rule 104(a), believing that it is more likely than not that there was an original, the judge will have effectively taken the only issue in the case—the existence of a written contract—away from the jury. The judge does not do that. Instead, the judge hears the plaintiff's evidence in favor of existence and any evidence the defendant offers to show non-existence and then applies the same test as is applied to a request for a judgment as a matter of law. Unless the judge can say that no reasonable jury could ever find that the contract existed, the judge admits the contract and leaves it to the jury to decide whether plaintiff can establish it is more likely than not that the original contract existed.

§ 1.05 Examination of Witnesses–To Lead or Not to Lead [FRE 611]

Examining witnesses is the lawyer's most common task during trial. The lawyer's skill in asking questions can have as much influence on the evidence that is admitted as can the law of evidence. Moreover, the lawyer's skill in asking questions can have a significant influence upon how the jurors assess the evidence that is admitted.

The form of a question asked of a witness can vary from a completely open question that asks for a narrative response–"What happened next?"–to a completely closed question that leads the witness directly to the answer–"You next opened the window, didn't you?" Most of the questions that lawyers ask are in between–more directive than "what happened," but less suggestive than a question that contains the answer.

27. See **Ch. 11**.

"What did you see?" is a less open question (more directive) than "What happened next?" because it limits the range of the witness' possible responses. What the witness smelled, thought, heard, felt, or was told by another are not proper responses. "What did you see behind the door?" is an even more directive question–narrowing the inquiry to a particular place–though still not so directive that it leads the witness to the answer. "Did you see a cat behind the door?" is so directive that it suggests the answer to the witness, even though the words of the question, alone, do not tell the witness whether the lawyer wants an answer of "yes" or "no". "You saw a cat behind the door, didn't you?" is beyond suggestive, almost demanding a positive response from the witness.

Most good trial lawyers believe that witnesses are more credible when important information comes from the witness' mouth, rather than from a mere affirmation by the witness of what the lawyer says. Conversely, a witness is more easily controlled and less likely to make a favorable impression on jurors when the witness is restricted to a one word response–such as "yes" or "no." As a result, good trial lawyers ask mostly open questions on direct examination of friendly witnesses and mostly leading questions on cross-examination of witnesses called by the opponent.

A question is leading when its words or its context suggest the answer to the witness.

This is a leading question, isn't it?

Is this a leading question?

A question is not leading just because it is one that can be answered "yes" or "no," though that is often a clue that the question may be leading. "Could you tell whether the driver was dead?" calls for a "yes" or a "no" answer, when asked of a person who saw an unconscious person pinned behind the steering wheel of a smashed car. It may not be leading, because the answer–the witness either could or could not tell–is not suggested by the words and may not be suggested by the context of the question.

Rule 611(c) reflects the trial lawyer's advocacy wisdom in establishing the evidence law for the norms of direct and cross-examination of witnesses at trial.

> (c) Leading questions. Leading questions should not be used on the direct examination of a witness except as may be necessary to develop the witness' testimony. Ordinarily leading questions should be permitted on cross-examination. When a party calls a hostile witness, an adverse party, or a witness identified with an adverse party, interrogation may be by leading questions.

By discouraging the use of leading questions during direct examination, the Rule forces the lawyer to ask questions that encourage the witness, rather than the lawyer, to tell the jurors what happened. This provides the jurors with a reasonable opportunity to assess the witness' credibility. By allowing leading questions on cross-examination, the Rule provides the cross-examiner, who is trying to identify specific weaknesses in the witness' testimony, with control of the organization and the flow of the inquiry. This provides the jurors with a reasonable opportunity to follow the inconsistencies the cross-examiner wants to explore.

The trial lawyer's wisdom and the rule of evidence–do not lead on direct, lead on cross–both grow out of the common law theory of adversary justice. One lawyer has the opportunity to prepare the witness and shape the delivery of the information from the witness to the jury. That lawyer does not need to suggest answers to the witness and, because the witness is friendly, should not be able to give the witness verbal cues when the witness is in front of the jurors. The other lawyer did not have an opportunity to prepare the witness and is charged with discrediting the witness' testimony. That lawyer, with whom the witness has no interest in cooperating, needs to control the inquiry in order to identify the problems with the witness' testimony.

There are some common exceptions to the general rule of trial craft and evidence that a lawyer should not lead on direct and should lead on cross. They arise out of the same approach to the adversary system of examination as the rule itself and are expressed in Rule 611(c).

On direct examination, leading questions are permitted "as may be necessary to develop the witness' testimony."[28] A child witness who freezes on the witness stand or who is not articulate is an obvious example.[29] If the normal direct examination method of examination proves ineffective in bringing the witness' testimony to the jurors, leading questions will often be permitted. This is consistent with the overall approach of modern evidence law, which is to treat rules about the form of questions as rules of preference, allowing the evidence to be presented in an inferior form and trusting the trier of fact to give it the proper weight. The jurors will have seen that open-ended questions were ineffective in eliciting information from the witness and will, therefore, have the information necessary to evaluate the use of the leading questions.

Transitional and preliminary questions are less dramatic but more common examples of the permissible use of leading questions on direct examination. When such questions will elicit facts that are not in dispute, they allow the lawyer "to develop the witness' testimony" more expeditiously without the risk that the lawyer will suggest answers to the witness on anything of consequence.

"Was there another meeting on June 13?" is a typical transition question that takes the witness to a new topic. In some cases there is no other way to turn to a new topic, in others it would take four or five more open questions to arrive at the same place.

---

28. Fed. R. Evid. 611(c).

29. *See* Rotolo v. United States, 404 F.2d 316, 317 (5th Cir.1968)

"You live right next door to the defendant, don't you?" is a leading question that will be permitted if it is preliminary and not in dispute. The fact, necessary to explain why the witness knows something about the defendant could be elicited by a number of non-leading questions: "Where do you live?" Who lives next door to the east?" But why bother? Over the course of a trial with a number of witnesses and many preliminary facts, direct examinations without leading questions on preliminary matters would consume more time than necessary or desirable.

Direct examination of witnesses who are not cooperative may often be conducted by using leading questions. This is most often the "adverse party or a witness identified with an adverse party," though it may be a witness who is "hostile" without being necessarily aligned with the adverse party.[30]

On cross-examination, leading questions may not be allowed, if the witness is one who might be favorable to the cross-examiner. The cross-examiner's client, called for adverse testimony or a witness who is identified with the cross-examiner's client are common examples.[31]

Whether a witness is hostile, identified with the adverse party, or is for some other reason so situated that the normal method of examination should not be followed is a question for the judge to decide.[32] There are many more circumstances of examination, witnesses, and relationships than the law of evidence can conveniently categorize. A witness called by a party may not wish to testify because the witness has been threatened, because the witness is fearful that some interest of the witness' may be compromised, or just because the witness does not like the party. Rule 611(a) handles the inevitable uncertainty of witnesses by placing the control of the mode and order of interrogation and presentation within the discretion of the trial judge–a discretion that is virtually never overturned on appeal.

Rule 611. Mode and Order of Interrogation and Presentation

(a) Control by court. The court shall exercise reasonable control over the mode and order of interrogating witnesses and presenting evidence so as to (1) make the interrogation and presentation effective for the ascertainment of the truth, (2) avoid needless consumption of time, and (3) protect witnesses from harassment or undue embarrassment.

Sometimes judges refuse the request to have a witness declared hostile or otherwise uncooperative,[33] and the lawyer must patiently try to

30. Fed. R. Evid. 611(c).

31. *See* Deshpande v. Ferguson Bros. Constr. Co., 611 So.2d 877, 878–79 (Miss. 1992) (defense may not ask leading questions in cross-examining a witness called by the plaintiff, but employed by the defendant)

32. *See, e.g.,* Ellis v. City of Chicago, 667 F.2d 606, 611–13 (7th Cir. 1981); United States v. Diaz, 662 F.2d 713, 719 (11th Cir. 1981); Riverside Ins. Co. of America v. Smith, 628 F.2d 1002, 1009 (7th Cir. 1980).

33. In the criminal trial of the Chicago Eight for conspiracy to riot during the 1968 Democratic National Convention, Judge extract the testimony with open-ended questions. Moreover, a lawyer who persists in asking improper leading questions in bad faith or in apparent defiance of the court is likely to find the examination terminated by the court.[34]

§ 1.06 Direct Examination

Direct examination is the examination conducted by the party calling the witness, whether the witness is friendly or not. Most direct examinations, however, are of friendly witnesses whom the lawyer would like the jurors to believe and who have more than one matter of importance to tell the jurors.

If a lawyer has a poised, articulate, and persuasive witness with knowledge of an important sequence of events, it is tempting to give the witness an opportunity to tell the jurors the story without interruption. After the witness has testified to name, address, and brief introductory information about standing on the corner when two cars collided in the intersection, the lawyer might try to give the witness the opportunity to narrate.

Example

Direct examiner: Tell the jurors, in your own words, what happened.

Witness: I was standing on the corner waiting to catch the bus I take to work every day. It was a nice day, though the weather report said it was going to rain. Rush hour traffic was pretty much over. There were not many people waiting for the bus. Just before the bus arrived, I saw a Chevrolet speed through the intersection—must have been going forty miles an hour—and smash into a Ford. The Ford got hit so hard it rolled over and landed on its roof. It was awful. The woman standing next to me said, "Did you see that? That idiot tried to beat the yellow light." I heard the driver of the Ford screaming, so I ran over to see if I could help. The driver was stuck behind the wheel. There was nothing I could do by myself, so I went to the phone and called for help.

Trial lawyers often disagree about the persuasive merits of a narrative that leaves the shape of the direct examination to the predilections of the witness, rather than the questions of the lawyer. The persuasive

Julius Hoffman refused to declare Mayor Richard Daly a hostile witness though it was clear he did not like nor did he wish to cooperate with the defendants. *See* David Dellinger, The Conspiracy Trial 386–89 (J. Clavir & J. Spitzer eds. 1970).

34. *See* United States v. Clinical Leasing Service, Inc., 982 F.2d 900, 905 (5th Cir.1992) (district court did not abuse discretion in terminating direct examination because of blatant and excessive leading questions).

value of an uninterrupted story can be undermined by cluttering the narrative with information that is not important (the weather forecast), by omitting information that may be important (the color of the light for the Ford when it entered the intersection), and by leaving the impression that all of the information given is of equal importance. On the other hand, the narrative response, followed by questions searching for detail, provides an opportunity for the lawyer to present the same information to the jury twice. The lawyer is able to provide emphasis, add detail, and have the witness tell, again, a story with which the jurors are already familiar, by following the narrative with questions such as: Where were you standing when you first saw the Chevrolet? Which of the traffic lights could you see? When did the Ford enter the intersection? What color was the light for the Ford when it started into the intersection?

Rule 611 leaves it within the judge's discretion whether a lawyer may conduct a direct examination using questions that call for a narrative from the witness. It is such a common issue at trial that judges develop individual tendencies to generally favor or disfavor the narrative. A narrative response may be more expeditious, generally, but it carries the potential for presenting information to the jurors that is not admissible under the rules of evidence. The lack of questions from the direct examiner makes it difficult for the opposing lawyer to object to the inadmissible material.

When a lawyer objects to a question that calls for a narrative response, the judge's general tendency to allow or disallow the narrative will be moderated by the nature of the narrative requested, the risk of inadmissible information in the particular circumstance, and the representation of the lawyers about what they expect and fear in the testimony. If the judge decides to allow the narrative and then discovers that the fear of inadmissible information was valid, the judge is free to stop the narrative and require the direct examiner to provide better direction for the examination through more specific questions.

Leading questions–at the other end of the question continuum from those that ask for a narrative response–provide another common problem in the mode of direct examination, but more for the lawyers than for the judge. Unlike questions that call for a narrative response, the normal rule about leading questions is set out in Rule 611(c). The judicial response to leading question objections, therefore, is more predictable and less dependent upon individual judicial preference than judicial responses to questions that call for a narrative response.

Lawyers, on the other hand, often have difficulty conducting a direct examination without using leading questions in violation of the Rule. Because direct examination is the lawyer's opportunity to present the client's story in as compelling a fashion as possible, the lawyer is eager to make sure the jurors hear all of the important detail of the client's entire story, and in the most persuasive words. The poised, articulate, and persuasive witness who knows all about a sequence of events that we posited in discussing narrative responses is, in fact, rare. More often than not, the lawyer, who knows the story, the right words, and the courtroom so well, is tempted to tell the story through the questions rather than through the witness' answers.

Example

Direct examiner:	You saw the defendant's Chevrolet enter the intersection at the end of the yellow light, didn't you?
Witness:	Yes.
Direct examiner:	When the Chevrolet entered the intersection, it was traveling about forty miles per hour, isn't that right?
Witness:	Yes.
Direct examiner:	It smashed into the plaintiff's Ford at that speed, didn't it?
Witness:	Yes.
Direct examiner	The Chevrolet smashed into the driver's side of the Ford, isn't that right?
Witness:	Yes.
Direct examiner:	The Ford had just entered the intersection with a green light, hadn't it?
Witness:	Yes.
Direct examiner:	The impact rolled the Ford over and pinned the poor plaintiff in under the steering wheel, didn't it?
Witness:	Yes.
Direct examiner:	You heard the witness cry out, saw blood all over the place, and could see the bone sticking out of the plaintiff's arm, couldn't you?
Witness:	Yes.

The jurors hear all of the facts, with the words the lawyer wants, but the examination is improper under Rule 611, and not very effective, to boot. The jurors have not heard anything from the witness except a witless "yes" that seems programmed. Each question suggested the answer to the witness and was, therefore, leading.

To present testimony effectively through the words of the witness and to avoid the natural temptation to lead the witness into telling the story as the lawyer would, many direct examiners try to begin their questions with the "who, what, where, when, why, and how" of the reporter's liturgy. It is difficult to make such a question leading and it provides the witness an opportunity to tell the story.

Rule 611(c) contains an exception to the normal prohibition against using leading questions in a direct examination. The direct examiner may use leading questions to move the testimony along smoothly and efficiently—in the words of the Rule "to develop the witness' testimony." Sometimes this can mean leading a young child or other witness who has difficulty in testifying. Its most common use, however, is to allow the direct examiner to lead a friendly witness as to preliminary or non-controversial matters and as a means of easy transition from one subject area or time to another, while asking non-leading questions in areas where the answer is important.

Example

Direct examiner:	Were you at the corner of Third and Sheridan at 3:00 p.m. on August 1 of last year? [Leading, but preliminary.]
Witness:	Yes.
Direct examiner:	Did you witness a collision? [Leading, but unless controverted, proper as a preliminary question.]
Witness:	Yes.
Direct examiner:	What did you see?
Witness:	I saw a Chevrolet race through an intersection trying to make a yellow light and slam into a Ford.
Direct examiner:	How fast was the Chevrolet going when it slammed into the Ford?
Witness:	Over the speed limit—at least forty miles per hour.
Direct examiner:	Where was the Ford when the Chevrolet ran though the red light and slammed into it?
Witness:	It had just entered the intersection, not even half way through.
Direct examiner:	What color was the light for the Ford when it entered the intersection?
Witness:	Green.

Direct examiner:	What happened when the Chevrolet slammed into the Ford?
Witness:	It hit the Ford hard enough to roll it over. The Ford came to rest on its top.
Direct examiner:	When things came to rest, did you go over to the Ford? [Leading, but transitional.]
Witness:	Yes.
Direct examiner:	Why did you go over to the Ford?
Witness:	I heard the driver screaming and I went over to see if I could help.
Direct examiner:	What did you see when you got there?
Witness:	The driver was pinned beneath the steering wheel. There was blood all over the place. I could see the upper bone in the driver's arm sticking out through the skin. It was awful.

Rule 611(c) recognizes that some witnesses called on direct examination will not be friendly, but rather, witnesses that would normally appear in the opponent's case—witnesses the lawyer did not prepare and who would normally be subject to cross-examination by the lawyer. The adverse party or witnesses identified with an adverse party are common examples. When such a witness is called, the direct examiner is usually allowed to proceed through the use of leading questions, in the fashion of a cross-examination.

§ 1.07 Refreshing Recollection [FRE 612]

Witnesses forget. It is often a long time between the event to which someone might have been a witness and the trial in which that person must testify. For someone who is not experienced in trials and familiar with the courtroom, the witness box can be a frightening place, not particularly conducive to recollection.

Refreshing the recollection of a witness is most often accomplished by showing the witness a document that will remind the witness of the forgotten information, but any question or device that will jog the witness' memory may be used, including a leading question. Rule 611(c) specifically provides for judicial discretion to allow leading questions on direct examination "to develop the witness' testimony."

Although a failure of memory can happen to any witness, it is, ironically, people familiar with trials and courtrooms who most often are in need of having their recollections refreshed. Witnesses who regularly perform similar tasks and are asked to testify in court about many of them often have difficulty sorting out the proper event months or years after it occurred. Police officers, who investigate hundreds of incidents and make written reports, are common examples.

The officer who investigated the collision between the Chevrolet and the Ford is likely to have investigated a hundred accidents between the time of the collision and the time of the trial of the Ford driver's claim against the driver of the Chevrolet. At trial, the officer is not likely to have a current detailed recollection of finding broken headlamp glass near where the Ford entered the intersection. The officer may not recall the headlamp damage to the Chevrolet or that the glass found in the intersection matched that of the Chevrolet headlamp.

If the direct examiner can establish the officer's lack of current recollection, the examiner will be able to use the officer's notes, a leading question, or any other device the judge will allow to refresh that recollection. The device used to refresh recollection need not be admissible evidence. It will neither be offered into evidence by the direct examiner nor admitted by the judge.[35]

Example

Direct examiner:	Officer, were you called to investigate an automobile collision between a Chevrolet and a Ford at the corner of Third and Sheridan on August 1st of last year?
Witness:	Yes.
Direct examiner:	What did you find at the scene of the collision?
Witness:	I'm sorry counsel, I investigate a lot of accidents in a year. I don't remember the details of this one.

Having demonstrated that the witness has no current recollection of the facts, the direct examiner must find out whether there is anything that will refresh that recollection and bring the once known information back up. If the officer wrote a report detailing where the glass was found, the damage to the Chevrolet, and the match, the direct examiner might use the report as a device to refresh the officer's recollection.

Direct examiner:	Did you make a report of your investigation of the collision at Third and Sheridan on August 1 of last year?
Witness:	Yes.

---

35. *See, e.g.,* State v. Schultz, 392 N.W.2d 305, 307 (Minn.App.1986) (recognizing that the use of an accident report to refresh a police officer's memory while testifying to facts within his knowledge permitted although the report was inadmissible under state statute).

Direct examiner:	Would reviewing that report refresh your recollection about what you found at the scene of the collision?

Witness:	Yes, I am sure that it would.

Once the officer has demonstrated lack of current memory and has said that something would assist in calling the information up, the direct examiner may show the item to the officer. After the officer has looked at the report, the direct examiner must determine whether it has, in fact, refreshed the officer's recollection.

Direct examiner:	Officer, does the report refresh your recollection about what you found at the scene of the collision?

Witness:	Yes, it does.

The direct examiner has now completed the foundation needed to repeat the question about what was found at the scene of the collision. Before asking the question, however, the lawyer must retrieve the report from the officer. The report may be used to refresh the officer's recollection, but it may not, upon this foundation, be used as a substitute for the officer's current recollection. (Use of the report, itself, if it does not refresh the officer's current recollection, raises hearsay issues. The use of a report as a substitute for a witness' failure of current recollection is called Past Recollection Recorded, which is discussed at § 7.15 and compared with refreshed recollection.)

The same kind of foundation must be demonstrated regardless of the device being used to refresh the witness' recollection. Showing the officer the glass collected from the intersection might refresh the officer's recollection as well as the report that says, "I found headlamp glass in the southeastern quadrant of the intersection." A leading question, "Did you find headlamp glass in the intersection?" might be equally as useful and much quicker than either the report or the glass. Just as with the use of the report, the object (the glass particles) or the leading question may only be presented after the direct examiner has shown that the officer cannot remember and that the device used will revive the memory. Some judges believe that the direct examiner should ask permission before using a leading question to refresh a witness' recollection, so that the opponent and the judge will have the same kind of notice as when the witness is shown the report.

Example

Direct examiner:	Officer, were you called to investigate an automobile collision between a Chevrolet and a Ford at the corner of Third and Sheridan on August 1st of last year?

Witness:	Yes.

Direct examiner:	What did you find at the scene of the collision?
Witness:	I'm sorry counsel, I investigate a lot of accidents in a year. I don't remember the details of this one.
Direct examiner:	May we approach?
Judge:	You may.
Direct examiner:	[At the bench.] Your honor, I am going to ask this witness a leading question about a fact set out in his written report to see if that will refresh his recollection. His report says that he found broken glass in the southeast quadrant of the intersection. That will be the subject of the leading question.

The direct examiner may wish to use the leading question instead of the report, if the report contains material that the direct examiner would rather not have before the jury. If the officer uses the report to refresh recollection during the trial, Rule 612 entitles the adverse party to have the report produced, to introduce into evidence those portions of the report that relate to the refreshed recollection, and to use the report to cross-examine the witness.

§ 1.08 Cross-examination

Cross-examination is the interrogation of a witness by a lawyer other than the lawyer who called the witness to testify. In most instances, cross-examination is of a witness whom the other side prepared and who has offered testimony harmful to the cause of the cross-examining lawyer's client. Neither preparation by the other side nor harmful testimony, however, is required. After one lawyer has called a witness and conducted a direct examination, the subsequent examination is called cross-examination, even if the witness is friendly toward the cross-examiner. The usual purpose of cross-examination, however, is to discredit the witness or to diminish the impact, in some way, of the witness' testimony.

The facts that might diminish a witness' testimony are often not facts that the witness is eager to divulge or that the lawyer calling the witness for direct examination wants the jurors to hear. The cross-examiner, therefore, usually employs leading questions to focus the examination on the witness' uncertainty, a previous contrary statement made by the witness, additional facts that raise questions about the witness' direct testimony, or other factors that discredit the witness or raise questions about the direct testimony. The leading question ensures that the jurors hear the discrediting or doubt-raising information, because it comes from the lawyer's mouth. It is in the question put to the witness. It does not depend upon the witness' willingness to volunteer it.

Leading questions also help the lawyer to control the witness and to limit the witness' response to an affirmation or denial of the cross-examiner's assertion.

Consider, again, the accident witness who, in the direct examination example, left the jurors with the impression that the witness saw clearly what happened. If at the time of the collision, the witness was preoccupied studying a memorandum for the first meeting of the day at work, that is information the witness is unlikely to offer. If the cross-examiner could not ask leading questions of the witness, the examination would probably not elicit the pre-occupation and not allow the lawyer to present information to the jurors that might cast some doubt on the witness' attentiveness.

Examples

A non-leading examination would reveal only the innocuous.

Cross-examiner: What were you doing just before seeing the accident?

Witness: Waiting for the bus.

If, on the other hand, the cross-examiner states the answer, which the witness does not want to offer, as a part of the question, the truthful witness will affirm the fact when confronted with it.

Cross-examiner: Just before seeing the accident, you were reading a memorandum for work, isn't that right?

Witness: Yes.

Cross-examiner: The memorandum was about a meeting to be held as soon as you arrived at work, wasn't it?

Witness: Yes.

Cross-examiner: That was an important meeting?

Witness: Yes.

Non-leading questions about the witness' estimate of the speed of the Chevrolet would be unlikely to elicit that the witness was not certain about the speed, was not experienced at judging the speed of cars, and was not in a position to see that the light for the Chevrolet was yellow.

Cross-examiner: How do you know the Chevrolet was going forty miles per hour?

Witness: It was right in front of me and going a lot faster than cars normally travel on this road.

Cross-examiner:	How fast do cars normally travel on that road?
Witness:	About the speed limit during rush hour.
Cross-examiner:	How do you know what color the light was for the Chevrolet?
Witness:	I could see it.

Leading questions, on the other hand, put the "answer" into the question. This allows the cross-examiner to "testify" (by asking the questions) to the witness' uncertainty about the exact speed, to the witness' lack of experience estimating the speed of passing cars, and to facts suggesting the witness did not actually see that the light was yellow for the Chevrolet.

Cross-examiner:	You said that the Chevrolet was going forty miles per hour, isn't that right?
Witness:	Yes.
Cross-examiner:	Could have been thirty-eight, couldn't it?
Witness:	Yes. [The Cross-examiner does not care what the witness answers. If the witness answers, "no," the Cross-examiner will argue that the witness is too precise to be credible on what is necessarily an estimate.]
Cross-examiner:	You were not looking at the speedometer, were you?
Witness:	No.
Cross-examiner:	You did not have some other kind of timing device at the time?
Witness:	No.
Cross-examiner:	You have no experience watching cars pass by you at different speeds and then comparing their times against a timing device, do you?
Witness:	No.
Cross-examiner:	There were no other cars driving in the same direction as the Chevrolet, so you could draw a comparison when you estimated the Chevy's speed, were there?
Witness:	No.

Cross-examiner:	Now, you know the light for the Ford was green when it entered the intersection?
Witness:	Yes.
Cross-examiner:	The traffic lights at the intersection have those black hoods that shield the light color from cars approaching from the side, don't they?
Witness:	Yes.
Cross-examiner:	You were facing the Ford's light directly, weren't you?
Witness:	Yes.
Cross-examiner:	So that black hood that shields the light color from those approaching from the side didn't interfere with your ability to see that the Ford's light was green, did it?
Witness:	No.

Leading questions may not be appropriate for every cross-examination. Rule 611 provides that "ordinarily leading questions should be permitted on cross-examination." When the witness is not prepared by and is not friendly to the direct examiner, the cross-examiner may not be allowed to lead the witness. This is the other side of the Rule 611(c) coin that allows a direct examiner to lead certain unfriendly witnesses. The cross-examiner's own client, witnesses closely identified with that client, and neutral witnesses from whom the potential cross-examiner is as eager to elicit information as the direct examiner are examples of witnesses for whom leading questions during cross-examination might not be appropriate. The judge has the discretion, but is not required, to prohibit leading questions if the examination is a cross-examination procedurally, but a direct examination in substance.

§ 1.09 Scope of Cross-examination and Other Subsequent Examinations [FRE 611(b)]

Rule 611(b), Scope of Cross-examination, limits cross-examination "to the subject matter of the direct examination and matters affecting the credibility of the witness." The Rule is based upon the same general assumption about the normal progress of a trial as is the rule that limits the plaintiff's rebuttal case to matters raised in the defendant's case-in-chief and the defendant's surrebuttal case to matters raised in the plaintiff's rebuttal case.

As a general proposition, lawyers are allowed to conduct subsequent interrogations of a witness until everything the witness can offer is before the jury. The direct examiner's subsequent examinations of the witness are called redirect examinations and the cross-examiner's subsequent examinations of the witness are called re-cross examinations. How many layers of redirect and re-cross are necessary to present the full testimony to the jurors is entirely within the discretion of the trial judge.

The language of Rule 611(b) addresses only cross-examination, but the principle expressed in the Rule—that the subsequent examination is limited to the subject matter of the preceding examination—is usually applied to redirect examinations, as well as to cross and re-cross examinations. The judge's discretion, pursuant to Rule 611(a), to promote the orderly presentation of evidence by restricting redirect examination to the scope of the cross-examination can, of course, be exercised in the other direction. The judge can allow the proponent on redirect to repair omissions in the direct examination, by allowing questions that go beyond the scope of the cross-examination.

A few jurisdictions do not follow the principle that a subsequent examination must relate to the subject matter of the preceding examination or to the credibility of the witness. Known as "wide open" cross-examination jurisdictions, they allow a cross-examiner to ask about any relevant matter within the witness' knowledge.[36] In most jurisdictions, however, the lawyers must pay attention to the scope of examination in determining what questions they may ask in a subsequent examination.

Example

If the lawyer for the driver of the Ford calls the investigating officer to testify only about the location of the Chevrolet headlamp glass in the intersection, the Chevrolet driver's lawyer can cross-examine the witness on the time of arrival at the scene; whether there was evidence that others had been in the intersection and moved the glass; whether the officer had measured accurately to locate the position of the glass; and the like—all within the scope of the direct.

If the officer happens to have more information—information the direct examiner elected not to present, for whatever reason—the cross-examiner might want to ask the following questions:

Q: Did the driver of the Ford say to you, "I should have been watching more carefully?"

Q: Isn't it true that the yellow light on the traffic signal at Third and Sheridan lasts for seven seconds?

Q: Officer, didn't you happen to see, quite by coincidence, the driver of the Ford about a month after the accident throwing a ball with the arm that was supposed to be broken?

---

36. *See, e.g.,* State v. Mincey, 687 P.2d 1180, 1193 (Ariz. 1984) (en banc), *cert. denied,* 469 U.S. 1040 (1984) (holding that cross examination may extend to any relevant matter within witness' knowledge); State v. Morgan, 367 So. 2d 779, 782 (La. 1979) (holding that if witness testifies to any single fact on direct, witness may be cross examined on the whole case); Dedeaux v. State, 519 So. 2d 886, 890 (Miss. 1988)(stating that scope of cross examination not confined to subjects testified to on direct); Arnold v. State, 679 S.W.2d 156, 159 n. 1 (Tex. App. 1984)(scope of cross examination not limited to scope of direct). *See also* Rogers v. State, 287 N.W.2d 774, 777 (Wis.1980).

If the direct examiner objects to these questions, which of them will be allowed will depend upon the judge's view of whether the question is within the subject matter of the direct examination.

It is difficult to state with precision a test for distinguishing between examination that does or does not go beyond the scope of the direct. A test sometimes cited says that in exercising discretion, the judge may permit cross-examination "as to all matters reasonably related to the issues put in dispute by . . . testimony on direct."[37]

If the judge believes that the subject matter of the direct examination, in the above example, was the location of broken headlamp glass, all of the additional questions are beyond the scope of the direct examination. If, on the other hand, the judge believes that the subject matter of the direct examination was the officer's investigation of the accident, some of the additional questions will be within the scope of the direct. The questions about the Ford driver's statement of fault and about the length of the yellow light at the intersection are probably part of the officer's investigation. The question about the officer's inadvertent observation of the plaintiff's use of a supposedly injured arm is probably beyond the scope of any characterization of the direct examination.

If the throwing incident is beyond the scope, that does not mean the defendant's lawyer may not ask the officer about it. The scope of examination issue is not whether the cross-examiner may ask about the throwing incident, but when and how. Rule 611(b) provides that the "court may, in the exercise of discretion, permit inquiry into additional matters as if on direct examination." The judge has discretion to allow the question during cross-examination or to require the defendant to wait and present the officer during the cross-examiner's case.

Judicial discretion on scope of the examination issues is likely to turn on questions of convenience for the witness, the length of the examination that the lawyer wants to conduct, how severely the examination will interfere with the orderly presentation of the proponent's case-in-chief, and similar factors that influence the orderly presentation of evidence—the flow of the trial.

§ 1.10 "Opening the Door," "Curative Admissibility," "Fighting Fire With Fire"

The theory of adversary justice and the notion that a trial should progress through a series of moves and related counter-moves are responsible, together, for the trial phenomena known as "opening the door," "curative admissibility," and "fighting fire with fire." These phrases are sometimes considered by courts and commentators to be merely different ways to colorfully express a single idea: that a party is allowed to do something or to present evidence that ordinarily would be improper only because the other party did it first. While each of the

---

37. United States v. Vasquez, 858 F.2d 1387, 1392 (9th Cir. 1988)(quoting United States v. Miranda–Uriarte, 649 F.2d 1345, 1353 (9th Cir. 1981); United States v. Green, 648 F.2d 587, 594 (9th Cir. 1981)).

phrases describes a situation in which "evening up" is an important consideration, there are differences that affect the possible consequences when the action of one party, be it appropriate or inappropriate, "opens the door" to reaction by the opponent.

"Curative admissibility," coined by Wigmore,[38] is the narrowest of the terms. It applies only to the circumstance in which one party's presentation of inadmissible evidence causes a problem that the judge will cure by allowing the other party to present inadmissible evidence. "Fighting fire with fire," McCormick's phrase,[39] is a broader concept. It includes "curative admissibility," but it also includes an otherwise improper action–such as an argumentative opening statement–that a party might take in response to the other party's initial improper action. "Opening the door" is the broadest of the terms. It describes what the initial party does that leads to "curative admissibility" and that prompts the other party to "fight fire with fire." But it also describes what happens when the initiating party offers admissible evidence and, as a result, the other party may offer previously inadmissible evidence.

It is worth noting that the three terms describe different actors. The party who begins the process by doing something "opens the door." In certain circumstances, that initial action will cause the judge to allow otherwise inadmissible evidence to go to the fact finder as an act of "curative admissibility." "Fighting fire with fire" describes what the responding party does in response to the initial action. The focus on the different actors can be helpful in sorting out the various situations that appear similar in some respects, but are analytically different.

A judicial determination that one party's action "opens the door" to action by the other party–action that could not be taken "but for" the door opening–is a universal precondition to rebuttal. The action, however, may vary widely from offering competent, admissible evidence to making an improper argument to a jury. Whether and what kind of retaliation will be permitted depends in part on which door was "opened," what was used to "open the door," and what the opponent did to avoid the draft.

The following examples represent three different door openings: 1) presenting competent evidence that increases the issues before the jury and makes otherwise inadmissible counter evidence admissible, 2) presenting inadmissible evidence that creates a problem that can be cured only by allowing other inadmissible evidence, and 3) taking inappropriate trial action that justifies retaliatory inappropriate action.

Example–"Opening the door" with admissible evidence

During a prosecution for possession and distribution of cocaine, the prosecution wants to elicit that the arresting agent set up the buy

38. *See* 1 John H. Wigmore, Evidence § 15 (3d ed. 1940) (Curative Admissibility).

39. *See* 1 McCormick on Evidence § 57 (4th ed. John W. Strong ed. 1994) (Fighting

Fire With Fire: Inadmissible Evidence as opening the Door).

from the defendant because she had received word from U.S. Customs that he was a major drug dealer. Defendant's hearsay objection is sustained. The court rejects the prosecution's argument that the statement is offered to show the agent's state of mind, saying that the agent's state of mind is not relevant.[40]

In his case-in-chief, the defendant claims that the agent framed him, because she held a grudge against him. He produces evidence of the grudge.

In rebuttal, the prosecution should be able to call the agent and elicit the hearsay testimony that was not admissible in the government's case-in-chief. The defendant has "opened the door" to the testimony by making the agent's motive (state of mind) relevant.

Expanding the issues is a common explanation for the phenomenon of "opening the door."[41] It happens so regularly in some contexts, that those situations have been codified. Rules 404 and 608 are examples of "opening the door" to otherwise inadmissible evidence by expanding the issues. Rule 404(a) prohibits offering evidence of a character trait to prove that someone acted in conformity with that trait. The prosecution, therefore, may not offer evidence that the defendant is someone with a long criminal history. Rule 404(a)(1), however, permits a criminal defendant to offer evidence of good character to show that the defendant did not do the action charged. If the defendant chooses to offer such evidence, the same rule "opens the door" for the prosecution to offer the defendant's long criminal history. Similarly, Rule 608(a) prohibits a party from offering proof of a witness' character for truthfulness. If, however, the other party offers evidence that the witness has a reputation for being an untruthful person, that party "opens the door" to the otherwise prohibited testimony about the witness' character for truthfulness.

Waiver is another common explanation for situations in which the action of one party "opens the door" to retaliatory evidence from the other party–evidence that would not be admissible, but for the door opening. In *State v. Banks*,[42] a prosecution for child molestation, defendant made an adamant and expansive denial: "As God is my witness, I have never had sexual contact with my daughter or with any child under the age of 18 years old." The *Banks* Court held that the denial constituted a waiver of the jurisdiction's statute prohibiting evidence of specific instances of sexual activity by either victims or defendants.[43] The defendant had "opened the door" to the prosecution's otherwise inadmissible evidence from two minor girls of their prior sexual activity with the defendant.

The "opening the door" concept is complex. Although expansion of the issues and waiver are common reasons for the door to be opened to

---

40. United States v. Hernandez, 750 F.2d 1256 (5th Cir. 1985).

41. *See,* Clark v. State, 629 A.2d 1239 (Md. 1993).

42. 593 N.E.2d 346, 349 (Ohio App. 1991).

43. *Id.*

otherwise inadmissible evidence, the door may be opened because the opponent holds some right. In *Government of Virgin Islands v. Jacobs*,[44] a rape victim's direct testimony that she was a virgin before the rape "opened the door" to cross-examination in which the defense was allowed to confront the witness with impeachment evidence of prior sexual conduct. The questions, not normally permitted by Rule 412, were allowed not because the government waived anything, but because of the defendant's constitutional right of confrontation.[45]

Example–"Opening the door" with inadmissible evidence

Defendant presents a witness who testifies that the plaintiff has a reputation for being untruthful.

Plaintiff calls a witness in plaintiff's rebuttal case who is prepared to testify to three separate and compelling instances in which the plaintiff was truthful, in an attempt to undercut the untruthful reputation presented in defendant's case-in-chief.

Rule 608(b) specifically prohibits testimony about specific instances of conduct for the purpose of attacking or supporting a witness' credibility. The rebuttal witness' testimony, therefore, will be inadmissible, if defendant objects.

Defendant does not object to the rebuttal witness' testimony about the three specific instances of truthfulness, but during its surrebuttal case, calls a witness who will testify to two separate and compelling instances in which the plaintiff was untruthful.

The same provision of Rule 608(b) that would have prohibited the rebuttal witness' testimony, had the defendant objected, prohibits the surrebuttal witness' testimony, unless the plaintiff "opened the door" for the surrebuttal testimony by offering specific instances of truthful conduct during the rebuttal case. The trial judge is likely– but may not be required–to allow the defendant to present a witness who will "even up" the specific instance evidence available to the jury.

If the judge allows the defendant's inadmissible specific conduct evidence, it is because it is the only way to cure the problem caused by the plaintiff's inadmissible specific conduct evidence. The basis for the court's discretion to admit inadmissible evidence to cure other inadmissible evidence is not obvious. The early cases upholding trial court decisions to allow retaliatory inadmissible evidence consider it a matter of simple fairness.[46] This common law rule that gives the judge discretion to

44.   634 F.Supp. 933 (D.V.I.1986).

45.   *Id* at 940. *But see* United States v. Duran, 886 F.2d 167 (8th Cir. 1989) (In sexual abuse trial, defendant's confrontation right not sufficient to allow cross-examination question about the identity of the father of a child the victim testified she had while living with defendant's family. *Jacobs* distinguished because the response to the cross-examination question about the father of the child would not go to the credibility of the witness.)

46.   *See, e.g.,* Bogk v. Gassert, 149 U.S. 17 (1893) ("manifestly unfair" to allow one party's inadmissible version of a conversation without allowing the other party to use fairness as the standard for admitting inadmissible evidence to "cure" other inadmissible evidence apparently was not superseded by the Federal Rules of Evidence. The advisory committee's note to Rule 611(a) suggests that many of the common law rules giving judges discretion to make trials fair are embodied in the judge's obligation to "make the interrogation and presentation effective for the ascertainment of the truth."[47] When and under what circumstances the judge should use what one court has described as a "nebulous and nodus so-called doctrine"[48] to admit otherwise inadmissible evidence is not so clear from jurisdiction to jurisdiction. "Evening up" is the goal, and "fairness" the mechanism in almost every jurisdiction, but the methods for obtaining the goal and for being fair differ.

Some courts will not allow inadmissible "curative" evidence from a party who has objected to the initial party's inadmissible evidence.[49] Other courts take the opposite position and will not allow inadmissible "curative" evidence from a party who seeks "to introduce whatever incompetent evidence it desires by the simple expedient of failing to object to the introduction of incompetent evidence by the opposing party."[50]

Few courts will allow bootstrapping. A party may not cross-examine on a subject beyond the scope of direct examination, elicit a response that is inadmissible, and then offer inadmissible evidence to "cure" the inadmissible evidence elicited on cross-examination.[51]

One federal court has stated succinctly the contours of the "curative admissibility" doctrine:

> The doctrine of curative admissibility allows a trial judge, in his discretion, to admit otherwise inadmissible evidence in order to rebut prejudicial evidence which has already been erroneously admitted. * * * The doctrine applies, therefore, only when inadmissible evidence has been allowed, when that evidence was prejudicial, and when the proffered evidence would counter that prejudice.[52]

Some jurisdictions enumerate circumstances under which the judge

---

give its equally inadmissible version of the conversation.)

47. Rule 611(a). The advisory committee's note states:

> The ultimate responsibility for the effective working of the adversary system rests with the judge.

> * * *

> Item (1) restates in broad terms the power and obligation of the judge as developed under common law principles. It covers ... questions arising during the course of a trial which can be solved only by the judge's common sense and fairness in view of the particular circumstances.

48. Daniels v. Dillinger, 445 S.W.2d 410, 415 (Mo. App. 1969).

49. *See, e.g., id.* (citing Wigmore for the proposition that "curative admissibility" should not be applied when an objection has been made to the original evidence because the objection will protect the party.)

50. Busch v. Busch, 262 N.W.2d 377, 387 (Minn. 1977).

51. *See e.g.,* United States v. Pantone, 609 F.2d 675, 681 (3d Cir. 1979).

52. United States v. Nardi, 633 F.2d 972, 977 (1st Cir. 1980).

must allow "curative admissibility."[53] Other jurisdictions leave "curative admissibility" to the discretion of the judge, if the proper circumstances exist. *Clark v. State*,[54] is an example of the kind of preconditions imposed in some jurisdictions. A judge has discretion to permit curative admissibility of inadmissible evidence if:

(1) prejudicial inadmissible evidence was admitted without timely objection or timely motion to strike;

(2) the failure to object or move to strike was not shown to be an intentional or tactical decision in order to admit the "curative evidence;"

(3) the inadmissible evidence is highly prejudicial and a motion to strike the previously admitted evidence and a cautionary instruction would not cure its prejudicial effect;

(4) the "curative" inadmissible evidence goes no further than neutralizing previously admitted inadmissible prejudicial evidence without injecting additional issues in the case and does not allow the curing party to gain a tactical advantage from the failure to object to inadmissible evidence;

(5) the curative inadmissible evidence is of the same character as the previously admitted inadmissible evidence; and

(6) the probative value of the otherwise inadmissible curative evidence outweighs the danger of "confusion of the issues or misleading the jury or . . . considerations of undue delay, waste of time [etc.]" See Fed. R. Evid. 403.

Basically, these rules can be distilled into a rather simple maxim which can be characterized by McCormick's cliché "fighting fire with fire."[55]

McCormick used "fighting fire with fire" to describe what Wigmore called "curative admissibility,"[56] but the phrase is useful to describe a kind of "evening up" that is common in trial courts, but does not necessarily involve "opening the door" with inadmissible evidence or curing a problem with inadmissible evidence. The closing arguments from *United States v. Young*,[57] present a too common example of improper argument by counsel.

Example–"Opening the door" and "fighting fire with fire" through improper trial activity

In a prosecution for mail fraud, the defendant's lawyer begins his closing argument by saying that the prosecution has unfairly pre-

---

53. *Busch*, supra note 50.
In order to be entitled as a matter of right to present rebutting evidence on an evidentiary fact: (a) the original evidence must be inadmissible and prejudicial, (b) the rebuttal evidence must be similarly inadmissible, and (c) the rebuttal evidence must be limited to the same

evidentiary fact as the original inadmissible evidence. *Id.*

54. 629 A.2d 1239 (Md.1993)

55. *Id.* at 1246.

56. 1 McCormick, *supra* note 39, § 57.

57. 470 U.S. 1 (1985).

sented the defendant and that from the beginning the prosecution's statements were designed to unfairly poison the minds of the jurors. The defense lawyer goes on to intimate that the prosecution deliberately withheld exculpatory evidence. He charges the prosecution with acting reprehensibly in attempting to cast a false light on respondent's activities, pointing to the prosecutor's table and saying: "I submit to you that there's not a person in this courtroom including those sitting at this table who think the defendant intended to defraud anyone." The defendant, he says, is "the only one in this whole affair that has acted with honor and with integrity."

The prosecutor does not object to defense counsel's summation, but rather, improperly presents his own views about the guilt of the defendant. He says, "I think defense counsel said that not anyone sitting at this table thinks that Mr. Young intended to defraud anyone. Well, I was sitting there and I think he did. I think he got 85 cents a barrel for every one of those 117,250.91 barrels he hauled and every bit of the money they made on that he got one percent of. So, I think he did. If we are allowed to give our personal impressions since it was asked of me. I don't know what you call that; I call it fraud." The prosecutor finished his closing by giving his opinion about the defendant's honor and integrity. "I don't know whether you call it honor and integrity, I don't call it that. If you feel you should acquit him for that it's your pleasure. I don't think you're doing your job as jurors in finding facts as opposed to the law that this Judge is going to instruct you. If you think that's honor and integrity then stand up here in this courtroom and say that's honor and integrity. I don't believe it."

The *Young* Court expressed concern for the "all too common occurrence in criminal trials–the defense counsel argues improperly, provoking the prosecutor to respond in kind, and the trial judge takes no corrective action."[58] It asserted that "two improper arguments–two apparent wrongs–do not make for a right result" and made it clear that courts "have not intended" by any means to encourage the practice of zealous counsel's going "out of bounds" in the manner of defense counsel here, or to encourage prosecutors to respond to the "invitation."[59] The Court went on to say that the prosecutor should have objected, rather than "fight fire with fire" and that "invited responses" might be diminished if trial courts would take prompt action. But it let the conviction stand.

Misconduct in argument is not restricted to criminal cases.[60] Examples of judges using their discretion to even things up by allowing aggrieved counsel to "fight fire with fire" after the other lawyer has done something improper are as common across all litigation as the *Young* Court thought true of criminal cases.

58. *Id.* at 11.
59. *Id.*
60. *See, e.g.,* Findlay v. Griffin, 484 S.E.2d 80 (Ga. App. 1997); Amador v. Lea's Auto Sales & Leasing, Inc., 916 S.W.2d 845 (Mo. App. 1996).

§ 1.11 Documents in Context [FRE 106]

Rule 106, Remainder of Related Writings or Recorded Statements, is another example of judicial discretion as the major factor in managing the proper flow of evidence at trial. The Rule allows the judge, upon motion by the other party, to require the proponent of a portion of a document or recording to offer the remainder of the document or recording at the same time. It is a matter of fairness. Depositions are the most common example. If a statement on page 3 is qualified by another statement on page 100, the judge might not allow the statement from page 3 to be admitted without the qualifying statement from page 100.

The Rule allows the same result when the proponent offers an entire document and its full context will not be understood without consideration of some other document, as, for example, when a letter purporting to be an acceptance is offered. If determining whether the letter is really an acceptance requires that the jurors see the offering letter at the same time, the judge might require the latter to be admitted with the former.

The Rule does not mean that if a party wants to offer a portion of a document the party must introduce the entire document, or when offering one document, all other related documents must be offered as well. There are reasons of emphasis, admissibility, and time economy, among other considerations, that might lead a party to introduce only a portion of a document or only one of a series of documents. The other side is often fully protected by the right to inquire about or offer the remainder of the document or related documents on cross-examination or through later examination of a different witness. When that is the case, the judge is not likely to compel a party to interrupt the flow if its case to offer the entire document or related documents.

Rule 106, a codification of the common law rule of completeness, allows the judge, upon complaint that admission of a portion of a document or a single document will be prejudicial, to require introduction of the entire document or related documents.

There is disagreement in the Federal circuits as to whether Rule 106 is merely a Rule about the order of proof,[61] or whether it authorizes admission of otherwise inadmissible evidence to demonstrate the context of a document or a portion of a document, in order to avoid misleading jurors.[62] In the 1988 case of *Beech Aircraft Corp. v. Rainey*,[63] a case better known for its discussion of the meaning of "factual findings" in the public records exception to the hearsay rule,[64] the Supreme Court discussed the common law Rule of Completeness as it was codified in Rule 106. The Court's discussion suggests that the rule allows the admission of an otherwise inadmissible portion of a document, if it is necessary to

---

61. United States v. Terry, 702 F.2d 299 (2d Cir.), *cert. denied,* 461 U.S. 931 (1983).

62. United States v. Sutton, 801 F.2d 1346 (D.C. Cir. 1986).

63. 488 U.S. 153 (1988).

64. See § **7.29**.

demonstrate the context of the admissible portion of the document offered by the opposing party.

In *Rainey*, the defendant called the plaintiff, husband of the deceased Navy pilot as an adverse witness and asked him about a portion of a letter he sent to the Navy concerning his wife's airplane accident. The plaintiff, a pilot himself, had written to the Navy expressing his opinion that the crash was a result of a power failure in the airplane. The portion of the letter that the defense elicited on direct examination of the adverse party made three points, suggesting the crash was the result of something other than a power failure. It said the plaintiff's wife had attempted to cancel the flight, partly because her student was tired and emotionally drained; that "unnecessary pressure" was placed on them to proceed with the flight; and that the plaintiff's wife or her student had abruptly initiated a hard right turn when the other aircraft unexpectedly came into view. On cross-examination, the plaintiff's lawyer attempted to ask about the remainder of the letter, which made clear the plaintiff's position that the crash was the result of power failure. The trial court would not allow the cross-examination on grounds that the testimony would constitute an opinion of a non-expert.

The Court of Appeals reversed and remanded for new trial because the trial court's refusal to allow the plaintiff to testify to the rest of the letter misled the jury as to the plaintiff's position. Even though the letter itself had not been offered, the Court of Appeals held that the rule of completeness as to documents as codified in Rule 106 applied. It held that the trial court had abused its discretion in not allowing examination about the remainder of the letter.

The Supreme Court found the "concerns underlying Rule 106" to be relevant and agreed with the Court of Appeals that the trial court abused its discretion in not permitting questions about the remainder of the letter:

> The common-law "rule of completeness," which underlies Federal Rule of Evidence 106, was designed to prevent exactly the type of prejudice of which Rainey complains. In its aspect relevant to this litigation, the rule of completeness was stated succinctly by Wigmore: "[T]he opponent, against whom a part of an utterance has been put in, may in his turn complement it by putting in the remainder, in order to secure for the tribunal a complete understanding of the total tenor and effect of the utterance." 7 J. Wigmore, Evidence in Trials at Common Law § 2113, p. 653 (J. Chadbourn rev. 1978). [65]

§ 1.12 Judicial Notice of Adjudicative Facts [FRE 201]

The witness testified that at eleven o'clock at night, by the light of a full moon, he saw the defendant kill a man in the middle of a field some hundred and fifty feet away. But the moon was not full on August 29,

---

65. 488 U.S. at 171.

1857, the night of the killing. It was barely past the first quarter. How would Abraham Lincoln, the lawyer for the defendant, prove the moon was not full, so that he could argue to the jurors that the supposed eyewitness was not believable? He might call as a witness someone who remembered looking up at the moon at eleven on August 29, 1857 and who could recall it was barely past first quarter. But who remembers the moon on a particular night? And why should the jurors believe one amateur stargazer over another? He might call an astronomer as an expert witness, if one were easily available in the pre-Civil War frontier of Illinois and if the Court would recognize the area of expertise. Lincoln chose, instead, to ask the sheriff to bring him a copy of the almanac for 1857. The Court took judicial notice of the moon phase information in the almanac.[66] By asking the Court to take judicial notice, Lincoln was taking advantage of a shortcut in proof that the common law had developed to reduce the time and expense required in proving something certain beyond argument.[67]

Judicial notice can be a powerful tool with which a lawyer can prove a fact that is not easily demonstrated through the traditional means of calling a witness, but which is a fact that "everyone knows" or is "beyond argument."

Rule 201 permits a lawyer to establish an "adjudicative fact"[68] that is "not subject to reasonable dispute"[69] merely by asking the Court to take judicial notice of it. If a fact is one "generally known within the territorial jurisdiction of the trial court" or is one capable of determination "by resort to sources whose accuracy cannot reasonably be questioned"[70] the judge may take judicial notice of it, even if no lawyer asks for it.[71] If a lawyer does ask a court to take judicial notice and supplies the trial court with the "necessary information," the judge must take judicial notice of the fact.[72]

In a civil case, a judicially noticed fact may be more powerful than a fact presented through the testimony of a witness. While jurors may refuse to accept what a witness says as fact, the judge instructs civil jurors that they must accept the judicially noticed fact as conclusive.[73] Judges may not instruct criminal jurors to accept anything offered against an accused, so the Rule requires judges in criminal cases to instruct jurors that they may, but are not required, to accept the judicially noticed fact.[74]

Rule 201 is limited to judicial notice of adjudicative facts as substitutes for presenting evidence to a fact-finder through witnesses and

66. Albert A. Woldman, Lawyer Lincoln 123 (1996).

67. For a thorough discussion of the history and rationale behind the development of common law judicial notice, see 2 McCormick, *supra* note 39 § 328.

68. Fed. R. Evid. 201(a).

69. Fed. R. Evid. 201(b).

70. *Id.*

71. Fed. R. Evid. 201(c).

72. *Id.*

73. Fed. R. Evid. 201(g).

74. *Id.*

exhibits. "Adjudicative facts"–"simply the facts of the particular case"[75]– and "legislative facts" are two terms coined by Professor Kenneth Davis to help to understand the two different functions of the court or agency– adjudication and law making. "Adjudicative facts" are the "facts that normally go to the jury in a jury case."[76] Professor Davis' definition, though arguably too narrow by its limitation to the parties, is repeated with approval by the advisory committee.

> When a court or an agency find facts concerning the immediate parties–who did what, where, when, how, and with what motive or intent–the court or agency is performing an adjudicative function, and the facts are conveniently called adjudicative facts. . . .[77]

"Legislative facts," on the other hand, are those that a court uses in the law making process. Courts are often required to interpret a statute or to define the limits of a common law rule. Such decisions often turn on policy, which, in turn, depends upon acceptance of some social, economic, or other hypothesis the court must adopt as "fact" to reach a decision.

The oldest and simplest basis for judicial notice is that the adjudicative fact to be established is one that is so universally known that there is no argument about it.[78] As a New York court said, "What everybody knows the courts are assumed to know. . . ."[79] For example, "everybody knows" that the Grand Canyon is in the United States; the Eiffel Tower is in Paris, France; and George Washington was the first President of the United States.

That "everybody knows," of course, has never actually been the test[80] and is not a requirement under Rule 201. A court may take judicial notice of a fact that is only "generally known" and that general knowledge need be only "within the territorial jurisdiction of the trial court."[81] The fact that the Chicago Cubs last won the World Series in 1908 and are never likely to win it again is probably not as well known as the fact that George Washington was the first President of the United States. The Cubs' almost century-long failure to win baseball's greatest prize might be, nevertheless, the subject of judicial notice in a court sitting on Chicago's north side–even if no one else in the country knows or cares when the Cubs last were supreme. ("Are never likely to win it again" is probably an opinion rather than a fact, except to the most dispirited of rabid Cub fans. See § 10.01 for a discussion of the lack of a clear dividing line between fact and opinion.)

Even a fact that is *not* "generally known within the territorial jurisdiction of the trial court" (or anywhere else, for that matter) may be

---

75. Advisory committee note, FRE 201(a).

76. Kenneth C. Davis, 2 Administrative Law Treatise § 15.03.

77. *Id.*

78. McCormick, supra, note 39 at § 329.

79. In re Buszta's Estate, 186 N.Y.S.2d 192, 193 (Sur.1959).

80. McCormick, supra, note 76.

81. Fed. R. Evid. 201(b).

judicially noticed. A court in New Mexico, for example, might take judicial notice that the Cubs last won the world series in 1908–four years before New Mexico became a state–because the fact is "capable of accurate and ready determination by resort to sources whose accuracy cannot reasonably be questioned."[82] Sometimes referred to as "almanac-type facts," these facts are often ones that "nobody knows" except through resort to the "sources." The Encyclopedia of Baseball, for example, might suffice as a source for the Cubs' near-century of despair.[83]

Judicial notice of an adjudicative fact that is critically important to a case "may be taken at any stage of a proceeding,"[84] even if no lawyer requests it.[85] When the plaintiff in the oft cited case of *Varcoe v. Lee*[86] forgot to prove that Mission Street was in a business district (in order to establish that speed in excess of fifteen miles per hour constituted negligence per se), the judge was free, nevertheless, to instruct the jury that Mission Street was in San Francisco's business district.

A party against whom a fact is judicially noticed is entitled "to be heard as to the propriety of taking judicial notice and the tenor of the matter noticed."[87] While this will often be easy to accommodate when one party asks for notice during a trial, it may not be so simple when the trial judge takes notice of a fact inadvertently, as in *Varcoe v. Lee*, or when it is an appellate court that takes the notice. The rule recognizes the problem and allows the party to be heard after judicial notice has been taken.[88]

Judicial notice of such standard reference material as when the Cubs last won the World Series is not particularly remarkable,[89] but what about Abraham Lincoln's use of the almanac to show that the moon was just past the first phase on August 29, 1857? The almanac writer did not spend every night walking outside to look up and record the phase of the moon–charting history, as it were. The phases of the

82. *Id.*

83. *Compare* Smith v. Pro Football, Inc., 593 F.2d 1173 (D.C.Cir. 1978). In defending the use of the use of Encyclopedia of Pro Football to notice when the Minnesota Vikings selected a player in the pro football draft, MacKinnon, C.J., a former All-American football player at the University of Minnesota, said:

> The majority complains of reference to facts disclosed in the Encyclopedia of Pro Football and to matters of common knowledge that can be readily verified by reference to encyclopedias, books and other publications of established authenticity. This however is clearly permissible and may be done for the first time on appeal as is recognized by the Federal Rules of Evidence, Rule 201(f) which states: "Judicial notice may be taken at any stage of the proceedings."

Id. at 1213, fn. 71 (MacKinnon, C.J., concurring and dissenting).

84. Fed. R. Evid. 201(f).

85. Fed. R. Evid. 201(c).

86. 181 P. 223 (Cal.1919).

87. Fed. R. Evid. 201(e).

88. *Id.*

89. *See, e.g.,* George v. Hilaire Farm Nursing Home, 622 F.Supp. 1349, 1354 (S.D.N.Y. 1985) (judicial notice of dates from a calendar); Hays v. National Elec. Contractors Ass'n, Inc., 781 F.2d 1321, 1324 (9th Cir. 1985) (judicial notice of American Automobile Association map of Alameda County); In re Marriage of Aud, 491 N.E.2d 894 (Ill. 1986) (statistics prepared by the United States Bureau of Census were the proper subject of judicial notice).

moon were undoubtedly derived from the work of an astronomer who used a scientific principle to produce the information. In spite of the almanac, should the judge have required Lincoln to bring in the astronomer for cross-examination?

The first time expert opinion was offered in court about ballistics, radar, genetic testing, and the like, lawyers undoubtedly produced substantial testimony in an effort to persuade the judge of the validity of the underlying scientific principles.[90] As the underlying scientific principles became well accepted, trial courts no longer required elaborate proof of the validity of the science, but rather took judicial notice of the validity of the theory and required evidence only of the particular application or of the qualifications of the particular expert. Appellate courts in various jurisdictions have at one time or another decided that the forensic science of "ballistics" can assist in the identification of the gun from which a bullet was fired,[91] that the speed of an approaching car can be measured by a radar gun,[92] and that genetic markers can be used to establish parentage.[93] Although many scientific principles have become so well accepted that they are judicially noticed, the process to reach that status is often difficult during the period in which the science is being developed.[94]

When a court takes judicial notice of the scientific principle underlying radar, for example, it is not clear whether that judicial notice is of an "adjudicative" or a "legislative fact." It is of some moment because "legislative facts," unlike "adjudicative facts," are not governed by Rule 201.

"Legislative facts" are often central to a court's determination of a legal issue, but the "legislative fact" is not always identified as something of which the court is taking judicial notice. A "legislative fact," unlike an "adjudicative fact," is often not "generally known," cannot be found in a source "whose accuracy cannot reasonably be questioned," and is not something the parties necessarily had an opportunity to address.

The scientific principles underlying radar, ballistics, DNA and the like seem to be "adjudicative facts" to the extent that they constitute evidence that without the judicial notice would normally go to a jury for its consideration. On the other hand, the scientific principle underlying radar is an hypothesis not unlike the social or economic hypotheses that are usually characterized as "legislative facts." The difference is that our

---

90. See **Ch. 10**.

91. Oliver Wendell Holmes, when he served on the Massachusetts Supreme Judicial Court, is credited by David Faigman, et al, Modern Scientific Evidence § 23–1.2 (1997) with the first decision admitting modern firearms identification–Commonwealth v. Best, 62 N.E. 748 (Mass.1902).

92. *See, e.g.,* People v. Magri, 147 N.E.2d 728 (N.Y. 1958) (no longer be necessary to require expert testimony in each

case as to the nature, function or scientific principles underlying radar).

93. *Compare* Clark v. Jeter, 486 U.S. 456 (1988) (Court ordered blood test to determine parentage accepted as a matter of course).

94. For a discussion of the current process by which DNA testing is becoming accepted in the courts, see Faigman, et al, *supra,* note 91 at Ch. 15.

belief in science allows us a greater certainty about the truth of the hypothesis.

In re Sealed Case[95] presents a clear example of "legislative fact." In trying to secure notes of conversations between a White House aide and the aide's lawyer, a prosecutor argued that the lawyer-client privilege did not survive the death of the White House aide. While recognizing the Supreme Court's earlier finding of a "legislative fact"–that the provision of legal advice "can only be safely and readily availed of when free from the consequences or apprehension of disclosure"[96]–the District of Columbia Court of Appeals found its own "legislative fact," though it did not denominate it as such. To support departing from the long established rule that the client's need to be "free from the consequence or apprehension of disclosure" required that the privilege survive the death of the client, the court said: "[I]t is surely true that the risk of post-death revelation will typically trouble the client less than pre-death revelation."[97]

The "fact" that post-death disclosure of privileged information will trouble the client less than pre-death disclosure is as subject to quarrel as is the "fact" that legal advice cannot exist without confidentiality in the first instance.[98] Both propositions are more properly characterized as "hypotheses" than "fact," but they are noticed and treated as facts by courts that are engaged in the law making, as opposed to the fact finding, process.

While the individual judge's "knowledge" of an hypothesis that the judge will notice as a "legislative fact" in support of legal reasoning is inevitable, the individual judge's "knowledge" of an "adjudicative fact" is neither necessary nor sufficient for judicial notice under Rule 201. A judge who does not know the Chicago Cubs from the fuzzy, brown four-footed creatures in the zoo will take judicial notice of the last year the Chicago Cubs won the World Series when shown the Encyclopedia of Baseball. But if that same judge should happen to know the ages of the children of the Cubs' current manager, the judge is not entitled to take judicial notice of them.

The adjudicative facts most trial lawyers will be concerned about in substituting for the testimony of witnesses may be called to the court's attention in any number of ways. The most common is: "Your honor, I ask the court to take judicial notice that the Chicago Cubs last won a World Series in 1908 and that the Boston Red Sox have been forlorn for almost as long, last winning the World Series in 1918."

95. 124 F.3d 230 (D.C. Cir. 1997), *rev'd sub nom.* Swidler & Berlin v. United States, 1998 WL 333019 (June 25, 1998). The Supreme Court expressed doubt about the validity of the lower court's conclusions concerning the likely effect of the loss of privilege. *Id.* at 5–6.

96. Hunt v. Blackburn, 128 U.S. 464, 470 (1888).

97. 124 F.3d at 233.

98. See David Louisell, *Confidentiality, Conformity, and Confusion: Privileges in Federal Court Today*, 31 Tul. L. Rev. 101, 112 (1956) for an argument that the effect of disclosure is speculative and cannot be proven scientifically.

Chapter 2

PROCEDURES FOR OFFERING AND OPPOSING EVIDENCE IN A COMMON LAW TRIAL

Analysis

§ 2.01 Lawyers as Evidence Police

The lawyers, who are primarily responsible for the content of an adversary system common law trial, have the privilege and the obligation to determine which evidence rules will be enforced and which will not—at least in the first instance. The trial judge may on a rare occasion exclude information *sua sponte*—when the United States Constitution prohibits the evidence, for example—but the lawyers are ordinarily responsible for rooting out inadmissible evidence.

Information offered by a proponent that does not meet the requirements of the evidence rules usually will be admitted as evidence, unless the opponent objects to it. Often the opponent knows the information is not admissible, but has no tactical or strategic reason to exclude it. Other times, both parties may have an equal interest in having the information before the jurors. Sometimes the opponent will be unaware that the information can be excluded. Occasionally the opponent will not be quick enough with an objection to keep it from the jurors' ears, and not interested in emphasizing the information by asking the judge to strike it and tell the jurors to disregard it.

Rule 103(a)(1) recognizes the importance of the lawyer as the enforcer of evidence law, by requiring an objection before admission of evidence can be appealed, unless the admission amounts to plain error.[1]

Lawyers enforce evidence law in two different ways. Some evidence issues are sufficiently obvious before trial and critical enough to the way the trial will proceed to be researched, briefed, and argued to the judge in the fashion of any major matter of law. This method of enforcing evidence law demands the same skills and effort as the presentation of any other legal position. Most evidence issues, however, pop up unexpectedly at trial. They require the trial lawyer to hear the issue in the examiner's question; recognize the applicable evidence law; gain the judge's attention, while quieting the witness; object precisely; and be prepared to argue evidence theory and its applicability to the facts presented—all in less than half a minute.

§ 2.02   Motions in Limine

A motion in limine is a common method for raising evidentiary matters of a substantial or highly prejudicial nature, the resolution of which will influence the conduct of and streamline the trial. This anticipatory motion, usually made in writing before the beginning of the trial, gives the lawyers an opportunity to ensure that objectionable and particularly prejudicial information will never be offered in front of, and, therefore, never heard by the jurors. Although the motion is most often used to exclude evidence, it also can provide a mechanism for a lawyer planning to offer controversial evidence to obtain a pre-trial ruling on admissibility.

Lawyers should be sure to obtain a clear ruling from the judge on the motion in limine and should make certain that the motion and the ruling are entered into the trial record. The record and the lawyer's understanding of the rationale for the judge's decision are important for the trial of the case as well as for any possible appeal. Denial of a motion in limine does not mean, necessarily, that the judge will exclude or admit the evidence in question at trial. In many cases, the judge will deny a motion in limine, not because the motion is wrong on the merits, but because a ruling is not possible without hearing the proffered evidence in the context of other evidence. Admission of a critical hearsay statement, for example, may depend upon the facts surrounding the utterance—facts that will not be apparent until the testimony of the person who heard the statement. Similarly, before trial a judge may not be confident enough of the context or of other evidence to exclude evidence for which it is claimed the prejudicial effect substantially outweighs the probative value.

If the denial of a motion in limine to exclude evidence is merely a postponement, the moving lawyer will make the objection at trial. A moving lawyer losing a motion to admit evidence will, similarly, offer the evidence at trial.

---

1.   On plain error, see § **12.04.**

A moving lawyer losing a motion to exclude evidence on the merits might be tempted not to object at trial—in order to avoid emphasizing the evidence in front of the jury—relying on the motion in limine to preserve the point for appeal. There is some risk that the point will not be preserved, if the lawyer fails to object during trial. Although some jurisdictions have held that reasserting the objection at trial is not necessary to preserve the point for appeal, there is a split of authority on the issue.[2] If in doubt about the law in the jurisdiction, the lawyer should obtain an express statement on the record at the in limine hearing that the trial judge considers the objection preserved. Otherwise, the objection should be put on the record during trial—during a bench conference outside the hearing of the jurors, if possible, but in open court if that is the only available method.

Sometimes a lawyer will lose a motion in limine to exclude evidence and then will want to bring out the damaging information on direct examination to blunt the effect. For example, upon losing a motion to exclude a defendant's criminal convictions, the lawyer might have the testifying defendant tell the jurors about the criminal record, so that it will not appear that the defendant is keeping something from the jurors. Although there is authority holding that bringing out the information on direct does not waive the right to appeal the denial of the motion in limine,[3] there is some risk.

In *Luce v. United States*,[4] the Supreme Court ruled that an in limine denial of a motion to prohibit the prosecution from impeaching the defendant with prior criminal convictions may not be raised as a ground for appeal unless the defendant actually testifies and is impeached with the criminal convictions. *Luce* was a non-constitutional ruling concerning the effect of an in limine decision about Rule 609.[5] The opinion has been rejected by some state jurisdictions.[6] The *Luce* Court's concern for having the defendant testify, so the reviewing court would be in a position to assess the extent of the prejudice, should give some pause to a lawyer who fails to obtain a ruling on a motion in limine to exclude evidence. If the lawyer decides to blunt the effect of the damaging evidence by offering it in the lawyer's own case, the logic of *Luce* is likely to result in a ruling that the motion in limine did not preserve the

---

2. Thronson v. Meisels, 800 F.2d 136, 142 (7th Cir.1986) (error preserved by motion *in limine* alone); Palmerin v. City of Riverside, 794 F.2d 1409, 1411–13 (9th Cir. 1986) (error preserved by motion *in limine*); Sheehy v. Southern Pacific Transportation Co., 631 F.2d 649 (9th Cir.1980) (held that a motion made *in limine* is preserved) *with* Collins v. Wayne Corp., 621 F.2d 777 (5th Cir.1980)(holding that objections overruled *in limine* are not preserved for review unless the objection is raised again at trial).

3. *See* United States v. Muscato, 534 F.Supp. 969, 973 (E.D.N.Y.1982)(Weinstein,

J.); Reyes v. Missouri Pac. R. Co., 589 F.2d 791, 793, n. 2 (5th Cir. 1979).

4. 469 U.S. 38 (1984).

5. *See also,* United States v. Witschner, 624 F.2d 840, 844 (8th Cir.), *cert. denied,* 449 U.S. 994 (1980)(held that the trial judge can refuse to rule on a motion *in limine* to bar prior similar acts until after the testimony of the defendant on direct examination is heard without violating the defendant's constitutional right to testify).

6. State v. Lamb, 353 S.E.2d 857 (N.C.App.1987); State v. McClure, 692 P.2d 579 (Or. 1984) (defendant not required to testify in order to preserve error).

matter for appeal. The lawyer may have to weigh the advantage of the tactic against the risk of losing the right to appeal the refusal to exclude. If it is most important to blunt the effect of the evidence by presenting it on direct, the lawyer should seek a stipulation that the point is not waived. Failing that, a statement for the record that no waiver is intended may help to preserve the point for appeal.

§ 2.03 Objections and Motions to Strike at Trial [FRE 103]

The lawyer's choices about and the procedure for making objections at trial can have an important influence on the outcome of the trial, as well as on whether evidence issues are preserved for appeal. The constant tension between the tactics that will be most effective at trial and the steps necessary to create a good record for appeal are never more apparent than when a lawyer is objecting to evidence.

The ability to appeal an evidentiary ruling can be waived by any number of actions or inaction. Failure to object constitutes a waiver.[7] Waiver also may result from an objection that is untimely,[8] an objection that is not sufficiently specific,[9] or an objection that is made on the wrong ground.[10] The purpose for requiring a timely objection that states the proper specific ground is to give the trial judge an opportunity to correct the error and to prevent a wasted trial. Moreover, it gives the proponent an opportunity to withdraw the matter and rely on other evidence or to cure the problem by laying a further foundation.[11] The plain error rule occasionally will preserve an evidentiary matter for appeal, irrespective of anything that may have occurred at trial,[12] but the trial lawyer cannot afford to rely on the chance that plain error will save a mistake in evidence advocacy. The effective evidence advocate must combine knowledge of the substance of the case with fluency in the language of the courtroom in order to make the most difficult judgment—whether to object to inadmissible evidence—and then to object in a timely and proper fashion.

Most accomplished trial lawyers relieve the tension between protecting the record and conducting the best possible trial by objecting to evidence only when the question is objectionable *and* the answer will be harmful to the objecting party's case. The lawyer who makes too many objections may be seen as an obstructionist who is trying to conceal information. Moreover, overruled objections can be harmful to the case.

7. United States v. Weed, 689 F.2d 752, 756 (7th Cir.1982).

8. In some courts, a timely objection requires objection during the opponent's opening statement if the proposed evidence is mentioned. *See* Reagan v. Brock, 628 F.2d 721, 723 (1st Cir. 1980); Bewley v. Allright Carpark, Inc., 617 S.W.2d 547, 552 (Mo. App. 1981).

9. *See* § 2.04.

10. United States v. Johnson, 722 F.2d 407, 409 (8th Cir. 1983); Ralston v. Plogger, 476 N.E.2d 1378, 1384 (Ill.App. 1985).

11. *See* United States v. Del Llano, 354 F.2d 844, 847–8 (2d Cir. 1965); 1 Weinstein's Federal Evidence § 103.02[2] (2d ed. Joseph M. McLaughlin ed. 1997).

12. *See* § 12.04 (discussing the plain error doctrine).

The jurors may give the admitted evidence more weight than it would otherwise receive, because attention has been drawn to it by the objection.

Sometimes failure to make a valid objection is sound because the opponent's evidence will open the door to devastating evidence that would not otherwise be admissible.

Technical objections to foundation may backfire. If the lawyer knows that the opposing party can lay the foundation, then the objection should ordinarily be withheld. Otherwise, the lawyer appears to be obstructing the trial for no reason. Moreover, the opponent's evidence may be more persuasive if the full foundation has been laid. The same principle applies to certain objections to the form of questions, such as objections to questions that are vague or over-broad. The re-phrased question may elicit testimony that is more persuasive than what would have been brought forth by the original testimony.

Technical objections, on the other hand, may break the flow of a cross-examiner's effective examination, and give the direct examiner's friendly witness time to think about what is coming next. Occasionally, a direct examiner will not be very adept. Posing technical objections may make it impossible for such an examiner to complete the direct examination, let alone make it persuasive.

The lawyer with a strong or sympathetic jury case should generally be less eager to make objections. The trial judge may err in sustaining the objection, thereby giving the opponent an appeal point with which to overturn the verdict.

Careful preparation and knowledge of the judge's individual predilections can help the lawyer to prepare for the quick give and take of trial evidence. Judges have vastly different attitudes about the admission and exclusion of evidence. Some give lawyers much more leeway than do others. Since most of the Rules rest upon the judge's discretion, the lawyer's conduct must be adjusted to take into account whether the judge is free and easy in receiving evidence, or extremely technical-minded about excluding it. Some judges, for example, have a strict attitude toward asking questions in proper form, and will frequently sustain objections to leading questions or to questions that call for a narrative response. Others are impatient with attorneys who make such objections and are likely to give the jury the impression that the objecting attorney is wasting everyone's time. Because a trial judge's rulings on matters of form almost never create reversible error, the individual judge's attitude is determinative.

Consideration of the potential objections to be made at trial is an important part of the lawyer's trial preparation, given the risk that error will be waived by failing to object, and the counter-danger that over-objecting will try the patience of the judge and the jurors. The lawyer should be able to anticipate and identify most of the opponent's damaging evidence before trial and should outline the legal grounds for exclusion and consider the language which will be most effective in persuading the judge without offending the jurors.

No lawyer, however, can anticipate every potential piece of damaging, but inadmissible, evidence the opponent might offer. In the heat of trial, the jurors might hear such evidence because the witness responds to the question either before the objecting lawyer can object or before the judge can instruct the witness not to answer. If that happens, the objecting lawyer must move, immediately, to have the question and answer stricken from the record and the jurors instructed to disregard them, in order to protect the record and preserve the matter for appeal.

Example

Proponent:	What happened next?
Witness:	My wife told me it was the same car that had been cruising around our house the day before.
Opponent:	Objection! Hearsay, irrelevant and prejudicial. I move to strike the answer, your Honor.
Judge:	Motion granted, the answer is stricken.
Opponent:	Move to instruct the jury to disregard.
Judge:	The jury will disregard the witness' answer to the question.

The separate motion for an instruction may not be necessary. Judges will often anticipate and instruct the jurors to disregard at the same time as striking the testimony.

Judge: Motion granted. The answer is stricken and the jury is instructed to disregard it.

The same motion to strike and for an instruction to disregard will protect the record if a witness volunteers damaging, inadmissible information without a question being posed; makes a non-responsive answer to a proper question; or has testified on direct, but is unavailable for cross-examination due to death, sickness, refusal to testify further, or some similar reason.

Whether a lawyer should make the motion to strike and for an instruction to disregard is subject to the same tactical considerations as whether the lawyer should object to evidence in the first instance. When jurors have already heard the information, there is the added consideration that a motion to strike and an instruction from the judge to disregard will only emphasize the information and ensure that the jurors will not forget it. The more prejudicial the information, the more likely the lawyer will want to preserve the point for appeal and will move to strike and for an instruction to the jury to disregard.

In some cases, the information may be so prejudicial that the lawyer will consider moving for a mistrial. Whether that is a wise course requires the lawyer to make a sophisticated analysis of, among other things, whether the case will try better a second time; if it is a criminal case, whether double jeopardy might bar a second trial; how the jurors are likely to decide the case, if the judge instructs them to disregard the prejudicial evidence and they take it to heart; and the cost to the client of delay and appeal.

§ 2.04   How to Phrase an Objection

It is not possible to give a formula of words that will work in every courtroom for all objections. Much depends upon the particular judge. When preparing a case to be tried before an unfamiliar judge, the attorney should try to learn the unwritten customs of the trial judge by talking to other lawyers or by sitting in the courtroom. Knowledge of the judge will tell the lawyer whether the judge is likely to rule on a general objection or will require articulation of a specific basis. If the judge requires a specific basis, the lawyer will learn whether it may be expressed by description, or whether a rule number is required. In courts where the judge prefers a description, the lawyer will learn whether the judge expects a short legal description, such as "hearsay" or "document has not been properly authenticated," or will allow longer objections aimed at letting the jurors know why the particular question is "unfair."

"Objection, your honor, the question calls for a hearsay response, depriving the jurors of the opportunity to hear the truth from the person who actually made the observation" will tell the jurors more about the reason for the lawyer's objection than does "Objection, hearsay." Many judges will not allow the lawyer to justify the objection to the jurors[13] for fear that the justification will persuade the jurors not to consider a type of evidence that the law of evidence has determined is entitled to consideration.

Although no two judges treat evidence issues in precisely the same fashion, the language of the courtroom has developed some general conventions of articulation that will work in most situations.

A lawyer who, upon hearing an objectionable question, stands and says, "Objection, your honor," and then states the precise reason for the objection, such as "hearsay," "leading," "calls for a narrative response," and the like will be on safe ground in most courtrooms. Anything more general runs the risk of not preserving the objection for appeal.

Rule 103, Rulings on Evidence concerns preserving evidence matters for appeal and Rule 103(a)(1), Objection, requires that "timely objection

---

13. *See* People v. Simpson, No. BA097211, 1995 WL 294282 (Cal. Super. Trans. Apr. 26, 1995) for Judge Ito's attempt, in a nationally televised case, to keep the lawyers from communicating to the jurors through their objections. "Speaking objections are forbidden. The proper procedure is to notify the court of the objection by standing and stating, 'Objection.' The court will then ask for a statement of the specific legal ground(s). Counsel may not expand beyond that specific and precise statement without leave of court."

or motion to strike appears of record, stating the specific ground of objection, if the specific ground was not apparent from the context."

The Rules' requirement of something more than a general objection to preserve the matter for appeal has made almost extinct the once common practice in some courtrooms of not allowing lawyers to say anything more than "objection," unless asked to give a reason by the judge. Because general objections will not preserve the issue for appeal, virtually all judges allow an objecting lawyer to articulate the specific reason.

Some reasons often used by lawyers are not sufficient to preserve an issue for appeal. They are general objections, even though the lawyer has said something more than just "Objection."

The time-honored objection "Irrelevant, immaterial and incompetent," despite its length remains a general objection that is not sufficient to preserve error, except, perhaps, when the only objection is that the evidence is irrelevant under Rule 401.[14]

"No foundation" is not a "specific ground" that will satisfy Rule 103(a)(1).[15] "No foundation" means only that opposing counsel has failed to do something that is a prerequisite for the admission of evidence. The objection could refer to a variety reasons for exclusion. It could refer, for example, to failure to lay a foundation establishing the authenticity of a document, a foundation for a hearsay exception, or a foundation showing the existence of personal knowledge.

That a general objection usually will not preserve a matter for appeal, does not mean that a lawyer should never lodge a general objection. When a lawyer hears a question that will lead to dubious evidence, but the lawyer cannot think of the specific ground for objection, a general objection is better than nothing at all.

"Objection" alone, or "objection" followed by a stock phrase such as "prejudicial," "no foundation," "not a proper question," or even "that can't be asked," will preserve the point for appeal, if the appellate court finds that the specific ground is "apparent from the context."[16] Moreover, the general objection may cause the evidence to be excluded at trial, because the trial judge may appreciate the specific ground for the objection, even if the objecting lawyer does not. The judge's exclusion of the evidence will be upheld on appeal if there was any ground to support it.[17] Ironically, when the general objection is sustained at trial, the objecting lawyer may be in a better position on appeal than if a specific objection had been made on the wrong ground and sustained by the judge.[18]

14. 1 Weinstein's Federal Evidence § 103.12[1] (2d ed. Joseph M. McLaughlin ed. 1997).

15. Boss & Bowen, Inc. v. Head Realty Co., 224 S.E.2d 459, 460 (Ga. App. 1976) ("[O]bjection to admission of documents on the ground 'no foundation has been laid' is not a proper objection.")

16. Fed. R. Evid. 103(a).

17. Fendley v. Ford, 458 N.E.2d 1167 (Ind. App. 1984).

18. Although in most cases an objection sustained on the wrong ground, when a

When a general objection is made and sustained, the attorney offering the evidence should consider asking that the ground for objection be specified. This is particularly true when the lawyer is unsure how to proceed to get the testimony into evidence in the face of the objection. Many objections can be obviated by changing the form of the question or by bringing out the evidence in another fashion. Inexperienced lawyers, however, sometimes give up from confusion or embarrassment and lose the benefit of admissible testimony, because of problems with the form in which it is being elicited. In cases like this, the lawyer should *not* issue the request for clarification as a challenge to the trial judge ("Judge, why specifically did you sustain the objection?"), but should respectfully ask the court's help.

Examples

Requesting that counsel give a specific ground.

Proponent:	Dr. Green, when did you first see the patient?
Witness:	[Refers to notes before answering.]
Opponent:	Objection.
Judge:	Sustained.
Proponent:	[Confused] Your honor, may I request that counsel state a specific ground for objection, so that I can ask the question in a proper form?
Judge:	What is the basis for the objection?
Opponent:	No foundation.
Proponent:	Your honor, that is still a general objection. Counsel should specify what type of foundational objection is being made.
Opponent:	No foundation has been laid for the witness's use of the notes to refresh memory or as past recollection recorded.

Asking the trial judge for help.

Proponent:	Mr. Green, would you indicate on the diagram where you were standing at the time of the collision?

proper ground exists, will not be reversed on appeal, commentators have suggested the result might be different if the proponent of the evidence could have cured the problem upon a proper objection, had it been made. *See* 1 Weinstein's Federal Evidence, *supra* note 14, at ¶ 103.12[4]; Edmund M. Morgan, Basic Problems of State and Federal Evidence 48 (5th ed. 1976); 1 McCormick on Evidence § 52 at 131 (4th ed. John W. Strong ed. 1994).

Opponent:	Objection, no foundation.
Judge:	Sustained.
Proponent:	[Having been stymied in this fashion on several similar questions] Your Honor, may I approach the bench?
Judge:	Yes.
Proponent:	Your Honor, I am having problems here. I think that the witness's testimony would be admissible if I could put the questions in the proper form. Could you give me some guidance about how to proceed? [Or simply, "Could you give me some help here, judge?"]

The words to articulate various specific grounds for objections may not be susceptible to formula, but ought to be chosen in mind of the two reasons that underlie the requirement of specificity. Hearing the specific ground for an objection allows the judge to make an intelligent ruling and provides the proponent of the evidence with an opportunity to cure the defect.

In jurisdictions in which the rules of evidence have been codified, the requirement of specificity can often be met by referring to rule numbers.[19] This is particularly true when there is no universally recognized catch phrase that describes the objection.

Examples

"Objection! The question asks about statements made during mediation. Those are excluded under Rule 408."

"Objection! Rule 407. That change was a subsequent remedial measure."

"Objection! Rule 403. Prejudicial, confusing, and a waste of time."

In other instances, the words describing the objection may be so familiar as to render reference to the rule number superfluous or pedantic.

"Objection! Hearsay. [No need to refer to Rule 801(c).]

"Objection! Attorney-client privilege. [No point in referring to Rule 501.]

When evidence is admissible in part and objectionable in part—for example, when the medical history portion of a hospital record is

---

19. *See* Jack Pope & Charles E. Hampton, *Presenting and Excluding Evidence*, 9 Tex. Tech L. Rev. 403 (1978). Even when rule numbers would be more precise, however, use of them is not required to preserve error. "Any expression which pointedly discloses the vulnerable quality of the proof or the character of the incompetency is sufficient.... [However,] care must be taken that the objection strike at the very heart of the infirmity." *Id.* at 445. *See also* Mason Ladd, *Objections, Motions and Foundation Testimony*, 43 Cornell L.Q. 543, 550–51 (1958).

admissible, but the portion of the history that contains plaintiff's description of the accident is not—the objecting lawyer must identify the portion of the offered or expected testimony that is objectionable. If the ground for objection is not applicable to the entire statement or document, the court can overrule the objection.[20]

In many instances, there are multiple grounds for objection to a single item of evidence. The objecting lawyer should raise *all* the legal grounds that apply. To make the grounds clear for the judge and to avoid confusion in the record, the grounds can be numbered as they are stated. Identifying multiple grounds not only avoids the risk of choosing the wrong ground, but one of several correct grounds may be more persuasive to the judge than others.

It is necessary to enumerate all specific grounds in order to be sure of preserving the objection on appeal. An objection that specifies the wrong ground is as bad as an insufficient general objection. If the trial judge overrules the objection on the specific ground stated, the appellate court will affirm, even if the evidence would be excludable on other grounds, unless that other ground is plain from the context.[21]

§ 2.05 Timing of Objections

The most perplexing problem for the lawyer learning the language of the courtroom is the speed with which it must be spoken. In a sense, the law of evidence has a very short life, from the time of an objectionable question until the witness answers. If the lawyer does not spot the evidence issue as the question is asked and voice the objection in that brief pause between question and answer, the law of evidence might have no effect. Courts have held that objections raised after the answer is given are not adequate, unless the answer was given so quickly that objection could not possibly be interposed.[22] Some trial judges are strict about requiring the objection before the answer, at least when the objection concerns a matter of form.

Example

Proponent:	Did Mr. Brown's vehicle cross the centerline?
Witness:	Yes.
Opponent:	Objection, leading question.
Judge:	Asked and answered, counsel. Next question.

Despite the best efforts of the objecting lawyer and the judge, there are a variety of reasons why a witness' inadmissible testimony may be

---

20. *See* Jones v. Petroleum Carrier Corp., 483 F.2d 1369, 1371–72 (5th Cir. 1973).

21. United States v. Johnson, 722 F.2d 407, 409 (8th Cir. 1983); Ralston v. Plogger, 476 N.E.2d 1378, 1384 (Ill. 1985).

22. 75 Am. Jur. 2d, *Trial* § 164 (1974); 1 McCormick, *supra* note 18, § 52.

heard by the jurors, before the operation of the law of evidence can avoid the problem. The witness might offer testimony without a question being posed. The witness might answer so quickly that there is no time to interpose an objection. The basis for an objection might not be apparent in the question, becoming obvious only with the witness' answer. The witness might respond to an unobjectionable question with a non-responsive answer. The witness might respond to the question, despite a timely objection, before the judge has an opportunity to rule. The judge might sustain an objection, but the witness might answer, anyway. To preserve the point for appeal in any of these situations, the lawyer must make sure the objection is of record and must make a motion to strike the testimony and for an instruction to the jurors to disregard it.

The motion to strike the testimony and for an instruction to the jurors to disregard might not actually cure the harm, as it relates to the outcome of the trial. It might even aggravate it by calling attention to the matter. But if the lawyer's judgment is that the client's cause will be better served by preserving the appeal point than it will be hurt by the added emphasis, the lawyer must make the motion.

There will be times when a lawyer anticipates objectionable evidence and wants to interpose the objection immediately, to avoid any danger that the jurors will hear the prejudicial and inadmissible information, because it comes out before the operation of the law of evidence prohibits it. Some trial judges will treat objections to preliminary questions as premature. For instance, if the examiner asks whether the witness has an opinion and the other lawyer objects because the opinion will be inadmissible, the trial judge might treat the objection as untimely until the witness has actually been asked to state the opinion. Similarly, some trial judges treat objections to questions about conversations as premature until the witness has actually been asked to state the contents of the conversation. If the court takes this tack, the objecting lawyer should be careful to renew the objection in order to exclude the evidence. The problem might not be with the nature of the objection, but only with its timing.

Example

Prosecutor:	Did you have a conversation with the victim?
Defense lawyer:	Objection—hearsay.
Judge:	Overruled. He hasn't asked what was said.
Witness:	Yes.
Prosecutor:	What did the victim say?
Defense lawyer:	Objection, hearsay.
Judge:	Sustained.

The defense lawyer might be making the early objection to avoid the common problem of a witness who does not respond to the first question with a "yes" or "no," but with a recitation of the conversation. If that is the case, the lawyer should ask the judge who overrules the objection to instruct the witness to answer precisely.

Example

Prosecutor:	Did you have a conversation with the victim?
Defense lawyer:	Objection—hearsay.
Judge:	Overruled. He hasn't asked what was said.
Defense lawyer:	Will your honor please caution the witness to answer "yes" or "no" and not to testify to the contents of the conversation?

A similar timing problem can arise when an exhibit is being marked, authenticated, and then offered into evidence. When the proponent begins the process by having the exhibit marked for identification, there is no question posed and, therefore, nothing about which to object. The handling of an exhibit can be cumbersome and can lead to the exhibit being seen by the jurors before it is admitted into evidence. If it is an exhibit the opponent expects to exclude, and even the mention of it might be prejudicial, the lawyer should raise the issue at the earliest possible time.

Example

Proponent:	Your honor, may I have an exhibit marked for identification.
Judge:	[Assents by nodding the head and pointing toward the clerk who will mark the exhibit.]
Opponent:	May we approach the bench?

Or

Objection, may we approach?

The request for a sidebar conference without the objection is likely to let the judge know that there is an evidentiary issue surrounding the exhibit. The judge will probably respond by asking the lawyers to approach for a discussion outside the hearing of the jurors. If the judge does not understand or does not agree to the sidebar, the lawyer will have to expand the request and let the judge know specifically that the lawyer wishes to lodge an objection outside of the hearing of the jurors.

An objection to the marking of an exhibit cannot be sustained—even if the judge is not going to allow its admission—because the exhibit must be marked for the record to be complete. The judge may, nevertheless, entertain the argument over admission, at the time the exhibit is being marked, particularly if the objection is one that can be settled without the judge first hearing the foundation testimony. By asking for the sidebar conference when the proponent first asks to have the exhibit marked, the objecting lawyer avoids making the objection in front of the jury, is not responsible for squelching the natural anticipation that jurors feel when they are about to see an exhibit, and avoids the jurors seeing the exhibit through inadvertent display.

§ 2.06 Sidebar Conferences (Bench Conferences); Excusing the Jury

Rule 103(c), Hearing of the jury, explicitly encourages lawyers and judges to use all available means "to prevent inadmissible evidence from being suggested to the jury by any means."

Pretrial conferences—before the jurors are even empanelled—and hearings conducted outside the presence of the jurors, when lengthy offers of proof are made by the question and answer method, are often employed to keep jurors from learning information that, ultimately, will be ruled inadmissible. Although many judges try to encourage settling as many evidence issues as possible in pre-trial conferences, particularly issues surrounding tangible exhibits, the sidebar conference is still the common device employed to further the ends of Rule 103(c). Much as lawyers anticipate and attempt to handle evidence matters before trial with motions in limine, there are always matters that arise at trial that should be discussed outside the presence of the jurors.

The sidebar (or bench) conference is an effective device for furthering the goals of Rule 103(c) and keeping matters from the jurors. The problem for the trial lawyer, and for the judge, to some extent, is that the jurors sit around bored—and maybe resentful about being left out—while the lawyers and the judge thrash out evidence law problems.

Lawyers may ask for a sidebar at anytime, but granting the request is within the discretion of the judge. Refusal to allow a sidebar is unlikely to be cause for a reversal, unless as a result, a party is denied the opportunity to make an offer of proof, or the jurors receive information so prejudicial that the side requesting the sidebar is denied a fair trial. When a lawyer wants a sidebar conference outside the hearing of the jurors to make an objection, to argue about an objection, or to make an offer of proof regarding evidence that the judge has ruled inadmissible, the lawyer requests a hearing. "Sidebar, your honor?" "May we approach?" "May we approach the bench, your honor?" "Bench conference, your honor?" are various ways a lawyer might signal the judge that the lawyer wishes to discuss a matter outside of the hearing of the jurors, but without excusing the jurors from the courtroom.

Judges, aware of jurors' impatience with discussions in their presence to which they are not privy, do not grant every request for a sidebar. Generalization about how any judge will handle requests for a sidebar is impossible, but there are some general clues to the exercise of judicial discretion.

Lawyers who want to make every objection at the bench are unlikely to be welcome at the bench for that purpose after their goal becomes apparent to the judge.

Lawyers who wish to argue every objection, irrespective of the importance of the proposed evidence or the rectitude of the argument, are unlikely to be welcome at the bench when the pattern becomes apparent.

When a real dispute about evidence is apparent, sidebars will almost always be granted.

"Offer of proof, your honor?" will almost always result in a sidebar conference, because it is specifically mentioned in Rule 103(c). If the offer is to be made by questioning a witness, the jurors will be excused, but often the offer can be made by narrative at the bench, without the disruption of removing the jurors from the courtroom.

When a question asks about character, criminal convictions, specific acts, or other matters that might have a prejudicial effect if they are heard by the jurors and not admitted into evidence, a request for a sidebar, following an objection made without stating a specific ground, is likely to be granted.

When the judge can tell from the context of a request for a sidebar that the articulation of an objection and a ruling might cause the jurors to give extraordinary weight to evidence they have heard or to speculate about excluded evidence, the request is likely to be granted.

During sidebar conferences, whether requested by the lawyers or initiated by the judge, the lawyer should be sure that the conference is conducted in the kind of hushed tones that will not be heard by the jurors *and that the conference is on the record*. Without the court reporter present to record the bench conference, anything said or done at the conference is beyond appellate review.

§ 2.07 Continuing Objections

The requirement that objections be specific, both as to the legal grounds and to the part of the evidence objected to, can require a lawyer to object to each one of a series of questions posed to a witness on the same topic. Because such repeated objections can antagonize both judge and jury, the objecting lawyer might want to request a continuing objection to a line of questioning.

When the objection is first raised and overruled by the judge, the lawyer may ask for a continuing objection that will obviate the need constantly to interrupt the examination in order to preserve the record.

Example

Proponent:	How many incidents did you discuss with the deceased?
Witness:	Seven.
Proponent:	Do you remember what the deceased said about the incident of March 2, 1998?
Witness:	Yes.
Proponent:	What did the deceased say about that incident?
Opponent:	Objection, hearsay.
Judge:	Overruled.
Opponent:	Your honor, if counsel is going to ask what the deceased said about all seven encounters, may I have a continuing hearsay objection to what the deceased said?
Judge:	You may.

The lawyer asking for the continuing objection must obtain the judge's consent on the record, in order for the continuing objection to preserve the issue for appeal.

If the testimony that is the subject of a continuing objection is likely to be critical to the outcome, the lawyer should take care in relying upon a continuing objection. If the ground for objection to a later question differs from the ground upon which the continuing objection is granted, the issue for the later question will not be preserved, because the continuing objection to the question will not have stated the proper specific ground for exclusion. It is often difficult to determine where the continuing objection should end, and differences of opinion on that point could result in the failure to preserve error.

At the end of a witness' testimony, for which a continuing objection has been taken, the objecting lawyer should renew the objection for the record, move to strike the entire line of testimony, and move to have the jurors instructed to disregard it.

§ 2.08 Voir Dire to Lay the Foundation for an Objection

There will be times when a lawyer believes that certain testimony will be improper, that the foundation is lacking for an exhibit, or that a witness is not qualified to testify, but the basis for the objection is not apparent from the questions posed by the direct examiner. When such a circumstance first becomes apparent to the lawyer, it is appropriate to object and to ask permission of the court to "take the witness on voir dire." The objecting lawyer is asking the judge to interrupt the direct examination and to allow a limited cross-examination for the purpose of laying the foundation for the objection. There are times when the lawyer will ask or the judge may prefer that the voir dire is conducted outside the hearing of the jurors, but more often, the jurors will hear the examination. A typical example is when a proponent has apparently qualified a witness as an expert, and the objecting lawyer has additional information that might change the judge's willingness to accept the witness as an expert in the field designated by the direct examiner.

Example

Proponent:	Your honor, plaintiff submits that Dr. Wissard is qualified as an expert in the design and and operation of radial tires.
Opponent:	Objection, your honor. May I take the witness on voir dire?
Judge:	You may.
Opponent:	Dr. Wissard, isn't it true that your Ph.D is from Western Atlantic University?
Witness:	Yes.
Opponent:	Western Atlantic University is a correspondence school located above a hardware store, isn't that right.
Witness:	Well, yes. But it is a good school.
Opponent:	Dr. Wissard, you have never designed a radial tire, have you?
Witness:	No.
Opponent:	Dr. Wissard, you have never run tests comparing the operation of the defendant's radial tires to those of other manufacturers, have you?
Witness:	No. But I have read the literature.
Opponent:	Your honor, defense believes that Dr. Wissard is not qualified as an expert in the design and operation of radial tires and objects to the court accepting him as an expert witness in that field.

The judge might disqualify the witness, believing that the points raised in the voir dire disqualify the witness from testifying to an expert opinion. On the other hand, the judge might believe that the points raised on voir dire affect the weight of the expert's testimony, but are insufficient to disqualify the witness as an expert. In the latter case, the judge is likely to say something like: "Counsel, the issues you have raised concerning the witness' education and experience go to weight. You may argue them to the jurors, but the court accepts Dr. Wissard as an expert in the design and operation of radial tires."

§ 2.09 Motion for Limiting Instruction [FRE 105]

Valid objections to evidence will often be overruled because the evidence is admissible in part, or for a limited purpose. A portion of an exhibit may be admissible while other portions are not. Where there are multiple parties on one side, evidence may be admissible against one party, but not against another. In any of these situations, the objecting lawyer must take steps to prevent prejudicial evidence from being used improperly by the jurors.

A motion for a limiting instruction might be the only precaution available to the lawyer who has not been able to persuade the judge to invoke remedies that will keep the information from the jurors.[23] If the lawyer believes the jurors are more likely to heed the judge's instruction than to be influenced by the emphasis that the specific instruction might give to the evidence, the lawyer should make the motion as soon as the evidence is presented.[24] The motion should be restated at the completion of the case, for inclusion in the judge's instructions to the jurors.

Example

Cross-examiner: Isn't it true that you previously said the light was green for the Chevrolet?

Direct examiner: Objection, hearsay.

Cross-examiner: Impeachment, your honor.

Judge: Overruled.

Direct examiner: Your honor, I request an instruction to the jurors regarding the limited use of the witness' answer.

Judge: Members of the jury. An out of court statement by a witness is not admissible in evidence to prove the contents of the statement. It may,

---

23. Oral testimony that is admissible for one purpose, but not for another may be excluded if the prejudice resulting from the inadmissible purpose substantially outweighs the probative value of the admissible purpose. Fed. R. Evid. 403. Some exhibits can have the inadmissible information redacted without ruining the proper use of the exhibit. However, other evidence might be so prejudicial that the party against whom it is not admissible will be entitled to a severance.

24. Many lawyers believe that an instruction to use something for one purpose and not for another is impossible to state and equally difficult to do. The lawyer who asks for a limiting instruction should be prepared to say something in closing argument to turn the emphasis to the lawyer's advantage. If no such argument is apparent to the lawyer, a motion for a limiting instruction might hurt more than it will help.

however, be admitted as it bears on the credibility of the witness. You may consider the answer you hear from the witness only as it bears on the witness' credibility.

Cross-examiner: You may answer.

Witness: Yes.

The judge might well wait until after the witness' answer to give the limiting instruction. The instruction at the end of the trial might be general with respect to using evidence only for the purpose offered or specific with respect to a piece of evidence when requested by the lawyer who asked for the limiting instruction.

§ 2.10 Offer of Proof

Rule 103(a)(2) provides for offers of proof. When an objection to evidence is sustained, the issue will not be preserved for appeal unless the proponent makes sure that the "substance of the evidence was made known to the court by offer or was apparent from the context within which questions were asked." Rulings sustaining objections to the form of the question or lack of foundation do not call for an offer of proof, because the examiner should simply proceed by asking the question in a different fashion or presenting the additional information that will complete the foundation. It is only when the judge has sustained an objection that excludes evidence and the lawyer cannot cure the problem, that an offer of proof is needed.

An offer of proof will further two of the examiner's goals. It will comply with Rule 103(a)(2), making it possible for an appellate court to evaluate the effect of the exclusion of the evidence on the proponent's case and, therefore, not invoke the common response that the trial judge's error does not justify reversal, because the error was harmless.[25] A solid demonstration of the importance of the evidence to the proponent's case might, also, persuade the trial judge to reconsider the ruling and admit the evidence. Even if the context within which the questions are asked gives the trial judge sufficient knowledge of the substance of the evidence to preserve the point for appeal,[26] the proponent of the evidence might wish to make an offer of proof, in hopes the judge will be persuaded to reverse the ruling and admit the evidence.

There are two usual forms of offer, both of which are conducted outside the hearing of the jurors, to comply with the mandate of Rule 103(c) to keep inadmissible evidence from being presented to the jurors. The narrative form—in which the lawyer who wants to offer the evidence tells the judge and the other lawyer what testimony would be produced from which witnesses—is usually conducted at sidebar. The question and answer form—in which the proponent puts the witness on

---

25. *See* United States v. Rayco, 616 F.2d 462 (10th Cir. 1980).

26. *See* Collins v. Wayne Corp., 621 F.2d 777 (5th Cir. 1980).

the stand and conducts the proposed examination—is usually conducted in the courtroom, after the jurors have been excused.

Before making any offer of proof, the proponent should be certain of the grounds for the objection so that the grounds may be addressed in the offer. If the specific ground is not clear, or if the court has sustained a general objection, the proponent should request the court to ask objecting counsel to state the specific grounds.

The showing required in an offer of proof in order to persuade a trial judge to admit the evidence is the same as is needed to persuade an appellate court to reverse, if the trial judge does not admit the evidence:

A pertinent question was asked of a witness who could have provided an answer.

What the answer would have been.[27]

Why the testimony was relevant.

How the testimony would benefit the proponent's case.

Why the evidence should be admitted under the rules of evidence.[28]

The offer of proof must be precise. Where more than one piece of testimony or more than one tangible item are the subjects of an offer, the lawyer must handle each piece as if it were a separate offer of proof. If the lawyer does not differentiate the bases and arguments for each piece, there is a risk of losing the point on appeal, even though some of the evidence should have been admitted, because one of the pieces was properly excluded.

When the proponent of excluded evidence makes an offer of proof at sidebar, that lawyer should ask the judge to excuse the witness. In the event the offer persuades the judge to admit the evidence, the witness will not have heard the offer and will not be able to tailor the testimony to be consistent with the offer. When a cross-examiner is making an offer of proof, it is even more important that the lawyer make sure the witness is excused so that the offer does not tip the witness to the direction of the cross-examination.

An offer of proof should do more than enumerate, if it is to be effective. It should inform the trial judge as to the exact nature of the testimony, the specific relation of the evidence to the claim or defense in the proponent's case, the evidence rule under which the evidence is admissible, the argument for its application, and the prejudice the proponent's case will suffer if the evidence is excluded.

27. *In re* Adoption of Baby Boy Irons, 684 P.2d 332, 338 (Kan. 1984)(proponent did not indicate what excluded testimony would have been, so error was not preserved).

28. The lawyer should state all grounds on which the evidence is admissible. This is particularly important when dealing with hearsay objections. *See* Huff v. White Motor Corp., 609 F.2d 286, 290 (7th Cir. 1979) (after hearsay objection, proponent should have alerted trial court to the statement against interest exception in order to preserve error on that ground).

Example

Defense lawyer: What did she say she saw?

Plaintiff lawyer: Objection, your honor, hearsay.

Judge: Sustained.

Defense lawyer: Offer of proof, your honor.

Judge: Approach.

Defense lawyer: [At sidebar, after plaintiff lawyer has requested that the judge ask the witness to stand down from the witness chair so the offer of proof is not overhead.]

Your honor, if allowed to answer the question about what she heard, the words used by the man who saw the accident will demonstrate why the testimony is admissible under two different exceptions to the rule against hearsay.

If allowed, the witness will testify that the man said, "Oh my God, my God. Did you see that? Did you see that? That blue car sped right through that red light and slammed into the white car. Is anybody hurt? What should we do? Can we call someone? Oh, my God."

The words, themselves, indicate that the man was very excited and that the statement was made immediately after he saw the accident. That makes the statement admissible under two separate exceptions to the hearsay rule: the excited utterance exception and the present sense impression exception.

This is the only available evidence we have to demonstrate that the plaintiff here, not the defendant, caused this accident.

In the rare case in which a trial judge will not allow an offer of proof to be made, error will be preserved if the lawyer puts the offer of proof in writing and requests that it be entered into the record before the close of trial.[29]

---

29. An offer of proof will not preserve a matter for appeal if it is not on the record. If the judge refuses to hear an offer of proof, the written offer (with copies given to opposing counsel, the judge, the clerk, and the court reporter) is likely to preserve the matter for appeal.

Chapter 3

OBJECTIONS TO THE FORM
OF THE QUESTION OR
THE ANSWER

Analysis

§ 3.01 The Rules of the Game

Objections to the form of the question or answer are rules about the conduct of the trial, rather than about the validity of various kinds of evidence. They relate not to what was asked or answered, but rather, how it was done. They are, in short, rules of the game. As a result, most good trial lawyers avoid making such objections, unless they believe that the objection will influence the effectiveness with which either the examiner or the witness is able to relate to the jurors. The trial lawyer uses the objections to the form of the question to influence the flow of the information to the jurors. As with presentation of any material, "how" the information is presented to the jurors can often be as influential as "what" the information is. Aside from issues of witness credibility, the effectiveness of presentation (or lack of it) can determine whether the information ever reaches the jurors ears or eyes. Just because something is said or shown does not mean it is heard or seen. Trial results come from what is heard and seen.

Objections to the form of the question or answer ask the judge to exercise the discretion provided by Rule 611 to control the mode of questioning witnesses. They invoke the universal understanding that lawyers and judges have about the language of the courtroom. Because the particular dialect of the trial judge determines almost entirely whether objections to form are sustained or ignored, the trial lawyer is well advised to be familiar with the judge's predilections about questions and answers that touch only on the "how" and not the "what" of the examination of witnesses. Except in the most egregious case (amounting to denial of a fair trial) the last word on how the evidence will be educed belongs to the trial judge.

There are many objections to form and more than a few ways to express each of them. This chapter contains some of the more common objections to form and the manner in which they are expressed.

§ 3.02 "Objection, Leading"

Leading questions are prohibited on direct examination, except for those questions that are preliminary, transitional, about non-controversial matters, or asked of an uncooperative witness or a witness designated in Rule 611(c).

A question is leading when its words or its context suggest the answer to the witness.

Q: You were in the hallway when the shot was fired, weren't you?

A complete discussion of the importance of leading questions in defining direct and cross-examination is found at § 1.03.

§ 3.03 "Objection, Calls for a Narrative."

Judges prohibit questions that call for an extensive narrative response, when they foresee that the narrative may make it impossible for the opponent to interpose a timely objection, with the result that the jurors will hear inadmissible and prejudicial evidence that will not be susceptible to cure by an instruction to disregard. Although some judges are sticklers about the objection, even if those dangers do not appear imminent, narratives are tolerated, if not encouraged, in some courtrooms because they often speed up a trial. The lawyer who wants to be successful in objecting to a question that calls for a narrative response should be prepared to illustrate the problem or the extremely prejudicial nature of the possible answer.

Some questions that call for a narrative are more likely to carry the dangers of the narrative response than are others. "What happened next?" is a question without limitation, except for the time of beginning. "Will you please tell us how the collision occurred?" is limited to a specific event and asks for a description. Either may be allowed or prohibited in the face of an objection that the question calls for a narrative, but the latter might carry less danger that the jurors will hear inadmissible evidence than the former, because the subject matter of the latter is known. "Will you please tell us what you know about the collision," though limited to a specific event, might carry a greater danger that the opponent cannot interpose a timely objection concerning the source of the witness' knowledge. The answer might well contain inadmissible evidence such as hearsay or opinion that the opponent cannot reasonably anticipate.

More than any other objection, the objection that a question calls for a narrative is a matter of feel and understanding of the trial judge's preferences, and Rule 611 gives the judge ample room to exercise judgment as to the most appropriate response in each situation.

§ 3.04   "Move to Strike, The Answer Is Not Responsive"

Witnesses often give narrative responses to questions that do not fairly call for a narrative and occasionally give specific answers that are not responsive to the question asked. The opposing lawyer should move to strike these answers and request an instruction to the jurors to disregard them. Although some judges maintain that the motion to strike a non-responsive answer belongs only to the lawyer asking the question, the better view is that either lawyer may make such a motion. The mistaken notion that the motion to strike as non-responsive belongs only to the questioner may have its origin in the fact that it is almost always the cross-examiner who gets a non-responsive answer and wants it stricken.

The cross-examiner uses leading questions to control what the witness can tell the jurors. Witnesses often attempt to thwart that control and offer an excuse or an explanation at the same time as their assent to a cross-examination question that does not put them or their testimony in a favorable light.

Example

Cross-examiner:	During your direct testimony you said that the Ford had the green light when it entered the intersection, didn't you?
Witness:	Yes.
Cross-examiner:	Two days after the accident you signed a statement under oath that the Chevrolet had the green light, didn't you?
Witness:	I was confused.
Cross-examiner:	Move to strike, your honor, as non-responsive, [and maybe add] and will your honor instruct the witness to answer the questions that are asked?
Judge:	The response is stricken; jurors, you are to disregard the witness' previous answer; [and

maybe, if the witness has been evasive and non-responsive to a series of cross-examination questions] and, witness, you should listen to the question and answer only what is asked. If there are explanations required, you may be asked about them on redirect examination.

The cross-examiner is using the motion to strike the non-responsive answer not so much to keep the information from the jurors, as to gain help in controlling the witness and in keeping the witness' answers to one word—"yes" or "no." Further, while the "explanation" will undoubtedly be part of the redirect examination, it may appear to be more of an after-the-fact excuse than an at-the-time reason for the difference between the testimony and the statement under oath.

A direct examiner may, also, receive non-responsive answers, but is not as likely as the cross-examiner to want the non-responsive answer stricken. The non-responsive answer is likely to be the answer to the next question or inadmissible evidence that the direct examiner cannot otherwise present to the jurors. The opponent, who will probably not object if the non-responsive answer results from a witness' innocent anticipation of the next question, will want the answer stricken if it is inadmissible evidence, if it constitutes a narrative, or if the issue of admissibility will turn on further information.

Example

Direct examiner: Did you see what happened?

Witness: I saw the Chevy speed into the intersection at the end of a yellow light and smash into the Ford.

The responsive answer to the question, "Did you see what happened," would be "yes." Neither lawyer, however, is likely to object that the answer is non-responsive, because it is a proper answer to the next question: "What did you see?"

Example

Direct examiner: What happened at the intersection of Third and Sheridan?

Witness: The Chevy sped into the intersection on a yellow light and smashed into the Ford. The driver of the Chevy was drunk.

Opponent: Move to strike that portion of the answer following "smashed into the Ford" as non-responsive and for an instruction to the jurors to disregard it.

The question did not ask for the witness' opinion about the condition of the driver of the Chevy. The part of the response that contains that opinion is non-responsive. The witness' opinion that the Chevy driver was drunk may be admissible, if the direct examiner can demonstrate that the opinion is the result of the witness' rational perception. The opponent should be entitled, however, to have the testimony struck, until the foundation for the opinion has been shown. The judge should strike the non-responsive testimony, even though it is the opponent, not the questioner, making the motion. Most judges will.

§ 3.05 "Objection, Assumes Facts Not in Evidence"

"When did you stop beating your wife?" as the first question to a witness on cross-examination, is the classic example of a question that assumes facts not in evidence. The first assumed fact is that the witness beat his wife. The second assumed fact is that he stopped.

A question that assumes facts not in evidence is particularly unfair on cross-examination. The assumed fact in the question is usually inadmissible or unavailable. Because the cross-examiner can place the fact into a leading question, there is some danger the jurors will remember the information, but not the source. In order to answer properly, the witness must make an explanation about why the assumed fact is untrue, when the form of the question does not call for an explanation. The process may make the witness appear evasive, when it is the form of the question, not the witness that is responsible for the explanation. If the direct examiner does not protect the witness by objecting to the question that assumes a fact not in evidence, the witness may seem less credible to the jurors.

Example

Plaintiff's witness in a wrongful death action came upon the accident at 12:30 in the morning. The witness was driving home from a dinner club after seeing the late show. There has been no evidence that the witness was drunk, or even drinking.

Cross-examiner:	What time was it when you were driving drunk on the loop highway?
Witness:	I wasn't drunk.
Cross-examiner:	You don't know what time it was?
Witness:	Yes, but I wasn't drunk.
Cross-examiner:	You had been drinking, isn't that right?
Witness:	No.
Cross-examiner:	You didn't have wine with dinner?

Witness:	Well, yes, but that was one glass at 7:30 in the evening.

By asking the first question, assuming the fact not in evidence—that the driver was drunk—the cross-examiner raises questions about the witness' ability to observe, because of alcohol consumption. The witness, trying to counter the assumed fact, ends up looking less than fully credible. If the direct examiner protects the witness by objecting, the witness' credibility will not be damaged.

Cross-examiner:	What time was it when you were driving drunk on the loop highway?
Direct examiner:	Objection, your honor. The question assumes a fact not in evidence.
Judge:	Sustained.
Direct examiner:	Will your honor instruct the jury that there is no basis in fact for the cross-examiner's assertion that the witness was drunk.
Judge:	Yes. Members of the jury, there has been no showing that this witness was under the influence of alcohol.

The direct examiner can, also, ask questions that assume facts not in evidence, though the opponent may not be as eager to object as when such a question is asked on cross-examination. When the direct examiner asks a question that assumes a fact not in evidence, the jurors, who have not heard the assumed fact, may be confused by the question and may not hear or understand the answer. In that circumstance, the opponent is unlikely to object and give the direct examiner an opportunity to dispel the confusion.

Example

The plaintiff's first witness is a person who saw the collision between the Ford and the Chevrolet. The person is called to the witness stand, takes the oath, and then gives name, address, and occupation.

Plaintiff's lawyer:	Where were you when the collision occurred?
Witness:	On the corner of Third and Sheridan.
Jurors:	[What collision? When? How many cars? Not much chance they will hear the witness' answer while they are trying to figure out what this is all about.]

Defense lawyer: [Does nothing and hopes the direct examiner does not remember to get back to the collision so that the jurors know what the witness is talking about.]

A direct examination question that assumes facts not in evidence is used sometimes as a means of leading a witness or of filling in facts that may not otherwise be available. The opponent will object if the evidence is important and unavailable.

Example

Police officer-witness testifies to arriving at the scene of a shooting and conducting an investigation, including the taking of photographs of the scene after the body had been removed. The pictures show some objects and some distance relationships that suggest the defendant was the shooter.

Prosecutor: After the body had been removed and everything was put back in place, did you take pictures?

Defense lawyer: Objection, your honor, assumes facts not in evidence.

In this case, where the objects and their locations are important, the picture will not be admitted, showing the objects and their relationships, unless the prosecution can show that things were moved away and replaced with great precision, when the body was moved. If care was not taken, if there were a number of officers moving things, so that no one person can say where everything was, the prosecution will not be able to make that showing. If the defense lawyer fails to object to the question that assumes the fact that "everything was put back in place," the prosecution will put valuable evidence before the jurors that would be unavailable otherwise.

Some questions that assume facts not in evidence are permissible on direct. If the fact assumed is a natural consequence of a previous answer, most judges will allow the question as a convenient way to move the testimony along.

Example

Direct examiner: Where did you go?

Witness: Into the bedroom.

Direct examiner: What did you see?

Witness: There was a body on the bed.

The question, "What did you see" assumes a fact not in evidence—that the witness saw something. Seeing something when one enters a room is a natural consequence of being in the room, absent some evidence of the unusual, such as that the room was dark, the witness was blind, or the witness' eyes were shut.

Direct examiners who are unaware that most judges will allow a question that assumes a fact of natural consequence often try to cure the problem of the assumed fact by adding an awkward and disingenuous, "if anything" somewhere in the question. "What did you see, if anything" or "what, if anything, did you see." The questions still assume that when people are wherever they are, they see things. For those concerned that some judge may disfavor a question that assumes a fact of natural consequence, an easier and less awkward sounding approach is to lead the witness with a transition question.

Example

Direct examiner: Did you see anything when you went into the bedroom? [Leading, but transitional or preliminary.]

Witness: Yes.

Direct examiner: What did you see? [No longer assumes a fact not in evidence.]

The objection that a question assumes a fact not in evidence should not be confused with the cross-examination question that asks about a specific fact not brought out during direct examination, but that is, nevertheless, within its scope. A cross-examination that brings out new facts is both proper and common.

Example

A police officer testifies on direct examination about the investigation conducted at the crime scene, but says nothing about fingerprints because none were found. The defense wishes the jury to know that the police did check for fingerprints and that the defendant's prints were not found at the scene.

Defense lawyer: You checked for fingerprints at the scene, didn't you?

Prosecutor: Objection. Assumes a fact not in evidence.

Judge: Overruled. You may answer.

Police officer: Yes.

Defense lawyer: When you checked for prints, you did not find my client's fingerprints at the scene of the crime did you?

Prosecutor: Objection. Assumes a fact not in evidence.

Judge: Overruled. You may answer.

Police officer: No.

Notice that had the second question, "When you checked for prints, you did not find my client's fingerprints at the scene of the crime did you?" been asked first, it would have improperly assumed a fact not in evidence. It would have *assumed* that the police "checked for prints"–a fact not brought out during direct examination and, without the first question, not brought out during cross-examination, either.

§ 3.06   "Objection, Argumentative"

An argumentative question is one that makes an argument to the jurors rather than posing a question to the witness.

Examples

Cross-examiner: Isn't that preposterous?

          or

Cross-examiner: Do you expect the jury to believe that you drove twenty miles home and back during the most important business day of the year solely to get your handkerchief?

"Objection, argumentative,' is the direct examiner's response to either question.

The argumentative objection often is made when counsel is harassing a witness. The harassment, however, is not the basis for the argumentative objection. The essential feature of the objection is that counsel is making an argument that should be saved for the summation. In the summation, counsel is free to draw inferences from the testimony, to characterize it as believable or ridiculous, to point out inconsistencies and improbabilities. Ordinarily, the questioning process should be limited to drawing information from the witnesses about what they observed. It should not be used to argue the believability of the testimony or the wisdom of drawing particular inferences from it.

§ 3.07   "Objection, Counsel Is Harassing the Witness"

This objection is not really about a particular question, but rather, about the cross-examiner's approach to the witness. The problem is often not the form of the question, but rather, the way the examiner is treating the witness. Cross-examination can be embarrassing, insulting, and unpleasant for the witness and still be permissible, if the questions are pertinent and not cumulative. But the cross-examiner may not make it ugly. In addition to using the kinds of questions that have an unfair form—argumentative, assume facts, and the like—harassment might include yelling at a witness, cutting off the witness' answer unreasonably, and getting up into the witness' face. Give or take a little, the objection is the equivalent of saying to the judge: "Please stop that lawyer from beating up my witness, enough is enough." Whether the objection is sustained will depend upon the judge's sensibilities.

§ 3.08   "Objection, Compound Question"

Cross-examiner:	As you approached the intersection, did you look down, change the radio station, and then look up and for the first time notice the oncoming car?
Opponent:	Objection, compound question.

§ 3.09   "Objection, Vague" (or Ambiguous or Confusing)

Direct examiner:	Did you turn left or right or not?
Opponent:	Objection, confusing.

Occasionally a question is so incomprehensible that a mere objection that the question is vague does not do the situation justice. Consider the following question and imaginative objection taken from an actual trial transcript.

Direct examiner:	When he went, had you gone and she, if she wanted to and were able, for the time being excluding all the restraints on her not to go, gone also, would he have brought you, meaning you and she, with him to the station?
Opponent:	Objection. That question should be taken out and shot.

§ 3.10   "Objection, Misstates the Evidence"

After a witness testifies on direct examination to hearing the fire truck make a noise like a foghorn, the following cross-examination occurs:

Cross-examiner:	When you first heard the fire truck siren, where were you?
Opponent:	Objection, misstates the evidence.

On cross-examination, the question that misstates the evidence can operate in the same fashion and with the same dangers as the question that assumes a fact not in evidence.

Questions that are compound, vague, or misstate the evidence exemplify the kind of question that can confuse the witness because of the form, producing answers that do not reflect what the witness knows or wants to say. While any of them might be asked as easily on direct examination as on cross-examination, they are most likely to draw objection on cross-examination. The direct examiner, who called the witness, makes the objection to protect the witness from appearing less than fully credible on cross-examination. The cross-examiner, upon hearing direct examination question that will confuse the witness, is usually pleased and unlikely to object. The unintelligible question on direct examination carries its own penalty.

§ 3.11 "Objection, Asked and Answered"; "Objection, Cumulative"

These objections both invoke the judge's discretion to prohibit questions that create a "needless consumption of time" under Rule 611 or constitute a "needless presentation of cumulative evidence" under Rule 403. They usually occur, however, in different circumstances.

The "asked and answered" objection is usually made by the direct examiner when a cross-examiner has asked the same question, or different questions about the same subject, a number of times. It is one of a number of objections that a direct-examiner uses to protect the witness from an unfair cross-examination.

Example

Cross-examiner:	You were drunk when you walked into that room, weren't you?
Witness:	No.
Cross-examiner:	You had consumed so much alcohol you didn't know where you were, isn't that right.
Direct examiner:	Objection, your honor, asked and answered.
Judge:	This is cross-examination, counselor. Overruled.
Witness:	No.
Cross-examiner:	Isn't it true that you had so much to drink that you were not even aware of what was going on.
Direct examiner:	Objection, your honor, asked and answered.
Judge:	Sustained. Move along, counsel.

The "cumulative" objection is usually made by the cross-examiner when a direct examiner has tried to drive a point home by having the witness or a succession of witnesses testify to the same thing a number of different times.

Example

Direct examiner:	What did you see at the intersection?
Witness:	I saw the Chevrolet speed into the intersection and slam into a Ford that was entering the intersection on a green light.
Direct examiner:	What color was the light for the Ford when it was entering the intersection?
Cross-examiner:	Objection, cumulative.
Judge:	Overruled.
Witness:	It was green.

[A number of intervening questions about other observations during the collision and the aftermath.]

Direct examiner:	Now what color was the light for the Ford when it entered the intersection?
Cross-examiner:	Objection, cumulative.
Judge:	Sustained.

Repeating questions on both cross and direct examinations is subject to the judge's tolerance for allowing lawyers to do things that they believe will help persuade the jurors and to the judge's patience with the pace of the trial at the time the objection is made. As a result, cross-examiners may often be allowed a couple of questions on the same subject and direct examiners are likely to be able to present important facts at least twice. When the repetition becomes obvious or the judge becomes irritated, the objection will be sustained the first time it is made.

§ 3.12 "Objection, Improper Opinion" (Calls for Speculation, or Too General)

Lay opinions rationally based upon perception and expert opinions[1] are admissible, but it does not follow that all opinion is admissible.

If a particular perception does not justify the opinion—that is, if it is not rationally based—the witness may not testify to the inference.

Direct examiner:	What was his condition?
Witness:	He was stoned on marijuana.
Cross-examiner:	Objection, improper opinion.

---

1. *See* **Ch. 10.**

Judge:	Sustained. [If the witness not only perceived the activity, but also perceived the use of marijuana preceding the activity, the opinion *might* be allowed.]
Cross-examiner:	Move to strike.

If an opinion is speculative because it is not based on perception, it is not admissible.

Direct examiner:	Where was the cow when you arrived?
Witness:	On the roof of the building.
Direct examiner:	How did it get there?
Cross-examiner:	Objection, calls for speculation.
Judge:	Sustained.

If an opinion is too broad to be helpful or can be communicated easily in more concrete terms, it may be inadmissible.

Direct examiner:	What was he doing?
Witness:	He was acting silly.
Cross-examiner:	Objection, too broad.
Judge:	Sustained.
Cross-examiner:	Move to strike.

§ 3.13 "Objection, The Document Speaks for Itself

Direct examiner:	I'm handing you what has been received in evidence as plaintiff's exhibit A. Are you familiar with it?
Witness:	Yes.
Direct examiner:	What is it?
Witness:	It's a memorandum telling the marketing department that . . .
Cross-examiner:	Objection, your honor, the document speaks for itself.

Having a witness read a document received in evidence is often the most effective way to present the information to the jury and is proper under most circumstances. Paraphrasing the document, however, can be misleading and confusing and violate Rule 403. Moreover, a paraphrase constitutes an opinion about the emphasis intended by the author of the document that, in the absence of some expertise needed for the interpretation, is not likely to be "helpful" to a jury capable of reading for itself.

§ 3.14 "Objection, Lack of Personal Knowledge"

Direct examiner: Where was Mr. Jones at 8:00 p.m. on July 12?

Cross-examiner: Objection, no showing of personal knowledge.

It may be that the witness does not know where Jones was, but it is more likely that the witness does know and the lawyer has used bad form in asking. Rule 602 provides that "[a] witness may not testify to a matter unless evidence is introduced sufficient to support a finding that the witness has personal knowledge of the matter." Had the lawyer first laid a personal knowledge foundation, there would have been no problem with the question. As it stands in the example, the judge should sustain the objection unless the direct examiner promises to establish the witness' personal knowledge.

The personal knowledge requirement is sometimes confused with the hearsay objection, because the witness' knowledge is sometimes based on what the witness heard. But the two objections are not the same. While the witness might be prepared to provide information based on what the witness heard—in which case either a hearsay or no personal knowledge objection would suffice—it may also be that the witness heard nothing and is merely engaged in speculation. If the answer is based on speculation, only the personal knowledge objection is appropriate.

§ 3.15 One Non-Objection—"Self-Serving"

"Objection, self-serving" is heard in many courtrooms. The form problem here is not with the question, but with the objection. As with "Incompetent, irrelevant, and immaterial," "self serving" is not a sufficient objection to preserve a matter for appeal. Although the "self serving" objection is often made in situations that are unlikely to produce reversible error, there are times when it will be made instead of a specific objection that would preserve an important issue for appeal.

Most evidence is "self serving." The adversary assumption is that each side presents evidence that will serve its purpose and hurt the other side. Far from being inadmissible, "self-serving" evidence is the whole idea.

There are two problems a lawyer might encounter by using the "self serving" objection. It might signal to the judge that the lawyer does not really understand the law of evidence. More importantly, it might substitute for an objection, which, if made, would preserve an important point for appeal, where the "self serving" objection may not.

The temptation to make the "self serving" objection may arise because "self serving" often describes the analytic problem with a piece of evidence, even though it does not describe the specific evidentiary problem. The specific evidentiary problem, however, is necessary to allow the judge to avoid the error by an exclusionary ruling or to allow the opponent to cure the problem or rely on other evidence.

Example

In a contest between two people who shared a house over the ownership of a painting that was assumed to be of minimal value when purchased and now is valued at $1,000,000, plaintiff calls a person who was a regular guest at the house.

Plaintiff's lawyer:	Have you ever seen what has been received in evidence as Plaintiff's exhibit #1?
Witness:	Yes.
Plaintiff's lawyer:	Under what circumstances?
Witness:	In plaintiff's bedroom. I saw it on the wall and asked plaintiff about it.
Plaintiff's lawyer:	What did the plaintiff say?
Defense lawyer:	Objection, self-serving.
Judge:	Overruled.
Witness:	The plaintiff said: "It's my favorite possession. I paid $20 dollars for it. Now it's worth a million.

The plaintiff's out-of-court statement offered to prove that the plaintiff owns the painting is hearsay. When offered by the other side, it would be an admission, not hearsay. When the party making the statement offers it, "self-serving" may be the idea, but hearsay is the specific objection that will exclude the statement.

Example

A personal injury action by automobile driver against trucking company, following a collision between driver's automobile and company's truck.

The company requires its drivers to file an accident report with the company after every incident. The statement is made immediately after the accident, if the driver is able. The statements are kept in an accident file and are reviewed regularly by the company in assessing the adequacy of its insurance, the progress of its training programs, and the position it should take in any lawsuit resulting from the incident. The report in this particular case includes the driver's recitation of the plaintiff's statement to the driver immediately after the accident: "It was my fault; I wasn't watching." The driver is no longer available to testify, so the company offers the report as a business record.

Defense lawyer:	[After laying the traditional business records foundation through the company record custodian]. Defense offers the report of the same date as the event as Defense exhibit #1.]
Plaintiff's lawyer:	Objection, self-serving.
Judge:	Overruled.

The self-serving objection will probably not preserve the matter for appeal. There is a substantial chance that the hearsay report does not fall within the business records exception to the rule against hearsay, because it does not satisfy the trustworthiness requirement of Rule 803(6). While the theory for failure to fall within the business records exception—prepared for litigation—is something akin to "self-serving,"[2] hearsay is the specific objection that will keep the report from being admitted and preserve the matter for appeal.

2. *See* Palmer v. Hoffman, 318 U.S. 109 (1943).

Chapter 4

BURDENS AND PRESUMPTIONS

Analysis

§ 4.01 Introduction

Few legal terms related to the law of evidence have engendered as much confusion as those to be considered in this brief chapter.[1] Perhaps this is partly because the entire subject of burdens of proof and presumptions is not clearly associated with any particular area of the law. The lion's share of evidence law, after all, is concerned with admissibility of particular classes of evidence, not with the *effect* that evidence has under given circumstances. Thus, evidence law does not determine which party

---

1. Referring to the confusion surrounding the term "burden of proof," one renowned evidence scholar wrote:

> Under our law the term burden of proof has been used to express two rather different ideas, and as might be expected this usage has led to a jumble. Incisive thinkers have framed a more particularized vocabulary, duly segregating the ideas, but have not managed to get their vocabulary into universal use.

John M. Maguire, Evidence: Common Sense and Common Law 175 (1947). Wigmore wrote of the "lamentable ambiguity of phrase and confusion of terminology under which our law has so long suffered." 9 John H. Wigmore, Evidence in Trials at Common Law § 2485, at 283 (James H. Chadbourn rev. 1981). McCormick's handbook calls the term presumption "the slipperiest member of the family of legal terms, except its first cousin, 'burden of proof.'" 2 McCormick on Evidence § 342, at 449 (4th ed. John W. Strong ed. 1994).

has a "burden of proof" with respect to a particular issue, nor is the *level* of that burden a function of the types of rules we normally associate with "evidence law." The same can be said for presumptions, which concern not particular classes of evidence, but the effect that certain evidence is to have if certain conditions are satisfied.

One must approach the subject with at least three understandings: (1) courts often describe issues involving burdens of proof and presumptions using variable and ill-defined terms; (2) courts often use the same term to mean different things and do not indicate clearly which meaning is intended in a particular context; and (3) even where courts have reached consensus about the meaning of certain terms, some key unresolved questions remain. With these admonitions in mind, we approach this chapter with the modest goals of setting forth some basic principles and pointing out where some of the land mines are hidden.

Although questions of "burden of proof" apply to bench trials as well as jury trials, throughout the discussion we will assume that the case is being tried to a jury.

§ 4.02 "Burden of Proof": Two Meanings

The term "burden of proof" is an umbrella term that's used to refer to both the burden of *persuasion* and the burden of *production*.[2] The burden of persuasion is a function of substantive law. It concerns the ultimate function of the factfinder, and involves two distinct things: the determination of the *quantum of evidence* (or standard of proof) required to establish an ultimate question of fact, and the *allocation of the risk* that the factfinder will not be persuaded to that prescribed degree of certainty.

The burden of production does not deal with proof in the sense of ultimate persuasion. It is of concern only to the trial judge, and its effect is expended before the case is submitted to the jury. This subcategory of "burden of proof" comes into play when one party claims that the other party has not offered sufficient evidence even to merit continuing with the case as to that issue or claim, and that the judge must grant a preemptive motion at that point. This concept is sometimes referred to as the burden of producing evidence, or the burden of "going forward," though the term burden of production will generally be used here.

§ 4.03 Burden of Persuasion

The burden of persuasion concerns the ultimate question in the trial: legally satisfactory proof of all elements of a claim or defense.[3] Two key questions related to the "burden of persuasion" must therefore be

---

2. *See* James B. Thayer, A Preliminary Treatise on Evidence at the Common Law 355 (1898); Larry L. Teply & Ralph U. Whitten, Civil Procedure 828 (1994).

3. *See* Cal. Evid. Code § 115 (1966) (using term "burden of proof" and stating

that the concept "means the obligation of a party to establish by a requisite degree of belief concerning a fact in the mind of the trier of fact or the court").

addressed any time a claim is made or a defense raised. First, to what degree must the factfinder be persuaded in order for the claim or defense to be "proven?" Second, which party must meet that burden of persuasion?

Before turning to those questions, it is necessary to stress that at law, claims or defenses are only "proven" if the factfinder believes that *each element* of the claim has been established by the requisite degree of proof. Thus, in a civil action for battery, the jury cannot find the defendant liable unless it believes that plaintiff has established each element of the claim (volitional act, unlawful intent to contact, and harmful or offensive contact)[4] by the prescribed degree of proof. If the jury is sufficiently persuaded that defendant acted volitionally and with unlawful intent, but that no contact occurred, it must find for the defendant. The same principle holds in criminal cases, and indeed more strongly; proof of each element beyond a reasonable doubt is constitutionally mandated before a person may be convicted of a crime.[5]

§ 4.04 Burden of Persuasion—Defining Burdens of Persuasion: Standards of Proof

Standards of proof exist "to instruct the factfinder concerning the degree of confidence our society thinks he should have in the correctness of factual conclusions for a particular type of adjudication."[6] Substantive law prescribes the various levels of proof that must be offered to establish particular claims or defenses–levels of confidence the factfinder must have in the correctness of the propositions at issue. Three degrees of proof are common. The first is best denoted "more likely than not," though the terms "greater weight of the evidence" and "preponderance of the evidence" are frequently used as well.[7] This is the least demanding burden to satisfy, as it requires the factfinder's mind be tipped only slightly in favor of the party with the burden. It is applied to the vast majority of civil claims and defenses. Thus, in a negligence case, plaintiff must offer enough evidence as to duty, breach, cause in fact, proximate cause, and damages to cause the jurors' minds to be tipped just slightly in favor of the existence of each element. The easiest way to understand this burden is to see it as one of risk: if after considering all the

---

4. *See* Restatement (Second) of Torts § 18 (1965).

5. In re Winship, 397 U.S. 358, 364 (1970) ("[T]he Due Process clause protects the accused against conviction except upon proof beyond a reasonable doubt of every fact necessary to constitute the crime with which he is charged.")

6. *Id.* at 370 (Harlan, J., concurring).

7. *See* Larry L. Teply & Ralph U. Whitten, Civil Procedure 828 (1994) ("In civil actions, the burden of persuasion is usually described as a requirement that there must be a *preponderance of evidence,* or that the *greater weight of the evidence*

must exist in favor of the party having the burden of persuasion. . . .") (emphasis in original). These terms can be misleading because they suggest that the jury need only be convinced of the truth of a proposition by the greater weight of the *evidence actually produced at the trial.* This quantum of evidence might not be sufficient, however, to persuade the jurors that the proposition is "more likely than not" true. *See* Norman Dorsen & Daniel A. Rezneck, *In re Gault and the Future of Juvenile Law,* Fam. L.Q. 1, 26–27 (Dec. 1967) (making similar point), quoted approvingly in *Winship,* 397 U.S. at 367–68.

evidence, the jurors either believe some element has not been proven by this amount, or are in "equipoise" (they cannot decide either way), the party with the burden of persuasion (here, plaintiff) must lose. This is why the burden of persuasion is sometimes referred to as the "risk of nonpersuasion."[8]

At the other end of the spectrum, the most onerous burden imposed by the law is that of proof "beyond a reasonable doubt," the standard applicable to criminal cases.[9] Defining the term reasonable doubt is of course difficult, and indeed there has been some debate about whether it is appropriate even to attempt to define the concept in an instruction to the jury.[10] Pattern instructions can give the flavor of "reasonable doubt,"[11] and jurisdictions have attempted to state their own definitions,[12] but in the end, the term is almost wholly subjective. Despite this lack of precision, courts scrutinize jury instructions on reasonable doubt with great care,[13] making it particularly important to frame instructions in accordance with existing statutory and judicial standards. In some jurisdictions, in fact, courts have approved of tendering no instruction defining reasonable doubt, or of instructions stating only a very general definition.[14] And in *Victor v. Nebraska*,[15] the Supreme Court approved of such an approach, holding that the Constitution does not prohibit trial courts from defining reasonable doubt nor does it require them to do so. As long as the court instructs the jury of the necessity that the prosecution prove defendant's guilt beyond a reasonable doubt, the Court held, no particular form of instruction is required.

8. *See, e.g.*, Fed. R. Evid. 301 (referring to the "burden of proof in the sense of the risk of nonpersuasion"); 9 John H. Wigmore, Evidence in Trials at Common Law § 2485 (James H. Chadbourn rev. 1981).

9. *Winship*, 397 U.S. at 364.

10. *See, e.g.*, Henry A. Diamond, Note, Reasonable Doubt: To Define or Not to Define, 90 Colum. L. Rev. 1716 (1990); Note, *Reasonable Doubt: An Argument Against Definition*, 108 Harv. L. Rev. 1955 (1995).

11. *See, e.g.*, Devitt et al., Federal Jury Practice and Instructions § 12.10 (4th ed. 1992):

> It is not required that the government prove guilt beyond all possible doubt. The test is one of reasonable doubt. A reasonable doubt is a doubt based upon reason and common sense—the kind of doubt that would make a reasonable person hesitate to act. Proof beyond a reasonable doubt must, therefore, be proof of such a convincing character that a reasonable person would not hesitate to rely and act upon it in the most important of his or her own affairs.

12. *See, e.g.*, Cal. Penal Code § 1096 (West 1985) (Reasonable doubt "is not a mere possible doubt; because everything re-lated to human affairs is open to some possible or imaginary doubt. It is that state of the case, which, after the entire comparison and consideration of all the evidence, leaves the minds of jurors in that condition that they cannot say they feel an abiding conviction of the truth of the charge.)

13. *See, e.g.*, United States v. Campbell, 874 F.2d 838, 842–43 (1st Cir.1989) (error to give instruction repeatedly using term "fair doubt"; such a term could impose a lower burden on the prosecution); Lanigan v. Maloney, 853 F.2d 40, 48 (1st Cir.1988), *cert. denied*, 488 U.S. 1007 (1989) (holding instruction stating that beyond a reasonable doubt meant "to a degree of moral certainty" constitutionally defective as potentially lightening prosecution's burden).

14. *See, e.g.*, United States v. Jorge, 865 F.2d 6, 10 (1st Cir.), *cert. denied*, 490 U.S. 1027 (1989) (Defendant claimed error in not giving instruction which contained no definition of reasonable doubt; while court affirmed conviction, it stated that "it may be prudent on the part of a trial court to consider seriously a defendant's request to define the concept only minimally, or not at all").

15. 511 U.S. 1 (1994).

A middle ground lies between "preponderance of the evidence" and "beyond a reasonable doubt." In some contexts,[16] proof must be "clear and convincing." That term, of course, is no more easily defined than the others, but it certainly falls between the extremes.[17]

§ 4.05   Burden of Persuasion—Allocating the Burden of Persuasion Between the Parties

Once the quantum of proof is defined, it remains to determine which party must "carry" that burden—which party must lose unless the jury finds that the burden has been met. This, too, is a matter of substantive rather than evidence law, and is affected by several factors. As one commentator has written:

> (1) *Caution* and *convenience* often result in the burden of proof being placed upon the party seeking change. (2) *Policy* may dictate charging one side or the other with a particular element as a means of encouraging or discouraging a given kind of litigation.... (3) *Fairness* may suggest placing the burden of an element upon the party within whose control the evidence lies.... (4) *Probabilities* may be estimated and the burden placed upon the party who will benefit by a departure from the supposed norm.[18]

Though each of these factors affect the allocation of the burden of persuasion, no one factor controls the determination. Instead, the courts appear to accord the various factors different levels of importance in different situations. As Wigmore wrote, "[t]he truth is that there is not and cannot be any one general solvent for all cases. It is merely a question of policy and fairness based on experience in the different situations."[19] Often, however, the burden is placed on the party who

---

16. For example, it is common for courts to hold that certain elements of a fraud case must be proved by clear and convincing evidence. *See, e.g.*, Kungys v. United States, 485 U.S. 759, 789 (1988) (under statute applicable to naturalization of citizens, proof of materiality of representation—that it was predictably capable of affecting decision to grant citizenship—must be shown by clear, unequivocal, and convincing evidence). Some jurisdictions provide that punitive damages cannot be awarded unless the jury makes the requisite finding by clear and convincing evidence. *See, e.g.*, Cal. Civ. Code § 3294 (West Supp. 1997) (punitive damages available if "it is proven by clear and convincing evidence that the defendant has been guilty of oppression, fraud, or malice"). *See also* Addington v. Texas, 441 U.S. 418, 431 (1979) (applying standard to civil commitment); Rosenbloom v. Metromedia, 403 U.S. 29, 52 (1971) (libel).

17. One state defines clear and convincing evidence as evidence that "leads you to a firm belief or conviction that the allegations are true. This is a higher standard of proof than proof by the greater weight of the evidence. The evidence presented need not be undisputed to be clear and convincing." N.D. Jury Instructions Civ. No. 41 (1991).

18. 1 Michael H. Graham, Handbook of Federal Evidence § 301.2, at 138 (4th ed. 1996) (emphasis in original). Wigmore listed several factors courts consider in allocating burden of persuasion: (1) the burden is on the party having the burden of pleading; (2) the burden is on the party to whose case the fact is essential; (3) the burden is on the party assumed to have "*peculiar means of knowledge*" of the facts. 9 John H. Wigmore, Evidence in Trials at Common Law § 2486 (James H. Chadbourn rev. 1981) (emphasis in original). Morgan offered a similar list. Edmund M. Morgan, *Some Observations Concerning Presumptions*, 44 Harv. L. Rev. 906, 910–11 (1931).

19. 9 Wigmore, *supra* note 18 § 2486, at 291.

wishes to disturb the status quo by asserting a claim for relief, or a party asserting an affirmative defense to a claim.[20] Thus, in a negligence case, the plaintiff has the burden of persuasion as to the elements of the prima facie case. Because the burden of persuasion is preponderance of the evidence, this means that if, after all deliberations have concluded, the jury either believes by a preponderance of the evidence that any or all elements have not been satisfied, or believes the evidence as to any or all elements is equally balanced, the jury must find for the defendant. By the same token, defendant has the burden of persuasion as to any affirmative defenses, such as contributory (or comparative) negligence. Unless the jury believes by a preponderance of the evidence that sufficient evidence has been offered to satisfy each element of the defense, it must find for the plaintiff on that issue.

The general principles just described apply regardless of the quantum of proof necessary to meet a burden of persuasion. So, in a criminal case, the prosecution bears the burden as to all essential elements of the crime.[21] The law regarding defenses is somewhat uncertain, however. There is no constitutional barrier against imposing a burden of persuasion on defendant as to certain excuses or justifications, including insanity, intoxication, and self-defense.[22] However, it is likely that principles of due process impose some limits on the gravity of the burden defendant must meet. It has been held, for example, that if the burden of proving insanity is placed on the defendant, defendant's burden cannot be greater than a preponderance of the evidence.[23] Moreover, about half the states place the burden on the prosecution to prove the defendant's sanity beyond a reasonable doubt.[24]

Once the law has placed the burden of persuasion on a party, that burden rarely shifts during the trial. In criminal cases, even in the face of overwhelming evidence of guilt, the state may never shift to the defendant the burden of persuasion as to any elements of the crime. The same is true in civil cases, with rare exceptions. One common exception holds that where two parties each acted negligently but only one caused

---

20. *See, e.g.,* Cal. Evid. Code § 500 (1966) ("Except as otherwise provided by law, a party has the burden of proof as to each fact the existence or nonexistence of which is essential to the claim for relief or defense that he is asserting.")

21. In re Winship, 397 U.S. 358 (1970). *See* 1 Wayne R. LaFave & Austin W. Scott, Jr., Substantive Criminal Law § 1.8(b) (1986).

22. *Id. See also* Medina v. California, 505 U.S. 437 (1992) (state may presume defendant competent to stand trial and require defendant to prove incompetence by preponderance of the evidence); Buzynski v. Oliver, 538 F.2d 6 (1st Cir.), *cert. denied*, 429 U.S. 984 (1976) (Maine rule requiring defendant to persuade jury of insanity by preponderance of the evidence did not deny due process).

23. Although the Supreme Court held in Leland v. Oregon, 343 U.S. 790 (1952) that a state may require a defendant to prove insanity beyond a reasonable doubt, the continuing validity of the decision is unclear. In Mullaney v. Wilbur, 421 U.S. 684 (1975), the Court held that the prosecution has the burden of overcoming a mitigating defense of heat of passion on sudden provocation beyond a reasonable doubt. And in Cooper v. Oklahoma, 517 U.S. 348 (1996), the Court held that an Oklahoma law providing that defendant is presumed competent to stand trial unless defendant proves incompetence by clear and convincing evidence violates due process.

24. *See* 1 LaFave & Scott, *supra* note 21 § 4.5.

the injury in question, the court may shift to each defendant the burden of showing that her conduct was not the cause in fact of the injury.[25] In some jurisdictions, the operation of a presumption can cause the burden of persuasion to shift.[26] Except in the case of these few exceptions, the burden of persuasion stays put.

§ 4.06   Burden of Production

The term "burden of proof" also includes a concept entirely different from the burden of persuasion. The burden of production does not define or assign the ultimate burden of convincing the jury. Instead, it is a function of the division of responsibilities between the judge and the jury; it refers to the judge's power to prevent a party from reaching the jury at all or as to particular elements of a claim or defense. The burden of production pinpoints, at key moments in the trial, whether a particular party is subject to a peremptory motion if that party does not produce further evidence to support its claim or defense. Put more simply, the party who bears the burden of production at any given point in the trial, if subjected to a motion to dismiss, a motion for directed verdict, or similar challenge, must satisfy the judge, that the party has offered sufficient evidence to merit submission of the case to the jury.[27] If that party does not convince the judge, the judge will declare that party's claim or defense unproven. Generally speaking, but not always, the burden of producing evidence begins with the party on whom the burden of persuasion falls.[28]

Because this concept is more easily understood by example than by definition, several examples follow.

Examples

P sues D for negligence following a collision between their two cars. At trial, P rests after producing evidence showing only that the two cars collided at an intersection, and that as a result of the collision, P suffered property damage and personal injury. D moves for a directed verdict. The court should grant the motion. In a negligence case, plaintiff has the burden of persuasion as to all elements of the

25. *See, e.g.,* Summers v. Tice, 199 P.2d 1 (Cal.1948) (where two negligent hunters each fired the direction of the plaintiff but only one shot caused the significant harm, burden of proof shifted to each defendant to prove that his shot did not cause that harm).

26. *See* § 4.10 (describing effect of Morgan-McCormick approach to presumptions).

27. *See* Cal. Evid. Code § 110 (1966) (defining burden of producing evidence as "the obligation of a party to introduce evidence sufficient to avoid a ruling against him on an issue"). *See also* 9 John H. Wigmore, Evidence in Trials at Common

Law § 2487, at 293 (James H. Chadbourn rev. 1981) (explaining concept).

28. *See* Cal. Evid. Code § 550 (1966) ("The burden of producing evidence as to a particular fact is initially on the party with the burden of proof as to that fact"). That this generalization is not always true is illustrated by the rule in some states that a criminal defendant who wishes to rely on the defense of insanity must both plead and initially produce evidence tending to prove insanity, but that the prosecution bears the ultimate burden of persuading the jury that the defendant was sane. *See* 1 Wayne R. LaFave & Austin W. Scott, Jr., Substantive Criminal Law § 4.5 (1986).

prima facie case (roughly speaking, duty, breach, causation, and damages). Plaintiff also has the burden of production as to each element. Because P failed to offer any evidence that the collision between the cars resulted from D's breach of a duty of reasonable care, P has not met the burden of production as to those elements. To allow the case to go forward would be to permit the jury to render a verdict based on speculation rather than evidence. This would be improper.

In the automobile collision case discussed in the previous example, P offers evidence sufficient to meet the burden of producing evidence as to all elements of the prima facie negligence case. D's answer to P's complaint alleged that the accident was partly P's fault, and that accordingly, P's recovery, if any, should be reduced by the proportion of fault attributable to P's conduct. At trial, D offers no evidence to support the comparative negligence claim, either during cross-examination of P's witnesses or during D's own case-in-chief.[29] If P moves to dismiss D's comparative negligence defense, the court must grant the motion. D had both a burden of persuasion and a burden of production as to the elements of the defense. Because D failed to produce any such evidence, the court must not permit the claim to go to the jury.

Following a barroom brawl, the state brings criminal charges against D for assault and battery. At trial, the prosecution fails to call a witness to testify that D was present in the bar at the time of the altercation. If D moves for a directed verdict at the close of the prosecution's case-in-chief, the court will grant the motion because the prosecution has failed to offer any evidence to support its contention that the person on trial was one of the participants in the brawl.

Unlike the burden of persuasion, the burden of producing evidence can shift back and forth during the trial. A party cannot cause the burden of production to shift to the opponent merely by offering evidence sufficient to meet the burden. However, the burden will shift to the opponent if the party who had the burden offers evidence strong enough to require a peremptory finding in favor of that party.[30]

The operation of the burden of production can be illustrated graphically:[31]

29. In addition, it will be assumed that D did not produce any evidence to support the claim during cross-examination of P's witnesses.

30. *See also* Larry L. Teply & Ralph U. Whitten, Civil Procedure 829 (making similar point).

31. This diagram can be found in Richard H. Field, Benjamin Kaplan, & Kevin M. Clermont, Civil Procedure: Materials For a Basic Course 672 (7th ed. 1997). It, in turn, is based on a diagram in 9 Wigmore, *supra* note 27 § 2487, at 298.

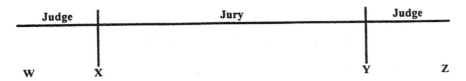

Now imagine the following case: P brings a negligence action against D following an intersection collision between their two cars. P claims D ran a red light, causing the collision. P has the burden of production as to evidence of D's negligence–in this case, that D ran a red light. At the commencement of trial, consider P's evidence to be at point W. Were P to offer no evidence of D's violation, the judge would grant D's motion for directed verdict. There being no basis for a jury finding that D was negligent (no reasonable jury could find, based on the evidence, that D was negligent) the judge's responsibility is to take the case from the jury.

Suppose, however, that P and P's friend, who was a passenger in the car, testify that P had the green light. This will likely meet P's burden of production on that issue, which moves P's evidence into the points between X and Y in the diagram. Should D move for a directed verdict at the close of P's case, the court will deny the motion because P has made out a case sufficient to reach the jury. Note that at this point, P is entitled only to reach the jury. The burden of production has not shifted to D. Even if D rested without offering any evidence to rebut the inference of negligence created by P's evidence, the judge would still let the jury decide the negligence issue. This makes very good sense. Particularly because P had an interest in the outcome, and because P's witness was an acquaintance who might have been biased in P's favor, the jury could rationally decide the case either way. This weighing of credibility is not for the judge; the judge's only role is to assess whether the evidence, if credible, could lead a rational jury to find for P on the negligence issue. If so, the case goes to the jury. This is the most common situation; the burden of production has not shifted, but has remained with P. And of course, P still has the burden of persuasion, which means convincing the jury that D was "more likely than not" negligent.

Suppose, however, that in addition to the testimony noted above, P calls a police officer who lays the foundation for admission of a videotape produced by a police camera mounted near the intersection for monitoring of traffic. The tape displays the date and time of the accident, and clearly shows P and D entering the intersection simultaneously, with the green light in P's favor. At this point, P has most likely produced sufficient evidence to move the evidence past point Y, and the burden of production will shift to D. Unless D offers evidence refuting D's illegal entry into the intersection, the court would almost certainly grant a directed verdict for P on the issue of D's negligence.[32] If D offers

---

32. *See* 2 McCormick on Evidence 1992):
§ 338, at 437 (4th ed. John W. Strong ed.

sufficient evidence to meet a burden of production on that issue, such evidence will have moved the case back between points X and Y, once again making a jury issue. On the facts, it is almost inconceivable that D could offer sufficient evidence to move the case back past point X; evidence already adduced by P remains before the jury, along with D's evidence of non-negligence.

An additional question is raised at this point: What does it take to "meet" a burden of producing evidence? For obvious reasons, this question has no quantifiable answer. As the previous discussion indicates, to satisfy the burden of production does not mean a party must offer enough evidence to *require* the jury to render a verdict in its favor on the issue. The party must merely offer evidence sufficient to *justify* a reasonable jury in rendering a verdict in its favor. Thus, if a directed verdict or similar motion is made against a party who has the burden of production, the court may grant the motion only if it finds that it would be unreasonable for the jury to decide in favor of the party with the burden.[33] If a verdict in favor of the party with the burden would be reasonable, it must deny the motion. The court does not become the factfinder on a motion to dismiss or for directed verdict; it merely decides whether only one verdict would be reasonable.

How much evidence, then, is enough? This is where no clear answer can be given. To say that "more than a scintilla" is required,[34] of course,

We have seen something of the mechanics of the process of "proceeding" or "going forward" with evidence, viewed from the point of view of the *first* party who is stimulated to produce proof under threat of a ruling foreclosing a finding in her favor. She may in respect to a particular issue pass through three states of judicial hospitality: (a) where if she stops she will be thrown out of court; (b) where if she stops and her adversary does nothing, her reception will be left to the jury; and (c) where if she stops and her adversary does nothing, her victory (so far as it depends on having the inference she desires drawn) is at once proclaimed. Whenever the first producer has presented evidence sufficient to get her to the third stage and the burden of producing evidence can truly be said to have shifted, her adversary may in turn pass through the same three stages. Her evidence again may be (a) insufficient to warrant a finding in her favor, (b) sufficient to warrant a finding, or (c) irresistible, if unrebutted.

33. One federal court wrote, in the similar context of a motion for judgment notwithstanding the verdict, that "if there is substantial evidence opposed to the [motion], that is evidence of such quality and weight that reasonable and fair-minded men in the exercise of impartial judgment might reach different conclusions, the [motion] should be denied." Boeing Co. v. Shipman, 411 F.2d 365, 374 (5th Cir.1969).

34. *See* 2 McCormick on Evidence, *supra* note 32 § 338, at 433 ("A 'scintilla' of evidence will not suffice. The evidence must be such that a reasonable person could draw from it the inference of the existence of the particular fact to be proved....") The caselaw contains many similar expressions. *See, e.g.,* United States v. Groessel, 440 F.2d 602, 606 (5th Cir.1971) (the burden of going forward means producing "more than a scintilla" of evidence; failure to do so means party is not entitled to have issue submitted to the jury). The Supreme Court has also used the term. In one case, it held that if the defendant in a civil case moves for summary judgment or directed verdict based on lack of proof of a material fact,

the judge must ask himself not whether he thinks the evidence unmistakably favors one side or the other but whether a fair-minded jury could return a verdict for the plaintiff on the evidence presented. The mere existence of a scintilla of evidence in support of the plaintiff's position will be insufficient; there must be evidence on which the jury could reasonably find for the plaintiff.

is only to utter an abstract expression, and the same is true of other similar phrases.[35] The decision can only be made in the context of each case, taking into account the state of the evidence at the time the motion is made.

More precision than this is rather difficult, though some guidance can be offered. First, most courts require that the party with the burden of production must offer some affirmative evidence of the propositions it is charged with proving–that reliance on the jury's disbelieving adverse witnesses is not enough. In *Chesapeake & O. Ry. Co. v. Martin*,[36] for example, plaintiff brought an action to recover damages for alleged misdelivery of a carload of potatoes. A crucial issue concerned the reasonableness of an eight-day delay in delivery. Plaintiff called an experienced witness who testified that forty-eight hours was a reasonable time for delivery, and this witness's testimony stood unimpeached. Nevertheless, the trial court allowed this issue to go to the jury. The Supreme Court held:

> We recognize the general rule ... that the question of the credibility of witnesses is one for the jury alone; but this does not mean that the jury is at liberty, under the guise of passing upon the credibility of a witness, to disregard his testimony, when from no reasonable point of view is it open to doubt. The complete testimony of the agent ... discloses no lack of candor on his part. It was not shaken by cross-examination; indeed, upon this point there was no cross-examination. Its accuracy was not controverted by proof or circumstances, directly or inferentially; and it is difficult to see why, if inaccurate, it readily could not have been shown to be so.[37]

The Court acknowledged that the witness was an employee of the party that called him, but held that "[i]n the circumstances ..., we are of opinion that this was not enough to take the question to the jury...."[38]

Another case illustrates the point. In *Dyer v. MacDougall*,[39] plaintiff brought a four-count complaint for libel and slander. Unfortunately, plaintiff could offer no affirmative evidence that defendant had made

---

Anderson v. Liberty Lobby, Inc., 477 U.S. 242, 252 (1986). *See also* Rodney L. Bean & Sean P. McGinley, *West Virginia's Very Own* Celotex *Trilogy: A Series of Recent Opinions By the Supreme Court of Appeals of West Virginia Reveals that the Rumors of Rule 56's Death Were Greatly Exaggerated*, 98 W. Va. L. Rev. 571, 597 (1996) (to defeat a motion for summary judgment, party "must demonstrate the ability to produce enough competent evidence at trial to enable a finding in his or her favor. A mere 'scintilla of evidence' will not suffice, nor will evidence which is 'conjectural,' 'problematic,' 'merely colorable,' or 'not significantly probative.' ") (footnotes omitted).

35. *See* Laura G. Kniaz, *Animal Liberation and the Law: Animals Board the Un-*

derground Railroad, 43 Buff. L. Rev. 765, 834 n.273 (1995) ("Across jurisdictions, the quantum of evidence required to satisfy a [criminal] defendant's burden of production have included the following standards: some evidence, more than a scintilla, slight evidence, evidence to support, some credible evidence, and evidence sufficient to raise a reasonable doubt") (citing 1 Paul H. Robinson, Criminal Law Defenses § 4(c), at 35–36 (1984)).

36. 283 U.S. 209 (1931).

37. *Id.* at 216.

38. *Id.*

39. 201 F.2d 265 (2d Cir.1952).

these statements, and defendant moved for summary judgment, supporting the motion with several affidavits and a deposition, all of which denied that the statements were ever made. Plaintiff's response to the motion was supported by affidavits the contents of which would be inadmissible at trial. Ultimately, the court granted summary judgment as to two counts, on the ground that plaintiff would have no evidence that the statements alleged in those counts were made, except the testimony of witnesses all of whom would deny their utterance.

On appeal from the dismissal of the two counts, plaintiff argued that he should be able to go to trial even without affirmative evidence because the jury would be entitled to disbelieve the evidence that no defamatory utterances had been made, and find, in fact, that the opposite was true. In other words, plaintiff wished to rely solely on the demeanor of the witnesses, and perhaps the plausibility of their testimony, to establish the truth of his claims. The Court of Appeals for the Second Circuit, Judge Hand writing for the majority, affirmed. In the court's view, failure to grant summary judgment under these circumstances would eviscerate the effectiveness of motions of this kind, as a party could always claim that a jury could find in her favor because it believed the opposing witnesses were lying and that the opposite of what they testify is true. The court was particularly struck by plaintiff's failure to exercise an opportunity to depose several witnesses prior to trial. *Dyer* thus tells us that satisfying a burden of production at trial means offering some affirmative evidence to support the allegations of the complaint.[40]

The rule in *Dyer* is followed by most courts,[41] although a few cases suggest that a witness's demeanor and the content of the witness's testimony can, in some instances, suffice to meet a burden of production.[42] Moreover, in *Dyer* itself, Judge Frank offered a persuasive argu-

40. *See also* Teply & Whitten, *supra* note 30, at 829 ("To satisfy the burden of production, a party must ordinarily introduce some affirmative evidence that the fact in question has occurred"). Although *Dyer* arose in the summary judgment context, rather than on a motion for directed verdict, the standards to be applied by the trial judge are essentially the same. *See id.* at 786.

41. "[T]here is virtual unanimity among the courts that have addressed the issue that a fact finder may not base its finding of fact on disbelief of a witness. The party with the burden of proof must introduce affirmative evidence to sustain its burden." J. Palmer Lockard, *Summary Judgment in Pennsylvania: Time for Another Look at Credibility Issues*, 35 Duq. L. Rev. 625, 682 (1997).

42. *See, e.g.,* In re Melnick, 360 F.2d 918, 920 (2d Cir.1966) (in bankruptcy proceeding in which debtor had burden of proving he did not knowingly and fraudu-

lently make a false oath as to a material matter, referee entitled to disbelieve debtor's testimony); Morrison v. Lefevre, 592 F.Supp. 1052, 1065 (S.D.N.Y.1984) (in civil rights action against prison officials arising from alleged planting of contraband, testimony of three defendants who "found" contraband established that one of them planted it, even though they did not so testify; court held that "[t]he stories told by the three officers and their demeanor on the stand strongly support the inference that they were responsible for 'planting' and then 'discovering the vial of florescent fluid. As Judge Learned Hand observed in Dyer v. MacDougall, . . .' a witness' implausible denials can lead a court to infer the true state of affairs. . . .'"); In re Bebar, 315 F.Supp. 841 (E.D.N.Y.1970) (similar). Note that because none of these cases involved jury trials, the propriety of directed verdicts was not in issue. Nevertheless, the courts' actions demonstrate a willingness to accept that a proposition may be sufficiently estabment that demeanor could, in some cases, suffice to allow a party to reach the jury:

> One can imagine a case in which a man would suffer a grave injustice, if it were the invariable rule that a plaintiff can never win a case when (1) he can offer only the oral testimony of the defendant, the one available witness, which is flatly and unswervingly against the plaintiff but (2) the jury (in a jury trial) or the judge (in a judge trial) is thoroughly convinced by the witness' demeanor that he is an unmitigated liar. On that account, I would oppose such a rule.[43]

In several opinions issued in 1986, the Supreme Court has signaled its strong support for the judge's power to grant summary judgment against the party who had the burden of production.[44] Though the Court may not have wished to increase plaintiffs' burden on summary judgment substantially,[45] the cases do demonstrate the Court's commitment to the trial court's close analysis of the allegations and proof, and the

---

lished even in the absence of affirmative evidence.

Some scholars have supported such an argument. *See, e.g.*, Richard D. Friedman, *Route Analysis of Credibility and Hearsay*, 96 Yale L.J. 667, 742 n.134 (1987) ("Indeed, it may be that in some cases a factfinder may find a proposition to be true solely on the basis of a witness' demeanor in testifying to the contrary of that proposition"); Edmund Morgan, *Admissions*, 12 Wash. L. Rev. 181, 185–86 (1937). *See also* Olin Guy Wellborn, III, *Demeanor*, 76 Cornell L. Rev. 1075, 1102 (1991) (distinguishing between relying on demeanor and relying on the content of the testimony itself to establish facts contrary to the witness's testimony).

43. *Dyer*, 201 F.2d at 272 (Frank, J., concurring). Judge Frank believed that the case at hand was not such a case, because in the relevant counts, plaintiff claimed to have been slandered in his absence and in the presence of only two other persons, both of whom would deny the slander. Thus, "only plaintiff's own suit serves to publicize the alleged slander." *Id.* In his majority opinion, Judge Hand also pointed out that plaintiff had failed to avail himself of the opportunity to depose the witnesses prior to trial. *Id.* at 267.

44. Anderson v. Liberty Lobby, Inc., 477 U.S. 242 (1986) (in libel action where plaintiffs were required to demonstrate actual malice, trial court properly granted summary judgment for defendants where defendants produced affidavit of author-employee detailing quality of research and variety of sources used in the articles; even though plaintiffs submitted affidavits demonstrating numerous inaccuracies in the stories and that several of defendants' sources were unreliable, the trial court must consider the heavy burden on plaintiffs of showing actual malice, and plaintiffs' showing was insufficient to defeat motion); Celotex Corp. v. Catrett, 477 U.S. 317 (1986) (in wrongful death action alleging exposure to asbestos manufactured by defendant, district court properly granted summary judgment where plaintiff was unable to produce evidence of exposure to defendant's products; after adequate time for discovery, party with burden of proof must be able to make showing sufficient to establish existence of element, and in the absence of such a showing, defendant was not obligated to come forward with materials outside the pleadings to negate plaintiff's claim); Matsushita Electric Industrial Co. v. Zenith Radio Corp., 475 U.S. 574 (1986) (in antitrust action alleging conspiracy to raise, fix, and maintain artificially high prices for television sets in Japan and artificially low prices for sets in United States, district court properly granted summary judgment for defendant on ground plaintiffs did not raise genuine issue of material fact; in antitrust action, plaintiff must present evidence showing that inference of conspiracy is reasonable, and the nature of predatory pricing conspiracies is such that defendants had no plausible motive to engage in conspiracy charged in complaint).

45. *See* Eastman Kodak Co. v. Image Technical Servs., Inc., 504 U.S. 451, 468–69 (1992) (*Matsushita* did not introduce special burden on plaintiffs in antitrust cases, but economic theory relied upon by plaintiffs in proving violation must not be "senseless").

need for the plaintiff to rely on meaningful evidence to support its claims. Because of the similarity of the standard for granting summary judgment and directed verdict,[46] these cases lend considerable support to the same conclusion in regard to motions for directed verdict. Thus, meeting a burden of production in modern civil litigation almost certainly means offering affirmative evidence to support one's claims.

A series of examples can illuminate somewhat further the problem of when a party has met a burden of production. Suppose P is a child who suffers from a form of leukemia. P sues the power company, claiming that its the illness was caused by electromagnetic fields (EMFs) generated by high tension lines 100 feet from P's home. There is no contest about the existence of P's illness; the only substantial issue in the case concerns causation. To prove causation, suppose P offers the following evidence:

1. Testimony that two children living in P's neighborhood have contracted this form of leukemia in the thirty years since the high tension lines were installed, compared with only one in the thirty years before installation.

2. A published study showing that worldwide, the incidence of this type of leukemia is ten percent higher among children living in homes within 100 feet of high tension lines than among children living further away.

3. A controlled scientific study demonstrating that laboratory rats exposed to EMFs have a greater incidence of a similar disease than do rats raised in an identical environment without EMF exposure.

If P only offers the evidence described in 1. above, and D moves for a directed verdict, the court almost certainly should grant it. Though it is not utterly irrational to causally relate the EMFs with the leukemia cases, the fallacy of *post hoc ergo propter hoc* applies to remind us that a correspondence between two events does not mean the first event caused the second. For the court to allow the jury to render a verdict for P on such speculative evidence almost certainly would be incorrect. P has not met the burden of production on the issue of causation.[47]

The evidence described in 2. above is somewhat stronger, though also fairly speculative. Leukemia, as with other forms of cancer, can be caused by many environmental and hereditary factors. Without any

---

46. *See supra* note 40.

47. A directed verdict for D might be justified for another reason. Given that there are, in fact, scientific studies studying the existence or nonexistence of a link between EMFs and childhood leukemia, it seems appropriate to place on P the burden of presenting evidence of those studies, and forcing P to bear the consequences of an ill-prepared case. *See, e.g.,* Smith v. Rapid Transit, Inc., 58 N.E.2d 754 (Mass.1945) (plaintiff's testimony that bus causing her to strike a parked car was a "great big, long, wide affair," and that defendant's buses were the only ones authorized to operate on that street at that time of night was insufficient to overcome defendant's motion for directed verdict; plaintiff's failure to develop any further evidence, such as testimony from bystanders or bus passengers, might have motivated court to affirm judgment for defendant).

effort to demonstrate that the children in the worldwide study constitute a valid proxy for P, the jury would again be speculating about the validity of the evidence for P's case. An appellate court would likely affirm a directed verdict for D.

The evidence described in 3. above is more probative and to the point in one sense: it would support the rational conclusion that EMFs *can* cause cancer, at least in laboratory animals. If the court finds that animal studies are relevant indicators of effects on humans,[48] the evidence probably will be admissible under the *Daubert* standard, and the evidence would satisfy at least one aspect of P's burden of production as to causation–that EMFs are capable of causing cancer. However, does the evidence advance the proposition that EMFs caused P's leukemia in this case? This is a more difficult proposition, as it is in many toxic tort cases, in which direct evidence of causation is elusive at best. It is likely that a ruling either way on D's motion for directed verdict would be affirmed on appeal.

Some further possibilities, also based on the EMF-leukemia example, are also instructive about the quantum of proof necessary to satisfy a burden of production. First, assume that P offers the evidence described in each of the scenarios listed above, and that the court denies D's motion for directed verdict. Now, in its case-in-chief, D calls an expert to testify to the existence of ten other published studies of the effects of EMFs on animals, none of which demonstrated any statistically meaningful correlation between EMF exposure and elevated levels of cancer.[49] If D renews its motion for directed verdict, what should the court do? The state of the causation evidence appears to be overwhelmingly against P. Only a single study reached a conclusion favorable to P's position; a mountain of studies stands against it. In such a case, the risk of inferential error is likely too great to justify allowing the jury to decide for P. Though it is always possible that P's allegations are true, a directed verdict would likely be required.[50]

48. For discussion of the *Daubert* test for admissibility of scientific evidence, see **§ 10.04**.

49. We will assume that all studies presented by both parties were conducted by reputable scientists whose funding derived from sources with no financial stake in their outcome.

50. *Cf.* Pennsylvania R. Co. v. Chamberlain, 288 U.S. 333 (1933). Plaintiff brought suit against a railroad to recover for the death of a brakeman struck by train cars. Plaintiff claimed that the accident was caused by the violent collision of one string of cars with the string on which the deceased was riding. At trial, three employees riding on the other string of cars testified that no collision occurred, and they were corroborated by all other employees in a position to see the event. The only witness favorable to plaintiff on this issue testified to hearing a loud crash and to seeing the two strings of cars together shortly afterward. The witness was standing 900 feet from where the deceased's body was found, and his angle of vision to the possible crash was such that he would not have been able to determine whether the two strings of cars were actually in contact. The district court directed a verdict for defendant. The Court of Appeals reversed, but the Supreme Court reinstated the judgment for defendant. The Court held that the testimony of plaintiff's witness was "wholly circumstantial, and the inferences which might otherwise be drawn from it were shown to be utterly erroneous unless all of petitioner's witnesses were willful perjurers." *Id.* at 338. The Court held that the evidence did not even raise a conflict: "It, of course, is true, generally, that where there is a direct conflict of testimony upon a matter of fact,

As discussed above, failure to offer evidence sufficient to meet a burden of production will result in the granting of a peremptory motion, generally leading to the dismissal of a claim or defense. Of course, the court has discretion to grant the party's motion to reopen its case to offer additional evidence if it believes that the interests of justice would be served by doing so.

§ 4.07 Presumptions; Introduction

The word "presumption" has perhaps suffered from more misuse and inconsistent use than any other evidentiary term. The next several sections will distinguish true presumptions from other devices and concepts, and will then explain how presumptions operate. Throughout, it will be the conventional wisdom that is presented.[51] Despite the articulation of arguments that there is no need for a distinct law of presumptions,[52] courts and commentators continue to use the term, and the language of presumptions is likely to be with us for the foreseeable future.

§ 4.08 Presumptions; Introduction—Presumptions Defined and Distinguished from Other Devices

A presumption is a rule providing that proof of a designated fact has a predetermined effect in establishing the existence of another fact. It thus expresses a legal relationship between certain facts (what we will call the "foundational" or "basic" facts) proved by a party and certain other facts (what we will call the "presumed facts").[53]

the question must be left to the jury to determine, without regard to the number of witnesses upon either side. But here there really is no conflict in the testimony as to the facts. The witnesses for petitioner flatly testified that there was no collision between the nine-car and the two-car strings. [Plaintiff's witness] did not say there was such a collision. What he said was that he heard a 'loud crash,' which did not cause him at once to turn, but that shortly thereafter he did turn and saw the two strings of cars moving together with the deceased no longer in sight...." *Id.* at 338–39.

51. *See, e.g.,* Fleming James, Jr. et al., Civil Procedure § 7.17 (4th ed. 1992); 2 McCormick on Evidence § 345 (4th ed. John W. Strong ed. 1994).

52. *See, e.g.,* Ronald J. Allen, *Presumptions, Inference and Burden of Proof in Federal Civil Actions—An Anatomy of Unnecessary Ambiguity and a Proposal for Reform,* 76 Nw. U.L. Rev. 892 (1982); Ronald J. Allen, *Presumptions in Civil Actions Reconsidered,* 66 Iowa L. Rev. 843 (1981) (arguing that presumption concept is artificial and should be replaced by a direct approach allocating burdens of proof and allowing careful judicial comment on evidence, and

that where proof adduced at trial is sufficiently strong to require shifting or reassigning a burden of persuasion, this can be done by means of a "conditional imperative"); Edward W. Cleary, *Presuming and Pleading: An Essay on Juristic Immaturity,* 12 Stan. L. Rev. 5 (1959) (suggesting elimination of concept of presumptions that transfer burden of proof). *But see* Kenneth S. Broun, *The Unfulfillable Promise of One Rule for All Presumptions,* 62 N.C. L. Rev. 697 (1984) (recognizing validity of argument that courts should discuss propriety of allocating burdens rather than technical application of presumptions, but noting that presumption concept is unlikely to be displaced and that "conditional imperative" suffers from same difficulties as current presumption language).

53. *See* Cal. Evid. Code § 600(a) (1966) ("A presumption is an assumption of fact that the law requires to be made from another fact or group of facts found or otherwise established in the action"). McCormick's handbook states that "a presumption is a standardized practice, under which certain facts are held to call for uniform treatment with respect to their effect as

A "true" presumption is rebuttable by evidence to the contrary of the presumed facts. When it is not rebutted, it is deemed conclusive in the sense that the jury will be informed that the fact at issue is proven. It is not that the law no longer demands that the underlying (presumed) fact be proven, but that the presumed fact should be deemed proven in the absence of contrary evidence.

A few examples will clarify the nature of true (rebuttable) presumptions.

Examples

A presumption states that a letter properly addressed, stamped, and deposited in an appropriate receptacle is presumed to have been received in the ordinary course of the mail.[54] Unless the presumption created by this rule is rebutted, the properly addressed, stamped, and deposited letter will be deemed to have been received in what is considered to be the ordinary amount of time needed in that delivery area.

A presumption states that money delivered to another person is presumed to have been due to that person.[55] Unless the presumption is rebutted, if delivery is proven, the money will be deemed to have been owed to the person to whom it was delivered.

A presumption provides that a writing is presumed to have been accurately dated.[56] Unless the presumption is rebutted, the writing in question will be deemed accurately dated.

Note that if a true presumption is not rebutted, the factfinder might be required to make a factual conclusion that does not accord with reality. The properly addressed, stamped, and mailed letter might actually not have been received in what is considered to be the ordinary course of the mail. The money delivered might have been a gift rather than payment of a debt. The writing might have been dated incorrectly. Nevertheless, this is the essential effect of presumptions, and the thing that separates them from mere inferences; if not rebutted, they will require a factual finding even if that finding is contrary to reality.

Just as several reasons support the law's determination to assign a burden of persuasion to one party or another, presumptions are also created for a variety of reasons. Among them are *fairness*—to "correct an imbalance resulting from one party's superior access to the proof."[57] Some presumptions are supported by reasons of *substantive policy*–to encourage or discourage certain "primary" (non-litigation) behavior, or

proof of other facts." 2 McCormick on Evidence § 342, at 449 (4th ed. John W. Strong ed. 1994).

54. *See* Legille v. Dann, 544 F.2d 1 (D.C.Cir.1976).

55. *See* Cal. Evid. Code § 631 (1966).

56. *See* Cal. Evid. Code § 640 (1966).

57. 2 McCormick on Evidence, *supra* note 53 § 343, at 454. An example would be the presumption that as between connecting carriers of goods, damage occurred while the goods were in the possession of the last carrier. *Id.* at n.4, citing Chicago & North Western Ry. Co. v. C.C. Whitnack Produce Co., 258 U.S. 369 (1922).

to effectuate a goal of the law.[58] Some presumptions are created simply to *resolve issues* otherwise difficult to resolve because of the absence of proof.[59] The most common reason for creating presumptions, however, is simply the *facilitation of the litigation process* by resolving matters in accordance with *high probability*. In other words, most presumptions are created for situations in which the presumed fact is very likely to be true. This both streamlines the process of proof of the fact and avoids the factfinding distortion that might occur were the jury to decide that the fact is not true.[60]

Individual presumptions often exist for a combination of reasons. For example, the common presumption that a person not heard from in a certain period of years is dead[61] does indeed facilitate proof of the person's death where the risk of error is slight, but it also does more. It reflects a social policy that the affairs of people who have been missing for a period of years should be wrapped up without the necessity of burdensome (and often practically unavailable) proof. Similarly, the presumption that a ceremonial marriage is valid[62] both facilitates proof that a marriage is lawful and effectuates a policy that the marriage of people who go through a marriage ceremony should not be subject to question except in unusual cases. Also, the common presumption that the official actions by public officers were regularly and legally performed[63] exists because the probability of regular and legal performance is high, because it is often difficult for a public official who conducts a great deal of repetitive business to remember exactly how the act at issue was performed, and because people should be confident that officials perform their duties correctly. Even the presumption of receipt of mail in the regular course is supported by more than probability; the presumption also facilities proof where, as is often true, the postal worker cannot be expected to remember delivering a particular piece of mail at a particular time.

Further support for the multi-faceted rationale for presumptions is provided by the existence of some presumptions in situations in which a logical inference would be difficult to draw—or, more precisely, where the probative value of the evidence is very slight. For example, the presumption that the driver of an automobile was the agent of the owner

---

58. A common example is the presumptions of the death of a person not heard from for a specified period of years, which serves the goal of settling issues of title and of estates. *See, e.g.,* Cal. Evid. Code § 667 (1966).

59. 2 McCormick on Evidence, *supra* note 53 § 343, at 454 (giving as an example presumptions resolving questions of who survived longest in a common disaster). Presumptions in Title VII employment discrimination cases are an important contemporary example. *See, e.g.,* Price Waterhouse v. Hopkins, 490 U.S. 228 (1989) (holding that once plaintiff proved that firm's failure to promote her to partner was motivated in part by her gender, burden of persuasion was placed on defendant to demonstrate lack of unlawful discrimination).

60. 2 McCormick on Evidence, *supra* note 53 at 454–55. For an illustrative list of such presumptions, *see* Cal. Evid. Code §§ 630–647 (1966).

61. *See, e.g.,* Cal. Evid. Code § 667 (1966) (five years); Green v. Royal Neighbors of America, 73 P.2d 1 (1937 (seven years).

62. *See, e.g.,* Cal. Evid. Code § 663 (1966).

63. *See* Cal. Evid. Code § 664 (1966).

exists where a rational inference is possible, but the probative value of the inference is often sufficiently slight that, in the absence of an agency presumption, the plaintiff will likely face dismissal of the claim against the owner. If presumptions only existed in situations where the probability of the presumed fact is high, the agency presumption would not exist.

True presumptions must be distinguished from other concepts, including the permissive inference and the "conclusive presumption."[64] A permissive inference is a factual conclusion that the factfinder *may*, but is not required to, draw from another fact or group of facts.[65] An inference is based on simple everyday logic—the factfinder's application of everyday experience to determine the likelihood that a given fact is true. Thus, one may infer that a person whose usual practice is to fasten the automobile seat belt did so on the relevant occasion. Similarly, one may infer that marks on a person's body matching the teeth of a particular dog living next door were made by the dog.

Note that inferences may not always be accurate. The driver might not have worn the seat belt on the occasion in question; the dog might not have bitten the person. But in each case, it is logical to assume, given the facts stated, that the events happened as initially indicated. In each case the court would not require the jury to reach a given conclusion; unless the evidence was so one-sided as to require the conclusion, the jury will be permitted to draw the inference but will not be compelled to do so. These types of inferences, then, are purely permissive in nature.

True presumptions must also be distinguished from so called "conclusive presumptions" or "irrebuttable presumptions." These devices are not actually presumptions at all, even though they operate in a mandatory fashion and even though they express a relationship between certain basic facts and a presumed fact. Instead, they are rules of law that change the nature of the facts needed to be proven. A few examples will demonstrate the nature of "conclusive presumptions."

Examples

A statute provides that except as provided in a separate statute, "the child of a wife cohabiting with her husband, who is not impotent or sterile, is conclusively presumed to be a child of the marriage."[66] This statute means that the biological facts are no longer important to the law. If a husband and wife are cohabiting, and if the husband is not impotent or sterile, the child is presumed to be the child of the marriage. Unless an exception applies, no evidence to the contrary would be admissible.

64. Another concept to be distinguished is the so-called "permissive presumption," a term the United States Supreme Court has used in the context of criminal cases, which raise special issues regarding presumptions. *See* § 4.15.

65. *See* Cal. Evid. Code § 600(b) (1966) ("An inference is a deduction of fact that may logically and reasonably be drawn from another fact or group of facts found or otherwise established in the action").

66. Cal. Fam. Code § 7540 (1994). *See also* In re Findlay, 170 N.E. 471, 473 (N.Y. 1930).

A statute provides that "[t]he facts recited in a written instrument are conclusively presumed to be true as between the parties thereto, or their successors in interest; but this rule does not apply to the recital of a consideration."[67] What this rule means is that unless the issue concerns consideration, all that matters is the facts recited in the written instrument. The law is no longer concerned about the "true" facts, and proof of those facts will not be heard.

A criminal statute provides that "[a] defendant who does not plead not guilty by reason of insanity shall be conclusively presumed to have been sane at the time of the commission of the offense charged...."[68] As a result of this rule, even a person who fails to meet the test for insanity under that state's law would be considered sane for purposes of the trial if she did not plead not guilty by reason of insanity.

"Conclusive presumptions" are not evidentiary devices. They are not evidence rules at all. They are new rules of substantive law. In virtually every case, they exist because of a policy-based determination that the existence of certain facts should establish a factual issue and that society would not be served by permitting contrary evidence. In the examples given above, this is easiest to understand with respect to the presumption of paternity. This presumption represents a legislative judgment that the legitimacy of children born under the specified circumstances should not be subject to challenge. In all likelihood, such a presumption is created in order to protect such children from ridicule or from the domestic battles of their now-estranged parents. Thus, while other legal issues concerning custody and support must still be resolved in circumstances involving paternity, the father's initial responsibility for the child will be beyond question. The presumption thus establishes a new substantive rule: that a child born to a married woman cohabiting with her husband, who is not impotent or sterile, is entitled to inherit from the mother's husband whether or not the child is the biological child of the husband.

§ 4.09 Presumptions; Introduction—Causing Presumptions to Take Effect

A presumption does not come into being in a given case until the party seeking to employ it has "proven" its foundational facts. Proof involves two steps. First, the party seeking to take advantage of the presumption must offer evidence sufficient to meet a burden of production as to each foundational fact. It is up to the trial court to determine whether this has occurred. Unless the opponent offers evidence that overwhelmingly rebuts those facts, the party using the presumption is entitled to reach the jury for a determination of the existence of those facts. The second step is the jury's decision whether the foundational facts are indeed true. If the proponent passes both steps, the presump-

---

67. Cal. Evid. Code § 622 (1966).   **68.** Cal. Penal Code § 1016 (1985).

tion comes into being. It will then have conclusive effect in the litigation unless the presumption is "rebutted."

A simple example will illustrate how presumptions come into being. Suppose P, a second-floor tenant in D's apartment building, suffers a fall on a dark stairway leading to the second floor. P sues D, the building's owner, claiming that D failed to maintain the stairway in a reasonably safe condition because several of its lights did not work. To prove notice to D of the stairway's condition, P wishes to prove that two weeks before the accident, she mailed a letter to D, who lived in the building, informing D that several of the lights in the stairway no longer worked.[69] At trial, P testifies that she addressed the letter properly, placed a first-class stamp on it, and took it to a United States Postal Service receptacle around the corner from the apartment building. P also offers testimony that letters sent from one address to another in the city normally arrive within two days.

As described, the testimony offered by P is sufficient to meet a burden of production as to each foundational fact necessary to raise the common presumption that a letter properly addressed, stamped, and mailed was received in the ordinary course of the mail. In the absence of substantial contrary evidence concerning those facts,[70] the court will instruct the jury that if it finds that those facts are true,[71] it must find that D received the letter well before the accident.

§ 4.10 Presumptions; Introduction—Rebutting Presumptions

How does one go about "rebutting" a presumption? The simple answer is by offering evidence attacking either its foundational (basic) facts or the presumed fact. The reality is somewhat more complicated.

A party against whom a presumption would operate actually has several choices. The party may:

1. offer no evidence challenging the existence of either the foundational facts or the presumed fact;

2. offer evidence challenging the existence of only the foundational fact;

3. offer evidence challenging the existence of only the presumed fact; or

69. Notice to D of the defect would make D's failure to repair the condition more likely unreasonable.

70. To prevent the issue from going to the jury, D will have to offer evidence not merely strong enough to meet a burden of production as to the nonexistence of the foundational facts, but so strong as to require that finding. This will not often occur, though one might imagine that if D asks the court to take judicial notice that there was a nationwide postal strike stopping all mail delivery during the entire relevant period, the court would hold that P did not notify D of the alleged defect in the manner to which P testified.

71. We are assuming at this point that D does not offer evidence attacking *receipt* of the letter. For discussion of what happens if D does offer evidence attacking the presumed fact, see § 4.10.

4. offer evidence challenging the existence of both the foundational and presumed fact.

To illustrate the consequences of these choices, the hypothetical discussed in the previous section, involving P's letter to D warning of the darkness of the stairway, will be used.

Challenging Neither Foundational Nor Presumed Facts

Suppose first that D chooses not to offer evidence challenging either the foundational facts (addressing, stamping, depositing) or the presumed fact (D's receipt of the letter well before the plaintiff's accident). In this situation, the court will simply instruct the jury that if it finds the foundational facts to be true, it *must* find that D received the letter in the ordinary course (about two days after P mailed it). Of course, P has the burden of persuasion as to these facts, because they form part of the basis of P's prima facie negligence case against D.[72] And P also has the burden of producing evidence of those facts.[73] But as long as P's evidence is sufficient to meet her burden of production, the question of the existence of the foundational facts will be for the jury. If the jury is even slightly more persuaded of the existence of the foundational facts than of their nonexistence, P will have met the burden of persuasion, and the jury must find that D received the letter well before the accident (thus making D more likely negligent in failing to take precautionary steps).

In the absence of evidence from D of the nonexistence of either the foundational or presumed facts, there are two possible outcomes: (1) In most instances, P will only have to meet a burden of production as to the existence of the foundational facts. This means that the court will merely leave the question of the foundational facts to the jury. This is the likely result in our hypothetical, where P's evidence, though compelling on the surface, comes from a witness (P) with an interest in the outcome of the case. Thus, it would not be irrational for the jury to disbelieve P, and find that the foundational facts are not true. (2) In some cases, the evidence of the existence of the foundational facts will be so strong as to compel a finding of their existence, and thus of the presumed fact. So, in the hypothetical case, assume that P's evidence of each of the foundational facts includes testimony from unimpeached, disinterested witnesses.[74] In such a case, P would be entitled either to a directed verdict as to an element of the case, or a binding jury instruction requiring the jurors to make a certain factual finding.[75]

---

72. *See* § 4.05.

73. *See id.*

74. For example, suppose P claims to have sent the letter by registered mail. To establish mailing to the correct address, P offers in evidence a telephone book listing D's address and a postal receipt showing that the letter, addressed to the same address, was deposited in the post office on a date two weeks before the accident.

75. *See, e.g.,* Chesapeake & O. Ry. Co. v. Martin, 283 U.S. 209 (1931) (where question concerned reasonableness of eight-day delay in delivery, trial court erred in failing to direct verdict on basis of witness's unimpeached, uncontradicted testimony that forty-eight hours was a reasonable time; even though witness was employed by party calling him, this was not enough to raise a jury question). In the hypothetical case, the

Challenging Only Foundational Facts

If D chooses only to challenge the existence of the foundational (basic) facts, the consequences are similar. Suppose, then, that D testifies that there is no United States Postal Service mailbox around the corner from the apartment building, or that P was on vacation out of state for more than a week beginning on the day P claims to have mailed the letter. In this instance, the court will almost certainly allow the jury to determine whether the foundational facts exist, and instruct the jury that if it finds that the facts do indeed exist, it *must* find that the letter was received in the ordinary course. Because D has done nothing to challenge the existence of the presumed fact—his receipt of the letter—the presumption will come into play and mandate a finding of receipt if proper addressing, stamping, and mailing are proven by the preponderance of the evidence.[76]

Challenging Only Presumed Fact

There is a long-standing debate about what happens when the party against whom the presumption would operate challenges the existence of the presumed fact.[77] To take our hypothetical as the starting point, suppose D does not challenge P's proper addressing, stamping, and mailing of the letter, but offers testimony to support a contention that he never received the letter. For example, D might testify that he picked up and read his mail diligently each day from the date on which P claims to have mailed the letter until the date of the accident, and that he never saw the letter. What happens to the presumption now? There are two distinct views, each associated with respected evidence scholars.

(1) The Thayer–Wigmore "bursting bubble" theory. If presumptions are nothing more than devices that facilitate proof and help to ensure that the correct factual conclusions are reached where the risk of error is very slight,[78] presumptions should have no effect once "rebutted" with evidence challenging the presumed fact. This was the view of the Missouri court, which in 1906 wrote that presumptions are "like bats of the law flitting in the twilight, but disappearing in the sunshine of actual facts."[79] This position also gave rise to the "bursting bubble" theory of presumptions, usually associated with Thayer,[80] and supported by Wig-

---

most likely outcome would be a jury instruction telling the jurors to assume that D received the letter more than a week in advance of the accident. Such notice, in turn, would increase the likelihood that the jury would find D to have been negligent in failing to remedy the danger before the accident.

76. In light of D's testimony attacking the foundational facts, there is virtually no chance that the court will instruct the jury to find that the foundational facts are true.

77. "The problem of the effect of a presumption when met by proof rebutting the presumed fact has literally plagued the courts and legal scholars." 2 McCormick on Evidence § 344, at 461 (4th ed. John W. Strong ed. 1994).

78. For discussion of the purposes of presumptions, *see* § **4.08**.

79. Mackowik v. Kansas City, St. Josephs & Council Bluffs R. Co., 94 S.W. 256, 262 (Mo.1906).

80. James B. Thayer, A Preliminary Treatise on Evidence at the Common Law ch. 8 (1898).

more[81] (though the positions of both authors were actually somewhat different from the pure "bursting bubble" theory).[82] The theory holds that a presumption does no more than shift to the opponent the burden of producing evidence, not the burden of persuasion. And when the opponent offers evidence sufficient to meet that burden of production, the presumption disappears from the case entirely. In other words, a presumption has spent its currency once proof is offered sufficient to meet a burden of production as to the nonexistence of the presumed facts—that is, sufficient to support a finding that the presumed fact is not true.

Under the "bursting bubble" theory, the disappearance of the presumption means that the jury should not be apprised about the presumption.[83] However, note the state of the evidence in our hypothetical: P has offered evidence concerning proper addressing, stamping, and mailing a warning letter. D has offered evidence that he never received the letter. If there had never been a presumption in the case, the jury would simply apply its sense of logic and experience and determine, as a matter of permissive inference, whether P mailed and D received a letter concerning the dark stairway. It would hardly be unreasonable to reach such a conclusion, nor would it be unreasonable in some cases to conclude that D did not receive any such letter. The same procedure applies under the "bursting bubble" theory; the question of D's receipt of a letter from P is simply left to the jury as a matter of logical inference. This being the case, there is no more reason to instruct the jury about applying its reasoning powers to this evidence than there is with respect to any other disputed fact; the jury will simply decide, guided by argument of counsel.[84]

Even under the "bursting bubble" theory of presumptions, it is possible that the evidence offered by the party against whom the

---

81. 9 John H. Wigmore, Evidence in Trials at Common Law § 2491(2) (James H. Chadbourn rev. 1981).

82. Thayer was not so unequivocal about the disappearance of presumptions upon the admission of evidence contradicting the presumed fact. *See* 2 McCormick on Evidence, *supra* note 77 § 344, at 462 n.7; 21 Charles A. Wright & Kenneth W. Graham, Jr., Federal Practice and Procedure: Evidence § 5122 (1977). As Wright and Graham state,

> neither Thayer nor Wigmore advocated the "bursting bubble" theory of presumptions, the notion that the judge was required to direct a verdict against the plaintiff once the presumption was rebutted, unless there was an underlying inference sufficient to take the case to the jury.... In fact, what both Thayer and Wigmore seem to have believed was that a presumption vanished in the face of rebuttal only in the sense that the proponent was no longer entitled to

a directed verdict; both Thayer and Wigmore seem to have assumed that the case would still go to the jury unless the evidence in rebuttal was such that no reasonable juror could find the nonexistence of the presumed fact.

Id. at 573 n.86, citing Thayer, *supra* note 80, at 336–37; James B. Thayer, *Presumptions and the Law of Evidence*, 3 Harv. L. Rev. 141, 165 (1889); 9 Wigmore, *supra* note 80 §§ 2487, 2491, 2493, 2494, 2498.

83. 2 McCormick on Evidence, *supra* note 77 § 344, at 462 (citing Orient Ins. Co. v. Cox, 238 S.W.2d 757 (1951); Ammundson v. Tinholt, 36 N.W.2d 521 (1949)).

84. Under Supreme Court Standard 107, it is permissible for the trial court to instruct the jury as to the permissive inference. The validity of the procedure is questionable given the large number of inferences possible in any given case and the fact that the trial judge gives no instruction as to the vast majority of them.

presumption would operate offers evidence so strong as to require a directed verdict or partial directed verdict in the absence of further evidence from the opponent. Such a result would be rather unlikely in our hypothetical case because the simple inference of receipt from proper mailing is so strong. But suppose instead that the presumption on which a party seeks to rely is artificial, in the sense that it gives rise only to a weak logical inference. For example, suppose the jurisdiction in which the case is tried adheres to the presumption that the driver of a vehicle owned by another is the agent of the owner. P, a pedestrian, is struck in a crosswalk by a dry cleaning delivery truck driven by X. It is firmly established that D owns the dry cleaning business and the truck, and that X is employed by D as a delivery driver. Suppose, however, that D calls X, who testifies that she was on her way to a midnight poker game when the accident occurred, and that P is unable to do anything to impeach the witness. This evidence almost certainly would do more than meet a burden of production. Rather, it is likely so strong as to require a directed verdict for D. Thus, even under the "bursting bubble" theory of presumptions, it is possible for the party against whom the presumption operates to rebut the presumption with evidence sufficient to meet a burden of production (which would leave the factual matter for the jury), but also to rebut the presumption with evidence so compelling as to require a directed verdict for that party.

(2) The Morgan–McCormick theory. Morgan, McCormick, and some other legal scholars reject the notion that presumptions are so fragile as to disappear when evidence is offered to rebut the existence of the presumed fact. They have emphasized that presumptions are more than simple procedural devices for the facilitation of proof, but also exist for reasons of policy.[85] As McCormick's handbook explains:

> Presumptions ... have been created for policy reasons that are similar to and may be just as strong as those that govern the allocation of the burdens of proof prior to the introduction of evidence. These policy considerations may persist despite the existence of proof rebutting the presumed fact.[86]

These scholars believe that the "bursting bubble" theory gives too "slight and evanescent" an effect to presumptions.[87] Thus, they reject the view that presumptions disappear on the presentation of evidence sufficient to support the non-existence of the presumed fact.[88] Instead, they assert that once a presumption is raised by proof of the foundational facts, the *burden of persuasion* as to the existence of the presumed fact

85. *See* § **4.08.**

86. 2 McCormick on Evidence, *supra* note 77 § 344, at 463.

87. Edmund M. Morgan & John M. Maguire, *Looking Backward and Forward at Evidence*, 50 Harv. L. Rev. 909, 913 (1937).

88. *See* Edmund M. Morgan, Some Problems of Proof 74–81 (1956); Edward W. Cleary, *Presuming and Pleading: An Essay on Juristic Immaturity*, 12 Stan. L. Rev. 5, 18 (1957); Alfred L. Gausewitz, *Presumptions in a One–Rule World*, 5 Vand. L. Rev. 324, 342 (1952); Morgan & Maguire, supra note 87, at 913.

shifts to the opponent.[89] To use the landlord-tenant hypothetical, if the jury finds that P properly addressed, stamped, and mailed the letter sufficiently in advance of the accident, D must now prove it is more likely than not that he never received the letter or suffer a finding that he did.

The battle between the Thayer–Wigmore and Morgan–McCormick views of presumptions is exemplified dramatically in Title VII employment discrimination cases. Even though the cases speak in the language of burdens rather than that of presumptions, pressing considerations of policy bear heavily on the process of proof, and the Court has dealt with the question of whether "prima facie" evidence offered by the employee shifts the burden of persuasion or only of production to the employer on the issue of discrimination. For a time, the Supreme Court's decisions might have supported a shifting of the burden of persuasion (consistent with the Morgan–McCormick theory of presumptions).[90] It now seems clear, however, that only the burden of production shifts to the employer.[91]

Because the burden of persuasion shifts under the Morgan–McCormick theory once the proponent offers sufficient evidence to meet a burden of production as the existence of the foundational (basic) facts, a jury instruction is needed in most situations. There are several possibilities, each described and then followed by an example of an instruction based on the hypothetical slip-and-fall case:[92]

89. McCormick agreed with Morgan in rejecting the Thayer–Wigmore theory, though he tended to emphasize the usefulness of jury instructions as a way to assure that presumptions retain their effectiveness even in the face of evidence challenging the presumed fact. He argued that the jury should be instructed about the existence of the presumption and about its power to make a factual finding consistent with the presumption even in the face of evidence challenging the presumed fact. Charles T. McCormick, Handbook on the Law of Evidence §§ 311, 316 (1954).

90. In McDonnell Douglas Corp. v. Green, 411 U.S. 792 (1973), the Supreme Court held that employee has the burden of proving by a preponderance of the evidence a "prima facie case" of discrimination. Upon such proof, the burden shifts to the employer "to articulate some legitimate, nondiscriminatory reason for the employee's rejection." *Id*. at 802. If the employer succeeds, the employee then has an opportunity to prove by a preponderance of the evidence that the employer's alleged reasons were pretextual. *Id*. at 804. Some years later, in Price Waterhouse v. Hopkins, 490 U.S. 228 (1989), the Court held that once the employee shows that her gender played a part in the decision not to promote her to partnership, the employer had the

burden of persuasion on the issue whether decision was unlawfully discriminatory.

91. In Texas Dept. of Community Affairs v. Burdine, 450 U.S. 248, (1981), the Court held that where the employee proves a prima facie case of discrimination, the employer bore only the burden of explaining clearly the nondiscriminatory reasons for its actions, and did not have burden of persuasion on issue of nondiscriminatory intent. The Court held that "[t]he ultimate burden of persuading the trier of fact that the defendant intentionally discriminated against the plaintiff remains at all times with the plaintiff." *Id*. at 253. *See also* St. Mary's Honor Center v. Hicks, 509 U.S. 502 (1993) (in race discrimination case where trier of fact rejected employer's asserted nondiscriminatory reason for demoting employee, employee was not entitled to judgment as matter of law); Wards Cove Packing Co. v. Atonio, 490 U.S. 642 (1989) (where employee offers statistical evidence to show disparate impact, only the burden of producing evidence of non-discriminatory purpose shifts to employer).

92. The examples are of instructions that do not directly mention the term "presumption" or instruct the jury to "presume" any facts. Other forms of instruction, including forms that address the

Examples

Description: If the proponent's evidence of the existence of the foundational facts is sufficient only to meet a burden of production, and the opponent's evidence of the nonexistence of the presumed fact is sufficient only to meet a burden of production, the court must instruct the jury that if it finds the foundational facts to be true, it must find the presumed fact to be true unless the opponent persuades the jury that it is more likely than not that the presumed fact is not true.

Application: If you find that the letter described by P was correctly addressed, stamped, and mailed two weeks before the accident, then you must find that D received the letter approximately two days after it was mailed unless D persuades you that it is more likely than not that he did not receive any such letter during the time in question.

Description: If the proponent's evidence of the existence of the foundational facts compels a finding of their existence, but the opponent's evidence concerning the nonexistence of the presumed fact is only strong enough to meet a burden of production, the court must instruct the jury that it must find the presumed fact to be true unless the opponent persuades the jury that it is more likely than not that the presumed fact is not true.

Application: I instruct you to find that P correctly addressed, stamped, and mailed to D two weeks before to the accident a letter as described in P's testimony. You must therefore find that D received the letter approximately two days later unless D persuades you that it is more likely than not that he did not receive the letter during the time in question.

Description: Regardless of whether the proponent's evidence of the existence of the foundational facts compels or merely allows a finding of their existence, if the opponent's evidence of the nonexistence of the presumed fact is so strong as to compel a finding of their nonexistence, the court need not mention a presumption, and need only instruct the jury that the presumed fact is not true.

Application: I instruct you to find that D never received from P during the time in question a letter describing the condition of the stairway.

(3) Compromise positions. As is often the case with long-standing academic debates, there is more than a thread of validity to each position. The reality is that most presumptions are overwhelmingly based in probability, and have little or no fairness or policy purpose, while some have deeper substantive than probability-based roots, and some are almost entirely policy-based. Because of this, there is no reason

---

matter in terms of presumptions, are possible. For extended discussion of alternative forms of jury instruction in the context of presumptions, see 2 McCormick on Evidence, *supra* note 77 § 344, at 467–69.

to treat all presumptions in the same way. A theoretically simple approach is to treat probability-based presumptions under the Thayer–Wigmore theory, and to treat presumptions created largely for substantive reasons under the Morgan–McCormick view. This, in fact, is the approach of the California Evidence Code,[93] and it is eminently sensible in some cases.[94] The problem with the California approach arises from the nature of presumptions. Though some are entirely or overwhelmingly based on one of consideration (generally probability, fairness, or policy), most exist for a mixture of reasons the relative importance of which is often not determinable. Different courts are likely to assign different levels of importance to the various factors, and thus treat the same presumptions differently.[95] Unless a legislature were to decide exactly how each presumption is to be treated,[96] the risk of inconsistency among courts is unavoidable.

If, then, the language of presumptions is to be maintained, there does not appear to be a perfect solution to determining their effect where the opponent offers evidence contesting the existence of the presumed fact. Though neither the Thayer–Wigmore nor the Morgan–McCormick approach operates satisfactorily in all cases, these approaches at least offer some degree of consistency and predictability. Middle-ground approaches such as that of the California Evidence Code are finer-tuned, but will often lead to less consistent and predictable results.

Challenging Both the Foundational and the Presumed Facts

If the jurisdiction follows the "bursting bubble" theory of presumptions, this situation creates no additional complications. Once the opponent offers evidence sufficient to satisfy a burden of production as to the assumed fact, regardless of the evidence offered concerning the foundational (basic) facts, the presumption simply disappears, leaving the jury to decide the question as a matter of permissive inference.[97]

In a jurisdiction employing the Morgan–McCormick theory of presumptions, the matter is considerably more complicated. The court must consider the evidence offered on both sides concerning both the founda-

---

93. The California Evidence Code divides presumptions into those affecting only the burden of production (§§ 630–647), and those affecting the burden of persuasion (denoted burden of "proof") (§§ 660–670).

94. An approach based on similar principles, but which required the opposite conclusions, was that taken by the original version of the Uniform Rules of Evidence. Uniform Rule 14 (1953) provided that if a presumption has "probative value" (if it gives rise to a reasonable inference as to the presumed fact), it shifts the burden of persuasion, but that if the presumption does not have probative value, it shifts only the burden of production and disappears when sufficient contrary proof is offered. The drafters of the Uniform Rules eventually

abandoned this approach in favor of a Morgan–McCormick position (all presumptions shift the burden of persuasion). Unif. R. Evid. 301 (1986).

95. See 2 McCormick on Evidence, *supra* note 77 § 344, at 471.

96. Note that although the California Evidence Code divides presumptions into two categories, its list is hardly exhaustive of all presumptions that can be found in the massive California Code, many of which are codified in Codes other than the Evidence Code.

97. Of course, the opponent's evidence as to the nonexistence of the presumed fact might be so strong as to require a directed verdict or partial directed verdict.

tional (basic) facts and the presumed fact. An unadopted Federal Rule of Evidence attempted to set forth the possibilities, and what the trial court must communicate to the jury:

> When evidence as to the existence of the basic facts is such that reasonable minds would not necessarily agree whether their existence is more probable than not and any evidence as to the nonexistence of the presumed fact is such that they would not necessarily agree that its nonexistence is more probable than not, the judge shall submit the matter to the jury with an instruction to find in favor of the existence of the presumed fact if they find from the evidence that the existence of the basic facts is more probable than not and unless they find the nonexistence of the presumed fact more probable than not, otherwise to find against the existence of the presumed fact.[98]

It is highly unlikely that jurors would understand the complex set of instructions mandated by this approach. As one author has written, the complexity of the proposed rule is "[t]he strongest single argument in favor of [the existing Federal Rule] and against the Morgan approach. . . . It is ventured to say that not only does such an instruction, if understood, by its very structure result in a greater burden of persuasion being placed upon the party opposing the presumption than if the identical burden of persuasion had been initially placed, but that there is not one juror in a hundred able to understand the instruction as presented at trial."[99]

§ 4.11 Presumptions; Introduction—The Problem of Conflicting Presumptions

What should a court do when two presumptions appear to be raised by the facts of a case, and the presumptions would require inconsistent factual findings? *Atkinson v. Hall*,[100] a paternity case, provides an illustration. To summarize a complicated set of facts, plaintiff claimed that defendant was the father of her child, which defendant denied. The child was born several months after plaintiff married another man, though the couple divorced less than a year after the child was born.

Both parties relied on presumptions. Blood tests performed on the defendant showed a 98.27 percent probability that he was the father. A Maine statute provided that when blood tests show a 97 percent or higher probability of paternity, a presumption of paternity is created that can only be rebutted by "clear and convincing evidence." Plaintiff asked the court to instruct the jury in accordance with this presumption. Defendant relied on a different statutory presumption that a child born during a lawful marriage is presumed to be the child of the husband

---

98. Proposed Fed. R. Evid. 303(c), 46 F.R.D. (paper edition) 161, 214 (1969).

99. 1 Michael H. Graham, Handbook of Federal Evidence § 301.13, at 164 (4th ed. 1996).

100. 556 A.2d 651 (Me.1989).

unless the party claiming otherwise proves the husband's nonpaternity beyond a reasonable doubt. The trial court ignored both presumptions and instructed the jury that plaintiff had the burden of proving paternity by a preponderance of the evidence.

The Maine Supreme Court affirmed. Maine evidence law provided that when two presumptions conflict, the court shall apply the presumption that is founded on weightier considerations of policy and logic, and that if neither satisfies this test, both presumptions are to be disregarded. The court examined the two presumptions raised by the facts, and noted that the presumption of paternity from the blood tests was based on weightier considerations of logic, but that the presumption of legitimacy from marriage was supported by weightier considerations of policy ("to minimize official intrusion into marital and family relations"[101]). The Court determined that the legitimacy presumption was at least as weighty as the paternity presumption, and hence that the trial judge did not prejudice the plaintiff's case by discarding both presumptions and sending the case to the jury with instructions that the plaintiff bore the burden of persuasion.

Many cases of conflicting presumptions have involved the validity of a second marriage. One presumption is that a ceremonial marriage is valid; another is that a person's original married status continued. In these cases, a court could disregard both presumptions and leave the question of the validity of the second marriage to the jury. Apparently, however, many courts do not disregard the conflicting presumptions in these cases, but hold that the presumption of the validity of a marriage is stronger, and validate the second marriage.[102]

No single approach to the conflicting presumptions problem can be ventured. Thayer believed that in such cases, both presumptions should be ignored and the jury left to weigh the logical inferences arising from the foundational facts.[103] In some circumstances, this seems to be the most appropriate course of action. In other cases, particularly where one of the presumptions is considerably more grounded in substantive policy than the other, perhaps it is better to give effect to the policy-based presumption, but to stress to the jury that it should examine the facts closely to determine whether the presumption has been rebutted.[104] Many courts have followed this type of approach, seeking to give effect to the "weightier" presumption.[105] Among the facts to be considered, of course, are the foundational facts supporting the other presumption, which may still be considered as a matter of logical inference. Such an

---

101. *Id*. at 653.

102. *See* 2 McCormick on Evidence § 344, at 466 (4th ed. John W. Strong ed. 1994) (citing cases).

103. Thayer, A Preliminary Treatise on Evidence at the Common Law 346 (1898). Wigmore agreed. 9 John H. Wigmore, Evidence in Trials at Common Law § 2493 (James H. Chadbourn rev. 1981).

104. Morgan favored giving effect to the presumption founded on stronger considerations of policy. Morgan, *Some Observations Concerning Presumptions*, 44 Harv. L. Rev. 906, 932 n.41 (1931).

105. *See* 2 McCormick on Evidence, *supra* note 102 § 344, at 466.

approach, however, suffers from the familiar problem of lack of predictability. Courts are likely to view particular presumptions differently, leading to different analyses in similar cases. Other approaches to this difficult problem have also been considered,[106] though none perfectly resolves all cases.

§ 4.12 Presumptions; Introduction—Presumptions in Criminal Cases

In the landmark case of *In re Winship*,[107] the United States Supreme Court held that the Due Process clause demands that a criminal defendant be convicted only "upon proof beyond a reasonable doubt of every fact necessary to constitute the crime with which he is charged."[108] In *Ulster County v. Allen*[109] and *Sandstrom v. Montana*,[110] the Court made clear that this requirement has left little or no room for the operation of true (mandatory) presumptions in criminal cases.

In *Ulster County*, four defendants were charged with illegal possession of handguns (among other items). Two of the handguns were found in the front of the car in a handbag belonging to one defendant, who was 16 years old. A New York statute provided that a firearm in an automobile is presumed to be possessed illegally by all occupants. The Supreme Court attempted to set forth clearly the difference between permissive devices and mandatory devices, and their treatment under the Constitution:

> Inferences and presumptions are a staple of our adversary system of factfinding. It is often necessary for the trier of fact to determine the existence of an item of the crime—that is, an "ultimate" or "elemental" fact—from the existence of one or more "evidentiary" or "basic" facts.... The value of these evidentiary devices, and their validity under the Due Process Clause, vary from case to case, however, depending on the strength of the connection between the particular basic and elemental facts involved and on the degree to which the device curtails the factfinder's freedom to assess the evidence independently. Nonetheless, in criminal cases, the ultimate test of any device's constitutional validity remains constant: the device must not undermine the factfinder's responsibility at trial, based on evidence adduced by the State, to find the ultimate facts beyond a reasonable doubt.[111]

Thus, the key question is whether the device, as applied, undercut the factfinder's role to determine guilt beyond a reasonable doubt based on the evidence. A device that operates in a mandatory fashion—one that *requires* the jury to reach a certain factual finding based on the presence

---

106. *See id.*

107. 397 U.S. 358 (1970).

108. *Id.* at 364.

109. 442 U.S. 140 (1979).

110. 442 U.S. 510 (1979). For a brief summary of the cases leading up to *Ulster County* and *Sandstrom*, see 2 McCormick on Evidence, *supra* note 102 § 547, at 485–87.

111. *Ulster County*, 442 U.S. at 156.

of certain foundational facts—will usually do so, while one that operates permissively—allowing the jury to reach conclusions it deems appropriate under the circumstances—will not. As the Court wrote:

> Because this permissive presumption leaves the trier of fact free to credit or reject the inference and does not shift the burden of proof, it affects the application of the "beyond a reasonable doubt" standard only if, under the facts of the case, there is no rational way the trier could make the connection permitted by the inference. For only in that situation is there any risk that an explanation of the permissible inference to a jury, or its use by a jury, has caused the presumptively rational factfinder to make an erroneous factual determination.[112]

Note that the Court spoke in terms of "mandatory presumptions" and "permissive presumptions." This usage can easily confuse the reader accustomed to thinking of "presumptions" as mandatory devices and "inferences" as permissive devices. Nevertheless, for criminal cases, the Court has chosen this terminology, dividing presumptions into permissive and mandatory types, and holding that the former is constitutional[113] while the latter is normally not.[114] As applied to the facts of the case before it, the Court scrutinized not simply the language of the presumption, but the way in which the trial court instructed the jury about the presumption. Analyzing the facts, the Court held that the device did not operate in a mandatory fashion because the court instructed the jury using permissive language.[115] This left only the question whether there was a rational basis for a finding of guilt beyond a reasonable doubt, which the Court held did exist.[116]

In *Sandstrom v. Montana*,[117] a homicide prosecution, the Court dealt with a presumption that a person intends the ordinary consequences of his voluntary acts. Defendant claimed that the degree of the offense should be reduced because he suffered from a personality disorder that was aggravated by his intoxication. The Supreme Court reversed defendant's conviction, holding that as applied in jury instructions, the jury could have believed that the presumption was mandatory or shifted the burden of persuasion on the intent issue to the defendant. Even if the

---

112. *Id.* at 157.

113. As the language quoted in text indicates, a permissive "presumption" will only be constitutionally infirm if the "presumption" allows a finding of fact where a rational inference is not even permissible. Such a situation would be unusual.

114. The Court's language left open the possibility that a mandatory presumption would be constitutional where the basic (foundational) facts, standing alone, would be sufficient to support the inference of guilt beyond a reasonable doubt. *Id.* at 167. It has been suggested that such a presumption would always be unconstitutional. *See, e.g.,* Ronald L. Allen & Lee Ann DeGrazia, *The Constitutional Requirement*

of Proof Beyond Reasonable Doubt in Criminal Cases: A Comment Upon Incipient Chaos in the Lower Courts, 20 Am. Crim. L. Rev. 1, 12 (1982). It is indeed difficult to visualize a mandatory presumption that could survive the *Ulster County* test.

115. *Id.* at 160–65. The trial court instructed the jury about the presumption but stated that it "need not be rebutted by affirmative proof or affirmative evidence but may be rebutted by any evidence or lack of evidence in the case." *Id.* at 161 n.20.

116. *Id.* at 167.

117. 442 U.S. 510 (1979).

trial court's instruction was subject to interpretation as creating a permissive "presumption," the Court held that the instruction was unconstitutionally infirm because it could also have been interpreted as mandatory or as imposing on the defendant the burden of persuasion as to intent.[118]

In 1985, the Court revisited the subject in *Francis v. Franklin*.[119] Defendant, convicted of murder during a prison escape, sought federal habeas corpus relief. The only contested issue at trial was intent. Defendant claimed constitutional error in the trial court's jury instruction (1) that "[t]he acts of a person of sound mind and discretion are presumed to be the product of the person's will, but the presumption may be rebutted"; and (2) that a "person of sound mind and discretion is presumed to intend the natural and probable consequences of his acts but the presumption may be rebutted." The Court examined whether the instructions were unconstitutional because they relieved the state of the burden of proving defendant's guilt by creating a mandatory presumption of intent upon proof of other elements, and held that the instructions were in fact unconstitutional.

Even though the Georgia Supreme Court had interpreted the offending language as creating no more than a permissive inference, the Court held that a reasonable juror could have understood the charge as creating a mandatory presumption shifting the burden of persuasion on the element of intent once the state had proved the underlying acts. The words of the charge were stated as a command; even though the court instructed the jury that the presumption could be rebutted, the jurors could reasonably have understood that they must find intent unless defendant persuaded them to the contrary. Though any ambiguity in the instructions can be cured by the particular context, in this case neither the instruction concerning the presumption of innocence nor an instruction telling the jury that a person will not be presumed to act with criminal intention were sufficient. As the Court explained, "a reasonable juror could ... have thought that, although intent must be proved beyond a reasonable doubt, proof of the firing of the gun and its ordinary consequences constituted proof of intent beyond a reasonable doubt unless the defendant persuaded the jury otherwise."[120] Nor was the error cured by a later instruction that "[a] person will not be presumed to act with criminal intention," because a reasonable juror could have understood the instruction to refer to a different element of the crime than intent. Even if not, the Court held, jurors might resolve the apparent conflict between this instruction and the invalid instructions "by choosing to abide by the mandatory presumption and ignore the prohibition of presumption."[121]

Finally, while not addressing the question whether this type of error could ever be harmless, the Court let stand the lower determination of

---

118. *Id.* at 516–19.

119. 471 U.S. 307 (1985).

120. *Id.* at 319.

121. *Id.* at 322.

the Court of Appeals that it was not harmless in this case.[122]

Although there remains much uncertainty even after *Ulster County,* *Sandstrom,* and *Francis,*[123] the cases do seem to establish certain propositions. That true (mandatory) presumptions are almost always unconstitutional as applied in criminal cases against the defendant. Counsel must scrutinize not only the language of the device itself, but the way in which it is explained to the jury and any other instructions that might have cured any defect, because even a presumption that appears mandatory on its face can be saved, under the circumstances, by an instruction that unambiguously leaves the matter to the jury's judgment as a matter of logical inference. A "permissive presumption," on the other hand, will be constitutional if a reasonable person could conclude that it is more likely than not that the "presumed" fact rationally follows from the foundational facts.[124]

§ 4.13   Presumptions; Introduction—The Federal Rules of Evidence and Presumptions

The Federal Rules of Evidence only address the subject of presumptions in civil cases. Rule 301 provides the basic rule:

> In all civil actions and proceedings not otherwise provided for by Act of Congress or by these rules, a presumption imposes on the party against whom it is directed the burden of going forward with evidence to rebut or meet the presumption, but does not shift to such party the burden of proof in the sense of the risk of nonpersuasion, which remains throughout the trial upon the party on whom it was originally cast.[125]

At first glance, it appears that the language of Rule 301 adopts the pure "bursting bubble" theory of presumptions, and some authorities have so stated.[126] Once a presumption goes into effect, it shifts to the opponent only the burden of going forward, not the burden of persuasion. However, the language and legislative history of Rule 301 leave

---

122. *Id.* at 325–26.

123. *See* 1 Michael H. Graham, Handbook of Federal Evidence § 303.4, at 186–93 (4th ed. 1996). For discussion of the use of presumptions against the criminal defendant, see Ronald J. Allen, *Structuring Jury Decisionmaking in Criminal Cases: A Unified Constitutional Approach to Evidentiary Devices,* 94 Harv. L. Rev. 321 (1980); Charles R. Nesson, *Rationality, Presumptions, and Judicial Comment: A Response to Professor Allen,* 94 Harv. L. Rev. 1574 (1981); Stephen Saltzburg, *Burdens of Persuasion in Criminal Cases: Harmonizing the Views of the Justices,* 20 Am. Crim. L. Rev. 393 (1983).

124. Special problems are also created by the use of affirmative defenses in criminal cases. The Supreme Court has held that

there are limits to the state's ability to create affirmative defenses, holding that such defenses are permissible as long as they do not simply negative an element of the crime. Patterson v. New York, 432 U.S. 197, 210 (1977). Determining when that is the case is a difficult question of interpretation; the law needs further development. For further discussion of affirmative defenses in this context, see 2 McCormick on Evidence, *supra* note 102 § 348.

125. Fed. R. Evid. 301.

126. *See, e.g.,* 1 Michael H. Graham, Handbook of Federal Evidence § 301.12, at 158 (4th ed. 1996). *See also* In re Yoder, 758 F.2d 1114, 1120 (6th Cir.1985) (stating that most commentators take the position that Rule 301 embodies the "bursting bubble" approach).

some room for doubt as to the drafters' intent. While it is clear that the drafters rejected the Morgan–McCormick view, but it is not so clear that they opted for full adoption of the "bursting bubble" theory, either. At one point, for example, the Conference Committee report states that "[i]f the adverse party does offer evidence contradicting the presumed fact, the court cannot instruct the jury that it may *presume* the existence of the presumed fact from proof of the basic facts. The court may, however, instruct the jury that it may infer the existence of the presumed fact from proof of the basic facts."[127] This appears to suggest that some remnant of the presumption may in fact outlive the admission of evidence contradicting the presumed fact. The authors of one treatise have argued that the Rule in fact adopt aspects of the Morgan–McCormick and "true" Thayer–Wigmore theory.[128]

Whatever the actual approach of Rule 301, it is undercut to some degree by Rule 302, which provides that "the effect of a presumption respecting a fact which is an element of a claim or defense as to which State law supplies the rule of decision" is to be decided in accordance with state law. Thus, in cases brought in federal court by virtue of diversity of citizenship, Rule 301 generally will not determine the effect of a presumption. Instead, the parties must look to the state's law.

As noted above, the Federal Rules do not address presumptions in criminal cases. The Advisory Committee proposed such a rule,[129] but Congress declined to adopt it. In federal criminal cases, therefore, the law of presumptions will be governed by judicial interpretation of the Constitution's demands, as discussed in a previous section.[130]

---

127. H.R. Fed. Rules of Evidence, Conf. Rep. No. 1597, 93d Cong., 2d Sess., at 5 (1974); 1974 U.S. Code Cong. & Ad. News 7098, 7099 (emphasis in original).

128. 21 Charles A. Wright & Kenneth W. Graham, Jr., Federal Practice and Procedure (Evidence) § 5122 (1977). The authors state:

> Rule 301 . . . creates a presumption that is neither Thayer–Wigmore nor Morgan–McCormick. Since the effect of Rule 301 is to increase the number of cases that are decided by the jury rather than the judge, it leans toward the Morgan–McCormick point of view. On the other hand, the mandatory effect of the Rule 301 presumption is limited to taking the case to the jury; thereafter, it has only such effect as the jury chooses to give it. In this respect, the Rule may be said to resemble the true Thayer–Wigmore theory. Since the Rule contemplates telling the jury about the presumption in most cases, it adopts a policy advanced by Professor McCormick. . . . The Rule 301 presumption operates only against the judge; insofar as the jury is concerned it is simply an authorized inference.

Id. at 572–73. For discussion the actual views of Thayer and Wigmore, see **§ 4.10.**

129. Proposed Fed. R. Evid. 303.

130. *See* **§ 4.12.**

Chapter 5

RELEVANCY AND ITS LIMITS

Analysis

GENERAL CONCEPTS OF RELEVANCY [FRE 401–403]

§ 5.01   The Minimal Relevancy Requirement of Rule 401

Federal Rules of Evidence 401 and 403 establish general principles of relevancy and general limits on the admission of relevant evidence. They are supplemented in many situations by more specific rules, such as those governing character evidence.[1]

Rule 401 provides that an item of evidence is relevant if it has "any tendency to make the existence of any fact that is of consequence to the determination of the action more probable or less probable than it would be without the evidence."[2] Rule 402 sets forth the general rule of admissibility of relevant evidence.[3] However, Rule 403 provides that even if relevant, evidence may be excluded if its probative value is substantially outweighed by considerations of unfair prejudice, waste of time, or confusion of issues.[4]

Rule 401 adopts a very broad conception of relevancy. Almost anything that a rational lawyer would attempt to offer into evidence would be "relevant" within the meaning of Rule 401 because it would have some minimal effect on the probability that a particular proposition of consequence to the case is true or false.[5] In a personal injury case, the fact that the defendant had a fight with his wife on the morning of the accident that is the subject of the suit might be minimally probative of a fact at issue (perhaps he was not paying attention to his driving because he was thinking about domestic problems). Yet though "relevant" within

---

1. Fed. R. Evid. 404–415.

2. Fed. R. Evid. 401.

3. The first sentence of Fed. R. Evid. 402 provides that relevant evidence is admissible except as otherwise provided by rule, statute, or constitution. For an expansive interpretation of this part of Rule 402, see Edward J. Imwinkelried, *Federal Rule of Evidence 402: The Second Revolution*, 6 Rev. Litig. 129 (1987) (arguing that the first sentence of Rule 402 abolishes common law rules, such as the *Frye* test, that Congress failed to codify in the Federal Rules of Evidence). The Supreme Court offered substantial support for this expansive interpretation of the Rules by ruling that the drafters did indeed intend to abolish the more restrictive *Frye* test for admissibility of novel scientific evidence, and replace that test with a standard of relevancy and reliability. Daubert v. Merrell Dow Pharmaceuticals, 509 U.S. 579 (1993). *See* **Ch. 10.** The second sentence of Rule 402 provides that "Evidence which is not relevant is not admissible."

4. Fed. R. Evid. 403.

5. *See* Fed. R. Evid. 401 advisory committee's note (evidence is relevant if it makes the existence of a fact " 'more probable or less probable than it would be without the evidence' "). *See, e.g.*, United States v. Rivera–Gomez, 67 F.3d 993, 996–97 (1st Cir.1995) (held, evidence of victim's death in attempted carjacking was admissible since it was relevant to proving the element of "force and violence" and was not overly prejudicial); United States v. Casares–Cardenas, 14 F.3d 1283, 1287 (8th Cir.), *cert. denied*, 513 U.S. 849 (1994) (in conspiracy case, evidence that woman with same surname as co-defendant was captured with defendant during case-related illegal entry was relevant, even though it did not conclusively show link to co-defendant); Conway v. Chemical Leaman Tank Lines, Inc., 525 F.2d 927, 930 (5th Cir.1976) (Rule 401's definition of relevant is "generous" and includes background information); International Merger & Acquisitions Consultants, Inc. v. Armac Enters., 531 F.2d 821, 823 (7th Cir.1976) (Rule 401 provides "rather liberal standard" of relevancy); David Crump, *On the Uses of Irrelevant Evidence*, 34 Hous. L. Rev. 1, 6 (1997) ("the relevancy 'standard' in Rule 401 is no standard at all, because it indiscriminately admits every arguable proposition no matter how low its probative value").

the meaning of 401, the court would almost certainly exclude the evidence as a waste of time (and possibly for reasons of unfair prejudice) under Rule 403.[6]

§ 5.02 Logical and Legal Relevancy

The term *logically relevant* has sometimes been used to refer to evidence that has any tendency in logic to establish a proposition, while *legally relevant* has sometimes been used to refer to evidence whose probative value is great enough to justify the delay, expense, prejudice, or confusion that is involved in considering it.[7] The Federal Rules of Evidence do not use these terms, but the concept of "logical relevancy" is in effect embodied in Rule 401, while evidence that previously might have been called "logically relevant but not legally relevant" could now be described as "relevant under Rule 401 but not admissible because of Rule 403."[8]

§ 5.03 Relevancy and Materiality

Relevancy is sometimes contrasted with *materiality*. While those two terms probably have as many meanings as they do users, the following distinction is as common as any. Evidence is irrelevant if it has no tendency in logic to establish the fact that the proponent asserts the evidence will help prove. Evidence is immaterial when, although it has a tendency in logic to establish the fact that it is offered to prove, that fact is not in issue.[9] For example, the fact might have been removed as an issue because of an admission in the pleadings.

To apply this terminology, imagine a slander case in which plaintiff alleges that defendant falsely called plaintiff a thief. If defendant offers evidence that plaintiff was seen on the street corner selling new gold watches for five dollars apiece, that evidence is relevant to show that the slanderous statement was true. However, if the defense of truth had been eliminated from the case because defendant admitted in the pleadings that the statement was false, then the evidence, though relevant, would be "immaterial" because it would have no bearing on any issue to be tried.

---

6. *See* Fed. R. Evid. 403 advisory committee's note.

7. *See, e.g.*, Cotton v. United States, 361 F.2d 673, 676 (8th Cir.1966) (although evidence that some people who pass counterfeit bills are innocent is logically relevant in counterfeiting trial, evidence is not legally relevant because it is potentially confusing). *See also* 1A John H. Wigmore, Evidence in Trials at Common Law § 28 (Peter Tillers rev. 1983) (stating that the standard for "legal relevancy" is higher than that for logical relevancy). To avoid creating confusion, we will eschew the term "legal relevancy" and instead discuss the precise principle under which logically rele-

vant evidence might be excluded in a given situation.

8. *See* Fed. R. Evid. 401, 403 advisory committee's note.

9. *See, e.g.*, 1 John H. Wigmore, Evidence In Trials at Common Law § 2, at 18 (Peter Tillers rev. 1983) (explaining distinction between materiality and relevancy); United States v. Williams, 545 F.2d 47, 50 (8th Cir.1976) (evidence concerning state insurance statutes and regulations relevant to insurance agent's knowledge of law, but inadmissible in mail fraud prosecution against insurance purchaser because agent's knowledge of law not a material issue).

The federal rules do not use the term "immaterial." Evidence that would previously have been described as "immaterial" is now "irrelevant" within the meaning of Federal Rule of Evidence 401 if, in the language of the Rule, it is not "of consequence" to the determination of the action.[10] Suppose, for example, that in a prosecution for forgery of a check, defendant admits signing another person's name to the check, but wishes to offer evidence that a week later, she "covered" the check with her own money. This evidence would be irrelevant—not "of consequence"—because it would not affect her guilt of the crime; evidence of later remorse has no bearing on defendant's state of mind at the time she forged the check.[11]

Where evidence is offered on an issue of consequence to the case, but which has been conceded, the Federal Rules take a somewhat different position. For example, suppose that in a personal injury case, plaintiff alleges that defendant's negligent driving caused permanent disability. Plaintiff makes no claim for punitive damages. Defendant, knowing that the evidence of negligence is overwhelming, and wishing to avoid having the jury hear damaging details of her conduct, admits negligence but disputes the amount of damages.[12] At trial, plaintiff offers evidence that the defendant was intoxicated at the time of the accident. Assuming that the evidence of intoxication has no bearing on any issue other than that of liability, which has been conceded, some jurists using pre-Federal Rules terminology would have excluded the evidence as irrelevant,[13] and a number of states would do the same today under their own codes.[14] The federal rules, however, would treat such evidence as relevant but exclude it as a waste of time or prejudicial under Rule 403.[15]

The importance of the Federal Rules' broad concept of relevance in relation to issues conceded by one party was made clear by the Supreme

---

10. *See* Fed. R. Evid. 401 advisory committee's note; 2 Weinstein's Federal Evidence § 401.04[3] (2d ed. Joseph M. McLaughlin ed. 1997).

11. Repayment is not a defense to a forgery charge. *See* United States v. Wilson, 28 C.M.R. 844, 850 (A.F.B.R. 1959) (military law); People v. Morris, 92 P.2d 644, 645 (Cal.App.1939). *See also* 37 C.J.S., Forgery § 41 (1943).

12. For results in cases in which this tactic has been used, see Annotation, *Admission of Liability as Affecting Admissibility of Evidence as to the Circumstances of Accident on Issue of Damages in a Tort Action for Personal Injury, Wrongful Death, or Property Damage,* 80 A.L.R.2d 1224 (1961); Jarvis v. Hall, 210 N.E.2d 414 (Ohio App.1964) (where defendant admits liability, evidence that defendant was driving while drunk inadmissible).

13. *See, e.g.,* 9 John H. Wigmore, Evidence in Trials at Common Law § 2591, at 824 (James H. Chadbourn rev. 1981) ("A

fact that is judicially admitted [e.g., by being admitted in the pleadings] *needs* no evidence from the party benefiting by the admission. But his evidence, if he chooses to offer it, *may* even be *excluded;* first, because it is now immaterial to the issues ..." [emphasis in original]).

14. *See, e.g.,* Cal. Evid. Code § 210 (West 1966) ("Relevant evidence" means evidence ... having any tendency in reason to prove or disprove any *disputed fact* that is of consequence to the determination of the action") (emphasis added).

15. Fed. R. Evid. 401 advisory committee's note ("[t]he fact to which the evidence is directed need not be in dispute. While situations will arise which call for the exclusion of evidence offered to prove a point conceded by the opponent, the ruling should be made on the basis of such considerations as waste of time and undue prejudice ..., rather than under any general requirement that evidence is admissible only if directed to matters in dispute").

Court in *Old Chief v. United States*.[16] In *Old Chief*, defendant was charged with being a felon in possession of a firearm, assault with a deadly weapon, and using a firearm in connection with a crime. He had previously been convicted of assault causing serious bodily injury, a felony that put him within the ambit of a federal statute prohibiting certain felons from possessing firearms. Prior to trial, defendant moved to prevent the government from mentioning any details of the prior conviction, except to state that he had been convicted of a crime punishable by imprisonment in excess of a year. In return, defendant offered to stipulate to the offense. The prosecutor refused the stipulation, arguing that he had a right to prove the essential facts of the case in his own way, despite defendant's offer to stipulate to one of the elements of the offense. The court denied defendant's motion, and at trial, the prosecutor introduced the record of conviction, which revealed defendant's prior conviction, including the nature of the crime and the sentence he received. Defendant was convicted, and the Ninth Circuit affirmed. In a 5–4 decision, the Supreme Court reversed. Though the Court rejected defendant's argument that the name of the prior offense was irrelevant,[17] it held that the trial court was obligated to grant defendant's motion pursuant to Rule 403.

Several aspects of the Court's discussion of Rules 402 and 403 have broad application.[18] In its discussion of relevance principles, the Court spoke broadly, emphasizing that "beyond the power of conventional evidence to support allegations and give life to the moral underpinnings of law's claims, there lies the need for evidence in all its particularity to satisfy the jurors' expectations about what proper proof should be."[19] As the Court explained:

> Unlike an abstract premise, whose force depends on going precisely to a particular step in a course of reasoning, a piece of evidence may address any number of separate elements, striking hard just because it shows so much at once; ... Thus, the prosecution may fairly seek to place its evidence before the jurors, as much to tell a story of guiltiness as to support an inference of guilt, to convince the jurors that a guilty verdict would be morally reasonable as much as to point to the discrete elements of a defendant's legal fault.[20]

This reasoning, in part, is what gives rise to the adage that the prosecution is entitled to prove its case by evidence of its own choice—that defendant has no right to "stipulate or admit his way out of the full

---

16. 117 S.Ct. 644 (1997).

17. *Id.* at 649. The Court held that the nature of the conviction "was a step on one evidentiary route to the ultimate fact, since it served to place Old Chief within a particular sub-class of offenders for whom firearms possession is outlawed by [the relevant federal statute]. A documentary record of the conviction for that named offense was thus relevant evidence in making Old's Chief's ... status more probable than it

would have been without the evidence." *Id.* The Court made clear that the availability of alternative means of proving the prior crime did not render the proof offered by the prosecutor relevant. *Id.*

18. For consideration of the Court's discussion of Rule 403, *see* § 5.04.

19. *Id.* at 654.

20. *Id.* at 653–54.

evidentiary force of the case as the government chooses to present it.''[21] Aphorizing that ''a syllogism is not a story,'' the Court wrote that the prosecution is entitled to the benefit of a colorful story with descriptive richness.[22] This led the Court to state a principle that, if carried to its logical extreme, would revolutionize the law of relevancy: in ruling on the admissibility of evidence, the court should take into account the prosecution's need to establish the ''human significance'' of a crime and to awaken a juror's ''obligation to sit in judgment.''[23] This suggests that the prosecution is entitled to offer evidence to show more than what is strictly necessary for logical inference when the extra evidence is needed to insure that the jury does not nullify substantive law and does not require greater certainty than proof beyond a reasonable doubt. The Court also noted, less adventurously, that in some cases the absence of proof can cause the jury to draw unfair inferences unfavorable to the prosecution.[24]

Nevertheless, the Court held that these principles had virtually no application in the case at bar, where the fact to be proved was the defendant's legal status, a decision to be rendered apart from the concrete facts of the present case but merely on the basis of some prior adjudicated events. As the Court stated, ''[p]roving status without telling exactly why that status was imposed leaves no gap in the story of a defendant's subsequent criminality, and its demonstration by stipulation or admission neither displaces a chapter from a continuous sequence of conventional evidence nor comes across as an officious substitution, to confuse or offend or provoke reproach.''[25] Here, then, the evidence the prosecution wished to offer carries the unfairly prejudicial risk that the jury will convict defendant because of his apparently bad character or simply to prevent him from committing future crimes regardless of his guilt in the present case. At the same time, the evidence has no greater probative value than the defendant's offered stipulation, which would have been ''seemingly conclusive evidence'' of an essential element of the crime.[26] Thus, in this situation, ''the only reasonable conclusion was that the risk of unfair prejudice did substantially outweigh the discounted probative value of the record of conviction, and it was an abuse of discretion to admit the record when an admission was available.''[27]

§ 5.04 Rule 403: The Universal Fall–Back Objection

Evidence that is otherwise admissible under the rules is still subject to the Federal Rule of Evidence 403 balancing test and can still be

21. *Id.* at 653. For example, in a pornography case, the prosecution would ordinarily be entitled to display the allegedly pornographic material to the jury, even if the defendant was willing to concede that the materials was pornographic and wanted merely to dispute the element of possession. *See* Parr v. United States, 255 F.2d 86, 88 (5th Cir.), *cert. denied*, 358 U.S. 824 (1958) (cited favorably in *Old Chief*).

22. *Id.* at 654.

23. *Id.* at 653–54.

24. *Id.* at 654.

25. *Id.* at 655.

26. *Id.* at 653.

27. *Id.* at 655. The Court left open the possibility that the error was harmless. *Id.* at 656 n.11.

excluded if its reception would be too unfairly prejudicial, too misleading, or waste too much time.[28] (The sole exception to the Rule 403 balancing test is evidence that impeaches a witness with a conviction for a crime of dishonesty, in which instance Rule 609 mandates admission without balancing.[29]) Rule 403 thus provides an almost universal "fall-back" argument for the attorney seeking the exclusion of evidence. The rule applies equally to all parties in both civil and criminal cases.[30] Rule 403 also provides a basis for arguing, when evidence is admissible for one purpose but inadmissible for another, that the evidence should be excluded in its entirety because of the danger that the jury will not follow a limiting instruction.[31]

The task of balancing probative value against the enumerated dangers in Rule 403 is hardly a precise one. Neither the rule itself nor its accompanying commentary offers specific guidelines for the judge. The court must consider the dangers not in the abstract, but in the precise context of the case at hand.[32]

Examples

Emotional appeal. Plaintiff offers a day-in-the-life film that not only depicts the plaintiff's daily activities, but also shows plaintiff in sentimental scenes with plaintiff's family. Rule 403 gives the trial judge discretion to edit out the portions of the film that are likely to

28. 2 Weinstein's Federal Evidence § 403.02[1][a] (2d ed. Joseph M. McLaughlin ed. 1997). *See, e.g.,* Trevino v. Gates, 99 F.3d 911, 922 (9th Cir.1996) (though jury could consider suffering of plaintiff's child as element of damages in suit based on killing of father by Los Angeles Police Department officers, it was nonetheless proper to prevent 5–year—old child from testifying; she had not been born at time of father's death and could contribute little to an understanding of her past or future suffering); United States v. Hicks, 103 F.3d 837, 842–44 (9th Cir.1996) (held, trial court did not abuse discretion in carjacking prosecution by admitting evidence of uncharged rape and murder of occupants; evidence went to "force and violence" element of carjacking offense); United States v. Merriweather, 78 F.3d 1070, 1077 (6th Cir.1996) (even though evidence of unrelated drug crime relevant to intent and identity, Rule 403 requires exclusion where prosecution had better means of proof).

29. *See* **Ch. 9.** On the doctrine of limited admissibility, see **§ 2.09.**

30. One author has argued that in criminal cases, Rule 403 is unconstitutional because it prescribes a balancing test that places the major risk of erroneous decision-making on the defendant. D. Craig Lewis, *Proof and Prejudice: A Constitutional Challenge to the Treatment of Prejudicial Evi-*

dence in Federal Criminal Cases, 64 Wash. L. Rev. 289 (1989). The author proposes revising the standard as applied to evidence offered against the defendant, requiring the prosecution to demonstrate that the probative value of its evidence substantially outweighs the danger of unfair prejudice (the opposite of the current standard).

31. *See, e.g.,* United States v. Beasley, 809 F.2d 1273, 1278–80 (7th Cir. 1987) (although evidence of prior drug offenses admissible to show intent in narcotics prosecution, trial court erred in admitting evidence without considering prejudicial effect because it was inadmissible to show defendant acted in conformity with prior conduct).

32. For discussion of the meaning and operation of the rule, see Victor J. Gold, *Limiting Judicial Discretion to Exclude Prejudicial Evidence*, 18 U.C. Davis L. Rev. 59 (1984); Victor J. Gold, *Federal Rule of Evidence 403: Observations on the Nature of Unfairly Prejudicial Evidence*, 58 Wash. L. Rev. 497 (1983); Edward J. Imwinkelried, *The Meaning of Probative Value and Prejudice in Federal Rule of Evidence 403: Can Rule 403 Be Used to Resurrect the Common Law of Evidence?*, 41 Vand. L. Rev. 879 (1988).

have an undue emotional appeal.[33]

Waste of time, confusion. The plaintiff in a personal injury action offers evidence about defects in shotgun shells manufactured by defendant corporation at a plant other than the one that manufactured the shell that injured the plaintiff. The evidence has some probative value, but evaluating it would require extensive examination of differences between the two plants, which would entail dangers of confusion of the jury and waste of resources. Rule 403 gives the trial judge authority to exclude.[34]

Ineffectiveness of limiting instruction. At a trial of D for murder by poison, where D claims that V, the alleged victim took her own life, the prosecution offers evidence that before her death, V accused D of poisoning her. The prosecution claims that the statement, though inadmissible to prove the truth of what it asserted, should be admitted for the limited purpose of showing that V was not in a suicidal state of mind.[35] In this situation, an instruction to the jury to consider the evidence in only to prove V's state of mind, and not

33. *See* Grimes v. Employers Mut. Liab. Ins. Co., 73 F.R.D. 607, 610, 612 (D.Alaska 1977). *See also* United States v. Lachman, 48 F.3d 586 (1st Cir.1995) (interlocutory appeal by government in case charging defendant with illegal export of prohibited goods; held, trial court properly excluded documents showing that importing country had nuclear missile program; evidence was confusing, prejudicial, and had little or no probative value on issue of defendant's scienter); Moreno v. State, 858 S.W.2d 453, 465–66 (Tex.Crim.App.1993) (in murder prosecution, trial court erroneously admitted contents of deceased victim's wallet, including photographs of friends, and a love poem written by his girlfriend; despite the "infinitesimally incremental" probative value of evidence, admission constitutes harmless error due to overwhelming evidence of defendant's guilt); State v. Smith, 857 S.W.2d 1 (Tenn. 1993) (no error in witnesses' description of crime scene as victim lying in a "pool of blood"); Uhr v. Lutheran Gen. Hosp., 589 N.E.2d 723, 744 (Ill.App.1992) (photographs of patient with sister and brother, and in hospital bed surrounded by presents before death during operation admissible to show close family relationship).

34. *See* Classen v. Remington Arms Co., 379 N.W.2d 133, 136 (Minn.App.1985) (interpreting Minn. R. Evid. 403, based on Fed. R. Evid. 403). *See, e.g.,* Rowan County Bd. of Educ. v. United States Gypsum Co., 407 S.E.2d 860, 870 (N.C.App.1991), *aff'd in part,* 418 S.E.2d 648 (1992) (evidence of risk assessment properly excluded; possible relevance outweighed by danger of confusing issues and misleading jury, and by con-

siderations of undue delay and waste of time); Strauss v. Springer, 817 F.Supp. 1211, 1222–23 (E.D.Pa.1992) (in civil action for excessive use of force by police officer, plaintiff's expert offered testimony based on a review of internal police investigations of shootings by other police officers, to show custom of indifference to use of excessive force; held, other shootings evidence excluded as confusing to jury).

But cf. United States v. Blackburn, 992 F.2d 666, 668–69 (7th Cir.), *cert. denied,* 510 U.S. 949 (1993) (held, in prosecution for bank robbery, district court did not abuse its discretion by allowing government to introduce testimony of exotic dancer that defendant gave her approximately one hundred one-dollar bills as birthday present shortly after robbery, despite fact that government admitted to court that the one-dollar bills were not the same bills as those taken from bank; moreover, though defendant's character may have been impugned by evidence that he frequented bar where the exotic dancer worked, testimony regarding defendant's patronage of bar supplied background narrative material linking him to the dancer).

See generally United States v. Thomas, 86 F.3d 647, 652–54 (7th Cir.1996) (in cocaine conspiracy case, evidence that defendants belonged to same Mafia Insane Vice Lords gang held admissible to illuminate relationship, but evidence of death threats by third parties should have been excluded as prejudicial).

35. *See* Shepard v. United States, 290 U.S. 96 (1933).

to prove that D poisoned V, would almost certainly be ineffective. The low probative value of the evidence for this limited purpose, combined with the great potential for prejudice against D, calls for exclusion of the evidence under Rule 403.

In the *Old Chief* case,[36] the Supreme Court attempted to clarify the trial court's task in applying Rule 403. The Court held that on objection, the trial judge should decide whether the questioned evidence raises a danger of unfair prejudice. If such a danger exists, the judge must "take account of the full evidentiary context of the case as the court understands it when the ruling must be made."[37] In particular, the judge should consider not just the evidence itself, but also the probative value and risk of prejudice of any available substitutes for that evidence. The Court continued:

> If an alternative were found to have substantially the same or greater probative value but a lower danger of unfair prejudice, sound judicial discretion would discount the value of the item first offered and exclude it if its discounted probative value were substantially outweighed by unfairly prejudicial risk.... The judge would have to make these calculations with an appreciation of the offering party's need for evidentiary richness and narrative integrity in presenting a case, and the mere fact that two pieces of evidence might go to the same point would not, of course, necessarily mean that only one of them might come in. It would only mean that a judge applying Rule 403 could reasonable apply some discount to the probative value of an item of evidence when faced with less risky alternative proof going to the same point.[38]

While Rule 403 gives the trial judge the discretion to exclude evidence on grounds that it will prejudice, confuse, or mislead the jury, one limitation should be noted. The trial judge must still respect the jury's role in assessing the credibility of witnesses and cannot exclude evidence on grounds that the testifying witness is unreliable. Weighing probative value against unfair prejudice under Rule 403 means accepting the accuracy of the witness's testimony and then assessing the probative value of the inferences to be drawn from it; the judge is not supposed to decide whether or not the witness is believable.[39]

Finally, it is not enough for the court to find that one of the enumerated dangers simply outweighs the probative value of the evidence; the danger must *substantially* outweigh the probative value. Thus, the greater the probative value of the evidence, the more difficult it will be to exclude it under this rule. And the converse is also true. If the probative value of the evidence is slight, the degree of danger necessary to satisfy the rule's standard need not be particularly great.

36. Old Chief v. United States, 519 U.S. 172 (1997). For discussion of the Court's relevance analysis, *see* § 5.03.

37. *Id*. at 651.

38. *Id*.

39. *See* Ballou v. Henri Studios, Inc., 656 F.2d 1147, 1154 (5th Cir.1981) (trial court erred in excluding results of blood alcohol test on ground that it did not find results credible).

CHARACTER AND OTHER MISCONDUCT EVIDENCE

§ 5.05 The Prohibition on Use of Character to Show Conduct: In General [FRE 404(a)]

A definition of the character evidence rule is a helpful starting point in grasping both its limits and its breadth, though the generalities of the definition can only define a starting point, not provide an invariable test for the decision of particular cases. In general, the rule against character evidence *prohibits the reception of evidence illuminating a person's general disposition, when that evidence is offered to show action in conformity with that disposition on a particular occasion.*[40] The rule is subject to exceptions that will be discussed later. *See* §§ **5.06–5.15.** At this point, we will examine the contours and limits of the general rule itself.[41]

Before considering how and when the rule operates, it is necessary to attempt to define "character." Interestingly, neither the language of Federal Rule 404 nor the official commentary to the rule define the term. However, in distinguishing "character" from "habit," the drafters wrote:

> Character is a generalized description of one's disposition, or of one's disposition in respect to a general trait, such as honesty, temperance, or peacefulness.... If we speak of character for care, we think of the person's tendency to act prudently in all the varying situations of life, in business, family life, in handling automobiles and in walking across the street.[42]

This description begins to explain the meaning of character, but does not complete the story. Not all general tendencies constitute character. For example, a stroke victim's propensity to forget would not be seen as a trait of character, but as a medical condition. And despite the Advisory Committee's reference to "temperance" as a character trait, one could argue that intemperate use of alcohol is a medical condition rather than a character trait—though admittedly this view has not achieved accep-

---

40. *Compare* Fed. R. Evid. 404(a), which states that, with enumerated exceptions, "evidence of a person's character or a trait of character is not admissible for the purpose of proving action in conformity therewith on a particular occasion...." *See generally* Bonilla v. Yamaha Motors Corp., 955 F.2d 150 (1st Cir.1992) (held, in case where personal injury plaintiff sued for design defect in motorcycle, trial court committed reversible error by admitting evidence of prior speeding offenses in support of defendant's claim that speeding was cause of accident; evidence not admissible either to show a predisposition to speed or to impeach plaintiff's denial of having a speeding record; to allow impeachment in this fashion would create a situation in which otherwise inadmissible evidence would inevitably come in (either because plaintiff admitted the prior speeding offenses, or because plaintiff denied them and they were received to impeach).

41. For general discussion of the character evidence rules, see H. Richard Uviller, *Evidence of Character to Prove Conduct: Illusion, Illogic, and Injustice in the Courtroom*, 130 U. Pa. L. Rev. 845 (1982); Richard C. Wydick, *Character Evidence: A Guided Tour of the Grotesque Structure*, 21 U.C. Davis L. Rev. 123 (1987).

42. Fed. R. Evid. 406 advisory committee's note (quoting Charles T. McCormick, Handbook of the Law of Evidence § 162 at 340 (1954)).

tance.[43] To constitute a character trait, one would think (though this is not settled) that the tendency must arise in some reasonable degree from the person's *moral* being—from traits over which the person has a substantial element of choice, and which cause observers to regard the person more favorably or less favorably upon learning of the individual's behavior.[44] This principle becomes more obvious when one observes the examples listed in the drafters' notes to the Federal Rule. The drafters list "honesty, temperance, [and] peacefulness" in one place,[45] and use the terms "violent disposition" and "honesty" in another.[46]

While the statement of the general prohibition offered here is necessarily general, it does provide guidelines to some of the principal features of the rule against character evidence:

1. The rule applies not only to evidence of reputation, but also to any evidence that illuminates character. Reputation is not character, but only one way of showing character. (One's reputation, after all, might be deserved or undeserved.) Evidence of a person's specific deeds, whether good or bad, is also character

---

43. *See* Reyes v. Missouri Pacific R. Co., 589 F.2d 791, 794 (5th Cir.1979) (evidence of plaintiff's "character trait of drinking to excess" to prove that he was drunk on night of accident inadmissible because it did not fall into any exceptions in Fed. R. Evid. 404(a)); 1 McCormick on Evidence § 195, at 825 (4th ed. John W. Strong ed. 1994) (describing "temperance" as a character trait). *See also* Quinto v. City and Borough of Juneau, 664 P.2d 630, 634 (Alaska App.1983) (in prosecution for driving while intoxicated, testimony that defendant had a community reputation for being "a cautious, sober individual" should not have been excluded because it demonstrated a relevant trait of character). One court took note of an Air Force regulation that apparently attempted to distinguish between character-based and medically-based causes of excessive alcohol consumption of alcohol. Rowe v. United States, 167 Ct.Cl. 468 (1964) (citing Air Force regulation giving authority to discharge personnel for "unfitness" on grounds including "evidence of habits or traits of character manifested by ... chronic alcoholism" not caused by psychiatric disease).

44. Unfortunately, the drafters of the Federal Rules did not attempt to define character, and the legal literature reflects little effort to do so. Wigmore defined character as "the actual moral or psychical disposition or sum of traits...." 1A John H. Wigmore, Evidence in Trials at Common Law § 52, at 1148 (Peter Tillers rev. 1983). Elsewhere, however, he did not appear to confine the concept of character to aspects of the person that reflect her moral qualities. For example, he defined "character or

disposition" as simply "a fixed trait or the sum of traits." *Id.* § 55, at 1159. The Model Code of Evidence offered a similarly broad definition of character as "the aggregate of a person's traits, including those relating to care or skill and their opposites." Model Code of Evidence, Rule 304 (1942). The authors of one treatise have noted the difficulty of defining character:

> The Evidence Rules do not define "character." That may seem quite justifiable; doesn't everyone know what the word means in this context? Perhaps. But suppose the prosecution in a criminal case offers evidence that the accused is a "professional gambler" or that the victim of an attempted rape was a "virgin." Is this evidence barred by Rule 404(a) when offered as circumstantial evidence of conduct? Or take a civil case in which it is proposed to prove that the defendant was "clumsy" or "colorblind" or "accident prone" or a "wealthy playboy." Are any or all of these evidence of "character"? Consider also testimony that the accused was "a member of the Mafia" or a "skillful practitioner of the martial arts" offered to show a motive for a murder or the ability to commit it or the identity of the perpetrator.

22 Charles A. Wright & Kenneth W. Graham, Jr., Federal Practice and Procedure (Evidence) § 5233, at 349–50 (1978).

45. Fed. R. Evid. 406 advisory committee's note.

46. Fed. R. Evid. 404 advisory committee's note.

evidence if offered to show a person's general disposition as described above.

2.   The rule only applies, however, to evidence offered to show a person's general disposition. When, for example, evidence of a prior bad act is offered not to show general disposition, but something other than general disposition, such as motive or opportunity to commit a crime, *see* § **5.16,** the ban on character evidence does not apply. Moreover, the ban does not apply when the trait shown by the evidence is too narrow and specific to be considered a trait of character. There is a varying and hard-to-define line between general character-based disposition, which embraces such traits as honesty, peacefulness, and the like, and specific disposition, which embraces evidence of "habit", evidence of modus operandi, and evidence of other relatively narrow tendencies of a person. *See generally* § **5.30.** Evidence of general disposition or proclivities is "character evidence" that falls under the ban; evidence of specific or narrow disposition is not "character evidence." The distinction, like many troublesome legal distinctions, is one of degree.

3.   The rule bans only character evidence that is offered for the purpose of showing action in conformity with character on a particular occasion—or, as it is sometimes put, character evidence is barred only when it is offered *circumstantially* to prove out-of-court behavior. When character is the ultimate issue, as in a defamation case in which truth is the defense, then the ban against character evidence does not operate, because the evidence is not offered to show action in conformity with character, but to show character as an end in itself. *See* § **5.29.**

The principles set forth above may be represented diagrammatically. Suppose that "E" in the diagram set forth below represents the testimony of a witness offered at trial. "C" represents a general character-based disposition of the person whom the testimony concerns, such as the disposition to generosity or lack of generosity, to violence or nonviolence, to care or carelessness, or to obey the law generally. "A" represents an act of that person that is sought to be proven at trial.

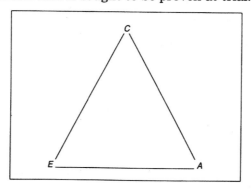

Evidence (E) falls within the character evidence ban only if it is offered to show a person's *general disposition* (C) en route to showing a specific act (A). If the evidence is offered to show general disposition without any further inference to a specific act (as is the case when character is the ultimate issue, see **§ 5.29**) then the character evidence ban does not apply. If the testimony leads to an inference that the act occurred *without the necessity* of any intermediate inference about general disposition, then the character evidence ban also does not apply. Examples of such testimony include testimony about habit (plaintiff always fastened his seat belt), modus operandi (defendant had previously robbed banks using an identical threatening note), or motive (defendant had debts from illegal gambling, and therefore had a motive to embezzle). Such testimony leads to an inference that the subsequent act was more likely to have occurred (the person was more likely to have fastened his seat belt, robbed the bank, or embezzled the money) without the necessity of drawing any inference about the person's general disposition of character. In other words, it is possible to go from "E" to "A" on the diagram without the necessity of a trip through "C." The ban on character evidence prohibits only the use of the route E–C–A; it does not prohibit a trip from E to C when C is the ultimate issue and no trip to A is necessary; and it does not prohibit a trip from E to A if that can be done without going through C. If evidence offered to prove a specific act tends to make the doing of the act more likely both because it throws light upon general disposition and because it shows something else, such as motive, then the doctrine of limited admissibility applies and the evidence will ordinarily be admitted with a limiting instruction. *See* **§ 2.09.** However, the limits of Rule 403 and its common law analogues apply here as elsewhere; if the value of the evidence, when considered for its legitimate purpose, is substantially outweighed by dangers of prejudice, confusion, or waste of time, then it may be excluded even though, in theory, it would be acceptable if its use were restricted to one purpose.

Purposes of the Rule Excluding Character Evidence

It has long been accepted that character evidence is relevant in the minimal sense of having some tendency to make a fact of consequence more likely or less likely than would be the case without the evidence.[47] The fact that a defendant had previously robbed banks makes it somewhat more likely that the defendant is guilty of the bank robbery charged in the present case. That is, we are generally willing to accept that a person who has robbed banks possesses a general disposition

---

47. As Wigmore wrote, "[a] defendant's character, then, as indicating the probability of his doing or not doing the act charged, is essentially relevant." 1A Wigmore, *supra* note 44 § 55, at 1157 (emphasis in original). *See also* John Jay McKelvey, Handbook of the Law of Evidence § 108, at 149 (1898) ("Where the question is whether X. did or did not do a certain act, his character, if proved, might throw a strong light upon the issue, and justify an inference as to the act charged"); James B.

toward this type of criminal behavior. Of course, the evidence is certainly not conclusive, but it does possess some probative value. Similarly, the opinion testimony of a close acquaintance of the defendant that defendant is the type of person who would rob banks is probative of defendant's relevant character trait and is circumstantial evidence of behavior. The same can be said for testimony concerning defendant's community reputation as a bank-robbing type of person. Yet, in contrast to some European systems, all of the evidence just discussed, whether in the form of specific instances of conduct, opinion, or reputation, would be excluded if offered to show defendant's disposition to rob banks.

The reason most commonly given for the character ban is that the trier of fact would be unduly prejudiced by the information[48] and might either overestimate the value of the evidence as proof that the defendant committed the crime charged[49] or decide to punish the defendant for being a bad person (or for the past misconduct) even if the trier was not convinced that the defendant was guilty of the crime charged.

Thayer, A Preliminary Treatise on Evidence at the Common Law 525 (1898) ("Undoubtedly, as a mere matter of reason, it often affords a good basis of inference").

48. *See, e.g.,* Michelson v. United States, 335 U.S. 469 (1948). Justice Jackson wrote:

The inquiry [into character] is not rejected because character is irrelevant; on the contrary, it is said to weigh too much with the jury and to so overpersuade them as to prejudge one with a bad general record and deny him a fair opportunity to defend against a particular charge. The overriding policy of excluding such evidence, despite its admitted probative value, is the practical experience that its disallowance tends to prevent confusion of issues, unfair surprise, and undue prejudice.

Id. At 475–76 (footnote omitted). *See also* 1 Wigmore, *supra* note 44 § 58.2 at 1212 (evidence of other acts is excluded, "not because it has no appreciable probative value, but because it has too much. The natural and inevitable tendency of the tribunal—whether judge or jury—is to give excessive weight to the vicious record of crime thus exhibited, and either to allow it to bear too strongly on the present charge, or to take the proof of it as justifying a condemnation irrespective of guilt of the present charge").

49. Empirical research suggests that "trait theory" is flawed. Trait theory relies on the notion that people possess relatively stable, general traits that manifest themselves consistently and predictably across situations. Today the more dominant theory, interactionism, posits that behavior in a given situation is governed both by a person's general tendencies and by the similarity of the situation to others the person has faced. Even with a large amount of data (an amount no trial court would presently allow), prediction is extremely difficult. For reviews of the psychological literature, *see* Susan M. Davies, *Evidence of Character to Prove Conduct: A Reassessment of Relevancy*, 27 Crim. L. Bull. 504 (1991); David P. Leonard, *The Use of Character to Prove Conduct: Rationality and Catharsis in the Law of Evidence*, 58 U. Colo. L. Rev. 1 (1986–87); Miguel Angel Mendez, *The Law of Evidence and the Search for a Stable Personality*, 45 Emory L.J. 221 (1996); Miguel Angel Mendez, *California's New Law on Character Evidence: Evidence Code Section 352 and the Impact of Recent Psychological Studies*, 31 UCLA L. Rev. 1003 (1984); Andrew E. Taslitz, *Myself Alone: Individualizing Justice Through Psychological Character Evidence*, 52 Md. L. Rev. 1 (1993). *See also* Michael R. Gottfredson & Travis Hirschi, A General Theory of Crime 85–91 (1990) (developing a new type of propensity-based theory, arguing that criminality is linked to lack of self-control and appreciation for long-term consequences of committing the crime; authors find much evidence of different crimes committed by criminals rather than specialization in particular crimes).

Unfair prejudice is not the only concern, however. Commentators have long stressed at least two other reasons to exclude evidence of other acts. First is simple fairness and surprise: the supposed unfairness of surprising the actor with such evidence. This consideration overlaps with that of unfair prejudice, but encompasses basic fairness concerns as well. Though surprise is less of a concern under modern rules,[50] it can still be a concern in some situations. Second is the fear of over-complicating the issues of the trial, leading to confusion and distraction of the jury and undue lengthening of the trial. The danger of over-complication of issues is very real. As one writer has noted, "particularly if there is a dispute about whether the defendant committed the other acts, introduction of evidence concerning those acts could be time-consuming and distract the factfinder from the central issues in the case."[51] Thus, in some situations, the character evidence rule promotes adjudicative efficiency by preventing the tribunal from pursuing side issues about whether other crimes or acts were in fact committed.

Another justification for the character rule is aspirational. The principle that guards against trial by character is deeply embedded in English and American history and practice. The rule thus represents a substantive value about how people *should* behave in relation to each other. It tells us that in making formal judgments that affect a person's life or freedom, some kinds of considerations should be out of bounds. To be sure, we use evidence of character in our daily lives when deciding such diverse matters whether to hire an individual as a caretaker for our children or whom to entrust with a bank deposit. Nobody would deign to tell us we should not do so, and any effort to regulate our behavior to prevent us from considering such qualities would fail utterly. Moreover, we can live comfortably with inaccuracy in this realm of private behavior. If it turns out that the information we received about the person's past behavior or general character is simply wrong, the error will usually cause only a relatively small degree of harm (though at times, the harm can be great, as in marriage or employment decisions). It would thus be both impracticable and of little actual value to try to regulate the use of character evidence in the private dealings of daily life. Decisions made in the courtroom are fundamentally different. In that public forum established for the formal resolution of disputes about past events, we are forced to adjudicate facts; we can seldom avoid making concrete and

---

50. The drafters of the Federal Rules of Evidence did not include "surprise" as among the dangers against which probative value should be measured when determining whether to exclude relevant evidence. The Advisory Committee appeared to believe that danger of surprise can be reduced by notice requirements and other procedural devices, and that its impact can be evaluated under the heading of "unfair prejudice." *See* Fed. R. Evid. 403 advisory committee's note. An amendment to Feder- al Rule 404(b), in fact, requires that in criminal cases, the prosecution provide the defendant notice of its intent to introduce evidence of the defendant's other acts, and of the general nature of the evidence it intends to offer. Fed. R. Evid. 404(b).

51. Richard B. Kuhns, *The Propensity to Misunderstand the Character of Specific Acts Evidence*, 66 Iowa L. Rev. 777, 777 (1981).

largely final decisions about events. In this context, the harms that can be engendered by character-based decision-making can be extremely costly for several reasons. First, even though we are aware that "truth" can never be determined with certainty, factfinding error can be very costly. Naturally, error can have significant impact on the parties, whose financial well being, freedom, and even life will depend upon the outcome. To the extent admission of character evidence creates a significant risk of inferential error, decisions based upon it can be highly dubious. Not only do judgments based on erroneous factfinding affect the parties in the case before the court, but they erode public confidence in the civil and criminal justice systems, creating a very real risk of disorder. Second, and regardless of the accuracy of character evidence in a given situation, its use in formal adjudication violates the common aspiration that people should not be judged based upon their characters. The trial can and should be a model for formal decision making. The types of evidence we find acceptable in that setting should represent our best, not our most base, instincts about how we *ought* to behave. If we believe that we should avoid decision based on character, then the trial process should reinforce that belief through regulation of character evidence. As such, it can model the kind of decision-making to which we aspire.

It would have been possible to leave the question of character evidence to the discretion of the trial court, under some general guideline such as that provided by Rule 403. However, the common law had built up a structure of specific rules dealing with this species of evidence, and the drafters of the Federal Rules decided to follow the common law tradition in almost all respects. The result is a series of familiar, but complicated and sometimes arbitrary, rules governing the reception of the evidence. In a leading case, the Supreme Court stated that much of the law is "archaic, paradoxical and full of compromises and compensations by which an irrational advantage to one side is offset by a poorly reasoned counter-privilege to the other." Nonetheless, the Court said, the system had proven workable if clumsy, and to "pull one misshapen stone out of the grotesque structure is more likely simply to upset its present balance between adverse interests than to establish a rational edifice."[52]

§ 5.06 Exceptions to the Rule Against Using Character Evidence to Show Conduct [FRE 404(a)(1)-(3)]

The rule against using character evidence to prove conduct is subject to exceptions. Before examining these exceptions, however, we should emphasize that most of the litigation concerning character evidence does not deal with the scope of the exceptions, but rather with whether the character evidence rule applies at all. The rule has limited scope, applying only to evidence of general disposition offered for the purpose of showing action in conformity with disposition. Evidence of other crimes, wrongs, and acts is often received, not under an *exception* to the

---

52. Michelson v. United States, 335 U.S. 469, 486 (1948).

character evidence rule, but under the theory that the character evidence rule simply does not apply, because the evidence is being received for some purpose other than showing conduct in conformity with character. See § **5.16**.

The character evidence rule, limited as it is, has long been subject to three exceptions, recognized both at the common law and under the Federal Rules. First, the defendant in a criminal case is permitted to offer character evidence, and if the defendant opens the door by offering this evidence, the prosecution may rebut it with contradictory character evidence. *See* §§ **5.07–5.08**. Second, with limits, the defendant and the prosecution may offer relevant evidence about the character of the victim of a crime. *See* § **5.09**. Third, the credibility of witnesses may be attacked or supported with certain types of character evidence. The present discussion will describe the first two exceptions. For discussion of the exception applicable to the credibility of witnesses, see § **5.11**.

Recently, a new exception to the general rule against character to prove conduct was added to the Federal Rules. This exception allows evidence of other similar misconduct of the defendant in prosecutions for sexual assault and child molestation, and for civil actions arising from such misconduct. This controversial exception, which has also been enacted in some states, will be discussed in § **5.10**.

§ 5.07 Exceptions to the Rule Against Character Evidence to Show Conduct [FRE 404(a)(1)–(3)]— Evidence of Defendant's Good Character in Criminal Cases [FRE 404(a)(1)]

Both the common law and the Federal Rules recognize an exception to the rules against character evidence for defendants who wish to offer witnesses to attest to their good character.[53] In this respect the defense has an advantage over the prosecution. The defense has an absolute right to offer character evidence as part of defendant's case in chief; the prosecution may offer character evidence only if the defendant "opens the door." The reason for different treatment is unclear. One reason might be that because our system has a built-in preference for freeing the guilty over convicting the innocent, the dangers inherent in bad character offered against the criminal defendant are considerably greater than the possible inferential error invited by the defendant's use of good character evidence to prove innocence. Perhaps the exception is just a merciful dispensation to the defendant, or a compensation for other features of a criminal trial that throw the balance in favor of the

---

53. *See* Fed. R. Evid. 404(a); Michelson v. United States, 335 U.S. 469, 476 (1948) (describing common law rule); David P. Leonard, *The Use of Character to Prove Conduct: Rationality and Catharsis in the Law of Evidence,* 58 U. Colo. L. Rev. 1 (1986–87) (reviewing common law and Federal Rule); Richard Uviller, *Evidence of* *Character to Prove Conduct: Illusion, Illogic, and Injustice in the Courtroom,* 130 U. Pa. L. Rev. 845 (1982) (reviewing entire structure of character evidence rules); Richard C. Wydick, *Character Evidence: A Guided Tour of the Grotesque Structure,* 21 U.C. Davis L. Rev. 123 (1987) (similar).

prosecution. Certainly the danger that a person who has led an unblemished life might become enmeshed in a web of incriminating circumstantial evidence through pure coincidence leads to the natural feeling there should be some way to show the jury what the person is really like, and some way for one's friends to help in an hour of need. For that matter, there may in fact be a difference in the probative force of evidence of good and bad character, on the theory that proof of good character is considerably more probative of character on a particular occasion than is evidence of bad character.[54] From a more cynical perspective, the rule allowing defendants to present character evidence is likely to favor persons who have status and connections, and this may have given the rule additional appeal to lawmakers who themselves would be able to present character witnesses if accused of crime.

Whatever the reason, it is well established that the defendant in a criminal case may offer evidence of good character. There are limits, however, on the form that the evidence may take. While evidence of actual good deeds by the defendant—for example, acts of honesty and kindness—might actually be the most persuasive evidence of character, it is universally excluded. Specific acts are not admissible to show character, though to a limited extent the defendant's attorney is entitled to introduce some "background" about such matters as the defendant's occupation, education, family, and military service.[55] Instead, at common law, character evidence had to take the relatively colorless form of evidence about community reputation. Under the Federal Rules, the permissible form of evidence has been expanded to include a knowledgeable witness's opinion of the defendant's character. *(See § 5.12* on methods of proving character.) Originally, reputation in the community was considered more probative than specific acts, representing as it did the community's collected wisdom, discussed and relied upon, about a lifetime of activity.[56] In modern society, where transient populations and breakdowns of community ties make it more difficult to derive reliable reputation testimony, evidence of specific acts is probably a better indicator of true character. Nonetheless, the limitation to reputation and opinion testimony is still a rational one, because restricting the testimony to that form saves time and avoids collateral conflicts about whether specific good or bad deeds actually took place.

A great deal of ink has been spilled discussing the question of what aspects of the defendant's character may be the subject of testimony. In general, the testimony has to concern a "pertinent" trait of character.[57]

---

54. *See* 22 Charles A. Wright & Kenneth W. Graham, Jr., Federal Practice and Procedure (Evidence) § 5236, at 380–81 (1978).

55. *See* State v. Stokes, 523 P.2d 364, 366 (Kan.1974) ("background information" and "biographical data" such as "place of birth, education, length of residence in the community, length of marriage, size of family, occupation, place of employment, service in armed forces and receipt of honorable discharge" not considered character evidence entitling prosecution to respond with evidence of bad character; defendant "entitled to let the jury know who he is").

56. *See* 5 John H. Wigmore, Evidence in Trials at Common Law § 1610, at 582 (James H. Chadbourn rev. 1974).

57. *See* Fed. R. Evid. 404(a)(1).

Thus, a defendant charged with a crime of dishonesty may not offer testimony about his character for peacefulness, but is limited to providing testimony about traits relating to honesty.[58] What about testimony about an extremely general trait, such as the defendant's proclivity to obey the law? Some common law courts permitted witnesses to testify about the defendant's reputation as a law-abiding person; others have required more specificity.[59] The exception for defense character evidence in the Federal Rules of Evidence refers to a the admissibility of a "pertinent trait of character"[60] and the advisory committee's note states that proof is limited to "pertinent traits of character, rather than character generally,"[61] so it would appear that under the Federal Rule specific traits, such as honesty and nonviolence, are admissible, but general testimony that a person has "good character" is not.

§ 5.08   Exception to the Rule Against Character Evidence to Show Conduct—Rebuttal by the Government of Defendant's Character Evidence [FRE 404(a)(1)]

There are two ways in which the defendant may open the door to attack by the prosecution on his or her character. The first is by producing favorable evidence about his or her own character. This may be called placing one's character *as a defendant* in controversy. The second is by taking the stand as a witness. This may be called placing one's character *as a witness* in controversy. The defendant in a particular case may do one without doing the other, or may do both or neither. The two forms of placing character in controversy lead to different consequences. By placing one's character *as a defendant* in question, the defendant opens the door to prosecution evidence about character traits relevant to the crime charged. When testifying, the defendant's character *as a witness* is in question, and the prosecution is permitted a different form of attack. Principally, this attack consists of introducing the prior convictions of the defendant that bear upon the defendant's credibility as a witness, though it may also take the form of putting on character witnesses who derogate the defendant's character for truthfulness. This attack on defendant's character *as a witness* is described elsewhere, under the rubric of impeachment of witnesses. *See* **Ch. 7**. The present section describes how the prosecution may attack the defendant's character *as a defendant*.

When the defendant offers character witnesses who attest to the defendant's good character, the defendant has opened the door to rebuttal by the prosecution. Although it is often said that by offering character evidence the defendant has put his or her "character in issue," this phrase is technically incorrect. Character does not become an ultimate

---

58. *See* 22 Wright & Graham, *supra* note 54 § 5236, at 385.

59. *See* 1A John H. Wigmore, Evidence in Trials at Common Law § 59 nn.1–2 (Peter Tillers rev. 1983).

60. Fed. R. Evid. 404(a)(1).

61. Fed. R. Evid. 404 advisory committee's note.

issue, in the sense that term is used in § 5.29, merely because the defendant has offered character evidence. The ultimate issue is still whether the defendant committed the crime charged, not whether the defendant had a good or bad character. Character is merely an evidentiary fact that bears upon this issue.

Once the defendant has opened the door, the prosecution may offer character evidence of its own, and it may do so in one of two ways. First, the prosecution may call its own witnesses to offer evidence of defendant's character. Like the defendant's witnesses, such testimony must be in the form of reputation or opinion. Second, the prosecution may cross-examine defendant's character witnesses, and such cross-examination may include questions about specific instances of defendant's conduct that bear on the traits of character to which the witness testified on direct examination.[62]

This second form of attack is likely to be the most potent. The defendant's character witnesses must testify in the form of opinion and reputation, and may not describe specific good deeds of the defendant; but on cross-examination the prosecution may bring out bad acts or prior crimes that the defendant is believed to have committed. For example, in *Michelson v. United States*,[63] the defendant's character witnesses testified favorably about his reputation for honesty and truthfulness and for being a law-abiding citizen. On cross-examination, the prosecutor asked certain of the character witnesses the following questions:

> "Did you ever hear that Mr. Michelson on March 4, 1927 was convicted of a violation of the trademark law in New York City in regard to watches?"

> "Did you ever hear that on October 11th, 1920, the defendant, Solomon Michelson, was arrested for receiving stolen goods?"

One of these questions concerned a 20-year old conviction; the other concerned an arrest which, so far as appeared, did not even result in conviction. Both involved specific acts, not general testimony about reputation or opinion. Nonetheless, the Supreme Court affirmed the conviction, indicating that the questions were proper.[64]

---

62. *See* Fed. R. Evid. 404(a)(1), 405(a). *See also* United States v. Smith–Bowman, 76 F.3d 634, 636 (5th Cir.), *cert. denied*, 518 U.S. 1011 (1996) (permissible to ask defendant's character witness whether he had heard that defendant, a Red Cross official, had used her Red Cross VISA card (a) to pay for a motel room for a rendezvous with her boyfriend and (b) to buy jewelry for herself); SEC v. Peters, 978 F.2d 1162, 1171–73 (10th Cir.1992) (trial court committed reversible error by allowing defendant to present impressive array of "good character witnesses" while refusing to allow SEC to cross-examine witnesses about sworn charges and past lawsuits against defendant for fraud and insider trading).

63. 335 U.S. 469 (1948).

64. The advisory committee's note to Rule 405(a) endorses *Michelson* and implies that the same questions would still be permissible. For cases presenting a different point of view about cross-examination on arrest records, see Commonwealth v. Scott, 436 A.2d 607 (Pa.1981); People v. Roberts, 479 N.E.2d 386 (Ill.App.1985); Kruse v. State, 483 So.2d 1383 (Fla.App.1986). *Cf.* United States v. Mason, 993 F.2d 406 (4th Cir.1993) (held, cross-examining character witness about whether witness would change mind if defendant guilty of instant crime was impermissible).

The theory on which the prosecution's questions were permitted in *Michelson* was that they were pertinent, not to the question of whether the defendant had actually committed the prior acts, but to the question whether the character witnesses were actually knowledgeable about the defendant's reputation. If they had not heard about the arrest and conviction, the character witnesses were not fully knowledgeable; if they had heard, then one might question their criteria for good reputation.

The presentation of character evidence by the defense therefore opens the door to potentially very harmful questioning of the character witnesses about prior acts of the defendant, whether or not they resulted in conviction. However, there are two significant limitations upon the prosecutor's freedom in using evidence of this nature. First, the prosecutor can only ask the questions, and must take the witness's answer. *Extrinsic evidence of the defendant's prior conduct is not admissible.* If the witness denies having heard of the prior conduct, the prosecution may not produce other witnesses to prove that the defendant in fact engaged in the character-destroying conduct.[65] Second, the prosecutor must have a good faith basis for asking the question. That is, the prosecutor cannot simply manufacture questions about prior convictions, arrests, or bad acts, but must actually have information indicating that these events occurred.[66]

If the prosecutor questions character witnesses about prior acts of the defendant, the defendant is entitled to a limiting instruction describing the way in which the jury is supposed to use the evidence.[67] Because the concept under which the evidence is admitted is a complicated one, the instruction is necessarily a hard one to understand and apply, but it should nevertheless be requested by the defense, if only to preserve the point on appeal if the instruction is not given. The instruction should state that the jury is not to assume that the incidents asked about

---

Because they are aimed at impeaching the witness, not showing the defendant's propensity, the questions must concern a matter about which the witness (in the case of an opinion witness) or the community (in the case of a reputation witness) might reasonably be expected to have heard. See United States v. Monteleone, 77 F.3d 1086, 1090 (8th Cir.1996) (question about whether character witness had heard that defendant perjured himself before grand jury improper since witness would not know what had happened in secret grand jury proceedings).

65. *See* Fed. R. Evid. 405(b), and advisory committee's note thereto.

66. Michelson v. United States, 335 U.S. 469, 481 n. 18 (1948); 1 McCormick on Evidence § 191, at 817 (4th ed. John W. Strong ed. 1992); United States v. Wells, 525 F.2d 974 (5th Cir.1976); United States v. Beno, 324 F.2d 582 (2d Cir.1963) *cert. denied*, 379 U.S. 880 (1964); State v. Keul,

5 N.W.2d 849 (Iowa 1942). Logically speaking, the prosecution should be permitted to ask defendant's reputation witnesses about the arrest as long as there is a good faith belief that rumors were circulating through the community that the arrest had occurred, even if such rumors were untrue. (If rumors were circulating, and the witnesses had not heard them, the jury might question the witnesses' knowledge; if the witnesses had heard the rumors but nevertheless testified favorably about defendant's reputation, the jury might question the witnesses' judgment.) The Court recognized this illogical aspect of the rule, but retained the common law requirement of a good faith belief that the arrest actually occurred, in order to prevent undue prejudice to the defendant. *Michelson*, 335 U.S. at 481 n.18.

67. *See* Fed. R. Evid. 105.

actually took place, but use the evidence only to test the witness's standard for evaluating the reputation of the defendant.[68]

§ 5.09 Exceptions to the Rule Against Character Evidence to Show Conduct—Character of the Victim in Criminal Cases [FRE 404(a)(2), 412]

The prosecution or defense will sometimes seek to offer evidence about the character of the victim in a criminal case. Such evidence is, of course, not admissible to show that the victim was a bad person who deserved to be a victim, but it may be admissible if it is relevant to a legal defense of the accused. Though it is possible for the issue to arise in other contexts,[69] the most common situations in which victim character is offered are homicide cases, in which the defendant claims that the victim was the first aggressor (and hence that the defendant should be acquitted on grounds of self-defense), and rape cases, in which the defendant claims that the victim consented to the sexual act, and seeks to introduce evidence of her prior sexual conduct to show a proclivity to consent.

Homicide Cases

A defendant raising the claim of self-defense may seek to introduce evidence that the victim had a violent or turbulent character in order to persuade the trier that the victim was the first aggressor. Similarly, the prosecution may seek to introduce evidence of the victim's peaceable character to show that victim did not attack the defendant.

In cases in which the victim's violent character was known to the defendant, the rule against character evidence erects no obstacle, and no exception is needed in order to make the evidence admissible. The evidence would be admissible, even in the absence of an exception to the character evidence rule, on grounds that it is not offered as evidence to show action in conformity with character; instead, it is being used to show the reasonableness of the defendant's belief in the necessity for violent resistance.[70] If the defendant believed that the victim had violent

---

68. One example of this instruction was given by the trial court in the *Michelson* case. The instruction stated:

> I instruct the jury that what is happening now is this: the defendant has called character witnesses, and the basis for the evidence given by those character witnesses is the reputation of the defendant in the community, and since the defendant tenders the issue of his reputation the prosecution may ask the witness if she has heard of various incidents in his career. I say to you that regardless of her answer you are not to assume that the incidents asked about actually took place. All that is happening is that this witness' standard of opinion

of the reputation of the defendant is being tested.

Michelson v. United States, 335 U.S. 469, 472 n. 3 (1948).

69. *See* 1A John H. Wigmore, Evidence in Trials at Common Law § 63 n.1 (Peter Tillers rev. 1983), suggesting that under the Federal Rule "in an embezzlement case, an accused might be allowed to put in the propensity of a victim to defraud insurers in order to show that the victim rather than the accused removed certain money from a safe."

70. In terms of the diagram in **§ 5.05,** the use of the evidence does not require either an inference from E to C (it is not necessary that the victim have actually had propensities, then that belief might form the basis for a claim that defendant's conduct was reasonable, whether or not the victim actually had that character, and whether or not the victim acted in conformity with it. The admissibility of evidence of the victim's violent character, when that character was known to the defendant prior to the incident, is clearly established.[71]

An exception to the rule against character evidence is needed when the defendant offers evidence of the victim's violent character, for the purpose of showing that the victim was the first aggressor, rather than for the purpose of showing defendant's belief in the victim's aggressiveness. Most jurisdictions, and the Federal Rules, provide for such an exception.[72] By use of reputation evidence or, in jurisdictions following the Federal Rules, by opinion testimony as well, the defendant may show that the victim had a violent character. In jurisdictions following the Federal Rules, specific instances of conduct are not admissible for this purpose, if the sole reason is to show that the victim had a general disposition toward violence.[73] (Of course, specific acts of violence by the victim are admissible if they are relevant for some other purpose, such as showing motive or a specific disposition to act violently toward a specific person.[74])

Once the defendant has opened the door by attacking the victim's character for peacefulness, or has otherwise offered testimony to support the claim that the victim was the first aggressor, the prosecution may support the victim's character with evidence that the victim had a peaceable disposition. In some circumstances, the character of a victim can be supported even if the defense has not attacked it with evidence of bad character. Under the Federal Rules of Evidence, the prosecution can also offer evidence of the good character of the victim if, in a homicide

---

a violent character, so long as the defendant believed it to be so) or a trip from C to A (it is not necessary that the victim have acted in conformity with character for the evidence to be probative of the defendant's subjective belief).

71. 1A Wigmore, *supra* note 69 § 63, at 1369; State v. Miranda, 405 A.2d 622 (Conn.1978); People v. Lynch, 470 N.E.2d 1018 (Ill.1984); State v. Jacoby, 260 N.W.2d 828 (Iowa 1977). *See also* Smith v. State, 606 So.2d 641, 642–43 (Fla.App.1992) (trial court erred by excluding evidence of victim's specific acts of violence against defendant, his family and others, when defendant knew about the attacks and defendant pleaded self-defense).

72. *See* Fed. R. Evid. 404(a)(2); 1A Wigmore, *supra* note 69 § 63.

73. Fed. R. Evid. 405(a); United States v. Keiser, 57 F.3d 847, 856–57 (9th Cir.), *cert. denied*, 516 U.S. 1029 (1995) (though relevant, character evidence of the victim was properly excluded under Rule 405; defendant had shot victim but claimed it was

done in self-defense; defense wanted to proffer evidence that in lobby outside courtroom, victim pointed to the defendant's brother and told his family and friends that he was "the fucker's brother" and to remember his face); United States v. Waloke, 962 F.2d 824, 830 (8th Cir.1992) (although evidence of victim's reputation for violence after drinking was properly allowed, danger of unfair prejudice and "collateral mini trials" warranted excluding evidence in assault case of specific violent acts by victim).

74. Thus, a husband's prior acts of beating his wife while intoxicated are admissible when offered to show, not that the husband was a generally violent person, but that he had a specific propensity to beat his wife, and hence that the wife acted in self-defense. *See, e.g.,* United States v. McIntire, 461 F.2d 1092, 1092–93 (5th Cir.1972); White v. State, 717 S.W.2d 784 (Ark.1986); Worthington v. State, 405 N.E.2d 913 (Ind. 1980).

case, the defendant has offered evidence that the victim was the first aggressor.[75] The defendant need not have supported the claim with character evidence; the right of the prosecution to support character is triggered by any evidence that the victim was the first aggressor, whether the evidence takes the form of character evidence or of testimony about what the victim did during the encounter that forms the basis for the prosecution.

Rape Cases

At common law, some courts admitted evidence of a woman's character for chastity, in the form of either reputation testimony or specific acts testimony, to show that she had a propensity to consent, for the further purpose of showing consent on a particular occasion.[76] This approach deterred the pursuit of rape complaints, because of the victims' fear of abuse and degradation in the courtroom. Moreover, its premise that consent on one occasion with one partner is worthy evidence of consent on another is untenable in an age in which "one can presume that a woman will freely choose her partners, picking some and rejecting others, in line with highly personal standards not susceptible of generalization."[77] As part of a reform effort supported by the women's movement and by law enforcement officials, almost all state legislatures and Congress adopted "rape shield" legislation in the 1970s that limited the use of evidence of prior sexual conduct in sexual assault cases.[78]

Rape shield legislation differs from state to state, but all statutes have at least one common feature: evidence of reputation and sexual behavior is not admissible purely for purposes of showing unchaste character, as the basis for a further inference that the complainant consented to sex on the occasion in question. The statutes generally do allow prior sexual behavior to be admitted for certain limited purposes. Two widely recognized examples of admissible behavior are (a) the complainant's prior sexual behavior with the defendant, as opposed to behavior with other persons, and (b) evidence of the complainant's sexual behavior with other persons, when offered for purposes of explaining the physical consequences of the alleged rape—e.g., injury, the presence of semen, pregnancy, or venereal disease.[79] Other examples of

---

75. *See* Fed. R. Evid. 404 (a)(2).

76. *See* 1A Wigmore, *supra* note 69 § 62; People v. Allen, 124 N.E. 329 (Ill. 1919); Graham v. State, 67 S.W.2d 296 (Tex.Crim.App.1933); Fry v. Commonwealth, 177 S.E. 860 (Va.1935).

77. Vivian Berger, *Man's Trial, Women's Tribulation: Rape Cases in the Courtroom*, 77 Colum. L. Rev. 1, 56 (1977).

78. For a thorough and insightful review of this legislation, see Harriett R. Galvin, *Shielding Rape Victims in the State and Federal Courts: A Proposal for the Second Decade*, 70 Minn. L. Rev. 763 (1986). Professor Galvin reports that 48 states and the federal government have adopted re-

form legislation. *Id.* at 808. *See also* Ann Althouse, *Thelma and Louise and the Law: Do Rape Shield Rules Matter?*, 25 Loy. L.A. L. Rev. 757 (1992).

In civil cases, a modified version of the "rape shield" rule excludes evidence of sexual predisposition or sexual behavior of an alleged victim unless "its probative value substantially outweighs the danger of harm to any victim and of unfair prejudice to any party." Fed. R. Evid. 412(b)(2), Pub. L. No. 103–322, 108 Stat. 1796 (1994).

79. *See, e.g.,* Fed. R. Evid. 412; Mich. Comp. Laws Ann. § 750.520j (West Supp. 1987); Mass. Ann. Laws ch 233, § 21B (1986); Minn. R. Evid. 404(c). If the proseadmissible behavior, though not universally recognized, are instances in which the evidence is offered to show a motive for fabrication by the complainant[80] or to show other behavior so nearly identical to the behavior on the occasion in question that it leads to a reliable inference of consent.[81] The statutes generally also have a procedural element, providing for hearings in limine on the issue of admissibility, and in some cases providing for in camera hearings to protect the woman's privacy.[82] Indeed, some statutes do little more than set up a procedural mechanism for pretrial decision and call attention to the problem, providing only some general standard of admissibility, such as weighing prejudice against probative value.[83] Others attempt a more radical approach to exclusion by providing that the evidence may be received only for specific purposes.[84] The more radical statutes have sometimes been challenged on grounds that they deny due process by preventing defendants from presenting legitimate exculpatory evidence.[85]

Other Criminal Cases

Under the Federal Rules of Evidence, and subject to the limitation for rape cases, the defendant is allowed to offer evidence of a "pertinent trait" of the victim's character.[86] Suppose, for example, defendant is charged with assault and battery, and claims self-defense, asserting that

---

cution seeks to prove rape by putting in evidence that, for example, the complainant became pregnant, it is only fair to allow the defense to rebut by showing that another man could have caused the pregnancy. But the defense is not entitled to put in evidence of disease, pregnancy, or semen where the prosecution has not benefited from the evidence and has done nothing to open the door. *See* United States v. White Buffalo, 84 F.3d 1052, 1054 (8th Cir.1996) (held, where government made no effort to introduce semen evidence, defendant not entitled to put in evidence of rape complainant's prior consensual intercourse solely to impeach her by showing that she made a false statement to hospital doctor that she had not had consensual intercourse within 72 hours of rape).

80. *See* Md. Code Ann. art 27, § 461A (1996). *See also* Olden v. Kentucky, 488 U.S. 227 (1988) (unconstitutional to prevent defendant from cross-examining accuser about fact that she lived with male friend R., when R. saw accuser disembarking from defendant's car after alleged rape, and defense was based on claim that accuser fabricated rape in order to protect relationship with R.); United States v. Platero, 72 F.3d 806, 814–16 (10th Cir.1995) (trial court erred in not allowing evidence of victim's affair with her co-worker, to whom victim reported the rape; defense alleged that victim engaged in consensual intercourse and that she had fabricated the rape to protect

her relationship with the co-worker; issue whether affair had occurred was for jury, not trial judge, to decide).

81. *See* Minn. R. Evid. 404(c).

82. *See* 23 Charles A. Wright & Kenneth W. Graham, Jr., Federal Practice and Procedure (Evidence) § 5391 (1980). *But cf.* United States v. Platero, 72 F.3d 806, 813 (10th Cir.1995) (held, issue whether rape victim had prior sexual relationship was for the jury, not the judge, to decide under amended Rule 412).

83. *See, e.g.,* R.I. Gen. Laws § 11–37–13 (1981) (providing for notice to court and discussion of admissibility "out of hearing of jury").

84. *See* Fed. R. Evid. 412.

85. *See, e.g.,* State v. Jalo, 557 P.2d 1359 (Or.App.1976) (unconstitutional to exclude evidence of child complainant's prior sexual conduct when adult defendant claimed that she had falsely accused him because he told her that he was going to inform her parents of her sexual conduct with his son and others); Commonwealth v. Black, 487 A.2d 396 (Pa.Super.1985) (unconstitutional to exclude sexual behavior evidence that shows bias). *See also* Clifford S. Fishman, *Consent, Credibility, and the Constitution: Evidence Relating to a Sex Offense Complainant's Past Sexual Behavior,* 44 Cath. U.L. Rev. 709 (1995).

86. Fed. R. Evid. 404(a)(2).

the victim attacked first. Because the case is not a homicide prosecution, the exception previously discussed relating to homicide cases does not apply, but the rule nevertheless permits the defendant to offer character evidence to show the victim's violent character, and thus the likelihood that the victim was the first aggressor.[87]

An important difference from the homicide exception is that, as with her own character, the defendant holds the key to the admissibility of character evidence of the victim in these cases. If defendant does not offer evidence of the victim's character to prove the victim's behavior on the occasion in question, the prosecution may not do so. Of course, the rule permits the prosecution to "rebut" defendant's character evidence, and in those circumstances the rule works identically with that governing the defendant's character. In examining its own witnesses, the prosecution is limited to evidence of reputation and opinion, but in cross-examining defendant's witnesses, the prosecution may inquire about relevant specific instances of conduct.

The key threshold question is what traits of the victim's character are "pertinent" to the defendant's claims. Obviously, a general tendency toward violence would be pertinent to the defendant's claim that the victim attacked first. But just as discussed above, such evidence would not be admissible to prove the subtly different self-defense claim based on the defendant's *belief* that the victim was violent, and thus to explain why *defendant* attacked first. In many criminal cases, the victim's character simply will not be pertinent to any issue. It is difficult to imagine, for example, how the victim's character could be relevant in prosecutions for robbery, burglary, or fraud. Unless the defendant can convince the court that a particular character trait is pertinent to her defense, this exception will not apply.

§ 5.10 Exceptions to the Rule Against Character Evidence to Show Conduct—Character of Defendant in Sexual Assault and Child Molestation Cases [FRE 413–415]

In 1994 new federal crime legislation was enacted that included three new evidence rules making evidence of other sexual misconduct admissible "on any matter to which it is relevant." Specifically, evidence of other sexual assaults is now admissible in prosecutions for sexual assault,[88] evidence of other acts of child molestation is now admissible in prosecutions for child molestation,[89] and the same types of misconduct are admissible in civil actions arising out of alleged sexual assault and child molestation.[90] Though case law will be needed to clarify the rules in

---

87. *See, e.g.,* United States v. Perez–Casillas, 607 F.Supp. 88 (D.Puerto Rico 1985) (in prosecution of police officers for perjury and conspiracy in killing two individuals, evidence that victims had reputation for violence and aggression admissible to prove alleged victims were first aggres-

sors in confrontation that led to their deaths).

88. Fed. R. Evid. 413.

89. Fed. R. Evid. 414.

90. Fed. R. Evid. 415.

many respects, it is clear that Congress intended to allow juries in these types of cases to employ the character reasoning forbidden by longstanding rules. In a prosecution for rape, for example, it will now be permissible for the government to offer evidence of other rapes or sexual assaults committed by the defendant, in order to establish defendant's character-based propensity to commit such crimes, and thus, the likelihood that defendant committed the charged offense.

The general admissibility of this evidence does not render futile all attacks upon it. Certainly, Congress did not intend to abolish the trial judge's discretion to exclude the evidence when its probative value is substantially outweighed by the danger of unfair prejudice.[91] Though the defendant will no longer be able to argue that the evidence is unfairly prejudicial in that it invites the jury to convict based upon the belief that he is the kind of person who would commit such a crime, the court may still exclude the evidence on the basis that the jury will convict based on emotional grounds, that it will overvalue the evidence, or on other bases.[92]

In addition, not all character evidence will be admissible under the new rules. Only specific instances of conduct are allowed, and, as noted above, the rules limit the prosecution to evidence of similar misconduct. Thus, acts of child molestation generally will not be admissible in prosecutions for rape.[93]

One can expect a number of states to follow the lead of the federal government and provide for admission of this kind of evidence. California, for example, enacted similar legislation in 1995,[94] and other states

---

91. *See* United States v. Guardia, 955 F.Supp. 115, 117 (D.N.M.1997) ("A common sense reading of Rule 403 . . . indicates that since it applies only to evidence otherwise admissible, it applies to evidence otherwise admissible under Rule 413"; court limited number of witnesses prosecution permitted to call to present evidence under Rule 413); Frank v. County of Hudson, 924 F.Supp. 620, 624 (D.N.J.1996) ("evidence proffered under [Rules 413 to 415] must still be shown to be relevant, probative and 'legally relevant' under FRE 403"; because probative value of questioned evidence was slight and potential for prejudice was high, court granted protective order against its use). *See also* David J. Karp, *Evidence of Propensity and Probability in Sex Offense Cases and Other Cases*, 70 Chi.-Kent L. Rev. 15, 19 (1994) (statement of author of legislation that "[t]he general standards of the rules of evidence would apply to evidence offered under these rules, including . . . the authority of the court to exclude relevant evidence under Rule 403").

In United States v. Enjady, 134 F.3d 1427 (10th Cir.1998) the court held that the trial court has authority, pursuant to Rule 403, to exclude evidence otherwise admissible under Rule 413, and that so understood the rule survives constitutional due process and equal protection challenges.

92. One issue left open by the new rules is whether the evidence is admissible against a non-human defendant. *See* Cleveland v. KFC Nat. Mgmt. Co., 948 F.Supp. 62, 65–66 (N.D.Ga.1996) (where Title VII party defendant was corporate employer, Rule 415 nevertheless applies to admit relevant sexual acts of defendant's manager despite language in rule referring to "a party's" other sex offenses).

93. *See* Fed. R. Evid. 413(a) ("In a criminal case in which the defendant is accused of an offense of sexual assault, evidence of the defendant's commission of another offense or offenses of sexual assault is admissible. . . ."); Fed. R. Evid. 414(a) ("In a criminal case in which the defendant is accused of an offense of child molestation, evidence of the defendant's commission of another offense or offenses of child molestation is admissible. . . .")

94. Cal. Evid. Code § 1108 (West Supp. 1997).

are sure to follow.[95] Whether the new rules will work a significant change in actual practice is unclear.[96] Many states have long followed lenient rules of admissibility of such evidence in sexually related crimes, sometimes on the theory that the evidence is not "character" as used in those cases. *See* § 5.24.

95. *See, e.g.,* Ind. St. Ann. § 35–37–4–15 (1994) (allowing similar crimes evidence in prosecutions for child molestation and incest if probative value of evidence is not substantially outweighed by danger of unfair prejudice); *cf.* Mo. Rev. Stat. § 566.025 (1995) (in prosecutions for some crimes against minors, allowing evidence of other crimes against minors to show propensity to commit such crimes).

96. The new rules have engendered substantial commentary, much of it critical. Among the many works criticizing the rules are Katharine K. Baker, *Once a Rapist? Motivational Evidence and Relevancy in Rape Law*, 110 Harv. L. Rev. 563 (1997); Craig R. Callen, *Proving the Case: Simpson, Fuhrman, Grice, and Character Evidence*, 67 U. Colo. L. Rev. 777 (1996); James J. Duane, *The New Federal Rules of Evidence on Prior Acts of Accused Sex Offenders: A Poorly Drafted Version of a Very Bad Idea*, 157 F.R.D. 95 (1994); Karen M. Fingar, *And Justice For All: The Admissibility of Uncharged Sexual Misconduct Evidence Under the Recent Amendment to the Federal Rules of Evidence*, 5 S. Cal. Rev. L. & Women's Stud. 501 (1996); Stephen R. Henley, *Caveat Criminale: The Impact of the New Military Rules of Evidence in Sexual Offense and Child Molestation Cases*, Army Law. 82 (March, 1996); Edward J. Imwinkelried, *Some comments About Mr. David Karp's Remarks on Propensity Evidence*, 70 Chi.-Kent L. Rev. 37 (1994); Edward J. Imwinkelried, *Undertaking the Task of Reforming the American Character Evidence Prohibition: The Importance of Getting the Experiment Off on the Right Foot*, 22 Fordham Urb. L.J. 285 (1995); David P. Leonard, *The Federal Rules of Evidence and the Political Process*, 22 Fordham Urb. L.J. 305 (1995); James S. Liebman, *Proposed Evidence Rules 413 to 415—Some Problems and Recommendations*, 20 U. Dayton L. Rev. 753 (1995); Louis M. Natali, Jr. & R. Stephen Stigall, *"Are You Going to Arraign His Whole Life?": How Sexual Propensity Evidence Violates the Due Process Clause*, 28 Loy. U. Chi. L.J. 1 (1996); Jeffrey G. Pickett, *The Presumption of Innocence Imperiled: The New Federal Rules of Evidence 413–415 and the Use of Other Sexual–Offense Evidence in Washington*, 70 Wash. L.

Rev. 883 (1995); Mark A. Sheft, *Federal Rule of Evidence 413: A Dangerous New Frontier*, 33 Am. Crim. L. Rev. 57 (1995); Anne Elsberry Kyl, Note, *The Propriety of Propensity: The Effects and Operation of New Federal Rulers of Evidence 413 and 414*, 37 Ariz. L. Rev. 659 (1995); Lisa M. Segal, Note, *The Admissibility of Uncharged Misconduct Evidence in Sex Offense Cases: New Federal Rules of Evidence Codify the Lustful Disposition Exception*, 29 Suffolk U.L. Rev. 515 (1995). In 1995, the American Bar Association adopted a resolution opposing the substance of the new rules. *See* Myrna S. Raeder, *American Bar Association Criminal Justice Section Report to the House of Delegates, reprinted in* 22 Fordham Urb. L.J. 343 (1995). The Judicial Conference, given an opportunity to comment on the proposed rules before they became effective, suggested revisions to "clarify drafting ambiguities and eliminate constitutional infirmities." Report of the Judicial Conference of the United States on the Admission of Character Evidence in Certain Sexual Misconduct Cases 1 (Feb. 1995).

There has been some commentary favorable to aspects of the new rules. *See, e.g.,* David P. Bryden & Roger C. Park, *"Other Crimes" Evidence in Sex Offense Cases*, 78 Minn. L. Rev. 529 (1994) (proposing a limited exception to the character bar in sexual assault cases involving acquaintances); Karen M. Fingar, *And Justice for All: The Admissibility of Uncharged Sexual Misconduct Evidence Under the Recent Amendment to the Federal Rules of Evidence*, 5 S. Cal. Rev. L. & Women's Stud. 501 (1996); Norman M. Garland, *Some Thoughts on the Sexual Misconduct Amendments to the Federal Rules of Evidence*, 22 Fordham Urb. L.J. 355 (1995) (supporting the policy of the new rules though sharply criticizing the drafting); Roger C. Park, *The Crime Bill of 1994 and the Law of Character Evidence: Congress Was Right About Consent Defense Cases*, 22 Fordham Urb. L.J. 271 (1995) (supporting the new rules in cases in which the accused raises a consent defense); Andrew E. Taslitz, *Patriarchal Stories I: Cultural Rape Narratives in the Courtroom*, 5 S. Cal. Rev. L. & Women's Stud. 387, 494–

§ 5.11　Exceptions to the Rule Against Character Evidence to Show Conduct [FRE 404(a)(3)]— Character of Witnesses

Another exception to the rule against using character to show action in conformity involves the firmly rooted rule allowing the impeachment of the credibility of witnesses by showing their prior convictions or by offering testimony about their bad character for truthfulness. For a discussion of this topic, see the sections on impeachment of witnesses in Chapter 9.

§ 5.12　Methods of Showing Character: Evidence of Reputation, Opinion, and Specific Acts [FRE 405]

As the previous discussion indicates, the rules governing the admissibility of character evidence to prove conduct specify the *form* of character evidence that may be offered. Though technical (and arcane), lawyers must take care to offer the evidence in its permissible form.

The most general rule is that the character of a person is ordinarily not provable through specific instances of a person's conduct,[97] but only through reputation or opinion. While reputation and opinion testimony may not carry as much flavor as specific act testimony, it is much less time-consuming and less likely to lead to confusing collateral issues.

The common law rule restricted evidence of character to testimony about reputation, which was thought to represent the accumulated wisdom of the community, and hence to be more reliable than the mere opinion of any particular person. This restriction was too hobbling; because of the transitory conditions of modern society, it is more difficult to acquire a broad, reliable reputation. At any rate, "reputation" evidence often merely represented the witness's opinion in disguise. The Federal Rules take a broader view, and allow the testimony to be given in the form of either reputation or opinion.[98]

Reputation and Hearsay

Evidence of reputation, when used to show character, is evidence of out-of-court statements offered for the truth of the matter asserted, and hence is hearsay. (Reputation, after all, is what the community *says* about a person.) However, the Federal Rules provide a special hearsay exception applicable to reputation testimony.[99] At common law, reputation for character was also, implicitly or explicitly, treated as falling

96 (1996) (favoring limited change while criticizing the new rules).

97. The exception to this rule occurs when character is an ultimate issue. *See* § 5.29.

98. Fed. R. Evid. 405(a).

99. Fed. R. Evid. 803(21). It should be noted that this exception does not guarantee the admission of all reputation evidence that meets the requirements of the exception, but only takes care of any hearsay objection that might be made to the testimony. The reputation-for-character evidence, even though not hearsay, must still fall into a category in which character evidence is admissible in order to be received. *See* Fed. R. Evid. 404(a). *Compare* United States v. Reveles, 1993 WL 135864, at *6 (A.F.C.M.R.1993), *aff'd.*, 41 M.J. 388 (1995) (trial court properly excluded bartender's testimony as to victim's reputation for intemperance, because reputation based upon within a hearsay exception, so the question was not whether the evidence was hearsay, but whether it was admissible under the rules governing character evidence.

Reputation in the Community or in the Workplace

Some common law cases restricted reputation evidence to evidence about a person's reputation in the community in which he or she lived, thereby preventing testimony about the person's reputation in the place of work.[100] As a hard-and-fast rule, this view never had much to recommend it; sometimes reputation at the place of work was more pertinent than reputation in the neighborhood. As one early source put it, when a schoolmaster is accused of beating schoolchildren, which reputation is more convincing, that of the schoolroom or that among his neighbors?[101] With the advent of suburbia and the apartment complex, and the modern separation of job and home, the view has become even less defensible, since a person may often have closer acquaintances in the place of work than in the place of residence. The Federal Rules accordingly provide for the admission of reputation evidence either "in the community" or "among associates."[102]

Personal Knowledge Requirement

When character evidence is offered in the form of reputation, the witness must have personal knowledge of reputation. The witness usually will also know the person whose reputation is the subject of testimony, but it is personal knowledge of reputation, not directly of the person's character, that is required. When the witness is testifying about his or her own opinion of a person's character (as is permitted in jurisdictions following the Federal Rules), he or she must have personal knowledge of the person about whom the opinion has been formed and enough experience with that person to justify entertaining an opinion; but it is not necessary for the opinion witness to know the reputation of the subject.

The reputation knowledge must be acquired by having heard the reputation discussed with a sufficient number of people, though the number is not precisely quantifiable.[103] A witness who reports reputation secondhand (that is, who reports what one other person says about reputation) is reporting hearsay that does not fall under an exception.

group of patrons at Officers' Club bar, not a "recognized community"; Rule 404(d) of Military Rules of Evidence defines reputation as the "estimation in which a person is generally held in the community").

100. *See* Williams v. United States, 168 U.S. 382 (1897) (reputation at place of work excluded, on grounds that it existed only among a limited number of people in a particular building).

101. Keener v. State, 18 Ga. 194, 221 (1855), excerpted in 5 John H. Wigmore, Evidence in Trials at Common Law § 1616, at 591 (James H. Chadbourn rev. 1974).

102. Fed. R. Evid. 803(21).

103. There is no precise number or percentage of people in a community who must discuss their opinion of a person for that opinion to be a "reputation." It is clear that it need not be a majority, See 5 Wigmore, *supra* note 101 § 1613; Girch v. State, 177 N.W. 798 (Neb.1920) (witness who heard 15 to 20 people in a community of 200 say that defendant had a bad reputation for truth competent to testify as to that reputation). *Cf.* United States v. Neff, 343 F.Supp. 978, 982 (E.D.Pa.1972) (witness talked to "seven or eight people" about

Can an investigator acquire knowledge of reputation specifically for purposes of a case, and then testify about reputation? Despite early cases to the contrary, the prevailing view appears to be that the investigators can acquire reputation knowledge for purposes of a particular case.[104] The partisanship of the investigator may throw some doubt upon the veracity of the evidence, but this is true of any facts discovered by an investigator, and of course the investigator is subject to cross-examination concerning his or her testimony about reputation. If the investigation was thorough and the investigator testifies truthfully, then the investigator's work product is as reliable as any testimony of a resident of the community.

Absence of Bad Reputation

The witness who testifies to having never heard anything about the reputation of the subject may be demonstrating a lack of personal knowledge about reputation. The testimony should not be received in this exact form. However, the witness who testifies to being acquainted with people who know the defendant, and is in a position to hear derogatory statements if any were made, is permitted to testify about not having heard anything unfavorable. The mere fact that a person who was in a position to hear unfavorable comments has never heard them, despite having been privy to conversations concerning the person whose reputation is the subject of testimony, is itself evidence of good character. Acts of misconduct are more a topic of conversation among one's associates than acts of ordinary rectitude, and the law recognizes that the person who has led an unstained life may show that to be so through the testimony of a witness who has "never heard anything against" the person.[105]

§ 5.13 Methods of Showing Character: Evidence of Reputation, Opinion, and Specific Acts [FRE 405]— Laying the Foundation for Character Evidence: Examples

The Federal Rules of Evidence permit character evidence to be presented either in opinion form or reputation form. Most pre-Rules

defendant; problem with testimony was that they did not know defendant, not that number was insufficient).

104. *See* 3 John H. Wigmore, Evidence in Trials at Common Law § 692 (James H. Chadbourn rev. 1970).

105. *See, e.g.,* Deschenes v. United States, 224 F.2d 688, 691 (10th Cir.1955) ("silence speaks in his favor and the fact that a character witness has never heard ill said of the defendant is evidence within itself of a good reputation"); State v. Foster, 665 S.W.2d 348 (Mo.App.1984); State v. Floyd, 289 S.E.2d 139 (N.C.App.1982); 5 Wigmore, *supra* note 79 § 1614. An interesting example of this problem arose in the celebrated murder trial of Harvard Medical College Professor John Webster in 1849. One of Webster's character witnesses testified that he had been defendant's neighbor for 15 years but had never heard his character for violence or inhumanity discussed. He was permitted to testify that he had "never heard any acts of violence, or inhumanity, imputed to him." Testimony of John G. Palfrey, Stone, Report of the Trial of Professor John W. Webster 145 (1850). *Cf.* SEC v. Peters, 978 F.2d 1162, 1171–73 (10th Cir.1992) (trial court erred by excluding "have you heard" cross-examination questions about defendant's prior misconduct to an opinion character witness for the defense).

common law jurisdictions allowed only opinion testimony.[106]

Example (Reputation)

Q. Do you know Mr. Smith [the defendant]?

A. Yes

Q. Is he here in the courtroom today?

A. Yes.

Q. Where is he sitting?

A. Right next to you, on your left.

COUNSEL: Let the record reflect that the witness has identified Mr. Smith.

Q. How long have you known Mr. Smith?

A. Four years.

Q. During that period, how often did you see him?

A. Every day during the weekends, then sometimes during the week.

Q. What is the nature of your association with him?

A. We are next-door neighbors.

Q. Anything else?

A. We served on the homeowners' association together, both on the Board of Directors for two years.

Q. Did you know other people who knew him?

A. Yes.

Q. How many?

A. Dozens, he is very well known.

Q. Did you discuss with these people, or hear discussed, the defendant's reputation for being a [law-abiding] [truthful] [peaceable and nonviolent] person?

A. Yes.

Q. What is his reputation for being a [law-abiding] [truthful] [peaceable and nonviolent] person?

A. It is excellent, the best.[107]

Example (Opinion)

Q. Do you know Mr. Smith [the defendant]?

A. Yes.

106. *See* 5 John H. Wigmore, Evidence in Trials at Common Law § 1610 (James H. Chadbourn rev. 1974).

107. Note that in this example, the witness testifies to knowing Mr. Smith per-sonally. This is not necessary for a reputa-tion witness. It is common for such a wit-ness to be quite familiar with a person's community reputation without knowing the individual personally.

Q. Is he here in the courtroom today?

A. Yes.

Q. Where is he sitting?

A. Right next to you, on your left.

COUNSEL: Let the record reflect that the witness has identified Mr. Smith.

Q. How long have you known Mr. Smith?

A. Four years.

Q. During that period, how often did you see him?

A. Every day during the weekends, then sometimes during the week.

Q. What is the nature of your association with him?

A. We are next-door neighbors.

Q. Anything else?

A. We served on the homeowners' association together, both on the Board of Directors for two years.

Q. Did you know him well enough to form an opinion as to his character for truth and veracity? [being a law-abiding person?] [being a peaceable and nonviolent person?]

A. Yes, certainly.

Q. What is your opinion?

A. He is an extremely truthful and honest person.

§ 5.14　Character Evidence in Civil Cases: In General

The Federal Rules of Evidence do not permit the use of character evidence in civil cases, except insofar as it may be used to impeach the credibility of witnesses.[108] The rule makers reasoned that character evidence is of slight probative value and may be very prejudicial. They recognized that the same could be said of character evidence in criminal cases, but stated the criminal rule was "deeply imbedded in our jurisprudence," while the admissibility of character evidence in civil cases was not, and "those espousing change [in civil cases] have not met the burden of persuasion."[109] Nevertheless, there is a dissenting view that the provision in Rule 404(a) allowing the "accused" to put in character evidence applies to a party in a civil action who is accused of crime-like conduct, such as a police officer in a federal civil rights action accused of killing a person,[110] or a defendant in a wrongful death action who has been accused of intentionally killing the victim.

---

108. *See* Fed. R. Evid. 404(a), which creates exceptions only for impeaching witnesses and for evidence offered for and against an "accused" person.

109. Fed. R. Evid. 404 advisory committee's note.

110. *See* 22 Charles A. Wright & Kenneth W. Graham, Jr., Federal Practice and Procedure (Evidence) § 5236, at 386–89

The rule against use of character evidence in civil cases must be understood in light of the limited nature of the character evidence ban. As noted in § **5.05,** the ban applies only to evidence of general disposition, when offered to show conduct in conformity with that disposition. It does not prohibit the use of habit evidence. *See* § **5.30.** Nor does it prohibit the use of evidence of prior acts when used for the purpose of showing something other than character, such as motive, opportunity, preparation, plan, or the like. *See* § **5.16.** Also, it does not prohibit the use of evidence of character when the evidence is not used to show action in conformity with character, as is the case when character is the ultimate issue. *See* § **5.29.** Moreover, the rule is subject to an exception, applicable in civil as well as criminal cases, permitting the impeachment of a witness by evidence of prior convictions or by opinion and reputation evidence concerning the witness's character for truthfulness. See § **5.11** and **Ch. 7**. It is also subject to Rule 415, which permits the use of evidence of specific instances of misconduct in civil actions involving allegations of rape or child molestation. *See* § **5.10.**

Rule 412, the federal "rape shield" rule, now applies in modified form to civil cases. As amended effective December 1, 1994, the rule generally excludes evidence offered to prove that an alleged victim engaged in other sexual behavior and evidence of the alleged victim's sexual predisposition.[111] However, the rule further provides that in civil cases, "evidence offered to prove the sexual behavior or sexual predisposition of any alleged victim is admissible if it is otherwise admissible under these rules and its probative value substantially outweighs the danger of harm to any victim and of unfair prejudice to any party."[112] Further, evidence of an alleged victim's reputation is admissible only if the alleged victim has placed that reputation in controversy.[113]

Not all jurisdictions follow the restrictive position of the Federal Rules concerning the use of character evidence in civil cases. In some jurisdictions, a party is permitted to offer evidence of good character in a civil case, in response to an allegation of criminal conduct or conduct involving moral turpitude. Once this evidence has been offered and received, the opposing party may meet it with evidence of bad character.[114]

§ 5.15 Character Evidence in Civil Cases: Other Claims, Other Frauds

A character evidence problem can arise in civil cases in situations in

---

(1978) which, though conceding that apparently the word "accused" was intended to refer to the defendant in a criminal case, argues that the word could be construed to embrace as well the party in a civil action who is accused of a criminal act. *See also* Perrin v. Anderson, 784 F.2d 1040, 1044–45 (10th Cir.1986) (victim character evidence would be admissible in a civil case in which defendant accused of unlawful killing; however, because plaintiff's evidence constitut-ed specific instances of conduct rather than opinion or reputation, such evidence was inadmissible).

111. Fed. R. Evid. 412(a).

112. Fed. R. Evid. 412(b)(2).

113. *Id.*

114. *See generally* 1A John H. Wigmore, Evidence in Trials at Common Law §§ 65–67 (Peter Tillers rev. 1983).

which a litigant wishes to prove that a civil plaintiff is "claim-minded."[115] For example, a defendant in a personal injury case might offer evidence that on one or more other occasions the plaintiff claimed to have been injured while boarding a bus. When offered to show that the plaintiff is litigious, it is character evidence that may prejudice the jury. Evidence of other claims is usually rejected.[116] However, it can be received if there is a showing of a distinct pattern of making false claims.[117] When such a showing is made, the evidence is not offered as character evidence to show a general disposition to make such claims, but is admitted under Rule 404(b) as evidence of intent, plan, or modus operandi.[118]

Civil cases in which a claim or defense turns on fraud can also raise potential character evidence problems. For example, the alleged victim of a misrepresentation by a real estate broker might wish to show that the broker made similar misrepresentations to other clients. In such instances, the party claiming fraud is usually allowed to put in evidence of similar past frauds by the opposing party.[119] This evidence would not be admissible if it were relevant only to show the bad character of a human adversary. However, it usually comes in for its bearing on some other issue that is at least semantically distinct, such as intent, knowledge, or lack of mistake or accident.[120]

§ 5.16　Evidence of Other Crimes, Wrongs, or Acts When Used for a Purpose Other Than Showing Action in Conformity With Character—In General [FRE 404(b)]

Suppose a defendant charged with bank robbery raises the defense of alibi. As part of its proof, the prosecution seeks to show that the defendant robbed a convenience store a year before the bank robbery.

---

115. *See generally* 3A John H. Wigmore, Evidence in Trials at Common Law § 963, at 808 (James H. Chadbourn rev. 1970) (courts divided on admissibility of evidence); 1 McCormick on Evidence § 196 (4th ed. John W. Strong ed. 1992) (admissibility of party's prior actions or defenses).

116. *See, e.g.,* Outley v. City of New York, 837 F.2d 587, 592 (2d Cir.1988) (in civil rights action against city and individual police officers alleging police brutality, evidence of plaintiff's prior lawsuits against police department inadmissible where previous claims not shown to be fraudulent); Lowenthal v. Mortimer, 270 P.2d 942, 945 (Cal.App.1954) (plaintiff's fifteen prior lawsuits inadmissible, prejudicial); 1 McCormick on Evidence, *supra* note 90 § 196, at 832 (evidence usually excluded when offered to show plaintiff is chronic litigant).

117. *See, e.g.,* Sessmer v. Commonwealth, 103 S.W.2d 647, 649 (Ky.1937) (prior unfounded claims admissible in disbarment proceeding for blackmailing physician with frivolous claim); 1 McCormick on Evidence, *supra* note 115 § 196, at 831–32 (party's previous similar claims admissible if fraudulent).

118. *See* Fed. R. Evid. 404(b).

119. *See, e.g.,* Edgar v. Fred Jones Lincoln–Mercury, 524 F.2d 162, 167 (10th Cir. 1975) (similar past conduct in tampering with odometer to falsify mileage on second-hand cars); 1 McCormick on Evidence, *supra* note 115 § 197, at 835 (evidence of similar frauds frequently admitted).

120. *See, e.g., Edgar,* 524 F.2d at 167 (past tampering with odometer admissible to show intent); Dial v. Travelers Indem. Co., 780 F.2d 520, 523–24 (5th Cir.1986) (plaintiff's association with two other intentionally set fires also destroying insured property admissible to show intent or plan); 1 McCormick on Evidence, *supra* note 115 § 197 (past frauds admissible to demonstrate intent, knowledge, lack of accident, or plan or scheme).

The inferential process most likely set in motion by this evidence is the following:

EVIDENCE: The defendant committed one armed robbery.

> **INFERENCE:** The defendant is the type of person who commits armed robberies.

> **CONCLUSION:** It is more likely that the defendant is guilty of the present crime than would otherwise be the case.

When offered on this reasoning, the evidence would be barred by the rule against character evidence.[121] First, it is evidence of a general disposition offered to show conduct in conformity with that disposition, and hence is barred by the general rule against character evidence. *See* § 5.05. Second, even if one of the exceptions to the rule against use of character evidence to show conduct applied—for example, even if the defendant had opened the door to evidence about character traits by putting on witnesses who testified that the defendant was honest and law-abiding—the evidence about the prior convenience store robbery would still be inadmissible, because it is evidence of a specific act offered to prove character, and character may only be proven by reputation and opinion testimony. *See* § 5.15.

How is it, then, that specific acts and specific prior crimes are often admitted in criminal cases (and sometimes in civil cases)? Of course, when the defendant testifies, prior convictions may be admitted, subject to restrictions, for the purpose of impeaching credibility. *See* § 5.11 and **Ch. 9.** Yet even when the defendant does not testify, and even when prior conduct has not led to a conviction, other instances of defendant's misconduct may be admissible, not to show a defect in credibility, but as substantive evidence of guilt. The theory of admission is that the evidence is not offered to show character, but to show something else— either a trait of personality that is too narrow to be called character, or something that is not a trait of personality at all. The Federal Rules of Evidence provide for admission under the following formula in Rule 404(b):

> Evidence of other crimes, wrongs, or acts is not admissible to prove the character of a person in order to show that he acted in conformity therewith. It may, however, be admissible for other purposes, such as proof of motive, opportunity, intent, preparation, plan, knowledge, identity, or absence of mistake or accident.[122]

---

121.   *See, e.g.*, United States v. Brown, 71 F.3d 1158, 1162 (5th Cir.1995) (in drug sale case, held error to admit, under Rule 404(b) to show identity, evidence that the defendant had previously been convicted of possession of cocaine with intent to distribute since prior conviction was only relevant to show bad character); United States v. Phillips, 599 F.2d 134 (6th Cir.1979) (prior bank robberies inadmissible when no showing of similarity of plan). For a case that, in the authors' opinion, violates this principle, see State v. Smith, 707 P.2d 289, 297 (Ariz. 1985) (robbery of other convenience stores admissible in prosecution for robbing convenience store).

122.   Fed. R. Evid. 404(b).

Suppose, therefore, that in the previous bank robbery hypothetical, the evidence suggests that the crime was committed by an individual wearing a clown mask and who handed the teller a note claiming to be Robin Hood, saying all the money would be given away to the "poor people on the streets," and instructing the teller to empty the drawer of all small bills. The prosecution wishes to prove that on several other occasions, defendant robbed banks in the same town using precisely the same method. Though the evidence would be inadmissible if offered to prove defendant's general character for unlawful behavior and thus her guilt of the present crime, it would likely be admissible to prove her *identity* as the bank robber on the following reasoning:

EVIDENCE: Defendant robbed other banks using exactly the same method.

INFERENCE: Defendant is a bank robber who uses that distinctive method to commit the crime.

CONCLUSION: Defendant is the person who committed the crime at issue.

Note that this reasoning does not involve an inference of or from a general disposition to commit crime, or even to rob banks. It is offered to establish defendant's identity as the bank robber solely through reasoning that does not require an inference that defendant possesses a general character trait. This does not mean the jury will not employ the forbidden reasoning; in many instances the danger that this will occur even with a limiting instruction is sufficiently great to merit exclusion.[123] But in the absence of too great a danger of that eventuality (and assuming exclusion is not required for other reasons), the evidence would almost certainly be admissible.

The list of purposes for which other crimes may be offered is a time-honored (though non-exclusive) one. Similar lists appeared in decisions and treatises long before the adoption of the Federal Rules of Evidence.[124]

The admissibility of other crimes and acts has been a hotly and exhaustively debated and litigated subject, and it is perhaps the most commonly asserted ground for appeal in criminal cases. Federal Rule 404(b) has generated more reported appellate litigation than any other subsection of the rules.[125]

---

123. For an excellent analysis and critique of the rule, particularly noting that the rule does not avoid all propensity inferences, see Richard B. Kuhns, *The Propensity to Misunderstand the Character of Specific Acts Evidence*, 66 Iowa L. Rev. 777 (1981).

124. H. Richard Uviller, *Evidence of Character to Prove Conduct: Illusion, Illogic, and Injustice in the Courtroom*, 130 U. Pa. L. Rev. 845, 877 (1982):

The entire list, obviously, arrived—complete—down the chute of history. A virtually identical version can be found in a famous decision of the New York Court of Appeals written in the second year of this century, and several earlier treatises recite a comparable catalogue. The origins are doubtless obscure in the mists antedating the great treatises.

(Footnotes omitted.)

125. *See* 22 Charles A. Wright & Kenneth W. Graham, Jr., Federal Practice and

In such litigious terrain, one might expect to find well-trodden paths furnished with helpful guideposts, and perhaps even a paved way to the most common destinations. To the contrary—the terrain is so vast, inconsistent, and full of different starting points that judges who travel it must find a way to their destinations mainly through a sense of what is fit for the particular case, with the language of case law and treatises serving more as soothing incantations than as guideposts. The ultimate question presented (when is specific past human conduct a reliable predictor of present action?) is so difficult, so susceptible to differences of opinion, and so dependent upon the peculiar facts of the individual case, that it is unlikely that any set of hard-and-fast rules will provide exact answers.

The decided cases do, however, provide some general guidelines. If the evidence is relevant only to show character, then its use is prohibited by Rule 404(a), Rule 404(b), and by the Rules' common law analogue. If the evidence is relevant for some other purpose—and, as noted, the list in 404(b) is merely a list of examples, not an exhaustive list—then the probative value of the evidence must be balanced against its prejudicial effect, as well as the danger of waste of time and confusion.[126] In other words, even if the evidence falls into one of the categories listed in Rule 404(b), it must still withstand scrutiny under Rule 403. Among the considerations that bear upon the Rule 403 determination is whether the prior crime has the capacity to arouse horror or sympathy or to invoke a desire to punish; the remoteness in time of the evidence of other crimes and bad acts;[127] and whether the fact sought to be proven by the uncharged crime is really in dispute and, if so, whether it might be proven with other evidence. As the Supreme Court made clear in *Old Chief v. United States*,[128] the trial court must consider the *context* in which evidence is offered, which includes the other evidence available to prove the fact.[129] Another factor mentioned by some courts is the strength of the evidence (aside from evidence of uncharged crimes or collateral bad acts) that is available against the defendant. If the evidence directly concerning the charged crime is very powerful, then the incremental probative value of the other crimes evidence is less, and there is therefore (under this line of reasoning) less reason for admitting it.[130] The basic task is one of balancing, and as the advisory committee's note to Rule 404(b) states, the rule offers no mechanical solution.

Procedure (Evidence) § 5239 (1978). One author has devoted an entire text to the subject. Edward J. Imwinkelried, Uncharged Misconduct Evidence (1984).

126. Fed. R. Evid. 404 advisory committee's note to subdivision (b); 2 Weinstein's Federal Evidence § 404.07[4] (2d Ed. Joseph M. McLaughlin ed. 1997).

127. *See* 1 McCormick on Evidence § 190, at 809–810 (4th ed. John W. Strong ed. 1992).

128. 117 S.Ct. 644 (1997).

129. *Id*. at 652 ("what counts as the Rule 403 'probative value' of an item of evidence, as distinct from its Rule 401 'relevance,' may be calculated by comparing evidentiary alternatives"). For discussion of *Old Chief, see* § **5.03.**

130. United States v. Beechum, 582 F.2d 898 (5th Cir.1978). One may question whether this is a proper consideration, since it seems to suggest that when the proof of the charged crime is weak, evidence the prejudicial effect of which would otherwise outweigh its probative value should be

It is also necessary for the court to consider the quantum of evidence that the defendant in fact committed the other misconduct which the prosecution offered. The Supreme Court has held that there need only be evidence sufficient to support a finding by a preponderance of the evidence that defendant committed the act, but not all states follow this permissive rule. *See* § **5.28**.

It should be noted that the evidence of other crimes, wrongs, or acts is not limited to evidence of convictions. Crimes or wrongs that did not result in conviction may be admissible if they are offered for a proper purpose. Indeed, even a crime that resulted in an acquittal may be admissible, provided that its commission is established in the present proceeding in accordance with the rules about quantum of proof that are in force in the jurisdiction. *See* § **5.28**. It should also be noted that the rules do not require that the other crimes, wrongs, or acts be previous crimes, wrongs, or acts. Uncharged misconduct that occurs after the crime charged in the instant case may also be admissible. For example, a defendant who used a distinctive modus operandi in a series of murders was charged with the murder that was first in time, but was identified as the murderer partly by evidence that he was linked with subsequent murders having a similar method.[131]

As a convenient shorthand, this book will refer to evidence of other crimes, wrongs and acts as *uncharged misconduct* evidence.[132] The term *uncharged* refers to the fact that the defendant in the instant case is not now charged with the other misconduct; it does not mean that he or she was never charged with the misconduct, since prior convictions can be one form of uncharged misconduct evidence. The term *misconduct* correctly emphasizes that the evidence offered need not be evidence of a crime, but may be evidence of some form of non-criminal misconduct. The term is not absolutely precise, for though the evidence will usually in practice be evidence of misconduct offered to show the commission of a crime, in theory (and occasionally also in practice) it might be evidence of a good act offered to show the commission of another good act. (The same principle applies to the latter as to the former; prior good acts are not admissible for an inference of good character en route to an inference of action in conformity with good character, but they may be admissible to show conduct if that can be done without relying upon an inference about character.)

admitted, thus putting the defendant with a good case on the facts of the particular crime charged in a worse position than one who is clearly guilty of the particular crime charged. Perhaps, however, in some cases the weighing of this factor can be justified on grounds that the other crimes evidence is simply a waste of time when the immediate evidence is overwhelming.

131. Rex v. Smith, [1914–15] All E.R. Rep. 262, the celebrated "Brides in the Bath" case described at § **5.19** was just such a case of the use of subsequent acts to prove an earlier crime.

132. In this respect, we have followed the usage of Imwinkelried, *supra* note 125.

§ 5.17 Specific Purposes for Which Uncharged Misconduct Evidence May Be Offered

This section will offer examples of particular purposes for which other crimes evidence may be admitted. As Rule 404(b) suggests, the list of specific purposes is not exhaustive; evidence of uncharged crimes may be admissible for other reasons not listed. In addition, the purposes listed below often overlap. For example, evidence that is offered to show intent may also show a common plan; evidence that is offered to show identity often does so by showing modus operandi. It is the obligation of the proponent of the prior misconduct evidence to specify the 404(b) exception under which the evidence falls.[133]

It is also important to recognize that the various possible purposes for which the evidence might be offered are not all of the same order. A close examination of the list in Rule 404(b) reveals that most of the potential uses of uncharged misconduct evidence are merely circumstantial evidence of other facts that must be proven to establish a claim or defense (ultimate facts). For example, motive, opportunity, preparation, and plan are not ultimate facts, but only facts that, if proven, offer circumstantial support to the existence or nonexistence of ultimate facts. Intent and identity, on the other hand, are usually ultimate facts; unless these facts can be proven, the facts necessary to sustain the charge will not have been proven. *Knowledge* is often in this category of ultimate facts as well.[134] Because relevance issues often arise with respect to uncharged misconduct evidence, counsel must not only identify the *immediate* purpose for which the evidence is offered, but also the *ultimate* fact such evidence tends to prove. While a person's conduct might well establish an evidentiary fact, unless that fact is relevant to an ultimate issue in the case, the evidence should be rejected. Suppose, for example, that in a prosecution for receiving stolen goods knowing them to be stolen, defendant admits knowingly possessing the goods but claims they were not stolen. If the prosecution offers evidence of other instances in which defendant received stolen goods, it is important to inquire why such evidence is relevant. If offered on a modus operandi theory to prove identity (that defendant was the person who possessed the goods), defendant should argue that the evidence should be rejected because identity is not a contested issue.[135] If offered to prove plan as a means to

---

133. *See* United States v. Sampson, 980 F.2d 883, 888 (3d Cir.1992) (prosecution may not list the "litany" of 404(b) exceptions without specifying which one(s) apply).

134. For example, in a prosecution for receiving stolen goods, it is not sufficient that the prosecution prove that defendant received goods and that the goods were stolen; the prosecution must also prove that defendant *knew* the goods were stolen. Without proof of this fact, defendant will prevail. For discussion of the use of un-

charged misconduct evidence to prove knowledge, see § 5.21.

135. Technically, the evidence would be relevant under Fed. R. Evid. 401, but should be rejected under Rule 403. *See* § 5.04. Some courts have held, however, that even if defendant does not contest the existence of an element of the crime, the prosecution may still offer evidence to prove that element. *See, e.g.*, United States v. Bastanipour, 41 F.3d 1178, 1183 (7th Cir. 1994); United States v. Gilliam, 994 F.2d 97, 102 (2d Cir.), *cert. denied*, 510 U.S. 927 (1993). Even so, when an issue is undisputshow intent, defendant should also argue for exclusion because defendant admits knowingly possessing the goods. Counsel should be prepared in advance to make and meet relevance arguments whenever the admissibility of uncharged misconduct evidence is at issue.

§ 5.18　Specific Purposes for Which Uncharged Misconduct Evidence May Be Offered—Motive

The uncharged misconduct may be received to show a motive for the charged crime. Though motive is not itself an issue in a criminal prosecution, motive can be relevant to an ultimate issue such as criminal intent or the identity of the perpetrator.

For example, if the defendant and another person previously committed a crime together, and the defendant knew that the other person was prepared to testify against him in a prosecution for the other crime, then the defendant would have a motive for murdering the other person, and the prior crime—though perhaps not all of its details—would be admissible for that purpose.[136] In such a case, motive could be offered to prove that defendant committed the crime (if defendant denies involvement), or that the killing was intentional (if defendant admits killing the victim but asserts lack of criminal intent). Similarly, some courts have admitted evidence of a defendant's drug addiction as showing a motive for a crime of theft, on grounds that the addiction would create an

---

ed, defendant can argue that the probable value of the uncharged misconduct evidence is slight when compared with the danger of unfair prejudice.

136. *See* United States v. Clark, 988 F.2d 1459, 1465 (6th Cir.), *cert. denied*, 510 U.S. 832 (1993) (evidence of defendant's car theft activities admissible to show his motive for killing his brother-in-law and former employee, who told FBI about defendant's illegal acts); United States v. McKinney, 954 F.2d 471, 480–81 (7th Cir.), *cert. denied*, 506 U.S. 1023 (1992) (evidence that victim had botched a drug transaction 20 months before the charged conspiracy to commit murder admissible to establish motive); United States v. Dunn, 946 F.2d 615, 617–18 (9th Cir.), *cert. denied*, 502 U.S. 950 (1991) (evidence that defendant had been dealing cocaine on evening of gun offense admissible to show defendant's motive for threatening security guard with gun); United States v. Felix–Gutierrez, 940 F.2d 1200, 1207 (9th Cir.1991) (prior drug trafficking offenses admissible to prove motive for charged offense of accessory after the fact to kidnapping, torture, and murder of DEA agent). *Cf.* United States v. Harvey, 526 F.2d 529 (2d Cir.1975) (boy's statements implicating defendant in crime jointly committed by boy and defendant admissible to show defendant murdered boy). *But see* United States v. Murray, 103 F.3d 310,

316–18 (3d Cir.1997) (held, reversible error to admit evidence of prior murder by defendant charged with drug-related murder; court noted lack of evidence that prior murder was part of some criminal scheme or committed in some distinctive fashion; dubious character of witness who purported to have knowledge of prior murder may have influenced court, though court did not expressly allude to that consideration as a basis for its decision).

Evidence of the uncharged crime can provide a motive for murder in a variety of ways. *See, e.g.,* State v. King, 468 S.E.2d 232, 239 (N.C.1996) (held, evidence proving defendant involved in drug operations was properly admitted in defendant's trial for first-degree murder and assault with a deadly weapon since prosecution's theory was that defendant threatened to murder victim because of his belief that victim had robbed one of defendant's "lieutenants" in his drug organization); United States v. Santiago, 46 F.3d 885, 889 (9th Cir.), *cert. denied*, 515 U.S. 1162 (1995) (held, evidence of defendant's dealings with the prison gang "the Mexican Mafia" was properly admitted to explain motive in killing an inmate who defendant was not acquainted with).

extraordinary need for money.[137] This, in turn, would generally tend to establish defendant's identity as the perpetrator. In an unusual case, the court admitted evidence that a doctor had patients perform fellatio while he wrote them prescriptions for Quaalude; the uncharged misconduct was received to show that the doctor was motivated by something other than a desire to provide legitimate medical treatment.[138] In a celebrated case growing out of the Watergate scandal, evidence of the break-in in the office of Daniel Ellsberg's psychiatrist was admitted to show a motive for a subsequent cover-up by Nixon administration officials Haldeman and Erlichman. Among other things, the court pointed out that the payment of money to one of the Watergate burglars, E. Howard Hunt, could have been motivated partly by a desire to conceal evidence of the Ellsberg break-in.[139]

Sometimes evidence of prior assaults is admitted in an assault case under the rubric of "motive." If the defendant has previously assaulted the same person, then these courts allow the prior assault to be used as evidence that the defendant disliked the person, providing a motive for a subsequent assault. Such evidence could be admissible to prove that defendant committed the crime,[140] or that the killing was intentional rather than the result of an accident.[141] Acts showing enmity toward a racial group can also be used as evidence of subsequent discrimination.[142] Similarly, enmity toward an opponent in corporate politics may be

137. United States v. Saniti, 604 F.2d 603 (9th Cir.), *cert. denied*, 444 U.S. 969 (1979); Archie v. State, 224 S.E.2d 64 (Ga. App.1976). *See also* United States v. Aramony, 88 F.3d 1369, 1376–77 (4th Cir.1996) (held, in prosecution of former CEO of United Way of America, where prosecution's theory was that defendant defrauded United Way in order to obtain sexual pleasure at no cost to himself, evidence of defendant's sexual advances and activities with United Way employees was relevant and admissible to show motive for charged crimes, even though charged crimes involved expenditures on other women); United States v. Robinson, 956 F.2d 1388, 1396–97 (7th Cir.), *cert. denied*, 506 U.S. 1020 (1992) (evidence of defendant's prior imprisonment admissible to show that raising money for his family was motive for charged cocaine distribution).

138. United States v. Potter, 616 F.2d 384 (9th Cir.1979). *Cf.*, United States v. Cunningham, 103 F.3d 553, 556–57 (7th Cir.1996) (Posner, J.) (in case in which nurse allegedly replaced Demerol with saline solution in syringes, thus depriving patients of pain medication, evidence of nurse's addiction admissible to show motive, Judge Posner conceded that "motives" derived from a taste for engaging in a crime or compulsion to do it, as here, "overlap" with propensity).

139. United States v. Haldeman, 559 F.2d 31, 88–91 (D.C.Cir.1976), *cert. denied*, 431 U.S. 933 (1977).

140. *See* United States v. Wynn, 987 F.2d 354, 356–57 (6th Cir.1993) (evidence of defendant's past threats and prior attempt to kill his ex-wife admissible in prosecution to solicit her murder); State v. Green, 652 P.2d 697, 700–01 (Kan.1982) (in prosecution for murdering wife, evidence of several prior violent altercations between defendant and wife, for one of which defendant had been convicted of battery, admissible to show relationship of parties giving rise to motive and intent and thus defendant's identity as killer).

141. State v. Hedger, 811 P.2d 1170, 1173–74 (Kan.1991) (in prosecution for murdering wife where defendant claimed he shot her accidentally, evidence of two prior violent incidents between defendant and wife admissible to prove "ongoing relationship between the parties").

142. *See* Johnson v. Hugo's Skateway, 949 F.2d 1338, 1345–46 (4th Cir.1991), *aff'd in relevant part*, 974 F.2d 1408 (4th Cir. 1992) (failure to abide by prior consent decree's nondiscrimination requirements, including failure to obey requirement that sign be posted on premises stating policy of equal access to persons of all races, admissible in case alleging defendant caused racially biased arrest of plaintiff).

shown by similar acts against another.[143] Also, in an incest or statutory rape case, some courts admit the defendant's prior unlawful sex acts, when committed with the same person as the person involved in the charged crime, to show motive, on the theory that the prior acts show a passion for illicit relations with that particular person.[144] As will be discussed later,[145] some courts have stretched even further to admit evidence of other misconduct in sexual misconduct cases. Applying theories such as these to particular cases often blurs the line between evidence offered to show a general bad character and evidence legitimately offered to show motive. Opponents of such evidence should be prepared to argue either that the line has been crossed, or that even if the evidence *in theory* is relevant to a purpose other than character, the jury is unlikely to use it in that permissible way.

§ 5.19 Specific Purposes for Which Uncharged Misconduct Evidence May Be Offered—Modus Operandi

Evidence that the defendant was involved in prior crimes accomplished by a distinctively similar method is often admissible for several purposes. "Modus operandi" is not specifically listed in Rule 404(b) as one of the "other purposes" for which evidence of uncharged crimes and acts may be admitted. However, Rule 404(b) does list "identity" as a purpose, and most often, evidence showing modus operandi is offered to identify the defendant as a perpetrator of the crime.[146] At other times it may be relevant to such matters as intent or lack of mistake or accident, which are listed as permissible purposes under Rule 404(b).[147] In any event, the list of purposes in 404(b) is expressly not exclusive; the words *such as* preceding the list of permissible purposes indicates that the list is merely a list of examples, not a complete list of all permissible purposes. Under 404(b), if evidence is offered for any purpose other than proving "the character of a person in order to show that he acted in conformity therewith," then it is admissible, providing, of course, that its probative value outweighs Rule 403 considerations of prejudice, confusion, and waste of time. A defendant's tendency to use a distinctive

---

143. *See* Duckworth v. Ford, 83 F.3d 999, 1001–02 (8th Cir.1996) (held, in civil suit based on premise that superior retaliated against employee for supporting rival, judgment against same defendant in favor or another employee based on same theory admissible to show motive and intent).

144. *See* State v. DeLong, 505 A.2d 803 (Me.1986) (father's prior sexual relations with same daughter admissible in incest case); Commonwealth v. Machado, 162 N.E.2d 71, 72–73 (Mass.1959) (evidence of intercourse with same victim admissible if not too remote in time); Collins v. State, 669 S.W.2d 505 (Ark.App.1984) (evidence of previous sexual overtures toward victim admissible in sexual abuse case). *See also* Heyne v. Caruso, 69 F.3d 1475, 1478–81

(9th Cir.1995) (defendant's acts of sexual harassment against other employees admissible to show that, in firing plaintiff, defendant was motivated by desire to retaliate because plaintiff had refused his sexual advance).

145. *See* § 5.24.

146. *See e.g.*, People v. Massey, 16 Cal. Rptr. 402, 405–06 (App.1961) (though court stated that similarities in crime charged and other offense were relevant to "intent," court likely meant identity); State v. Williams, 670 P.2d 1348, 1352 (Kan.1983).

147. *See e.g.*, United States v. Woods, 484 F.2d 127 (4th Cir.1973).

modus operandi is too narrow a tendency to be considered a trait of character, and evidence of it is therefore not excluded by Rule 404.

In one of the most celebrated examples of the use of uncharged misconduct evidence, the "Brides in the Bath" case, the evidence was used both to show that a crime had been committed (in particular, that the death of the defendant's wife had not been accidental) and that the defendant was the perpetrator. The defendant, under a false name, married a woman who had inherited a small trust fund.[148] After the couple had made out joint wills, the wife was found drowned in the bathtub. The defendant soon thereafter married another woman under another name in another county; she also made out a will to him (and named him the beneficiary of a life insurance policy) and also drowned in the bathtub in similar circumstances. A third wife died in the same fashion, after making out an appropriate will and taking out insurance, only one day after having gone through the marriage ceremony with the defendant. In the trial for the murder of the first victim, the issue turned upon the admissibility of the second and third drownings. The evidence against the defendant was otherwise scant: there was no proof he was with the victim at the time of the drowning; the victim had previously consulted a doctor about seizures, which might account for an accidental drowning; and there was no sign of violence or of a struggle. The crucial issue was the admissibility of the strikingly similar other drownings.[149] The evidence was admitted,[150] and the defendant, protesting to the end that he was an innocent victim of coincidence, was convicted and hanged.

It has sometimes been said that evidence of modus operandi must be extremely distinctive, so as to amount to the equivalent of the defendant's signature. The degree to which courts have been willing to require this degree of similarity has varied. Sometimes uncharged crime evidence is admitted even though the degree of similarity is minimal—in one case, for example, the only similarity noted by the court between the uncharged crimes and the charged crime was that the crimes all involved robberies of similar convenience stores.[151] Other courts have taken a stricter view. For example, the Fifth Circuit has held that the similarities between two bank robberies were not great enough to justify admission of the second robbery in a trial for the first, despite similari-

---

148. Rex v. Smith, [1914–15] All E.R. Rep. 265. Technically, the defendant did not legally marry any of the victims with whom he went through the marriage ceremony; he was already married, a fact that he did not reveal to the victims.

149. One observer has written that "throughout the trial the atmosphere of the court was not, 'is this man innocent or guilty' but 'is there sufficient evidence in law to convict this undoubtedly guilty man.' "? E. Marjoribanks, For the Defense: The Life of Sir Edward Marshall Hall 312 (1931).

150. Rex v. Smith, [1914–15] All E.R. Rep. 265. For a comparable recent case, see United States v. Woods, 484 F.2d 127 (4th Cir.1973) (defendant's child mysteriously died, possibly smothered; evidence that nine other children in defendant's care had each suffered twenty or more episodes of cyanosis (blue coloration due to lack of oxygen) held admissible).

151. State v. Smith, 707 P.2d 289, 297 (Ariz.1985). *Cf.* People v. Massey, 16 Cal. Rptr. 402 (App.1961) (evidence of similar burglary admitted, though similarities hardly enough to justify analogy to "signature").

ties in time of day (late afternoon), disguise (gloves and stocking masks), weapons (revolvers), and location of bank (outlying, on a highway).[152] Of course, the less similarity there is between the uncharged misconduct and the charged crime, the more likely the evidence is more properly characterized as impermissible character evidence; and, even where the evidence in theory is relevant for the non-character purpose, the greater the chance the defendant will be unfairly prejudiced by the jury's employing the evidence for its forbidden (character) purpose.

Another potential problem with the modus operandi theory for admission of uncharged misconduct evidence arises with respect to what has been called the "doctrine of chances." As Wigmore described the theory, the relevance of similar misconduct

> derives purely from the point of view of the doctrine of chances-the instinctive recognition of that logical process which eliminates the element of innocent intent by multiplying instances of the same result until it is perceived that this element cannot explain them all. Without formulating any accurate test, and without attempting by numerous instances to secure absolute certainty of inference, the mind applies this rough and instinctive process of reasoning, namely that an unusual and abnormal element might perhaps be present in one instance, but that the oftener similar instances occur with similar results, the less likely is the abnormal element likely to be the true explanation of them.[153]

152. United States v. Myers, 550 F.2d 1036 (5th Cir.1977). The court may have been influenced partly by the fact that the earlier robbery involved a single robber, while the later one involved multiple robbers. Nevertheless, even these supposedly distinctive factors could describe many typical bank robberies. *See also* United States v. Smith, 103 F.3d 600, 603–04 (7th Cir. 1996) (held, similarities between two bank robberies justified admitting evidence of other robbery to show identity through modus operandi; court listed several similarities, the most distinctive of which was that both robbers held a knife vertically when entering bank) (authors' note: *query* appropriateness of court's listing fact that both robberies were "committed by young white males with slender builds"; such evidence goes only to whether defendant was guilty of other robbery, a matter not in dispute, and not to the *modus* of the robberies). A case displaying a stricter attitude is Sutphin v. Commonwealth, 337 S.E.2d 897 (Va.App. 1985). In *Sutphin*, defendant was charged with burglary. Entry during the charged burglary had been accomplished by throwing a cinder block through a glass door. The trial court admitted evidence that earlier in the same day, the defendant had used a brick to break a glass door and enter anoth-

er establishment. The appellate court reversed on grounds that the similarities between the two crimes were not great enough; breaking in with a cinder block, brick, or similar object was not distinctive enough to justify admission under a modus operandi rationale. *See also* United States v. Carrillo, 981 F.2d 772 (5th Cir.1993), *cert. denied*, 513 U.S. 901 (1994) (held, prior sales of drugs in balloon not sufficiently distinctive to satisfy modus operandi requirements in case where defendant charged with sale of drugs in balloon). *But see* United States v. Sanchez, 988 F.2d 1384, 1393–94 (5th Cir.), *cert. denied*, 510 U.S. 878 (1993) (evidence of subsequent offense of drugs sold in pink balloons admissible to counter defendant's misidentification defense because act was sufficiently similar to charged crime to qualify as modus operandi evidence); United States v. Wesley, 990 F.2d 360, 366 (8th Cir.1993) (held, evidence of defendant's five-month-old prior convictions for possession of firearm and possession of crack cocaine properly admitted where defendant in subsequent case denied possession of seized revolver and seized cocaine base).

153. 2 John H. Wigmore, Evidence in Trials at Common Law § 302 (James H. Chadbourn rev. 1979).

To put it more simply, the doctrine of chances asks us to inquire how likely it is that the defendant would be involved innocently in so many similar acts. In the "Brides in the Bath" case,[154] for example, how likely is it that so many of defendant's wives would have died in such a similar manner unless defendant had killed them? Though applicable to the "modus operandi" theory for admissibility of uncharged misconduct evidence, the "doctrine of chances" has also been applied to a number of other admissibility routes described here.[155] The reasoning behind the theory seems compelling, and has been embraced quite broadly.[156] No doubt, it helps us to understand the small likelihood of innocence in many cases. But the reasoning can also be dangerously misleading, and potentially violative of the character prohibition.[157] The tendency to "round up the usual suspects"[158] can often lead to undue suspicion of people who have been guilty of similar crimes in the past but who were not involved in the crime under consideration. In some cases, "it is not so unlikely that an innocent person would be repeatedly charged falsely."[159] The doctrine should therefore be used with care to avoid possible inferential error.

§ 5.20 Specific Purposes for Which Uncharged Misconduct Evidence May be Offered—Opportunity

Evidence of uncharged misconduct may be used to show that the defendant had the opportunity to commit the charged offense. For example, evidence that the defendant had previously stolen a key to the premises that were later burglarized would be admissible, in trial for the burglary, to show opportunity.[160] Other examples include evidence that the defendant had, shortly before the crime, escaped from prison in the

154. Rex v. Smith, [1914–15] All E.R. Rep. 265. *See supra* notes 148–50 and accompanying text.

155. For a careful review of some of the many potential uses of "doctrine of chances" reasoning in a class of cases, see Mark Cammack, *Using the Doctrine of Chances to Prove Actus Reus in Child Abuse and Acquaintance Rape: People v. Ewoldt Reconsidered*, 29 U.C. Davis L. Rev. 355 (1996).

156. *See, e.g.*, Edward J. Imwinkelried, *The Evolution of the Use of the Doctrine of Chances as Theory of Admissibility for Similar Fact Evidence*, 22 Anglo–Am. L. Rev. 73 (1993).

157. Paul F. Rothstein, *Intellectual Coherence in an Evidence Code*, 28 Loy. L.A. L. Rev. 1259, 1260–64 (1995) (arguing that the doctrine relies on prohibited propensity reasoning). *But see* Myrna S. Raeder, *The Admissibility of Prior Acts of Domestic Violence: People v. Simpson and Beyond*, 69 S. Cal. L. Rev. 1463, 1491 & n.152 (1996) (questioning Rothstein's position). *See also* Edward J. Imwinkelried, *The Use of Evidence of an Accused's Uncharged Misconduct to Prove Mens Rea: The Doctrines that Threaten to Engulf the Character Evidence Prohibition*, 130 Mil. L. Rev. 41, 54–56 (1990) (characterizing "doctrine of chances" reasoning as non-character reasoning).

158. For the most famous use of the phrase, see "Casablanca" (Warner Bros. 1942). In the movie's climactic scene, after the hero has killed a Nazi officer, a police officer lets the hero go and orders another officer to "round up the usual suspects" to hold responsible for the killing.

159. Rothstein, *supra* note 158, at 1263.

160. *See, e.g.*, State v. Uthe, 542 N.W.2d 810, 814 (Iowa 1996) (in prosecution for forgery of checks from a stolen checkbook, Evidence that defendant forged another check from same checkbook a few days after last charged forgery admissible to show possession of checkbook and therefore opportunity to commit earlier forgeries; opportunity tended to prove defendant's identity as perpetrator).

vicinity of the crime charged;[161] this evidence shows opportunity (the defendant was free in the area of the crime) as well as motive (a fugitive has a motive to commit crimes to obtain the means of avoiding capture, especially since obtaining funds and transportation by legitimate means may be more difficult for a fugitive than for other persons). The fact that the defendant was previously seen in an area where the defendant had no right to be also shows access and therefore opportunity.[162]

Prior criminal activity that puts defendant in contact with an organization or mechanism for committing the prior crime may also be admissible to prove opportunity.[163]

Defense counsel faced with a claim that a prior crime is relevant to opportunity should seek to avoid prejudice by pointing out other ways in which the prosecution could prove that the defendant had access to the area in which the crime was committed, by stipulating to access, or by offering ways in which the evidence could be received in a redacted fashion. Doing so could prevent the prejudice likely to occur in situations such as that of the prison break just discussed; it is not very difficult to prove access to the area in which the crime was committed without mentioning that defendant was present there as a result of the escape. *See* §§ 5.34.

§ 5.21   Specific Purposes for Which Uncharged Misconduct Evidence May be Offered—Knowledge

Another purpose for which uncharged crimes evidence may be admitted is to show guilty knowledge. In fact, this is one of the oldest uses of uncharged misconduct evidence.[164] One who tries to deduct a

161. United States v. Stover, 565 F.2d 1010 (8th Cir.1977) (escape from prison, to show presence in area).

162. *See* United States v. DeJohn, 638 F.2d 1048 (7th Cir.1981) (testimony about defendant's presence and taking of checks at other times in mailbox area of YMCA admissible to show access).

163. *See, e.g.,* United States v. Robinson, 956 F.2d 1388, 1395–96 (7th Cir.), *cert. denied,* 506 U.S. 1020 (1992) (marijuana distribution conspiracy in the 1970s admissible to show opportunity in prosecution for cocaine distribution, where nearly identical organizational scheme was used for both offenses; prior offense Evidence also relevant to establish intent and motive). *But see* United States v. Hill, 953 F.2d 452 (9th Cir.1991) (evidence that co-conspirator used small amounts of cocaine five years earlier inadmissible even though it explained why co-conspirator approached defendant about financing drug transaction).

164. The most common use of other misconduct evidence in the English cases through the nineteenth century was to prove that a person possessed a particular kind of guilty knowledge that would constitute an element of a crime or tort. Many of the cases were prosecutions for forgery and uttering of forged instruments, where, to prove the uttering charge, it was necessary to demonstrate that the defendant knew the instrument was forged. *See, e.g.,* Rex v. Whiley, 168 Eng. Rep. 589 (1804), also reported at 127 Eng. Rep. 393 (1804) as Rex v. Wylie. Such evidence was also admitted in fraud cases, where it was necessary to demonstrate not only the defendant's intent to defraud, but also quite often, as a necessary part of this, that the defendant knew the true nature of the item she sought to transfer to the alleged victim. *See, e.g.,* Regina v. Roebuck, 7 Cox C.C. 126 (1856). Courts also admitted evidence of other misconduct to prove guilty knowledge in prosecutions for receiving stolen goods, where defendant's knowledge that the goods in question were stolen was an essential element of the charge. *See, e.g.,* Rex v. Davis, 172 Eng. Rep. 1196 (1833). Early American case authority, which relied heavily on English law, was very similar. *See* Samuel March Phillipps, A Treatise on the Law of roommate as a dependent cannot claim good faith if the Internal Revenue Service warned her against doing the same thing in a previous year, and evidence of the spurious deduction that led to the warning would be admissible even though it necessarily suggests a prior crime. Similarly, if a defendant found in possession of a quantity of heroin claimed that he did not know that the substance was heroin, then evidence that he had previously used or sold heroin would be admissible to show guilty knowledge.[165] Or suppose again that defendant claims not to have known that substance he possessed was an illegal drug, and the prosecution offers evidence of a previous arrest for possession of that same drug. Regardless of the outcome of the prior case (no trial, trial and conviction, or even an acquittal), the evidence would likely be admissible in the present case because of the likelihood that defendant would have become familiar with the appearance of heroin through the prior experience.[166] Similarly, where a person is charged with committing a crime using a sophisticated technique or device, evidence that defendant had at another time committed a similar crime using the same method would be admissible to prove defendant knew how to use such a device or method, and thus might have been involved in the crime.[167] In many cases, the

Evidence 137 (John A. Dunlap ed. 1816); Thomas Starkie, A Practical Treatise on the Law of Evidence 378 (Theron Metcalf ed. 1826).

165. *See* United States v. Francesco, 725 F.2d 817 (1st Cir.1984); United States v. Wixom, 529 F.2d 217 (8th Cir.1976). *See also* United States v. Obiuwevbi, 962 F.2d 1236, 1240–41 (7th Cir.1992) (evidence that defendant withdrew large amounts of money five times in the previous five years before making trips to Nigeria admissible "other acts" evidence to show knowledge and intent in present prosecution for violation of currency reporting requirement); *In re* Korean Air Lines Disaster of Sept. 1, 1983, 932 F.2d 1475, 1483–84 (D.C.Cir.), *cert. denied,* 502 U.S. 994 (1991) (in suit arising from shooting down of flight over Soviet airspace, evidence of prior instances of airline's commercial flights straying into Soviet airspace properly admitted to show knowledge of consequences of straying and to rebut certain defense evidence); United States v. Osum, 943 F.2d 1394, 1403–04 (5th Cir.1991) (subsequent fraudulent claims of injury from bus accidents admissible against bus driver charged with fraudulent claim, when bus driver claimed that he was genuinely injured and had not known that codefendants were making false claims). *See generally* 2 Weinstein's Federal Evidence § 404.08[2] (2d ed. Joseph M. McLaughlin ed. 1997).

166. *See* United States v. Rocha, 553 F.2d 615 (9th Cir.1977) (where defendant was charged with possession of marijuana

with intent to distribute and defendant claimed he thought the sacks he was loading onto a truck contained furniture, evidence of prior acquittal for possession of marijuana was properly admitted to prove knowledge). *See also* 22 Charles A. Wright & Kenneth W. Graham, Jr., Federal Practice and Procedure (Evidence) § 5245, at 505 (1979).

167. *See, e.g.,* United States v. Jones, 982 F.2d 380, 382 (9th Cir.1992) (where defendant charged with conspiracy involving large drug smuggling operation, evidence that defendant had been involved in similar operations in previous years was admissible to prove, *inter alia,* defendant's knowledge and intent with regard to the present scheme). (In slip opinion, court stated: "[I]n light of the similarity in the modus operandi . . . the testimony was relevant as tending to show that appellant had the requisite knowledge and intent to commit the crimes with which he was charged." United States v. Jones, No. 90–10501, slip op. At 3335 (9th Cir. Apr. 6, 1993).) *See also* United States v. Andonian, 29 F.3d 634 (9th Cir.1994) (unpublished disposition), *cert. denied,* 513 U.S. 1128 (1995) (in prosecution for conspiracy to commit money laundering and for money laundering, evidence that defendants had been involved in identical scheme admissible to prove, *inter alia,* defendants' knowledge and intent to commit charged crimes).

evidence could also be characterized as proving opportunity; the categories overlap significantly.[168]

Not all cases in which evidence is ostensibly offered to show guilty knowledge are so easy. For example, suppose that the search of a vehicle reveals a suitcase full of heroin in the trunk. The owner of the vehicle claims never to have seen the contents of the suitcase at all, asserting that the offending suitcase belonged to a passenger who told the vehicle owner nothing about its contents. Here, evidence that the vehicle owner had previously been involved in drug dealings would seem to be evidence of character; it shows "knowledge" only through the inferential route of showing that the defendant has propensity to possess quantities of drugs, and hence that he is more likely to have been guilty on this particular occasion. The evidence does not show something narrower than character (such as familiarity with the physical characteristics of a drug). In terms of the diagram set forth in § 5.05, it is necessary to take the forbidden inferential route through general propensity in order to reach the desired conclusion. Nonetheless, courts have not always drawn such fine distinctions, particularly in drug cases, and the evidence is sometimes admitted to show knowledge of the presence of a drug even when there is no claim that the defendant was naive about the drug's characteristics.[169] Such cases blur the line between character and non-character uses of uncharged misconduct evidence.

§ 5.22 Specific Purposes for Which Uncharged Misconduct Evidence May Be Offered—Intent; Absence of Mistake or Accident

Evidence of uncharged misconduct is sometimes relevant to show that the defendant had the requisite intent to commit the crime charged—for example, the intent to steal in a larceny case, or the intent to kill in a murder case. This use of the evidence differs from use to show motive, in that it seeks not to show the reason why the defendant might

---

168. *See, e.g.,* State v. Campbell, 367 N.W.2d 454 (Minn.1985) (evidence of prior criminal act of using mace admissible to show defendant's knowledge of the use of mace and to show that defendant had opportunity to use the substance).

169. *See* State v. Garza, 735 P.2d 1089 (Idaho App.1987) (held, defendant's large money transactions with person shown to be drug dealer was evidence that he knew of existence of marijuana in residence he shared with his wife). *But see* United States v. Garcia–Orozco, 997 F.2d 1302, 1303–04 (9th Cir.1993) (prior incident in which defendant, a passenger in car, fled car containing hidden drugs not admissible to show knowledge in subsequent case in which defendant prosecuted for importing drugs); United States v. Harrison–Philpot, 978 F.2d 1520, 1527 (9th Cir.1992), *cert. denied,* 508 U.S. 929 (1993) (tape recording or drug negotiations between defendant and undercover agent admissible to show defendant's knowledge of drug distribution ring when defendant claimed drugs were for personal use only); United States v. Bakke, 942 F.2d 977, 980–83 (6th Cir.1991) (held, reversible error to admit evidence of unrelated subsequent drug transaction involving defendant accused of being member of drug conspiracy; only issue was membership in conspiracy, not knowledge or intent). *But cf.* United States v. Beasley, 809 F.2d 1273 (7th Cir.1987) (Easterbrook, J.) (denying proposition that any drug offense can be used to show intent to commit another drug offense, and remanding for reconsideration of admission of other crimes evidence in case in which defendant was alleged to have fraudulently obtained prescriptions from physician to obtain drugs for sale).

have committed the crime, but the existence of the state of mind that is a prerequisite for the commission of the crime. The category does, however, overlap with some of the other categories listed, since intent may be shown by demonstrating a similar modus operandi[170] or by showing the absence of mistake or accident.

Sometimes the use of uncharged misconduct evidence to show intent can be non-controversial. The defendant's claim that he shot his wife on sudden impulse is less plausible if, on the way to shooting his wife, the defendant shot his wife's lover.[171] Yet in other circumstances the showing of intent is very close to a showing of character. To show that a defendant intended to kill, one might argue that prior killings by the defendant of unrelated persons throw light upon intent. And so they do, but only by showing that the defendant has a violent, murderous character—exactly the sort of inferential process that is prohibited by the first sentence of Federal Rule of Evidence 404(b), which prohibits evidence of other bad acts to prove a person's character, and that the person acted in conformity with that character trait on the occasion in question. Some opinions recognize this principle, and restrict the use of this type of evidence,[172] while others tend to ignore the principle or show

170. *Modus operandi* and *intent* are not parallel categories, but describe different matters: modus operandi describes the nature of the circumstantial evidence (similarity of method) that causes us to infer guilt by inferring intent or identity, whereas intent describes not the evidence, but the ultimate inference that is sought to be drawn from the evidence.

171. *Compare* State v. Shackford, 506 A.2d 315 (N.H.1986) (defendant accused of stabbing and killing a stranger in a shopping center; held, evidence that shortly before he attacked the victim, he accosted and threatened another woman was admissible on issues of premeditation and intent).

172. *See* State v. Robtoy, 653 P.2d 284, 292 (Wash.1982) (prior unrelated murder inadmissible to show premeditation; jury "could well have interpreted the evidence of the prior killing as proof that Robtoy acted in conformity therewith on this occasion"). For an example of a restrictive attitude toward admitting evidence to show intent under Rule 404(b), see Sparks v. Gilley Trucking Co., 992 F.2d 50, 52 (4th Cir. 1993). The plaintiff was injured when he lost control of his Corvette while driving up a mountain road and struck a tree. He sued the defendant for negligence, alleging that its truck had run his car off the road. At trial, the defendant argued that the plaintiff had been racing another car and thus had been contributorily negligent. In support of this contention, the defendant offered evidence that the plaintiff had received six speeding tickets in the preceding

three years. The district court admitted evidence of the speeding tickets under Rule 404(b) "to show intent, preparation, plan or motive to race or speed on the day in question." The Fourth Circuit held that the evidence of the tickets virtually presented speeding as the plaintiff's character trait and, hence, was inadmissible. The court noted that the Circuit had approved the admission of such evidence when *intent to commit a crime* was at issue. However, in this case, the defendant merely sought to prove the plaintiff was negligent, and "proof of negligence does not require a showing of intent or plan." *See also* Hynes v. Coughlin, 79 F.3d 285, 290–92 (2d Cir. 1996) (where prison inmate denied kicking guard, error to admit evidence of inmate's prior assaults and threats against prison staff because intent not in issue); United States v. Merriweather, 78 F.3d 1070, 1074 (6th Cir.1996) (held, under Fed. R. Evid. 404(b), taped conversation showing defendant's involvement in unrelated drug conspiracy not admissible where prosecution had better means of proving intent and identity).

The dangers of the "intent" theory of admissibility under Rule 404(b) are discussed in Edward J. Imwinkelried, *The Use of Evidence of an Accused's Uncharged Misconduct to Prove Mens Rea: The Doctrines Which Threaten to Engulf the Character Evidence Prohibition*, 51 Ohio St. L.J. 575 (1990).

a rather lenient attitude toward admitting evidence to show intent under Rule 404(b).[173]

Because intent is often proven by showing the commission of similar crimes, one finds statements in opinions that the similarities must be marked, or that the crimes must show the same intent, or even that they must show the same physical elements.[174] These requirements make sense if the only basis for showing intent is the inference that the defendant had the state of mind to commit that sort of crime—that is, if intent evidence is offered as a sort of narrow character evidence, in which the defendant has a behavioral tendency that is deemed not to constitute a trait of character. Yet in appropriate cases, intent may be shown even by producing evidence of a quite different crime. For example, if the defendant claims that he robbed a bank with X because of duress, proof that the defendant shortly afterward committed another crime with X under circumstances in which duress was obviously absent throws reflected light upon the claim of duress, without committing the sin of defaming the defendant's character in general.[175]

173. For a case that appears to ignore the principle, see State v. Harris, 726 P.2d 943 (Or.App.1986) (prior assaultive behavior with rifle, unrelated to present incident, admissible to show intent to kill in murder case). For an example of a lenient attitude toward admitting evidence to show intent under Rule 404(b), see United States v. Neely, 980 F.2d 1074 (7th Cir.1992). The trial court admitted evidence of a prior insurance fraud scheme involving breaking up cars when the instant case involved faking automobile accidents. The Seventh Circuit held that the evidence was admissible even though the defendant claimed intent was not an issue. See also United States v. Donovan 984 F.2d 507 (1st Cir.), reh'g. en banc, 984 F.2d 493 (1993), cert. granted & jmt. vacated, 510 U.S. 1069 (1994) (banker's subsequent conduct in missing bank funds admissible to show willfulness in earlier failure to file required currency transaction report for same account; the later acts "reflected a conscious disregard of any legal requirements that might hinder Donovan's ability to use Saba's property for his immediate benefit"). See also United States v. Long, 86 F.3d 81, 82–85 (7th Cir.1996) (defendant, charged with possession of crack cocaine with intent to distribute, claimed cocaine found in his car belonged to another person; held, evidence that defendant on another occasion had traded crack cocaine for goods admissible; court states that uncharged crime need not be a "duplicate" of the charged crime to be admissible, an understatement in view of the lack of similarity between the two crimes).

Some cases display a receptive attitude toward evidence of prior drug offenses to show intent. See United States v. Butler, 102 F.3d 1191, 1195–96 (11th Cir.1997) (held, in an opinion citing cases on both sides, evidence of personal drug use more than three years before an unrelated prosecution for distribution conspiracy is admissible to prove intent); United States v. Moore, 98 F.3d 347, 350 (8th Cir.1996) (Loken, J.) (a "mere presence" defense to a drug charge puts intent in issue, so other drug offenses are admissible to show intent); United States v. Perkins, 94 F.3d 429, 433–34 (8th Cir.1996) (prior contact of defendant with crack cocaine admissible to show his knowledge and intent); United States v. Broussard, 80 F.3d 1025, 1039–40 (5th Cir.1996) (no abuse of discretion to admit prior drug offenses, despite remoteness in time as to one defendant and lack of similarity as to another); United States v. Bermea, 30 F.3d 1539, 1562 (5th Cir.1994), cert. denied, 513 U.S. 1156 (1995) (noting general receptiveness toward drug offenses as 404(b) evidence). But see United States v. Beasley, 809 F.2d 1273, 1279–81 (7th Cir. 1987) (Easterbrook, J.) (one drug offense not always admissible to prove another, even when intent is in issue; remanded for on-the-record 404(b) balancing).

174. See United States v. Beechum, 582 F.2d 898 (5th Cir.1978) (abandoning same physical element requirement, but retaining same intent requirement).

175. See United States v. Daniels, 948 F.2d 1033, 1035 (6th Cir.1991), cert. denied, 503 U.S. 912 (1992) (held, defendant's request to acquaintance to call in bomb threat against employer admissible against defendant in case in which defendant, a striking

The difficulties inherent in the separation of intent and character evidence are displayed in the well-known case of *United States v. Beechum*.[176] Beechum, a substitute letter carrier, was accused of unlawfully possessing a silver dollar that he knew to be stolen from the mails. To establish that Beechum intentionally and unlawfully possessed the silver dollar, the prosecution introduced evidence that two Sears credit cards were found in Beechum's wallet when he was arrested. Neither card was issued to Beechum, neither was signed, and both were mailed some ten months earlier to addresses on routes Beechum had serviced. Beechum claimed that the silver dollar fell out of the mailbox as he was raking out the mail and that he planned to turn it in. The fact that he kept the credit cards suggested he intended to keep the silver dollar. The crucial question was whether the inference of intent must be derived from a forbidden inference about character, or whether the evidence can be viewed as something other than character evidence. An en banc majority of the Fifth Circuit viewed the evidence as related to intent, not character, and held it to be admissible. According to the majority, the evidence would show a larcenous state of mind even in the absence of proof that the credit cards had been stolen from the mail. A forceful dissent charged that the court's concept of intent was really propensity in disguise, and that the evidence was inadmissible character evidence. The case illustrates the very thin line between permissible and impermissible uses of uncharged misconduct evidence. There is no obviously "correct" answer; different courts employ different reasoning.

In addition to "intent," Rule 404(b) lists "absence of mistake or accident" as one of the permissible purposes for which evidence of uncharged crimes may be offered. This category seems to be merely a way of stating a subcategory of the intent category, since the defense of mistake or accident is a defense based on the absence of criminal intent.[177] Examples of using uncharged misconduct to rebut a claim of mistake or accident include the case in which the defendant claims that a death caused by him was accidental,[178] that sexual touching of a child

worker, was charged with shooting at bus belonging to employer; prior act showed specific intent to do harm to employer during strike); United States v. Hearst, 563 F.2d 1331 (9th Cir.1977) (subsequent criminal activity of Patricia Hearst admissible to show her intent at time of original bank robbery, thus rebutting duress defense).

176. 582 F.2d 898 (5th Cir.1978).

177. *See, e.g.,* United States v. Pless, 79 F.3d 1217, 1220 (D.C.Cir.), *cert. denied,* ___ U.S. ___, 117 S.Ct. 251 (1996) (defendant charged with bank fraud; defendant owned corporation which held bank accounts at two different financial institutions, and to obtain more expendable funds, defendant overdrew the accounts in both banks, hiding overdrafts by cross-depositing checks in the two banks; held, trial court properly received evidence of defendant's

failure to pay corporate, employment withholding, and personal federal taxes to rebut defendant's defense that he believed that those overdrafts would be treated as loans).

178. *See* United States v. Harris, 661 F.2d 138 (10th Cir.1981) (prior battering of child admissible to show death, which father claimed occurred because he tripped while holding child, was not accidental). *Cf.* Kopf v. Skyrm, 993 F.2d 374, 380–81 (4th Cir.1993) (in civil litigation claiming excessive force by defendant police officer, allegedly in retaliation for plaintiff's attack on defendant's police dog, trial court erred by excluding evidence of prior incident in which defendant shot and killed a fleeing burglary suspect after the suspect killed another police dog); United States v. Marion, 977 F.2d 1284, 1288 (8th Cir.1992) (prosecution may refute defendant's arguwas inadvertent,[179] that property was destroyed by accident, rather than by arson,[180] or that illegal dumping of waste was inadvertent.[181]

§ 5.23 Specific Purposes for Which Uncharged Misconduct Evidence May Be Offered—Preparation

Evidence of uncharged crimes may be admissible to show preparation for the charged crime. For example, the prosecution may show that the defendant stole a car (the uncharged crime) to use as a getaway car for the charged crime, or that the defendant broke into a store to steal tools to use in the charged burglary.[182] In these cases, preparation is offered to prove the ultimate fact of identity—that defendant in fact participated in the charged crimes. Preparation can also be relevant to the ultimate issue of intent. For example, if in a murder prosecution

ment that failure to appear to serve sentence was mistake with evidence that defendant previously failed to appear in court and fled the state).

179. *Cf.* Findley v. State, 577 P.2d 867 (Nev.1978).

180. *See* Hammann v. Hartford Accident & Indem. Co., 620 F.2d 588 (6th Cir. 1980) (prior incendiary fires on plaintiff's property, in conjunction with evidence that plaintiff had concealed information about fires from insurance company, admissible to show arson).

181. *See* United States v. Paccione, 949 F.2d 1183, 1198–99 (2d Cir.1991), *cert. denied,* 505 U.S. 1220 (1992) (held, evidence of attempt to bribe state officials who called buried garbage to defendant's attention, admissible in mail fraud RICO prosecution arising from illegal dumping of garbage in illicit landfill, to show that dumping was not accidental or mistaken).

On the issue of intent generally, see also United States v. Hadley, 918 F.2d 848 (9th Cir.1990), *cert. dismissed as improvidently granted,* 506 U.S. 19 (1992). Hadley, a teacher, was accused of sexually abusing a male student. Evidence of similar acts with other students was admitted by the trial judge on the issue of intent. Hadley argued that the acts were inadmissible because he did not contend that he lacked intent, but instead denied participation in the acts charged. The Ninth Circuit held that the evidence was admissible because the government still had the burden of proof on intent whether the defendant relied on that defense or not.

On the use of prior drug-related acts to show intent, see United States v. Parziale, 947 F.2d 123 (5th Cir.1991), *cert. denied,* 503 U.S. 946 (1992). There, the defendant was the pilot of a stolen amphibious aircraft

that flew from Louisiana to Montego Bay, Jamaica, and then attempted to make a return trip. He took off from Montego Bay but crashed at sea. Though the defendant was rescued the aircraft was not, and its contents were lost. The government sought to put in prior acts of the defendant to show intent. The other crime was an attempt to smuggle four and one-half pounds of marijuana into the country from Jamaica on a prior occasion. On the prior occasion, he had carried the marijuana in his clothing. The court held that the evidence was admissible because it showed intent, not character. It rejected the argument that uncharged misconduct evidence was inadmissible because the defendant had not put intent in issue. It held that in a conspiracy case the mere entry of a not guilty plea raises the issue of intent sufficiently to justify the admission of uncharged misconduct evidence.

182. *See* Lewis v. United States, 771 F.2d 454, 456 (10th Cir.), *cert. denied,* 474 U.S. 1024 (1985) (defendant broke into one establishment to steal cutting torch and oxygen for use in second burglary; prior crime admissible in trial for second). *But cf.* People v. Zackowitz, 172 N.E. 466 (N.Y. 1930) (Cardozo, J.), where the defendant whose wife had been insulted by a bystander, went home and returned with a pistol, which he used to shoot the bystander. The prosecution sought to introduce evidence that defendant had other weapons in his home, in rebuttal of defendant's claim that he shot the bystander in self-defense after an altercation started upon his return to the scene. In dictum, Justice Cardozo distinguished a hypothetical case in which the defendant purchased the weapons in preparation for the particular crime; had that been the case, the evidence would have been admissible.

defendant claims lack of premeditation, evidence that she broke into a gun store prior to the killing and stole what would become the murder weapon would tend to prove premeditation.

§ 5.24 Specific Purposes for which Uncharged Misconduct Evidence May Be Offered—Other Acts of Sexual Misconduct

Evidence of other sex offenses in cases involving charges of rape, sexual assault, child abuse, or incest may be admissible under traditional theories, that is, under the categories described above. Thus, prior sexual contact with a particular person may be received on the theory that it shows motive, because it shows sexual passion for that person; or prior rapes of unrelated persons may be admitted on grounds that they show a particular modus operandi. Nonetheless, sex crimes deserve special treatment here, because some courts have shown a greater willingness to admit evidence of uncharged misconduct in cases involving sexual offenses. In addition, as discussed in **§ 5.10**, recent legislation has broadened admissibility of other acts of sexual misconduct by the defendant, making separate consideration of this type of evidence particularly pertinent.

Even in the absence of such legislation, other offenses and prior sexual acts with the same victim are usually admissible. For example, when a defendant is accused of incest, other acts of incest with the same child are admissible, not as showing character but as showing an inclination to engage in sexual activity with that particular victim.[183] Where defendant denies that any crime occurred, evidence of other sexual misconduct with the same victim has been admitted to prove that the charged crime was in fact committed.[184] When the uncharged crimes evidence relates to sexual acts with other persons, the evidence is, of course, admissible if the prior acts show a distinctive pattern that

---

183. *See, e.g.,* State v. DeLong, 505 A.2d 803 (Me.1986) (father's prior acts with same daughter admissible in prosecution for incest); Commonwealth v. Machado, 162 N.E.2d 71, 73 (Mass.1959) (broad statement that when defendant is charged with illicit sexual intercourse, evidence of similar crimes against the same victim, if not too remote in time, is admissible as " 'relevant to show the probable existence of the same passion or emotion at the time in issue' "); Brown v. State, 736 P.2d 1110 (Wyo.1987) (testimony of victim and her half-sister implicating defendant in prior sexual abuse was properly admitted); State v. Cameron, 349 S.E.2d 327, 331 (N.C.App.1986) (trial court admitted evidence of prior sexual acts with same victim; on appeal, court notes that in sexual offense cases, state's courts have "liberally permitted the introduction of evidence of prior sexual acts committed by the defendant upon the same prosecuting witness"); 1 McCormick on Evidence § 190, at 803 n.24 (4th ed. John W. Strong ed. 1992).

184. *See, e.g.,* People v. Ewoldt, 27 Cal. Rptr.2d 646, 867 P.2d 757 (1994) (in prosecution for child molestation, evidence of similar misconduct with victims was admissible to prove design or plan, which in turn is admissible to prove that the defendant in fact engaged in the alleged criminal conduct); Brown v. State, 817 P.2d 429, 433–35 (Wyo.1991) (in prosecution for sexual abuse of two stepdaughters where defendant claimed the charges were fabricated, evidence of prior sexual misconduct between defendant and stepdaughters was admissible to prove course of conduct and motive; court held motive was important to case given defendant's claim of fabrication).

amounts to a modus operandi.[185] Some courts have shown an inclination to go further, admitting, for example, prior acts of rape to rebut a consent defense, even when the only clear commonality between different incidents was the forced nature of the intercourse.[186] Cases liberally admitting this evidence are difficult to reconcile with the general rule against character evidence.

Some jurisdictions have recognized a specific exception to the rule against character evidence for evidence of uncharged misconduct to show "lustful disposition" or "depraved sexual instinct" in cases involving sex crimes against children.[187] Other courts have rejected such an exception.[188] Where the courts reject the exception, change may come from legislatures; the most obvious example is the 1994 federal crime legislation adding several new evidence rules (Rules 413 to 415) making evidence of other sexual misconduct admissible "on any matter to which it is relevant."[189] Specifically, evidence of other sexual assaults is now admissible in prosecutions for sexual assault,[190] evidence of other acts of child molestation is now admissible in prosecutions for child molesta-

185. State v. Coen, 382 N.W.2d 703, 705–08 (Iowa App.1985) (prior offense admitted when similar modus operandi of flattening tire, then asking to fix it and get ride with woman in order to rape her); State v. Bennett, 672 P.2d 772 (Wash.App.1983) (defendant had enticed teenage runaways into exchanging sex for food and shelter; prior conduct with unrelated runaways admitted in statutory rape case as showing plan to take advantage of runaways).

186. For example, in Carey v. State, 715 P.2d 244, 248 (Wyo.1986), the court took a broad view of the admissibility of prior crimes in rape cases involving defense of consent. It held that two prior assaults (one sexual assault and one mugging), one resulting in acquittal and other resulting in dismissal of charges, were admissible on the issue of consent in a rape case, stating that "in cases involving sexual misconduct prior conduct consisting of bad acts is of increased pertinency," and:

> In an instance such as this, when the accused denies the use of force and claims consent, evidence which contradicts his denials of previous use of force in sexual encounters is of assistance to the trier of fact in evaluating his testimony with respect to motive, knowledge and intent in resolving the issue of fact and in evaluating his credibility.

See also State v. DeBaere, 356 N.W.2d 301, 305 (Minn.1984) (enunciating and applying a broad test for admissibility); State v. Crocker, 409 N.W.2d 840 (Minn.1987) (similar); United States v. Sneezer, 983 F.2d 920, 924 (9th Cir.1992), cert. denied, 510

U.S. 836 (1993) (broad standard). For a case taking a more restrictive approach, see State v. Saltarelli, 655 P.2d 697 (Wash. 1982) (held, in rape case with consent defense, that evidence of a prior attempted rape of another woman four and a half years earlier was not admissible to show motive or intent to rape).

187. See, e.g., State v. Tobin, 602 A.2d 528 (R.I.1992) ("lewd disposition" exception to rule against character evidence recognized in case in which evidence of prior acts involved same victim); State v. Raye, 326 S.E.2d 333, 335 (N.C.App.1985). See generally Edward J. Imwinkelried, Uncharged Misconduct Evidence § 4:14 (1984).

188. See, e.g., Lannan v. State, 600 N.E.2d 1334 (Ind.1992) (overruling Indiana "depraved sexual instinct" exception to character evidence rule). But see Ind. Code 35–37–4–15 (1993) (legislative reinstatement of Indiana exception). Some of these courts have construed the Federal Rules of Evidence as precluding the reception of evidence of a "lustful disposition" or "depraved sexual instinct" theory. See, e.g., Getz v. State, 538 A.2d 726, 733–34 (Del. 1988) ("[t]he sexual gratification exception proceeds upon the assumption that a defendant's propensity for satisfying sexual needs is so unique that it is relevant to his guilt. The exception thus equates character disposition with evidence of guilt contrary to the clear prohibition of DRE Rule 404(b)").

189. See § 5.10.

190. Fed. R. Evid. 413.

tion,[191] and the same types of misconduct are admissible in civil actions arising out of alleged sexual assault and child molestation.[192] However wise or unwise the policy behind the new rules might be,[193] it is clear that Congress intended to allow juries in these types of cases to employ the character reasoning forbidden by longstanding rules. That being the case, in federal trials[194] and in states enacting similar legislation,[195] it will no longer be necessary to make the fine distinctions demanded by the character bar when such evidence is offered. Nevertheless, common law and more recent federal and state treatment of uncharged sexual misconduct remains relevant today, and counsel should be aware of the alternate theories on which such evidence might be offered.

§ 5.25 Specific Purposes for Which Uncharged Misconduct Evidence May Be Offered—Common Plan or Scheme

Evidence of uncharged misconduct may also be admissible to show a common plan or scheme leading to the charged crime. This route to admission or exclusion of uncharged misconduct evidence has proven especially challenging for the courts, and diverse views prevail.

Where a person commits several acts in pursuit of a single, pre-established goal, the theory operates in a straightforward and uncontroversial manner. Thus, if the defendant is trying to reconstitute a gun collection previously owned by his father, evidence that defendant committed one burglary in which one gun was recaptured would be admissible to show the defendant's involvement in another burglary in which another was recaptured.[196]

Note that in applying this reasoning, there is no need for a great degree of similarity in the *manner* in which the person committed the various acts. In the gun collection situation, for example, the evidence would be admissible even if the first gun was obtained by using a passkey to obtain entry to an apartment, while the second was obtained by using a hatchet to break down the door of a house in broad daylight. Indeed, defendant need not have obtained the guns in both cases by means of burglary. If, for example, the first gun was obtained by burglary, and the charged crime by fraud, evidence of the burglary would likely still be admissible.

It is important to distinguish the use of uncharged misconduct to prove common plan or scheme from its use to prove modus operandi. There is, of course, some overlap between the theories.[197] Some cases fall

---

191. Fed. R. Evid. 414.

192. Fed. R. Evid. 415.

193. The new rules have engendered substantial scholarly commentary. *See* § 5.10.

194. The new rules became effective on July 9, 1995. *See* 108 Stat. 1796 (1994).

195. *See, e.g.,* Cal. Evid. Code § 1108 (West Supp. 1997).

196. *See* State v. Wallace, 431 A.2d 613 (Me.1981).

197. In fact, federal modus operandi cases sometimes use the phrase "common plan" because "plan" is listed as one of the specific purposes for which uncharged misinto both categories. The man who makes a practice of marrying women of means and then drowning them in the bathtub may be said to have both a modus operandi (bathtub drowning) and a plan (to acquire wealth by marrying and murdering). In others, the plan theory applies though the modus operandi theory does not. That is true of the gun case in which the guns were obtained using different means. Another example is provided by the film *Kind Hearts and Coronets* (EAL/GFD 1949), in which a character plotted to acquire a title by killing off the eight people (all eight were played by Alec Guinness) with a superior claim. Each of the bizarre killings was different, but each was in pursuit of the same goal. They showed a common plan but not a common method. In still other cases, modus operandi theory applies though there is no common scheme. A defendant may have committed multiple crimes with a distinctive method without planning more than one crime at a time. For example, a person may have committed two unconnected spite killings at different times and places, having no idea that the occasion for the second killing would arise at the time of the first, but finding it convenient to use exactly the same distinctive method when the occasion did arise.

The most controversial common scheme or plan cases are those in which the evidence fails to establish a single, persistent plan leading to a clear goal and covering both the uncharged acts and the crime for which the person is on trial. It is in these situations that the cases are most diverse and difficult to categorize. Some are very liberal in finding a common plan in similar offenses. For example, prior acts of accepting kickbacks from different persons have been admitted to show a common scheme to use one's position to get kickbacks;[198] other activity involving drug offenses has been admitted liberally in some cases on the theory that selling drugs is a continuous business involving a common plan.[199]

conduct evidence may be offered, while "modus operandi" is not. There is no need to try to force the modus operandi cases into the common plan category, however, since the Rule 404(b) list of permissible purposes for which other misconduct evidence may be offered is not exclusive, and hence modus operandi evidence may be admissible even though not specifically listed.

198. Commonwealth v. Schoening, 396 N.E.2d 1004, 1009 (Mass.1979) (held, evidence that defendant took kickbacks on two other occasions, even if from a different party, is admissible to show motive, plan, common scheme—"The defendant's use of his position to guarantee contracts to particular firms and thus to guarantee kickbacks to himself provided the common or general scheme underlying all three transactions"). *Cf.* United States v. Powers, 978 F.2d 354, 361–62 (7th Cir.1992), *cert. denied*, 507 U.S. 935 (1993) (prior convictions for bank robbery and attempted bank robbery admissible as "plan" evidence when

perpetrator wore wide-brimmed hat, dark glasses, a business suit, had a moustache, and carried a briefcase in all incidents). *But see* United States v. O'Connor, 580 F.2d 38, 42 (2d Cir.1978) (bribes taken from third parties not sufficiently probative of "definite project" of committing present crime).

199. *See* United States v. Carson, 702 F.2d 351, 368–69 (2d Cir.), *cert. denied*, 462 U.S. 1108 (1983). *But see* United States v. Beasley, 809 F.2d 1273 (7th Cir.1987) (Easterbrook, J.) (denying proposition that any drug offense can be used to prove another drug offense); *cf.* United States v. Mejia–Uribe, 75 F.3d 395, 398–99 (8th Cir.), *cert. denied*, ___ U.S. ___, 117 S.Ct. 151 (1996) (held, error to admit evidence of defendant's 17–year-old drug conviction in trial for possession of cocaine with intent to distribute; the two different crimes were not linked as such to be considered part of one common scheme, since the earlier crime involved a single sale whereas the charged

As Weinstein and Berger have stated, "The cases reveal a continuum ranging from situations close to the common design, to cases where the boundaries of the scheme are astonishingly wider."[200]

The different approaches to these controversial cases is exemplified by recent authority from the California courts. In *People v. Tassell*,[201] the California Supreme Court held that common design or plan could not be established by evidence of even extremely similar misconduct unless all of the acts were part of a single, continuing conception or plot. A decade later, in *People v. Ewoldt*,[202] the court overruled *Tassell*, holding that *Tassell* had failed to recognize that evidence of similar misconduct could be relevant to prove not only intent or identity, but a common scheme or plan, which in turn is relevant to prove that the defendant engaged in the charged offense. The court announced a new, far less restrictive rule that "evidence of a defendant's uncharged misconduct is relevant where the uncharged misconduct and the charged offense are sufficiently similar to support the inference that they are manifestations of a common design or plan."[203] The validity of the respective views has been the subject of spirited debate.[204]

§ 5.26 Specific Purposes for Which Uncharged Misconduct Evidence May Be Offered—Identity

Under Federal Rule of Evidence 404(b), another purpose for which uncharged misconduct evidence may be offered is to show the identity of the person who committed a certain act. Like intent, identity is usually an ultimate fact rather than merely a fact offered to prove an ultimate fact. In a criminal case, for example, the prosecution must prove not only that a crime was committed, but that it was the defendant who committed it. Sometimes, other misconduct evidence tends to prove another fact, and from that, identity. Most commonly, evidence tends to prove identity by means of modus operandi.[205] For another example, uncharged

crime involved large scale, ongoing operations).

200. 2 Weinstein's Federal Evidence § 404.08[5][b], at 404–123 to 404–125 (2d ed. Joseph M. McLaughlin ed. 1997) (footnote omitted).

201. 679 P.2d 1, 201 Cal.Rptr. 567 (1984).

202. 867 P.2d 757, 27 Cal.Rptr.2d 646 (1994).

203. *Id.* at 769, 27 Cal. Rptr. At 657.

204. *See, e.g.*, Mark Cammack, *Using the Doctrine of Chances to Prove Actus Reus in Child Abuse and Acquaintance Rape:* People v. Ewoldt *Reconsidered*, 29 U.C. Davis L. Rev. 355 (1996); Edward J. Imwinkelried, *Using a Contextual Construction to Resolve the Dispute Over the Meaning of the Term "Plan" in Federal Rule of Evidence 404(b)*, 43 U. Kan. L. Rev. 1005

(1995); Miguel A. Mendez & Edward J. Imwinkelried, People v. Ewoldt: *The California Supreme Court's About–Face on the Plan Theory for Admitting Evidence of an Accused's Uncharged Misconduct*, 28 Loy. L. A. L. Rev. 473 (1995); Jeannie Mayre Mar, Note and Comment, *Washington's Expansion of the "Plan" Exception After State v. Lough*, 71 Wash. L. Rev. 845 (1996).

205. *See, e.g.*, United States v. Tai, 994 F.2d 1204, 1208 (7th Cir.1993) (in prosecution of extortion scheme, evidence of threats against others and assaults by defendant's employee admissible to show defendant's identity); *see also* State v. Rehberg, 919 S.W.2d 543, 548–50 (Mo.App. 1995) (where defendant charged with stealing plumbing equipment by placing it in an opened lamp box, sealing the box with tape and later purchasing the box, paying only for the lamp, evidence that defendant had been stealing equipment in such a manner misconduct might be offered to prove that defendant had a motive, and thus that she was the person who committed the crime.[206]

Sometimes, the uncharged misconduct evidence proves identity more directly. For example, evidence that defendant threatened prospective prosecution witnesses or attempted to bribe a witness or juror tends to evidence a consciousness of guilt, which serves to identify the defendant as the perpetrator of the crime in question.[207]

Of course, there must be limits to the degree to which evidence of uncharged misconduct can be admissible to prove identity. Otherwise, whenever there was an issue whether the defendant was the person who committed the crime charged, the door would open to evidence of other crimes by the defendant. The mere fact that the defendant committed prior robberies, for example, does have some probative value in identifying the defendant as the one who committed the robbery involved in the instant case; all else being equal, a person who has robbed before is part of a population that is more likely to commit robbery than the general population. Yet to allow that reasoning to prevail would be to admit character evidence. It seems clear from the structure of Rule 404(b) that, while evidence of uncharged crimes is admissible to prove identity if the chain of reasoning can bypass inferences about the general character of the defendant, it is not admissible if identity is sought to be proven by means of showing the defendant to have a bad character and to have acted in conformity with that bad character. To hold otherwise would vitiate the first sentence of Rule 404(b).[208]

§ 5.27 Res Gestae; Background; Complete Story Principle

Sometimes incidental crimes are admitted simply because the testimony of witnesses would be unduly hamstrung by attempting to avoid reference to them, and the incidental crimes have no particular prejudicial effect. This would be true, for example, if a witness mentioned that the defendant and his cohorts smoked some marijuana while negotiating

for the past four years was held admissible since the crimes were so nearly identical and the methodology so distinctive that it showed a signature); Commonwealth v. Madyun, 458 N.E.2d 745 (Mass.App.1983) (subsequent rapes by defendant admissible to prove identify, when there were "striking similarities in the unconnected crimes and the subject crime"); United States v. Hamilton, 684 F.2d 380, 384 (6th Cir.), *cert. denied*, 459 U.S. 976 (1982) (prior crime with similar modus operandi admissible on issue of identity of defendant charged with circulating altered currency); State v. Williams, 670 P.2d 1348, 1352 (Kan.1983). *Cf.* United States v. Williams, 994 F.2d 1287, 1288 (8th Cir.1993) (in prosecution for drug distribution, evidence that defendant "showed up" during a later drug deal admissible to show his identity); State v. Speer, 501 N.W.2d 429 434 (Wis.1993) (held, in burglary prosecution, trial court properly admitted evidence of defendant's prior burglary conviction to establish identity; both burglaries occurred during daylight at houses with "For Sale" signs posted nearby).

206. *See* § **5.18.**

207. *See, e.g.*, United States v. Meling, 47 F.3d 1546, 1557 (9th Cir.), *cert. den'd*, 516 U.S. 843 (1995) (in prosecution for product tampering, evidence that defendant threatened his father-in-law and uncle to intimidate them into withholding information from the FBI admissible to demonstrate consciousness of guilt).

208. Fed. R. Evid. 404(b). *Cf.* 1 McCormick on Evidence § 190, at 808 (4th ed. John W. Strong ed. 1992).

a cocaine sale, or that the defendant stole an (uncharged) item from B at the same time that a (charged) item was stolen from A. The concept behind admissibility is that the witness should be permitted to tell the story in an natural fashion. The trier should get the full flavor of the happenings at the time of the crime; and the evidence is being admitted for this purpose, not for the purpose of saying anything about the character of the defendant. This route of admissibility is sometimes designated as *res gestae*, though perhaps it would be better to avoid the vagueness of the Latin term and refer to the "complete story" principle.[209]

Though evidence often should be admitted under this theory if it helps provide the trier with a complete picture, it is also necessary to exercise great care to avoid prejudice. The less probative value the evidence has in establishing the full story, and the more likely the evidence is to cause unfair prejudice, the more likely the court should exclude the evidence under Rule 403.

§ 5.28 Quantum of Proof Required for Evidence of Uncharged Misconduct

Evidence of uncharged misconduct may include not only evidence of prior convictions, but also evidence of crimes or misconduct that did not

---

209. *See* United States v. Rivera (Reynaldo Vazquez), 83 F.3d 542, 546 (1st Cir. 1996) (Coffin, J.) (in case charging carjacking, not error to admit evidence that defendant raped victim during carjacking; it might help explain, inter alia, why she heard but did not see firearm); United States v. Richards, 967 F.2d 1189, 1193–94 (8th Cir.1992) (evidence of incriminating items seized from trunk at the same time officers seized firearms is admissible as part of the res gestae of the firearms possession), citing United States v. Moore, 735 F.2d 289, 292 (8th Cir.1984) (per curiam) (res gestae exception to Rule 404(b) permits "introduction of evidence of other criminal activity" occurring at the time and place of arrest "for the purpose of providing the context in which the crime occurred"); Atkins v. Singletary, 965 F.2d 952, 960 (11th Cir.1992), *cert. denied*, 515 U.S. 1165 (1995) (evidence of confession to uncharged sexual battery admissible as part of the res gestae of the charged homicide); United States v. Dudley, 941 F.2d 260, 262–63 (4th Cir.1991), *cert. denied*, 502 U.S. 1046 (1992) (no error in allowing evidence of uncharged offense as part of the "res gestae"; "The jury is entitled to know the setting of a case. It cannot be expected to make its decision in a void—without knowledge of the time, place and circumstances of the acts which form the basis of the charge"); State v. Price, 598 P.2d 985, 987 (Ariz.1979) (in trial for aiding and abetting sale of heroin, evidence that

defendant asked for a "taste" of substance admissible, *inter alia*, under "complete story" theory. *See also* United States v. Hill, 953 F.2d 452, 457 (9th Cir.1991) (doctrine allowing introduction of other crimes where it is inextricably intertwined with charged crime should be applied narrowly to avoid overly broad, so-called res gestae exception); Hurns v. State, 616 So.2d 313, 321 (Miss.1993) (in prosecution for murder of inmate, evidence of sexual assaults admissible to show "complete story" of defendant's "total domination over all the inmates"); United States v. Vizcarra–Martinez, 66 F.3d 1006, 1012–13 (9th Cir.1995) (held, evidence of defendant's possession of small "personal-use" amount of methamphetamine when arrested should not have been admitted under aegis of complete story principle in case whether defendant charged with more serious crime of possessing substance knowing it would be used to manufacture methamphetamine); *cf.* United States v. Forcelle, 86 F.3d 838, 842 (8th Cir.1996) (where defendant charged with illegally obtaining corporate funds to purchase drag racing chassis and make home improvements, trial court improperly admitted evidence that defendant stole platinum from corporation, since it was distinct from the charged crimes; however, trial court properly admitted evidence of defendant's home improvements since such activity could be construed to be intertwined with the charged crimes).

result in conviction, including, in proper cases, crimes that resulted in an acquittal. This result is not illogical; acts that, when taken in isolation, might not be enough to convict beyond a reasonable doubt may, when joined with proof of other acts, provide convincing evidence of guilt.[210]

The fact that the prior misconduct need not have resulted in conviction does not, of course, mean that no proof that the prior misconduct occurred is required. Some courts require that the prosecution, as a preliminary matter, convince the judge by a preponderance of the evidence or even by clear and convincing evidence that the defendant committed the crime,[211] and a substantial number of lower federal courts followed a similar practice.[212] However, in *Huddleston v. United States*,[213] the Supreme Court unanimously rejected this line of authority as stating the rule under the Federal Rules of Evidence.

Huddleston was a case in which the defendant was accused of selling stolen goods in interstate commerce. The charge was based on defendant's sale of 5,000 blank video cassette tapes at a price below the cost of manufacture. The defendant did not deny selling the tapes, but did deny knowing that they were stolen. As evidence of the defendant's guilty knowledge, the government offered, and the trial judge received, evidence that the defendant had at other times sold large quantities of stolen or apparently stolen consumer goods for extremely low prices.

The Court rejected the argument that the government was required to make a preliminary showing by a preponderance of the evidence that the defendant had committed the prior similar acts. Instead, it held that all that was required was a showing of evidence sufficient to allow a reasonable jury to conclude that the defendant had committed the prior acts. The decision was based upon the Court's view that the admissibility of the evidence was governed by the "conditional relevancy" theory embodied in Federal Rule of Evidence 104(b), which provides that when "the relevancy of evidence depends upon the fulfillment of a condition of fact," the court shall admit it if there is evidence sufficient to support a finding that the condition has been fulfilled. In sending the evidence to the jury, the court should inform the jury of its obligation to consider the

---

210. *See* People v. Massey, 16 Cal. Rptr. 402 (App.1961) (evidence about alleged burglary, of which defendant had been acquitted, admitted in trial for another burglary; similar modus operandi); Dowling v. United States, 493 U.S. 342, 348–50 (1990) (held, not violation of double jeopardy to use conduct resulting in acquittal as other crime evidence).

211. Holmes v. State, 394 N.W.2d 818, 822 (Minn.App.1986); Ali v. United States, 520 A.2d 306, 310 & n. 4 (D.C.1987).

212. Prior to *Huddleston*, several circuits followed this rule. *See, e.g.*, United States v. Leight, 818 F.2d 1297, 1302 (7th Cir.), *cert. denied*, 484 U.S. 958, (1987);

United States v. Weber, 818 F.2d 14 (8th Cir.1987); United States v. Vaccaro, 816 F.2d 443, 452 (9th Cir.), *cert. denied sub nom.* Alvis v. United States, 484 U.S. 914, (1987). For a summary of the pre-*Huddleston* practice in the various circuits, see *Huddleston* at 685 n. 2.

213. 485 U.S. 681 (1988). *See also* United States v. Anderson, 933 F.2d 1261, 1267–74 (5th Cir.1991), *aff'd*, 976 F.2d 927 (5th Cir.1992) (proponent need show only that a reasonable jury could conclude that defendant committed the prior acts; remanding for on-record determination of whether standard of proof for preliminary facts was met.

evidence only if it decides (by a preponderance of the evidence) that the fact at issue is true.

In the authors' opinion, Rule 104(b) does not really answer the question confronted by the Court. By its reference to "sufficient" evidence, the Rule implicitly incorporates reference to an unstated, externally established burden of persuasion; what is "sufficient" to support a reasonable verdict when the burden of persuasion is a mere preponderance of the evidence may not be "sufficient" when the burden is proof beyond a reasonable doubt. While Rule 104(b) may be enough to suggest that the judge should defer to the jury in a jury trial, it is not enough to state exactly what the level of deference should be. If common law principles otherwise require that the jury be convinced by an extraordinary quantum of proof, then the judgment of what is "sufficient" must be altered accordingly.

In addition, the Court arguably did not give sufficient consideration to the problem of prejudice. Any time a jury is informed of a person's other misconduct—particularly serious criminal activities—there is a very real danger that the jury will employ the evidence for its improper (character) purpose and not for the more narrow purpose for which it might properly be considered. The standard adopted by the court takes a significant amount of filtering power out of the hands of the judge; it stands to reason that in the vast majority of cases, the prosecution can offer at least some evidence to support the defendant's participation in the uncharged misconduct, and courts will generally find this evidence "sufficient to support a finding" that defendant was in fact involved.[214] The court's ability to control the jury's very natural (though impermissible) tendency to employ the evidence for the wrong reason is quite limited. Moreover, if defendant decides seriously to contest her commission of the uncharged misconduct, the trial on the charged activities will often be sidetracked along a time-consuming and confusing course. This, too, creates the risk of injustice.

The Supreme Court has spoken for the federal system. It is likely, though, that some states will continue to adhere to a stricter standard of proof, even where the Federal Rules of Evidence have been used as a model for corresponding state rules.

In states in which a more demanding standard is applied, it is appropriate to consider all of the charged and uncharged misconduct together in deciding whether the standard has been met. Even if the defendant's commission of a prior crime, *when considered by itself*, has not been established by clear and convincing evidence, the suspicious prior circumstances, when taken together with the circumstances of the

---

214. In a footnote, the Court rejected defendant's contention that in performing the Rule 403 balance, the court must find that the prejudicial impact of the evidence outweighs its probative value unless the court concludes by a preponderance of the evidence that the defendant committed the uncharged act. The Court conceded, however, that "the strength of the evidence establishing the similar act is one of the factors the court may consider when conducting the Rule 403 balancing." 485 U.S. at 689 n.6.

charged crime, may be enough to prove the charged crime beyond a reasonable doubt. For example, it might be impossible to establish by clear and convincing evidence that the defendant had drowned his previous wife in the bathtub when the facts of that transaction are considered in isolation, but when the facts are considered in conjunction with evidence that the defendant drowned his second wife in the bath, the two crimes corroborate each other and ought to be considered together.[215]

§ 5.29   Character as an Ultimate Issue [FRE 405(b)]

Evidence of a party's character is not admissible, under the general rule, to show action in conformity with character. In such cases, character is not the ultimate issue; it is merely an evidentiary fact that is offered to prove something else (the action in conformity). Sometimes, however, character is not offered to prove any action; character itself is an ultimate issue (in the language of the Federal Rule, character is itself "an essential element of a charge, claim, or defense"[216]). The substantive law makes the rights and liabilities of the parties turn on a trait of character. When that is the case, character evidence is freely admissible. In fact, the character evidence need not be in the form of reputation and opinion testimony; evidence of specific acts of conduct is also admissible.[217]

Examples

The fitness of a parent, in custody litigation.[218]

The predisposition of a defendant, when the defendant relies upon the entrapment defense. For example, if the defendant claims that he was entrapped by the government into selling drugs, the government may freely introduce prior drug sales to show that the defendant was predisposed.

---

215. *Cf.* Rex v. Smith, [1914–15] All E.R. Rep. 265. For a case that apparently ignores this principle, see Tucker v. State, 412 P.2d 970 (Nev.1966), a case that suggests, if nothing else, that the rules of character evidence are not just dressed-up common sense. In May, 1957, Tucker phoned the police station and asked someone to come to the Tucker home in North Las Vegas. When the police arrived, they noticed that Tucker had been drinking. Tucker led them to the dining room where one Kaylor was laying dead on the floor, having been shot several times. Tucker explained that he had awakened and found Kaylor there. No one was ever charged with the crime. In October, 1963, Tucker again called the police. He had again been drinking. He led police to a dead man on the living room sofa. the man had been shot. Tucker explained that he had awakened and found the man dead on the couch. He was convicted of second-degree murder,

with the evidence of the Kaylor killing being admitted over objection. The Nevada Supreme Court reversed, reasoning that there was nothing in the record to establish that Tucker killed Kaylor. It announced a rule that before evidence of a collateral offense is admissible for any purpose, the prosecution must first establish by plain, clear, and convincing evidence that the defendant committed that offense.

216. Fed. R. Evid. 405(b).

217. *See* Fed. R. Evid. 405(b); 2 Weinstein's Federal Evidence §§ 404.03[2], 405.05[4] (2d ed. Joseph M. McLaughlin ed. 1997); United States v. Sonntag, 684 F.2d 781 (11th Cir.1982); Crumpton v. Confederation Life Ins. Co., 672 F.2d 1248 (5th Cir.1982).

218. *See* 1A John H. Wigmore, Evidence in Trials at Common Law § 69.1 (Peter Tillers rev. 1983).

The relevant trait of character that forms the basis for a defamation action, when truth is raised as a defense. For example, if the defendant called the plaintiff a thief, and in a defamation action admits making the statement but claims that it was true, the defendant is free to produce evidence showing the plaintiff to be a thief. (There are limits to the principle. Suppose D published an article that alleged that P stole a car on a certain date. If P sues for libel and D asserts truth as a defense, evidence to show that P stole the car would of course be admissible. However, evidence of P's general reputation as a car thief, or the opinion of one who knows P that P is the kind of person who steals cars, would not be admissible to prove truth because even though P's character is to some extent "in issue," the evidence would be offered as circumstantial evidence of P's conduct, for which purpose it is not admissible.)

§ 5.30 Character and Habit [FRE 406]

In most jurisdictions, character evidence is not admissible in civil cases as circumstantial evidence of conduct, and it is admissible in criminal cases only under prescribed exceptions. However, evidence of *habit* is freely admissible. The distinction between character and habit is largely a matter of degree. In describing the distinction, the advisory committee to the Federal Rules of Evidence quoted McCormick's classic definition:

> Character and habit are close akin. Character is a generalized description of one's disposition, or of one's disposition in respect to a general trait, such as honesty, temperance, or peacefulness. "Habit," in modern usage, both lay and psychological, is more specific. It describes one's regular response to a repeated specific situation. If we speak of character for care, we think of the person's tendency to act prudently in all the varying situations of life, in business, family life, in handling automobiles and in walking across the street. A habit, on the other hand, is the person's regular practice of meeting a particular kind of situation with a specific type of conduct, such as the habit of going down a particular stairway two stairs at a time, or of giving the hand-signal for a left turn, or of alighting from railway cars while they are moving. The doing of the habitual acts may become semi-automatic.[219]

---

219. Fed. R. Evid. 406 advisory committee's note (quoting Charles T. McCormick, McCormick on Evidence § 162, at 340 (1954)). *See also* Jones v. Southern Pac. R.R., 962 F.2d 447, 449 (5th Cir.1992) (habit evidence is superior to character evidence "because the uniformity of one's response to habit is far greater than the consistency with which one's conduct conforms to character"); Estate of Keys v. City of Harvey, 1996 WL 34422, at *2 (N.D.Ill.1996) (in wrongful death action stemming from killing by police sergeant, records of the ser-

geant's disciplinary and personnel files inadmissible under Fed. R. Evid. 406; records could only show a tendency to react violently to challenges to his authority, not conduct semi-automatic in nature; the degree of "specificity and frequency" of the action distinguishes habit evidence from impermissible character evidence); *cf.* Mobil Exploration & Producing U.S., Inc. v. Cajun Const. Servs., Inc., 45 F.3d 96, 100 (5th Cir.1995) (in suit claiming supplier had short-loaded its deliveries of limestone, trial court erroneously excluded evidence of sup-

The rules provide not only for the admission of habit evidence about human beings, but also for admission of evidence of the *routine practice* of a corporation or other organization. In contrast to the earlier practice of some jurisdictions, the Federal Rules contain no requirement that habit or routine practice be corroborated by other evidence; it can itself be sufficient to prove the doing of an act. Nor is there any rule that habit evidence is admissible only if eyewitness testimony is not available. One's habit—say, a habit of using seat belts—is admissible under the Federal Rules whether or not eyewitnesses are also available who could testify that the person wore the seat belt on the occasion in question.

Examples of habit or routine practice include a doctor's regular practice of advising patients of risks of joint replacement surgery, to show that the advice was given on a particular occasion involving ankle replacement surgery;[220] a bar's regular practice of serving intoxicated persons, to support the inference that it did so on a particular occasion;[221] a drinker's habit of getting drunk at a particular social club nearly every weekend, to show intoxication at the time of a hit-and-run accident;[222] a railroad crew's practice of not blowing a whistle at a particular crossing,[223] or of operating a switch engine without a flagman in the street;[224] an undercover agent's routine practice of marking and sealing illicit drugs seized during an investigation, to show that the practice was followed on a particular occasion;[225] a nurse's routine practice of taking blood samples;[226] a business's routine practice of stamping mail with sufficient postage;[227] and a hospital's routine practices concerning the presentation and signing of medical malpractice arbitration forms.[228]

In general, habit evidence has tended to be evidence of responses, often semi-automatic, to relatively narrow specific situations. The evidence is sometimes rejected on grounds that the conduct is not sufficiently regular or that the trait in question is actually a trait of character.[229] On the other hand, where the need is great enough and the

plier's method of loading its trucks; supplier's method of loading amounted to habit under Fed. R. Evid. 406 since the same procedure was used with such regularity as to amount to a routine business practice).

220. Bloskas v. Murray, 646 P.2d 907, 911 (Colo.1982). *See also* Meyer v. United States, 464 F.Supp. 317, 321 (D.Colo.1979) (dentist's practice of informing patients of the risks involved in extraction of third molars).

221. Tommy's Elbow Room, Inc. v. Kavorkian, 727 P.2d 1038 (Alaska 1986).

222. State v. Radziwil, 563 A.2d 856, 861 (N.J.Super.1989), *affirmed*, 582 A.2d 1003 (1990). *See also* Loughan v. Firestone Tire & Rubber Co., 749 F.2d 1519, 1522–24 (11th Cir.1985) (worker's habit of bringing cooler of beer to work on back of truck and drinking from it while working admissible

as evidence of drunkenness on a particular occasion).

223. Bradfield v. Illinois Central Gulf R.R., 505 N.E.2d 331 (Ill.1987).

224. Williams v. Union Pac. R.R., 465 P.2d 975 (Kan.1970).

225. State v. Van Sickle, 434 A.2d 31 (Me.1981).

226. State v. Shelton, 176 N.W.2d 159, 161–62 (Iowa 1970).

227. Swink & Co. v. Carroll McEntee & McGinley, Inc., 584 S.W.2d 393 (Ark. 1979).

228. McKinstry v. Valley Obstetrics–Gynecology Clinic, PC, 405 N.W.2d 88 (Mich.1987).

229. *See* Neuren v. Adduci, Mastriani, Meeks & Schill, 43 F.3d 1507 (D.C.Cir.

testimony convincing, some courts have treated rather broad traits as being "habit" traits.[230] There is much room for disagreement about just how much specificity is enough to establish habit.[231]

Habit evidence is often offered in civil cases to show a careful or careless habit. (In such instances, the evidence must actually demonstrate a habit, and not just a general tendency toward care or its opposite.) It should be noted, however, that although use of the habit concept is one way of justifying the receipt of other acts evidence in civil cases, it is not the only way. As already discussed, in both civil and criminal cases, evidence of uncharged misconduct (or of good conduct) may be admitted for one of the other purposes listed in Rule 404(b), as long as it is not offered for an inference about character. Thus, in a civil case in which a fire insurance company offers a defense of arson, the company may wish to offer evidence that other property belonging to the defendant had been destroyed by the defendant's arson. The commission of arson can hardly be regular enough to be considered a "habit," but if a distinctive modus operandi was involved, or if the arson was part of a common scheme or plan, it would be admissible under the principles of Rule 404(b).[232] *See* §§ **5.19.**

1995) (in an employment discrimination case, defendant's evidence that the plaintiff had experienced similar work-related problems, such as tardiness, on another job was inadmissible character evidence; court made no allusion to the "habit" theory of admissibility); Jones v. Southern Pac. R.R., 962 F.2d 447, 450 (5th Cir.1992) (evidence of nine violations in 29–year career as railroad engineer not admissible to prove habit of driving negligently); Smith v. State, 601 So.2d 201 (Ala.Crim.App.1992) (picking up prostitutes in certain area is not habit); Henry v. Cline, 626 S.W.2d 958 (Ark.1982) (testimony that witness had seen party drive on a road a dozen times and that party was speeding half the time not sufficient to establish habit; behavior not "nearly or completely involuntary"); Ritchey v. Murray, 625 S.W.2d 476 (Ark.1981) (tendency of driver to weave across centerline when reaching for chewing tobacco or delivering newspapers not sufficiently regular to constitute habit; no evidence that driver was delivering newspapers on occasion in question); Stapleton v. Great Lakes Chem. Corp., 616 So.2d 1311, 1317–18 (La.App. 1993), *vacated in part on other grounds,* 627 So.2d 1358 (1993) (harmless error for trial court to admit testimony of defendant's good driving record and awards for safe driving as habit evidence); State v. Lagasse, 410 A.2d 537, 542 (Me.1980) ("The tendency of a person to engage in violent acts while under the influence of intoxicating liquor does not establish 'the regular response to a repeated specific situation' necessary to constitute habit under M. R. Evid.

406"); De Matteo v. Simon, 812 P.2d 361, 362–63 (N.M.App.1991) (defendant's post-accident driving record not admissible to show a habit of negligence).

230. *See, e.g.,* Derring v. State, 619 S.W.2d 644 (Ark.1981) (regularity, reliability, and promptness of supposed victim admissible as habit evidence to show he would not have disappeared without foul play; query whether some of the traits described as habit should really be considered character).

231. *Compare* Loughan v. Firestone Tire & Rubber Co., 749 F.2d 1519, 1522–24 (11th Cir.1985) (evidence that employee regularly drank on the job from cooler of beer he carried on his truck was admitted at trial for purposes of showing that employee was impaired at time of accident; held, showing of regularity was sufficient to establish habit under Rule 406, and evidence was admissible despite absence of direct evidence that employee drank on day of accident) *with* Reyes v. Missouri Pac. R.R., 589 F.2d 791 (5th Cir.1979) (four prior convictions for intoxication held *inadmissible* to show action in conformity; evidence was evidence of character, not habit, and hence forbidden). *See* 1 McCormick on Evidence § 195, at 826 n.8 (4th ed. John W. Strong ed. 1992) (probative force of habitual intoxication to prove intoxication on particular occasion depends on regularity of details of characteristic behavior).

232. *Cf.* Hammann v. Hartford Accident & Indem. Co., 620 F.2d 588 (6th Cir.

§ 5.31　Procedural Aspects of Character and Other Crimes Evidence

Because of its potentially inflammatory nature, procedural safeguards are sometimes used to prevent the jury from learning about character evidence, before it has been formally admitted, from using character evidence for an improper purpose, and from receiving more details than absolutely necessary. The following sections deal with those safeguards.

§ 5.32　Procedural Aspects of Character and Other Crimes Evidence—Notice; Motions in Limine; Voir Dire Hearings

Since December, 1991, the Federal Rules of Evidence have required that the prosecution provide notice of intent to offer uncharged misconduct evidence. Fed. R. Evid. 404(b) provides that "upon request by the accused, the prosecution in a criminal case shall provide reasonable notice in advance of trial, or during trial if the court excuses pretrial notice on good cause shown, of the general nature of any such evidence [of other crimes, wrongs, or acts] it intends to introduce at trial." No such requirement is imposed on the defendant in criminal cases, or on either party in civil actions.

Some state jurisdictions require that the prosecutor notify defense counsel prior to trial of intent to use uncharged misconduct evidence. For example, the Minnesota Rules of Criminal Procedure require the prosecution to disclose any additional offenses that may be offered in evidence at trial,[233] and the admissibility of the prior offenses may be explored at the "omnibus hearing" prior to trial. Florida, Alaska, and Vermont also provide for notice and pretrial hearings on uncharged misconduct evidence.[234]

When the defendant learns of the possibility that the prosecution will use uncharged misconduct evidence, a motion in limine may be used to attempt to obtain a pretrial ruling on admissibility, so that an effective response can be planned against potentially very damaging evidence. The motion may be particularly useful, for example, when the prosecution does not plan to offer extrinsic evidence of other acts, but to cross-examine the defendant about them, since this may influence the defendant's decision whether to take the stand. The trial judge is under no obligation, however, to determine the issue prior to trial, even where delaying a ruling until the issue arises during trial may put the defendant in a bind.[235]

1980) (prior incendiary fires on plaintiff's property admissible). *See also* Gail A. Randall, Note, *Product Liability Litigation: Impact I of Federal Rule of Evidence 404(b) Upon Admissibility Standards of Prior Accident Evidence,* 61 Wash U.L.Q. 799 (1983).

233. Minn. R. Crim. Proc. 7.05.

234. *See* Fla. Stat. Ann. § 90.404 (West 1979); Alaska R. Evid. 404; Vt. R. Crim. Proc. 26(c).

235. *See* United States v. Lutz, 621 F.2d 940 (9th Cir.1980), *cert. denied,* 449 U.S. 1093 (1981).

In any event, the defendant, upon request, is entitled to a hearing outside the presence of the jury to determine the admissibility of other crimes evidence.[236] The hearing may occur prior to trial, during trial with the jury excused, at the sidebar, or in chambers.

§ 5.33 Procedural Aspects of Character and Other Crimes Evidence—Limiting Instructions

When evidence that is offered for a limited purpose, such as showing motive or intent, also reflects upon a defendant's character, the defendant is entitled to an instruction informing the jury of the limited purpose of the evidence. Often, the limiting instruction is likely to have little practical significance. An example of this sort of limiting instruction is contained in the account of the trial of Smith in the "Brides in the Bath" case. According to the account by Marjoribanks:

> The judge, however, admitted the evidence [that other wives of the defendant had been found drowned in the bath], warning the jury that they must not use it to infer that the prisoner was a man of bad character and infamous acts, likely to have committed the murder, but to help them to decide whether the death of Miss Mundy was accidental or designed by the prisoner.[237]

A juror, or anyone for that matter, would need a remarkably compartmentalized mind to be able to use the evidence solely on the issue of whether the defendant "designed" to kill his wife, and not whether the defendant was "likely to" have committed the murder. Yet even in these circumstances it might be worthwhile to seek a limiting instruction, if only to preserve a point for appeal.

In addition, limiting instructions can be made more effective than the one given in the "Brides" case, and counsel should be prepared to offer the court alternative language that better communicates to the jury the purpose for which the evidence may be considered and that for which it is not admissible.[238] Where they are effective, limiting instructions may be worth reiteration in final argument. One such case was the Seddon trial, in which Mr. and Mrs. Seddon were accused of poisoning a lodger, Miss Barrow. One of the motives was supposed to be acquiring a sum of about £300 which Miss Barrow supposedly kept in a lockbox in the house, and which disappeared after her death. There was strong evidence that the Seddons had taken the money and other possessions of Miss Barrow, but the evidence that they had poisoned her was less convincing. The evidence that they stole her money was, of course,

236. *See* Fed. R. Evid. 104(c); United States v. Beechum, 582 F.2d 898 (5th Cir. 1978).

237. E. Marjoribanks, For the Defense: The Life of Sir Edward Marshall Hall 324 (1931).

238. For discussion of the factors that make jury instructions difficult to understand and of ways to improve their compre- hensibility, *see* Amiram Elwork, Bruce D. Sales & James J. Alfini, Making Jury Instructions Understandable (1983); Robert P. Charrow & Veda R. Charrow, *Making Legal Language Understandable: A Psycholinguistic Study of Jury Instructions*, 79 Colum. L. Rev. 1306 (1979); Peter Meijes Tiersma, *Reforming the Language of Jury Instructions*, 22 Hofstra L. Rev. 37 (1993).

admissible as evidence providing a motive for the murder. Marshall Hall's closing argument pointed out the limited purpose for which the evidence could be used:

> [This] is one of those curious cases where, by reason of the fact that it is necessary in law to prove a motive for the poisoning, for the object of providing a motive, this man and this woman have been exposed to merciless cross-examination on the suggestion that they were thieves. In no other circumstances would that have been possible. If this man had been charged with any other crime, he could never have been cross-examined, nor could the woman have been cross-examined, as my learned friend the Attorney–General frankly admitted, to carry out the suggestion that they had robbed this woman. We are not trying these people on a charge of robbery. You will have to take the greatest care in this case that you do not allow the prejudice which has been brought into it to influence you unduly.... The only possible thing in which the matter might be dangerous, so far as your honest deliberations are concerned, is that you might think that the proposition is, "We have cross-examined these people to show they are thieves. If you think they are thieves therefore you must think they are murderers." It is a fallacy. It is a proposition which will not hold water in a Court. It has nothing to do with the question we have to deal with."[239]

In general, a limiting instruction should inform the jury that the only purpose of the evidence is to shed light on the defendant's possible motive (or intent, or whatever forms the basis for admission), and that it may not be used as evidence that the defendant had a bad character and was likely to commit crimes of the nature charged.[240]

Another situation in which a limiting instruction is appropriate is that in which the prosecution has cross-examined a defense character witness about uncharged misconduct by the defendant, in order to impeach the witness's knowledge of the defendant's reputation. This topic is discussed in § **5.08.** One form of limiting instruction, suggested by a well-known guide, reads as follows:

> On direct examination, _____, a witness for Defendant _____, testified that [he] [she] was familiar with the reputation of Defendant _____.

> The attorney for the government now proposes to ask certain questions on cross examination of this witness, as to events in the defendant's past.

> I caution you that these questions will be permitted solely for the limited purpose of testing the testimony of this witness that [he] [she] was familiar with the reputation of Defendant _____ in the

239. F. Young, Trial of the Seddons 281–82 (1914).

240. *Cf.* United States v. Adcock, 558 F.2d 397, 401 (8th Cir.1977), *cert. denied,* 434 U.S. 921 (1977).

community. The answers to these questions are to be considered by you only for the purpose of testing the credibility of the witness.

The questions and answers in this area are not to be considered as any evidence that the defendant committed the crime[s] charged in this indictment.[241]

While the instruction is technically accurate, defense counsel should request that the forbidden purpose be more specifically described, by telling the jury that "Regardless of [the witness's] answer you are not to assume that the incidents asked about actually took place. All that is happening is that this witness' standard of opinion of the reputation of the defendant is being tested."[242]

§ 5.34 Procedural Aspects of Character and Other Crimes Evidence—Partial Exclusion; Redaction; Limited Inquiry

The fact that evidence of uncharged misconduct is relevant to some permissible purpose, such as demonstrating motive or opportunity, does not mean that the full facts concerning the uncharged misconduct must be admitted. The court can sometimes limit inquiry or exclude evidence in part to avoid prejudice. In *United States v. Sims,*[243] for example, the defendant's failure to return to a halfway house was offered to identify him as one of the robbers of a savings bank. The trial court admitted the evidence, but in neutered form. In affirming the conviction, the court noted approvingly the care with which the trial court had attempted to avoid prejudice:

> Sims is correct in his assertion that the jury may have inferred from his residency in the halfway house that he had previously been involved in some other criminal activity. However, the trial judge carefully confined the jury's consideration of this matter and thus mitigated any possible prejudice. The testimony was limited to a showing that Sims was a resident of the halfway house, was required to return, and had failed to return on the day of the robbery. There was absolutely no mention made of any of Sims' prior criminal activity. Additionally, there was no testimony that only convicted criminals resided at the halfway house.[244]

241. 1 Edward J. Devitt *et al.*, Federal Jury Practice and Instructions § 11.15 (4th ed. 1992).

242. This was part of the instructions given by the trial judge, and implicitly approved by the Supreme Court, in Michelson v. United States, 335 U.S. 469, 473 n. 3 (1948).

243. United States v. Sims, 617 F.2d 1371, 1378–79 (9th Cir.1980). *See also* Unit-

ed States v. Beasley, 809 F.2d 1273 (7th Cir.1987) (Easterbrook, J.) (trial court criticized for allowing evidence of missing witness's addiction and hospitalization, possibly because witness had obtained drugs from defendant; it would have been sufficient to tell jury that witness was missing through no fault of the prosecution).

244. 617 F.2d at 1378–79.

THE SUBSEQUENT REMEDIAL MEASURES RULE [FRE 407]

§ 5.35 The Subsequent Remedial Measures Rule: Definition and Rationale

Under the subsequent remedial measures rule, evidence that after an accident the defendant made repairs or took other remedial measures is not admissible to prove negligence or other culpable conduct.

Example

Plaintiff, who slipped and fell on defendant's stairs, alleges that defendant was negligent in not providing a handrail and in allowing the stairs to become slick and worn. After the accident, defendant added an abrasive surface and a handrail to the stairs in question. Evidence of the defendant's subsequent improvements is not admissible to prove that defendant was negligent at the time of the accident.

A typical formulation of the subsequent remedial measures rule may be found in Rule 407 of the Federal Rules of Evidence. A majority of states have adopted rules based on Federal Rule 407, and even those states that have yet to adopt an evidence code or have addressed the subsequent remedial measures problem with different statutory language, the policy of the Federal Rule is usually followed.[245] This Rule, which codifies conventional doctrine, provides that:

When, after an injury or harm allegedly caused by an event, measures are taken which, if taken previously, would have made the event less likely to occur, evidence of the subsequent measures is not admissible to prove negligence, culpable conduct, a defect in a product, a defect in a product's design, or a need for a warning or instruction. This rule does not require the exclusion of evidence of subsequent measures when offered for another purpose, such as proving ownership, control, or feasibility of precautionary measures, if controverted, or, impeachment.

The conventional view is that subsequent remedial measures are relevant as an implied recognition of responsibility or fault.[246] Thus, in

---

245. Maine and Rhode Island have rejected the policy of the Federal Rule in favor of a rule freely admitting evidence of subsequent remedial measures. For a review of the states' provisions, see David P. Leonard, The New Wigmore: A Treatise on Evidence: Selected Rules of Limited Admissibility §§ 2.3.4, 2.5 (1996).

246. Wigmore wrote:

The opponent's conduct in taking precautions to prevent an apprehended injury, or to remedy one already inflicted, may sometimes indicate a consciousness of wrong, in respect either to the party's identity as the wrongdoer or to his culpability in doing the act.

2 John H. Wigmore, Evidence in Trials at Common Law § 282, at 146 (James H. Chadbourn rev. 1979). It is often said that the conduct constitutes an implied "admission" of fault, see Fed. R. Evid. 407 advisory committee's note, but we do not use that term here in order to avoid confusion with the hearsay rule. To be an admission, the conduct must constitute a "statement," which is defined in this context as assertive conduct. Fed. R. Evid. 801(a) (defining a "statement" as "(1) an oral or written assertion or (2) nonverbal conduct of a person, if it is intended by the person as an assertion"). Because people generally do not undertake subsequent remedial measures in order to *assert* their belief in the dangerousness of the condition, their conduct is not assertive and thus not hearsay. As such, the admissions rule, which exempts statements

the example given above, it is likely that at least one motivation behind defendant's improvement of the stairway was defendant's belief that the stairway was not sufficiently safe at the time of the accident. Because as the owner of the stairs, defendant is likely in a position to know if the stairs are safe, defendant's conduct is relevant.[247]

The subsequent remedial measures rule is often applied in cases in which a defendant made physical repairs after an accident. It is not, however, limited to evidence of repairs or physical improvements. Any remedial measure that would have made the accident less likely to occur falls under the scope of the rule. For example, if a defendant fired a careless employee who caused an accident, the termination of the employee is a remedial measure that is inadmissible to prove negligence. A change in manufacturing procedures, in training of employees, or in the design of a product can also be a remedial measure within the meaning of the rule. A manufacturer's recall letter to product purchasers can qualify. So, too, can a hospital's post-accident self-evaluative study made to find ways to improve patient care.[248]

The primary purpose of the remedial measures rule is to encourage defendants to make needed improvements or repairs by removing the danger that evidence of improvements or repairs will be used against them in litigation. Though the real-world validity of this rationale has not been sufficiently tested, it is generally assumed that the absence of an exclusionary rule might discourage the taking of precautionary measures and thus increase overall societal harm.

The rule also has secondary purposes. One purpose is to exclude evidence of doubtful relevancy or that even if relevant, has very low probative value. The fact that, with hindsight, a defendant decided to take additional precautionary measures often does not provide the jury with much assistance in deciding whether the defendant was negligent at the time of the accident. As one court put it, it is fallacious to assume that "because the world gets wiser as it gets older, therefore it was foolish before."[249] Another purpose of the rule is to promote fairness to the repairing party. To put it simply, it seems unfair to punish a party that engaged in useful, accident-prevention conduct by turning that conduct against it in subsequent litigation.[250]

---

of parties from the definition, is not implicated.

247. The existence of alternative explanations for defendant's conduct (such as that defendant improved the stairs merely in order to make them more attractive) does not make the evidence irrelevant for its offered purpose unless under the circumstances it would be irrational for the jury to conclude that defendant was motivated at least in part by a belief in the stairway's danger. *See* Leonard, *supra* note 245 § 2.2.

248. *See generally id.* § 5.6.1.

249. Hart v. Lancashire & Yorkshire Ry. Co., 21 L.T.R. (N.S.) 261, 263 (1869).

250. *See* 2 Christopher B. Mueller & Laird C. Kirkpatrick, Federal Evidence § 127, at 26 (2d ed. 1994); 23 Charles A. Wright & Kenneth W. Graham, Jr., Federal Practice and Procedure (Evidence) § 5282, at 96 (1980).

§ 5.36 Remedial Measures Evidence That Falls Outside the Rule

The subsequent remedial measures rule excludes evidence of safety measures only when the evidence is offered for one of the forbidden purposes—e.g., showing negligence through an inference that the conduct reflects the actor's belief that the pre-measures condition was unreasonably dangerous. If the evidence is offered for any other purpose or through any other reasoning, it falls outside the scope of the rule and will not be excluded unless other evidence rules so require. If evidence of remedial measures is relevant both to the issue of negligence and to some other issue, such as whether the measures were feasible, then the trial judge must make a Rule 403 determination whether the probative value of the evidence when offered for its permissible purpose is substantially outweighed by its possible prejudicial effect. If the trial judge admits the evidence, the objecting party has the right to a limiting instruction informing the jury that the testimony may not be used as evidence of negligence.[251]

The following sections contain a nonexclusive list of other purposes for which the evidence may be offered. The list cannot be exclusive because subsequent remedial measures evidence is admissible when it is offered for any purpose other than showing negligence, culpable conduct etc., by means of reasoning involving an implied recognition of responsibility.[252] Therefore, the purposes listed in the following sections are only examples.

Before turning to the particular purposes, several preliminary issues must be considered. First, subsequent remedial measures evidence will only be admissible for these purposes if the issue on which the evidence is offered is "controverted." Most states follow the same rule. Generally, courts have held that the controversion requirement applies to all alternate uses of subsequent remedial measures evidence, whether or not the purpose at issue is listed in the rule. This is a wise position, as there is no principled reason to risk discouraging repair conduct and potential prejudice to the defendant when the evidence is offered on an undisputed point.[253]

---

251. *See* Fed. R. Evid. 105 (providing that on request, the court "shall restrict the evidence to its proper scope and instruct the jury accordingly").

252. For example, some courts have held that remedial measures by third parties fall outside the rule. *See* Buchanna v. Diehl Machine, Inc., 98 F.3d 366, 370 (8th Cir., 1996) (Rule 407 does not preclude evidence of remedial measures by nonparties, since admitting such evidence does not deter safety measures); TLT–Babcock, Inc. v. Emerson Elec. Co., 33 F.3d 397, 399 (4th Cir.1994) (held, evidence of subsequent remedial measures properly admitted when performed by third parties). *But see* In re Air Crash Disaster, 86 F.3d 498, 528–30 (6th Cir.1996) (held, defendant Northwest not entitled to put in evidence of its own safety improvements on aircraft to show that manufacturer's original version was unsafe; Rule 407 is not limited to remedial measures by party who originally manufactured product). For discussion of whether the acts of non-parties are covered by the exclusionary principle, see David P. Leonard, The New Wigmore: Selected Rules of Limited Admissibility § 2.6.3 (1996).

253. The credibility of witnesses is always "controverted" in the sense that the jury will weigh the value of each witness's testimony.

There is also a question whether the subsequent remedial measures rule only excludes evidence of action taken *after the accident at issue* occurred. Rules that track original Federal Rule 407 provide for exclusion when measures are taken "after an event." Suppose plaintiff is injured in an automobile accident and brings a product liability action against the automobile's manufacturer alleging defective design of the braking system. Plaintiff learns that after she bought the car, but *before* the accident occurred, defendant altered the design of its braking system in a way that would have prevented the plaintiff's accident. Plaintiff argues that the exclusionary rule should not apply because the "event" at issue was the accident, and the design change was made before the accident. Although the literal language of the rule supports the plaintiff, some courts have held that the exclusionary rule can apply even if the remedial measure was not taken after the accident at issue.[254] Others, perhaps a majority, have held that for the exclusionary rule to apply, the remedial conduct must have been undertaken after the accident that give rise to the action.[255]

If the primary purpose of the rule is to encourage remedial measures, thus reducing accidents, it is difficult to discern why it should matter whether or not the accident in question has occurred. Especially if *some* accident has already occurred, or where the occurrence of accidents is a reasonably foreseeable event, application of the rule would encourage parties to take remedial measures without concern that doing so will be used against them. It is true that applying the rule to cases such as this will result in a loss of relevant evidence in some cases, but if the policy behind the rule is to prevail, it is difficult to identify a meaningful distinction between post-accident measures and pre-accident measures. On the other hand, there is little evidence that the exclusionary rule is needed in defective product cases, as a means of encouraging the taking of remedial measures. It does not seem very likely that a product manufacturer would forego the remedial measure solely to avoid

254. *See, e.g.,* Mills v. Beech Aircraft Corp., 886 F.2d 758, 763 (5th Cir.1989) (rejecting claim that rule only applies to measures taken in response to accident at issue); Petree v. Victor Fluid Power, Inc., 831 F.2d 1191, 1197–98 (3d Cir.1987) (in product liability action, trial court properly excluded evidence that after defendant sold machine at issue, but before plaintiff suffered injury, defendant added warning decal to machine; court rested decision on policy purpose of the rule, holding that the policy is "equally as supportive of exclusion of safety measures taken before someone is injured by a newly manufactured product. . . . ").

255. *See, e.g.,* Roberts v. Harnischfeger Corp., 901 F.2d 42, 44 n. 1 (5th Cir.1989) (Federal Rule 407 inapplicable where change in policy concerning equipment sold along with a crane occurred one month before accident); Chase v. General Motors

Corp., 856 F.2d 17, 21–22 (4th Cir.1988) (rule inapplicable where automobile manufacturer changed brake design occurred after sale of car at issue but before accident occurred); Arceneaux v. Texaco, Inc., 623 F.2d 924, 928 (5th Cir.), *cert. denied,* 450 U.S. 928 (1981) (Federal Rule 407 inapplicable where accident occurred after design change; but trial court did not err in excluding evidence because it was irrelevant under circumstances of case). *Cf.* Foster v. Ford Motor Co., 621 F.2d 715, 720–21 (5th Cir.1980) (in wrongful death action against truck manufacturer, trial court excluded evidence of redesign of trucks manufactured after truck in question but before accident; court was uncertain whether general exclusionary rule applies in products liability cases and whether "after the event" language in Federal Rule 407 applies to manufacture of product or accident involving it).

liability in the instant case. Rather, it seems more likely that the manufacturer would take the measure in order to avoid future mishaps. [256]

A 1997 amendment to Federal Rule 407 makes clear that the rule only applies to post-accident remedial measures.[257] The evidence could still be excluded under Rule 403, however.[258]

§ 5.37   Remedial Measures Evidence That Falls Outside the Rule—Evidence Offered to Show Ownership or Control

Evidence of subsequent remedial measures is admissible when it is offered, not to show negligence, but to show that the defendant owned or controlled the instrumentality of injury.

Example

Plaintiff is injured by a truck driven by a construction worker. A dispute arises about whether the truck was owned by the worker who was driving it or by the construction company that employed the worker. Evidence that the company subsequently had the truck repaired would be admissible to show the company's ownership and control of the truck.

A typical case of the use of remedial measures to show control is *Huxol v. Nickell.*[259] The plaintiff in *Huxol* sought to recover for injuries sustained when he fell into a hole at a construction site. The general contractor and the subcontractor each took the position that the other was responsible for safety measures at the site. This opened the door to the admission of evidence that, after the accident, the general contractor erected a barrier around the hole.[260]

---

256. For discussion of the lack of empirical support for the incentive effects of the exclusionary rule, see Leonard, *supra* note 252 § 2.4.1.

257. As amended, Rule 407 provides for exclusion only if the remedial measures were taken "after an injury or harm allegedly caused by an event." For detailed discussion of the "after an event" problem, see *id.* § 5.6.4.

258. *See* Bogosian v. Mercedes–Benz of North America, Inc., 104 F.3d 472, 480–81 (1st Cir.1997) (though Rule 407 does not apply to post-manufacture, pre-accident design modifications, such evidence may still be excluded under Rule 403.

259. 473 P.2d 90 (Kan.1970). *See also* Clausen v. Sea–3, Inc., 21 F.3d 1181, 1191 (1st Cir.1994) (held, in personal injury suit, admission of evidence of subsequent remedial measures undertaken on ramp where plaintiff slipped and fell was not plain error; control over the ramp was an unre-

solved issue in the case, evidence was admissible for limited purpose of showing that defendant controlled ramp area at time of accident); Eoff v. Hal & Charlie Peterson Found., 811 S.W.2d 187, 197 (Tex.App. 1991) (excluding evidence of sign subsequently placed in hospital emergency room notifying patients that physicians were not employees of hospital, where ownership of emergency room was uncontroverted, and where agency and control were issues in establishing liability).

260. *See also* Wallner v. Kitchens of Sara Lee, Inc., 419 F.2d 1028 (7th Cir.1969) (employee of company that installed conveyor unit at defendant's plant fell on slippery floor near conveyor and suffered injury when caught hand in machine as he tried to break his fall; held, evidence that after accident, defendant installed metal guard on conveyor, added drain lines, and took other steps that would have prevented injuries admissible to prove defendant was responsible for repair and daily maintenance of con-

Note that when subsequent remedial measures evidence is used to prove ownership or control, the reasoning by which the evidence is relevant to that issue still depends on acceptance of the proposition that the repair conduct evidences the party's belief that the condition at the time of the accident was unsafe. However, because the actor's belief is not offered to prove that the condition was unsafe but only to prove that the condition was under the actor's control, the evidence is not excluded by the rule. In a case such as *Huxol*, the evidence is offered to prove the existence of a *duty*, not whether that duty was *breached*. Nevertheless, the permissible reasoning is only subtly different from the forbidden "negligence or culpable conduct" reasoning. For that reason, counsel should be prepared to request a limiting instruction, or, in cases raising serious questions of unfair prejudice from improper use of the evidence by the jury, to ask that the evidence be excluded under the probative value/unfair prejudice rule.

§ 5.38 Remedial Measures Evidence That Falls Outside the Rule—Evidence Offered to Impeach a Witness

Evidence of remedial measures is sometimes admitted on the theory that it is being received not to show negligence, but to impeach a witness.[261]

Example

After falling down a flight of stairs, plaintiff sues the owner of the stairs, claiming that the stairs were negligently maintained in a slick and worn condition. At trial, defendant testifies that the stairs had an "excellent" surface at the time of plaintiff's fall and that the surface would "never need to be replaced." This testimony opens the door to evidence that, shortly after the accident, defendant covered the stairs with a more abrasive surface.[262] In theory, the testimony is not offered to show defendant's negligence at the time of the injury, but to impeach defendant's credibility as a witness by showing that defendant engaged in conduct that is inconsistent with his or her testimony or that defendant attempted to mislead the jury with the testimony. Thus, the evidence impeaches the witness by a type of impeachment by contradiction; the witness's own prior

veyor, where there was dispute concerning who was responsible for maintenance).

261. See, e.g., Dollar v. Long Mfg., N.C., Inc., 561 F.2d 613, 618 (5th Cir.1977) (although letter warning of dangers of product was subsequent remedial measure, it should have been received to impeach the trial testimony of the expert who wrote it); Rimkus v. Northwest Colo. Ski Corp., 706 F.2d 1060, 1065 (10th Cir.1983) (alternative holding) (evidence that rocks on which plaintiff was injured while skiing were subsequently marked with bamboo poles ad-

missible to impeach defense witness who testified that rocks were visible for 200 feet).

262. See Pierce v. J.C. Penney Co., 334 P.2d 117 (Cal.App.1959) (plaintiff alleged that fall on steps in defendant's store occurred because abrasive strip on step was worn, making step too slippery; evidence that after the accident, manager authorized installation of new abrasive slips on stairs admissible to impeach manager's testimony that steps were neither worn nor slippery).

behavior evidences facts different from those to which the witness has testified, casting doubt on the credibility of the witness's testimony.

The rule that evidence of subsequent remedial measures can be used for impeachment purposes opens large potential gaps in the exclusionary rule. For one thing, if interpreted too broadly, this route to admissibility of subsequent remedial measures evidence threatens to destroy the exclusionary principle. To be sure, the evidence should be admissible when defendant has taken unfair advantage by presenting testimony that creates a misleading impression. That is true when defendant testifies as in the example above, or has stated that she never made any changes to the instrumentality of the accident after its occurrence. In such instances, plaintiff should be permitted to offer evidence to neutralize defendant's unfair advantage. But suppose defendant merely testifies that the instrumentality was safe or in "normal condition" at the time of the accident.[263] Does this open the door to evidence of the subsequent remedial measure? If it does, the exclusionary effect of the rule is narrow indeed, for one should expect just this kind of testimony from a party accused of negligence. Forcing the defendant to deny danger (and thus invite evidence of the subsequent remedial measure) or forgo evidence to support that defense (and risk an inference that her lack of denial constitutes an admission of danger), places defendant in an untenable position.[264] In the end, the admissibility of the evidence under this kind of impeachment theory must be decided in the context of each case.

Another risk created by allowing "impeachment" use of subsequent remedial measures evidence is one of abuse by the plaintiff rather than the defendant. In some cases, plaintiff's counsel might be able to maneuver the defendant's witnesses into saying something that could be "impeached" by evidence of subsequent measures when the main goal is not truly to impeach, but to place the subsequent measures before the jury as evidence of negligence. For example, in *Daggett v. Atchison, Topeka, & Santa Fe Ry. Co.,*[265] a case arising from a train-auto collision,

263. *See* Wilkinson v. Carnival Cruise Lines, Inc., 920 F.2d 1560, 1568–69 (11th Cir.1991) (reversible error to admit for impeachment purposes evidence that cruise ship line kept sliding glass door locked in open position after accident; ship's officer testified that the door appeared to be in normal condition on the day of the accident and appeared to have been properly maintained but did not testify that the line had exercised "all reasonable care" in maintaining the door, or that the door was the "safest" or in the "best" condition).

264. *See* Kelly v. Crown Equipment Co., 970 F.2d 1273 (3d Cir.1992). Defendant's expert testified that design of forklift involved in accident was excellent and proper. The court held that this testimony was not contradicted by the design alteration

made after the accident because "alteration did not compel the conclusion that the first design was defective." *Id.* at 1278. *See also* Flaminio v. Honda Motor Co., Ltd., 733 F.2d 463, 468 (7th Cir.1984) (making similar point).

265. 313 P.2d 557 (Cal.1957). *See* Blythe v. Sears, Roebuck & Co., 586 So.2d 861, 864–65 (Ala.1991) (evidence of subsequent remedial measures may be introduced to impeach testimony when witness testifies in superlative that the condition was "the safest" or "the best"; but evidence is admissible to impeach only if testimony sought to be impeached is initiated by defendant, the witness authorized or directed the remedial measures, the evidence is offered for a material purpose, evidence is relevant to issue at hand, and the prejudithe plaintiffs succeeded in introducing evidence that the railroad had installed new signals after the accident and that the railroad had changed the speed limit for trains going through the intersection. The evidence of the new speed limit was introduced after the engineer who was operating the train at the time of the accident testified, during adverse examination by the plaintiff, that the speed limit "is 90" in the area. Over objection by the defense, the plaintiff was permitted to ask "Well, Mr. Benton, the restriction now is 50 miles an hour, isn't it?" The California Supreme Court sustained this line of questioning on grounds that it impeached the credibility of the engineer. The court also sustained the reception of the evidence about the new signals on impeachment grounds. The evidence impeached the testimony of a defense expert that the signal in use at the time of the accident was the "safest type of signal."

Whenever subsequent remedial measures evidence is offered to impeach, the court should weigh the impeachment value of the evidence against its possible prejudicial effect (i.e., the possibility that the jury will use the testimony as evidence of negligence). In some situations, the evidence should be excluded.

Example

In a wrongful death action based upon a fall down a stairway, the defendant-landowner is questioned during a deposition about the condition of the stairway. In response to a question by plaintiff's attorney, the owner answers that the stairway is now in the same condition that it was at the time of the accident. In fact, a handrail had been added after the plaintiff's fall. Subsequently, defendant notifies plaintiff that this answer was incorrect, claiming that the witness had misunderstood the question. In view of the negligible impeachment value of the witness' inaccurate deposition answer, the trial judge would have discretion to exclude evidence about the witness' inaccurate answer to the deposition question. The impeachment value of the evidence is substantially outweighed by the prejudice that would result from revealing the remedial measure.[266]

cial effect does not substantially outweigh the probative value). For a narrow interpretation of the impeachment exception to Rule 407, see Harrison v. Sears, Roebuck & Co., 981 F.2d 25 (1st Cir.1992). Harrison claimed to have been injured by a joint-planer manufactured by the defendants. An in-house expert testified for a defendant that there was no hazardous area on the joint-planer where the plaintiff's hand could unintentionally make contact with the cutter head. The trial judge refused to allow the plaintiff to impeach the witness with evidence that the witness had later made a design change that closed up the aperture through which the plaintiff's finger allegedly came into contact with the blade. The First Circuit upheld the decision on appeal, indicating that the impeachment use had to be strictly limited because of Rule 407.

266. *See* Hanson v. Roe, 373 N.W.2d 366 (Minn.App.1985). *See also* Agostinho v. Fairbanks Clinic Partnership, 821 P.2d 714, 716–17 (Alaska 1991) (trial court committed reversible error by failing to balance probative value against potential prejudice before determining whether to admit evidence of subsequent sanding and salting to impeach defense witness's testimony that walks did not appear to be icy when plaintiff fell).

§ 5.39 Remedial Measures Evidence That Falls Outside the Rule—Evidence Offered to Explain Exhibit Illustrating Scene of Accident

In appropriate situations, evidence revealing that safety measures were taken after an accident will be admissible because it is offered, not to show negligence, but to prevent the jury from being confused by an exhibit that depicts the scene of the accident after the measures were put into place.

Example

In an action to recover for injuries caused by falling down stairs, plaintiff claims that the defendant was negligent in maintaining stairs that were slick and worn, and that had no handrail. At trial, defendant introduces a photograph of the stairs to show that the stairs were not slick and worn. The photograph shows a handrail that was installed after the accident. The plaintiff is entitled to point out that the handrail was installed after the accident, in order to give the jury an accurate picture of the condition of the stairs at the time of the accident. (The same principle would apply if the jury had taken a view of the scene of the accident.)

In such a case, the evidence that the handrail was installed after the accident is admissible on the theory that it is not being used to prove "negligence or culpable conduct," but merely to prevent the jury from being confused about the condition of the stairs at the time of the accident. The defendant is entitled to a limiting instruction telling the jury not to use the testimony as evidence of negligence.

Can the plaintiff open this avenue of admissibility by offering a photograph that shows subsequent repairs and then offering evidence that the repairs were made after the accident? Clearly this should not be permitted in cases in which the plaintiff's photograph does not serve to give the jury a clearer understanding of the physical facts at the time of the accident than could otherwise be obtained.[267] However, the issue should be resolved, not by an absolute rule excluding photographs showing repairs when they are offered by plaintiffs, but by a flexible rule that weighs whether the evidence is needed for some purpose other than showing negligence. If, for example, a photograph of the scene taken after the repairs were made is the only means available to help the jury visualize how the accident occurred, then the photograph should be admitted, with a limiting instruction, even if it unavoidably shows the existence of repairs.[268] If, however, the condition of the scene at the time of the accident can be satisfactorily illustrated in some other fashion, then the photograph should be excluded. For example, if plaintiff has

267. See Gignoux v. St. Louis Public Serv. Co., 180 S.W.2d 784, 785–87 (Mo.App. 1944), and cases cited therein.

268. See, e.g., Lebrecht v. Bethlehem Steel Corp., 402 F.2d 585, 592 (2d Cir.1968) (plaintiff entitled to put in photo of site of accident, even though it showed planking added as safety improvement; photo illustrated conditions at time of accident and jury was instructed to ignore the added planking).

access to photographs or other evidence that adequately illustrate the scene without revealing that safety measures have been taken after the accident, then a photograph showing the safety measures should be excluded. Similarly, if the photograph could, without distorting the condition of the scene at the time of the accident, be cropped so that it does not show the subsequent repairs, then the photo should be cropped to avoid prejudice.

§ 5.40 Remedial Measures Evidence That Falls Outside the Rule—Evidence offered to Show Feasibility of Precautionary Measures

Although evidence of subsequent remedial measures is not admissible to show negligence or culpable conduct, it is admissible to show that the remedial measures were feasible, if feasibility is controverted.

Example

Plaintiff was injured while operating a drill press in defendant's plant. Plaintiff claims that the drill press should have been protected by a finger guard. Defendant asserts that installing a finger guard was not feasible; the workers would not have been able to operate the drill press properly because a finger guard would have interfered with their access to it. Evidence that the defendant subsequently installed a finger guard would be admissible to show feasibility.

Most claims that remedial measures were not feasible do not involve claims that it would have been physically impossible to take the proposed safety measure. Rather, the defendant will concede that safety measures were physically possible, but claim that they would be so costly or burdensome that they were not required by ordinary prudence. In such circumstances, evidence of remedial measures is admissible on the issue of feasibility. For example, in *Whitehead v. St. Joe Lead Co.*,[269] the court stated that evidence showing that after plaintiff's injury, defendant had affixed warning labels to its product should be received as evidence that warnings were not too costly, and hence that precautions were feasible under the circumstances.

Obviously, the question of feasibility overlaps with the question of "negligence or culpable conduct" to some extent. The evidence ultimately leads to the same conclusion on the same issue as it would if offered for the forbidden purpose. Obviously, there is a thin line between offering evidence of the subsequent remedial measure to prove that it was feasible to take those steps (and thus that defendant had a duty to take them), and offering the evidence to prove that defendant was aware of the danger (and thus had a duty to correct it sooner). Ultimately, the court must determine whether the evidence has much probative value on the issue of feasibility, and whether the jury is likely to understand and abide by a limiting instruction.

269. 729 F.2d 238, 247 n. 6 (3d Cir. 1984).

The federal rule makers included a provision that subsequent repairs evidence is inadmissible when the issue of feasibility is not "controverted." Suppose defendant claims that it was not negligent because the safety measures were so costly that the prudent person would not undertake them. In that instance, feasibility is controverted and the rule permits the admission of evidence to rebut the claim that the measures were impracticable because too costly. In other situations, however, it is possible to deny negligence without controverting feasibility. For example, when the defendant claims that the lack of safety devices was not the cause of the plaintiff's injury, or that the need for safety devices could not have been foreseen at the time of the accident, then it is possible to defend against a negligence claim without "controverting" the feasibility of safety devices. The defendant should also be able to avoid controverting the issue of feasibility by conceding that additional safety measures were economically feasible, while maintaining that its original measures were adequate and acceptable.[270]

The scope of the exclusionary rule will also be affected by the definition of "feasibility" applied by the courts. Although a number of cases have excluded evidence despite an argument that the evidence should be admitted to show feasibility, others have taken a very broad view of the admissibility of evidence on the issue of feasibility. For example, in *Anderson v. Malloy*,[271] the defendant did not contend that additional safety measures would have been too costly, but merely claimed that they would have been superfluous. The principal plaintiff had been raped by a stranger while alone in a room in a motel owned by the defendants. She had opened the door in response to a knock by the assailant, who spoke to her in a muffled voice that she thought was her husband's. She claimed that the motel should have installed peepholes and chain locks on the doors, and sought to introduce evidence that after the rape the defendants did install these devices. The trial judge exclud-

---

270. *See* Grenada Steel Indus. v. Alabama Oxygen Co., 695 F.2d 883, 888 (5th Cir.1983), which notes that while it is true that feasibility may "almost always" be in question in design defect cases, that is not always so; sometimes the manufacturer does not claim that another design was impracticable, but "only that it adopted an acceptable one."

271. 700 F.2d 1208, 1213 (8th Cir. 1983). For a case that takes a similarly broad view of feasibility, see Lewis v. Cotton Belt Route–Saint Louis Southwestern Ry., 576 N.E.2d 918, 929–30 (Ill.App.1991) (allowing evidence that injured lone worker was replaced by a worker plus a spotter, to impeach and controvert defense witness's testimony that using a spotter was not feasible, although witness apparently used the word "feasible" to mean "not necessary under the circumstances" rather than "impossible"). *See also* Wilkinson v. Hyatt Corp., 1993 WL 121287, at *2–3 (E.D.La.

1993) (plaintiff may introduce evidence of subsequent security changes when report by defendant's expert witness stated defendant should not be expected to do what society itself cannot do, to prevent all crime); Ross v. Black & Decker, Inc., 977 F.2d 1178, 1184 (7th Cir.1992), *cert. denied*, 507 U.S. 917 (1993) (defendant's "tactical error" in failing to stipulate feasibility of remedial measures makes post-manufacture remedial measures admissible). On feasibility in general, see Southland Enter., Inc. v. United States, 24 Cl. Ct. 596, 603 (1991) (allowing evidence that the Park Service redesigned road well after plaintiff completed construction, where parties contested feasibility); Phar–Mor, Inc. v. Goff, 594 So.2d 1213, 1218 (Ala.1992) (excluding photograph of baskets in store, stacked a different way after slip-and-fall accident, feasibility of stacking baskets differently not controverted).

ed the evidence, and on appeal, the Eighth Circuit reversed, holding that the evidence was admissible.

The Eighth Circuit alluded to certain testimony by defendant Malloy, one of the owners of the motel. Malloy had been called as an adverse witness by the plaintiffs. He testified that he had talked to the village police chief about security measures for the hotel. According to his testimony, the officer had told him that because the motel had six-foot picture windows right next to the doors (through which the guests could look to see who was knocking) peepholes were unnecessary. Also, chains would be "false security." In the view of the Eighth Circuit, this testimony raised an issue of the "feasibility" of peepholes and chains. The court held that "feasible" means not only "possible," but also meant "capable of being utilized ... or dealt with successfully." For the defense witness to say that peepholes and chains would only provide a false sense of security was to say that they could not be "utilized successfully," and hence to challenge the feasibility of the security measure.

The dissenting opinion by Judge Gibson questioned the majority's definition of feasibility. To him, a claim that a safety measure was not feasible had to be a claim that adopting the safety measure would be impossible or overly costly. Here, the defendants did not claim that the safety measures would not be feasible, only that they would not be desirable.

The *Anderson* majority takes a very broad view of the concept of feasibility, making it more difficult for a defendant to claim that its failure to use certain safety measures was not negligent without at the same time opening the door to an assertion that the defendant has challenged the feasibility of the safety measures, and hence that evidence of subsequent use of the measures is admissible. If the defendant claims that the reasonable person would not have used the safety measures because they were impracticable or too costly, then defendant has challenged feasibility under the *Whitehead* line of cases previously discussed. If the defendant claims that a reasonable person would not have used the safety measures because they were not necessary, then defendant has challenged feasibility under the *Anderson* case.

Other courts have taken a much narrower view than that taken in the *Anderson* case, and have held that a defendant can maintain that safety measures were not necessary without putting feasibility into issue. For example, in *Gauthier v. AMF, Inc.,*[272] the defendant conceded that the safety devices in question were technologically and economically feasible, but argued it had been justified in deciding that the questionable benefit of the device did not outweigh such factors as the consumer

---

272. 788 F.2d 634, 637–38 (9th Cir. 1986), *amended on denial of reh'g*, 805 F.2d 337 (9th Cir. 1986). *See also* Flaminio v. Honda Motor Co., 733 F.2d 463, 468 (7th Cir.1984); *In re* Joint E. Dist. and S. Dist. Asbestos Litigation, 995 F.2d 343, 345 (2d Cir.1993) ("'feasibility' is not an open sesame whose mere invocation parts Rule 407 and ushers in evidence of subsequent repairs and remedies ... to read it that casually will cause the exception to engulf the rule....").

frustration that would arise from the inconvenience caused by it. The court held that this position did not constitute a challenge to the feasibility of the safety devices, and hence did not open the door to evidence that they had later been installed.

§ 5.41   Remedial Measures Evidence That Falls Outside the Rule—Evidence Offered to Show Causation of Accident

Some courts have allowed plaintiff to offer evidence of subsequent remedial measures to prove that defendant's negligence was a cause of the injury or harm. In *Kuhn v. Illinois C. R.R.*,[273] for example, plaintiff alleged that his property was damaged by emissions from smokestacks on defendant's roundhouse. To prove causation, plaintiff was allowed to offer evidence that after the smokestacks were heightened, the damages ceased. Even though admission risked unfair prejudice to defendant, the evidence in *Kuhn* appears to have been highly probative of causation.[274]

§ 5.42   Remedial Measures Evidence That Falls Outside the Rule—Evidence Offered in Strict Liability Cases

Before the 1997 amendments, the applicability of Federal Rule of Evidence 407 in strict liability cases was a matter of dispute. By its terms, Rule 407 only prohibited the use of remedial measures to show "negligence or culpable conduct." A minority of the courts that interpreted the Rule took the position that because "negligence or culpable conduct" is not an issue in a strict liability action, the Rule did not apply.[275] They reasoned that the policy of Rule 407 did not require that it be extended to strict liability cases, since the typical defendant in a strict

---

273. 111 Ill.App. 323 (1903).

274. *See also* George v. Morgan Construction Co., 389 F.Supp. 253, 264 (D.Pa. 1975) (evidence of post accident change in mill design admissible to prove, *inter alia*, that condition at time of accident was a proximate cause of accident).

275. *See* Herndon v. Seven Bar Flying Serv., 716 F.2d 1322, 1331 (10th Cir.1983), *cert. denied*, 466 U.S. 958 (1984); Robbins v. Farmers Union Grain Terminal Assn., 552 F.2d 788, 792–93 (8th Cir.1977). *Accord* Unterburger v. Snow Co., 630 F.2d 599, 603 (8th Cir.1980). The Eighth Circuit modified its position in the subsequent case of DeLuryea v. Winthrop Labs., 697 F.2d 222 (8th Cir.1983). In *DeLuryea,* the plaintiff sued for damages allegedly suffered as a result of tissue damage and drug dependence caused by the drug Talwin. The trial judge admitted evidence of a change in warnings concerning Talwin's side effects that defendants had issued after plaintiff stopped taking Talwin. The court noted that cases admitting remedial measures evidence in strict liability actions had been

based on the theory that proof of negligence or culpable conduct is not required in a strict liability action because the issue is the product's defect rather than the manufacturer's conduct. Here, however, where the product was unavoidably unsafe (all prescription drugs are capable of doing harm if misused), the issue turned upon whether the manufacturer had failed to give "reasonable and adequate warnings" of dangers that were "reasonably foreseeable." This standard was similar to a negligence standard. *Id.* at 227–28. Therefore, the evidence of subsequent alterations in the warnings was offered for purposes of showing "negligence or culpable conduct" within the meaning of Rule 407, and should have been excluded. *Accord* Werner v. Upjohn Co., 628 F.2d 848, 858 (4th Cir.1980), *cert. denied*, 449 U.S. 1080 (1981). Recently, the Eighth Circuit further modified its position in Burke v. Deere & Co., 6 F.3d 497, 506–07 (8th Cir.1993), *cert. denied*, 510 U.S. 1115 (1994). In *Burke*, a strict liability case, the court held that the district court abused its discretion by admit-liability case is a mass producer of goods that will not forgo making improvements, and thereby risk innumerable lawsuits, merely to prevent evidence from being introduced in a lawsuit commenced prior to the improvement.[276]

Other courts disagreed, holding that Rule 407 did apply to strict liability actions.[277] For example, in *Gauthier v. AMF, Inc.*,[278] the court took issue with the public policy basis for decisions holding that Rule 407 did not apply, saying that "it is precisely the large manufacturers who are defendants in many product liability suits who are most likely to know about Rule 407 and be affected by the decision whether to apply it.[279] The court also apparently considered a strict liability claim that the defendant had marketed a defective product to be a claim of "culpable conduct" that fell within the language of original Rule 407.[280] The court noted that nearly all the circuits that had reached the issue had decided that Rule 407 applies to strict liability cases.[281]

In 1997, Rule 407 was amended, making clear that the exclusionary provision does in fact apply in all three main kinds of product liability cases (manufacturing defect, design defect, and failure to warn cases).[282]

§ 5.43 Practice Considerations

The remedial measures rule has sometimes been characterized as ineffective because evidence of repairs is so commonly admissible to for

ting evidence of subsequent remedial measures on the issue of punitive damages. The court reasoned that the evidence was admitted as ostensibly relevant to the defendant's state of mind relating to the imposition of a punitive award; the evidence of subsequent remedial measures was used, therefore, to show the defendant's "culpable conduct in connection with the event" and, hence, fell within the prohibitions of Rule 407.

276. *See* Robbins v. Farmers Union Grain Terminal Assn., 552 F.2d 788, 792–93 (8th Cir.1977). The California Supreme Court reached the same conclusion in applying California's subsequent remedial measures rule. Ault v. International Harvester, 528 P.2d 1148 (Cal.1974).

277. *See* Raymond v. Raymond Corp., 938 F.2d 1518, 1522 (1st Cir.1991) (explicitly holding for the first time that Rule 407 applies to strict liability cases; noting that the majority of sister circuits apply the rule to strict liability cases); *see also* Wood v. Morbark Indus., Inc., 70 F.3d 1201, 1206–07 (11th Cir.1995) (Rule 407 applies in strict products liability cases when plaintiff alleges that a product is defective because the design is unreasonably dangerous); Gauthier v. AMF, Inc., 788 F.2d 634 (9th Cir.1986), *amended on denial of reh'g*, 805 F.2d 337 (9th Cir.1986); Flaminio v. Honda

Motor Co., 733 F.2d 463 (7th Cir.1984); Grenada Steel Indus. v. Alabama Oxygen Co., 695 F.2d 883 (5th Cir.1983); Josephs v. Harris Corp., 677 F.2d 985, 990 (3d Cir. 1982); Cann v. Ford Motor Co., 658 F.2d 54 (2d Cir.1981), *cert. denied,* 456 U.S. 960 (1982); Werner v. Upjohn Co., 628 F.2d 848 (4th Cir.1980), *cert. denied,* 449 U.S. 1080 (1981); Bauman v. Volkswagenwerk Aktiengesellschaft, 621 F.2d 230 (6th Cir. 1980). For a discussion of the arguments that admitting subsequent remedial measures evidence in strict liability cases chills product improvement, see 2 Richard A. Givens, Manual of Federal Practice § 7.11, at 271–73 (Shepard's/McGraw–Hill 4th ed. 1991).

278. 788 F.2d 634 (9th Cir.1986), *amended on denial of reh'g,* 805 F.2d 337 (9th Cir.1986).

279. *Id.* at 637.

280. *Id.* at 636–37.

281. *Id.* at 636, and authorities cited therein.

282. As amended, Federal Rule 407 provides for exclusion of evidence of subsequent remedial measures to prove "negligence, culpable conduct, a defect in a product, a defect in a product's design, or a need for a warning or instruction."

other purposes of showing ownership, control, or feasibility, or for impeachment. Nevertheless, precautions can be taken to preserve the objection or to mitigate the effect of admission of the evidence.

Defense counsel should consider giving specific pretrial notice to plaintiff that the feasibility of remedial measures is not controverted. Removing feasibility from contention eliminates one common way of placing into evidence the fact that defendant took remedial measures after an accident.

In preparing defense witnesses, counsel who wish to preserve the objection should bear in mind that testimony of defense witnesses may open the door to evidence of remedial measures. This can occur if the witness testifies that a given way of preventing an accident is not practical (even though the measure was later taken), if the witness states that the safety measures in effect at the time of the accident were the best available, or if the witness states or implies that conditions have not changed since the accident. Testimony of this nature opens the door to use of remedial measures evidence to show feasibility or to impeach the witness. Defense counsel should object to exhibits, such as photographs, that show the existence of remedial measures. The court should be asked to crop photographs so that repairs or safety measures are not shown. When this is not practical, counsel should point out that evidence about the condition of the premises could be presented in another fashion—for example, by use of drawings or diagrams or by oral testimony. If other evidence of the condition of the premises has already been introduced by plaintiff, defense counsel should argue that reception of the photograph showing the safety measure is redundant and prejudicial.

Counsel should be prepared to argue that even if evidence of remedial measures fits one of the categories for which it is admissible, such as impeachment or showing feasibility, its value for this purpose is substantially outweighed by Federal Rule of Evidence 403 considerations—prejudice, confusion, and waste of time. In making this argument, it is helpful to point out that the fact the evidence is ostensibly offered to prove could be proven in some other fashion, or that other evidence on the point has been introduced and evidence showing safety measures is merely cumulative. When evidence is offered on a feasibility theory, counsel can point out that defendant does not dispute the practicality of the safety measure, but only claims that the measures in effect at the time of the accident were adequate.

If the court overrules an objection to evidence of safety measures, defense counsel should request a limiting instruction. The instruction will be most effective if it explains the policy of the rule to the jury. For example, if repairs appear on a photograph offered to show the condition of the premises, the court could be requested to give the following instruction:

> Members of the jury, you should disregard the fact that safety measures were taken after the accident. The law provides that repairs cannot be used as evidence against the defendant, because

the making of repairs and improvements is something to be encouraged and supported.

If evidence of subsequent repairs has been offered and received, the defendant may wish to deal with the evidence in final argument. Defense counsel can point out that the law does not require perfection. The defendant's concern for safety caused it to make improvements after the accident, but the fact that improvements were made does not mean that the defendant was careless before.

§ 5.44   Form of Objection

At trial, when opposing counsel asks a question or offers an exhibit that would reveal the existence of safety measures taken after an accident, the objection may be made as follows:

> Objection! Plaintiff is offering evidence of remedial measures taken after the accident.

If the objection is overruled, counsel should request a limiting instruction:

> Your Honor, I request a limiting instruction telling the jury that evidence that [name of defendant] took additional precautions after the accident may not be used as evidence of negligence at the time of the accident.

Whatever the practical value of the limiting instruction in convincing the jury, it should be requested to preserve the issue for appeal. Counsel should also request that the judge, in the final instructions, explain the reason for the remedial measures rule. Compare the instruction described in § 5.51.

Even if objection is made and sustained at trial, the jury may infer the existence of remedial measures from the nature of the questions asked by plaintiff's counsel prior to the objection. When remedial measure evidence is important, defense counsel should consider making a pretrial motion asking the court's assistance in preventing the jury from learning, directly or indirectly, of the remedial measures.

Example (Motion in Limine)

The defendant respectfully moves the Court to instruct the plaintiffs' counsel to refrain from offering any evidence that, subsequent to the accident that is the subject of this suit, the defendant modified the design of any of its snowblower models or other products to incorporate control devices that would stop the engine from running when the user left the operator's position.

The defendant also moves that the Court instruct plaintiffs' counsel to refrain from asking any question, making any statement, offering any exhibit, or otherwise indicating to the jury, directly or by innuendo, that these design changes in the defendant's product were planned, discussed, or made after the accident in which plaintiff was injured. Defendant further moves that plaintiffs' counsel be instructed to caution every witness called by them to refrain from any direct or indirect reference to design changes in defendant's product after the accident.

This motion is made on grounds that evidence of the design change would be evidence of a remedial measure offered in violation of Rule 407. The defendant concedes and will stipulate that the design change adding the above described control devices was feasible. Because feasibility is not controverted, there is no legitimate basis for offering evidence of the design change. If the design change becomes known to the jury, the defendant will be prejudiced even if the court were to sustain an objection and instruct the jury not to consider the evidence.

If the trial judge denies the motion in limine, on grounds that events at trial may open the door to remedial measures evidence, defense counsel may request that the court admonish the plaintiff not to introduce evidence of remedial measures without first clearing such evidence with the court in a conference held out of the hearing of the jury.[283]

THE OFFERS IN COMPROMISE RULE (SETTLEMENT NEGOTIATIONS AND AGREEMENTS) [FRE 408]

§ 5.45   Exclusion of Evidence of Settlement Agreements and Settlement Offers

A settlement offer or settlement agreement is generally inadmissible to prove the validity or invalidity of a claim or its value. This exclusionary rule applies not only to settlements or settlement efforts between the parties to the litigation in which the evidence is offered, but also to settlements between a party and a nonparty.

Examples

Offer of settlement to opposing party. Plaintiff, a condominium homeowners' association, sued defendant, a general contractor, claiming damages for allegedly defective work on the condominium's heating system. Defendant offered a substantial settlement. Plaintiff declined the offer. At trial, plaintiff seeks to introduce testimony about defendant's offer, arguing that the size of defendant's offer is evidence that defendant was conscious that the work was in fact defective. The evidence is inadmissible.

Completed settlement with a nonparty. Plaintiff, a motorcyclist, sues defendant, a motorcycle manufacturer, after being injured in a motorcycle accident in which plaintiff's motorcycle collided with a car. In a previous settlement, plaintiff had received a payment from the driver of the car and released the driver from liability. At trial, defendant offers plaintiff's settlement agreement with the third

---

283. This was the procedure employed by the trial court, and noted with approval by the appellate court, in Rimkus v. North- west Colo. Ski Corp., 706 F.2d 1060, 1065 (10th Cir.1983).

party into evidence, on the theory that the agreement is evidence that plaintiff believed that the accident was caused by the car driver, not by any defect in the motorcycle. The agreement is inadmissible if offered solely to show the plaintiff's belief that the claim against the motorcycle manufacturer is invalid,[284] though it may be admissible if offered for another purpose. For example, if the driver testifies as a witness,[285] or remains as a party in the case under a Mary Carter agreement,[286] the prior settlement may be admissible to show the bias of a witness or to explain trial conduct.

Settlement offers and settlement agreements, when offered as evidence of liability or nonliability on the underlying claim, are inadmissible both at common law and under the Federal Rules.[287] Federal Rule of Evidence 408 states, in relevant part:

> Evidence of (1) furnishing or offering or promising to furnish, or (2) accepting or offering or promising to accept, a valuable consideration in compromising or attempting to compromise a claim which was disputed as to either validity or amount, is not admissible to prove liability for or invalidity of the claim or its amount.[288]

Rule 408 has proven very influential. Many states have adopted language substantively identical or nearly identical to the Federal Rule, and a number of others have followed most aspects of the rule. No states reject the basic premise that evidence of compromises or compromise offers should be excluded when offered to prove validity or invalidity of a claim or defense.[289]

Several theories have been advanced in support of the exclusionary rule. One theory is that the evidence is simply irrelevant; an offer of settlement is not probative of the validity of the underlying claim, because the offeror may only have been seeking peace, rather than admitting that his or her legal position was weak.[290] While this theory may be valid in some situations, it does not explain a blanket rule of exclusion; an offer of settlement for more than the cost of litigation has some probative value as an indication of the party's belief in the strength or weakness of its legal position. For example, an offer to settle for 90

---

284. *See* McInnis v. AMF, Inc., 765 F.2d 240 (1st Cir.1985). The court in *McInnis* noted that the jury's verdict could be reduced by the amount of the payment received in the settlement.

285. *See* § 5.49.

286. *See* General Motors Corp. v. Simmons, 558 S.W.2d 855, 857 (Tex.1977) (evidence of agreement admissible because it gave settling parties an interest in the outcome that might affect their testimony or conduct). There has been extensive case law concerning both the validity and the admissibility of Mary Carter and similar types of agreements. For review of the problems raised by these agreements, see David P. Leonard, The New Wigmore: A Treatise on

Evidence: Selected Rules of Limited Admissibility §§ 3.7.4–3.7.5 (1996).

287. For a full discussion of common law theories under which settlement evidence was excluded, see Esser v. Brophey, 3 N.W.2d 3 (Minn.1942). *See also* Leonard, *supra* note 286 § 3.3.

288. Fed. R. Evid. 408. The rule may not apply in criminal cases. *See* Manko v. United States, 87 F.3d 50, 54–55 (2d Cir. 1996) (in tax fraud prosecution, not error to admit evidence of defendant's prior settlement with IRS; Rule 408 not applicable in criminal cases).

289. For examination of state provisions, see Leonard, *supra* note 286 § 3.6.

290. *See id.* § 3.3.2.

per cent of the claim would certainly suggest that the offeror believed that he or she had a weak case. A sounder basis for a blanket rule of exclusion is public policy: evidence of settlement offers is excluded in order to encourage settlement, in the belief that settlement of disputes serves the useful function of relieving court congestion and bringing peace to litigants. Whether the rule serves this purpose, or whether offers would be made even in the absence of an exclusionary rule, remains unclear. Nevertheless, the policy rationale is the most commonly cited reason for the rule.[291] The rule also tends to discourage tricky pretrial tactics, such as inveigling the other party into making an offer solely for the purpose of acquiring evidence at trial.[292] Finally, the rule arises from considerations of fairness—from a desire not to punish a party that acts in a socially useful way by seeking to resolve disputes without the necessity of trial.[293]

§ 5.46 Exclusion of Statements Made During Settlement Negotiations: Common Law and Federal Rule Approaches

At common law, offers of settlement and settlement agreements were inadmissible, but statements made during settlement negotiations were admissible.[294] For example, if a party or party's representative made an admission of fault during negotiations, that admission could be received into evidence, although the offer of settlement itself was inadmissible.[295] This result was consistent with the view, advocated by Wigmore,[296] that the true reason for excluding settlement offers was that

291. For full discussion of the policy rationale, see *id.* §§ 3.3.3, 3.4.

292. *See* Fed. R. Evid. 408 advisory committee's note; George M. Bell, *Admissions Arising Out of Compromise—Are They Irrelevant?* 31 Tex. L. Rev. 239, 241–42 (1953). *See also* Pierce v. F.R. Tripler & Co., 955 F.2d 820 (2d Cir.1992) (plaintiff in age discrimination case entitled, under circumstances, to have fact that defendant offered him job during subsequent settlement negotiations excluded; court rejects argument that policy of Rule 408 does not support exclusion when offeror of settlement seeks to have evidence admitted, on grounds that free admission of such offers would result in rash of disqualification of counsel motions, because counsel would need to be witness in order to prove making of offer and settlement purpose of offer, and counsel who plans to be witness must often withdraw under rules of professional responsibility; language of Rule 408 itself does not support exception for evidence proffered by maker of settlement offer).

293. *See* Leonard, *supra* note 286 § 3.3.4.

294. For discussion of evolution in the treatment of statements of fact made in

connection with compromise discussions, see David P. Leonard, The New Wigmore: A Treatise on Evidence: Selected Rules of Limited Admissibility § 3.5.2 (1996). The earliest case admitting statements of fact in connection with compromise discussions appears to have been Waldridge v. Kennison, 1 Esp. 143, 170 Eng. Rep. 306 (1794), in which defendant's admission during settlement negotiation that certain document was in his handwriting admissible. The court stated that admission not connected with merits of case and that facts easily could be proved by other evidence). The rule represented by *Waldridge* was not followed by all earlier courts, however. *See* Leonard, *supra* this note § 3.3.4, at 3:47 & n.8.

295. *See* 2 McCormick on Evidence § 266, at 195–96 (4th ed. John W. Strong ed. 1992); Albert Hanson Lumber Co. v. United States, 261 U.S. 581, 588–89 (1923).

296. *See* 4 John H. Wigmore, Evidence in Trials at Common Law § 1061 (James H. Chadbourn rev. 1972).

212 RELEVANCY AND ITS LIMITS Ch. 5

they were not probative of the fault of the offeror, who might be making an offer solely for the purpose of buying peace. A statement admitting fault was clearly relevant and hence was not excluded. Because statements in conjunction with settlement offers were often admitted at common law, counsel often sought to protect clients by noting during settlement negotiations that all statements were made hypothetically, or "without prejudice," or for purposes of discussion only.[297]

Contemporary law has taken the opposite position, holding that statements of fact made in connection with compromise discussions are generally inadmissible. This position is most consistent with the policy rationale for the rule excluding offers of compromise. Achieving compromise requires candor; if parties were aware that their opponents would be permitted to offer into evidence portions of the compromise discussions, they would be less likely to begin compromise discussions, or, even if they did enter into such discussions, they might be less forthcoming. The fairness rationale for the compromise rule also demands exclusion of statements of fact made in the course of compromise discussions. It is unfair to punish a candid party genuinely seeking compromise by admitting such statements.

The Federal Rules of Evidence follow this rationale, excluding both compromise offers and statements made during negotiations. Rule 408[298] expressly states that "Evidence of conduct or statements made in compromise negotiations is ... not admissible." The drafters of the Rules reasoned that uninhibited freedom of expression was necessary to facilitate settlement. A good example of the operation of the Federal Rule may be found in *Ramada Development Co. v. Rauch*,[299] an action in which Ramada sued for the balance due under a construction contract with Rauch. Rauch claimed defects in Ramada's construction of the project. Ramada retained an architect to study the alleged defects, and to prepare a report to be used as a tool in attempting settlement. The report was submitted to Rauch during settlement negotiations, There was no pretrial agreement between the parties about whether the report would be admissible or not. At trial, Rauch offered the architect's report as evidence because it confirmed the existence of many of the alleged defects. The trial judge excluded it on grounds that it was inadmissible under Rule 408. The Third Circuit upheld the exclusion.

Not all documentary evidence exchanged during compromise negotiations will be protected even by the expansive approach of Rule 408. Rule 408 expressly provides that it "does not require the exclusion of any evidence otherwise discoverable merely because it is presented in the course of compromise negotiations." The purpose of this provision is to prevent parties from immunizing pre-existing documents by turning

---

297. By analogy to contract law, common law courts were willing to treat an unaccepted offer as having no effect, Evidential or otherwise, if it was made "without prejudice." *See id.* § 1061, at 35. The contract rationale for the exclusionary rule

never took hold in the United States. *See* Leonard, *supra* note 294 § 3.3.1.

298. For the full text of Rule 408, see **App. A.**

299. 644 F.2d 1097, 1106 (5th Cir. 1981).

them over to the opposing party during negotiations. For example, a party cannot turn over its business records during negotiations and later claim that the opposing party could not use them at trial because of Rule 408. The opposing party would be entitled to use the discovery rules to obtain the records and then would be entitled to introduce them at trial. The case of *Ramada Development Co. v. Rauch,* discussed in the previous paragraph, is distinguishable from the situation in which the party seeks to immunize pre-existing documents. The Rauch court held that Rule 408's exception for documents "otherwise discoverable" did not apply to cases in which the document would *not have existed but for the negotiations.* In such cases, negotiations are not being used to frustrate discovery by making existing documents unreachable.

§ 5.47 Settlement Evidence That Is Admissible Despite the Rule of Exclusion

Settlement evidence is sometimes admissible despite the rule of exclusion. First, the rule of exclusion applies only to offers of compromise and statements made in seeking compromise;[300] it does not apply when there is no dispute about the validity or amount of the claim (and hence no effort at real compromise), nor does it apply to business negotiations that are not directed at achieving settlement of a legal claim, or to other situations that do not constitute "compromise negotiations." The rule is sometimes deemed inapplicable, for example, because the statement was made in a sort of discussion of rights and liabilities that fell short of the court's conception of a "compromise negotiation."[301]

Some of the more difficult cases arise when one party claims certain communications are subject to the rule's exclusionary force and the other claims that the communications were "business negotiations" and not the kind of conduct that falls within the rule.[302] These cases cannot be resolved with a simple rule governing when parties have ceased operating in a business mode and begun the type of dispute covered by the rule, but several factors can affect the decision, the most important of which is the timing of the discussions at issue. Though it is clear that communications can be excluded pursuant to the rule even if no formal

---

300. Of course, the rule also applies to completed compromises, as the language of Rule 408 makes clear. *See also* David P. Leonard, The New Wigmore: A Treatise on Evidence: Selected Rules of Limited Admissibility § 3.7.1(a) (1996).

301. *See* S.A. Healy Co. v. Milwaukee Metro. Sewerage Dist., 50 F.3d 476, 480 (7th Cir.), *cert. denied,* 516 U.S. 1010 (1995) (Posner, J.) (plaintiff, who had made a request or "claim" to city for adjustment of payment as provided in its contract with city, sought to introduce evidence that city engineer had remarked that plaintiff's "claim" probably had merit; held, engineer's statement admissible over a Rule 408 objection because no dispute had arisen at

time of statement; a claim is not a dispute until it has been rejected); Sage Realty Corp. v. Insurance Co. of N. Am., 34 F.3d 124, 128 (2d Cir.1994) (letter presenting party's version of obligations under lease not a statement made in settlement negotiations and hence admissible); Davidson v. Prince, 813 P.2d 1225, 1232 (Utah App.), *cert. denied,* 826 P.2d 651 (Utah 1991) (plaintiff's letter to defendant's insurance company describing circumstances of injury and demanding compensation not an "offer in compromise"; narrow interpretation of rule).

302. For extended discussion of this issue, see Leonard, *supra* note 300 § 3.7.5.

claim has been made at the time they took place, if the discussions occurred before it was apparent to the parties that there was a genuine dispute, they are likely to be admissible despite the rule. Some courts have gone quite far, holding that discussions constitute business communications if they take place before litigation had been threatened,[303] though this is unlikely to become the majority position.[304]

Secondly, the rule of exclusion applies only when the evidence about settlement or negotiations is offered to show the validity or invalidity of the underlying claim; it does not apply when the evidence is offered for some other purpose. For example, evidence about a settlement agreement is admissible in a suit to enforce the terms of the settlement; the evidence is not offered to prove the validity of the underlying (settled) claim, but rather to enforce the settlement contract itself.

§ 5.48 Settlement Evidence That Is Admissible Despite the Rule of Exclusion—Settlement of an Undisputed Claim

The purpose of Federal Rule of Evidence 408, and of many of its common law cognates, is to promote compromise when claims are genuinely disputed. The rulemakers did not intend to protect defendants who do not genuinely contest claims but who merely seek an extension of time or a discount for the nuisance value of litigation. Rule 408 provides no protection to the debtor who tells his creditor, "You'll have to take 50 cents on the dollar on what I owe you—if you don't like it, sue me." Such statements are admissible because they do not reveal any dispute; the debtor's reference to "what I owe you" demonstrates that she is not seeking compromise, but merely avoidance of part of a proper obligation. Rule 408 specifically provides that the rule of exclusion only applies to claims that are "disputed as to either validity or amount." The rulemakers reasoned that the policy considerations that favor settlement negotiations are not applicable to a debtor who seeks to get a creditor to settle an admittedly due amount for lesser sum.

---

303. *See* Big O Tire Dealers, Inc. v. Goodyear Tire & Rubber Co., 561 F.2d 1365, 1368 (10th Cir.1977), *cert. denied,* 434 U.S. 1052 (1978) (because discussions took place before litigation had been threatened in trademark dispute, they were not subject to exclusion under Rule 408; decision might be justified on ground that there were indications defendant was using the negotiations to buy time and take advantage of trademark during pendency of the talks and possible litigation).

304. *See* Affiliated Mfrs., Inc. v. Aluminum Co. of America, 56 F.3d 521 (3d Cir. 1995), for example, Affiliated argued that for there to be a "dispute" within the meaning of Rule 408, there must have been at least "a threat or contemplation of litiga-tion, that goes beyond conduct or statements made to resolve differences of opinion as to the validity or amount of a claim." *Id.* at 526. Affiliated relied on several cases, including *Big O.* The court held that if *Big O* stands for the proposition that Rule 408 applies only if there has been a threat of litigation, the case is too restrictive. *Id.* at 527. Rule 408 is invoked, the court held, "where an actual dispute or a difference of opinion exists, rather than when discussions crystallize to the point of threatened litigation." *Id. See also* Alpex Computer Corp. v. Nintendo Co., 770 F.Supp. 161 (S.D.N.Y.1991) (also rejecting had rejected such a narrow reading of exclusionary scope of Rule 408).

Note that the rule *does* apply if the claim is disputed as to *either* validity or amount. In tort actions, and in contract actions not involving a debt for a sum certain, the amount of the claim will almost always be disputed even if its validity is not. Thus, if counsel for a personal injury defendant says "O.K., there's no doubt about liability, but your damages demand is too high. Let's try to arrive at a reasonable figure for damages," the statement is not admissible because, though liability is conceded, the plaintiff's damage claims are not.

The common law rule about settlement offers is consistent with this aspect of Rule 408. To be affected by the rule of exclusion, the offer had to be an offer of compromise, not a concession that the full amount was due. Thus, for example, when the sales representative of an herbicide manufacturer told a farmer whose crop had been damaged by the herbicide that the company would pay for the damage, the statement was held admissible on grounds that it was not an offer of compromise.[305] Of course, there is a gray area between offers of compromise and noncompromise offers, and an admission of liability accompanied by an offer to pay for damage can still be an offer of compromise if there is an express or implicit dispute about the amount of the damages.

§ 5.49 Settlement Evidence That Is Admissible Despite the Rule of Exclusion—Evidence Offered for a Purpose Other Than Showing the Validity or Invalidity of the Underlying Claim

Federal Rule of Evidence 408 prohibits use of statements made during compromise negotiations when the purpose is to show the validity or invalidity of the plaintiff's claim, but not when the evidence is offered for another purpose. When a settlement offer or completed settlement is offered to show the *bias of a witness,* it is not offered to show the validity or invalidity of the underlying claim, and hence is admissible. For example, if the plaintiff has settled with one of the codefendants, and that codefendant testifies in the case, the settlement may be introduced into evidence because the payment to the codefendant may have influenced the testimony.[306] Of course, the impeachment value of the evidence must be weighed against its prejudicial effect, and in cases where impeachment value is slight, counsel opposing the offer should argue that the evidence should be excluded on Rule 403 grounds. A fair settlement arguably has little impeachment value, since the recipient of

305. Perzinski v. Chevron Chem. Co., 503 F.2d 654, 658 (7th Cir.1974).

306. *Cf.* John McShain, Inc. v. Cessna Aircraft Co., 563 F.2d 632 (3d Cir.1977) (not error to receive evidence of plaintiff's pretrial settlement with third party, where expert associated with third party testified in favor of plaintiff). *See also* Johnson v. Hugo's Skateway, 949 F.2d 1338, 1345–46 (4th Cir.1991), *superceded on other grounds at* 974 F.2d 1408 (4th Cir.1992) (evidence of prior consent decree admissible; evidence was not offered to show validity of claim that resulted in consent decree, but to show later racial bias by showing that provisions of decree, such as posting sign on premises announcing policy of equal access to all races, were not followed; requirements, such as posting equal access sign, admissible in case alleging defendant caused racially biased arrest of plaintiff); Reichenbach v. Smith, 528 F.2d 1072, 1075 (5th Cir.1976).

the settlement is not getting paid anything more than he or she lost.[307] In any event, the party objecting to the testimony is entitled to a limiting instruction to the effect that the evidence may only be used for its bearing on the credibility of the witness, and not as evidence of liability.

Evidence of statements made during settlement negotiations is sometimes offered on the theory that the statements are being used for *impeachment of a witness with inconsistent statements,* and not to prove the validity or invalidity of the underlying claim. For example, if the plaintiff's accountant submits information about lost profits for a settlement conference, the defendant may later seek to use the document if the accountant testifies inconsistently at trial. The literal language of Rule 408 suggests that the evidence should be admitted because it is not offered directly on the issue of the claim's validity, but merely for the purpose of showing that a witness is not reliable. Yet use of evidence of statements made during settlement negotiations for impeachment purposes would impede the frank and free discussion that the rulemakers sought to promote. A difference of opinion has arisen about the admissibility of such statements.[308] Of course, counsel can always argue that the impeachment value of the evidence is outweighed, under Rule 403, by its prejudicial effect.[309]

Evidence of statements made during settlement negotiations may be introduced for a variety of other purposes that do not involve use of the evidence to prove or disprove the validity of the underlying claim. These include use of the evidence to negate a claim of unnecessary delay, to show that defendants engaged in dilatory negotiations that prevented

---

307. *Cf.* Paster v. Pennsylvania RR, 43 F.2d 908, 911 (2d Cir.1930) (Hand, J.).

308. *See* Stainton v. Tarantino, 637 F.Supp. 1051 (E.D.Pa.1986) (holding evidence admissible for impeachment); Wayne D. Brazil, *Protecting the Confidentiality of Settlement Negotiations,* 39 Hastings L.J. 955, 978 (1988) (arguing that because perfect consistency is almost impossible, allowing use of prior statements somewhat inconsistent with trial testimony would undercut exclusionary rule). *See also* Davidson v. Prince, 813 P.2d 1225, 1233 n. 9 (Utah App.1991) (even if statements are part of offer in compromise, they are admissible to impeach maker's inconsistent trial testimony) (alternative holding). In the authors' opinion, the holding in *Davidson* might undermine the goal of encouraging settlement. Of course, the cautious lawyer can avoid the danger by measures such as getting a stipulation before entering negotiations or stating that factual assertions are "hypothetical" or "without prejudice." Nonlawyers negotiating on their own behalf will probably be the people most hurt by decisions such as *Davidson.*

For a further analysis of inconsistent statements made during settlement negotiations for impeachment, see the discussion of Rule 408 in ABA Section on Litigation, Emerging Problems Under the Federal Rules of Evidence 61 (2d ed. 1991) (see Appendix II of West's Federal Rules of Evidence pamphlet); Michael H. Graham, Handbook of Federal Evidence § 408.1 (4th ed. 1996); 1 Stephen A. Saltzburg, Michael M. Martin & Daniel J. Capra, Federal Rules of Evidence Manual 512–13 (6th ed. 1994). As these sources indicate, courts and commentators are divided on the appropriateness of allowing this use of statements made during settlement negotiations.

309. For a more detailed examination of the strengths and weaknesses of the different impeachment theories under which compromise evidence might be offered, see David P. Leonard, The New Wigmore: Selected Rules of Limited Admissibility § 3.8.2 (1996). One other such theory is that the evidence is admissible to impeach *by contradiction. Id.*

plaintiffs from mitigating their damages,[310] or to show that a party engaged in an unfair labor practice during the settlement negotiations.[311]

§ 5.50   Practice Considerations

In the few jurisdictions that follow the common law rule, statements of fact made during settlement negotiations are admissible when offered by the opposing party, though settlement offers are not. Counsel who wish to discuss the facts of a case during negotiations should either make clear during settlement negotiations that any statements of fact are made without prejudice for the purpose of achieving settlement or obtain an agreement with opposing counsel that statements made during negotiations will not be offered in evidence. In the absence of an express agreement, factual statements should be made hypothetically, or counsel should note that statements are being made "without prejudice."

Because the Federal Rules of Evidence expressly provide protection for statements of fact as well as for offers, such precautions might not seem necessary in jurisdictions that follow the Federal Rules. However, an express agreement not to offer statements during negotiations as evidence or a statement that negotiations are "without prejudice" does no harm, and may serve a function even under the Federal Rules. For example, in *S. Leo Harmonay, Inc. v. Binks Mfg. Co.*,[312] plaintiff's attorney sent defendant a letter that stated: "In accordance with our prior discussions and without prejudice to our clients' respective legal positions, I am taking the liberty of setting forth below a summary of the damages suffered by Harmonay. . . ."

Defendant offered the letter in evidence at trial in order to impeach the testimony of one of plaintiff's witnesses. In deciding that Rule 408 barred admission of the letter, the court noted that the words *without prejudice,* were no longer absolutely dispositive. However, it stated that the words "may still be evidence of the intent of the speaker which we may rely upon to determine whether the statement was made 'in compromise.'" Thus, use of the phrase *without prejudice,* which cost nothing, seems to have contributed to a decision in favor of excluding the evidence, even under the Federal Rules.

Because the exclusionary rule only applies to discussions aimed at compromising disputed claims,[313] and because in hindsight it can sometimes be questionable whether certain communications were of this type, counsel who wish to take advantage of Rule 408 should clarify the nature of the negotiation at the time the negotiation takes place in order to lay the foundation for invoking the rule.

310. Urico v. Parnell Oil Co., 708 F.2d 852 (1st Cir.1983).

311. For discussion of alternate routes to admissibility, see Leonard, *supra* note 309 §§ 3.8.3–3.8.5.

312. 597 F.Supp. 1014, 1023 (S.D.N.Y. 1984), *aff'd,* 762 F.2d 990 (2d Cir.1985).

313. *See* § 5.45.

§ 5.51 Form of Objection; Request for Limiting Instruction

At trial, the objection may be made as follows:

> Objection! The question calls for testimony about [a settlement offer] [an offer in compromise] [a statement made during settlement negotiations].

If the objection is overruled on grounds that the evidence is offered for some purpose other than showing the validity or invalidity of the claim, then the objecting party should request a limiting instruction. For example, in instances where the basis for admission is that the evidence shows the bias of a witness, counsel could request the following instruction:

> Your Honor, I request that a limiting instruction be given informing the jury that this evidence may be used only for the purpose of assessing credibility, and that it may not be used as evidence that the plaintiff's claim is valid or that the defendant is liable.

If the evidence is admitted for a limited purpose, counsel should request a further instruction at the close of the case explaining the policy of the rule against use of settlement offers. For example, counsel might request the following instruction:

> Members of the jury, evidence that a settlement offer was made was admitted for the limited purpose of assisting you in assessing the credibility of a witness. You should not use this evidence as proof of the validity of plaintiff's claim or as evidence that defendant is liable. The settlement of cases before trial is something that the law seeks to encourage and promote. For that reason, the law protects persons who make settlement offers by providing that a settlement offer may not be used at trial as evidence that the person making the offer is legally liable. Otherwise, people would hesitate to make offers and the chances of settlement would be reduced.

OTHER OBJECTIONS BASED ON RELEVANCY AND ITS LIMITS

§ 5.52 Evidence of Payment of Medical and Similar Expenses [FRE 409]

Suppose that after a traffic accident, one of the parties offers to pay the hospital expenses of the other. If the offer is part of an offer to settle the case, then the evidence would be inadmissible under Rule 408.[314] But even if the offer or payment is made without settlement in mind, Rule 409 makes the evidence inadmissible. Under Rule 409, the furnishing or offering or promising to pay medical, hospital, or similar expenses occasioned by an injury is not admissible to prove liability for the injury.[315]

---

314. Fed. R. Evid. 408.   **315.** Fed. R. Evid. 409.

There are several rationales for the rule.[316] The primary rationale is one of policy—that humane acts should be encouraged, not punished. Another purpose is one of relevancy—that a payment of medical expenses is often not an expression of belief in fault, but merely an expression of human kindness.[317] As with evidence of subsequent remedial measures and compromise, there is also the consideration of fairness—that it would be unfair to use a party's humanitarian behavior against her at trial.[318]

Though the general rule of exclusion is followed almost universally,[319] the rule has attracted little attention. Either it has rarely been invoked to exclude evidence, or the rule is so clear that it has not created the interpretive problems that beget reported decisions.

The rule does not apply to statements made in conjunction with payment of medical expenses.[320] Thus, the party who pays medical expenses and apologizes for an accident is likely to be faced with the apology in court.[321] This aspect of the rule contrasts with Rule 408, which covers not only offers in compromise but statements in conjunction with the offers.[322] The rationale for the difference is that offers in compromise come as part of settlement negotiations and statements of fact are an indispensable part of such negotiations. The nonnegotiator who does the good deed of paying medical expenses could do the deed just as effectively without commenting on the events that led to the injury, and hence is stripped of the protection that belongs to the negotiator on grounds that beneficial conduct is not being deterred by receiving evidence of the statements.[323]

As with evidence of subsequent remedial measures and compromise, evidence concerning payment of medical expenses is admissible if offered for purposes other than to prove an implied recognition of responsibility.

316. *See* David P. Leonard, The New Wigmore: A Treatise on Evidence: Selected Rules of Limited Admissibility § 4.4 (1996).

317. Fed. R. Evid. 409 advisory committee's note. *See also* 2 Weinstein's Federal Evidence § 409.02, at 409–4 (2d ed. Joseph M. McLaughlin ed. 1997) (traditional theory: offer to pay medical costs usually made from humane impulses, not admission of liability; and also stating policy rationale).

318. *See* 2 Christopher B. Mueller & Laird C. Kirkpatrick, Federal Evidence § 139, at 114 (1994) ("it would be unseemly to receive evidence that one who felt responsible had paid such expenses in a responsible manner, if he objected to the evidence"); 23 Charles A. Wright & Kenneth W. Graham, Jr., Federal Practice and Procedure (Evidence) § 5321, at 298 (1980) (it is "considered unfair to pervert a generous act into a confession of fault").

319. Nearly half of the states have adopted the language of Rule 409 verbatim,

and several have adopted rules with only minor differences. Though other states have enacted rules somewhat less similar in structure to Rule 409, these rules are likely to have the same scope as Rule 409. *See* Leonard, *supra* note 316 § 4.7.

320. Fed. R. Evid. 409 advisory committee's note.

321. *See, e.g.,* Sims v. Sowle, 395 P.2d 133, 135 (Or.1964) (defendant's apology to plaintiff accompanying offer to pay medical expenses admissible); Weinstein's Federal Evidence, *supra* note 317 § 409.03[3] (admissions of liability accompanying offer of assistance admissible if severable from offer).

322. Fed. R. Evid. 408.

323. Fed. R. Evid. 409 advisory committee's note. For more detailed discussion of the admission of statements of fact made in connection with payment of medical expenses, see Leonard, *supra* note 316 § 4.6.2.

For example, the evidence might be offered to prove control of an instrumentality, identity of the apparatus causing the injury, or defendant's status as an employer or principal of the person who caused the injury.[324]

§ 5.53 Plea Bargaining Statements; Withdrawn Guilty Pleas; Pleas of Nolo Contendere [FRE 410]

Under Federal Rule of Evidence 410, statements made during plea bargaining are inadmissible.[325] The primary purpose of the rule is to encourage full disclosure during negotiations for a plea.[326] In this sense, the rule is analogous to the rule covering statements of fact made in the course of compromise discussions.

A withdrawn guilty plea is also inadmissible.[327] The permission to withdraw must have been granted for a reason—such as involuntariness, lack of true understanding of the nature of the charges or the consequences of conviction, or the denial of assistance of counsel—and whatever reason is good enough to permit withdrawal is considered good enough to keep the plea out of evidence.[328] The rule is thus based strongly in considerations of fairness.[329] Its primary purpose, however, is to encourage the settlement of criminal cases, which is necessary in order to prevent the criminal justice system from collapsing under the weight of contested trials.[330]

Like any other statement of a party, a guilty plea not withdrawn is admissible as an admission.[331] However, where the plea is to a minor traffic offense—especially where the "plea" is made by mail—the inference that the statement shows consciousness of guilt may be too weak to permit it to be received in evidence. Persons accused of traffic violations often make such pleas simply for convenience, to avoid going to court. Use of the plea as evidence of guilt may be misleading.[332] Nevertheless,

---

324. *See id.* § 4.13.

325. Fed. R. Evid. 410(4).

326. Fed. R. Evid. 410 advisory committee's note.

327. Fed. R. Evid. 410. *But cf.* United States v. Greene, 995 F.2d 793, 798 (8th Cir.1993) (held, defendant not entitled to introduce evidence that he had rejected favorable plea agreement; defendant argued that his rejection of agreement was evidence of "consciousness of innocence").

328. Fed. R. Evid. 410 advisory committee's note (citing Kercheval v. United States, 274 U.S. 220 (1927)) (admitting withdrawn guilty plea would undermine purpose of allowing defendant to withdraw plea); 2 McCormick on Evidence § 257, at 152 (4th ed. John W. Strong ed. 1992) (where plea withdrawn to correct injustice, admission would undermine effectiveness of remedy).

329. *See* David P. Leonard, The New Wigmore: A Treatise on Evidence: Selected Rules of Limited Admissibility § 5.4.2 (1996). Another rationale for the exclusionary rule are prevention of unfair prejudice. *Id.* § 5.4.3.

330. *See id.* § 5.4.4.

331. *See, e.g.,* Taylor v. Whitley, 933 F.2d 325, 327 (5th Cir.1991), *cert. denied,* 503 U.S. 988 (1992) (guilty plea is an admission that defendant committed charged offense); Jacobs v. Goodspeed, 429 A.2d 915, 917 (1980) (plea of guilty to following too closely admissible as admission in negligence action); Teitelbaum Furs, Inc. v. Dominion Ins. Co., 375 P.2d 439, 441, 25 Cal. Rptr. 559 561 (Cal.1962) (guilty plea admissible in civil action as admission).

332. *See, e.g.,* Hannah v. Ike Topper Structural Steel Co., 201 N.E.2d 63, 65 (Ohio App. 1963) (plea of guilty to failing to yield signed on form attached to traffic tickthe party pleading guilty will usually have the opportunity to explain to the fact finder why he or she did so, potentially minimizing the misunderstanding that could result from admission of the evidence.

A plea of nolo contendere is not admissible in either a civil or criminal suit.[333] The trial judge who allowed the plea–which cannot be made as of right[334]–determined in allowing the plea that this consequence should not attach to the conviction.[335] Indeed, in many cases the most compelling motivation to utilize the nolo contendere plea is precisely to dispose of the case without creating adverse evidence for subsequent civil or criminal litigation.[336]

Unlike the federal rules governing evidence of subsequent remedial measures, compromise evidence, and evidence of payment of medical expenses, Rule 410 generally does not allow the use of plea evidence to impeach.[337] Some state codes expressly permit such use.[338]

The Supreme Court has issued an important decision concerning *waiver* of the protections of Rule 410. In *United States v. Mezzanatto*,[339] the Supreme Court held that a person may waive protection of Rule 410. Defendant was arrested on narcotics charges. Shortly after his arrest, defendant and his attorney met with the prosecutor to discuss cooperation. The prosecutor informed defendant that he would not continue with the discussion unless defendant agreed that any statements he made during the meeting could be used to impeach his testimony by contradiction should he testify at trial. After consultation with his attorney, defendant agreed to the prosecutor's terms, and then made evasive and false statements during the discussion. The prosecutor terminated the meeting on the basis that defendant was not being truthful, and when defendant testified inconsistently with certain statements he made during the session, the prosecutor offered the prior statements into evidence to impeach his credibility. The Supreme Court held that the trial court's admission of the evidence was proper, relying primarily on the theory that criminal defendant may waive many rights by voluntary agreement. Defendant argued that the disparity of bargain-

---

et inadmissible; cost of defense and inconvenience of court appearances compared to fine motivating factor for plea); 2 McCormick on Evidence, *supra* note 328 § 257, at 151–52 (recognition that collateral consequences as opposed to guilt often controlling factor in traffic violation guilty pleas has led to some tendency to exclude plea); *But see* Duvall v. Borough of Oxford, 1992 WL 59163, at *4 n. 6 (E.D.Pa.1992) (rejecting argument that guilty plea to underage drinking charge should be inadmissible as an admission because "like traffic violations, this charge is regularly 'admitted' even when false, because the costs of contest outweigh the punishment"); Ando v. Woodberry, 168 N.E.2d 520, 521, 203 N.Y.S.2d 74, 76 (N.Y. 1960) (plea of guilty to failing to signal and making improper turn admissible in negligence action; plea

was made in court, however, so inconvenience explanation not available).

333. Fed. R. Evid. 410(2).

334. *See* Fed. R. Crim. Proc. 11(b).

335. 1 McCormick on Evidence, *supra* note 328 § 257, at 152 & n.31 (judge assumedly considers admissibility of plea as factor in deciding whether to permit plea of nolo contenders).

336. For discussion of the application of the exclusionary rule to pleas of nolo contendere, see Leonard, *supra* note 329 § 5.8.3. Many states do not permit the entry of nolo pleas. *See id.* § 5.2.3.

337. *See id.* § 5.10.

338. *See id.*

339. 513 U.S. 196 (1995).

ing power makes such agreements "inherently unfair and coercive." In response, the Court acknowledged that the plea bargaining process exerts pressure on defendants to plead guilty and that there is potential for prosecutorial abuse. But, the Court wrote, such potential for abuse "is an insufficient basis for foreclosing negotiation altogether.... Instead, the appropriate response to [defendant's] predictions of abuse is to permit case-by-case inquiries into whether waiver agreements are the product of fraud or coercion."[340]

The scope of *Mezzanatto* is not yet clear. Justice Thomas' opinion for the Court strongly hinted that *any* of the protections of Rule 410 could be waived, but three concurring Justices distanced themselves from this position, and there were two dissenters. Because *Mezzanatto* was decided largely as a matter of statutory interpretation, the states are free to interpret their own rules as they deem just.

Even in the absence of waiver, statements made to prosecutors in hopes of obtaining lenience can fall outside the protection of the rule. The Eighth Circuit has held that revelations of incriminating information by the defendant, made during preliminary discussions with the prosecutor about the benefits of cooperation, did not occur during the "course of plea discussions" and hence did not qualify for protection.[341]

§ 5.54 Evidence of Liability Insurance [FRE 411]

Federal Rule of Evidence 411 prohibits evidence of the presence or absence of liability insurance, when offered on the issue whether the insured party acted negligently or wrongfully.[342] The general rule is followed almost universally. Some states have adopted language identical or virtually identical to Federal Rule 411, others have codified somewhat different versions of the rule. The few remaining common law states also tend to follow the general principles of Rule 411.[343]

The rule has three rationales. First, the relevance of insurance to the issue of liability is questionable. While it is conceivable that a person who buys insurance will act carelessly because there is less risk of economic loss, it is also possible that those who buy insurance are more careful by nature.[344] Second, the evidence about insurance has obvious potential for prejudice. If the jury finds out that a defendant is insured, it might be more likely to hold the party liable because of the presence of

---

340. *Id.* at 210.

341. United States v. Morgan, 91 F.3d 1193, 1196 (8th Cir.1996) (interpreting Rule 410's counterpart in Fed. R. Crim. Proc. 11(e)(6)(D)).

342. Fed. R. Evid. 411. *See, e.g.,* Rozark Farms, Inc. v. Ozark Border Elec. Coop., 849 F.2d 306, 309 (8th Cir.1988) (defendant's attorney asked plaintiff "And was this property damage insured by you?"; question abandoned after objection; trial judge did not rule on objection or give curative instruction; held, reversible error).

343. For discussion of state law, see David P. Leonard, The New Wigmore: A Treatise on Evidence: Selected Rules of Limited Admissibility § 6.6 (1996). Interestingly, Louisiana appears to reject the general exclusionary rule. *See id.* at 6:80. In light of Louisiana's direct action statute permitting the liability insurer to be made a party to the action, an exclusionary rule would serve little purpose.

344. *See* Fed. R. Evid. 411 advisory committee's note.

a deep pocket. If the jury finds out that a defendant is not insured, then the jury may make a finding of nonliability because it is afraid that a contrary verdict will bring financial ruin.[345] Similarly, if it finds out that a plaintiff is not insured for a loss such as destruction of property by fire, then the jury might make a lawless assignment of liability because of a defendant's greater resources.[346] Finally, the rule is occasionally supported by a policy rationale—that excluding evidence of liability insurance encourages people to carry such insurance.[347]

Of course, in many situations jurors will assume that parties are insured in the absence of evidence. For example, jurors will ordinarily assume some level of insurance when a case involves an automobile accident or destruction of property by fire. In this situation, it can be argued that revealing the true state of affairs when there is no insurance merely counteracts prejudice caused by this erroneous assumption, rather than injecting prejudice. This argument, however, cannot be accepted in jurisdictions following the Federal Rules of Evidence, because it is contrary to the plain language of Rule 411. In other jurisdictions, the argument has had scant success.[348] The uninsured party can, however, request an instruction that at least suggests the possibility of no insurance. For example, the instruction could state:

> There has been no evidence in this case about whether [the party] was covered by liability insurance. The reason is that the law does not permit evidence of the absence or presence of liability insurance to be presented to you. The evidence is inadmissible because you are not supposed to consider insurance one way or the other in this case. When deciding the case, you should put out of your mind the possibility that the loss in this case was covered, or was not covered, by liability insurance.

Although evidence of liability insurance is inadmissible when offered to show negligence or wrongful conduct, it is admissible when offered for another purpose. For example, it is admissible to show agency, ownership, or control[349] or to show the bias or prejudice of a

---

345. On the other hand, there is the possibility that the jury might wish to punish a party who, contrary to law, fails to carry automobile liability insurance.

346. See Fed. R. Evid. 411 advisory committee's note. *See also* Falkowski v. Johnson, 148 F.R.D. 132, 136 (D.Del.1993) (plaintiff's statements in closing argument implying that defendant's employer would pay personal injury damages constitutes reversible error).

347. *See, e.g.,* 2 Weinstein's Federal Evidence § 411.02[2] (2d ed. Joseph M. McLaughlin ed. 1997) (the exclusionary rule "seeks to implement a general policy favoring insurance. Both insurers and insured are, in effect, encouraged to enter into contracts of insurance with the implied promise that they will not, as a result of their

forethought, have what they believe to be the somewhat harmful inference of carelessness used against them"). Weinstein's text also states the prejudice rationale. *See id.* § 411.02[1].

348. 1 McCormick on Evidence § 201, at 857 (4th ed. John W. Strong ed. 1992) (few courts will allow defendant to demonstrate lack of insurance; instruction on insurance suggested).

349. Fed. R. Evid. 411. *See, e.g.,* Hunziker v. Scheidemantle, 543 F.2d 489, 495 n. 10 (3d Cir.1976) (insurance admissible to prove agency relationship between owner and pilot of aircraft which crashed in wrongful death action by survivors of passenger); Newell v. Harold Shaffer Leasing Co., 489 F.2d 103, 110 (5th Cir.1974) (plain-witness.[350] Thus, when there is a dispute about whether landlord or tenant is responsible for the maintenance of an elevator in an office building, evidence that the tenant maintained liability insurance on the elevator would be admissible. Similarly, when an insurance investigator testifies, evidence that the investigator works for the insurer of one of the parties is often admitted to show the witness's possible bias.[351] Some trial judges, however, will seek to eliminate possible prejudice by requiring that the question be neutered. Thus, the judge might require that the investigator be asked whether he or she is an investigator for the defense, without mention of the insurance company. Defense counsel should ask for a ruling before the question is asked.

Rule 411 sets forth certain purposes for which evidence of insurance may be received.[352] This list, however, is not exclusive. Insurance evidence is admissible for any relevant purpose not specifically prohibited by Rule 411, that is, on any issue other than showing that the insured acted negligently or otherwise wrongfully.[353] Thus, for example, evidence of insurance sometimes comes in incidentally in the impeachment of the credibility of a witness, even if the impeachment is based on grounds other than the listed purpose of showing bias. If a witness has filed a claim of loss that is inconsistent with the witness's in-court testimony, it is permissible to impeach the witness with the prior inconsistent statement.[354] Of course, if liability insurance is itself an essential element of a claim or defense, evidence of the insurance must be admitted.[355]

The fact that insurance evidence circumstantially tends to prove something other than negligence or wrongful conduct does not automatically make it admissible. As with other evidence that is admissible for

tiff's car damaged in accident with truck; draft from insurance company to plaintiff for amount of damages naming defendant as insured, admissible to show ownership); Dobbins v. Crain Bros., 432 F.Supp. 1060, 1069 MD Pa 1976), *aff'd in part, revd in part*, 567 F.2d 559 (3d Cir.1977) (defendant's insurance coverage on barge admissible to prove ownership).

350. Fed. R. Evid. 411. *See, e.g ..,* Charter v. Chleborad, 551 F.2d 246, 248 (8th Cir.), *cert.* denied, 434 U.S. 856 (1977) (plaintiff not permitted to show impeachment witness for defense employed by same insurance company representing defendant; held, reversible error).

351. *See, e.g.,* Ouachita Natl. Bank v. Tosco Corp., 686 F.2d 1291 (8th Cir.1982), *modified on rehg,* 716 F.2d 485 (8th Cir. 1983) (en banc) (defendant could inform jury of insurance coverage when it intended to call insurance adjuster as witness); Filloon v. Stenseth, 498 N.W.2d 353, 355 (N.D. 1993) (held, in tort action arising from automobile-bicycle accident, trial court committed reversible error in automatically barring evidence that key witness also worked for driver's insurance carrier; trial

court should have admitted evidence under state's Rule 411, subject to probativeness versus prejudice balancing under state's Rule 403); 1 Stephen A. Saltzburg, Michael M. Martin & Daniel J. Capra, Federal Rules of Evidence Manual 553 (6th ed. 1994) (where insurance adjuster testifies, permissible to demonstrate relationship between witness and employer).

352. The purposes are agency, ownership, control, and bias or prejudice of a witness. Fed. R. Evid. 411.

353. For extended discussion of permissible uses of liability insurance evidence, see Leonard, *supra* note 343 §§ 6.9–6.15.

354. *See* Rozark Farms, Inc. v. Ozark Border Elec. Coop., 849 F.2d 306, 309 & n. 2 (8th Cir.1988) (dictum) (stating that an amount set forth on a proof of loss form can be used to impeach testimony by insured that greater loss was suffered, and noting that it is not always possible to avoid reference to insurance in the process of this impeachment).

355. *See* Leonard, *supra* note 343 § 6.11.

one purpose but not for another, the trial judge must weigh the danger of prejudice against the probative value of the evidence in deciding whether to admit it.[356] When the court determines that admission is justified, it should issue a limiting instruction informing the jury of the limited purposes for which the evidence is admitted.

If the trial judge sustains an objection to the interjection of insurance, counsel should typically request a mistrial and then, if the request is denied, request a curative instruction telling the jury to ignore the evidence. These steps will protect the right to reversal on appeal. Of course, they may not be tactically wise in every situation. Getting a mistrial from the trial judge is no victory when the present jury is favorable.

In jurisdictions that allow substantial questioning of jurors on voir dire, insurance is sometimes brought in through the back door by questions to the jurors. For example, the plaintiff in a personal injury case might be permitted to ask jurors whether they work for an insurance company or whether they own stock in a liability insurance company.[357] In such jurisdictions, counsel may still be able to object successfully if the questions become too pointed. For example, one can argue that asking about employment with a specific insurance company is too suggestive, and that a question about general insurance employment is sufficient. Commentators have also suggested that the information about insurance be obtained from the venire by questionnaire prior to assignment to any particular case, but this solution does not appear to have been widely adopted.[358] In any event, the court must seek an appropriate balance between the conflicting rights to an unbiased jury and to avoidance of prejudice to the insured party.[359]

§ 5.55   Collateral Source Rule

A number of jurisdictions provide that the defendant's liability for damages caused by an injury is not diminished by the fact that the plaintiff has collected partial compensation from a collateral source.[360]

---

356. *See, e.g.,* Posttape Assocs. v. Eastman Kodak Co., 537 F.2d 751, 757–58 (3d Cir.1976) (trial court erred in excluding as prejudicial otherwise admissible evidence of plaintiff's insurance; evidence not prejudicial).

357. Drickersen v. Drickersen, 604 P.2d 1082, 1084–85 (Alaska 1979) (attorney entitled to ask prospective jurors if they had interest in, or connection with, any insurance company); 2 Weinstein's Federal Evidence, *supra* note 347 § 411.04[4] (jury panel may be questioned concerning interest in, or connection with, insurance company involved in litigation).

358. *See* Boos, *Recent Decisions, Practice and Procedure–Under What Circumstances May Counsel Ask Jurors Regarding Their Interest in Insurance Companies on*

Trial of a Case Against an Insured Defendant, 43 Mich. L. Rev. 621, 623 (1944) (give every member of jury panel questionnaire concerning relations with insurance companies); *Recent Cases, Jury—Competency of Jurors—Questioning Jurors on Voir Dire as to Their Connections with Insurance Company,* 52 Harv. L. Rev. 166, 166 (1938) (examine entire jury panel concerning connections to insurance companies before trial of any cases during term).

359. For further discussion of the problem of revealing evidence of liability insurance during jury selection, see Leonard, *supra* note 343 § 6.7.4.

360. *See, e.g.,* Gypsum Carrier, Inc. v. Handelsman, 307 F.2d 525, 535 (9th Cir. 1962) (benefits to injured seaman under

For example, under this rule, the plaintiff whose hospital bills were paid by health insurance is still entitled to recover the amount paid to the hospital from the party whose negligence caused the injury.[361] The rationale behind the collateral source rule is that the wrongdoer should not benefit from the injured person's expenditures or relationships that may exist between the injured person and third parties.[362]

The collateral source rule is not really a rule of evidence, but a rule of substantive law that causes certain evidence to be irrelevant.[363] If the substantive law prevents the collateral payments from diminishing recovery, evidence of collateral payments should be excluded as irrelevant.[364]

In recent years, however, the collateral source rule has come under attack. Many scholars have argued the rationale of the collateral source rule is outdated. Some have argued that the rule stymies what would otherwise be an economically sensible form of loss spreading.[365] In

compensation plan not deductible from Jones Act recovery; federal courts generally follow collateral source rule); Helfend v. Southern California Rapid Transit Dist., 465 P.2d 61, 63 (Cal.1970) (compensation for injuries received from source independent of tortfeasor may not be deducted from damages injured party would otherwise recover); Wilson v. Hoffman Group, Inc., 546 N.E.2d 524, 530 (Ill.1989) (benefits received by injured party from source independent of and collateral to tortfeasor will not diminish damages); Restatement (Second) of Torts § 920A (1979) ("Payments made to or benefits conferred on the injured party from other sources are not credited against the tortfeasor's liability although they cover all or a part of the harm for which the tortfeasor is liable").

Alabama's recent tort reform yielded a statute that allows admission of evidence that an outside source has paid or will pay or reimburse a plaintiff for certain medical or hospital expenses. Ala. Code § 12–21–45 (1995). An Alabama district court has found the statute inapplicable in federal diversity cases (Killian v. Melser, 792 F.Supp. 1217 (N.D.Ala.1992)) and has noted that, in the absence of an authoritative ruling by the Alabama Supreme Court, many state trial courts apparently allow the evidence accompanied by an instruction that the jury "may consider" it.

361. See, e.g., Carter v. United States, 982 F.2d 1141, 1145 (7th Cir.1992) (veterans' benefits not considered collateral source payments); Berg v. United States, 806 F.2d 978, 985–86 (10th Cir.1986) (Medicare benefits for injuries suffered at veterans' hospital could not be deducted from damages against federal government under Federal Torts Claim Act, 28 U.S.C § 267 1,

for medical malpractice); Helfend, 465 P.2d at 69, 84 Cal. Rptr. at 181 (defendant could not mitigate damages by medical insurance payments to injured plaintiff); Restatement (Second) of Torts § 902A comment c (1979) (collateral benefits from insurance policies not subtracted from plaintiff's recovery).

362. See, e.g., Wilson, 546 N.E.2d at 524 (wrongdoer should not benefit from injured party's expenditures or take advantage of contacts or other relations between injured party and third parties); Greenwood v. Hildebrand, 515 A.2d 963, 968 (1986), appeal denied, 528 A.2d 602 (1987) (wrongdoer should not receive benefit of fortuitous existence of collateral remedy).

363. As a rule of substantive law, one would expect that federal courts in diversity cases would be required to follow the state's collateral source rule. See Erie R. Co. v. Tompkins, 304 U.S. 64 (1938); Bradford v. Bruno's Inc., 94 F.3d 621 (11th Cir.1996), (Alabama's statutory modification of its common law collateral source rule was substantive law that must be applied in federal diversity action); In re Air Crash Disaster Near Chicago, Illinois, on May 25, 1979, 803 F.2d 304, 308 (7th Cir.1986) (holding that federal court in diversity case must apply collateral source rule of state whose law governs case).

364. See Jones on Evidence: Civil and Criminal § 4.48, at 480–81 (Spencer A. Gard 6th ed. 1972) (evidence of plaintiff's financial condition including receipts of benefits from collateral sources inadmissible as irrelevant to issue of compensatory damages).

365. See, e.g., Fleming, The Collateral Source Rule and Loss Allocation in Tort addition, the proliferation of medical malpractice suits and the rising cost of insurance led the American Medical Association to campaign for a variety of tort reforms including abolition of the collateral source rule.[366] In recent years, several jurisdictions have modified or abolished the collateral source rule in medical malpractice cases.[367] Although such laws have been attacked on both equal protection and due process grounds, the courts generally have held them constitutional.[368]

§ 5.56　Other Accidents, When Offered by Personal Injury Plaintiffs

A personal injury plaintiff may seek to introduce evidence of similar accidents involving the defendant's property or product. For example, in a slip-and-fall case involving a fall on a carpet, the plaintiff might offer evidence that other customers had previously fallen on the same carpet, to support a claim that the carpet was loose.[369] Such evidence is relevant if the conditions under which the other accidents occurred were sufficiently similar to the accident at issue to make it more likely either that the prior accidents were caused by the same defect or that the prior accidents would have given a reasonable property owner notice of a possible defect. Whether the evidence will in fact be admissible in a given

---

Law, 54 Calif. L. Rev. 1478, 1547 (1966) (moral postulates yielding to modern economic value system; "question is not so much whether a wrongdoer deserves to be relieved as which of several competing 'risk communities' should bear the loss"). Fleming argues that the collateral source rule is no longer justified in light of the high cost of shifting the loss to the tortfeasor from some form of collectivized risk-bearing regime which has already paid for the loss and could absorb it as well or even better than the tortfeasor. *Id.* at 1547–48.

366. *See* Banks McDowell, *The Collateral Source Rule—The American Medical Association and Tort Reform,* 24 Washburn L.J. 205, 215–16 (1985).

367. *See* Bernier v. Burris, 497 N.E.2d 763, 774–75 (Ill.1986) (listing state laws modifying or abrogating collateral source rule in medical malpractice cases permitting recovery to be reduced by amounts received from private or public sources).

368. *See, e.g.,* Fein v. Permanente Med. Group, 695 P.2d 665, 685–86, 211 Cal.Rptr. 368, 388–89 (Cal.1985), *appeal dismissed,* 474 U.S. 892 (1985) (statute allowing defendant to introduce evidence of collateral payments to injured party in medical malpractice suit does not violate due process or equal protection); *Bernier,* 497 N.E.2d at 775 (provision allowing judgment in medical malpractice cases to be reduced by up to 50 per cent for benefits received from collateral sources does not violate due

process). *See generally,* McDowell, *supra* note 366, at 215–19 (discussing general reform movement and constitutional challenges to abrogation of rule).

369. *See, e.g.,* Beck v. City of Pittsburgh, 89 F.3d 966, 973–75 (3d Cir.1996) (error to exclude other complaints against police officer to show defendant city's tolerance of excessive force); Tait v. Armor Elevator Co., 958 F.2d 563, 568–69 (3d Cir. 1992) (excluding evidence of prior accidents in other elevators in same elevator bank, where plaintiff failed to substantiate argument that accidents arose from similar cause); Wyatt v. Otis Elevator Co., 921 F.2d 1224, 1228 (11th Cir.1991) (allowing evidence of prior accidents involving failure of elevator doors to reverse and detract; discussion in court of other types of elevator accidents cured by jury instruction); Robitaille v. Netoco Community Theatres, 25 N.E.2d 749, 751 (Mass.1940) (held, reversible error to admit evidence of other fall two or three weeks earlier in same spot; no sufficient showing of similar conditions or similar conduct by victims of fall); Gable v. Kroger Co., 410 S.E.2d 701 (W.Va.1991) (excluding evidence of two previous slip-and-fall accidents, where neither accident occurred in same area of store or arose from a similar problem). *Cf.* Bitsos v. Red Owl Stores, Inc., 459 F.2d 656, 659–60 (8th Cir. 1972) (earlier falls on steps; admissible to demonstrate presence of foreign substance on steps).

case turns on a Federal Rule of Evidence 403 balancing of probative value against prejudice, confusion, and waste of time, with a measure of discretion accorded to the trial judge.[370]

In exercising discretion, the trial judge should consider whether a convincing showing of similar conditions has been made.[371] Also, the trial judge should consider whether the prior accidents are offered merely to show that a condition was dangerous—something that could be shown by other evidence with less waste of time or danger of prejudice—or whether the evidence is also relevant to the issue whether the defendant was on notice of the existence of the dangerous condition. If the evidence is relevant to notice, then the requirement of similar conditions is applied less strictly. All that is required is that the prior accident be similar enough to alert the defendant to the danger.[372]

When the evidence of other accidents is offered to show the carelessness of a human being, rather than merely to show the dangerousness of a thing, then the rules against character evidence come into play. The evidence is admissible only if it can be received under Rule 404(b) as probative of something other than a propensity to be negligent. *See* § 5.14.

§ 5.57 Absence of Other Accidents, When Offered by Personal Injury Defendants

Just as the plaintiff may wish to offer evidence of prior accidents to establish the dangerousness of a condition or notice to the defendant of possible danger, the defendant may wish to offer evidence that *no* accidents had occurred in the manner claimed by the plaintiff, even though the conditions had remained essentially unchanged. While some

370. *See, e.g.,* Simon v. Kennebunkport, 417 A.2d 982, 986 (Me.1980) (Me. R. Evid. 403 abolishes former Maine rule of exclusion and leaves admissibility of prior falls on same sidewalk to discretion of trial judge).

371. *See, e.g., id.* (error to exclude evidence of earlier falls; as many as one hundred people fell under similar circumstances). *See also* Drabik v. Stanley-Bostitch, Inc., 997 F.2d 496, 508 (8th Cir. 1993) ("for other accidents evidence to be admissible, the proponent of the evidence must show that the facts and circumstances of the other incident are substantially similar to the case at bar"); Lolie v. Ohio Brass Co., 502 F.2d 741, 745 (7th Cir.1974) (evidence that other metal clips failed inadmissible; no offer of proof that other clips were comparable to clips in issue).

372. *See, e.g.,* Exum v. General Elec. Co., 819 F.2d 1158, 1159–60 (D.C.Cir.1987)

(prior accident in which fast food employee burned by appliance; court states that higher degree of similarity is required when issue is dangerousness than when issue is notice); Gardner v. Southern Ry. Sys., 675 F.2d 949, 952 (7th Cir.1982) (prior railroad collision, to show notice of hazard at grade crossing; court indicates that it is appropriate to relax requirement of similar conditions when purpose is to show notice); City of Taylorville v. Stafford, 63 N.E. 624–25 (Ill.1902) (other people stumbled on sidewalk; admissible to show notice of dangerous condition). *See also* Four Corners Helicopters, Inc. v. Turbomeca, S.A., 979 F.2d 1434 (10th Cir.1992) (held, other failures of helicopter screws admissible to show notice; where issue is notice, lesser showing of similarity is sufficient); Cooper v. Firestone Tire & Rubber Co., 945 F.2d 1103, 1105 (9th Cir.1991) (noting that the circuits are split concerning whether evidence of similar accidents is admissible when relevant to witness credibility).

jurisdictions forbid receipt of such evidence,[373] most appear to recognize that evidence of the absence of accidents can be relevant in various types of actions including basic negligence and product liability cases.[374] As with evidence of prior accidents, the issue is first one of relevance, and then of balancing the probative value of the evidence against its potential for undue prejudice or jury confusion. At times, the evidence should be excluded, particularly because of its tendency to confuse the jury. In other cases, however, the evidence has substantial probative value. Where, for example, a condition has remained static for a number of years and nobody has suffered an injury, plaintiff's claim that the condition represents an undue danger is particularly weak. Depriving the jury of the evidence of the lack of accidents in such a case would be misleading.

The authorities have generally supported admission, and this appears to be the modern trend.[375] At least one authority suggested, in fact, that evidence of favorable safety history carries more probative value than plaintiff's evidence of prior accidents.[376]

373. *See, e.g.,* Jones v. Pak–Mor Mfg. Co., 700 P.2d 819, 821 (Ariz.1985) (stating a categorical rule in Arizona forbidding receipt of evidence of the absence of prior accidents to prove lack of defect, lack of danger, or similar issues); Paulison v. Chicago, M., St. P. and P.R.R., Inc., 392 N.E.2d 960, 965–66 (Ill.App.1979) (in wrongful death action against railroad for failure to provide automatic gates at crossing, evidence of only three minor accidents in prior fifteen years not admissible to prove lack of danger; prior Illinois authority had held such evidence admissible only to prove lack of notice, which was not an issue in this case).

374. *See, e.g.,* Benson v. Honda Motor Co., Ltd., 32 Cal.Rptr.2d 322, 325–28 (Cal. App.1994) (in product liability action alleging both negligence and failure to warn, manufacturer may offer evidence of absence of similar prior accidents); Carbin v. National Super Markets, Inc., 823 S.W.2d 93 (Mo.App.1991) (in negligence action by grocery store customer alleging injury from striking eye on display rack, held, defendant may offer evidence that manager was not aware of any prior similar accidents in the store; evidence admissible to prove store lacked knowledge, or reason to know, of dangerous condition); Reiger v. Toby Enterprises, 609 P.2d 402, 404 (Or.App.1980) (in product liability action by employee of meat processing plant against manufacturer of meat slicer for hand injuries, evidence of absence of prior accidents admissible to prove product not unreasonably dangerous).

375. *See, e.g.,* 1 McCormick on Evidence § 200, at 848–51 (4th ed. John W. Strong ed. 1992); 2 John H. Wigmore, Evidence in Trials at Common Law §§ 443–44, at 528–32 (James H. Chadbourn rev. 1979).

376. Clarence Morris, Studies in the Law of Torts 87–89 (1952).

Chapter 6

COMPETENCY

Analysis

§ 6.01 Rules of Competency in General [FRE 601]

Rules of competency are rules that disqualify a witness from testifying. Usually the ground of disqualification is that the witness has some personal defect that will prevent the testimony from being accurate. Some competency rules, however, are based upon considerations of extrinsic policy. Rules rendering jurors incompetent to impeach their own verdicts, for example, are based on a desire for stability and an end to litigation, not upon concerns about accuracy of testimony.[1]

The common-law rules of incompetency, which persisted in many jurisdictions until the middle of the nineteenth century or later, are to the modern lawyer bizarre and arbitrary. On grounds of preventing perjury, parties and others with an interest in a lawsuit were prohibited from testifying.[2] A criminal defendant, for example, could not testify in his or her own behalf, though the rule was mitigated in many jurisdictions by allowing an unsworn statement that did not amount to "testimony."[3] One spouse could not testify on behalf of the other.[4] A convicted felon could not testify at all.[5]

Rules of this nature are contrary to the modern approach to trials, which is to allow evidence to come in for what it is worth, and to trust the trier of fact to recognize its impurities and separate the grain from the chaff. For the most part, the rules of incompetency have given way to

---

1. *See* Fed. R. Evid. 606(b) advisory committee's note.

2. 2 John H. Wigmore, Evidence in Trials at Common Law § 577, at 817 (James H. Chadbourn rev. 1979).

3. *See id.* § 579, at 826–27.

4. *See id.* § 600, at 856.

5. *See id.* § 519, at 725.

230

rules allowing witnesses to testify, subject to being impeached by the same facts (e.g., bias, convictions) that would previously have made the witness incompetent.[6]

Some of the ancient rules of incompetency, however, persist in qualified form. Some states maintain rules against testimony by children or the insane, unless they can be shown to be of sufficient understanding.[7] Others maintain "dead man's statutes" that prevent interested survivors from testifying in their suits against a dead person's estate.[8] Some of the rules of competency—those prohibiting testimony by judges and jurors—have not been affected by the modern trend, because they rest on a basis other than that of protecting the trier from inaccurate evidence.[9] Finally, a new sort of incompetency rule seems to be taking hold in states that have barred the reception of testimony by a witness whose memory has been hypnotically refreshed.[10]

Rule 601 provides that "[e]very person is competent to be a witness except as otherwise provided in these rules." When state law provides the rule of decision, however, the state competency law governs in federal court.[11] As a practical matter, it is rare that a judge finds, pursuant to Rule 104(a), that a witness is incompetent. The competency bar is very low. Considerations that might affect competency—a child's inability to distinguish between the truth and a lie, a person's inability to perceive well, a failure of memory, and the like—are more appropriately matters of weight and credibility for the jury.[12] When a witness of questionable competency is offered, a lawyer might be well advised to object even if the objection is likely to fail in the end. The judge will allow the lawyer to conduct a voir dire examination on competency that may help the lawyer to develop facts that can be used to impeach the witness when the witness is allowed to testify.

§ 6.02   Incompetency of Insane Person

The Federal Rules of Evidence do not disqualify an insane person. The insanity may be shown to impeach, but may not be used to keep the witness off the stand.[13] Some state jurisdictions still allow objections to testimony to be based on the insanity of the witness.[14] Where incompetency by virtue of mental illness is a ground for objection, however, the objection will not succeed simply on a showing that the proposed witness is mentally ill. Typically, the state will provide that the insane person

---

6. *See* Fed. R. Evid. 601 advisory committee's note.

7. *See* § 6.03.

8. *See* § 6.04.

9. *See* § 6.05.

10. *See* § 6.07.

11. Fed. R. Evid. 601.

12. Fed. R. Evid. 601 advisory committee's note, citing Henry Weihofen, Testimonial Competence and Credibility, 34 Geo. Wash. L. Rev. 53 (1965).

13. Fed. R. Evid. 601 advisory committee's note.

14. *See, e.g.,* Mich. R. Evid. 601 (witness must have mental capacity or sense of obligation to testify truthfully and understandably); Ohio R. Evid. 601(A) (persons of unsound mind incapable of receiving just impressions or relating them truthfully not competent); Tex. R. Evid. 601(a)(1) (persons insane at time offered as witness or when event occurred about which they are offered to testify are incompetent).

may testify if able to understand the duty to tell the truth, or able to express thought in an understandable manner, or both.[15]

§ 6.03 Incompetency of Child

The Federal Rules of Evidence do not contain restrictions on testimony of child witnesses.[16] Many states, however, do have restrictions at least in theory on the testimony of children, and in those federal cases in which state law provides the substantive rule of decision the state law applies.[17]

Typically, a state statute on incompetency of children will provide that a child under a certain age is incompetent unless shown to understand the duty to tell the truth and to be of sufficient understanding to be able to testify accurately.[18] In recent years, concern for prevention of child abuse has led to relaxation of competency requirements in some states.[19] Minnesota's statute, for example, now provides that a child under ten years is competent unless shown to lack the capacity to remember facts correctly or to testify truthfully, a reversal of the prior burden of persuasion on competency.[20]

§ 6.04 Dead Man's Statute

The dead man's statute is a rule of evidence that, broadly speaking, prohibits an adverse party from testifying against a dead person's estate about transactions or conversations with the dead person.[21] The theory behind the statute is that it is unfair to allow the party to give self-

15. *See, e.g.,* Mich. R. Evid. 601 (witness must have mental capacity or sense of obligation to testify truthfully and understandably); Minn. Stat. Ann. § 595.02(1)(f) (West 1988) (persons of unsound mind not competent if they lack capacity to remember or to relate facts truthfully); N.C. R. Evid. 601(b) (witness disqualified if incapable of testifying in understandable manner or incapable of understanding duty to tell truth).

16. *See* Fed. R. Evid. 601; 3 Weinstein's Federal Evidence § 601 App.102[8] (2d ed. Joseph M. McLaughlin ed. 1997) (Rule 601 codified judicial practice in federal courts against indiscriminately disqualifying witnesses based on age).

17. Fed. R. Evid. 609; State v. Warden, 891 P.2d 1074 (Kan.1995) (held, trial court properly allowed autistic child witness to testify through a "facilitator" who guided witness' hands while he typed; however, since child was capable of signing "yes" or "no" by gesturing he should have been required to make those "yes" and "no" responses independently of facilitator; moreover, facilitator should generally be prevented from hearing questions asked to child in order to ensure that answer comes from child, not facilitator). *Compare* In re

Basilio T., 5 Cal. Rptr. 2d 450, 456 (Cal. App. 1992) (Cal. Evid. Code §§ 700–701 (1966) provide that regardless of age, witness is competent as long as he or she understands duty to tell truth and can express self); State v. Roman, 622 A.2d 96, 100 (Me.1993) (holding that "[a] child of any age is presumed competent to testify as a witness unless disqualified under [Maine] Rule 601(b)" as incapable of expressing herself or of understanding duty to tell truth, or lacking "reasonable ability" to perceive or remember the issue).

18. *See, e.g.,* Ohio R. Evid. 601(A) (children under ten years old, who appear incapable of perceiving facts correctly or of relating them truthfully incompetent); Sizemore v. State, 416 S.E.2d 500, 502 (Ga. 1992) (Ga. Code Ann. § 249–9–5 excepts children who are victims of crime from competency challenge based on allegations that child does not understand nature of oath).

19. John E.B. Myers, Child Witness Law and Practice § 3.11, at 73–74 (1987).

20. Minn. Stat. Ann. § 595.02(1)(*l*) (West 1988).

21. *See* 1 McCormick on Evidence § 65 (4th ed. John W. Strong ed. 1992).

serving testimony when the lips of the dead person are sealed.[22] There are competing values and not all states have adopted a dead man's statute. Those jurisdictions with dead man's statutes have given primary consideration to the risk that unscrupulous people will take advantage of the death of others to make false claims against their estates. Those jurisdictions that have rejected the notion have given primary consideration to the risk that honest creditors will not be able to prove up legitimate debts of the decedent. The differences among dead man's statutes are so substantial that it is difficult to generalize about them, and of course it is essential to consult the local statute and case law.

The Federal Rules of Evidence do not recognize the dead man's statute.[23] There is no prohibition against the testimony in federal cases, unless state substantive law governs and the state maintains a dead man's statute. The danger of self-serving perjury is something that goes to the weight of the testimony, not its admissibility.[24]

§ 6.05   Testimony by Judge or Juror [FRE 606]

The Federal Rules of Evidence contain an absolute prohibition against testimony by a judge in a case over which the judge is presiding.[25] No objection is necessary to preserve the error. To save the lawyer from the awkwardness of challenging the presiding judge, the rules provide for an automatic objection.[26] Occasionally a judge will do the equivalent of testifying by making a comment from the bench based on personal knowledge. Unless the statement concerns a matter that is an appropriate subject for judicial notice,[27] this conduct is objectionable.[28]

The Federal Rules also provide that jurors may not testify in cases in which they are sitting.[29] When a juror is called to testify, it is necessary to make an objection in order to preserve error. The lawyer must be given an opportunity, however, to make the objection outside the hearing of the jury.[30]

The long-respected doctrine that jurors may not be heard to impeach the verdict is carried forward in the Federal Rules.[31] This means that

22. *See id.* at 159–60.

23. Fed. R. Evid. 601 advisory committee's note.

24. *Id.*

25. Fed. R. Evid. 605.

26. *Id.* & advisory committee's note.

27. *See* Fed. R. Evid. 201(b), which defines a judicially noticeable fact as "one not subject to reasonable dispute in that it is either (1) generally known with the territorial jurisdiction of the trial court or (2) capable of accurate and ready determination by resort to sources whose accuracy cannot reasonably be questioned."

28. *See, e.g.,* Fox v. City of West Palm Beach, 383 F.2d 189, 191 (5th Cir. 1967) (judge's frequent statements based on own

extrajudicial experience reversible error); 3 Weinstein's Federal Evidence § 605.07[1] (2d ed. Joseph M. McLaughlin ed. 1997) (judge may not introduce personal experience under guise of judicial notice). *See also* United States v. Maceo, 947 F.2d 1191, 1200 (5th Cir. 1991), *cert. denied*, 503 U.S. 949 (1992) (judge's interruption of cross-examination with objection that counsel had misstated law of plea bargains was not improper judicial testimony).

29. Fed. R. Evid. 606(a).

30. *Id.*

31. *See* Fed. R. Evid. 606(b).

after verdict, jurors may not testify that the verdict was produced by an unlawful method, such as a coin toss or by agreeing to write down numbers and accept the average as the figure for recovery.[32] They may testify, however, that there was a mistake in reporting the actual verdict.[33] The Federal Rules do provide that jurors may testify about the introduction of extraneous prejudicial information or improper outside influence.[34] Thus, jurors would be able to testify that one of the jurors brought a newspaper describing the case into the jury room, or that a juror was bribed.[35] The Supreme Court has interpreted the exception for outside influence narrowly, holding in *Tanner v. United States*,[36] that jurors could not testify about other jurors' use of alcohol or drugs during the trial.[37]

32. *Id.*; *see, e.g.*, United States v. Straach, 987 F.2d 232, 242 (5th Cir. 1993) (defendant not entitled to mistrial when two jurors signed statements that they believed defendant's innocence throughout the jury deliberations, but were "pressured" into accepting a verdict of guilty); Dallas v. Arave, 984 F.2d 292, 296 (9th Cir. 1993) (trial court properly denied defendant's motions to supplement the record with jurors' testimony that by finding the defendant guilty of voluntary manslaughter, they found the defendant initially acted in self-defense); Scogin v. Century Fitness, Inc., 780 F.2d 1316, 1319–20 (8th Cir. 1985) (trial court properly refused to inquire whether jury reached its verdict by quotient method); People v. Morris, 807 P.2d 949, 995–98 (Cal.), *cert. denied*, 502 U.S. 959 (1991); (trial court properly refused to admit testimony by juror that the juror found erroneously typed sentencing instruction confusing); Bly–Magee v. Budget Rent–A–Car Corp., 24 Cal. App. 4th 318, 325–26 (1994) (juror affidavits stating confusion surrounding special verdict forms are inadmissible and at most suggest deliberative error; counsel should have devoted closing argument to clarifying the verdict forms if there was danger of confusion); Hartley *ex rel* Hartley v. Guthmann, 532 N.W.2d 331, 335–36 (Neb. 1995) (statute prohibiting use of "juror's affidavit to impeach verdict on basis of discussions during deliberations which enter into verdict" renders inadmissible affidavits containing juror's allegation that jury member brought in brochures dealing with issues in medical malpractice case; however, brochure discussing detrimental effects of smoking on fetus in suit alleging malpractice during birth is sufficient evidence of juror misconduct to affirm grant of new trial).

33. Latino v. Crane Rental Co., 630 N.E.2d 591 (Mass. 1994) (trial judge suspecting variation in verdicts properly in-

quired whether jury agreed on special verdicts announced in open court by limiting questions to what jury decided, not why); State v. Williquette, 526 N.W.2d 144, 145 (Wis. 1995) (after discharge, jurors competent to testify to clerical error in jury verdict).

34. Fed. R. Evid. 606(b); United States v. Walker, 1 F.3d 423 (6th Cir. 1993) (reversible error where transcripts of taped depositions, including parts deemed inadmissible, were inadvertently sent to jury room with other exhibits and court refused to order hearing concerning impact on jurors); Powell v. Allstate Ins. Co., 652 So. 2d 354, 357 (Fla. 1995) (juror allegations that all white jury made racial jokes about black plaintiffs during deliberations); Castaneda *ex rel* Correll v. Pederson, 518 N.W.2d 246, 252–253 (Wis. 1994) (juror's misconduct in researching and reporting average malpractice award).

35. Fed. R. Evid. 606(b) advisory committee's note (citing Mattox v. United States, 146 U.S. 140 (1892)). *See also* United States v. Swinton, 75 F.3d 374, 381 (8th Cir.1996) (juror revelation that defendant had a criminal record is "extraneous prejudicial information"); Haugh v. Jones & Laughlin Steel Corp., 949 F.2d 914, 916–919 (7th Cir. 1991) (new trial proper where marshal told jurors they would be locked up until they reached a verdict, but trial court was wrong to ask juror whether consent to verdict was result of agreement or desire to go home).

36. 483 U.S. 107 (1987).

37. *Id.* at 121–25. *See also* United States v. Griffith, 17 F.3d 865 (6th Cir.) *cert. denied*, 513 U.S. 850 (1994) (juror attempt to discuss case with deputy marshal not an extraneous influence); United States v. Martinez–Moncivais, 14 F.3d 1030, 1036 (5th Cir. 1994) (that two jurors mentioned that if defendant were innocent he

§ 6.06   Witness Has Not Taken Oath [FRE 603]

Occasionally a witness who does not want to testify will simply refuse to take the oath. Other witnesses may refuse to take an oath on religious grounds. The federal rules and most state codes permit the witness to take either an oath or affirmation.[38] The affirmation omits the word "swear" and references to "God" from the oath. A witness might be asked, for example, "Do you affirm that the evidence you shall give is the truth, the whole truth, and nothing but the truth?" A witness who refuses to take the oath or affirmation is not eligible to testify.[39] The trial judge should be willing to tailor the affirmation to avoid scruples of the witness, so long as the witness is willing to agree to tell the truth under penalty of perjury.[40]

§ 6.07   Hypnotically Refreshed Testimony

Sometimes witnesses, particularly victims in criminal cases, will undergo hypnosis in order to aid in recollecting the facts. This procedure, while it may provide useful leads for investigation, creates great danger of inaccuracy in testimony. The hypnotized person is highly suggestible, and can easily be influenced by unintentional cues from the hypnotist.[41] Moreover, a witness who has been hypnotized previously to refresh memory is likely to manufacture false memory or confabulate true memory in a way that is undetectable either to the hypnotist or to the subject.[42] To compound the problem further, the subject's memory tends to harden after hypnosis, creating an artificially high level of certainty.[43]

Despite the absence of any specific provision in the Federal Rules of Evidence prohibiting hypnotically refreshed testimony, a number of state and federal courts have either excluded it or placed limits upon it.[44] This

---

would have testified was not improper external influence).

38. *See* Fed. R. Evid. 603; Gregory P. Joseph, Stephen A. Saltzburg & Trial Evid. Comm., ABA, Evidence in America: The Federal Rules in the States § 37.2, at 1 (1987) (at least 31 states follow Rule 603 or comparable rule).

39. *See* Fed. R. Evid. 603; United States v. Fowler, 605 F.2d 181, 185 (5th Cir. 1979), *cert. denied*, 445 U.S. 950 (1980) (court did not err in refusing to allow defendant to testify after he refused to swear or affirm that he would tell truth).

40. *See* Fed. R. Evid. 603 advisory committee's note; Society of Separationists v. Herman, 939 F.2d 1207, 1215–17 (5th Cir. 1991) (trial court erred by not adjusting oath when witness objected to "affirmation" as being religious statement, even though there was no mention of God in the tendered oath); Gordon v. Idaho, 778 F.2d 1397, 1400 (9th Cir. 1985) (any statement indicating that witness is impressed with

duty to tell truth and understands that she is subject to penalty of perjury, sufficient).

41. *See, e.g.*, State ex rel Collins v. Superior Court, 644 P.2d 1266, 1269–70 (Ariz. 1982) (common characteristic of subject under hypnosis is hyper-suggestibility).

42. *See, e.g.*, State v. Hurd, 432 A.2d 86, 92–93 (N.J..1981) (quoting Martin T. Orne, *The Use and Misuse of Hypnosis in Court*, 27 Int'l J. Clinical & Experimental Hypnosis 311, 317–18 (1979)) (subject under hypnosis experiences need to fill gaps in memory and may create facts; impossible to distinguish truth from fiction without independent verification).

43. *Id.* at 93–94, citing Orne, *supra* note 42, at 318–20 (subject tends to be incapable of distinguishing prior memory from hypnotic recall and to have strong subjective confidence in validity of post-hypnotic recall).

44. *See, e.g.*, United States v. Valdez, 722 F.2d 1196, 1203 (5th Cir. 1984) (where approach is arguably in conflict with the spirit of the notion in Rule 601 that "[e]very person is competent." If insane persons who have delusions should be allowed to testify, why not persons who were once hypnotized? The courts have seemed to focus on the great danger that the hypnotically refreshed witness, who will seem both sane and confident, will mislead the jury. These courts have relied on Rule 403 to exclude such evidence as misleading and a waste of time.

There are at least three possible approaches to hypnotically refreshed testimony, each of which has some support in the case law:

1. Admit the witness' testimony without restriction, treating hypnosis as going to weight, not admissibility.[45]

2. Exclude the testimony, or at least the portion of it that was generated by hypnosis.[46]

3. Admit the testimony, but only if certain safeguards have been followed during the process of hypnosis.[47] These safeguards can include a

hypnotized witness first identifies person whom witness already knew was under suspicion, post-hypnotic testimony inadmissible); Collins, 644 P.2d at 1294 (hypnotically refreshed testimony inadmissible); People v. Shirley, 723 P.2d 1354, 1384 (Cal.), cert. denied, 458 U.S. 1125, and 459 U.S. 859 (1982) (testimony concerning events hypnotically refreshed inadmissible as to all matters relating to events); Bennett v. Saeger Hotels, Inc. 619 N.Y.S.2d 424, 425 (N.Y.A.D. 1994) (extending rule which precludes testimony as to hypnotically enhanced recollection in criminal cases to civil cases).

45. See, e.g., Kline v. Ford Motor Co., 523 F.2d 1067, 1069–70 (9th Cir. 1975) (per curiam) (that witness' testimony was hypnotically refreshed goes to credibility of testimony, not competence of witness); Pearson v. State, 441 N.E.2d 468, 472–73 (Ind. 1982) (hypnosis goes to weight of testimony, not to qualification of witness).

46. See also People v. Clark, 3 Cal. 4th 41, 50, 10 Cal. Rptr. 2d 554, 615 (1992), cert. denied, 507 U.S. 993 (1993) (reversing attempted murder and mayhem convictions when alleged victim's photographic lineup and in-court identification of defendant succeeded her hypnotic session); State v. Dreher, 598 A.2d 216, 223 (N.J. Super.1991), cert. denied, 606 A.2d 374 (N.J. 1992) (noting the "nearly unanimous body of sister-state decisions" allowing witnesses to testify to events that court finds are "recalled and related" before hypnosis); Commonwealth v. Kater, 592 N.E.2d 1328, 1330 (Mass. 1992) (trial court properly suppressed testimony from three hypnotized witnesses with respect to identifying the defendant's car because the prosecution

failed to show that the witnesses could identify the car before their hypnotic session); State v. Annadale, 406 S.E.2d 837, 845 (N.C. 1991) (witness who has been hypnotized may testify to facts related before hypnotic session); Odem v. State, 483 N.W.2d 17, 20 (Iowa App. 1992) (under Iowa law, post-hypnotic testimony is admissible where it is substantially the same as pre-hypnotic testimony); Hall v. Commonwealth, 403 S.E.2d 362, 366–71 (Va. App. 1991) (same; recommends that hypnosis be conducted according to *Hurd* guidelines (see *infra* note 47); State v. Armstrong, 329 N.W.2d 386, 396 (Wis. 1983) (to determine whether hypnosis session renders subsequent statements by hypnotized subject unreliable "there should be a determination of whether there was unnecessary suggestiveness in hypnotic process; and second, court should take into account the fact that some confabulation may occur during hypnosis").

47. See, e.g., White v. Ieyoub, 25 F.3d 245, 248 n. 13 (5th Cir. 1994) (although not mandated by due process, as check on suggestion it is preferable that hypnosis be performed by professional, independent hypnotist with little knowledge of case and that the session be recorded); Sprynczynatyk v. General Motors Corp., 771 F.2d 1112, 1122–23 & n. 14 (8th Cir. 1985), cert. denied, 475 U.S. 1046 (1986) (hypnotically refreshed testimony admissible if certain safeguards followed); Borawick v. Shay, 842 F. Supp. 1501, 1505,1508 (D. Conn. 1994) (court excluded testimony on post-hypnotic memories because the hypnotist who held no educational degree beyond high school, served apprenticeship abroad researching "faith healers," and spent time in Europe and South America as a "stage hypnotist" requirement that the hypnotist has certain qualifications, the witness's recollection of the event before hypnosis be recorded, the hypnotic sessions be recorded, and only the hypnotist and the subject be present.[48]

The New Hampshire Supreme Court has required a validity demonstration similar to that suggested for scientific expert testimony by the United States Supreme Court in the landmark scientific evidence case of *Daubert v. Merrell Dow Pharmaceuticals*.[49] In *New Hampshire v. Hungerford*,[50] the court concluded that recovered memory was not generally accepted by the psychological community, that it is a phenomenon unfamiliar to the average juror, and that to be admissible, the trial judge must be persuaded of its validity, partly as a matter of competence and partly as a matter of expert scientific evidence. The proponent of recovered memory in a sex crime case must show "a reasonable likelihood that the recovered memory is as accurate as ordinary human memory." The Court identified eight relevant factors for the trial judge to consider: 1) the level of peer review and publication on the phenomenon of recovered memory, 2) whether the phenomenon has been generally accepted in the psychological community, 3) whether it can be and has been empirically tested, 4) the potential or known rate of false recovered memories, 5) the age of the complainant at the time the memories were made, 6) the length of time between the event and the recovery of the memory, 7) the presence or absence of objective, verifiable corroboration of the event, and 8) the circumstances attending the witness' recovery of memory.[51]

on tour boats, nightclubs and resorts, was not appropriately qualified; despite fact that memories of sexual abuse arrived one year after last hypnosis session court "could not discount the causal connection between the two"); Haislip v. Roberts, 788 F. Supp. 482, 486 (D. Kan. 1992), *affd*, 992 F.2d 1085 (10th Cir. 1993) (hypnotically refreshed testimony is not per se inadmissible, as long as proper safeguards protect the reliability of the testimony; the opponent of the testimony must show that hypnosis accounts for any differences in the witness's pre-and post-hypnotic statements); State v. Lopez, 887 P.2d 538, 540 (Ariz. 1994) (in aggravated assault case, police officers who were hypnotized could not testify despite concurring pre-hypnosis reports because no records of safeguards used during hypnosis survived); State v. Hurd, 432 A.2d 86, 95–97 (N.J. 1981) (hypnotically refreshed testimony admissible only if certain safeguards followed); People v. Lozado, 620 N.Y.S.2d 32, 33 (N.Y. App. Div. 1994) (where eyewitness descriptions of the perpetrator remained consistent before and after hypnosis sessions and police could not have suggested improperly that defendant was the perpetrator because they did not have a suspect at the time, the state "established by clear and convincing evidence that the hypnosis had virtually no effect on the witnesses' pre-hypnotic recollection" and witness could testify); State v. Cook, 605 N.E.2d 70, 77–78 (Ohio 1992) (if testimony enhanced by hypnosis revealed no new, significant evidence, the hypnotized witness may testify without a hearing to determine the reliability of the testimony); State v. Evans, 450 S.E.2d 47, 51 (S.C. 1994) ("If post-hypnotic testimony is shown to be independent of the dangers associated with hypnosis, [suggestibility, confabulation, and memory hardening] the admission of the testimony does not violate the Confrontation Clause"; a court must examine whether trial testimony is "generally consistent" with pre-hypnotic statements, considerable circumstantial evidence corroborates post-hypnotic testimony, and responses to cross-examination).

48. *See, e.g., Sprynczynatyk*, 771 F.2d at 1123 n. 14; *Hurd*, 432 A.2d at 545–46.

49. 509 U.S. 579 (1993).

50. __ N.H. __, 697 A.2d 916 (1997).

51. *Id.*

Excluding the testimony of a defendant in a criminal proceeding whose memory has been hypnotically refreshed may violate the defendant's constitutional right to testify. In *Rock v. Arkansas*,[52] the accused in a murder case had undergone hypnosis to help remember the events on the night of the fatal shooting. The trial judge excluded the hypnotically refreshed testimony. The Supreme Court reversed, holding that the rigid Arkansas rule absolutely excluding such testimony violated the constitutional right to testify in one's own defense.[53] The Court left open the possibility that a more narrowly prescribed rule excluding hypnotically refreshed testimony taken without adequate precautions would be constitutional.[54] The hypnotist in *Rock* had taken certain precautions, such as making a tape recording of the session to show that the hypnotist did not suggest responses.[55]

52.   483 U.S. 44 (1987).
53.   *Id.* at 57–58.
54.   *Id.* at 61.

55.   *Id.* at 46–47.

Chapter 7

THE HEARSAY RULE AND ITS EXCEPTIONS

Analysis

THE DEFINITION OF HEARSAY [FRE 801]

EXCEPTIONS TO THE HEARSAY RULE

EXCEPTIONS THAT APPLY WHETHER OR NOT THE DECLARANT IS AVAILABLE [FRE 803]

THE DEFINITION OF HEARSAY [FRE 801]

§ 7.01 Definition of Hearsay; Out-of-Court Statements That Are Not Hearsay

Why is hearsay excluded? There are many answers to that question, and this text is not the place to canvass them all.[1] One answer is sufficient for most purposes: hearsay is excluded because the out-of-court declarant has not been subjected to the test of cross-examination. The absence of cross-examination creates an unacceptable danger that the trier of fact will give too much value to the declarant's statement.

There is no need to cross-examine the out-of-court declarant when the trier of fact can use the declarant's out-of-court statement without relying on the credibility of the declarant—that is, without relying on the sincerity, perception, memory, or narrative ability of the declarant. For example, when the out-of-court statement "Help me!" is offered solely for the purpose of showing that the declarant was alive at the time of making the statement, the trier is not being asked to rely upon the declarant's credibility. Nothing is lost by the fact that the out-of-court declarant was not subjected to cross-examination. What is important is that the statement was made, not the credibility of the person making it. Hence, the hearsay rule does not exclude the statement. In fact, the statement would not be considered hearsay at all. The same would be

---

1. For a critical examination of the standard explanation for excluding hearsay, and a suggestion that other reasons for excluding hearsay may also be important, see Roger C. Park, *A Subject Matter Approach to Hearsay Reform*, 86 Mich. L. Rev. 51 (1987). For other analyses of the basis and theory of the hearsay rule, see Craig R. Callen, *Hearsay and Informal Reasoning*, 47 Vand. L. Rev. 43 (1994); Richard D. Friedman, *Toward a Partial Economic, Game–Theoretic Analysis of Hearsay*, 76 Minn. L. Rev. 723 (1992); Eleanor Swift, *A Foundation Fact Approach to Hearsay*, 75 Cal. L. Rev. 1339 (1987); Glen Weissenberger, *Reconstructing the Definition of Hearsay*, 57 Ohio St. L.J. 1525 (1996).

ₙn if the statement had been "I'm alive!" The relevance of the ₋ₑnt derives from its having been made, not by its contents.

Some jurisdictions follow a declarant-oriented definition of hearsay. Under this definition, an out-of-court statement is hearsay if its use by a trier of fact will require reliance upon the credibility of the declarant.[2] Specifically, four factors are usually identified as affecting the declarant's credibility: *perception* (the accuracy of the declarant's perception of the event); *memory* (the accuracy of the declarant's recollection of the event); *narration* or *ambiguity* (the comprehensibility of the declarant's statement about the event); and *sincerity* (the honesty of declarant in making the statement).[3] However, the Federal Rules of Evidence and most common law jurisdictions follow the more familiar assertion-oriented definition. Under this definition, a statement is not hearsay unless it is being offered to show the truth of the matter asserted in the statement.[4] Usually, when a statement is not offered to show the truth of an assertion contained within the statement, the trier is not being asked to rely upon the credibility of the declarant, and therefore there is no reason to treat the statement as hearsay.[5] This is not always the case,[6] but it is usually so, and perhaps the existence of the exceptional situations in which it is not so do not justify departing from this familiar definition.[7]

Utterances that are not hearsay under the assertion-oriented definition generally fall into one of the following three categories:

Statements Offered to Show Their Effect on the Hearer or Reader

If a statement is not offered for the truth of what it asserts, but to show its effect upon the hearer or reader of the statement, then it is not hearsay.

---

2. *See* 2 Jones on Evidence § 8:1, at 159 (6th ed. Spencer A. Gard rev. 1972).

3. *See* Laurence H. Tribe, *Triangulating Hearsay*, 87 Harv. L. Rev. 957, 959 (1974). *See also* Paul Bergman, *Ambiguity: The Hidden Hearsay Danger Almost Nobody Talks About*, 75 Ky. L.J. 841 (1987).

4. Fed. R. Evid. 801 (c).

5. The sentence begins with "usually" because a few statements that are not offered to prove the truth of what they assert nevertheless involve a degree of reliance on credibility. This is true of statements offered as circumstantial evidence of the declarant's state of mind, such as those set forth later in this section. For an explanation, see Roger C. Park, *McCormick on Evidence and the Concept of Hearsay: A Critical Analysis Followed by Suggestions to Law Teachers*, 65 Minn. L. Rev. 423, 427–31 (1981).

6. For example, statements offered for their falsity are clearly not offered for the truth of the assertion, but they often rely on the credibility of the witness. Suppose that X is charged with robbery in Boston and X's wife tells police that on the date in question X was with her in Denver, even though her statement is demonstrably false. The prosecution offers the wife's statement against X for the inference that she lied because she knew X was guilty. Because the wife's statement is not offered for its truth, it is not hearsay; yet in order to accept the inference of X's guilt, the factfinder must rely on the wife's memory, perception, and narrative ability. *See also* Anderson v. United States, 417 U.S. 211, 219–20 (1974) (admitting testimony about false statements made by defendant's associate); Park, *McCormick on Evidence and the Concept of Hearsay, supra* note 5, at 424–41.

7. *See* Roger C. Park, *"I Didn't Tell Them Anything About You": Implied Assertions as Hearsay Under the Federal Rules of Evidence*, 74 Minn. L. Rev. 783 (1990).

Examples

The out-of-court statement, "Do it or I'll kill you," offered to show that the hearer acted under duress.[8]

"Please don't step in that ketchup," to show that the listener had been warned.[9]

"The sponge count came out wrong" to show that the surgeon, upon hearing this statement in the operating room, was negligent in not checking for a sponge in the patient's body.[10]

"Dr. Salinsky is incompetent," to show that a hospital was negligent in hiring Dr. Salinsky after being told of Dr. Salinsky's incompetence.[11]

"There's somebody poking around in your neighbor's garage," offered to explain the hearer's reason for checking out the garage of her absent neighbor.

Sometimes both the truth of the matter asserted and the effect on the hearer are relevant to issues in a lawsuit. When a statement has this sort of double relevancy, a limiting instruction should be given to the effect that the statement should not be used for its truth.[12]

For example, suppose a mechanic tells a customer, "the brakes on your car are bad." This statement is not hearsay when offered to show that the customer had notice that the brakes were bad, but is hearsay

---

8. *See* United States v. Williams, 952 F.2d 1504 (6th Cir.1991) (declarants' statements to alleged victim suggesting adverse economic consequences to victim if victim did not cooperate not hearsay because offered to show effect on victim's state of mind, i.e., victim's fear and the reasonableness of that fear); Martinez v. McCaughtry, 951 F.2d 130 (7th Cir.1991) (threats and verbal abuse by defendant's brother toward third person admissible to show why defendant, who was present, shot third person); United States v. Herrera, 600 F.2d 502, 504 (5th Cir.1979); Subramaniam v. Public Prosecutor, 100 Solicitor's Journal 566 (Privy Council, Malaya, 1956).

9. *See* Safeway Stores, Inc. v. Combs, 273 F.2d 295, 296 (5th Cir.1960); United States v. Calhoon, 97 F.3d 518, 533–34 (11th Cir.1996) (Schwarzer, J.) (held, corporate outside counsel's advice that defendant's method of collapsing advertising into single account was improper was admissible over hearsay objection because not offered to show truth, but merely to show that defendant was on notice that he had reason to question propriety of his action; evidence was relevant to question whether he had knowingly filed false Medicare claims). *But cf.* United States v. Sallins, 993 F.2d 344,

346 (3d Cir.1993) (police radio dispatch call alerting officers to whereabouts of black male suspect wearing black clothes and carrying gun held inadmissible hearsay even when statement offered to explain officers' reasons for suspecting defendant and not for its truth; officers' conduct could be explained through other non-hearsay testimony; moreover, in closing arguments prosecutor used statement for its truth).

10. *See* Smedra v. Stanek, 187 F.2d 892, 894 (10th Cir.1951).

11. Johnson v. Misericordia Community Hosp., 97 Wis.2d 521, 549–51, 294 N.W.2d 501, 515–16 (Wis.App. 1980). *See also* In the Matter of the Marriage of Fromdahl, 840 P.2d 683, 690 (Or.1992) (held, in custody case where mother alleged to be insane, polygraph examiner's reports whose contents were known to the mother, saying father had sexually abused children admissible to show that mother's belief in father's abuse was not an insane delusion).

12. *See* Fed. R. Evid. 105. *But see* United States v. Mancillas, 580 F.2d 1301, 1309–10 (7th Cir.), *cert. denied*, 439 U.S. 958 (1978) (excluding such a statement on grounds of prejudice). For a discussion of limiting instructions, see **§ 2.09.**

when offered to show that the brakes were, in fact, bad. A limiting instruction should be given.

Legally Operative Language

Legally operative language is language that itself establishes a new legal relationship or that establishes a new legal relationship if uttered with a certain intent. It is considered not to be an assertion, and hence not to be hearsay. It is not offered for what it says, but for what it does. In essence, the words uttered or written are not a statement about something, but the thing itself. They create a legal right, duty, power, privilege, or other legal relationship. Legally operative language is often characterized as a "verbal act"[13] or a "verbal part of an act,"[14] though these terms have been avoided in this text because they are indeterminate and because they suggest that speech explaining or substituting for conduct is generally not hearsay.[15]

Examples

"Take this as a gift," to show a gift.[16]

"This is a loan," to show a loan.

"I offer you $3000 a carload for your widgets," to show a contract offer.[17]

"This is my property," to show adverse possession.[18]

"We guarantee the loan," to prove a guarantee.[19]

Legally operative language is not hearsay even if it sets forth the exact proposition to be proved. Thus, "I am making you an offer of $3000 a carload" is not hearsay when offered to show the making of an offer of $3000 a carload. Superficially, the utterance seems to be a statement "offered for the truth of the matter asserted" within the meaning of the assertion-oriented definition. Commentators have reconciled the result with the definition by saying that the statement is not an "assertion" or that it is not offered for its truth because it cannot be false.[20] Another way to view the problem is to recognize that if the courts

---

13. *See, e.g.,* 2 Michael H. Graham, Handbook of Federal Evidence § 801.5, at 208–14 (4th ed. 1996).

14. *See* 6 John H. Wigmore, Evidence in Trials at Common Law § 1772 (James H.Chadbourn rev. 1976).

15. *See* Park, *McCormick on Evidence and the Concept of Hearsay, supra* note 5, at 441–49.

16. *See* 6 Wigmore, *supra* note 14, § 1777.

17. *Cf.* Mueller v. Abdnor, 972 F.2d 931, 937 (8th Cir.1992) (contracts offered to show how much a party had received and paid admissible as verbal acts); California Trucking Assn. v. Brotherhood of Teamsters, 679 F.2d 1275, 1291–92 n. 20 (9th

Cir.1981), *cert. denied,* 459 U.S. 970 (1982) (holding evidence of contract rejection admissible as nonhearsay).

18. *See* 6 Wigmore, *supra* note 14, § 1778.

19. *See* Ries Biologicals, Inc. v. Bank of Santa Fe, 780 F.2d 888, 890 (10th Cir. 1986); NLRB v. H. Koch & Sons, 578 F.2d 1287, 1290–91 (9th Cir.1978); see generally 2 McCormick on Evidence § 249 (4th ed. John W. Strong ed. 1992).

20. *See* Jack H. Friedenthal & Michael Singer, The Law of Evidence 83–84 (1985); E. Kimball, Programmed Material on Problems in Evidence 273 (1978).

were to exclude legally operative language as hearsay, they would render virtually impossible the proof of claims recognized by substantive law. Thus, if the court refuses to allow a party seeking to prove the existence of an oral contract to testify that she said "I am making you an offer of $3000 a carload," the only way to prove the contract would be by circumstantial evidence of the behavior of the parties, something that would be virtually impossible, given that at least one of the parties no doubt acted as though there were no contract, giving rise to the action itself.[21] One commentator has argued that "words need not be hearsay when they have important performative aspects and are offered to prove other acts, events, or conditions in the world."[22] Whatever the explanation, the nonhearsay status of legally operative language is established beyond dispute.[23]

Legally operative language is nonhearsay only when it is offered to show the legal relationship that it creates. If it is offered to show something else, then it might be hearsay. For example, language in a pleading (a complaint or answer in a civil case) is not hearsay if it is offered only to show what the issues are in a lawsuit. When used for purposes of defining issues and limiting proof, the language in pleadings is legally operative. Thus, an allegation of negligence in a complaint would not be hearsay when offered to show that the issue of negligence had been raised, but it would be hearsay when offered to show that the defendant was in fact negligent.

Circumstantial (Indirect) Evidence of Declarant's State of Mind

Within this category are utterances that are considered not to be hearsay because they can be used to show the declarant's own state of mind without accepting the truth of what is asserted in the utterance. These statements would technically be hearsay under a strict application of the declarant-oriented definition, but they are not hearsay under the assertion-oriented definition.[24]

Examples

"My husband beats me," offered to show that the declarant hated her husband. One can believe that declarant hated the husband without believing the truth of the matter asserted, that is, without believing that the husband actually beat the declarant. In fact, a false accusation might be more persuasive evidence of the declarant's hatred than a true one would be.[25]

21. *See* David P. Leonard, *Rules of Evidence and Substantive Policy*, 25 Loy. L.A. L. Rev. 797, 804–07 (1992).

22. Christopher B. Mueller, *Incoming Drug Calls and Performative Words: They's Not Just Talking About It, Baron Parke!*, 16 Miss. C.L. Rev. 117, 117 (1995).

23. *See, e.g.*, United States v. DiMaria, 727 F.2d 265, 270 n. 4 (2d Cir.1984).

24. For discussion of the distinction between the declarant-oriented and assertion-oriented definitions of hearsay, *see* **§ 7.01**.

25. *Cf.* Loetsch v. New York City Omnibus Corp., 291 N.Y. 308, 311, 52 N.E.2d 448, 449 (1943) (holding admissible, in husband's wrongful death action against streetcar company, wife's testamentary statement

"Daddy tried to kill me," to show the declarant's fear of her father, as evidence in a custody dispute that being with the father was not in the best interest of the child.[26]

A false alibi, offered to show that the person providing the alibi was trying to cover up for the beneficiary of the alibi, and hence that the beneficiary was guilty of a crime. E.g., the defendant's wife tells police that her husband was with her on the day of the crime, and the prosecution offers her statement in evidence, knowing that it can prove that it is a fabrication. Her statement is not offered to show its truth; indeed, the prosecution's whole theory is based upon the supposition that it is false.[27]

In an apparent application of the principle that circumstantial evidence of declarant's state of mind is not hearsay under the assertion-centered definition of the Federal Rules of Evidence, a number of cases have admitted drug ledgers into evidence on the theory that they were not being offered for the truth of anything asserted in the ledger, but merely to show that drug activity was taking place on the premises.[28] The theory under which this evidence is received is arguably wrong, since the ledgers could be viewed as assertions that quantities of drugs or money changed hands. If the ledgers make that general assertion, then they are being offered for the truth of that assertion when used to show drug activity.

Another example of cases offered as circumstantial evidence of the declarant's state of mind are cases in which evidence of intercepted telephone calls is used to show that the premises were being used for an illegal purpose. One example of this type of case arises when the police raid a suspected bookmaker and receive calls asking to place bets, or raid a suspected drug dealer and receive calls from persons who want to buy drugs. Most courts have treated these calls as admissible on grounds that they are not hearsay, despite the existence of some conceivable hearsay dangers.[29] Under the assertion definition of hearsay, it can be argued that a call asking to place a bet is not an "assertion," but a question or command.[30]

In another class of cases, verbal utterances have been received solely to show contact or association between two people, or between a person

accusing husband of cruelty to show that wife would not have given husband full comfort and support had she survived).

26. *See* Betts v. Betts, 473 P.2d 403, 407–09 (1970).

27. *Cf.* Anderson v. United States, 417 U.S. 211, 219–20 (1974). Statements of this nature do involve some reliance upon the credibility of the declarant, *see* Park, *McCormick on Evidence and the Concept of Hearsay, supra* note 5, at 426, but this reliance has generally been ignored.

28. *See, e.g.,* United States v. Huguez–Ibarra, 954 F.2d 546, 552–53 (9th Cir.1992).

See also cases cited in Park, *Implied Assertions, supra* note 7, at 817 n.220.

29. *See id.* (collecting cases).

30. One area of controversy concerns whether a statement should be classified as hearsay if offered for an unintended implication of the statement. For an analysis of this issue, see Paul R. Rice, *Should Unintended Implications of Speech Be Considered Nonhearsay? The Assertive/Nonassertive Distinction Under Rule 801(a) of the Federal Rules of Evidence,* 65 Temp. L. Rev. 529 (1992).

and a thing. The typical example is the instance in which, while searching a person who is in custody, the police find the name and telephone of another person. The evidence is offered to show that the two are acquainted. Applying the assertion definition, the court is likely to say either that the name and number were not offered to prove what they were asserting (that a certain person had a certain number) or that they were not offered assertively at all, but rather as circumstantial evidence of association.[31] Thus, the following utterances have been deemed not to be hearsay under the assertion definition: (1) an address book, when used to show that the holder knew the people listed therein; (2) a receipt for rent or goods, to show linkage between a person named in the receipt and the premises or goods; (3) a letter addressed to the defendant at a certain street address, to link the defendant with the house at that address; (4) a name mentioned in conversation, when used to show that the defendant knew the person named; (5) car papers, when used to show a link between the car and those named in the papers. These utterances are not offered for the truth of anything they assert, but to show something else.[32]

§ 7.02 Nonverbal Conduct as Hearsay

Nonverbal conduct can sometimes amount to a statement offered for the truth of what it asserts. For example, when a person points at another in response to the question "who did it?," the pointing amounts to an assertion that the person pointed at was the perpetrator. If done out of court, and offered into evidence to show who did do the act, the pointing would be hearsay.

Under the Federal Rules of Evidence,[33] whether nonverbal conduct is hearsay depends upon whether it was intended as an assertion, and if so, whether it is being offered to prove the truth of the matter asserted. If nonverbal conduct was not intended as an assertion, then it is not

---

31. An interesting example of this type of case is United States v. Arteaga, 117 F.3d 388 (9th Cir.1997). Defendants were charged with involvement in a scheme of drug money laundering. One defendant (Arteaga) allegedly used Western Union to wire drug money from Alaska to another defendant (Arrango–Laverde), who was in California. The prosecution offered evidence of Western Union "to-send-money" forms, used by Western Union on the sending end, and "to-receive-money" forms, issued on the receiving end. Copies of two "to-send-money" forms were found in defendant's apartment. They listed the recipient as "Linda Arce," allegedly an alias of Arrango–Laverde. The trial court instructed the jury that it was not permitted to consider the forms to prove the truth of the matters asserted. On appeal, the court explained the nonhearsay use of the evidence, stating that the piece of paper found in Arteaga's possession

is evidence that he had knowledge necessary to commit the criminal acts. Since the name Linda Arce was an alias, proven by independent evidence to have been used by Laverde in a drug conspiracy, it is unlikely that anyone not involved in that conspiracy would have had knowledge of, or reason to use, that name. In other words, . . . the pieces of paper provided strong circumstantial evidence that the defendant had the knowledge necessary to commit the act, and, therefore, that he likely did commit the act.

Id. at 398.

32. *See* Park, *Implied Assertions supra* note 7 at 817–23 (collecting cases). *See also* United States v. Jaramillo–Suarez, 950 F.2d 1378 (9th Cir.1991) (inscription "Garnika, Spain" on pistol not hearsay when offered to prove that pistol came from Spain).

33. *See* Fed. R. Evid. 801(a).

hearsay, even if its use in evidence requires the trier of fact to rely upon the credibility of the declarant.

Examples

In response to a question about who saw the accident, declarant raises his or her hand. The hand-raising gesture is assertive, and if offered to show that declarant saw the accident, would be hearsay.

To prove that it was raining, the proponent offers into evidence the fact that the witness saw pedestrians walking about with open umbrellas. Because the pedestrians did not intend to make a statement by opening the umbrellas, the evidence is not hearsay, even though its value depends upon the assumption that the pedestrians believed it was raining and were correct in that belief.

As evidence of innocence, defendant offers testimony that after the crime a third person fled the jurisdiction. The purpose of the offer is to show that the third person committed the crime. The testimony is not hearsay, because the third person's act of fleeing was not intended as an assertion; the person was merely trying to escape, not to assert guilt. Note that the evidence is categorized as nonhearsay despite the fact that its value depends upon inferences about the state of mind of the third person (that the fleeing was based upon belief in self-guilt, and that the belief was accurate). The fact that it would be helpful to put the third person on the stand to explore the reasons for the conduct was not considered by the rule makers to be a sufficient reason to classify the conduct as hearsay.[34] The rule makers thought that because the trier does not rely upon the sincerity of the declarant when drawing inferences from nonassertive conduct, the conduct should be treated as nonhearsay. The existence of other dangers, they felt, should affect the weight accorded to the evidence, not its admissibility.[35]

In the example just given, it is conceivable, though unlikely, that the third person's reason for fleeing was actually to draw suspicion away from someone else. Where there is a dispute about whether conduct was intended as an assertion, the trial judge decides the question of intent as a preliminary question of fact under Rule 104(a). The opponent of the evidence has the burden of proving that the conduct was intended as an assertion.[36]

34. *See* John M. Maguire, *The Hearsay System, Around and Through the Thicket,* 14 Vand L. Rev. 741, 766 (1961). For an argument that such statements should be considered hearsay, see Ted Finman, *Implied Assertions as Hearsay: Some Criticisms Of the Uniform Rules of Evidence,* 14 Stan. L. Rev. 682, 687–88 (1962).

35. *See* Fed. R. Evid. 801(a) advisory committee's note (citing Judson F. Falknor,

The "Hear–Say" Rule as a "See–Do" Rule, 33 Rocky Mt. L. Rev. 133 (1960); *see also* Finman, *supra* note 33, at 691–93 (discussing reliance as a substitute for cross-examination). For criticism of the advisory committee's view, see 2 Graham, *supra* note 13 § 801.3.

36. *See* Fed. R. Evid. 801 (a) advisory committee's note.

§ 7.03 Prior Statements of Witnesses

The mere fact that a person is on the witness stand does not automatically mean that that person's out-of-court statements become admissible. To put it another way, the hearsay rule sometimes operates to exclude statements made out of court even when the declarant has testified under cross-examination in the very action in which the out-of-court statements were offered. The hearsay rule, in other words, applies even when the witness and the declarant are the same person. Yet there are many ways in which the witness/declarant's statement may become admissible. First, of course, it may fall under one of the traditional hearsay exceptions. Second, it may be admissible on the theory that it is not offered to prove the truth of the matter asserted, but to accredit or discredit the witness. Third, it may fall under one of the special categories of nonhearsay created by the Federal Rules of Evidence—categories applicable to prior inconsistent statements, prior consistent statements, and prior statements of identification.[37]

§ 7.04 Prior Statements of Witnesses—Prior Inconsistent Statements [FRE 801(d)(1)(A)]

Under the Federal Rules of Evidence, there are two separate bases for receiving the prior inconsistent statement of a witness despite a hearsay objection.[38] The first is Rule 801(d)(1)(A), which provides:

> A statement is not hearsay if.... [t]he declarant testifies at the trial or hearing and is subject to cross-examination concerning the statement, and the statement is.... inconsistent with the declarant's testimony, and was given under oath subject to the penalty of perjury at a trial, hearing, or other proceeding, or in a deposition.[39]

If the prior inconsistent statement falls under Rule 801(d)(1)(A), then it is admissible as substantive evidence (to prove the truth of the matter asserted).

Rule 801(d)(1)(A) is not the only route of admissibility, however. Many inconsistent statements are routinely admitted even though they do not meet the requirements of Rule 801(d)(1)(A). For example, witness statements taken by police officers or insurance investigators are not made under oath or at a "proceeding," but nonetheless are routinely admitted. They are received under the second theory of admission, a traditional theory that was available at common law long before the advent of the Federal Rules. The theory is that prior inconsistent statements offered *solely to impeach* are not offered to prove the truth of the matter asserted, and hence are not hearsay within the traditional definition stated in Rule 801(c). For example, suppose that the prior statement, "The light was red," is offered to impeach a witness who has

---

37. *See* Fed. R. Evid. 801(d)(1).

38. Of course, the statement can also be received if it falls under an exception to the hearsay rule. The statement in text applies to prior inconsistent statements that do not fall under any of the enumerated exceptions.

39. Fed. R. Evid. 801(d)(1)(A).

testified at trial that the light was green. The statement is considered not to be hearsay because it is offered to impeach credibility. The fact that the declarant said different things at different times reflects poorly on the declarant's credibility, whether the original statement was true or not. The opposing party is entitled to a limiting instruction informing the jury that the statement is not admissible as evidence of the truth of the matter asserted, but only for the light it may throw upon the credibility of the person who made it.

One consequence of receiving the prior inconsistent statement under the common law theory, rather than under Rule 801(d)(1)(A), is that the opponent is entitled to a limiting instruction. The limiting instruction informs the jury that it may use the statement for its bearing on the credibility of the witness, but not as evidence of the truth of the matter asserted. Another consequence, perhaps one with more impact than the limiting instruction, flows from the concept that the evidence may not be used to prove its truth. Thus the prior statement, because it is not substantive evidence, may not be used to overcome a motion for a directed verdict. If elements A, B, and C are essential elements of the plaintiff's case, and the only evidence that plaintiff has on element C is the prior inconsistent statement of a witness who now testifies to Not–C, then the defendant is entitled to a directed verdict. The only admissible evidence on the point is the witness' courtroom testimony affirming Not–C; the only purpose for which the prior statement may be used is to impeach the testimony; even if the impeachment is complete, there is still no evidence affirming C. In this manifestation, the rule has an impact even in nonjury trials.[40] If the only evidence to support the verdict in a nonjury trial is evidence of a prior inconsistent statement that can be used only to impeach, then there is no admissible evidence to support the verdict and the trial judge's verdict in favor of the plaintiff must be overturned.

A final consequence of the need to rely upon the common law theory in cases in which 801(d)1)(A) does not apply is that evidence should sometimes be excluded on grounds that the limiting instruction would be ineffective. If the theory that the evidence is not received to prove its truth is taken seriously, then the evidence should be excluded under Rule 403 when the danger that it will be used for the truth outweighs its probative value for impeachment. The proponent should not be able to put on a witness known to be worthless merely to get in a prior inconsistent statement, in hopes that the jury will ignore the limiting instruction and accept the prior statement as true. For example, when a prosecutor knows that the witness will deny any knowledge of a criminal transaction, the prosecutor should not be able to call the witness and put in a prior statement incriminating the defendant, because the statement cannot possibly help the prosecution if used properly (if the jury believes

---

40. Normally, the impact of the hearsay rule is minimal in nonjury trials, because of the rule that even when the trial judge errs in admitting hearsay, the trial judge's verdict will stand if there is enough admissible evidence to support the verdict. *See* 1 McCormick on Evidence § 60, at 238 (4th ed. John W. Strong ed. 1992).

that the witness is not credible, what does the witness contribute?), and can only be helpful if the jury ignores the limiting instruction and puts the statement to a forbidden use, that is, only if the jury accepts the statement as true, as substantive evidence of guilt.[41]

§ 7.05 Prior Statements of Witnesses—Prior Consistent Statements [FRE 801(d)(1)(B)]

Suppose a witness testifies on the stand that the light was red, and the proponent of the witness wishes to put the witness' prior out-of-court statement that the light was red into evidence. The Federal Rules of Evidence do not require that the prior statement have been made under oath or at a proceeding in order for it to qualify as substantive evidence, but Rule 801(d)(1)(B) does require that the prior consistent statement be "offered to rebut an express or implied charge against the declarant of recent fabrication or improper influence or motive"[42] in order to be admissible under that provision.

Prior consistent statements are admissible only when they either (a) are helpful in assessing the credibility of the witness, or (b) fall under a hearsay exception. Sometimes prior statements do not fall into either category. The mere fact that a witness has said the same thing out of court does not necessarily aid in assessing credibility. In cases in which the prior statement is offered, pursuant to Rule 801(d)(1)(B), to rebut inferences drawn from the existence of a possibly improper motive, the statement does not reveal anything about credibility if it was made at a time when the witness labored under the same motive. For example, when a witness is attacked at trial on grounds that the witness is bending his or her testimony in return for leniency from the prosecution, a prior statement made before trial, but after the motive arose—after the deal with the prosecution—has no real probative weight and should be excluded by the trial judge. Recently, the Supreme Court approved this position when it held in *Tome v. United States*[43] that unless the prior consistent statement was made before the alleged improper motive arose, it is not admissible under Rule 801(d)(1)(B). Presumably, the same result could be obtained without this limitation on the exemption from the

41. *See* United States v. Hogan, 763 F.2d 697 (5th Cir.), *modified* 771 F.2d 82 (5th Cir.1985) (government called witness it knew would testify favorably toward defendants, they offered prior inconsistent statements of witness and called several other witnesses to contradict him; because none of this impeaching matter was substantively admissible, and because government's primary purpose in calling witness was to place impeaching matter before the jury, court should not have permitted government to call witness) (modification did not affect issue under consideration here). *See also* Michael H. Graham, *Employing Inconsistent Statements for Impeachment and as Substantive Evidence: A Critical Review and Proposed Amendments of Federal Rules of Evidence 801(d)(1)(A), 613, and 607*, 75 Mich. L. Rev. 1565, 1613–15 (1977).

42. Fed. R. Evid. 801(d)(1)(B). *See also* Gaines v. Walker, 986 F.2d 1438, 1444 (D.C.Cir.1993) (held, in civil rights action, plaintiff's cross-examination of defendant police officer regarding supposed omission in latter's police report is implied claim of fabrication; district court abused discretion in preventing defendant from rebutting fabrication claim by introducing actual police report as evidence of prior consistent statement). *See also* § **7.12** for a discussion of rehabilitation of witnesses through the introduction of prior consistent statements.

43. 513 U.S. 150 (1995).

hearsay rule, on grounds that unless the prior statement was made before the alleged motive arose, it is cumulative and a waste of time, and hence subject to exclusion under Rules 403 and 611.[44]

The statement in Rule 801(d)(1)(B) concerning admissibility of prior consistent statements offered to rebut a charge of fabrication or impropriety sometimes leads to the assumption that unless the prior consistent statement is offered to rebut a charge of fabrication or impropriety, then it is not admissible. That is not the case. Just as in the case of the prior inconsistent statement, a common law theory of admissibility is available, as long as the statement is relevant to the declarant's credibility.[45] One instance in which a prior consistent statement is relevant to the declarant's credibility (even in the absence of a charge of fabrication or impropriety) is the instance in which the declarant made a "prompt complaint" of a crime such as rape. Were the jury not informed of the prompt complaint near the time of the occurrence, it might draw inferences against the declarant's credibility even without attack by opposing counsel. Thus the evidence can be received as not offered for the truth of the matter asserted, but only for its bearing on the declarant's credibility.[46] This limitation on its use has relatively trivial consequences. It can lead to a truly unintelligible limiting instruction, telling the jury not to use the prior statement that the light was red as evidence of the truth of the matter asserted (that the light was red), but only for its bearing on the witness' credibility (in testifying that the light was red). The only effect of treating a prior consistent statement as substantive evidence under Rule 801(d)(1)(B), instead of as evidence not offered for its truth under the common law theory, is to eliminate the need for the limiting instruction.[47]

44. *Cf.* Mills v. Scully, 826 F.2d 1192, 1196 (2d Cir.1987) (noting that prior statements may be excluded as cumulative).

45. The Minnesota rule explicitly allows for admission of prior consistent statements that are "helpful to the trier of fact in evaluation the declarant's credibility as a witness." Minn. R. Evid. 801(d)(1)(B).

46. *See* Roger C. Park, *McCormick on Evidence and the Concept of Hearsay: A Critical Analysis Followed by Suggestions to Law Teachers*, 65 Minn. L. Rev. 441 (1981). The prompt complaint rule (also referred to as the "fresh complaint" rule) is explored in the following cases: Nitz v. State, 720 P.2d 55, 62–63 (Alaska App.1986); People v. Bailey, 532 N.E.2d 587, 590 (Ill.App.1988); State v. Hesse, 281 N.W.2d 491, 492 (Minn. 1979); State v. Campbell, 705 P.2d 694, 722 (Or.1985); Commonwealth v. Stohr, 522 A.2d 589, 592–93 (Pa.Super.1987); State v. Murray, 375 S.E.2d 405, 410 (W.Va.1988); State v. Golden, 336 S.E.2d 198, 203 (W.Va. 1985). The prompt complaint rule is distinct from Fed. R. Evid. 801(d)(1)(C) under which prior identification of the assailant is admissible as nonhearsay. *See* § 7.07. For commentary on the prompt complaint rule see Michael H. Graham, *The Cry of Rape: The Prompt Complaint Doctrine and the Federal Rules of Evidence*, 19 Willamette L. Rev. 489 (1983).

47. In contrast to the prior inconsistent statement, the fact that a prior consistent statement is not substantively admissible under Rule 801(d)(1)(B) (but is instead admitted under the common law theory that it is not offered to prove its truth) cannot lead to a directed verdict or the overturning of a judgment on appeal. The witness has testified in court to the existence of the element that was the subject of the out-of-court statement. The in-court testimony provides the basis for overcoming the directed verdict motion or for supporting the nonjury trier's verdict on appeal. The prior statement merely bolsters credibility for the trier.

Rules 403 and 611 also give the trial judge authority to prevent the witness from reading a prepared statement before giving oral testimony or to prevent the proponent from using direct examination of the witness merely as a vehicle for having the witness vouch for the accuracy of a written report prepared by the witness.[48]

§ 7.06 Prior Statements of Witnesses—Prior Identification Statements [FRE 801(d)(1)(C)]

Under the Federal Rules of Evidence, a witness' prior statement of identification is not hearsay and is admissible under Rule 801(d)(1)(C).[49] Prior identification is often more reliable than identification made at trial, because at trial "suggestions of others and the circumstances of the trial may have intervened to create a fancied recognition in the witness' mind."[50] The prior identification does not have to have been made close to the time of the occurrence; an identification from a photo display or a line-up made several days or weeks after the crime is just as admissible as a victim's identification at the scene of the crime.[51]

As with other prior witness statements governed by Rule 801(d)(1), prior identification statements are admissible only if the witness testifies in court and is subject to cross-examination on the statement.[52] A witness' identification can be admitted at trial either through that witness or through the testimony of another witness who observed the out-of-court identification.[53] For instance, a witness who identified the defendant from a photo display can testify to that fact, and the testimony can be corroborated by the police officer who observed the identification.[54] In addition, testimony about the prior identification will be admissible even though the witness is not able to make an identification in court.[55] Furthermore, under the Federal Rules of Evidence, if the witness cannot remember, or perhaps even denies, having made the out-of-court identification, another witness can testify to the prior identification.[56]

48. *See* Roger C. Park, *A Subject Matter Approach to Hearsay Reform*, 86 Mich. L. Rev. 120 (1987).

49. Fed. R. Evid. 801(d)(1)(C). *See* People v. Johnson, 701 P.2d 620, 622 (Colo. App.1985).

50. Gilbert v. California, 388 U.S. 263, 272 n. 3 (1967) (quoting People v. Gould, 354 P.2d 865, 867, 7 Cal.Rptr. 273, 275 (Cal.1960)); *see also* United States v. Barbati, 284 F.Supp. 409, 413 (E.D.N.Y.1968) (noting that in-court identifications are generally "an almost worthless formality"); *see generally* Annotation, Admissibility of Evidence as to Extra–Judicial or Pretrial Identification of Accused, 71 A.L.R.2d 449 (1960 & Later Case Service).

51. *See* 5 Weinstein's Federal Evidence § 801.13[3], at 801–35 (2d ed. Joseph M. McLaughlin ed. 1997).

52. Fed. R. Evid. 801(d)(1); *see* United States v. Owens, 484 U.S. 554, 561–64 (1988).

53. *See* Thomas A. Mauet, *Prior Identification in Criminal Cases: Hearsay and Confrontation Issues*, 24 Ariz. L. Rev. 29, 43–49 (1982).

54. *See* United States v. Elemy, 656 F.2d 507, 508 (9th Cir.1981); United States v. Miller, 381 F.2d 529, 538 (2d Cir.1967), *cert. denied*, 392 U.S. 929 (1968).

55. *See* United States v. DiTommaso, 817 F.2d 201, 212–14 (2d Cir.1987); United States v. Lewis, 565 F.2d 1248, 1252 (2d Cir.1977), *cert. denied*, 435 U.S. 973 (1978).

56. *See* United States v. Owens, 484 U.S. 554 (1988); United States v. O'Malley, 796 F.2d 891, 899 (7th Cir.1986); United States v. Jarrad, 754 F.2d 1451, 1456 (9th Cir.), *cert. denied*, 474 U.S. 830 (1985).

Admission of an out-of-court identification is independent of the restrictions of 801(d)(1)(A) and 801(d)(1)(B).[57] Thus, even if the out-of-court identification is inconsistent with the in-court identification, the former will be admitted and no allegation of fabrication is required for its admission. The out-of-court identification statement, thus, may be admitted before the in-court identification takes place.

The hearsay rule is not the only basis for objecting to identification evidence. When the police have used a suggestive identification procedure, defense counsel can challenge the admissibility of the identification on due process grounds. Identifications can also be challenged on grounds that the sixth amendment right to counsel was violated because of absence of counsel at a line-up or show-up.

§ 7.07 Admissions   of   a   Party–Opponent   [FRE 801(d)(2)(A)-(D)]

Admissions of a party-opponent are deemed nonhearsay by Federal Rule of Evidence 801(d)(2). The theory behind saying that admissions are not hearsay at all, as opposed to saying that they are hearsay that falls within an exception, is rather abstruse and perhaps over-refined. The advisory committee evidently accepted the following line of reasoning: The exceptions to the hearsay rule apply to admit hearsay when surrounding circumstances provide guarantees of reliability. There are no guarantees of reliability in the case of an admission. Therefore, admissions do not qualify for an exception to the hearsay rule. Nevertheless, admissions have been received into evidence since time immemorial. If they do not qualify as an exception, then they must have been received because they are not hearsay at all.[58]

If admissions are not reliable, why are they allowed into evidence? The standard view is that simple notions of fairness are involved and requiring a party to be stuck with his or her own statement is just. As Morgan said, "A party can hardly object that he had no opportunity to cross-examine himself or that he is unworthy of credence save when speaking under sanction of an oath."[59] One might add that while there is no requirement that the admission be against interest or that the party be available to rebut it, these two features are usually present. The first

---

57. *See* United States v. Lewis, 565 F.2d 1248, 1251–52 (2d Cir.1977), *cert. denied*, 435 U.S. 973 (1978).

58. *See* Fed. R. Evid. 801(d)(2) advisory committee's note ("Admission by a party-opponent are excluded from the category of hearsay on the theory that their admissibility in evidence is the result of the adversary system rather than satisfaction of the conditions of the hearsay rule"). For commentary on the rationale of the admissions rule, see Roger C. Park, *The Rationale of Personal Admissions*, 21 Ind. L. Rev. 509 (1988); *see also* Edmund M. Morgan, Basic Problems of Evidence 265 (1962); Edmund

M. Morgan, *Admissions as an Exception to the Hearsay Rule*, 30 Yale L.J. 355 (1921); John S. Strahorn, *A Reconsideration of the Hearsay Rule and Admissions*, 85 U. Pa. L. Rev. 484, 493, 569–88 (1937); 5 Weinstein's Federal Evidence § 801.20[1] (2d ed. Joseph M. McLaughlin ed. 1997) (discussing theory of the rule on admissions); United States v. United Shoe Machinery Corp., 89 F.Supp. 349, 352 (D.Mass.1950) (stating that admissions are outside the hearsay rule).

59. Morgan, Basic Problems, *supra* note 58, at 231.

gives added reliability to the admission, the second compensates for lack of cross-examination at the time. Since the two features are usually present, perhaps the virtues of having a simple rule justify not trying to make exceptions for the rare cases in which the features are not present.

The federal approach to admissions is found in Fed. R. Evid. 801(d)(2), which provides that a statement is not hearsay if

> [t]he statement is offered against a party[60] and is (A) the party's own statement in either an individual or a representative capacity or (B) a statement of which the party has manifested an adoption or belief in its truth, or (C) a statement by a person authorized by the party to make a statement concerning the subject, or (D) a statement by the party's agent or servant concerning a matter within the scope of the agency or employment, made during the existence of the relationship, or (E) a statement by a coconspirator of a party during the course and in furtherance of the conspiracy.

As applied to individual admissions, the Federal Rule is very broad. It means that any statement by a party, offered by an opponent, overcomes the hearsay hurdle. Use of the admission may encounter some other obstacle, such as privilege, but the admission is not hearsay. It does not matter whether the statement was against interest when made.[61] Nor does the statement have to be made based upon personal knowledge.[62] Furthermore, the opinion rule is no obstacle.[63]

Examples

"It wasn't my fault—the brakes went out." (not against interest when made, but admissible if offered by the opposing party)

"It was all my fault." (opinion, but still admissible)

"My wolf bit a little girl." (admissible even if no personal knowledge)[64]

---

60. The quoted language apparently does not allow admissions to be used against successors in interest. *See* 2 McCormick on Evidence § 260, at 171–72 (4th ed. John W. Strong ed. 1992). *But cf.* Hilao v. Estate of Marcos, 103 F.3d 767, 775 (9th Cir.1996) (in class action by torture victims against estate of dictator, held, torturer's statements admissible against estate as admission of agents; no reference to problem that Fed. R. Evid. 801(d)(2) does not provide for admissions to be used against successors in interest).

61. *See* Russell v. United Parcel Serv., Inc., 666 F.2d 1188, 1190 (8th Cir.1981); 2 McCormick, *supra* note 60 § 254.

62. *See* United States v. Lindemann, 85 F.3d 1232, 1237–39 (7th Cir.1996) (held, not necessary to show declarant's personal knowledge as part of foundation for admission of co-conspirator's statement); Mahlandt v. Wild Canid Survival & Research Center, Inc., 588 F.2d 626, 630–31 (8th Cir.1978); *see also* United States v. Haldeman, 559 F.2d 31, 110 (D.C.Cir.1976), *cert. denied*, 431 U.S. 933 (1977) (stating that opinion rule and lack of firsthand knowledge do not bar admissions under co-conspirator exception to hearsay rule).

63. *See* Russell v. United Parcel Serv., Inc., 666 F.2d 1188, 1190 (8th Cir.1981); Owens v. Atchison, Topeka & Santa Fe Ry. Co., 393 F.2d 77, 79 (5th Cir.), *cert. denied* 393 U.S. 855 (1968).

64. *See* Mahlandt v. Wild Canid Survival & Research Center, Inc., 588 F.2d 626, 630–31 (8th Cir.1978) (no requirement of personal knowledge).

Admissions by Silence

An admission by silence occurs when a party hears a statement and fails to deny it, in circumstances in which the party would naturally deny the statement were it untrue. By failing to deny the statement, the party adopts it.

Examples

After an accident involving Driver A and Driver B, Driver A accuses Driver B of crossing the centerline. Driver B hangs his head and says nothing. Driver B has adopted Driver A's statement as his own admission, assuming the absence of circumstances (such as severe injury, or fear of provoking an attack) that would inhibit him from answering.

Defendant's girlfriend mentions to a visitor, in front of defendant, that they have "sacks" of money in the house. If defendant doesn't say anything, he has adopted her statement.[65]

Sometimes a statement is not an admission by silence by reason of the defendant's reliance on the Fifth Amendment. The clearest example is when the defendant relies on *Miranda* rights during custodial interrogation; but the principle that invocation of the right to remain silent cannot be used against the defendant has been held by the Tenth Circuit to apply even to pre-arrest noncustodial interrogation.[66]

Agency Admissions

The Federal Rules of Evidence remove some of the common law restrictions on the admissibility of agency admissions. In many common law jurisdictions, the statement of an agent was not admissible against the principal unless the agent was authorized to speak for the principal.[67] This rule was sometimes expressed by saying that the agent had to be a "speaking agent." Under the "speaking agent" rule, if a truck driver admitted fault after an accident, the driver's admission was not admissi-

---

65. *See* United States v. Hoosier, 542 F.2d 687 (6th Cir.1976). *See also* United States v. Schaff, 948 F.2d 501, 505 (9th Cir.1991). There, the defendant's sister was being questioned by police officers in the presence of defendant. His failure to contradict her was held to be an admission by silence of the statements she made, such as the statement that she had made entries in a suspicious notebook at his direction.

66. *See* United States v. Burson, 952 F.2d 1196, 1200 (10th Cir.1991), *cert. denied*, 503 U.S. 997 (1992) (defendant's adamant attitude in refusing to answer investigator's questions constituted invocation of right to remain silent, even though defendant did not specifically mention constitutional rights).

67. Kelly v. Diesel Const. Div. of Carl A. Morse, Inc., 315 N.E.2d 751, 358 N.Y.S.2d 685 (1974) (elevator accident, allegedly due to overcrowding; superintendent's statement to inspector that there were 22 men on the elevator not admissible against superintendent's principal because superintendent was not authorized to speak on the subject); 4 John H. Wigmore, Evidence in Trials at Common Law § 1078 (James H. Chadbourn rev. 1982). *See also* United States v. Sokolow, 91 F.3d 396, 402–03 (3d Cir.1996), *cert. denied*, ___ U.S. ___, 117 S.Ct. 960 (1997) (held, changes made to documents by insurance company formed by defendant were not made with the defendant's consent and thus not an admission by an agent of the party-opponent); United States v. Brandon, 50 F.3d 464 (7th Cir. 1995) (attorney responding to subpoena is an agent of the client "so long as important policies concerning effective assistance or the counsel of one's choosing are preserved") (citing United States v. Harris, 914 F.2d 927 (7th Cir.1990)).

ble against the trucking company, because the truck driver was only authorized to drive trucks, not to speak for the company. In contrast, the Federal Rules provide that an agent's admission is admissible if either (a) the agent was authorized to speak for the principal, or (b) the agent was speaking about a matter within the scope of his employment. Under this approach, the truck driver's admission of fault would be admissible against the trucking company.[68] However, a driver's statement about something outside his job responsibilities, such as a statement about the safety of elevators at the company's main office, would not be admissible against the company.[69]

A statement is not admissible against a party as an agent's admission if the declarant, though hired by the party to work for the party's benefit, was an independent contractor instead of an agent. An outside expert is normally an independent contractor.[70]

A number of courts have admitted statement by interpreters as statements of agents of the person speaking, even when the person speaking did not hire the interpreter. Thus, when the opposing party spoke through an interpreter, the opponent's statement was admissible as the personal admission of a party opponent, while the interpreter's translation was admissible as the statement of an agent.[71] In many

68. Woodman v. Haemonetics Corp., 51 F.3d 1087 (1st Cir.1995) (held, in a case in which plaintiff claimed to have been terminated because of age, that a statement made by plaintiff's supervisor, after the supervisor attended a management discussion of terminations, that "these damn people" in higher management wanted younger employees, was admissible against the company as the admission of an agent; even if the declarant was merely a "first-line" supervisor with no authority to make final termination decisions, the statement was still within the scope of her employment, and it was not necessary that she be acting at the instance of her employer for her statement to qualify as an agent's admission).

69. *See, e.g.,* In re Air Crash Disaster, 86 F.3d 498, 536 (6th Cir.1996) (held, airline maintenance employee's out-of-court statement about what airline vice president said on inspecting crash site not admissible as agent's admission because it was not part of job of maintenance employees to investigate or report on accidents); Wilkinson v. Carnival Cruise Lines, 920 F.2d 1560, 1564–67 (11th Cir.1991) (trial court erred in admitting statement of cruise line steward about condition of sliding doors on passenger deck; the statement did not qualify as an agent's admission because the steward did not have responsibility for doors and was not authorized to be in area where the doors were located) (collecting cases); Precision Piping and Instruments, Inc. v.

E.I. Dupont de Nemours and Co., 951 F.2d 613, 617–18 (4th Cir.1991) (in antitrust action, trial court properly excluded statement of employee of rival company, where employee's statement concerned company's decision not to deal with plaintiff and where employee, who was responsible for engineering matters, had influence over which contractors were used but no actual authority to hire or discharge them; held, the statement was not within the scope of employment of the employee of an opponent).

70. *See* Kirk v. Raymark Industries, Inc., 61 F.3d 147, 163 & n. 20 (3d Cir.1995), *cert. denied,* 516 U.S. 1145 (1996) (testimony of expert witness for party in one case is not admissible in later unrelated case as admission of party because expert is not necessarily either an "agent authorized to speak on [the party's] behalf" or an agent speaking about a matter within the scope of employment).

71. *See, e.g.,* United States v. Nazemian, 948 F.2d 522 (9th Cir.1991), *cert. denied,* 506 U.S. 835 (1992). *See generally* DCS Sanitation Mgmt., Inc. v. Occupational Safety & Health Rev. Com'n, 82 F.3d 812, 814–16 (8th Cir.1996) (hearsay-within-hearsay problem in which one level of alleged hearsay was out-of-court translator's rendition of declarant's statements from Spanish to English; court describes various approaches to translators' statements and admits the evidence).

situations, this expansive interpretation of the concept of agency is unnecessary, since the interpreter's statement would be admissible as the interpreter's present sense impression of the statement just made by the opponent.

The common law requirement that the agent be authorized to speak could be construed to mean that statements of the agent to the principal were not admissible against the principal.[72] Thus, if a company authorized one of its officers to conduct an internal investigation, the officer's report of the investigation would not be admissible. The Federal Rules contain no such restriction on the admissibility of internal reports. Of course, the lawyer attempting to acquire an internal report may encounter work product or privilege objections, but the hearsay rule will pose no obstacle to admission.

What is an agent for the purposes of the rule? The most common approach to answering this question involves looking to the substantive law of agency, borrowing from it distinctions between "agents" and "independent contractors," and treating statements by "independent contractors" as inadmissible.[73] The general rule is that an agent is one "employed by a master to perform service in his affairs whose physical conduct in the performance of the service is controlled or is subject to the right to control by the master."[74] An independent contractor "is a person who contracts with another to do something for him but who is not controlled by the other nor subject to the other's right to control with respect to his physical conduct in the performance of the undertaking."[75] Despite the general rule that a person is an "agent" for purposes of this rule when the person would qualify as an employee rather than an independent contractor, there is some authority supporting the application of the agency admissions rule to non-employees.[76]

Courts are split on whether admissions by government agents are admissible against the government. Though Rule 801(d)(2) is silent on the issue and, if literally interpreted, would admit the evidence, some federal authority follows earlier law and excludes it.[77] In 1993, the Third

---

72. *See* Morgan, Basic Problems, *supra* note 58, at 236–37 ("an agent whose duty is to make statements to the principal or master cannot be said to be representing or speaking for him in performing that duty"; hence statements to principal not admissible because of common law "speaking agent" requirement).

73. For an example of this approach, see United States v. Wiedyk, 71 F.3d 602, 606 (6th Cir.1995). *See also* American Eagle Ins. Co. v. Thompson, 85 F.3d 327, 332–33 (8th Cir.1996) (common-law master-servant doctrine provides definition of "agent" for purposes of Fed. R. Evid. 801(d)(2)(D); under facts presented, insurance agent was not "agent" of insurance company for purposes of rule); Sanford v. Johns–Manville Sales Corp., 923 F.2d 1142, 1149–50 (5th

Cir.1991) (held, plaintiffs failed to prove that a doctor testifying as an expert for the defendants was an agent of the defendants since he was merely an independent contractor and not under the control of the defendants). Among the factors used by the courts in determining the agency issue.

74. Restatement (2d) of Agency § 2(2).

75. *Id.* at § 2(3).

76. *See* United States v. Chappell, 698 F.2d 308, 311 (7th Cir.1983) (held, statement by defendant's accountant, who was no longer on defendant's general payroll but still acting as company's accountant, admissible under Rule 801(d)(2)(D)).

77. *See* cases cited in Christopher B. Mueller & Laird C. Kirkpatrick, Evidence § 904, at 34–35 (1995); Murrey v. United

Circuit addressed the issue of whether a police informant may serve as an agent of the law enforcement officer for the purposes of Rule 801(d)(2)(D). In *Lippay v. Christos*,[78] the plaintiff sued the defendant police officer under § 1983 for malicious prosecution. At trial, the district court admitted, as an agency admission, testimony by the plaintiff's witness regarding out-of-court statements allegedly made by the defendant's police informant. The Third Circuit held that the informant was not an agent within the meaning of Rule 801(d)(2)(D). In reaching this conclusion, the court interpreted the term "agent" using federal common-law principles of agency law, reasoning that an agency relationship is established only where the party-opponent personally directed the declarant's work on a continuing basis. The court declined to adopt a per se rule that an informant can never serve as an agent of a police officer within the meaning of the rule; rather, the court merely held that in the instant case, the plaintiff failed to establish that the informant was an employee directly controlled by the defendant. Some courts have gone much further, holding simply that the admissions rule is inapplicable against the government in criminal cases.[79]

Under the 1997 amendments to Federal Rule 801(d)(2),[80] the contents of an alleged agency statement may be considered in deciding whether the agency or employment relationship existed and whether the statement falls within the scope of the agency or employment. However, independent evidence must also be offered on that point to justify the court's finding; the statement will not alone support its own admissibility.

States, 73 F.3d 1448, 1455 (7th Cir.1996) (Posner, J.) (held, statement by Secretary of Veterans Affairs that poor care at VA hospital had contributed to death of patient admissible in malpractice suit by patient's estate against government). *Cf.* United States v. Rioux, 97 F.3d 648, 660–61 (2d Cir.1996) (held, statements of defendant sheriff's subordinates admissible as agency admissions in prosecution of sheriff for extortion; agency relationship existed even if sheriff did not control daily tasks of declarants).

78. 996 F.2d 1490, 1497 (3d Cir.1993), *aff'd without opinion*, 61 F.3d 895 (3d Cir. 1995)

79. *See, e.g.,* United States v. Santos, 372 F.2d 177 (2d Cir.1967). The court wrote:

> Though a government prosecution is an exemplification of the adversary process, nevertheless, when the government prosecutes, it prosecutes on behalf of all the people of the United States; therefore all persons, whether law enforcement agents, government investigators, complaining prosecuting witnesses, or the like, who testify on behalf of the prosecution, and who, because of an employment relation or other person interest in the outcome of the prosecution, may happen to be inseparably connected with the government side of the adversary process, stand in relation to the United States an in relation to the defendant no differently from person unconnected with the effective development of or furtherance of the success of, the prosecution.

Id. at 180. Though *Santos* was a pre-Federal Rules case, it has been followed by some courts since the advent of the Rules. *See, e.g.,* United States v. Durrani, 659 F.Supp. 1183, 1185 (D.Conn.1987) (finding nothing in legislative history of Rules or judicial decisions since Rules became effective that would alter the *Santos* rule). For sharp criticism of the refusal of many courts to apply the admissions rule to government agents, see Edward J. Imwinkelried, *Of Evidence and Equal Protection: The Unconstitutionality of Excluding Government Agents' Statements Offered as Vicarious Admissions Against the Prosecution,* 71 Minn. L. Rev. 269 (1986).

80. *See* § 7.08.

§ 7.08 Admissions of a Co-conspirator [FRE 801(d)(2)(E)]

The statements of a member[81] of a conspiracy are admissible against the co-conspirators.[82] Under the Federal Rules of Evidence, and in most states, the statements must have been made in *furtherance of* the conspiracy and during the course of the conspiracy.[83] To be *in furtherance*, a statement must advance the main objectives of the conspiracy.[84] The *furtherance* requirement means that idle chatter or bragging about the conspiracy, or about the members of it, is not admissible.[85] Sometimes statements about who is a member of the conspiracy may be in furtherance of the conspiracy, as, for example, when their purpose is to induce another person to participate by showing the range and power of the conspiracy. Though the reliability of such statements may be in question, some courts have admitted them.[86] The *course of* requirement

81. The declarant must be a co-conspirator at the time the statement is made. Fed. R. Evid. 801(d)(2)(E). *See also* United States v. Lum, 466 F.Supp. 328, 335 (D.Del.), *aff'd without opinion*, 605 F.2d 1198 (3d Cir.1979) (preconspiracy statements are outside the rule); United States v. Abrahamson, 568 F.2d 604, 606 (8th Cir. 1978) (statements made to co-conspirator by unidentified informant not admissible); *cf.* State v. Stanley, 753 P.2d 182, 185 (Ariz. App.1988).

However, statements made by a co-conspirator during the conspiracy are admissible against conspirators who join after the statement was made. United States v. United States Gypsum Co., 333 U.S. 364, 393 (1948). For criticism of this rule, see 5 Weinstein's Federal Evidence § 801.33[2], at 801–62 to 801–63 (2d ed. Joseph M. McLaughlin ed. 1997).

82. *See generally* Ethyl R. Alston, Annotation, *Admissibility of Statement of Co-conspirator Under Rule 801(d)(2)(E) of Federal Rules of Evidence*, 44 A.L.R. Fed. 627 (1979). The co-conspirator exception applies whether or not conspiracy is one of the charged offenses. United States v. Stratton, 779 F.2d 820, 829 (2d Cir.1985), *cert. denied*, 476 U.S. 1162 (1986). It applies in civil as well as criminal cases. SEC v. Tome, 638 F.Supp. 629, 633–36 (S.D.N.Y.1986); Filco v. Amana Refrigeration, Inc., 709 F.2d 1257, 1267 (9th Cir.), *cert dismissed*, 464 U.S. 956 (1983).

83. Fed. R. Evid. 801(d)(2)(E); *see* United States v. Tombrello, 666 F.2d 485, 490 (11th Cir.), *cert. denied*, 456 U.S. 994 (1982).

84. 5 Weinstein's Federal Evidence, *supra* note 81 § 801.34; United States v. Hamilton, 689 F.2d 1262, 1269–70 (6th Cir. 1982), *cert. denied*, 459 U.S. 1117 (1983) ("need not actually further the conspiracy

... enough that they be intended to promote the conspiratorial objectives"). *Cf.* United States v. McConnell, 988 F.2d 530, 533 (5th Cir.1993) (while "the determination of whether a statement was made in furtherance of the conspiracy can, in appropriate circumstances, be made by reference to the statement alone," the conspiratorial nature of the statement must be "obvious from the statement itself").

85. *See* United States v. Means, 695 F.2d 811, 818 (5th Cir.1983) (holding that statement was "mere idle conversation" and should have been excluded); *cf.* United States v. Guerro, 693 F.2d 10, 12 (1st Cir. 1982) (holding comments not idle and therefore conversation admissible); United States v. Piccolo, 696 F.2d 1162, 1169 (6th Cir.1983), *cert. denied*, 466 U.S. 970 (1984) (holding statement not "mere conversation").

Idle chatter is sometimes found admissible under the "against penal interest" provision of Fed. R. Evid. 804(b)(3), or the state-of-mind exception to the hearsay rule. *See, e.g.*, United States v. Paone, 782 F.2d 386, 390–91 (2d Cir.), *cert. denied*, 479 U.S. 882 (1986).

86. *See* United States v. Watchmaker, 761 F.2d 1459, 1472 (11th Cir.1985), *cert. denied*, 474 U.S. 1100 (1986) (recognizing that "[s]tatements made to a non-conspirator in order to induce him to become part of a conspiracy come within the exception as furthering the purposes of the conspiracy"); United States v. Gibbs, 739 F.2d 838, 846 (3d Cir.1984); *cert. denied*, 469 U.S. 1106 (1985) (statements to induce continued participation); United States v. Goodman, 605 F.2d 870, 878 (5th Cir. 1979) (holding admissible statement made to induce hearer to join conspiracy); United States v. Nelson, 603 F.2d 42, 46 (8th Cir.1979); United means that the statement must have been made before the conspiracy has terminated.[87] Under federal law, a conspirator's participation in the conspiracy normally terminates with his or her arrest for the offense,[88] and, therefore, statements made by the arrestee to jailhouse informers are *not in the course of the conspiracy* and are not admissible against other co-conspirators.[89] Some courts have held that once the defendant is arrested, ending his or her participation in the conspiracy, statements made after the defendant's arrest by other co-conspirators are not admissible against the defendant.[90] Statements made after arrest may be

States v. Patton, 594 F.2d 444, 447 (5th Cir.1979) (statements identifying participants could be "intended to affect future dealings between the parties"); United States v. Dorn, 561 F.2d 1252, 1256–57 (7th Cir.1977) (holding admissible statement enlisting co-conspirators), overruled on other grounds, United States v. Read, 658 F.2d 1225 (7th Cir.1981).

87. The termination of a conspiracy is sometimes defined as occurring after the time of the last "overt" act of the conspirators. *See* United States v. Lewis, 759 F.2d 1316, 1346–48 (8th Cir.), *cert. denied,* 474 U.S. 994 (1985) (citing Fiswick v. United States, 329 U.S. 211, 216 (1946)); United States v. Barnes, 586 F.2d 1052, 1059 (5th Cir.1978); United States v. Sisto, 534 F.2d 616, 622 n. 7 (5th Cir.1976).

88. Wong Sun v. United States, 371 U.S. 471, 490 (1963) ("out-of-court declaration made after arrest may not be used against one of the declarant's partners in crime"); United States v. Postal, 589 F.2d 862, 888 (5th Cir.) *cert. denied,* 444 U.S. 832 (1979). *See also* United States v. Garate–Vergara, 942 F.2d 1543, 1553 (11th Cir.1991), *modified on other grounds in* United States v. Lastra, 991 F.2d 662 (11th Cir.1991), *cert. denied,* 502 U.S. 1110 (1992) (held, statements by captain of drug vessel to coast guard vessel, made before boarding in an attempt to deflect suspicion, were made during course of conspiracy).

89. United States v. Alonzo, 991 F.2d 1422, 1427 (8th Cir.1993) (in narcotics prosecution, trial court committed reversible error by admitting arrested co-conspirator's statement that he still owed defendant, his "source," money); United States v. Taylor, 802 F.2d 1108, 1117 (9th Cir.1986), *cert. denied,* 479 U.S. 1094 (1987); *cf.* United States v. Guerro, 693 F.2d 10, 12 (1st Cir. 1982) (noting each case is decided on its facts, where defendant, arrested for unrelated crime, continued to be involved in conspiracy, co-conspirator statement admissible); United States v. Smith, 623 F.2d 627, 631 (9th Cir.1980) (conspiracy ended as to co-conspirator when he turned informer);

United States v. Smith, 578 F.2d 1227, 1233 (8th Cir.1978) (statements of arrested co-conspirator acting as informant not admissible); United States v. Williams, 548 F.2d 228, 232 (8th Cir.1977).

90. *See* United States v. Smith, 578 F.2d 1227, 1233 & n. 12 (8th Cir.1978); United States v. Mardian, 546 F.2d 973, 978 n. 5 (D.C.Cir.1976) (stating that if the defendant had withdrawn from the conspiracy, "the declarations of co-conspirators uttered after the date of his withdrawal would not be admissible against him") (citing Lutwak v. United States, 344 U.S. 604, 617–18 (1953)). *But see* United States v. Williams, 87 F.3d 249, 253–54 (8th Cir.1996) (arrest of conspirator does not end conspiracy where other conspirator continued illegal acts and arrested conspirator's statements were aimed at furthering the conspiracy); United States v. Taylor, 802 F.2d 1108, 1117 (9th Cir.1986), *cert. denied,* 479 U.S. 1094 (1987) (statements made by an unarrested coconspirator after the arrest of a conspirator can be introduced against the arrested conspirator); United States v. Saavedra, 684 F.2d 1293, 1298 (9th Cir. 1982); United States v. Killian, 639 F.2d 206, 209 (5th Cir.), *cert. denied,* 451 U.S. 1021 (1981) (stating that "a member of a conspiracy continues to be responsible for acts committed by coconspirators even after the former's arrest unless he has withdrawn from the conspiracy"); United States v. Wentz, 456 F.2d 634, 637 (9th Cir.1972) ("unarrested coconspirator still operating in furtherance of the conspiracy may say and do things which may be introduced against the arrested one if the conspiracy is still in operation"); United States v. Marques, 600 F.2d 742, 750 n. 4 (9th Cir.), *cert. denied,* 444 U.S. 858 (1979), *cert. denied,* 444 U.S. 1019 (1980).

When a conspirator legitimately withdraws from the conspiracy, his or her postwithdrawal statements are not admissible against the remaining conspirators. *Cf.* United States v. Smith, 578 F.2d 1227, 1233 (8th Cir. 1978). Legitimate withdrawal re-admissible in some states if, for instance, their purpose is to cover up the conspiracy.[91]

There is a division of authority about whether statements of an alleged co-conspirator can be admitted against the defendant even if the district court decides to enter a judgment of acquittal for the alleged co-conspirator. In *United States v. Peralta*,[92] a kidnapping case, the acquittal of the alleged co-conspirator was apparently based on his defense that he was merely seeking to negotiate the release of the victim, and was not a kidnapper. The case could be read as one saying merely that the exception applies whether or not the goal of the "conspiracy" is lawful, i.e., that if the co-conspirator is acquitted on the ground that he or she did nothing unlawful, the exception still applies if the co-conspirator was acting as agent of the defendant in a lawful joint venture. It does, however, contain language suggesting that the decision turns on the notion that the burden of proof for the exception (preponderance of the evidence) is lower than the burden of proof required for conviction (beyond a reasonable doubt). This seems questionable, since all that is required to let the case go to the jury is evidence *sufficient to support a finding* beyond a reasonable doubt, and it seems that such evidence would exist when the judge is convinced of guilt by a preponderance of the evidence.

The co-conspirator exception to the hearsay rule has led to some complex procedural doctrine. Among the questions that have arisen are:

quires "affirmative action to defeat or disavow the purpose of the conspiracy ... [m]ere cessation of the activity in furtherance of the conspiracy does not constitute withdrawal." United States v. Garrett, 720 F.2d 705, 714 (D.C.Cir.1983), *cert. denied*, 465 U.S. 1037 (1984); *see also* United States v. Hamilton, 689 F.2d 1262, 1268 (6th Cir. 1982) (without affirmative action to withdraw or terminate it, conspiracy is presumed to continue), *cert. denied*, 459 U.S. 1117 (1983).

The arrest of some of the co-conspirators does not necessarily end the whole conspiracy. United States v. Ammar, 714 F.2d 238, 253 (3d Cir.), *cert. denied*, 464 U.S. 936 (1983); *cf.* United States v. Gullett, 713 F.2d 1203, 1212–13 (6th Cir.1983), *cert. denied*, 464 U.S. 1069 (1984) (finding error in admission of recording from meeting held between two co-conspirators to discuss primarily concealment was not "in course" of conspiracy because two other co-conspirators had already been arrested and others were under grand jury investigation).

91. *See* R.A. Horton, Annotation, *Admissibility of Statements of Coconspirator Made after Termination of Conspiracy and Outside Accused's Presence*, 4 A.L.R.3d 671, at § 15(b)(1965); People v. Meagher 388 N.E.2d 801, 805 (Ill.App.1979) (subsequent efforts at concealment are part of conspiracy if proximate in time); Reed v. People, 402 P.2d 68, 71 (Colo.1965) (holding admissible statements made while trying to cover up crime); *cf.* Romani v. State, 528 So.2d 15, 23 (Fla.App.1988) (holding that meetings of conspirators after murder to arrange payments were during the course of the conspiracy); State v. Elam, 328 N.W.2d 314, 319 (Iowa 1982); State v. Clevenger, 733 S.W.2d 782, 784–85 (Mo.App.1987).

For the federal rule regarding concealment activities, see Grunewald v. United States, 353 U.S. 391, 405–06 (1957) (statements made during concealment phase are admissible under co-conspirator exception if concealment is "done in furtherance of main criminal objectives of the conspiracy"). *See also* Dutton v. Evans, 400 U.S. 74, 81 (1970) (contrasting broader Georgia exception for concealment with federal *Krulewitch* rule); Krulewitch v. United States, 336 U.S. 440 (1949) (rejecting concealment as part of conspiracy); *cf.* Mares v. United States, 383 F.2d 805, 810 (10th Cir.1967), *cert. denied*, 394 U.S. 963 (1969) ("acting in concert to conceal the crime and avoid detection" is activity in course of conspiracy).

92. 941 F.2d 1003, 1005–08 (9th Cir. 1991), *cert. denied*, 503 U.S. 940 (1992) (collecting cases).

1. Who decides whether the exception applies—the judge or the jury?

2. What is the quantum of proof for the foundational requirements for the exception? That is, does the existence of a conspiracy, and membership in the conspiracy, need to be proven beyond a reasonable doubt before the exception applies, or is some lesser amount of proof, such as proof by a preponderance of the evidence, sufficient?

3. Is "bootstrapping" allowed, so that for purposes of deciding whether the defendant was a member of the conspiracy to determine the application of the co-conspirator hearsay rule, the judge can take into account the very statements that are sought to be admitted under the rule? For example, if the defendant's alleged co-conspirator said out of court that the defendant was a member of the conspiracy, can that statement be used to show the defendant's membership as a foundation for the exception? If the linkage evidence is not supplied, then the judge is supposed to strike the earlier evidence, or perhaps even grant a mistrial if the prejudice cannot be cured.[93] Whether the judge makes the determination before admitting any evidence of statements or whether the statements are admitted subject to a later foundation, it is still the judge who determines whether the requirements of the co-conspirator exception have been met.

1. Who decides?

In the federal system, the judge decides whether the requirements for the co-conspirator rule have been satisfied.[94] Some states allow the jury to decide. Under this approach, the statements are admitted and the jury is instructed to disregard them if it fails to find that there was a conspiracy, that the defendant was a member, and that the statement was made in the course of and in furtherance of the conspiracy.[95] Even in

---

93. *See* United States v. Grassi, 616 F.2d 1295, 1300–01 (5th Cir.), *cert. denied*, 449 U.S. 956 (1980); United States v. Lyles, 593 F.2d 182, 194 (2d Cir.), *cert. denied*, 444 U.S. 847 (1979); see *also* 2 Michael H. Graham, Handbook of Federal Evidence § 801.25, at 336–38 (4th ed. 1996) (discussing order of proof issues); 1 Weinstein's Federal Evidence, *supra* note 81 § 801.35 (same); *cf.* People v. Montoya, 753 P.2d 729, 734 (Colo.1988) (en banc) (discussing order of proof).

94. Bourjaily v. United States, 483 U.S. 171, 175 (1987) (existence of a conspiracy and defendant's involvement in it are preliminary questions of fact that the court must resolve pursuant to Rule 104(a)).

95. *See, e.g.*, Cal. Evid. Code § 1223 (West 1966); Fla. Stat. Ann. § 90.803(18)(e) (West Supp. 1997); see *also* People v. Smith, 231 Cal.Rptr. 897, 905–06 (Cal.App.

1986) (noting requirement that jury make preliminary finding of conspiracy); State v. Morales, 460 So.2d 410, 413 (Fla.App.1984) (discussing the "Apollo instruction" which defense counsel can request to be given to the jury "that the conspiracy and each member's participation in it must be established by independent evidence," and noting that despite the instruction, the trial court has the responsibility for determining the admissibility of hearsay evidence); Eaton v. State, 438 So.2d 822, 824 (Fla.1983) (discussing the "Apollo instruction"); Commonwealth v. Beckett, 373 366 N.E.2d 1252, 1259 (Mass.1977) (stating that "jury must be instructed that, before they may consider the statements of one coconspirator against another, they must make definite findings on the same questions which the judge must pass on before he may permit the jury to consider whether that evithe states where the jury decides, the judge must exclude the statement if no reasonable jury could decide that the foundational requirement had been met.

2. What is the quantum of proof?

In the federal system, the prosecution must show the judge by a preponderance of the evidence that the foundational requirements have been met.[96] This is in accordance with the standard generally applied to preliminary fact determinations under Rule 104(a).[97] In some state jurisdictions, a different standard of proof may apply.[98] In states where the jury essentially decides the admissibility of a co-conspirator statement, all that the judge must do is determine that there is evidence sufficient to support a finding by the jury.[99]

3. Is "bootstrapping" permissible?

Suppose that the statement of A is offered against alleged co-conspirator B, and the hearsay issue to be decided is whether the statement is admissible under the co-conspirator exception to the hearsay rule. Can the statement itself be considered in making this determination? Before the enactment of the Federal Rules of Evidence and for many years afterwards, many federal courts answered "no" to this question. They required that the existence of the conspiracy, and B's part in it, be shown by "independent evidence," exclusive of the co-conspirator statement, as part of the foundation for the hearsay statement.[100] The Supreme Court abandoned this requirement

dence may be used against all"); People v. H, 449 N.Y.S.2d 605, 609 n. 1 (N.Y.Sup. 1982) (indicating that jury must be instructed to make preliminary finding of conspiracy before using co-conspirator's statements); People v. Pontani, 306 N.Y.S.2d 240, 241 (1969) (approving a similar charge).

For an argument that having the jury make the preliminary fact determination makes more sense in the context of the co-conspirator exception than in other contexts, see John Kaplan, *Of Mabrus and Zorgs*, 66 Cal. L. Rev. 987, 997–98 (1978). Kaplan's argument is that, at least in the case where the preliminary fact issue is whether the defendant was a member of the conspiracy, that we should not be overly disturbed by the relegation of the preliminary fact determination to the jury, since the jury will surely not act on the evidence without determining that the fact exists, since the jury must determine that the defendant is a member of the conspiracy in order to convict. This is true, but from the standpoint of those who believe that the peril of hearsay is that the jury cannot properly evaluate it, then the contemplation of the jury possibly using hearsay to deter-

mine whether a hearsay exception applies should still be disturbing.

For an argument that it is preferable for the judge to make the preliminary determinations of admissibility, see Christopher B. Mueller, *The Federal Coconspirator Exception: Action, Assertion, and Hearsay*, 12 Hofstra L. Rev. 323, 365–70 (1984).

96. Bourjaily v. United States, 483 U.S. 171, 175–76 (1987); United States v. Chaney, 662 F.2d 1148 1153 (5th Cir.1981); United States v. Shelton, 669 F.2d 446, 465 (7th Cir.), *cert. denied*, 456 U.S. 934 (1982).

97. Fed. R. Evid. 104(a).

98. *See, e.g.*, McDowell v. State, 746 P.2d 149, 150 (Nev.1987) (slight evidence of conspiracy required before statement is admitted); State v. Lassiter, 354 S.E.2d 595, 601 (W.Va.1987) (fair preponderance standard); Burke v. State, 746 P.2d 852, 855 (Wyo.1987) (requiring prima facie evidence "sufficient . . . to permit the trial court to reasonably infer that a conspiracy existed").

99. *See supra* note 95 and accompanying text.

100. *See* United States v. Simpson, 709 F.2d 903, 909 (5th Cir.), *cert. denied*, 464 in 1987,[101] referring to Rule 104(a) and noting that otherwise inadmissible evidence may be used by the judge in making preliminary fact determinations.

In *Bourjaily*, the Court left open the question whether the co-conspirator's statement could be the only basis for a trial court finding that the defendant was a member of the conspiracy; in the case before it there was other evidence in addition to the statement. A 1997 amendment to the Rule resolves the issue by making clear that while the court shall consider the contents of the co-conspirator's statement in deciding whether the foundation for the exception has been laid, the proponent must also produce independent evidence.[102] The amendment codifies the result reached by most of the circuits.[103] Some states also still embrace

U.S. 942 (1983); United States v. Dean, 666 F.2d 174, 179 (5th Cir.), *cert. denied*, 456 U.S. 1008 (1982); United States v. Lyles, 593 F.2d 182, 194 (2d Cir.), *cert. denied*, 444 U.S. 847 (1979); United States v. Chaney 662 F.2d 1148, 1153 (5th Cir.1981); United States v. James, 590 F.2d 575, 581, 588 (5th Cir.) (en banc), *cert. denied*, 442 U.S. 917 (1979); United States v. Martorano, 561 F.2d 406, 406 (1st Cir.1977), *cert. denied*, 435 U.S. 922 (1978) (canvassing other circuits); *see generally* John J. Michalik, Annotation, *Necessity and Sufficiency of Independent Evidence of Conspiracy to Allow Admission of Extrajudicial Statements of Co–Conspirators*, 46 A.L.R.3d 1148 (1973).

101. Bourjaily v. United States, 483 U.S. 171, 176–81 (1987). In Bourjaily, the Court did not reach the question whether a preliminary finding of the existence of a conspiracy could be based solely on the co-conspirator statement, as the facts of the case included some other evidence of the conspiracy. *Id.* at 181. The First Circuit has interpreted Bourjaily to require "some" independent evidence. *See* United States v. Tarvers, 833 F.2d 1068, 1078 (1st Cir.1987).

In the years since the Supreme Court decided *Bourjaily*, a number of the federal circuits have held that a co-conspirator's statement standing alone is insufficient to meet the foundation requirement for rule 801(d)(23)(E); in these circuits, there must be some other proof of the declarant's involvement in a conspiracy. *See, e.g.*, United States v. Sepulveda, 15 F.3d 1161, 1181–82 (1st Cir.1993), *cert. denied*, 512 U.S. 1223 (1994); United States v. Gambino, 926 F.2d 1355, 1361 n. 5 (3d Cir.), *cert. denied*, 502 U.S. 956 (1991); United States v. Garbett, 867 F.2d 1132, 1134 (8th Cir.1989); United States v. Zambrana, 841 F.2d 1320, 1344–45 (7th Cir.1988); United States v. Daly, 842 F.2d 1380, 1386 (2d Cir.), *cert. denied*, 488 U.S. 821 (1988).

See also United States v. Castaneda, 16 F.3d 1504, 1507 (9th Cir.1994) (held, foundation for co-conspirator statement must include "fairly incriminating" independent evidence, aside from proffered statement, showing defendant to be a member of a conspiracy).

102. Fed. R. Evid. 801(d)(2). This rule also makes this concept applicable to the issue of the declarant's authority under the authorized admissions rule and the agency or employment relationship and their scope under the agency admissions rule. As amended, the Rule reads as follows:

(2) Admissions by party-opponent. The statement is offered against a party and is (A) the party's own statement, in either an individual or representative capacity or (B) a statement of which the party has manifested an adoption or belief in its truth, or (C) a statement by a person authorized by the party to make a statement concerning the subject, or (D) a statement by the party's agent or servant concerning a matter within the scope of the agency or employment, made during the existence of the relationship, or (E) a statement by a coconspirator of a party during the course and in furtherance of the conspiracy. The contents of the statement shall be considered but are not alone sufficient to establish the declarant's authority under subdivision (C), the agency or employment relationship and scope thereof under subdivision (D), or the existence of the conspiracy and the participation therein of the declarant and the party against whom the statement is offered under subdivision (E).

For a discussion of the wisdom of certain amendments to the co-conspirator rule, see James Joseph Duane, *Some Thoughts on How the Hearsay Exception for Conspirators' Statements Should—and Should Not—Be Amended*, 165 F.R.D. 299 (1996).

103. *See, e.g.*, United States v. Sepulveda, 15 F.3d 1161, 1181–82 (1st Cir.

the independent evidence requirement, requiring that the trial judge not consider the statement as part of the evidence that the defendant was a member of the conspiracy.[104]

Confrontation Issues

Even if a statement fits under the co-conspirator rule, the defendant may still claim that his or her right to confrontation was violated. This claim is unlikely to succeed in federal court, since the Supreme Court has held that neither a showing that the declarant is unavailable nor a particularized showing of reliability is necessary if a statement meets the requirements of the co-conspirator rule.[105] The argument may still be available under the confrontation clause of state constitutions, however-er.[106]

EXCEPTIONS TO THE HEARSAY RULE

§ 7.09 Exceptions to the Hearsay Rule—Introduction

Under the traditional common law approach to hearsay, the question whether the hearsay rule barred the reception of a statement could be reduced to two questions:

1. Was the statement being offered for the truth of the matter asserted? If not, it was not hearsay, and the hearsay rule posed no obstacle.

2. If the statement was hearsay, did it fall under an exception?

1993); United States v. Gambino, 926 F.2d 1355, 1361 n. 5 (3d Cir.), *cert. denied*, 112 S. Ct. 415 (1991); United States v. Garbett, 867 F.2d 1132, 1134 (8th Cir.1989); United States v. Silverman, 861 F.2d 571, 577 (9th Cir.1988); United States v. Zambrana, 841 F.2d 1320, 1344–45 (7th Cir.1988); United States v. Daly, 842 F.2d 1380, 1386 (2d Cir.), *cert. denied*, 488 U.S. 821 (1988).

104. *See, e.g.,* State v. Edwards, 536 So.2d 288, 294 (Fla.App.1988) (specifically rejecting the rule of Bourjaily and requiring independent evidence); People v. Woodland Oil Co., 396 N.W.2d 541, 544 (Mich.App. 1986) (requiring independent evidence); State v. Scanlon, 268 N.W.2d 63, 64 (Minn. 1978) (requiring "independent prima facie proof"); State v. Riggins, 519 N.E.2d 397, 403 (Ohio App. 1986); *see also* State v. Frederickson, 739 S.W.2d 708, 711 n. 3 (Mo.1987) (en banc) (recognizing Bourjaily and noting that Missouri law probably requires some independent evidence in addition to the co-conspirator statement); State v. Florie, 411 N.W.2d 689, 696 (Iowa 1987) (requiring some independent proof in addition to the statement); People v. Montoya, 753 P.2d 729, 734–36 (Colo.1988) (en banc) (statement can be considered in determin-

ing admissibility, but "cannot be the sole basis for establishing" admissibility).

105. Bourjaily v. United States, 483 U.S. 171, 181–84 (1987); United States v. Inadi 475 U.S. 387, 399–400 (1986) (unavailability is not a necessary condition to admission of extrajudicial co-conspirator's statement).

See United States v. Paris, 827 F.2d 395, 400 (9th Cir.1987) (stating that after *Bourjaily*, "Sixth Amendment requirements for admitting coconspirator statements [are] identical' to those of Rule 801(d)(2)(E)"). *Cf.* Dutton v. Evans, 400 U.S. 74, 78 (1970) (upholding admission of evidence under state co-conspirator exception against confrontation clause challenge). For fuller discussion of the confrontation clause and co-conspirator statements, see § 7.67.

106. *Cf.* Arnold v. State, 751 P.2d 494, 504–05 (Alaska App.1988) (listing four indicators of reliability to be established before hearsay is admitted under the co-conspirator doctrine, based on United States and Alaskan constitutions); Nunez v. People, 737 P.2d 422, 424–26 (Colo.1987) (en banc) (citing the two-step formulation from Ohio v. Roberts, 448 U.S. 56 (1980)).

The Federal Rules of Evidence complicated this system of organization.[107] Instead of treating admissions and statements of co-conspirators as statements that are hearsay but admissible under exceptions to the hearsay rule, they treated them as statements that were not hearsay at all even though offered to prove the truth of the matter asserted. Some commentators have referred to them as "exemptions" or "exclusions" from the hearsay rule, as opposed to "exceptions." The advisory committee's reason for adopting this approach has been explained in an earlier section.[108] Whether or not one agrees with this approach, the Federal Rules have become so pervasive that it makes sense to follow the committee's organizing principles. Therefore, under the Federal Rules the following questions should be asked in determining whether an out-of-court statement is barred by the hearsay rule:

1. Is the statement offered to prove the truth of the matter asserted? If not, it is not hearsay under the definition of Rule 801(c), and the hearsay rule poses no obstacle to receiving it.

2. If the statement is offered to prove the truth of the matter asserted, does it nonetheless fit into one of the special categories of nonhearsay described in Rule 801(d), such as admissions, statements of coconspirators, and prior statements of witnesses? If so, it is likewise not hearsay.

3. If the statement is hearsay within the definition of Rule 801(c), and does not fall into any of the special categories of nonhearsay described in Rule 801(d), does it nevertheless fit one of the exceptions described in Rules 803 and 804, so that it is admissible even though it is hearsay?

The preceding sections of this chapter have dealt with the first two questions. The remainder of this chapter is devoted to the third question: whether an out-of-court statement fits an exception to the hearsay rule.

EXCEPTIONS THAT APPLY WHETHER OR NOT THE DECLARANT IS AVAILABLE [FRE 803]

§ 7.10 Exceptions That Apply Whether or Not the Declarant Is Available

The Federal Rules of Evidence divide the exceptions to the hearsay rule into two categories, those that apply only when the declarant is unavailable (Rule 804 exceptions), and those that apply whether or not the declarant is available (Rule 803 exceptions). By far the larger number of exceptions fall into the latter category, permitting hearsay to be offered whether or not the declarant's testimony can be obtained. The only exceptions that require unavailability are the exceptions for dying

---

107. *See* James W. McElhaney, *Hidden Rules*, A.B.A.J., May 1989, at 92.

108. *See* § 7.07. For a critical examination of the advisory committee's approach to admissions, and suggested

justifications for treating admissions as exceptions to the hearsay rule, see Roger C. Park, *The Rationale of Personal Admissions*, 21 Ind. L. Rev. 509 (1988).

declarations,[109] for statements against interest[110] for former testimony,[111] and for statements of personal and family history.[112] Although one might expect a more widespread use of the idea that the declarant should be called if available,[113] the more than twenty exceptions in Rule 803 do not have this requirement, so that one can put into evidence excited utterances, business records, statements for medical diagnosis or treatment, and many other statements even if one has failed to call a declarant who is sitting in the back of the courtroom.

§ 7.11 The Present Sense Impression Exception [FRE 803(1)]

Federal Rule of Evidence 803(1) provides a hearsay exception for "[a] statement describing or explaining an event or condition made while the declarant was perceiving the event or condition, or immediately thereafter."[114] Examples of utterances falling under 803(1) include the following:

"I can't seem to turn the wheel," offered to show that the declarant, who was then attempting to do so, could not turn the wheel.[115]

"There's a mouse in the bottle," offered to show that declarant, who was then looking in the bottle, saw a mouse.[116]

"The license number of that car was FJY 644," offered to show that the license number was in fact FJY 644.[117] (The statement need not be made exactly at the time of observing the event; substantial contemporaneity is all that is required.)[118]

The rationale of the present sense impression exception is that (1) there is no substantial danger that defects in the declarant's memory will affect the value of the statement, (2) the declarant would not have had much time to fabricate before making the statement, and (3) in many cases, the person to whom the statement was addressed would have been in a position to check its accuracy; hence, declarant would speak with care.

109. *See* § 7.51.

110. *See* § 7.52.

111. *See* § 7.47.

112. *See* § 7.46.

113. *See generally* Daniel Stewart, Jr., *Perception, Memory, and Hearsay: A Criticism of Present Law and the Proposed Federal Rules of Evidence*, 1 Utah L. Rev. 1 (1970).

114. Fed. R. Evid. 803(1).

115. *See* Fratzke v. Meyer, 398 N.W.2d 200, 204 (Iowa App.1986) (statement by boy just before being struck by car, "Hurry up there is a car coming," admissible as present sense impression).

116. *See* Hall v. De Saussure, 297 S.W.2d 81, 89–90 (Tenn.App.1956) (doctor's statement while looking at x-ray, "He certainly did take a big chunk out of your spine," held admissible as present sense impression).

117. *See* State v. Smith, 285 So.2d 240, 244–45 (La.1973) (slip of paper on which bystander wrote license number of robbery getaway car offered to prove the license number of the car admissible as present sense impression or excited utterance).

118. *See* Fed. R. Evid. 803(1) advisory committee's note; *see also* United States v. Peacock, 654 F.2d 339, 350 (5th Cir.1981), *cert. denied*, 464 U.S. 965 (1983) (statements made by declarant immediately after phone conversation describing the conversation admissible under 803(1); the underlying conversation was admissible as the statement of a coconspirator.)

When determining whether to admit a statement as a present sense impression, the trial judge must determine, as a preliminary question under Fed. R. Evid. 104(a), whether the statement was made at the time of the event or immediately afterward. The word "immediately" in Rule 803(1) is not defined, and one court has held that the immediacy requirement was satisfied even though the statement might have been made as long as 23 minutes after the event.[119] Another has suggested, however, that 15 or more minutes after the event is too long.[120] In deciding whether a given period satisfies the requirement of contemporaneity under 803(1), the trial judge should take into account the rationale of 803(1), and decide whether the lapse of time provided an opportunity, under the circumstances, for fabrication or memory loss.[121] The question whether the lapse of time also eliminated the opportunity for the person who heard the declarant's statement to observe what the declarant was describing is also relevant. Although independent observation is not an absolute requirement for admission as a present sense impression,[122] one of the justifications for the exception is that the person to whom declarant addressed the statement would often have a chance to check on the validity of the statement by observing the same thing, and therefore the declarant would have a motive to be accurate. Where a lapse of time has removed this opportunity for independent observation by the addressee, the court may consider that fact in deciding whether to find that the statement was made "immediately" after the event.[123]

A statement offered as a present sense impression is not admissible unless the proponent demonstrates that the declarant had personal knowledge. For example, in *Bemis v. Edwards*,[124] the court rejected the argument that statements made in a 911 call were admissible as a present sense impression, stating that the proponent had failed to show that the declarant had firsthand knowledge. It noted that in fact the declarant's statement contained an affirmative indication that he lacked firsthand knowledge of the events described. The court stated that the

119. United States v. Blakey, 607 F.2d 779, 785–86 (7th Cir.1979).

120. Hilyer v. Howat Concrete Co., 578 F.2d 422, 426 n. 7 (D.C.Cir.1978).

121. *See* Fed. R. Evid. 803(1) advisory committee's note; *see also* Houston Oxygen Co. v. Davis, 161 S.W.2d 474, 476–77 (Tex. Com.App.1942); United States v. Campbell, 782 F.Supp. 1258, 1259–61 (N.D.Ill.1991) (call to 911 dispatcher, from declarant who stated that he was in a store that had "just" been scene of shooting, admissible as present sense impression under Rule 803(1) or as excited utterance under Rule 803(2); 4 Christopher B. Mueller & Laird C. Kirkpatrick, Federal Evidence § 438, at 483–85 (1992).

122. It is possible, therefore, that a statement can be admitted as a present sense impression even if not made in the immediate presence of another person. *See,*

e.g., Booth v. State, 508 A.2d 976 (Md.1986) (statement made over the telephone that a woman was talking to "some guy" behind the door admissible as a present sense impression; person on other end of telephone did hear a door open). For discussion of the corroboration issue, see Jon R. Waltz, *The Present Sense Impression Exception to the Rule Against Hearsay: Origins and Attributes,* 66 Iowa L. Rev. 869, 898 (1981) (stating that corroboration by an equally percipient witness should not be required, and that the event itself and the circumstances surrounding it event will often supply adequate information regarding the accuracy of the statement).

123. *See* 5 Weinstein's Federal Evidence § 803.03[2] (2d ed. Joseph M. McLaughlin ed. 1997).

124. 45 F.3d 1369, 1373–74 (9th Cir. 1995).

proponent has the burden of proving by a preponderance of the evidence that the declarant had firsthand knowledge. (In the authors' opinion, the requirement of proof by a "preponderance" may be correct when the exception being applied is the present sense impression exception, since the exception by its terms requires a preliminary showing that the declarant personally sensed the matter being described. However, the "preponderance" test cannot be generalized to other instances in which a showing of personal knowledge is required. As to that more general requirement of a showing of firsthand knowledge, the Advisory Committee's Note to Rule 602 indicates that the appropriate standard is whether there is *evidence sufficient to support a finding* of personal knowledge, not the higher standard of proof by a preponderance of the evidence.)

§ 7.12 The Excited Utterance Exception [FRE 803(2)]

Federal Rule of Evidence 803(2) provides an exception for "a statement relating to a startling event or condition made while the declarant was under the stress of excitement caused by the event or condition."

A core example of an excited utterance is a statement concerning a startling event or condition made while the event or condition is occurring or immediately thereafter. For example, a statement such as "My God! The car is on fire!", made while looking at the burning car and offered to show that the car is on fire, would fit comfortably within the exception. A more difficult example is a statement such as "He's the one who did it!", offered to prove that the person referred to did the act, and made upon seeing the person at some later time. In this second example, because of the lapse of time between the act to which the statement refers and the statement itself, one must determine whether the excited utterance exception should apply even though the declarant was not under the stress of excitement caused by the startling event itself. If the declarant was not suffering the stress of excitement caused by *any* startling event or condition, the exception obviously should not apply. On the other hand, if the court finds in our example that seeing the person referred to was itself a startling event, and that the declarant spoke while suffering from the stress of excitement caused by the new event, the excited utterance exception should apply. [125]

The rationale of this exception is that excited utterances are reliable because excitement suspends the capacity to fabricate. This reliability theory has been questioned on grounds that excitement, while it suspends fabrication, may also weaken the ability to perceive and report the event accurately. Despite convincing experimental support for this criticism,[126] the rule makers decided to retain the exception, basically on

---

125. *See* United States v. Napier, 518 F.2d 316, 317–18 (9th Cir.1975) (brain damaged victim said "he killed me!" when shown photograph of defendant long after event; court upholds admission as excited utterance); *but cf.* People v. Grubbs, 492 N.Y.S.2d 377 (1985) (testimony that claimant recoiled when she first saw defendant in identification lineup held inadmissible, with no explicit hearsay analysis; dissenting opinion cites *Napier* and states that evidence should have been admitted as excited utterance).

126. *See* Daniel Stewart, Jr., *Perception, Memory, and Hearsay: A Criticism of Present Law and the Proposed Federal*

grounds that it was well established in precedent.[127] The question whether the declarant was under the stress of excitement at the time that the utterance was made is a question for the judge to determine under Rule 104 (a). In deciding the question, all of the circumstances can be taken into account, including the contents of the utterance itself.[128] In other words, the fact that the utterance contains words like "My God!" can be used by the trial judge as evidence on the preliminary determination of fact about excitement. As is the case with other preliminary determinations of fact under Rule 104(a), the judge is not bound by the rules of evidence (except privilege) in making a determination whether a factual foundation has been laid for admission of an utterance under a hearsay exception.[129]

The exception for excited utterances is closely akin to the exception for present sense impressions.[130] There are, however, three differences between the two exceptions:

1. The excited utterance exception has no specific time limit,[131] while the present sense impression statement must be made while observing the event or "immediately" thereafter.

2. The present sense impression exception does not require that the declarant be excited.

3. The excited utterance can embrace a broader subject matter. An excited statement by a bystander "That has been on the floor for a couple of hours" would be admissible under the excited utterance exception even though it does not describe the exciting

---

Rules of Evidence, 1 Utah L. Rev. 1, 27–29 (1970), and authorities cited therein; Robert M. Hutchins & Donald Slesinger, *Some Observations on the Law of Evidence: Spontaneous Exclamations*, 28 Colum. L. Rev. 432, 437–39 (1928).

127. *See* Fed. R. Evid. 803(2) advisory committee's note.

128. When the declarant is an unidentified bystander, courts sometimes do not admit the statement as proof of the event due to insufficient proof of firsthand knowledge. *See* Fed. R. Evid. 803(1) advisory committee's note; *see also* Garrett v. Howden, 387 P.2d 874, 876–78 (N.M.1963) (not an abuse of discretion to reject testimony of unidentified bystander concerning speed of car prior to collision). *But cf.* United States v. Medico, 557 F.2d 309, 315–16 (2d Cir. 1977). In the *Medico* case, an unidentified bystander described the license plate number of a getaway car, and testimony about the bystander's statement was admitted at trial. The trial judge, Judge Jack Weinstein, admitted the evidence under the residual exception created by Rule 804(b)(5). The Court of Appeals opinion notes that the statement fits the requirements of the pres-

ent sense impression exception, and speculates that Judge Weinstein may have avoided that exception because of caveats about unidentified bystanders set forth in the advisory committee's note to Rule 803(1). It then examines admissibility under Rule 804(b)(5), since that was the rule that the trial judge used, and decides that the statement is admissible under that exception.

129. See Fed. R. Evid. 803(2) advisory committee's note; *see also* United States v. Obayagbona, 627 F.Supp. 329, 338–39 (E.D.N.Y.1985); United States v. Phelps, 572 F.Supp. 262, 265–66 (E.D.Ky.1983).

130. *See* § 7.12.

131. *See* United States v. Rivera, 43 F.3d 1291 (9th Cir.1995) (held, not an abuse of discretion for district court to admit as excited utterance testimony that victim said at least half an hour after event that the defendant raped and threatened the victim; in determining whether a statement was made under stress of excitement, court should consider not only lapse of time but declarant's age, characteristics of the event, and subject matter of the statements).

event (someone falling on the substance on the floor.)[132] The excited utterance need only "relate to" the exciting event; the present sense impression must "describe or explain" the event. Hence, the advisory committee suggests, the quoted statement would not qualify as a present sense impression.

§ 7.13 Statements About the Declarant's Present State of Mind or Body [FRE 803(3)]

Federal Rule of Evidence 803(3) provides an exception for a statement of the declarant's then existing state of mind, emotion, sensation, or physical condition (such as intent, plan, motive, design, mental feeling, pain, and bodily health), but not including a statement of memory or belief to prove the fact remembered or believed unless it relates to the execution, revocation, identification, or terms of declarant's will.[133]

Examples

"My back hurts" (to show pain)

"I hate him" (to show hatred)

"I'll kill him" (to show intent to kill)

"I'm going to my uncle's house" (to show intent to go to the uncle's house)

The rationale behind this exception is that the declarant's defects of memory will not affect the validity of the statement, since there has been no lapse of time between the condition being described and the description of it.[134] Also, there is a diminished danger of fabrication because there has been less time to fabricate in many instances—although, of course, in some cases, such as that of a personal injury plaintiff saying "my back hurts," there may be a preexisting motive to fabricate.[135]

---

132. *See* Fed. R. Evid. 803(2) advisory committee's note.

133. Fed. R. Evid. 803(3). *See* United States v. Tokars, 95 F.3d 1520, 1535–36 (11th Cir.1996) (in prosecution of husband for murdering wife, wife's statements to other persons about her intent to divorce husband and take away his money admissible to show her state of mind, which was probably manifested to him in some way, thus giving him a motive to kill); United States v. DiNome, 954 F.2d 839, 846 (2d Cir.), *cert. denied*, 506 U.S. 830 (1992) (held, murder victim's statement prior to crime that he was going to see a lawyer about his suspicion that his competitor was dealing in stolen cars admissible under Fed. R. Evid. 803(3) to show victim-declarant's intent and hence to show competitor's motive to murder declarant to keep him quiet; statement was not made in the presence of competitor, but court evidently assumed

that competitor might have heard of statement or of similar conduct by declarant); United States v. Veltmann, 6 F.3d 1483, 1494–95 (11th Cir.1993), *aff'd on remand*, 87 F.3d 1329 (11th Cir.1996) (held, in arson-murder prosecution, trial court erred by excluding witness' videotaped deposition testimony on prior alleged suicide threats by murder victim; testimony was admissible in light of relevance to defense that victim had committed suicide).

134. *Cf.* Fed. R. Evid. 803(3) advisory committee's note (arguably incorporating rationale of present sense impression exception). For an analysis of the concepts underlying the exception, see Glen Weissenberger, *Hearsay Puzzles: An Essay on Federal Evidence Rule 803(3)*, 64 Temp. L. Rev. 145 (1991).

135. Unlike the Federal Rule, the California rules governing statements of mental or physical state explicitly provide for exclu-

The exception for statements of present state of mind includes statements of present intent to do a future act, offered to show that the declarant did the future act. In the leading case on the subject, *Mutual Life Insurance Co. v. Hillmon*,[136] the declarant's statement that he was going to Colorado with Hillmon was held admissible to show that he had in fact done so.

However, the exception does not cover statements of present state of mind that are statements of memory or belief offered to show the fact remembered or believed.[137] Such statements of memory or belief are inadmissible unless they "relate to the execution, revocation, identification, or terms of declarant's will."[138]

A potential objection arises whenever a statement expressly or implicitly describes the intent of some person other than the declarant. Suppose that the statement "I'm going out with Harry" is offered against Harry to prove that the declarant, a murder victim, did go out with Harry, who is charged with her murder. This statement shows the intent of the declarant to go out with Harry, but it also relies upon her memory about what Harry himself said about Harry's plans; the statement would have little evidentiary value unless Harry had said he was going to go out with her. During the congressional process, the House Committee on the Judiciary issued a report asserting that Rule 803(3) should be construed "so as to render statements of intent by a declarant admissible only to prove his future conduct, not the future conduct of another person."[139] In a jurisdiction that follows the view set forth in the House Report, a statement like "X and I are going to rob a bank" would be inadmissible when offered against X to show that X participated in the robbery—unless, of course, some other basis for receiving the statement could be found, such as the rule receiving statements of co-conspirators. The statement "I'm going out with Harry" is more problematic. It is arguably admissible even if one accepts the view in the House Report. The theory of admission would be that it is offered not to show Harry's intent, but for the limited purpose of showing declarant's intent to go out with Harry should Harry come. Under this theory the defense would be entitled to a limiting instruction to the effect that the statement could be used to show that the declarant was planning to go out with Harry but not that Harry was planning on going out with the declarant. Courts have generally favored the reception of these state-

sion "if the statement was made under circumstances such as to indicate its lack of trustworthiness." Cal. Evid. Code § 1252 (1966).

136. 145 U.S. 285, 295–300 (1892).

137. *See, e.g.*, United States v. Neely, 980 F.2d 1074, 1082 (7th Cir.1992) (trial court properly excluded defendant's letter denying any involvement with fraudulent schemes written two and one-half weeks after defendant received letter from government witness detailing defendant's role in insurance fraud scheme); United States v.

Soghanalian, 777 F.Supp. 17 (S.D.Fla.1991) (self-exculpatory statement by defendant who did not testify at trial, made hours after plane arrived in Iraq with illegal cargo, that arms in cargo were supposed to have been off-loaded in Switzerland, was not made admissible by Rule 803(3) because it was a statement of memory or belief offered to prove the fact remembered or believed).

138. Fed. R. Evid. 803(3), final clause.

139. Fed. R. Evid. 803(3) advisory committee note.

ments despite the danger that the jury would use them to show another's intent.[140]

Moreover, one can argue that the House Report does not set forth the proper way to interpret Rule 803(3). To accept the House Report's view would be to reject the common law foundation for Rule 803(3). The leading Supreme Court case, *Mutual Life Insurance Co. v. Hillmon*,[141] was a case in which the declarant spoke not only about the declarant's own intent but about the intent of another (though the statement was admitted solely to prove the intentions of the declarant), and the advisory committee noted the Hillmon case favorably.[142] Though the House Report suggests a different legislative intent,[143] it is only the report of one House, not a statute adopted by Congress, and courts that have given a generous scope to the exception cannot be said to be ignoring any clear statement of uniform legislative intent.[144]

§ 7.14 Statements for Medical Diagnosis or Treatment [FRE 803(4)]

Federal Rule of Evidence 803(4) creates an exception for statements made for purposes of medical diagnosis or treatment and describing medical history, or past or present symptoms, pain, or sensations, or the inception or general character of the cause or external source thereof insofar as reasonably pertinent to diagnosis or treatment.[145]

Rule 803(4) creates a relatively broad exception. In contrast with the common law rules of some jurisdictions, note the following features of Rule 803(4):

140. *See* United States v. Pheaster, 544 F.2d 353, 374–80 (9th Cir.1976), *cert. denied*, 429 U.S. 1099 (1977) (canvassing arguments, and deciding in favor of admission). For a leading case from a non-Rules jurisdiction, see People v. Alcalde, 148 P.2d 627 (Cal.1944). However, some courts will only admit these statements if there is independent evidence of the other person's participation. *See* United States v. Cicale, 691 F.2d 95, 103–04 (2d Cir.1982) (admitting statement); United States v. Badalamenti, 794 F.2d 821, 825–26 (2d Cir.1986) (admitting statement); United States v. Delvecchio, 816 F.2d 859, 863 (2d Cir.1987) (excluding statement).

141. 145 U.S. 285, 288 & 295–300 (1892) (admitting statement "I expect to leave Wichita on or about March the 5th, with a certain Mr. Hillmon" for the truth of the matter).

142. *See* Fed. R. Evid. 803(3) advisory committee's note.

143. *See* House Comm. on the Judiciary, H.R. Rep. No. 650, 93d Cong., 1st Sess. 5 (1973).

144. Nevertheless, it is worth noting that the party in Hillmon against whom the evidence was offered, though objecting to the statement's admission for any purpose, would not have objected to the statement being used to prove Hillmon's intentions, once the statement was found admissible to prove the declarant's intention. The issue is whether a body found at Crooked Creek was that of Hillmon. To the extent the statement was offered to show the body might have been that of Walters, the declarant, it also increases the likelihood that the body was that of Hillmon. Thus, once Walters' statement was admitted, the opponent logically would have *wanted* the reference to Hillmon to be heard by the jury. The same would not be true in the case of the person who announces that she intends to go out with Harry. It is unlikely that there would be any real issue as to the declarant's having gone out; the real question would be with whom. To the extent the statement mentions the defendant, defendant will obviously object to its admission to prove his intention to go out with the declarant.

145. Fed. R. Evid. 803(4).

1. The Rule does not require that the statement be made to someone who is going to provide treatment. For example, statements made to forensic physicians whose only function is to provide testimony fall within the ambit of the Rule because of the Rule's reference to "diagnosis." This result seems inconsistent with the rationale of the exception (that persons who make statements for treatment will be careful to be accurate, since their health depends upon it). However, the advisory committee reasoned that pre-Rule courts would have allowed a non-treating expert to describe the patient's statements anyway, in order to bolster his or her credibility by showing a basis for the diagnosis. The theory was that the statements are admissible not for the truth of the matter asserted, but to show that the doctor was diligent in forming the diagnosis. If admissible under this theory, then a limiting instruction would be appropriate. As the advisory committee pointed out, the limiting instruction would be rather difficult to follow.[146] One could handle this problem by deciding that this type of credibility bolstering is not permissible because the jury could not follow the limiting instruction. Instead, the advisory committee elected to remove the need for the limiting instruction by providing that the statements made to the forensic expert are admissible without limit, on the same basis as statements made to a treating physician.[147] Doctor-to-patient statements generally are not covered by this rule,[148] though they often may be admissible under another exception.

2. The Rule does not require that the statement be made to a physician. So long as it is made for purposes of obtaining diagnosis or treatment, it could be made to anyone—an ambulance attendant, a nurse, or even a family member.[149]

3. The statement need not even be made by the person who was injured or who suffers from the condition being treated or diagnosed. For example, if a mother brings in a child and describes the child's accident from her firsthand knowledge, her statement falls under the Rule.[150]

146. Fed. R. Evid. 803(4) advisory committee's note.

147. *Id. See also* United States v. Whitted, 11 F.3d 782, 785 (8th Cir.1993) (trial court properly admitted government doctor solely retained as a trial witness to repeat statements made by alleged child victim of sex abuse).

148. Bombard v. Fort Wayne Newspapers, Inc., 92 F.3d 560, 564 (7th Cir.1996) (doctor's statement to patient recommending course of treatment not admissible under Rule 803(4), which was not designed to cover statements by the person providing the medical attention).

149. *Id. See also* United States v. Armstrong, 36 M.J. 311, 314 (C.M.A. 1993)

(held, statements made by child sex abuse victim during interview with psychologist and trial counsel inadmissible because statements were made by victim to trial counsel in preparation for trial, not by victim to doctor for purposes of medical treatment).

150. *See* Lovejoy v. United States, 92 F.3d 628, 631–32 (8th Cir.1996) (mother's statement to care provider on behalf of handicapped child describing abuse of child witnessed by mother admissible under exception); United States v. Yazzie, 59 F.3d 807, 812 (9th Cir.1995) (held, parent's note declaring "Step-dad brainwashed" victim and "I ask help, please" deemed admissible in child sex abuse case because the state-

4. The Rule is not limited to statements of present symptoms. If made for purposes of medical diagnosis or treatment, statements of past symptoms ("My back has been hurting for three years") are admissible. So are statements about the cause of an injury ("I drank a beer that had a mouse in it") if reasonably pertinent to diagnosis or treatment. However, a statement that "I got hit by a car that went through a red light" would not be admissible in full because the statement about the red light is not pertinent to diagnosis and treatment.[151] A statement such as "I slipped on a banana peel" is problematic; the fact that the patient slipped on a banana peel arguably tends to rebut the theory that the patient had a balance disorder or was intoxicated, and hence is relevant to diagnosis and treatment. However, one can argue that the statement should be redacted so that only the portion saying that the declarant "slipped" is admissible.[152]

A number of courts have used Federal Rule 803(4) as a basis for admitting the statements of sexual assault victims to physicians who have examined them after the assault, including statements identifying the perpetrator or describing the details of the incident. One justification has been that the physician must treat the whole patient, psychologically as well as physically, and that what the perpetrator said to the victim and the identity of the perpetrator can be relevant to treatment in the broader sense.[153]

ment were apparently made to aid medical treatment of child). Weinstein explains that as the relationship between the affected person and the declarant becomes less close, the statement will be less reliable and courts might exclude under Rule 403 balancing test. 5 Weinstein's Federal Evidence § 803.09[3], at 803–43 (2d ed. Joseph M. McLaughlin ed. 1997).

151. *See* Fed. R. Evid. 803(4) advisory committee's note.

152. *See* United States v. Pollard, 790 F.2d 1309, 1313–14 (7th Cir.1986) (reversible error to exclude portion of medical record relating to cause, though portion relating to fault clearly inadmissible); Roberts v. Hollocher, 664 F.2d 200, 204–05 (8th Cir. 1981) (excluding portion of hospital report, based on patient's statements, that said the patient's injuries were "consistent with excessive force" because statement was a "a conclusion going to fault rather than the cause of the condition and does not serve to promote diagnosis or treatment"). Statements regarding identity of individual responsible for injuries or condition are seldom pertinent to treatment or diagnosis. United States v. Iron Shell, 633 F.2d 77, 84 (8th Cir.1980), *cert. denied*, 450 U.S. 1001 (1981). However, statements by child abuse victim that abuser is member of victim's immediate household are reasonably perti-

nent to treatment and therefore admissible. The key is the need for psychological treatment. *See* United States v. Renville, 779 F.2d 430, 436–38 (8th Cir.1985); *Iron Shell*, 633 F.2d at 82–85.

153. *See* United States v. Cherry, 938 F.2d 748, 756–57 (7th Cir.1991) (in case arising from sexual abuse on military base, court concluded that district court did not abuse discretion in admitting statements of victim to doctor in which victim said to doctor, "He held my arms so I couldn't do anything. He laid me on the floor and had intercourse with me. He said not to tell anyone"); United States v. Moreno, 36 M.J. 107, 120 (C.M.A. 1992) (statement of teenager hospitalized for suicide attempt, that depression was partly due to sexual activity with his stepfather, admissible under exception); Eleanor Swift, *The Hearsay Rule at Work: Has It Been Abolished De Facto by Judicial Decision?*, 76 Minn. L. Rev. 473, 498 (1992) (describing permissible decisions which use hearsay exceptions (excited utterances, statement for diagnosis or treatment, and residual hearsay exception) to admit out-of-court statements made by child victims of sexual abuse). *Cf.* White v. Illinois, 502 U.S. 346 (1992) (no violation of confrontation clause for Illinois to take broad view of its medical diagnosis exception).

The exception for statements made for diagnosis or treatment is only one possible route for admission of statements relevant to medical condition. Some statements admissible under this exception are also admissible under other exceptions. For example, the statement, "my leg hurts" is probably admissible under Rule 803(3) as a statement of then existing physical condition. The same statement might also be admissible as a present sense impression under Rule 803(1) or, if made under the stress of excitement caused by a startling event, under Rule 803(2) as an excited utterance.

Statements of patients that are described in hospital records raise the special problem of hearsay within hearsay. To be admissible under the Rules, each statement must fall within an exception to the hearsay rule.[154] The patient's statement is admissible under Rule 803(4), and the statement of the person who records the patient's statement is admissible under the business records exception.[155] If either statement is not relevant to diagnosis or treatment, its opponents may challenge its admissibility.[156]

Another possible route for admitting statements related to medical care is the special hearsay exception applicable to expert witnesses. Under Rule 703, experts may rely, in forming their opinions, upon hearsay that is not otherwise admissible in evidence, so long as the hearsay is the type of data that experts in the field reasonably rely upon in forming their professional opinions.[157] Thus, experts may rely upon the statements of patients and their families in making a diagnosis and testifying to an expert opinion based upon the hearsay. However, there is case law supporting the position that Rule 703, while it may allow an expert to rely upon hearsay, does not necessarily allow the expert to repeat the hearsay statements.[158] Thus, according to some courts, while

Compare Ring v. Erickson, 983 F.2d 818, 819–20 (8th Cir.1992) (held, admission of videotaped interview between alleged child victim of sexual abuse and physician violated defendant's rights under the confrontation clause; government failed to establish reliability of victim's statement where victim's mother, not victim, sought medical treatment, where victim did not realize she spoke with a doctor, and where victim's statements lacked "particularized guarantees of trustworthiness"); State v. Haslam, 663 A.2d 902, 908 (R.I.1995) (held, a prior statement by a counselor, who testified that a minor patient had previously identified the defendant as her molester, was inadmissible as a prior consistent statement because the prior statement was not made before the motive to lie arose).

For an especially expansive interpretation of the medical treatment exception in sex abuse cases, see United States v. Yazzie, 59 F.3d 807, 812 (9th Cir.1995) (held, although statements assigning blame for an injury are not normally admissible under the medical treatment exception, they are admissible in sexual abuse cases because the physician must treat emotional as well as physical injuries; in this case, a parent's note declaring "Step-dad brainwashed" victim and "I ask help, please" was apparently made to aid medical treatment of child). *See also* United States v. Tome, 1995 WL 448878 (10th Cir.1995) (10th Circuit decision following Supreme Court reversal and remand) (held, sexual abuse victim's out-of-court statements to three pediatricians identifying her father as her abuser were properly admitted under Fed. R. Evid. 803(4) as reasonably pertinent to the victim's treatment or diagnosis).

154. Fed. R. Evid. 805.

155. *See* Fed. R. Evid. 803(6).

156. *See* § **7.27.**

157. *See* § **10.08.**

158. *See, e.g.,* Rose Hall, Ltd. v. Chase Manhattan Overseas Banking Corp., 576 F.Supp. 107, 158 (D.Del.1983), *affd,* 740

the expert may rely on the hearsay in forming an opinion, the hearsay is not itself rendered admissible in evidence.

§ 7.15 Past Recollection Recorded [FRE 803(5)]

Federal Rule of Evidence 803(5) provides a hearsay exception for:

A memorandum or record concerning matter about which a witness once had knowledge but has insufficient recollection to enable the witness to testify fully and accurately, shown to have been made or adopted by the witness when the matter was fresh in the witness' memory and to reflect that knowledge correctly. If admitted, the memorandum or record may be read into evidence but may not itself be received as an exhibit unless offered by an adverse party.

This exception allows a writing or recording to be received for the truth of its contents.[159] The rationale for Rule 803(5) is threefold: (1) necessity—the witness has insufficient memory to testify fully and accurately; (2) trustworthiness—the memorandum or report was made while the matter was fresh in the witness' memory and was embodied in a writing or recording;[160] and (3) opportunity for cross-examination of the witness—a witness who made or adopted the memorandum is available for testimony.

The foundational requirements of the past recollection recorded exception must be satisfied before a writing or recording may be received as substantive evidence.[161] Rule 803(5) requires that: (1) the witness once had sufficient personal knowledge of the underlying events to meet the

F.2d 958 (3d Cir. 1984), *cert. denied*, 469 U.S. 1159 (1985) (holding that while expert on value of land could base opinion partly on information gleaned from telephone conversation with surveyor, the expert could not repeat the contents of the conversation); State v. Towne, 453 A.2d 1133 (Vt. 1982) (excluding testimony by expert witness that he had talked to author of learned treatise and that author agreed with him). *See also* Gacy v. Welborn, 994 F.2d 305, 315–16 (7th Cir.), *cert. denied*, 510 U.S. 899 (1993) (trial court properly excluded as hearsay testimony by psychiatrists and psychologists repeating murder defendant's comments, but allowed experts to paraphrase defendant's remarks). *See generally* Ronald L. Carlson, *Experts, Judges, and Commentators: The Underlying Debate About an Expert's Underlying Data*, 47 Mercer L. Rev. 481 (1996); Ronald L. Carlson, *Policing the Bases of Modern Expert Testimony*, 39 Vand. L. Rev. 577, 584 & n.23 (1986); Ronald L. Carlson, *Collision Course in Expert Testimony: Limitations on Affirmative Introduction of Underlying Data*, 36 U. Fla. L. Rev. 234 (1984).

159. *See, e.g.*, 5 Weinstein's Federal Evidence § 803.10[1] (2d ed. Joseph M. McLaughlin ed. 1997).

160. Note that the witness does not have to make the record. A record adopted while the matter was fresh in the witness' mind may be admissible under Rule 803(5). Moreover, the advisory comments to Rule 803(5) state that multiple person involvement in the process of observing and recording is entirely consistent with the exception. Fed. R. Evid. 803(5) advisory committee's note.

161. *See, e.g.*, United States v. Riccardi, 174 F.2d 883 (3d Cir.), *cert. denied*, 337 U.S. 941 (1949). The Third Circuit stated:

[W]hether the record is directly admitted into evidence, or indirectly by the permissive parroting of the witness, it is nevertheless a substitute for his memory and is offered for the truth of its contents. It assumes a distinct significance as an independent probative force, and is therefore ordinarily required to meet certain standards. These requirements are [necessary because] the court is . . . determining whether the writing may be safely received as a substitute for the witness' memory and for the truth of the matter asserted.

Id. at 887–88 (footnotes omitted).

personal knowledge requirement of Rule 602 if testifying about these matters; (2) the record was made when the matter was fresh in the witness' memory; (3) the record accurately reflects the witness' knowledge;[162] (4) the witness cannot testify from present memory[163] (counsel must lay the foundation showing lack of present memory because if the witness has a present memory of the facts recited in the record, the witness' memory is considered superior to the hearsay record);[164] and (5) the testifying witness "made or adopted" the record. The "made or adopted" requirement of Rule 803(5) would seem to require that the person whose recollection has been recorded either make the record or examine and approve it. However, that interpretation of the rule has not been universal.[165]

Counsel opposing the admission of a past recollection recorded should challenge the memorandum's foundation under Rule 803(5). Once

---

162. *See* United States v. Edwards, 539 F.2d 689 (9th Cir.), *cert. denied*, 429 U.S. 984 (1976) (concluding that declarant's intoxication at time he made statement bears heavily on weight to be given statement, but not on its admissibility where declarant testified that he believed the statement accurately reflected his recollection at the time it was made, statement was signed and acknowledged by declarant, and government agent who was present at the interview testified that declarant's answers were "fairly detailed narrations"). *Cf.* United States v. Porter, 986 F.2d 1014, 1017 (6th Cir.), *cert. denied*, 510 U.S. 933 (1993) (at trial, defendant's girlfriend repudiated her prior statement implicating defendant, claiming she was confused and on drugs when statement was made; held, statement admissible because, among other things, witness signed and made corrections to statement immediately after events giving rise to prosecution).

Rule 803(5) attempts to ensure that the witness accurately recorded his knowledge when the witness remembered what he perceived. 5 Weinstein's Federal Evidence, *supra* note 159 § 803.10[4[c], at 803–52 to 803–53. A witness who does not remember the facts recorded cannot be cross-examined about his or her perception and, thus, direct testimony about what the witness perceived cannot be obtained. A criminal defendant may claim that the confrontation clause is violated if the witness has no recollection about the underlying event because the witness' perception cannot adequately be tested by cross-examination. *See* California v. Green, 399 U.S. 149, 155 (1970) (recognizing that hearsay exceptions and the confrontation clause are not necessarily congruent and expressing doubts about the constitutionality of the overlap between hearsay exceptions and the Sixth Amend-

ment); *But see* United States v. Kelly, 349 F.2d 720, 770 (2d Cir.1965), *cert. denied*, 384 U.S. 947 (1966) (stating that virtually all of the hearsay exceptions, including the past recollection recorded, do not involve any deprivation of the defendant's right of confrontation under the sixth amendment).

163. *See, e.g.,* United States v. Felix–Jerez, 667 F.2d 1297, 1300 (9th Cir.1982) (error to admit marshal's written statement based on his notes of an interview with defendant where there was no showing marshal had insufficient recollection to testify); United States v. Judon, 567 F.2d 1289, 1294 (5th Cir.1978) (error to admit statement under Rule 803(5) where there was no showing of witness' insufficient recollection). Thus, the proponent of a recorded recollection must show that the witness' memory was not refreshed by the record.

164. *See* Meder v. Everest & Jennings, Inc., 637 F.2d 1182, 1185–86 (8th Cir.1981) (police report that contained information officer did not personally know but obtained from someone else constituted hearsay within hearsay and was not admissible under Rule 803(5)).

165. *See* Boehmer v. LeBoeuf, 650 A.2d 1336 (Me.1994), which, in interpreting a Maine rule identical in wording to Fed. R. Evid. 803(5), stated that a person whose recollection is recorded by another in a "jointly produced past recollection recorded" need not have physically adopted or verified the record in order for the exception to apply. Under the facts of the case before it, however, the court held that the trial court did not abuse its discretion in excluding an investigator's notes of a child witness' recollection of the accident made two months after the accident, because it was reasonable for the court to find that there had not been a sufficient showing that the notes were accurate when made.

counsel establishes a document's foundation under Rule 803(5), it may be read into evidence but cannot be received as an exhibit or sent to the jury unless offered by the opposing party.[166] The rationale for limiting the admission of a recorded recollection is that the memorandum is a substitute for oral testimony, and offering the memorandum into evidence may encourage the jury to give it undue emphasis in relation to other oral testimony.[167]

Establishing the Foundation for a Past Recollection Recorded

Suppose a case in which counsel's witness is expected to testify about the contents of a warehouse, but on the stand the witness cannot remember everything that was in the warehouse. Counsel attempts to proceed as follows with a list of what was in the warehouse:

Q: I show you plaintiff's Exhibit 1. What is it?

A: A list of the items in the warehouse.

Q: Now, please tell us what was in the warehouse.

A: [Witness reads list]

This procedure is objectionable and the witness should not be permitted to read from the list because the foundational requirements of Rule 803(5) have not been satisfied.

To present the testimony in admissible form:

1. After showing the witness the list, have the witness testify that the witness' memory is not refreshed. Although the witness' recollection must be impaired, it need not be wholly exhausted before the record is admissible as evidence.[168] If the witness' memory is refreshed, take the list back and proceed to question the witness about the items in the warehouse. Testimony of a witness who can recollect the events recited in the record does not have to satisfy Rule 803(5) because the witness is testifying

---

166. *See, e.g.*, United States v. Ray, 768 F.2d 991, 995 (8th Cir.1985) (recognizing transcript of defendant's prior attorney's statement was properly admitted under Rule 803(5), but holding admission of transcript as an exhibit constituted reversible error where the statement was the only evidence on a crucial element of the charged offense).

167. *See* Jack R. Jelsema *et al.*, Comment, *Hearsay Under the Proposed Federal Rules: A Discretionary Approach*, 15 Wayne L. Rev. 1077, 1139 (1969).

168. A judge should admit pertinent portions of a recorded recollection which fail to refresh the witness' present memory. *See, e.g.*, United States v. Williams, 571 F.2d 344 (6th Cir.), *cert. denied*, 439 U.S. 841 (1978) (admitting statement made to

government agent with where witness' memory sufficient to testify generally about his conversations with defendant but did not recall whether defendant told him how the defendant acquired the forged government checks); United States v. Senak, 527 F.2d 129, 137–38 (7th Cir.1975), *cert. denied*, 425 U.S. 907 (1976) (admitting statement made to FBI agent where witness told part of conversation and cannot remember the rest); Fortier v. Dona Anna Plaza Partners, 747 F.2d 1324, 1332 (10th Cir.1984) (admitting subsurface report referred to by an expert witness in a negligent construction case as the recorded recollection of an expert witness as it enabled the expert to testify fully and accurately).

from present memory and is not putting the contents of a hearsay record into evidence.

2. After showing the witness the list, have the witness testify:

a. The witness made or adopted the list;

b. The list was made when the witness' memory of the warehouse's contents was fresh. Many factors affect whether the matter was sufficiently fresh to guarantee the memory's trustworthiness: time when list was made, quality of memory in the list, and whether the list was made before litigation commenced. Under Rule 803(5), courts have discretion to expand the concept of "freshness";[169]

c. The list was accurate when made;

d. The witness does not now remember what was in the warehouse. Although the witness cannot remember the warehouse's contents, the witness can remember being careful in making the list of items. The witness must testify either that the witness recalls making an accurate list or that, although the witness does not specifically recollect the witness' state of mind when making the list, the witness would not have made it unless it were correct.[170]

Now, the list may be read into evidence but is not received as an exhibit unless offered by the adverse party.

Refreshing Memory

The technique of refreshing a witness' memory[171] is sometimes confused with the hearsay exception for past recollection recorded. The Third Circuit described the distinction between refreshing memory and past recollection recorded in *United States v. Riccardi*:[172]

The primary difference between the two classifications is the ability of the witness to testify from present knowledge; where the witness' memory is revived, and he presently recollects the facts and swears to them, he is obviously in a different position from the witness who cannot directly state the facts from present memory and who must ask the court to accept a writing for the truth of its contents because

---

169. *See, e.g.,* United States v. Patterson, 678 F.2d 774, 778 (9th Cir.), *cert. denied*, 459 U.S. 911 (1982) (holding trial judge's finding, that witness' memory was fresh at the time he testified before grand jury about his conversation with defendant although 10 months elapsed between the conversation and grand jury appearance, did not abuse the broad discretion intended by Rule 803(5)); see 5 Weinstein's Federal Evidence, *supra* note 159 § 803.10[4][b], at 803–51 to 803–52.

170. *See, e.g.,* 3 John H. Wigmore, Evidence in Trials at Common Law § 747 (James H. Chadbourn rev. 1970) (stating that "the witness must be able now to assert that the record accurately represented (the witness') knowledge at the time . . . the witness [must] affirm that [he] knew it to be true at the time").

171. *See* § 1.06.

172. 174 F.2d 883 (3d Cir.), *cert. denied*, 337 U.S. 941 (1949).

he is willing to swear, for one reason or another, that its contents are true.[173]

One of the consequences of the concept that documents used to refresh memory are not evidence is that otherwise inadmissible documents may be used to refresh memory. For example, if a state statute provides that accident reports are inadmissible, counsel can still use the accident report to refresh the memory of a witness on the stand.[174] Because the report is not being used as evidence, and the witness is on the stand at the trial or hearing, the hearsay rule is not implicated.

The differences between refreshing memory and using a writing as past recollection recorded are:

1. Counsel can use anything to stimulate or refresh the witness' memory, regardless of whether the thing was prepared by the witness or somebody else. The stimulant need not be a writing; it may be anything that might help to jog the witness' memory.

2. The witness' memory must actually be refreshed before the witness can testify; the witness must testify independently from memory because the witness cannot read from a writing on the witness stand without first satisfying Rule 803(5).

3. A writing or recording used to refresh the witness' memory is not admissible into evidence, unless the opponent offers it.

4. The witness does not have to testify that the document is accurate because the document is only being used to awaken the witness' memory, not as evidence, (note: if counsel uses the witness' notes to refresh memory and the notes differ from the witness' testimony, opposing counsel can use the notes to impeach the witness under Rule 612).

§ 7.16   The Business Records Exception [FRE 803(6)]

Federal Rule of Evidence 803(6) creates an exception for

[a] memorandum, report, record, or data compilation, in any form, of acts, events, conditions, opinions, or diagnoses, made at or near the time by, or from information transmitted by, a person with knowledge, if kept in the course of a regularly conducted business activity, and if it was the regular practice of that business activity to make the memorandum, report, record, or data compilation, all as shown by the testimony of the custodian or other qualified witness, unless the source of information or the method or circumstances of preparation indicate lack of trustworthiness. The term "business" as used in this paragraph includes business, institution, association,

---

173. *Id.* at 886 (footnote omitted). *See* United States v. Rinke, 778 F.2d 581, 587–88 (10th Cir.1985) (holding trial judge properly permitted witness to use notes of telephone conversations with defendants to refresh his memory while testifying).

174. *See, e.g.,* State v. Schultz, 392 N.W.2d 305, 307 (Minn.App.1986) (recognizing that use of accident report to refresh a police officer's memory while testifying to facts within his knowledge permitted although report inadmissible under state statute).

profession, occupation, and calling of every kind, whether or not conducted for profit.[175]

The rationale of the business records exception is that there is a motive to be accurate for the business' sake; that regularity breeds habits of precision; that systematic checking is likely, and careless employees may be fired. Furthermore, it would be impractical to have each employee who participated in the creation of a business record testify in court.[176]

§ 7.17 The Business Records Exception [FRE 803(6)]— Regular Practice of the Business

Part of laying the foundation for a business record is showing that the record was made in the course of a regularly conducted business activity and that it was the regular practice of that business activity to make the record.[177] Occasionally, a record made in the course of business will be rejected on the ground that the proponent failed to demonstrate that it was the "regular practice" to make such records. For example, in *United States v. Freidin*,[178] the defendant, a tax partner in a large accounting firm, was charged with filing false income tax returns and making a false statement to the IRS in connection with those returns. The defendant received a substantial fee from a client, which he allegedly deposited in his personal account at his firm without reporting the fee on his income taxes. During his IRS audit, he claimed to have turned over the fee to his firm. One of the crucial pieces of government evidence was an internal office memorandum of the accounting firm memorializing Freidin's directive to place the fee in his own personal account. The memo, which was prepared by the secretary to the controller, stated that

175. Fed. R. Evid. 803(6). Note that the quoted language includes "opinions" and "diagnoses." Despite this language, opinions in business records are sometimes excluded. *See* § **7.27.** *See also* Vance v. Peters, 97 F.3d 987, 995 (7th Cir.1996). A female prison inmate brought a civil suit to recover for damages allegedly caused by excessive force by guard. The finding of the employee review officer, signed by the warden, that the guard had used excessive force was held inadmissible even though the requirements of Rule 803(6) were met. The court held that Rule 403 required exclusion because the jury should make up its own mind. (In the authors' view, the decision deprives plaintiff of valuable evidence by persons quite capable of forming a judgment on the subject, and who are unlikely to make such a finding unless it was true. Note also the possible application of the public records exception, Fed. R. Evid. 803(8), and the agency admissions rule, Fed. R. Evid. 801(d)(2).

176. Fed. R. Evid. 803(6) advisory committee's note; 2 McCormick on Evi-

dence § 286 (4th ed. John W. Strong ed. 1992); United States v. Snyder, 787 F.2d 1429 (10th Cir.1986).

177. *See* Fed. R. Evid. 803(6) advisory committee's note; *see also* 2 McCormick on Evidence § 288 (4th ed. John W. Strong ed. 1992). *See also* United States v. Chatman, 994 F.2d 1510, 1516 (10th Cir. 1993) (trial court properly admitted records of calls made from cellular phone when records routinely printed for billing purposes).

178. 849 F.2d 716 (2d Cir.1988). For examples of records held admissible, see Malek v. Federal Ins. Co., 994 F.2d 49, 53 (2d Cir.1993) (social worker's case notes admissible); United States v. Linn, 880 F.2d 209, 216 (9th Cir.1989) (computer printout of telephone call admissible); United States v. Versaint, 849 F.2d 827, 831–32 (3d Cir. 1988) (police report admissible); United States v. Catabran, 836 F.2d 453, 457 (9th Cir.1988) (computer printouts of accounting data admissible); City of Idaho Falls v. Beco Constr. Co., 850 P.2d 165, 172–73 (Idaho 1993) (computer printout summary of labor and equipment costs admissible).

Freidin had given her a check for $22,000 and told her that it was to go into his personal account. There was no testimony at trial that it was the regular practice of the business to make such memoranda. Instead the testimony was that only the partners' secretaries normally made directives about depositing money in personal accounts, and only at the direction of a partner. Rejecting the argument that the record need not be a routine record if it was made in the regular course of business, the court found this record to be an "isolated document" and held that it should have been excluded on grounds that it was not the regular practice of the business to make this type of record. The court acknowledged that it was taking a narrow view of the "regular practice" requirement and noted the existence of authority taking a broader view.

§ 7.18   The Business Records Exception [FRE 803(6)]— Nature of the Testifying Witness

The federal rules are liberal, allowing the custodian or other qualified witness to lay the foundation for a business record. The witness need not have made the record or have custody of it, but must be able to testify that they are made as a regularly conducted business activity, that it is the practice of that business to make that type of record, that the source of the information was a person with knowledge, and that the record was made at or near the time of the event.[179]

Applying a rule identical to Federal Rule 803(6), the Minnesota Supreme Court has allowed a witness who was not an employee of the business to lay the foundation for a business record. The record in question was an Underwriters' Laboratory report, and the witness laying the foundation demonstrated that he was familiar with the operations and procedures employed by the organization for product certification.[180]

§ 7.19   The Business Records Exception [FRE 803(6)]— The Business Duty Requirement

In the leading pre-Rules case of *Johnson v. Lutz*,[181] the plaintiff in a wrongful death action offered a police officer's report of the accident involved. The police officer had not been present at the accident; his report was based on statements by third persons about what had happened.

The New York statute purported to eliminate any requirement of personal knowledge. Nevertheless, the New York court held that the business records exception does not apply to third-party hearsay from someone who has no business duty to report.

179. *See* 2 McCormick on Evidence § 292 (4th ed. John W. Strong ed. 1992).

180. National Tea Co. v. Tyler Refrigeration Co., 339 N.W.2d 59, 61–62 (Minn. 1983); *But see* Karme v. Commissioner, 673 F.2d 1062, 1064 (9th Cir.1982) (records not admissible since government agent not a custodian or qualified witness capable of testifying that bank records were kept as regularly conducted business activity).

181. 170 N.E. 517 (N.Y.1930).

The Advisory Committee for the Federal Rules of Evidence reached the same conclusion. *Johnson v. Lutz* was specifically cited and approved by the committee, which wrote that "If ... the supplier of the information does not act in the regular course [of business], an essential link is broken; the assurance of accuracy does not extend to the information [supplied]."[182]

In the years since the Federal Rules became effective, the courts have tended to water down the business duty requirement in at least two ways. First, some cases hold that information provided by customers of the business is admissible if the business made an effort to verify its accuracy.[183] Second, if a business record contains records of another business, some courts have admitted the entire record even if the proponent does not call a witness to lay the foundation for the records within. For example, in *United States v. Duncan*,[184] the proponent offered into evidence certain hospital records that contained documents from an insurance company. The court admitted the records even though the proponent did not call a witness to verify that the insurance company records satisfied all foundational elements of the business records exception.

Not all courts have been eager to weaken the business duty requirement. For example, in *NLRB v. First Termite Control Co.*,[185] the NLRB sought to introduce a carrier's freight bill for transportation of lumber through an employee of the buyer of the lumber for the purpose of establishing the lumber's origin. The Ninth Circuit held that the freight bill was *not* admissible under the business records exception because the witness knew nothing about how the carrier prepared the freight bill and the company employing the witness did not rely upon or use the information concerning the lumber's origin. Other courts have also held firm to the business duty requirement.[186]

182. Fed. R. Evid. 803(6) advisory committee's note; *see also* Ramrattan v. Burger King Corp., 656 F.Supp. 522, 529 (D.Md.1987) (court excluded bystander's statement to police at site of auto accident because bystander was not acting in the regular course of business).

183. *See, e.g.*, United States v. Sokolow, 91 F.3d 396, 403–04 (3d Cir.1996), *cert. denied*, ___ U.S. ___, 117 S.Ct. 960 (1997) (held, insurance company documents containing unpaid insurance claims admissible under business records exception, even though some of the people documenting the information were not under a business duty, since insurance company had standard practice of verifying information); United States v. Emenogha, 1 F.3d 473, 482 (7th Cir.), *cert. denied*, 510 U.S. 1080 (1994) (trial court properly admitted Currency Transaction Reports to rebut defendant's claim that an impostor used his name; obtaining identification before commencing

transaction was a regular business practice and bank employees testified as eyewitnesses to the transactions with defendant); *cf.*, United States v. McIntyre, 997 F.2d 687, 692 (10th Cir.1993), *cert. denied*, 510 U.S. 1063 (1994) (held, motel arrival and departure log inadmissible as business record when guest supplied relevant information, employee only recorded it, and motel had no specific policy asking guests to show identification). *See also* United States v. Arteaga, 117 F.3d 388 (9th Cir.1997) (collecting cases).

184. 919 F.2d 981, 985–87 (5th Cir. 1990), *cert. denied*, 500 U.S. 926 (1991).

185. 646 F.2d 424 (9th Cir.1981).

186. *See, e.g.*, Cameron v. Otto Bock Orthopedic Indus., 43 F.3d 14 (1st Cir.1994) (Boudin, J.). Plaintiff alleged that he had been injured by a defective artificial leg manufactured by the defendant. In upholding the trial judge's rulings on admissibili-

Of course, if the statement contained within the business record is admissible under another hearsay exception, then the business record exception and the other exception can combine to provide a route of admission.[187] For example, in *Kelly v. Wasserman*,[188] the New York courts held that an entry in the records of the welfare department by a caseworker who had talked to one of the parties to a lawsuit was admissible. The entry stated that the defendant had promised to allow the plaintiff to live rent-free in an apartment plaintiff had conveyed to him. The caseworker's statement was a business record, and the defendant's statement was the admission of a party.[189]

§ 7.20 The Business Records Exception [FRE 803(6)]— Transmitted By a Person With Knowledge

Strict personal knowledge is not required when admission is sought under the business records exception. For example, when a ledger entry made by a bookkeeper is offered, it is not necessary that the bookkeeper have personal knowledge of the underlying transactions represented by the entry. However, the rule does require *either* personal knowledge or that the information have been transmitted by a person with knowledge.[190] Several layers of hearsay can be involved without transgressing this rule, so long as the foundation is laid showing that the original source was a person with knowledge. For example, if employee one observes the transaction, reports it in the regular course of business to employee two, who transmits the information to employee three in the regular course, then the record comes from information that has been transmitted by a person with knowledge and is admissible.[191]

ty, the Court of Appeals held (1) that pre-accident "product failure reports" sent by prosthetists to defendant were admissible as nonhearsay evidence of notice of defect, but (2) that post-accident "product failure reports" were inadmissible hearsay that did not fall under the business records exception. The reports had been prepared by prosthetists based partly upon reports from patients. The court remarked that "[w]hile the reports may be part of the business records of Otto Bock in a colloquial sense, that does not render admissible information contained in the records whose source is a non-party to the business. Under Fed. R. Evid. 803(6), the report must be made by a person acting 'in the course of a regularly conducted business activity.' It is quite clear that the prosthetists' patients are not part of Otto Bock's business." Cameron, 43 F.3d at 16.

187. *See* Fed. R. Evid. 805 (hearsay within hearsay admissible if each statement falls within an exception); *see e.g.*, United States v. Baker, 693 F.2d 183 (D.C.Cir. .. 1982).

188. 158 N.E.2d 241 (1959).

189. *See also* In re Fleet, Inc., 95 Bankr. 319, 330–31 (E.D.Pa.1989) (records admissible since OCA record was business record and statements within record were admissions of party opponents).

190. For an example of a case in which plaintiff failed to satisfy the rule, see Petrocelli v. Gallison, 679 F.2d 286, 289–91 (1st Cir.1982). There, the plaintiff offered a hospital record that stated that plaintiff had suffered a severed nerve in earlier surgery at another hospital. The source of knowledge was not apparent from the record and it appeared unlikely that the physician or nurses at the second hospital would have personally observed the injury. The evidence was excluded for failure to show that the information was transmitted by a person with knowledge. *See also* Ricciardi v. Children's Hosp. Medical Center, 811 F.2d 18, 21–23 (1st Cir.1987) (handwritten notation, not by doctor with personal knowledge of operation, inadmissible to show what happened during operation).

191. *See* 2 McCormick on Evidence § 290 (4th ed. John W. Strong ed. 1992); United States v. Baker, 693 F.2d 183, 188

Issues involving transmission by a person with knowledge have become more complicated with the advent of computerized record-keeping.[192] Today, businesses of all sizes make extensive use of spreadsheets, databases, and other complex software, and locating the source of a particular item within a record is a considerably more daunting task than with handwritten ledgers. Indeed, even defining a "record" is complicated by the way computers store information and the fact that human input—often by a person with no knowledge of the data's accuracy—is necessary in order to retrieve information in a form that can be interpreted by a factfinder. As a result, while computerized record-keeping can be (and generally is) very accurate, some attention must be paid to the way in which the information presented to the court has been prepared, entered into the computer's storage system, and retrieved. One should not simply assume that because information was retrieved for trial from a computerized spreadsheet, database, or the like, it is reliable. The careful lawyer must always remain a skeptic.[193]

§ 7.21 The Business Records Exception [FRE 803(6)]—At or Near the Time

Federal Rule of Evidence 803(6) requires that the business record be made "at or near the time" of the event recorded. Thus, for example, where a telex describing bank deposits was made two years after the deposits, it did not satisfy this requirement of substantial contemporaneity.[194]

§ 7.22 The Business Records Exception [FRE 803(6)]— Lack of Trustworthiness

The final clause of Federal Rule 803(6) provides that even if a record otherwise qualifies as a business record, it can be excluded by the trial judge when "the source of information or the method or circumstances of preparation indicate lack of trustworthiness."[195]

Probably the most common examples of records excluded for lack of trustworthiness are those that were prepared in anticipation of litigation.[196] However, occasionally other records are found that lack the requisite trustworthiness.[197]

(D.C.Cir.1982) (discussing double hearsay problem in employment context).

192. For discussion of authentication of computer-generated records, see § 11.11.

193. *See* Rudolph J. Peritz, *Computer Data and Reliability: A Call for the Authentication of Business Records Under the Federal Rules of Evidence,* 80 Nw. U.L. Rev. 956 (1986) (suggesting expanded foundation for admission of computerized business records).

194. United States v. Kim, 595 F.2d 755, 760–63 (D.C.Cir. .. 1979); *cf.* Gulf South Machine, Inc. v. Kearney & Trecker

Corp., 756 F.2d 377, 381 (5th Cir.1985) (logbook of machine malfunctions admissible where similar books kept for other machines and entries logged within 24 hours of problem).

195. Fed. R. Evid. 803(6).

196. *See* § 7.23.

197. *See* Pan–Islamic Trade Corp. v. Exxon Corp., 632 F.2d 539, 560 (5th Cir. 1980) (excluding record prepared originally as partisan document for presentation to Algerian oil agency); Schaps v. Bally's Park Place, Inc., 58 Bankr. 581, 583 (E.D.Pa. 1986) (books and records of debtor inadmis-

The mere fact that a business record is self-serving does not mean that it will be excluded as untrustworthy. For example, a record showing that a department store customer owes money on a credit card is, when offered by the department store in a collection action, a self-serving statement. Yet if it was prepared in the regular course of business, not for litigation, and if the other requirements of the rule are met, it would be admitted routinely.[198]

§ 7.23 The Business Records Exception [FRE 803(6)]— Statements Prepared for Litigation

In another leading pre-Rules case, *Palmer v. Hoffman*,[199] the United States Supreme Court interpreted the federal business records statute to exclude from evidence a report prepared for a railroad by an engineer describing an accident in which the engineer had been involved. The Court held that statements prepared by parties in anticipation of litigation were not admissible under the exception, even if the business made a regular practice of collecting such reports. Searching for a way to exclude the report, the Court said that the railroad was in the railroad business, not the accident-reporting business, and therefore the accident report was not a business record.

The Advisory Committee for the Federal Rules of Evidence spoke approvingly of *Palmer v. Hoffman* in its note, but it did not adopt the Court's reasoning. Instead, it provided generally that the business records exception would not apply when the circumstances of preparation "indicate lack of trustworthiness." The mere fact that the record was prepared in anticipation of litigation might not always mean that it was untrustworthy, though the advisory committee seems to have expected that usually this would be the case. [200]

One example of a statement prepared for litigation that nevertheless qualifies as a business record is described in *Yates v. Bair Transport, Inc.*[201] There, reports to an insurance company concerning the plaintiff's injuries and prepared by doctors retained by the insurance company were admitted. The reports were offered by the plaintiff, not the company, and the court found the fact that they had been prepared for a company whose interests would be harmed if they were favorable to

---

sible because they were not submitted by the regular custodian and party admitted that the records were not kept in business like manner, thus the records were untrustworthy), *aff'd*, 815 F.2d 693 (3d Cir.1987).

198. *See* Matador Drilling Co. v. Post, 662 F.2d 1190, 1198–99 (5th Cir.1981) (plaintiff's daily drilling records admissible despite claim that they were self-serving); Downing v. Overhead Door Corp., 707 P.2d 1027, 1031 (Colo.App.1985) (error to exclude insurance adjuster's report even though it was claimed to be prejudicial and self-serving).

199. 318 U.S. 109, 111–15 (1943).

200. *See* Fed. R. Evid. 803(6) advisory committee's note.

201. 249 F.Supp. 681, 688–92 (S.D.N.Y.1965); State v. Therriault, 485 A.2d 986, 994–95 (Me.1984) (police report prepared in anticipation of litigation admissible when offered by other party). *But see* United States v. Blackburn, 992 F.2d 666, 670 (7th Cir.), *cert. denied*, 510 U.S. 949 (1993) (report prepared for FBI was not admissible under Rule 803(6) as a record of regularly conducted business activity; report was specially prepared at FBI's behest, with knowledge that any information it supplied would be used in an ongoing criminal investigation).

plaintiff to be a sufficient guarantee of trustworthiness when they were offered by plaintiff. The court, however, did not permit the plaintiff to offer reports prepared by doctors he retained.

As discussed previously,[202] computerized business records can sometimes present special foundational problems. One should not lose sight of the fact that reports prepared for litigation from computers can be no less self-serving than any other types of records. Both proponents and opponents of such reports should be prepared to consider carefully the foundational issues raised by computer-based records.

§ 7.24 The Business Records Exception [FRE 803(6)]— Special Problems With Hospital Records

Hospitals are businesses under the business records exception, whether they are for-profit or nonprofit institutions. However, that they are businesses does not automatically mean that everything in their records is admissible.

Hearsay Within Hearsay in Hospital Records

Sometimes hospital records contain hearsay within hearsay. For example, the hospital record might repeat what the plaintiff told the doctor, nurse, or other hospital employee. Suppose, for example, that the hospital record contains a statement by plaintiff describing the plaintiff's symptoms and the cause of plaintiff's injury.

If the record is offered in favor of the plaintiff, then a hearsay within hearsay problem arises because the plaintiff was under no business duty to the hospital, hence the business records exception does not cover the plaintiff's statement. The plaintiff's statement may, however, be covered by another exception, such as the Federal Rule of Evidence 803(4) exception for statements for medical diagnosis or treatment.[203] This exception would apply if the plaintiff's statements repeated within the record were reasonably pertinent to diagnosis or treatment. Statements by the plaintiff that his leg hurt or that he had been hit by a car would fit the exception. A statement by the plaintiff that the car that hit him went through a red light would not fit it.[204]

If the record is offered against the plaintiff, then there is no problem with fitting the plaintiff's statement into a hearsay exception-it is the

---

202. *See* § **7.20.**

203. *See* § **7.17.** *see also* Elmer v. Tenneco Resins, Inc., 698 F.Supp. 535, 543–45 (D.Del.1988) (medical records containing plaintiff's statements regarding 1952 surgery admissible).

204. *Cf.* Cook v. Hoppin, 783 F.2d 684, 689–90 (7th Cir.1986). In that case the court held that the trial judge committed reversible error by admitting a statement in a hospital record that an injury had been caused by a "shoving or wrestling match." The anonymous source of the statement was not under any business duty to make it, so Rule 803(6) did not apply to it; Rule 803(4) could not be used as a basis for receiving the evidence because Rule 803(4) does not apply to "statements relating to fault which are not relevant to diagnosis or treatment." *See also* Brown v. St. Paul City Ry. Co., 62 N.W.2d 688, 695–96 (Minn. 1954) (statement in hospital record that plaintiff's injury occurred when she fell from a step after streetcar door "was closed suddenly in her face" held inadmissible).

admission of a party opponent. However, the record that repeats the plaintiff's statement—the out-of-court declaration of the doctor or nurse asserting that the plaintiff made the statement—must also fit within an exception to be admissible. The obvious candidate is the business records exception. That exception will work for statements that are pertinent to diagnosis or treatment, such as statements that the plaintiff's leg hurt or that the plaintiff had been hit by a car, since the foundation showing that it is the regular practice of the hospital to make such records can be laid. However, the foundational requirements might not be met in cases in which the hospital employee-declarant recorded something that had no direct connection with medical treatment, such as a statement that the plaintiff had been hit by a car that went through a red light.[205] Hospitals do not regularly record assessments of whether the patient was the victim of a traffic law violation, and a hospital that did would be creating records that might be excluded under the final "lack of trust-worthiness" clause of the business records rule. That the patient was injured by a car violating the law is not closely connected with the hospital's business; the hospital employee has no particular reason to record any such statements accurately. Thus, that part of the record would be excluded for lack of trustworthiness.

Diagnoses in Hospital Records

The business records exception specifically provides for the reception of "opinions" and "diagnoses" that are contained in hospital records. This provision would appear to undermine a series of pre-Rule cases that excluded hospital records containing expert opinions on grounds that the expert should be subject to cross-examination and the qualifications should be explored.[206] However, courts have sometimes found another way to exclude diagnoses or opinions in medical records. For example, in *Fowler v. Carrollton Public Library*,[207] the plaintiff offered hospital records on the issue of damages. The records contained a statement that

---

205. *See* Williams v. Alexander, 129 N.E.2d 417, 418–20 (N.Y.1955) (hospital record offered against plaintiff stated that plaintiff said "he was crossing the street and an automobile ran into another automobile that was at a standstill, causing the standing car to run into him"; trial court reversed for admitting statement on the grounds that it is not the business of the hospital to determine how the accident occurred); *see also* Wagner v. Obert Enterprises, 396 N.W.2d 223, 228 (Minn.1986) (excluding hospital record containing plaintiff's version of accident when offered by defendant on basis that such a record lacks trustworthiness).

206. For examples of pre-Rules cases excluding medical opinions, see Raycraft v. Duluth, Missabe & Iron Range Ry. Co., 472 F.2d 27, 31 (8th Cir.1973) (stating that lack of opportunity to cross-examine expert medical witness may indicate lack of trustwor-

thiness); England v. United States, 174 F.2d 466, 468 (5th Cir.1949) (excluding reports containing doctor's individual opinions about defendant's mental capacity); Mullican v. United States, 252 F.2d 398, 404 (5th Cir.1958) (hospital records concerning defendant's mental condition ruled expert opinions and excluded due to lack of opportunity to cross-examine). For post-Rules cases admitting diagnosis from hospital records, see Norton v. Colyer, 828 F.2d 384, 386–87 (6th Cir.1987) (medical records concerning plaintiff's alleged drug abuse as hospital diagnosis admissible under 803(6)); Pieters v. B–Right Trucking, Inc., 669 F.Supp. 1463, 1464–66 (N.D.Ind.1987) (hospital record of blood alcohol level admissible); Manko v. United States, 636 F.Supp. 1419, 1425 (W.D.Mo.1986) (medical diagnosis admissible under 803(6)).

207. 799 F.2d 976, 983 (5th Cir.1986).

plaintiff had been hospitalized for three days with a diagnosis of "transient global amnesia." They were offered by plaintiff on the theory that the hospitalization was caused by the stress of mistreatment on the job. The court of appeals reversed on other grounds, and went on to discuss the issue to give guidance on retrial. It wrote that

> the district court here abused its discretion in admitting medical records from Fowler's brief hospital stay with no accompanying expert explanation of their significance. The fact of hospitalization in establishing pain and suffering is equivocal, at best, because no expert witness appeared to support Fowler's subjective belief that her "transient global amnesia" was caused by stress at work. The court sustained an objection preventing Fowler from testifying as a layman to the causal connection. This court as well as the jury remains completely unenlightened by the record evidence as to the cause and nature of transient global amnesia. The records could lead only to unwarranted speculation by the jury and inferences in favor of Fowler, and their prejudicial impact manifestly outweighed the benefit of verifying such uncontested facts as the hospitalization. This court has held, in a 1983 case, that where a plaintiff attempted to prove that racially motivated harassment proximately caused a fatal heart condition, speculation will not suffice. *Hamilton v. Rodgers*, 791 F.2d at 444–45. So should it be on retrial.

Though the court did not make specific reference to Rule 403 in its decision, perhaps this case could be viewed as one in which the record got over the hearsay ban by reason of Rule 803(6), only to run afoul of Rule 403 because, without the help of an expert to explain it, it was confusing and misleading.[208]

Another case excluding a diagnosis in a hospital record is *Petrocelli v. Gallison*.[209] In Petrocelli, the plaintiff's medical record, created for his second hernia surgery, contained a statement that in his first hernia surgery, the plaintiff's ilioinguinal nerve had been severed. The plaintiff was suing the physician who had allegedly severed the nerve. It was not clear where the statement in the medical record had come from; the plaintiff himself might have told the recordkeeper that the nerve had been severed in prior surgery. The court upheld the trial judge's exclusion of the record, noting that there was no foundation showing that the information had been transmitted by a "person with knowledge" as required by Rule 803(6). The court recognized that Rule 803(4) theory had not been advanced as a basis for letting in hearsay within hearsay if the source of information was the patient himself, but since the Rule 803(4) theory had not been advanced at trial it refused to allow it to be used on appeal.[210]

---

208. *See also* Nauni v. State, 670 P.2d 126, 131 (Okla.Crim.App.1983) (excluding psychiatric opinions and diagnosis in hospital record under Rule 403 when doctors were not available for cross-examination, to clarify otherwise speculative and subjective process).

209. 679 F.2d 286, 289–91 (1st Cir. 1982).

210. *Id*: *see also* Ricciardi v. Children's Hosp. Medical Center, 811 F.2d 18, 21–23

§ 7.25 The Business Records Exception [FRE 803(6)]— Police Records as Business Records

As a regularly conducted activity, the police qualify as a "business" within the meaning of the business records rule. Moreover, unlike Federal Rule of Evidence 803(8), Rule 803(6) contains no express prohibition of use of police records against a criminal defendant. However, the difference in language may have been inadvertent. It seems unlikely that Congress intended to exclude police records from use under Rule 803(8), while allowing them to be routinely admitted under Rule 803(6). For this reason, some courts have refused to allow them to be used against criminal defendants under either Rule,[211] though not all courts have reached this conclusion.[212] One could justify exclusion in terms of the language of Rule 803(6), by saying that when suspicion has focused upon a particular person, a police report incriminating that person is subject to dangers of bias that disqualify it under the final "trustworthiness" clause of the business records exception.

§ 7.26 The Business Records Exception [FRE 803(6)]— Absence of Entry in Business Record [FRE 803(7)]

Federal Rule of Evidence 803(7) provides for admission of testimony about absence of an entry in a business record. The proponent must lay the foundation by showing that the record involved was kept in the regular course of business, from information transmitted by persons with knowledge, and that it was the regular practice of the business to make entries such as the one missing in this case. The foundation must also show that an adequate search was made for the missing record. Examples of the use of this provision include testimony about the absence of records of orders for fishing reels, to show that the orders had not been received;[213] the absence of records showing receipt of money, to

(1st Cir.1987) (handwritten note by doctor with no knowledge of operation inadmissible).

211. One leading case on the subject is United States v. Oates, 560 F.2d 45, 78 (2d Cir.1977), *on remand* 445 F.Supp. 351 (E.D.N.Y.), *aff'd without opinion*, 591 F.2d 1332 (2d Cir.1978). The Oates court reversed a conviction because the trial judge had admitted a laboratory report identifying a substance as heroin without requiring testimony of the chemist who performed the analysis. The court reasoned that the congressional intent not to allow law enforcement reports to be used against the defendant in criminal cases under Rules 803(8)(B) and (C) required that they be excluded when offered as business records under Rule 803(6). *See also* United States v. Cain, 615 F.2d 380, 382 (5th Cir.1980) (per curiam) (reversible error to receive prison

escape report under 803(6); United States v. Ruffin, 575 F.2d 346, 356 (2d Cir.1978) (error, though harmless, to receive IRS investigator's file note describing phone call by defendant). However, in dicta the *Oates* court suggested that law enforcement records are not admissible under any of the other hearsay exceptions. For discussion of the admissibility of police reports, see § 7.28.

212. Some courts have also held that where the author testifies, Rule 803(8)(C) does not require exclusion of reports that satisfy Rule 803(6). *See, e.g.*, United States v. Sokolow, 91 F.3d 396, 404–05 (3d Cir. 1996); United States v. Hayes, 861 F.2d 1225, 1230 (10th Cir.1988); United States v. King, 613 F.2d 670, 672–73 (7th Cir. 1980).

213. Fury Imports, Inc. v. Shakespeare Co., 554 F.2d 1376, 1381 (5th Cir.1977).

show that the money was not received;[214] and the absence of any record of an offer to donate property, to show that no such offer was made.[215]

§ 7.27   The Public Records Exception [FRE 803(8)]

Federal Rule of Evidence 803(8), the public records exception, is one of the most complicated portions of Rule 803. The exception is divided into three sections, each of which covers a slightly different type of public record.

Part (A) of the Rule covers records and reports setting forth the activities of an office or agency. It applies to both civil and criminal cases. Any party, whether plaintiff, prosecution, or defendant, whether governmental or nongovernmental, can take advantage of the exception.[216]

Examples of matters falling under part (A) include payroll documents, personnel records, records of receipts and disbursements, and so forth.[217] More exotic examples include a report of the Department of Commerce about the usual ease of expediting defense deliveries, offered to show approval of a "jawboning" policy that gave defense orders informal priority,[218] and a report of the Center for Disease Control to show the existence of vaccine-induced polio cases,[219] though one might argue that these reports would fit more readily under part (B) or (C) of the Rule than part (A).

Part (B) of the Rule covers matters observed pursuant to a duty imposed by law when there is also a duty to report. The rule contains an exception, however, applicable to criminal cases. Read literally, it prohibits use by any party in a criminal case, whether government or defense, of police or law enforcement reports. There is case authority, however, which supports the use of 803(8)(B) reports by a criminal defendant.[220] The rule permits either party in criminal cases to use the public records exception when the report is not a law enforcement report.[221] And in civil cases, reports falling within Part (B) of the rule can be offered by either party.

Examples of matters falling under part (B) include weather records, maps, a court reporter's transcript, an officer's letter describing the circumstances of a refusal to accept induction, a federal "warrant of

214. United States v. Zeidman, 540 F.2d 314, 319 (7th Cir.1976).

215. United States v. 34.60 Acres of Land, More or Less, In the County of Camden, 642 F.2d 788, 790 (5th Cir.1981).

216. Glen Weissenberger, Weissenberger's Federal Evidence § 803.42, at 495 (2d ed. 1995).

217. *See* e.g., Major v. Treen, 574 F.Supp. 325, 330 n. 6 (E.D.La.1983) (records of joint committee and subcommittee sessions of Louisiana legislature admissible under 803(8)(A)); Needham v. United States, 564 F.Supp. 419, 421–22 (W.D.Okla.

1983) (IRS computer printout of mailing admissible under 803(8)(A)).

218. Eastern Air Lines, Inc. v. McDonnell Douglas Corp., 532 F.2d 957, 983 n. 79 (5th Cir.1976).

219. Givens v. Lederle, 556 F.2d 1341, 1346 (5th Cir.1977).

220. *See* United States v. Smith, 521 F.2d 957, 968 (D.C.Cir.1975) (permitting defense use of police report despite literal language of Rule 803(8)(B)).

221. *See* 2 McCormick on Evidence § 296 (4th ed. John W. Strong ed. 1992).

deportation," routine INS records, and a police property receipt for a weapon.[222]

Part (C) of the Rule covers findings resulting from an investigation made pursuant to legal authority. It applies both in civil and criminal cases, but only the defendant may take advantage of the exception in criminal cases. Apparently the rule makers made a judgment that in fairness the government ought not to be able to suppress its own prior findings, but that the defendant is entitled to confront an accuser in a criminal case.[223]

Examples of findings falling under part (C) include a Coast Guard report containing conclusions about the causes of the grounding of an oil tanker, a report by state police authorities containing factual information and opinions about certain racial disturbances, administrative findings about sex discrimination or employment discrimination, and FAA findings about the safety of the plane that injured the plaintiff.[224]

Like the business records exception embodied in Rule 803(6), the public records exception allows the court to exclude evidence otherwise satisfying any part of the rule if the court finds that "the sources of information or other circumstances indicate lack of trustworthiness." This is an important part of the rule; the opponent of a party offering a public record should be prepared to demonstrate lack of trustworthiness, and the offering party should be prepared to defend the report's accuracy.

The rationale for the public records exception is (1) government officials are considered trustworthy, (2) the legal duty to be accurate is considered to provide incentive to be careful, and (3) the exception is considered necessary because public officials handle many matters and may forget facts important to the determination of the suit.[225]

222. *See* Fed. R. Evid. 803(8) advisory committee's note; United States v. Contreras, 63 F.3d 852, 857 (9th Cir. 1995) (warrant of deportation); United States v. Agustino–Hernandez, 14 F.3d 42, 43 (11th Cir. 1994) (routine INS records); United States v. Brown, 9 F.3d 907, 910–11 (11th Cir. 1993) (police property receipt for a weapon); United States v. Torres, 733 F.2d 449, 455 n. 5 (7th Cir.1984) (tribal rolls establishing defendants as American Indians admissible under 803(8)(B)); United States v. Grady, 544 F.2d 598 (2d Cir. 1976) (police records which routinely log serial numbers of guns recovered in Ireland admissible under 803(8)(B)).

223. *See* 2 McCormick on Evidence, *supra* note 221 § 296.

224. *See* In re Complaint of Nautilus Motor Tanker Co., Ltd., 85 F.3d 105 (3d Cir.1996) (Coast Guard report concerning grounding of oil tanker); Clark v. Clabaugh, 20 F.3d 1290, 1294–95 (3d Cir.1994) (Pennsylvania State Police report about circum-

stances surrounding certain civil disturbances); Chandler v. Roudebush, 425 U.S. 840, 863 n. 39 (1976) (administrative findings regarding claims of discrimination generally admissible under 803(8)(C); Melville v. American Home Assurance Co., 443 F.Supp. 1064, 1129 (E.D.Pa.1977) (FAA directives concerning safety of plane admissible), *rev'd on other grounds*, 584 F.2d 1306 (3d Cir.1978); 3 Stephen A. Saltzburg, Michael M. Martin & Daniel J. Capra, Federal Rules of Evidence Manual 1422–26 (6th ed. 1994).

225. *See* Fed. R. Evid. 803(8) advisory committee's note; 2 McCormick on Evidence, *supra* note 223 § 295. Note that the burden of proof is on the party opposing the introduction of public records to overcome their presumed trustworthiness. *See* Montiel v. City of Los Angeles, 2 F.3d 335, 341 (9th Cir.1993) (in § 1983 action, district court erred by failing to presume the trustworthiness of the Report of the Independent Commission on the Los Angeles Police

Many public records are also business records, since the government is a business within the meaning of the business records exception. However, the public records exception serves an important function because it covers matters that are not recorded with regularity. For example, a civil defense official might only once record observations about nuclear damage, but the recorded observations would be public records.[226] In addition, Rule 803(8)(C), admitting investigative findings, does not contain a "business duty" requirement analogous to that applied to business records. This will permit the admission of some public records containing factual findings based on hearsay within hearsay. Finally, the public record, unlike the business record, can be admitted over objection without a foundation witness. If it meets the self-authentication requirements of Rule 902 (which makes certified copies, etc., self-authenticating), then the foundation for the public records hearsay exception will usually be adequate, because the record will show on its face that it meets the requirements of 803(8).[227]

§ 7.28   The Public Records Exception [FRE 803(8)]—Police Records

The public records exception contains specific language prohibiting the use of law enforcement records in most criminal cases.[228] Yet there are still some bases for arguing that certain law enforcement records are admissible against the defendant in criminal cases.

First, a law enforcement record could be offered not as a public record, but as a business record. There is no doubt that law enforcement agencies are businesses within the meaning of the business records rule. The rule is not restricted to profit-making private activity, but applies to any regularly conducted activity, whether it is public, charitable, or otherwise.[229]

However, the legislative intent of the public records exception indicates a strong purpose to prevent the police officer's report from taking his or her place on the witness stand. Apparently Congress simply overlooked the fact that police reports and other law enforcement records would also qualify as business records. Because of the intent to

Department (Christopher Commission Report) and by not shifting the burden of establishing the report's untrustworthiness to the defendant city); Ellis v. International Playtex, Inc., 745 F.2d 292, 302 (4th Cir. 1984).

226. *See, e.g.,* United States v. Harris, 446 F.2d 129, 131 (7th Cir.1971), *cert. denied* 404 U.S. 994 (1971) (letter from state hospital stating that defendant had failed to appear for alternative service admissible); United States v. Versaint, 849 F.2d 827, 831 n. 9 (3d Cir.1988) (police report admissible under 803(8), thus not necessary to determine if report would meet 803(6) requirements of reliability and regularity).

227. *See* Zambito v. Blair, 610 F.2d 1192, 1198 (4th Cir.1979) (certified "Order Finding Probable Cause" admissible under Rules 902(*l*) and 803(8)(A)); United States v. Hart, 673 F.Supp. 932, 934 n. 2 (N.D.Ind. 1987) (government exhibit self-authenticating under 902(*l*) and admissible under 803(8)). Note also that Rule 803(8) does not require record to be created contemporaneously with the event recorded, as in 803(6). *See* Weissenberger, *supra* note 216 § 803.41, at 426–26.

228. *See* Fed. R. Evid. 803(8)(B), (C).

229. *See* Fed. Rules of Evidence, H.R. Conf. Rep. No. 1597, 93d Cong., 2d Sess. 11 (1974).

exclude law enforcement records when offered under the public records exception, some courts have held that they are likewise not admissible as business records, though other courts have reached the contrary conclusion.[230]

Second, some recent case law has supported the admission of law enforcement records under Rule 803(5), the exception for past recollection recorded. This result has been justified on grounds that Congress, in excluding law enforcement records, was concerned about the danger that the defendant would lose the right to cross-examine the officer who made the report. This danger is not present when the past recollection recorded exception is used, because under that exception the person who made or adopted the record must testify in order to lay the foundation for the admission of the report.[231]

Third, courts have allowed law enforcement records into evidence under other exceptions, including Rule 803(10) (the exception for evidence of absence of a public record),[232] and Rule 803(24) (one of the residual hearsay exceptions).[233]

Finally, some courts have created an exception for routine, non-adversarial law enforcement reports. Rule 803(8) does not specifically distinguish between routine reports of objective facts, such as records of serial numbers, or fingerprint records, and reports prepared during an investigation that incriminate a particular defendant. However, a number of courts have made a distinction of this nature. They have used words such as "routine," "non-adversarial," "ministerial," "objective," and "non-evaluative" to describe law enforcement records deemed admissible against the defendant despite the restrictions of Rule 803(8).[234]

230. *See* § 7.25.

231. *See* United States v. Picciandra, 788 F.2d 39, 44 (1st Cir.), *cert. denied*, 479 U.S. 847 (1986) (DEA agent's report was admissible against criminal defendants under Rule 803(5)); United States v. Sawyer, 607 F.2d 1190, 1193 (7th Cir.1979), *cert. denied*, 445 U.S. 943 (1980) (reports excluded under Rule 803(8)(B) may be received under Rule 803(5)).

232. *See, e.g.,* United States v. Metzger, 778 F.2d 1195, 1201 (6th Cir.1985), *cert. denied*, 477 U.S. 906 (1986) (certificate that defendant had not registered a destructive device or paid tax on one admissible under 803(10) even if record kept by law enforcement official); United States v. Neff, 615 F.2d 1235, 1241 (9th Cir.1980) (IRS certificate admissible under 803(10)); United States v. Yakobov, 712 F.2d 20, 25 (2d Cir.1983) (upon a proper showing of diligent search, ATF certificate stating that there was no record that defendant had applied for or received a firearms license would be admissible).

233. *See, e.g.,* United States v. Blackburn, 992 F.2d 666, 672 (7th Cir.), *cert.*

denied, 510 U.S. 949 (1993) (report prepared for FBI investigation admissible under Rule 803(24)).

234. *See* United States v. Wiley, 979 F.2d 365, 369 (5th Cir.1992) (in action for passing counterfeit IRS obligations, reports indicating that IRS agents investigated and froze third-party's account admissible under public records hearsay exception because law enforcement actions occurred within "routine, non-adversarial setting"); United States v. Gilbert, 774 F.2d 962, 964–65 (9th Cir.1985) (report on location of latent print admissible; court notes non-evaluative, routine, nonadversarial nature of report); United States v. Wilmer, 799 F.2d 495, 500–01 (9th Cir.1986), *cert. denied*, 481 U.S. 1004 (1987) (calibration certificate for breathalyzer admissible); United States v. Puente, 826 F.2d 1415, 1417–18 (5th Cir. 1987) (held, Customs Service records of license plates of cars crossing from Mexico to United States admissible under 803(8), even though Customs officers are law enforcement officers; 803(8)(B) does not apply to routine, objective factual observations).

Typically, these courts have reasoned that routine non-adversarial reports are not subject to the same dangers of bias and clouded perception as are other police reports.[235] To put it another way, in these cases the cross-examination is most unlikely to yield information that would be helpful to the defendant. In some limited circumstances, routine police activities, such as the recording of serial numbers, might be considered "activities of the office" and hence under part (A).[236]

§ 7.29   The Public Records Exception [FRE 803(8)]—The Concept of "Factual Findings"

Section (C) of Federal Rule of Evidence 803(8) permits the admission, in civil suits and against the government in criminal cases, of reports containing "factual findings" derived from investigations made under authority of law.[237]

Before *Beech Aircraft v. Rainey*,[238] there was a conflict of authority in the federal courts on the question whether opinions contained in Rule 803(8)(C) reports were also admissible. For example, the Second Circuit excluded an FDA finding that a drug was dangerous on grounds that it was a medical opinion, not a factual finding.[239] However, the Sixth Circuit admitted a finding by an administrative law judge that a tow boat captain had not been negligent, saying that "[a]lthough a finding that [the captain's] actions were reasonable is somewhat conclusory, we do not believe that such a label is controlling. . . . In our view a finding that amounts to an inference drawn from subsidiary findings is admissible under Rule 803(8)(C)."[240]

In *Beech Aircraft v. Rainey*, the United States Supreme Court came down on the side of free admission of opinions. *Beech Aircraft* was a wrongful death action against an aircraft manufacturer by the survivors of two naval aviators who had been killed in a crash during a training exercise. A naval investigator had issued a JAG report describing the surrounding facts and also offering the opinion that the most probable cause of the crash was pilot error. The Court held that the opinion was admissible, interpreting Rule 803(8)(C) to permit reception of opinions

---

235. *See* United States v. Gilbert, 774 F.2d 962, 965 (9th Cir.1985).

236. *Cf.* United States v. Grady, 544 F.2d 598, 604 (2d Cir.1976) (police records of routine nature, such as recording of serial numbers, are admissible under 803(8); in putting limits on admissibility of police records, Congress did not have this sort of routine function in mind); United States v. Orozco, 590 F.2d 789, 793–94 (9th Cir.1979) (computer cards recording vehicle license plate numbers admissible under 803(8)).

237. *See* Fed. R. Evid. 803(8)(C).

238. 488 U.S. 153 (1988).

239. Lindsay v. Ortho Pharmaceutical Corp., 637 F.2d 87, 94 (2d Cir.1980); *see also* Matthews v. Ashland Chemical, Inc.,

770 F.2d 1303, 1309–10 (5th Cir.1985) (memo outlining future inquiries into safety measures and offering opinions on expected results inadmissible under 803(8)(C)).

240. *See* Complaint of Paducah Towing Co., Inc., 692 F.2d 412, 420 (6th Cir.1982); *see also* Kehm v. Procter & Gamble Mfg. Co., 724 F.2d 613, 619–20 (8th Cir.1983) (reports analyzing statistical relationship between tampon use and toxic shock syndrome admissible); Zenith Radio Corp. v. Matsushita Elec. Indus. Co., 505 F.Supp. 1125, 1145 (E.D.Pa.1980) (factual findings as used in the Rule encompass evaluative reports of public agencies).

contained in investigative reports so long as the reports also contain factual findings.[241]

Note that even in a jurisdiction that excludes the public record from direct admission because it contains opinions and not findings, the record still might be the basis upon which an expert could rely in forming his or her opinion under Rule 703, which allows experts to rely upon data not admissible in evidence.[242]

§ 7.30   Absence of Public Record or Entry [FRE 803(10)]

Federal Rule of Evidence 803(10) provides an exception for evidence that data was not contained in a public record, provided that certification or testimony shows that a diligent search was made.

Examples of the operation of this exception include reception of a certificate from the IRS reciting its failure to find income tax returns, as evidence of failure to file,[243] and use of a certificate from the Navy reciting failure to find a record of registration, to show that a vehicle was not registered.[244]

At common law, evidence of a diligent search through public records was admissible to show the absence of a record, but some courts would not allow the search to be established by a certificate from a public official reciting that the diligent search had been made.[245] Rule 803(10) cures that omission.

241.   488 U.S. 153 (1988); Distaff, Inc. v. Springfield Contracting Corp., 984 F.2d 108, 111–12 (4th Cir.1993) (held, report by naval investigator about cause of fire admissible, even though Navy refused to permit him to testify subject to cross-examination). Note that the evidence may still be inadmissible if there is reason to suspect it lacks trustworthiness. *See generally* Anderson v. City of New York, 657 F.Supp. 1571, 1578 (S.D.N.Y.1987); 5 Weinstein's Federal Evidence § 803.13[4][b], at 803–93 to 803–94 (2d Ed. Joseph M. McLaughlin ed. 1997). *See* Nipper v. Snipes, 7 F.3d 415, 417 (4th Cir. 1993) (held, judicial findings of fact are not "public records" within the meaning of Rule 803(8)); Cortes v. Maxus Exploration Co., 977 F.2d 195, 201 (5th Cir.1992) (held, trial judge did not err in excluding conclusory EEOC document containing determination that plaintiff had not been sexually harassed; though government reports are presumptively reliable under Rule 803(8) in the absence of an affirmative showing of untrustworthiness by the opponent, here the danger of prejudice substantially outweighed the probative value, justifying exclusion under Rule 403); Ake v. General Motors Corp., 942 F.Supp. 869, 877 (W.D.N.Y.1996) (tentative "findings" of Na-

tional Highway Traffic Safety Administration excluded under Rule 803(8)'s trustworthiness proviso; they might have been changed after public hearing); Kemper Architects v. McFall, Konkel, 843 P.2d 1178, 1188 (Wyo.1992) (held, trial court properly excluded exhibit prepared by Army Corps of Engineers under state's version of Rule 803(8)(C); exhibit lacked indicia of trustworthiness because it contained multiple hearsay-within-hearsay statements, impermissible legal conclusions, and appeared to have been prepared with a view towards possible litigation).

242.   *See* § **10.08**.

243.   *See* United States v. Penes, 577 F.2d 754, 761 (1st Cir.1978) (certificate from computer check showing defendant had not filed tax returns admissible under Rule 803(10)).

244.   United States v. Martinez, 700 F.2d 1358, 1364–65 (11th Cir.1983) (under Rule 803(10), no error to admit naval certificate concluding that vessel was not registered).

245.   5 John H. Wigmore, Evidence in Trials at Common Law § 1678 (James H. Chadbourn rev. 1974).

The opponent of the record can seek to rebut the claim that a diligent search occurred. Because the certification provision allows the substitution of a certificate for the person who did the search, this can be difficult unless the opponent has affirmative witnesses. However, in some instances lack of diligence may appear from the face of the certificate, as when the certificate uses incorrect names or contains other mistakes.[246]

The public records exception, Rule 803(8), prohibits use of police and other law enforcement records as evidence against criminal defendants. Rule 803(10) does not contain any such prohibition, and there is substantial authority for allowing evidence of the absence of a law enforcement record to be used against a criminal defendant. For example, in *United States v. Yakobov*,[247] the Second Circuit ruled that upon a proper showing of diligent search, an ATF certificate stating that there was no record that defendant had applied for or received a firearms license would be admissible, even though the record was a law enforcement record.[248]

§ 7.31 Records of Vital Statistics; Death Certificates [FRE 803(9)]

Federal Rule of Evidence 803(9) provides a hearsay exception for "[r]ecords or data compilations, in any form, of births, fetal deaths, deaths, or marriages, if the report thereof was made to a public office pursuant to requirements of law."

This exception allows official records of birth, death, and marriage to be received in evidence even if someone other than a public official prepares the records.[249] Thus, a death certificate is admissible whether it is prepared by a private doctor, mortician, or public coroner; a marriage certificate is admissible whether it was prepared by a judge or by a minister. In the absence of Rule 803(9), these records might be considered admissible under a generous reading of Rule 803(8)(B) (the public records exception), but the present exception resolves any doubt about whether the private status of the record-makers affects admissibility.

Many states also have statutes providing for the admission of death certificates. These statutes often provide that death certificates are prima facie evidence of the facts stated in them.[250]

---

246. *See* United States v. Yakobov, 712 F.2d 20 (2d Cir.1983).

247. *Id.* at 25.

248. *See also* United States v. Metzger, 778 F.2d 1195, 1201 (6th Cir.1985), *cert. denied*, 477 U.S. 906 (1986) (held, certificate that defendant had not registered a destructive device or paid tax on it was admissible under 803(10) even if record kept by law enforcement official); United States v. Neff, 615 F.2d 1235, 1241 (9th Cir.1980) (IRS certificate admissible under Rule 803(10)).

249. *See, e.g.*, 5 Weinstein's Federal Evidence § 803.14[1], at 803–102 (2d Ed. Joseph M. McLauglin ed. 1997).

250. D.E. Evins, Annotation, *Official Death Certificate as Evidence of Cause of Death in Civil or Criminal Action*, 21 A.L.R. 3d 418, 422 n.5 (1968 & Supp. 1996). If a narrow state statute predates the adoption of a state version of Rule 803(9), Rule 803(9) supersedes the statute or at least expands the limits of admissibility-provided the state supreme court adopted Rule 803(9) under an enabling act that renders

Death certificates have been offered in evidence in a wide variety of situations.[251] These include the prosecution's offer of a death certificate to show the victim in a murder case died of gunshot wounds;[252] an insurance defense counsel's offer, in a suit to recover on a life insurance policy, of a statement that the cause of death was suicide;[253] the government's offer of death certificates in a tax case to show that the death of two taxpayers was not simultaneous, and therefore one inherited from the other;[254] and a plaintiff's offer, in an asbestosis wrongful death action, of a death certificate to show that plaintiff's decedent died of adenocarcinoma of the lung.[255]

The reception of statements from death certificates may raise dangers of unreliability. For example, a death certificate may contain assertions based on hearsay or speculation by a record-maker who does not have firsthand knowledge of the facts stated in the certificate; or a lay coroner may express a medical opinion in the certificate that only a qualified expert could state with confidence. In these situations, cross-examination of the person who prepared the death certificate would be useful. Counsel faced with an unreliable statement in a death certificate could object on several possible grounds:

1. An objection might assert that the certificate contains statements not based on personal knowledge or contains hearsay

prior inconsistent statutes ineffective after implementation of Rule 803(9).

251. *See generally id.* (discussing the admissibility of death certificates in wrongful death actions, actions on life insurance policies, will contests, personal injury actions, actions to recover property, and criminal homicide prosecutions).

252. *See, e.g.,* Stevens v. Bordenkircher, 746 F.2d 342 (6th Cir.1984). *But see* 2 Michael H. Graham, Handbook of Federal Evidence § 803.10, at 519 (4th ed. 1996) (stating that if a record concerning cause of death is offered against a criminal defendant, it should not be received because admission would violate the policy of Rule 803(8)).

253. For cases excluding such statements, see Security Life Ins. Co. v. Blitch, 270 S.E.2d 349, 352 (Ga.App.1980) (holding trial court did not err in deleting "homicide" from death certificate before receiving certificate in double indemnity insurance recovery case); Hestad v. Pennsylvania Life Ins. Co., 204 N.W.2d 433, 436 (Minn.1973) (indicating courts should redact portion of death certificate saying that suicide or accident was cause of death). In Hestad, the Minnesota Supreme Court stated:

[D]eath certificates are not admissible to show the manner in which the death occurs, such as by accident or suicide, but may be admitted only to

show the immediate cause of death, which, in this case, was carbon monoxide poisoning. Statements as to the manner of death in a death certificate constitute conclusions and hearsay.

Id. Accord State v. Jurgens, 424 N.W.2d 546, 552 (Minn.App.1988) (dictum).

254. *See, e.g.,* Vaughn v. United States, 536 F.Supp. 498 (W.D.Va.1982). In Vaughn, an assailant shot and killed a father and daughter in their home. *Id.* at 500. According to the death certificate, the father died at home and the daughter died about an hour later at the hospital. *Id.* The court admitted the certificate as evidence that the deaths were not simultaneous, and thus the daughter's estate owed additional taxes because she inherited money from her father upon his death. *Id.* at 501–02.

255. *See, e.g.,* Burton v. Johns–Manville Corp., 613 F.Supp. 91 (W.D.Pa.1985). In *Burton,* the district court explains why a death certificate stating that the decedent died of adenocarcinoma of the lung was admitted in an asbestos case. The court applied a Pennsylvania statute making a death certificate prima facie evidence of its contents. *Id.* at 93 n.2. The court also noted that, in any event, reception of the death certificate did not harm the defendant because a medical expert with firsthand knowledge was cross-examined about the cause of death.

within hearsay. Courts often confound the personal knowledge objection and the problem of hearsay within hearsay. (For a distinction between the two, see § 7.57.) The advisory committee's comments to Rule 803 state that neither Rule 803 nor Rule 804 dispenses with the requirement of personal knowledge.[256] Thus, when a death certificate describes something that the coroner clearly did not observe, the personal knowledge objection should prevent reception of the evidence.[257]

2. Where the death certificate expresses an expert opinion, an objection may claim that the declarant was not qualified as an expert, or at least that the declarant should be produced for cross-examination about qualifications.[258] When the record-maker is not a qualified medical expert and the certificate is admitted, counsel can argue that the medical conclusions stated in it are insufficient to get the opponent past a directed verdict.[259]

3. Where the death certificate contains extraneous matter, counsel can argue that Rule 803(9)'s prerequisite that the record be made "pursuant to requirements of law" is not satisfied as to the extraneous matter, because its inclusion is not required by law. Similarly, where the argument for admission rests on a state statute that admits death certificates as prima facie evidence of the "facts" stated in them, some courts have redacted the certificates to exclude matters deemed to be opinion or speculation rather than fact.[260]

When an unreliable death certificate is offered in a criminal case, the confrontation clause furnishes another basis for objection. In a

256. Fed. R. Evid. 803 advisory committee's note (paragraph 3, preceding discussion of Rule 803(1)).

257. *See* Bowman v. Redding & Co., 449 F.2d 956, 961 (D.C.Cir.1971) (statement in death certificate describing how decedent' fall occurred inadmissible); State v. Gould, 704 P.2d 20 (Mont.1985) (admission of portion of death certificate containing statement that decedent was in a pickup truck which left roadway and overturned, ejecting decedent, was error because statement was based on hearsay; error harmless under circumstances). *But see* Shell v. Parrish, 448 F.2d 528, 531 (6th Cir.1971) (statement in death certificate that "victim fell in ditch" admissible). One eminent authority has suggested, however, that, in accordance with prior precedent, courts should admit such statements for what they are worth. 5 Weinstein's Federal Evidence, *supra* note 249 § 803.14[4], at 803–107.

258. *See, e.g.,* Charleston Nat. Bank v. Hennessy, 404 F.2d 539, 542 (5th Cir.1968) (holding lay coroner's opinion that decedent

"apparently had heart attack" would not be admissible if offered in live testimony and statement did not become admissible because included in official death certificate).

259. *See* De Courcy v. Trustees of Westminster Presbyterian Church, Inc., 134 N.W.2d 326, 328–29 (Minn.1965) (holding death certificate prepared by nonexpert insufficient substitute for expert testimony regarding cause of death, and concluding trial court should have directed verdict for defendant hospital where death allegedly occurred as a result of fracture caused by hospital's negligence).

260. *See* Carswell v. State, 320 S.E.2d 249, 253 (Ga.App.1984) (excluding statement that "auto struck pedestrian"). *See also* Lockwood v. Travelers Ins. Co., 498 P.2d 947, 952 (Colo.1972) (error to admit death certificate containing conclusory statement that death resulted from accident rather than suicide or homicide); People v. Fiddler, 258 N.E.2d 359, 361 (Ill.1970) (coroner's statement about cause of death not a "fact" within meaning of state statute making facts in death certificates admissible).

leading federal case, *Stevens v. Bordenkircher*,[261] the Sixth Circuit Court of Appeals held that the reception of a death certificate of questionable reliability in lieu of live testimony violated the confrontation clause. *Stevens* was a habeas case arising from a state court murder conviction. One of the issues at trial was whether the alleged victim was murdered or simply disappeared. The state claimed that bones found in a sawdust pile were those of the victim. The state's principal evidence of murder consisted of the testimony of a highly questionable witness who described alleged inculpatory statements the codefendants made to him. The state also introduced a death certificate that identified the body recovered from the sawdust pile as the victim's, stated that gunshot wounds to the thorax caused the victim's death, and noted the approximate date of death. This information, on the surface, corroborated the story of the state's chief witness. Although the coroner who prepared the death certificate had been subpoenaed, the prosecutor released him from the subpoena as a personal favor and, over objection, produced the death certificate instead. The death certificate purported to be an autopsy that revealed the identity of the body, the cause of death, and the approximate date of death. The state court trial resulted in the petitioner's conviction. At the federal evidentiary hearing on the habeas motion, the coroner stated that only fifteen pounds of bones remained when he examined the body. The coroner also admitted that he did not find any metallic fragments or other evidence of gunshot death, and that he obtained the information stated in the certificate from the police. The Sixth Circuit held that receiving the death certificate under these circumstances violated the petitioner's constitutional right to confrontation. Citing the Supreme Court's decision in *Ohio v. Roberts*,[262] the court

---

261.   746 F.2d 342 (6th Cir.1984).

For a case raising similar confrontation issues in the context of medical records, see Pickett v. Bowen, 626 F.Supp. 81, 83–85 (M.D.Ala.1985) (holding medical record describing ruptured hymen inadmissible in child sexual abuse case as confrontation clause violation; examining doctor testified at habeas hearing to facts that, if brought out on cross, would have shown vagina's condition required 3–5 minutes of manipulation, not merely one touch as described in child's testimony).

262.   448 U.S. 56 (1980). The *Roberts* Court established a two-pronged test for determining whether the introduction of hearsay violates the confrontation clause.

The first prong of the *Roberts* test requires that the prosecution produce the hearsay declarant or demonstrate that the declarant is unavailable. *Id.* at 65. This requirement, however, is not absolute: it only applies in the "usual" case and the prosecution need not demonstrate unavailability if the utility of confrontation is "remote." *Id.* at 65 n.7.

The second prong of the *Roberts* test requires that the hearsay have "adequate 'indicia of reliability.'" *Id.* at 65. In some cases, this prong requires "a showing of particularized guarantees of trustworthiness." *Id.* at 66 & n.9. The Supreme Court, however, apparently recognized the need for certainty in criminal trials and provided more specific guidance. The Court indicated that courts should defer to established hearsay exceptions by stating reliability can be inferred "without more" where evidence falls within a "firmly rooted" hearsay exception. *Id.* at 66.

Cf. Manocchio v. Moran, 919 F.2d 770 (1st Cir.1990) (although finding no confrontation violation under the circumstances, court finds Roberts requires a finding of adequate "indicia of reliability" and because 803(a) is not "firmly rooted" the government must show "particularized guarantees of trustworthiness").

For extended discussion of the Supreme Court's analysis of hearsay and the confrontation clause, see §§ 7.65–7.66.

concluded that the death certificate's assertions lacked the required indicia of trustworthiness, and also noted that the death certificate's maker was available for cross-examination but was excused by the prosecutor.[263]

§ 7.32 Learned Treatise Exception [FRE 803(18)]

Federal Rule of Evidence 803(18) provides a generous exception for learned treatises and other expert publications. The exception allows the introduction of passages from books, scholarly journals, technical magazines, and other published works on any science or art, once a foundation has been established that the work is a reliable authority.

The exception is based on the theory that most learned publications are reliable enough to be helpful. The author has no bias or interest in any particular case. In addition the author realizes that the work will be read and evaluated by other members of the same profession. Thus the author is highly motivated to be accurate and complete.[264]

The federal rule makes substantial changes in the common law. The common law theory was that learned treatises were admissible solely for purposes of impeaching experts.[265] In some jurisdictions, the expert could not be impeached with the treatise unless the expert had testified that he or she had relied upon the treatise in preparing an expert opinion. This theory was based upon the view that the treatise was not being used to prove the truth of what it asserted, but only to show that the expert was unreliable. For example, suppose a case in which plaintiff's expert testified that a patient's spleen should be removed only if severely damaged. Suppose also that the defense attorney has in hand a treatise stating that the spleen should be removed whenever it has suffered the slightest trauma. The defense attorney could ask the opposing expert whether the expert had relied on the treatise. If the expert claimed reliance on the treatise in preparing the opinion, then the attorney could read the damaging passage to the jury or require the expert to do so.[266]

---

263. It should be noted that since *Stevens* was decided in 1984, the Supreme Court has interpreted *Roberts* rather narrowly. Under the Court's current analysis, if Montana's broad interpretation of the hearsay exception is "firmly rooted," no further confrontation analysis would be required.

264. Fed. R. Evid. 803(18) advisory committee's note; 2 McCormick on Evidence § 321 (4th ed. John W. Strong ed. 1992); *see also* Schneider v. Revici, 817 F.2d 987, 991 (2d Cir.1987).

265. *See generally* 2 McCormick on Evidence, *supra* note 264 § 321; *see also* Brown v. United States, 419 F.2d 337, 341 (8th Cir.1969) (medical treatises may be used in cross-examination "but are not admissible to prove the probative facts of opinions in the treatise"); United States v. One Device, 160 F.2d 194, 198–99 (10th Cir.

1947) (medical books and treatises are not admissible to prove the truth of the statements they contain); Annotation, *Medical Treatises; Rule of Inadmissibility*, 84 A.L.R.2d 1341 (1962). Courts refused to recognize the exception primarily because the author was not subject to cross-examination and was not under oath, and because of the difficulty in determining whether the author was an authority in the field. Also courts expressed concern that jurors would become confused and that trials might devolve into conflicts between authors that jurors would not be equipped to resolve fairly. *See* 2 McCormick on Evidence, *supra* note 264 § 321; Annotation, *supra* this note, at 1347.

266. *See* Carter Prods., Inc. v. FTC, 201 F.2d 446, 449 (9th Cir.1953) (noting that many courts hold that learned treatises cannot be used in cross-examination un-

The theory was not that the treatise was being admitted under a hearsay exception, but that it was not hearsay at all. The treatise was not being used to prove the truth of anything that it asserted, but to show that the expert was untrustworthy or careless because the expert claimed to have relied upon an unsupportive treatise.

The impeachment of an expert who claims to have relied upon a treatise can be highly impressive. Wellman's classic work on cross-examination contains a pungent example from his own experience. Wellman was examining an adverse medical expert. He reported that he asked the expert whether anyone agreed with the expert's diagnosis, and the expert testified that Ericson on the Spine agreed with him. Wellman asked who Ericson was, and the expert answered patronizingly that Ericson was probably one of the most famous surgeons that England has ever produced. Wellman then posed the following question:

Wellman: "Well, how is it that a man, whose time is so much occupied as you have told us yours is, has leisure enough to look up medical authorities to see if they agree with him?"

To which he got the dream answer:

Doctor: [fairly beaming on counsel]. "Well, Mr. Wellman, to tell you the truth, I have often heard of you, and I half suspected that you would ask me some such foolish question; so this morning after my breakfast, and before starting for court, I took down from my library my copy of Ericson's book, and found that he agreed entirely with my diagnosis in this case."

Wellman then reached under the counsel table and took out his own copy of "Ericson on the Spine" and asked the doctor to find the place at which Ericson agreed with him. The doctor said "I have not time to do it now." Wellman responded "Time!—why, there is all the time in the world." The witness sat in pained silence until excused by the trial judge.[267]

This form of impeachment can still be used under the Federal Rules. If the witness will say that he or she has relied on a treatise, then the impeachment will be very successful if the treatise does not support the witness' position. Undoubtedly there are lawyers who encounter such witnesses, just as there are poker players who draw royal flushes. But most experts will not fall into this trap. They will deny relying upon the

less witness has relied on treatise in forming opinion, and citing authority); Ullrich v. Chicago City Ry. Co., 106 N.E. 828, 829 (Ill.1914) (scientific books not admissible to impeach witness unless witness has relied upon that particular work in forming opinion); Percoco's Case, 173 N.E. 515, 516 (Mass.1930) (error to admit medical books when expert, though stating he had read the books, was not shown to have relied on them in forming opinion).

267. Francis L. Wellman, The Art of Cross–Examination 69–70 (1923).

disagreeable treatise, perhaps upon any treatise. The problem with the common law rule was that the expert could always short-circuit the cross-examination by denying reliance on the treatise in forming the opinion.[268]

Some common law courts allowed broader use of the treatise to impeach. Even if the expert was not willing to testify that the expert had relied upon the treatise, the treatise could be used in evidence if the expert was at least willing to concede that the treatise was a reliable authority in the field.[269] This approach, however, still allowed the expert witness to block cross-examination simply by refusing to concede that the treatise was authoritative.[270]

The common law position was not completely uniform. Some courts were far more liberal in allowing cross-examination on treatises. Some allowed it even when the opposing expert neither relied on the work nor recognized it as an authority, on grounds that the cross-examination was still a valuable way to test the expert's knowledge, credibility, and accuracy.[271] But many courts imposed restrictions that severely hampered the use of learned treatises.

Liberalization in the Federal Rules

The federal rule makers thought that the learned treatise ought to be admissible if its reliability was established by any means, whether or not the opposing expert conceded that it was authoritative. The rule makers said that the testing of professional knowledge was incomplete without exploration of the witness' knowledge of, and attitude toward, established treatises in the field.[272]

Because of the danger that the treatise, even if reliable in itself, might be misleading and confusing without the guidance of an expert, the rule makers did require that an expert be available and that the treatise be shown to the expert on the stand.[273] The expert is not

---

268. *See* Percoco's Case, 173 N.E. 515, 516 (Mass.1930); De Haan v. Winter, 241 N.W. 923, 925 (Mich.1932) ("If a medical witness refers to a textbook as his authority, then the book may be used to contradict him").

269. *See, e.g.,* Shaw v. Duncan, 194 F.2d 779, 783 (10th Cir.1952) (error to exclude cross-examination upon treatise when witness testified he had read the treatise in question); Lawrence v. Nutter, 203 F.2d 540, 543 (4th Cir.1953) (error to exclude cross-examination of witnesses from treatise recognized by witnesses as authority).

270. Hastings v. Chrysler Corp., 77 N.Y.S.2d 524, 527 (1948) ("If the expert witness does not concede the authoritativeness of the literature attempted to be resorted to, it may not be used on cross-examination"); *see also* Nutter, 203 F.2d at 543.

271. *See* Atlanta Corp. v. Olesen, 124 F.Supp. 482, 488 (S.D.Cal.1954) (reading portions of medical texts proper method to test knowledge, accuracy, and credibility of expert witness, and to determine if expert agreed with the text); Reilly v. Pinkus, 338 U.S. 269, 275–76 (1949) (prejudicial error not to allow cross-examination concerning statements in medical texts to test expert's testimony).

272. Fed. R. Evid. 803(18) advisory committee's note.

273. *Id.*; *see* Tart v. McGann, 697 F.2d 75, 78 (2d Cir.1982) (medical literature admissible as long as called to the attention of expert witness and established as authoritative); Schneider v. Revici, 817 F.2d 987, 991 (2d Cir.1987).

required to actually explain the treatise, but the expert is available if either party wishes to ask questions about it.[274]

§ 7.33   Learned Treatise Exception [FRE 803(18)]—Foundation for Use of Learned Treatise

Established as Reliable Authority

The treatise must be shown to be authoritative. This can be done in a number of ways.[275] The treatise may be established as reliable authority through the testimony of the proponent's own expert witness.[276] Or the opposing expert can be used to establish that the work is authoritative when the opponent's expert is willing to concede the point. Even a grudging concession that the treatise is "somewhat" authoritative may be enough to support admission.[277] Or the treatise can be established as authoritative through judicial notice.[278] It seems that this would rarely be appropriate, but Judge Weinstein suggests that

> In a medical malpractice case ... if plaintiff cannot get an expert to testify on the standard of care, it is equally unlikely that an expert will testify about authoritative treatises. If defendant's experts refuse to concede the qualifications of a particular work, the trial judge should be liberal in allowing other proof of the treatise's authoritativeness so long as it indicates that the book is recognized by the medical professional. For example, reading lists used in medical school courses or postgraduate seminars might be admissible as market reports or commercial publications and a court might take judicial notice of books admitted in the course of other litigation.[279]

274. Note this also helps reduce the danger of passages of learned treatises being taken out of context. *See* 5 Weinstein's Federal Evidence § 803.23[1] (2d ed. Joseph M. McLaughlin ed. 1997).

275. *See* Fed. R. Evid. 803(18) advisory committee's note; see also Johnson v. William C. Ellis & Sons Iron Works, 609 F.2d 820, 822 (5th Cir.1980) (treatises may be established as reliable authority by either testimony or admission of an expert witness, or by other expert testimony, or by judicial notice).

276. *See* Burgess v. Premier Corp., 727 F.2d 826, 834 (9th Cir.1984) (books on cattle investment offered by proponent's expert witness admissible where expert testified that author was the pre-eminent industry expert).

277. *See* Allen v. Safeco Ins. Co., 782 F.2d 1517, 1519–20 (11th Cir.1986) (opposing expert testified that fire investigation magazine was "somewhat" authoritative and that he had used it himself; authority of magazine sufficiently established; no error by trial judge in admitting evidence); Dawson v. Chrysler Corp., 630 F.2d 950,

961 (3d Cir.1980) (reports inferentially conceded by opposing experts as authoritative properly established). The trial judge, of course, always has discretion under Rule 403 to exclude prejudicial or confusing evidence. For a decision that, on unusual facts, appears to go beyond the rule by requiring that a testifying expert *rely* upon the learned treatise, see Conde v. Velsicol Chem. Corp., 804 F.Supp. 972, 990 (S.D.Ohio 1992), *aff'd*, 24 F.3d 809 (6th Cir.1994) (in products liability action, scholarly article alleging manipulation of health data by defendant corporation inadmissible when plaintiffs failed to show any expert relied on it and article author did not testify at trial; however, letter to editor, in medical journal, discrediting study upon which defense relied admissible).

278. *See* Hemingway v. Ochsner Clinic, 608 F.2d 1040, 1047 (5th Cir.1979) (medical text written by registered nurses could not be established by judicial notice).

279. Weinstein goes on to note that the finding of authoritativeness goes only to admissibility; it is up to the jury to decide

A learned treatise might be admitted conditionally, with the expert laying the foundation after it has already been used in cross-examination.[280] However, if the expert being cross-examined says that the treatise is worthless and if there has been no prior testimony establishing that it is authoritative, the judge ought to be reluctant to admit it conditionally.[281] In any event, when there is a controversy about whether the treatise is a reliable authority, the issue is a preliminary question of fact for the trial judge to resolve in determining whether the evidence is admissible.[282]

Shown to Expert

The treatise must be shown to an expert, either one's own expert or the opponent's, on the witness stand. Even if the authoritative nature of the treatise is established by judicial notice, as opposed to expert testimony, it is still necessary that an expert witness testify in order for the excerpt from the treatise to be admissible. The reason for this requirement is that the trier ought to have the aid of an expert in interpreting the treatise, however authoritative it may be.[283]

Limitation: Treatise Is Not an Exhibit

Federal Rule of Evidence 803(18) provides, "If admitted, the statements may be read into evidence but may not be received as exhibits."[284] The advisory committee wrote:

> The rule avoids the danger of misunderstanding and misapplication by limiting the use of treatises as substantive evidence to situations in which an expert is on the stand and available to explain and assist in the application of the treatise if desired. The limitation upon receiving the publication itself physically in evidence, contained in the last sentence, is designed to further this policy.[285]

what weight to give to the treatise. 5 Weinstein's Federal Evidence § 803.23[14], at 803–122 to 803–123 (2d ed. Joseph M. McLauglin ed. 1997) (footnotes omitted).

280. *Cf.* Fed. R. Evid. 104(b); *see* Maggipinto v. Reichman, 481 F.Supp. 547, 550–52 (E.D.Pa.1979) (treatise used for impeachment purposes properly excluded for substantive purposes where treatise not offered and established as reliable authority).

281. *See* Dawsey v. Olin Corp., 782 F.2d 1254, 1263–64 (5th Cir.1986) (no error in prohibiting use of government publication in cross-examination where no experts testified that publication was reliable authority and one testified that it was unreliable).

282. *See* Fed. R. Evid. 104 (a).

283. *See* Fed. R. Evid. 803(18) advisory committee's note; *see also* 2 McCormick on Evidence § 321, at 352 (4th ed. John W. Strong ed. 1992) (the restriction is "designed to ensure that materials are used only under the sponsorship of an expert who can assist the fact finder and explain how to apply the materials").

284. Fed. R. Evid. 803(18).

285. Fed. R. Evid. 803(18) advisory committee's note; see also Dartez v. Fibreboard Corp, 765 F.2d 456, 465 (5th Cir. 1985):

> The reason for the Rule's restrictions on the use of learned treatises is to avoid the possibility that the jury will misunderstand and misapply the technical language within such an article if they are allowed to consider the publication itself instead of receiving the information through the testimony of an expert in the field.

In other words, the lawyer or witness can read a passage from the treatise to the jury once the foundation has been established, but the jurors cannot take the treatise into the jury room and read it themselves.

§ 7.34 Ancient Documents [FRE 803(16)]

The exception for statements in ancient documents is recognized both at common law and under the Federal Rules.[286] It applies to allow the reception of documents that have been in existence for a certain period of time–20 years under the federal rules. Common law exceptions often contained a requirement that the document be found in a place where it would naturally be expected to be found.[287] The Federal Rule simply affirms that the document must be authentic.[288] Courts appear to admit evidence under Federal Rule of Evidence 803(16) as long as it is properly authenticated under Rule 901.[289] It is at least arguable, however, that the burden of proof for admission under 803(16) is different than that for authenticating evidence under 901. Under Rule 803(16) the document must be shown to be authentic by a preponderance of the evidence;[290] under Rule 901 evidence sufficient to support a finding would have been enough.[291] Of course, one of the ways to show that a document is authentic under the Federal Rules is to show that it was found where it would most likely be if authentic, and that it is in a condition that raises no suspicion as to its authenticity.[292]

An example of the operation of the rule appears in *In re Rhode Island Asbestos Cases*.[293] In that case, plaintiff offered records of an asbestos company that were prepared more than 20 years before the action. Noting the age of the documents and the fact that their origin and storage had been adequately accounted for, the court admitted them under the ancient documents exception.[294]

286. *See generally* 5 Weinstein's Federal Evidence § 803.21 (2d ed. Joseph M. McLaughlin ed. 1997); 2 McCormick on Evidence § 323 (4th ed. John W. Strong ed. 1992).

287. *See, e.g.,* Sinkora v. Wlach, 35 N.W.2d 40, 47–48 (1948) (66–year-old passport found where expected admissible); Tillman v. Lincoln Warehouse Corp., 423 N.Y.S.2d 151, 153 (1979) (30–year-old inventory shown to have come from proper custody admissible).

288. Fed. R. Evid. 803(16).

289. *See, e.g.,* DeWeerth v. Baldinger, 658 F.Supp. 688, 695 n. 12 (S.D.N.Y.1987) ("The relevant exhibits, specifically the 1943 photograph . . . have been in existence 20 years or more and thus contain hearsay admissible under the ancient documents exception of Fed. R. Evid. 803(16)"); Dartez v. Fibreboard Corp., 765 F.2d 456, 464 (5th Cir.1985) ("The authentication requirement is governed by the standards set forth in Fed. R. Evid. 901(a)").

290. It is arguable that the foundation for any hearsay exception must be shown by a preponderance. *See* Bourjaily v. United States, 483 U.S. 171, 175–76 (1987) (holding that the preliminary facts necessary to establish the foundation for evidence under 801(d)(2)(E) must be proven by a preponderance of the evidence).

291. *See* Fed. R. Evid. 901(a); the requirement of authentication is satisfied by "evidence sufficient to support a finding that the matter in question is what its proponent claims."

292. *See* Fed. R. Evid. 901(b)(8).

293. 11 Fed. R. Evid. Serv. (Callaghan) 444 (D.R.I.1982).

294. *Id.* at 447. *See also* United States v. Stelmokas, 100 F.3d 302, 312 (3d Cir. 1996) (held, Nazi and Soviet records showing Stelmokas membership in Lithuanian unit that murdered Jews admissible as ancient documents despite allegations of policy of spoliation and forgery by such au-

Another modern case admitting an ancient document as an exception to the hearsay rule is *Fulmer v. Connors*.[295] In the *Fulmer* case, the court admitted cash books and time and payment books of a company to establish that certain wages were paid in 1941. The books were over 20 years old, had been found as expected in the company's records, and did not appear suspect.[296]

For a case in which the exception did not apply because of problems of showing that the document was authentic, see *Dartez v. Fibreboard Corp.*.[297] *Dartez* involved intracompany correspondence about employees possibly injured by exposure to asbestos. The plaintiff failed to introduce evidence that the documents came from the company's records, and the court considered that the requirement of authentication had not been satisfied because the documents were not found in the expected place. While finding the documents in the expected place is not an invariable requirement (they can be authenticated by other means, so long as they are shown to be what they purport to be), the absence of other admissible evidence to authenticate the documents in this case made the failure to make that showing fatal.[298]

The use of an ancient document to prove the truth of its assertion involves hearsay dangers. The maker of the document might have been insincere or deficient in some other way. However, the age of the document at least provides assurance that it was not prepared in a self-serving manner with the present controversy in mind. Also, there is a special need for the hearsay, because memories of persons who lived at the time may have faded, or it might be difficult to find other evidence. Finally, the fact that the document is in writing at least removes dangers that the in-court witness might have misunderstood the hearsay statement or manufactured it.[299]

§ 7.35 Family History Exceptions and Related Matters [FRE 803(19), 804(b)(4)]

Classroom teachers sometimes startle students by asking them whether asking a witness "How old are you?" is objectionable. The witness has no personal knowledge, at least not of the exact date of birth. The witness' knowledge is derived from the statements of others, and those statements are out-of-court statements that are offered for the truth of the matter asserted. So the rules requiring personal knowledge and banning hearsay seem to stand in the way of this everyday testimony.[300]

thorities; Holocaust experts vouched for authenticity of documents).

295. 665 F.Supp. 1472 (N.D.Ala.1987).

296. *Id.* at 149.

297. 765 F.2d 456 (5th Cir. 1985).

298. *Id.* at 464–65.

299. *See* 5 Weinstein's Federal Evidence, *supra* note 286 § 803.21[1]; 2

McCormick on Evidence, *supra* note 286 § 323, at 358; Roger C. Park, *A Subject Matter Approach to Hearsay Reform*, 86 Mich. L. Rev. 51, 71–73 (1987).

300. For an example of taking this idea to its logical extreme, see Mary Morton, Note, *The Hearsay Rule and Epistemological Suicide*, 74 Geo. L.J. 1301 (1986) (when witness testifies that the witness saw a

The question is not entirely a silly classroom exercise. Sometimes a fact such as age can be a crucial fact in the litigation. This is the case, for example, when the defendant is accused of a sexual crime that can only be committed against a victim who is underage.[301] Ideally one might want to require the best evidence available, such as a birth certificate or even the testimony of someone present at the birth. However, that degree of strictness has not usually been observed. The testimony of a witness about the witness' own age is admissible in evidence, both at common law[302] and under the Federal Rules of Evidence.[303] The hearsay exceptions governing statements about family history cover not only testimony about name and birthdate, but also about adoption, marriage, divorce, legitimacy, family relationship (by blood, marriage, or adoption), ancestry, and similar facts of personal or family history. They apply not only to testimony by the witness on the stand about the witness' own family history, but also about the family history of others.

The modern family history exceptions are descendants of the common law pedigree exception. The pedigree exception is one of the first established exceptions to the hearsay rule. Chief Justice John Marshall listed it in 1813 as one of the four exceptions "said to be as old as the [hearsay] rule itself."[304]

---

chair, the testimony is hearsay because the witness only knows what a chair is by having been told by others).

301. *See* Government of Virgin Islands v. Joseph, 765 F.2d 394, 397 n. 5 (3d Cir. 1985) (held, victim may testify about her own age over hearsay objection). Of course, where age is a crucial fact, the party seeking to prove the person's age will have an incentive to offer stronger evidence of the victim's age. In cases such as *Joseph*, for example, the jury might well discount the victim's own testimony.

302. *See* 5 John H. Wigmore, Evidence in Trials at Common Law § 1493 (James H. Chadbourn rev. 1974); United States v. Austrew, 202 F.Supp. 816, 822 (D.Md. 1962). However, common law courts were occasionally quite strict. *See* Pickering v. Peskind, 183 N.E. 301, 305–06 (1930) (plaintiff not allowed to testify about own birthdate, as told to her by her grandmother); National Aid Life Assn. v. Wiles, 41 P.2d 655 (1935) (daughter of insured not allowed to testify to family reputation about insured's age). The latter case can perhaps be explained on policy grounds as a case in which age was crucial, the statements were self-serving, and better evidence should have been available.

303. *See* Government of Virgin Islands v. Joseph, 765 F.2d 394, 397 n. 5 (3d Cir. 1985) (held, victim may testify about her own age over hearsay objection).

304. Mima Queen & Child, Petitioners for Freedom v. Hepburn, 11 U.S. (7 Cranch) 290, 296 (1813) (Marshall, J.):

> To this rule there are some exceptions which are said to be as old as the rule itself. These are cases of pedigree, of prescription, of custom, and in some cases of boundary. There are also matters of general and public history, which may be received without that full proof which is necessary for the establishment of a private fact.

The *Mima Queen* case was a petition for freedom by persons held in slavery. Chief Justice Marshall refused to extend the pedigree exception to allow reception of evidence that the petitioners' ancestors had been free, holding that hearsay evidence on this subject should be excluded, and stating that "this Court is not inclined to extend the exceptions further than they have already been carried." *Id.* at 297. An able dissent by Justice Duvall argued that hearsay evidence was admissible

> Upon the same principle, upon which it is admitted to prove a custom, pedigree and the boundaries of land;—because from the antiquity of the transactions to which these subjects may have reference, it is impossible to produce living testimony. To exclude hearsay in such cases, would leave the party interested without remedy.... It appears to me that the reason for admitting hearsay evidence upon a question of freedom is much stronger than in cases of pedigree or

We have referred to "family history exceptions." The Federal Rules of Evidence actually contain four separate exceptions dealing with family history.

The first is the exception created by Rule 803(19) for reputation about family history. It allows a witness to testify about reputation with regard to marriage, birth, and similar facts of personal or family history. The reputation must be either among the family members, among associates, or in the community. The foundation for the testimony is similar to the foundation laid for reputation as to character. For example, the basic foundation for showing through a witness that Julie Curran is the daughter of James Curran could be laid as follows:

Example of Foundation

Did you know James Curran?

How long did you know him?

What was the nature of your association with him?

Do you know Julie Curran?

How long have you known her?

What is the nature of your association with her?

Do you know other persons who have known both James and Julie Curran?

Who are those other persons?

What is their relationship to James and Julie Curran?

[The reputation sources can be members of the family, the community, or other associations, such as co-workers.]

Have you talked to those persons about the family relationship of Julie Curran and James Curran?

Are you familiar with the reputation for family relationship of John Curran and Julie Curran among those persons?

What is that reputation?

When proceeding under this exception, there is no need to show that the declarants (the persons making the statements that collectively make up the reputation) are unavailable. However, it is necessary to show the existence of general reputation. The fact that the witness has been told by one person that X was the child of Y does not constitute a reputation.[305]

An exception for statements of family history is recognized by Federal Rule of Evidence 804(b)(4). This exception covers oral or written statements about birth, marriage, adoption, and the like. It does not require a showing of reputation. The statement of one person is enough.

in controversies relative to the boundaries of land. It will be universally admitted that the right to freedom is more important than the right of property.

305. *See* § **7.37**.

However, either that one person must be the person whose family history is sought to be proven (e.g., the statement of declarant about where she was born)[306] or the statement must be that of someone related by blood or marriage or otherwise "so intimately associated with the other's family as to be likely to have accurate information concerning the matter declared."[307] Moreover, the declarant must be unavailable. In contrast, the reputation-based family history exception, Rule 803(19), does not require any showing of unavailability.

The common law version of the exception for statements of family history required that the statement be made *ante litem motam*, that is, before the controversy arose. Once the controversy arose, the danger of fabricated evidence was considered to be too great.[308] This requirement was intentionally omitted from the Federal Rule. The advisory committee considered that this and other motives to fabricate should go to weight, not to admissibility.[309]

The third family history exception recognized by the Federal Rules of Evidence relates to family records, such as statements in family Bibles or on tombstones.[310] The fourth relates to judgments of family history.[311] These exceptions are described in separate sections of this hornbook.[312]

§ 7.36 Market Reports and Commercial Publications [FRE 803(17)]

Federal Rule of Evidence 803(17) recognizes a hearsay exception for market reports and commercial publications. The exception applies to stock market quotations, telephone directories, business directories, commercial compilations, lists, tabulations, and similar publications. The rule requires that the compilations be published and that they be generally used and relied upon by the public or by persons in particular occupations.

The rationale of the exception is that there is ordinarily no motive to deceive and that reliance upon the publications by the public or by business users is an assurance of trustworthiness. In any event, it would usually not be feasible to call all of the people involved in making a compilation, so if the information is to be received at trial at all, it must be received in its published form.[313]

The exception overlaps with the business records exception to some extent. Often the foundation for reception as a business record could be laid in the case of a commercial publication. For example, in *United*

---

306. For examples of statements involving place of birth, decided under the common law precursors to the federal exceptions, see 5 Wigmore, *supra* note 302 § 1501.

307. *See* Fed. R. Evid. 804(b)(4) and advisory committee's note.

308. *See* 5 Wigmore, *supra* note 302, at § 1483.

309. *See* Fed. R. Evid. 804(b)(4) advisory committee's note.

310. *See* Fed. R. Evid. 803(13).

311. *See* Fed. R. Evid. 803(23).

312. *See* §§ **7.37 and 7.43**.

313. *See* 5 Weinstein's Federal Evidence § 803.22[1], at 803–115 (2d Ed. Joseph M. McLaughlin ed. 1997).

States v. Grossman,[314] the defendant was charged with knowingly receiving stolen property. The property in question was 300 stolen Colibri cigarette lighters. At trial, a Colibri catalog was admitted to prove the retail price and to show that the lighters in evidence were the same models as those listed in the invoice of a stolen shipment. The court held that the catalog was admissible under the business records exception. In the view of the court, a sufficient foundation had been established through the testimony of a witness who was a purchasing agent for Colibri Corporation. The court went on to note that the trial judge could have admitted the catalog as a commercial publication under Rule 803(17), because "the catalog was a published compilation generally used and relied upon by retailers of Colibri lighters."[315] The exception specifically requires both that the report be published and that it be generally relied upon. There is some authority for a third requirement, that the report concern objective facts not requiring interpretation or analysis.[316]

Reports that fail to meet both these requirements may nonetheless be used by experts in forming opinions if they meet the reasonable reliance requirements of Rule 703.[317]

§ 7.37 Reputation Concerning Boundaries, Land Customs, and General History [FRE 803(20)]

Rule 803(20) of the Federal Rules of Evidence creates what amounts to two exceptions. The first is an exception for reputation in the community as to boundaries or customs affecting lands. As to this exception, the Rule specifically requires that the reputation arise before the controversy, though it does not require that the reputation be ancient.[318] The second is an exception for reputation in the community as to events of general history. As to this exception, the Rule does not specifically require either that the reputation be ancient or that it arise before the controversy. However, the Rule's reference to general "history" may cause courts to infer that the information must be non-contemporary. For example, in *State ex rel Abrams v. Ocean Club, Inc.,*[319] the court refused to admit, under the exception, a club's relatively contemporaneous reputation for being anti-Semitic as evidence of discrimination, on grounds that the reputation should be either ancient or at least not likely to be provable with living witnesses. This interpretation is supported by the reason that the advisory committee gave for not requiring, in the second part of the rule, that the reputation arise before the controversy-that "the historical character of the subject matter

---

314. 614 F.2d 295, 296–97 (1st Cir. 1980).

315. *Id.* at 297.

316. *See* White Indus. v. Cessna Aircraft Co., 611 F.Supp. 1049 (W.D.Mo.1985) (rejecting prospectus filed with SEC as evidence, and noting both publication requirement and requirement that the publication concern objective facts).

317. *See* § 10.08.

318. *See* Fed. R. Evid. 803(19)-(21) advisory committee's note (stating "The reputation is required to antedate the controversy, though not to be ancient").

319. 602 F.Supp. 489 (E.D.N.Y.1984).

dispenses with any need that the reputation antedate the controversy with respect to which it is offered."

Like other reputation evidence, the supposed guarantee of trustworthiness for this type of evidence is that the community will have discussed and scrutinized the matter carefully, so that its conclusion is likely to be reliable.[320] It has been said that to be probative the reputation must concern "such facts as have been of interest to all members of the community as such, and therefore have been so likely to receive general and intelligent discussion and examination by competent persons, so that the community's received opinion on the subject cannot be supposed to have reached the condition of definite decision until the matter had gone, in public relief, beyond the stage of controversy and had become settled with fair finality.[321]

In both parts of the exception, the reputation involved must be community reputation, not merely the word of one person or reputation among a narrow slice of the community. This requirement was examined in *Ute Indian Tribe v. Utah*,[322] in which the court held that the reputation in the non-Indian community about tribal boundaries was admissible, but noted that it would be given little probative weight in the bench trial because of the adverse attitude of the non-Indian community to the Indian community.

As to most events of history, the "general history" part of the exception is not needed. Most historical events are offered not as adjudicative facts, which relate to the issues of who did what in the particular lawsuit, but as legislative facts, which relate to how to interpret law or what the law should be. Legislative fact issues may be resolved by judicial notice. that is, even if there is a reasonable dispute about the accuracy of a legislative fact, a court may resolve the dispute without taking testimony, by referring to whatever sources the court deems reliable.[323] Even as to adjudicative facts, many historical facts are

---

320. Fed. R. Evid. 803(19)-(21) advisory committee's note; Ute Indian Tribe v. Utah, 521 F.Supp. 1072 (D.Utah 1981), *revd on other grounds* 773 F.2d 1087 (10th Cir. 1985), *cert. denied*, 479 U.S. 994 (1986).

321. 5 John H. Wigmore, Evidence in Trials at Common Law § 1598, at 564–65 (James H. Chadbourn rev. 1974); *see also id.* §§ 1583–1597.

322. 521 F.Supp. 1072 (D.Utah 1981), *rev'd. on other grounds* 773 F.2d 1087 (10th Cir.1985), *cert. denied*, 479 U.S. 994 (1986).

323. Kenneth C. Davis, Administrative Law Treatise 296 (3d ed. 1972):

The cardinal distinction which more than any other governs the use of extra-record facts by courts and agencies is the distinction between legislative facts and adjudicative facts. When a court or an agency finds facts concerning the im-mediate parties—who did what, where, when, how and with what motive or intent—the court or agency is performing an adjudicative function, and the facts are conveniently called adjudicative facts. When a court or agency develops law or policy, it is acting legislatively. The courts have created the common law through judicial legislation, and the facts which inform the tribunal's legislative judgment are called legislative facts.... The exceedingly practical difference between legislative and adjudicative facts is that, apart from facts properly noticed, the tribunal's findings of adjudicative facts must be supported by evidence, but findings or assumptions of legislative facts need not be, frequently are not, and sometimes cannot be supported by evidence.

(Footnotes omitted.)

generally known within the territorial jurisdiction of the trial court or capable of accurate and ready determination by resort to sources whose accuracy cannot reasonably be questioned, and hence are judicially noticeable under Rule 201(b).

The "general history" aspect of the exception is little used. Facts of general history are likely to be derived from information that qualifies for another hearsay exception, such as the exceptions for ancient documents, learned treatises, and business records, or to be a proper subject for judicial notice, as is the case when the historical fact is being used for lawmaking or law interpretation.[324]

The exception was used, or at least alluded to as one possible basis for receiving evidence, in *Pan American World Airways v. Aetna Casualty & Surety Co.*[325] This case involved insurance claims arising out of the hijacking of a Pan Am jet by persons aligned with the Palestine Liberation Organization. To allocate the insurance liability between the "all risk" and the "war risk" carriers, the court had to consider facts about the nature of the PLO and the Middle East conflict. It noted that in hearing the case it had generally taken a liberal view of the admissibility of hearsay, on grounds that it would have to consider hearsay or be in the dark about many issues. It alluded to the predecessor common law general history exception, as exemplified by what was then Proposed Rule 803(20), and to judicial notice as possible bases for admitting the evidence.

§ 7.38 Use of Prior Convictions to Prove the Convicted Person Committed the Acts Charged and Related Matters [FRE 803(22)]

Records of prior convictions can be offered for a variety of reasons.

Examples

1. The judgment of conviction can be offered for impeachment of a witness in a civil or criminal case, as an attack on the witness' character for truth and veracity. This use of the prior conviction is dealt with in the section of this Hornbook that deals with impeachment of witnesses under Federal Rule of Evidence 609(a)(2).

2. The judgment of conviction can be offered as circumstantial evidence of another crime that the convicted person is alleged to have committed. For example, suppose that the prior conviction is a conviction for distributing cocaine. It is offered as evidence in a subsequent case arising from a separate occurrence. In the

---

324. *See* 5 Weinstein's Federal Evidence § 803.26[3] (2d ed. Joseph M. McLaughlin ed. 1997) (noting that there has always been a dearth of authority under the exception, and that under the Federal Rules there is probably less need of the

exception than before because of the learned treatise exception).

325. 368 F.Supp. 1098 (S.D.N.Y.1973) (although Federal Rule 803(20) was not in effect at the time of this case, the court alluded to the proposed version of the rule).

new case, the defendant is charged with possessing cocaine with intent to distribute. The defendant claims that the cocaine possessed in the second case was for the defendant's own personal use, and that he or she had no intent to distribute. Most courts would admit the prior conviction as evidence of intent to distribute. (For that matter, most would admit evidence of prior sales of cocaine that did not lead to conviction on the same theory.) This hornbook discusses this basis for receiving prior convictions in the sections of the character evidence chapter that deal with admissibility of other crimes, wrongs, and acts under Rule 404(b). *See* **Ch. 5**.

3. A judgment of conviction may be offered because a fact determined in a criminal case is in issue in a subsequent civil action that arises from the same transaction or occurrence. The convicted defendant is seeking to relitigate in the civil case a fact necessarily determined in the criminal case. The prior conviction is being used to establish, in the civil case, one of the very facts that was at issue in the criminal case. This way of using prior convictions is the subject of the present section.

    One example of this third type of proffer of a prior conviction occurs when, in a personal injury action, plaintiff offers evidence that defendant was convicted of driving under the influence, the conviction arises from the accident that caused the plaintiff's injury, and the conviction is offered to show that defendant was driving under the influence at the time of the accident.[326] Another example is the action to recover on a fire insurance claim, where the defendant insurance company offers evidence that the claimant was convicted of arson in the burning of the property that forms the basis for the claim.[327]

The use of records of convictions to establish facts essential to the conviction has undergone dramatic changes in modern law. Until relatively recently, the general rule was that the prior conviction was not even *admissible* in evidence.[328] In recent decades, the courts have moved toward treating these convictions not only as admissible (but rebuttable) evidence, but as being *conclusive* on the facts established in the first case under the principles of collateral estoppel. We will turn first to this strongest use of the prior conviction.

---

326. *See, e.g.,* Scott v. Robertson, 583 P.2d 188 (Alaska 1978) (held, drunken driving conviction admissible in subsequent civil action, and conclusive on issue of whether defendant was driving when intoxicated). For cases adopting a more restrictive view, see W.E. Shipley, Annotation, *Conviction or Acquittal as Evidence of the Facts on Which It was Based in Civil Action,* 18 A.L.R.2d 1287 (1951).

327. *See, e.g.,* Schindler v. Royal Ins. Co., 179 N.E. 711 (N.Y.1932) (insurer allowed to introduce conviction for making fraudulent insurance claim, not preclusive but admissible as evidence).

328. *See* Annotation, *supra* note 326, for numerous citations to cases supporting the traditional view.

§ 7.39 Use of Prior Convictions to Prove the Convicted Person Committed the Acts Charge and Related Matters [FRE 803(22)]—Principles of Collateral Estoppel and the Prior Conviction

Historical Doctrine

The offering of a prior conviction as rebuttable evidence must be distinguished from the offering of a prior conviction as precluding relitigation under the principles of collateral estoppel, or to use a term favored by many modern proceduralists, under the principles of issue preclusion.[329] Take, for example, the case in which a convicted arsonist brings a civil action to recover on a fire insurance policy. If the prior conviction is merely admissible in evidence, then the plaintiff is entitled to present countervailing evidence and to go to the jury on the issue of whether the fire was caused by the plaintiff's arson. If the prior conviction has preclusive effect because of the doctrine of collateral estoppel, then the arson cannot be contested at trial and the insurance company is entitled to summary judgment on the issue.

The traditional reason for declining to give collateral estoppel effect to a prior conviction is the doctrine of mutuality. In the arson example, the insurer would not have been bound by a decision in the criminal case in favor of the alleged arsonist because it was not a party.[330] (It would not be fair to bind the insurer with the results of a case in which it was not represented. In any event, it could not be bound by an acquittal, which is merely a decision that there was a reasonable doubt, not a decision that the accused did not commit arson. When the standard of proof changes from proof beyond a reasonable doubt to some lower requirement, then collateral estoppel does not apply if the party against whom it is sought to be used is the beneficiary of a more favorable standard of proof in the second action.[331]) Under the doctrine of mutuality of estoppel, if the first judgment went in favor of the insurance company, then the convicted arsonist would not be bound in the second case. A person who had not been a party to the prior lawsuit was neither bound by the prior suit nor permitted to take advantage of any determinations made in the prior action.[332]

The traditional mutuality rule was based on the notion that it was unfair to allow someone to take advantage of findings in an action in

---

329. Fleming James, Geoffrey Hazard & John Leubsdorf, Civil Procedure § 11.3 (4th ed. 1992) (stating that the "effect traditionally known as collateral estoppel now is called issue preclusion.").

330. *See, e.g.,* Show–World Center v. Walsh, 438 F.Supp. 642 (S.D.N.Y.1977); Restatement (Second) of Judgments § 34(3) (1980). For exceptions to the rule that nonparties are not bound by a judgment, see *id.* §§ 34–61 (codifying privity exceptions); Teitelbaum Furs, Inc. v. Dominion Ins. Co.,

375 P.2d 439, 25 Cal.Rptr. 559, (Cal. 1962) (en banc; Traynor, J.) (closely held corporations collaterally estopped from recovering alleged insurance loss after president convicted of crimes arising from false insurance claims based on same loss).

331. *See* Restatement (Second) of Judgments § 28(4) (1980) and cases cited in Reporter's Note thereto.

332. James, Hazard & Leubsdorf, *supra* note 329, § 11.25.

which that person was not a party, since that person was not bound by any adverse determination. The doctrine's appeal to notions of equal treatment was based on an oversimplification. It treated persons equally when in fact they were in quite different situations. It treated the party who had an opportunity to litigate in the first action in the same way that it treated a nonparty who had no opportunity.

The mutuality rule never appealed to scholars. Bentham said that the rule was more appropriate to the gaming table than the law court.[333] Other scholars have maintained his attack upon the doctrine, and the courts seem to have listened. They made repeated incursions on the mutuality doctrine. It became riddled with exceptions, and then itself became the exception. The prevailing modern view is that if a party had a full and fair opportunity to litigate in the first action, that party ought generally to be bound in subsequent litigation, in the absence of special circumstances.[334]

The once-prevalent ban on prior criminal convictions as collateral estoppel in subsequent civil cases was a specific application of the mutuality doctrine, though other considerations, such as the absence of discovery in criminal actions and procedural differences between criminal and civil cases, may also have had an impact.[335]

Issue Preclusion Where Mutuality Exists

Cases in which a criminal action is followed by a civil suit by the government are simpler than those in which the civil litigant is a private party, because they do not present the same problems of mutuality. The same parties are present in both actions. An example of issue preclusion in a case not raising mutuality problems is *United States v. Killough*.[336] *Killough* was a civil action in which the United States sued to recover money lost to contractors who had worked on disaster relief in the wake of Hurricane Frederic in 1979. The contractors had submitted fraudulently inflated invoices for mobile home set-ups. They had been involved in a scheme under which they would pay kickbacks to officials, and then would inflate the amount charged the government to recoup the kick-

---

333. 7 Works of Jeremy Bentham 171 (U. Bowring ed. 1843), as quoted in Brainerd Currie, Mutuality of Collateral Estoppel.-Limits of the Bernhard Doctrine, 9 Stan. L. Rev. 281, 284 (1957):

Another curious rule is, that, as a judgment is not evidence against a stranger, the contrary judgment shall not be evidence for him. If the rule itself is a curious one, the reason given for it is still more so:—"nobody can take benefit by a verdict, who had not been prejudiced by it, had it gone contrary": a maxim which one would suppose to have found its way from the gaming table to the bench.

334. *See, e.g.,* Parklane Hosiery Co. v. Shore, 439 U.S. 322 (1979) (permitting of-

fensive issue preclusion in favor of plaintiffs seeking to take advantage of determination in prior action, brought by SEC, that defendant had issued a materially misleading and false proxy statement); Restatement (Second) of judgments § 29 (1980).

335. *Cf.* Annotation, *Conviction or Acquittal as Evidence of the Facts on Which it was Based in Civil Action,* 18 A.L.R.2d 1287, 1291–98 (1951) (describing reasons given by common law courts, both for not giving preclusive effect and for excluding evidence of the conviction); Scott v. Robertson, 583 P.2d 188 (Alaska 1978) (describing reasons for cautious attitude in course of adopting much more adventuresome one).

336. 848 F.2d 1523 (11th Cir.1988).

backs. The officials and the defrauding contractors were convicted after a guilty plea of conspiracy to defraud the United States.

The government sued the contractors and two officials. It filed a motion for partial summary judgment, claiming that preclusive effect should be given to the guilty pleas. The trial court granted summary judgment on all issues except damages. On appeal, the court noted that "when an issue is resolved in favor of the United States in a criminal prosecution, that issue may not be contested by the same defendant in a subsequent civil suit brought by the government." The prior judgment was not merely evidence of guilt, it conclusively established guilt.[337] On the general question of preclusion when there are successive suits by the government to impose a criminal penalty and then recover the proceeds of crime, the *Killough* case represents established law. There appears to be general agreement under modern law that when the government seeks to recover the proceeds of a crime, the prior conviction precludes relitigation.[338]

Issue Preclusion Despite Lack of Mutuality

In *Killough*, the parties were the same in both cases, so the dangers of unfair preclusion were reduced.[339] Cases in which a third party seeks to obtain preclusive effect from a criminal conviction are more difficult. However, the trend seems to be in favor of preclusion even when mutuality is lacking, that is, even when the conviction is sought to be used by a third party, not by the government. The preclusion is most likely to be granted in cases in which the convicted party is seeking to benefit from the crime, as in cases in which the arsonist sues for the proceeds of the fire insurance policy[340] or the murderer sues as the beneficiary of the life insurance policy.[341] There is also ample authority for allowing a victim of crime to use preclusion to recover from the perpetrator the proceeds of the crime.[342] In other situations, the law is

337. *See id.* at 1528 and cases cited therein. The prior judgment was conclusive on the guilt of the defendants and on the fact that they had paid at least $577,400 in kickbacks. *Id.*

338. *See* Hiroshi Motomura, *Using Judgments As Evidence*, 70 Minn. L. Rev. 979, 990 & n.39 (1986).

339. Arguably, there was a problem of unequal treatment because had the defendants been acquitted in the first action, the government would not necessarily have been bound. *See* United States v. Killough, 848 F.2d 1523 (11th Cir.1988). However, some of the other problems that arise when the parties are different were missing in *Killough*. There was no danger of unforeseeability of the second action, and there was no danger that the first action was influenced by sympathy for a now-absent party.

340. *See* Eagle, Star & British Dominions Ins. Co. v. Heller, 140 S.E. 314 (Va.

1927) (after conviction for arson, arsonist barred from recovering on policy). Compare Breeland v. Security Ins. Co., 421 F.2d 918 (5th Cir.1969) (held, under Louisiana law applicable in diversity case, prior criminal conviction for fraud in reporting value of fire loss precludes civil suit and justifies summary judgment). *See generally* Jonathan C. Thau, *Collateral Estoppel and the Reliability of Criminal Determinations: Theoretical, Practical, and Strategic Implications for Criminal and Civil Litigation*, 70 Geo. L.J. 1079 (1982).

341. *See* Travelers Ins. Co. v. Thompson, 163 N.W.2d 289 (Minn.1968) (held, husband's conviction for murdering wife preclusive in his later action to recover proceeds from her life insurance policy).

342. Motomura, *supra* note 338, at 990.

more muddled, but the trend seems to be toward greater and greater use of the doctrine of preclusion, at least when there was a full and fair opportunity to litigate in the first action and the loser in that action cannot point to any obvious defect in the proceeding.[343]

An example of the modern trend toward allowing issue preclusion even though mutuality is lacking is *Scott v. Robertson*.[344] There, the plaintiff in a personal injury action arising from an automobile accident had been convicted of drunken driving in the very accident that gave rise to the civil action. The Alaska court expressed the view that the defendants in the civil action should be permitted not only to introduce the conviction into evidence, but to have it be given preclusive effect on the issue whether the plaintiff had been driving while intoxicated at the time of the accident. The court was willing to do this despite the absence of mutuality (the party seeking to take advantage of preclusion in the second action was not a party in the first action, and hence could not have been bound by any result of the first action). It noted that the prior conviction was for a relatively serious offense, punishable by a year's incarceration for the first offense, and that the defendant had in fact had a full and fair trial at the first hearing. It noted that its result might have been different had defendant lacked some significant procedural right, such as the right to jury trial.[345]

Though the trend seems to be toward preclusion, the result reached by cases like *Scott* is by no means firmly established. There are likely to continue to be jurisdictions that give prior convictions lesser effect, with a good deal of local variation in a field that is in so much flux.[346]

When considering whether a conviction has preclusive effect, one of the traditional requirements of collateral estoppel should be borne in

---

343. *See* Restatement (Second) of Judgments § 85(2)(a) comment e (1980) thereto, and authorities cited in comment e. Section 85(2)(a) provides, "A judgment in favor of the prosecuting authority is preclusive in favor of a third person in a civil action ... [a]gainst the defendant in the criminal prosecution as stated in § 29. Section 29 provides generally that a party precluded from relitigating an issue with an opposing party is precluded against third parties, with certain exceptions designed to protect public policy or avoid unfairness. Most of the exceptions, for example, the exception for cases in which the party seeking to use preclusion could have effected joinder in the first action, see § 29(3), would appear not to be applicable in the usual criminal case. However, the exception for cases in which there are procedural opportunities in the second action that might have significantly affected the outcome, see § 29(2) and comment d, might apply in some cases involving criminal convictions (*e.g.*, the traffic court conviction followed by the million dollar civil action).

344. 583 P.2d 188 (Alaska 1978).

345. *Id.* at 193.

346. *See, e.g.*, Brown v. Green, 738 F.2d 202 (7th Cir.1984) (under Illinois law, where defendant is convicted on the merits at trial, conviction not preclusive, but evidence surrounding prior conviction admissible in subsequent civil proceeding as prima facie evidence of facts on which conviction based; citing, *inter alia*, Thornton v. Paul, 384 N.E.2d 335 (Ill.1978). *See also* Aetna Cas. & Surety Co. v. Niziolek, 481 N.E.2d 1356 (Mass.1985) (under Massachusetts law, insured who was conviction at trial of burning property to collect insurance proceeds was collaterally estopped from relitigating issues in civil action; but conviction of second defendant of arson, entered on guilty plea, did not collaterally estop that party from litigating issues in later civil action, though conviction was admissible in evidence).

mind. The doctrine of collateral estoppel traditionally applies only to issues that were actually litigated and determined in a prior action. This traditional requirement has also undergone some erosion. Where followed, however, the requirement of actual litigation imposes a severe limit upon the preclusive effect of prior convictions. It would mean not only that prior convictions resulting from a plea of nolo contendere are not preclusive, but also that prior convictions resulting from a guilty plea are not preclusive. The *Killough* case, described above, seems to represent the current trend in the federal courts, at least in cases in which the government brings a civil action after having prevailed in a criminal action. In *Killough*, the prior convictions were treated as preclusive even though they arose from guilty pleas, not from actual litigation. The defendants were precluded from contesting the facts that they had admitted in the guilty pleas. They were not even allowed to put in evidence explaining why they made the pleas.[347] There is, however, authority to the contrary.[348] The traditional view was well stated by Judge Traynor:

> A plea of guilty is admissible in a subsequent civil action on the independent ground that it is an admission. It would not serve the policy underlying collateral estoppel, however, to make such a plea conclusive. "The rule [of collateral estoppel] is based upon the sound public policy of limiting litigation by preventing a party who has had one fair trial on an issue from again drawing it into controversy." ... "This policy must be considered together with the policy that a party shall not be deprived of a fair adversary proceeding in which fully to present his case." ... When a plea of guilty has been entered in the prior action, no issues have been "drawn into controversy" by a "full presentation" of the case. It may reflect only a compromise or a belief that paying a fine is more advantageous than litigation. Considerations of fairness to civil litigants and regard for the expeditious administration of criminal justice ... combine to prohibit the application of collateral estoppel against a party who, having pleaded guilty to a criminal charge, seeks for the first time to litigate his cause in a civil action.[349]

§ 7.40 Use of Prior convictions to Prove the Convicted Person Committed the Acts Charged and Related Matters [FRE 803(22)]—Use of Prior Convictions as Evidence

Even if a prior conviction is not preclusive under the doctrine of collateral estoppel, it may still be admissible as evidence of the facts

347. *See* United States v. Killough, 848 F.2d 1523, 1528 (11th Cir.1988) (trial judge did not abuse discretion in excluding the evidence).

348. *See* David L. Shapiro, *Should a Guilty Plea have Preclusive Effect?*, 70 Iowa L. Rev. 27 (1984).

349. Teitelbaum Furs, Inc. v. Dominion Ins. Co., 375 P.2d 439, 441 (Cal.1962) (dictum) (citations omitted).

necessary to support the judgment.[350] Though rebuttable, it is likely to be persuasive.

Traditionally, courts have not favored this use of the prior conviction. They have cited some of the same concerns about lack of mutuality that have impeded acceptance of the prior conviction as collateral estoppel. They have also expressed concern that the evidence would be too powerful, that jurors would tend to treat it as conclusive even if told not to do so.[351] Finally (and perhaps least important) the prior conviction is technically hearsay. When offered to prove guilt of the prior crime or to establish a fact essential to the judgment, the record of prior conviction is hearsay. It is the unsworn, uncross-examined statement of the trier of fact that the accused committed the crime charged. For the answer to the question whether the judgment is admissible to prove the truth of what it asserts, we must turn to the hearsay exception covering judgments of prior convictions, which in jurisdictions following the Federal Rules of Evidence is Rule 803(22).[352]

Although Rule 803(22) technically addresses only the hearsay problem, leaving open the possibility of exclusion of a prior conviction on Rule 403 grounds if the jury is likely to be over-influenced by it, in practice the prior conviction that meets the requirements of Rule 803(22) is likely to be admitted.

Under Rule 803(22), the prior conviction must have been for a crime punishable by death or imprisonment for more than a year.[353] Note, however, that when a prior conviction results from a guilty plea, the guilty plea may be independently admissible as the admission of a party-opponent.[354] On the other hand, Rule 803(22), which specifically provides

---

350. For an example of a prior conviction that was admissible but not given preclusive effect, see Brown v. Green, 738 F.2d 202 (7th Cir.1984). Brown v. Green arose in federal court in a state that did not give preclusive effect to prior convictions. The federal court applied state preclusion law but admitted the conviction as rebuttable evidence under Fed. R. Evid. 803(22).

351. For a useful discussion of the rationale for the traditional view, by a court that departs from it drastically, see Scott v. Robertson, 583 P.2d 188 (Alaska 1978).

352. The use of prior convictions solely to impeach the credibility of a witness is not affected by Rule 803(22). If a prior conviction-satisfies the requirements of Rule 609, then it is not required separately to satisfy the requirements of Rule 803(22). For example, Rule 803(22)'s provision that only convictions for crimes punishable by more than a year are admissible is not applicable when the conviction is for a crime of dishonesty within the meaning of Rule 669(a)(2). In such an instance, even though the conviction is still hearsay and even though it is being offered to prove the

truth of the matter asserted, Rule 609 itself creates an exception that supplements the exception created in Rule 803(22).

353. Some courts have allowed convictions for lesser crimes to be admitted under Rule 803(8) despite the apparent intent of this rule. See Stroud v. Cook, 931 F.Supp. 733, 736 (D.Nev.1996) (misdemeanor conviction that did not qualify under Rule 803(22) nevertheless admissible as public record under Rule 803(8) (alternative holding). Accord, United States v. Loera, 923 F.2d 725, 730 (9th Cir.1991). Contra Nipper v. Snipes, 7 F.3d 415, 417 (4th Cir.1993).

354. Guilty pleas to very minor offenses, such as traffic offenses, may not be highly probative on the issue of guilt, because of the possibility that the defendant merely wanted to dispose of the problem without bothersome proceedings. Yet there are undoubtedly some cases in which a guilty plea to even a minor traffic offense has substantial probative value. In addition, when the defendant had a real chance to contest the proceedings, the willingness to plead guilty seems at least relevant, and an exception for evidence of a final judgment entered after a trial or upon a plea of guilty, so long as the crime is punishable by a year or more, could be construed to carry a negative implication. What would be the point of excluding the prior conviction resulting from the plea of guilty if the guilty plea itself could come in?[355]

The hearsay exception, by the express terms of Rule 803(22), does not apply to guilty verdicts that are the result of pleas of nolo contendere, but only to verdicts that follow a trial or guilty plea. The rule preserves the traditional characteristics of a nolo plea, which was created essentially to avoid some of the consequences of an admission of guilt but to allow the case to be disposed of without trial.[356]

§ 7.41   Records of Religious Organizations [FRE 803(11)]

Federal Rule of Evidence 803(11) creates an exception for regularly kept records of religious organizations. These records may be used to show births, marriages, divorces, deaths, legitimacy, ancestry, relationship by blood or marriage, or other similar facts of personal or family history.

Most of this information would be admissible under the business records exception. A religious organization would be a "business" within the meaning of Rule 803(6), which covers institutions and callings of every kind, whether or not conducted for profit. However, the advisory committee decided to supplement the business records exception with the present exception because the business records exception requires that persons contributing to an entry be part of the business or activity (the "business duty" requirement).[357] Were the business records exception the only exception available, many but not all of the records admissible under the present exception would still be admissible. For example, a baptismal certificate could be used to show the fact of baptism, but the business records exception might not provide a basis for using the baptismal certificate to show the date of birth, since that information would have been contributed by the parents or by someone

---

explanations can always be weighed by the trier of fact. *See* Ando v. Woodberry, 168 N.E.2d 520 (1960) (rejecting argument that guilty plea to traffic offense should be inadmissible because people who believe themselves innocent often plead guilty merely to avoid expenditure of time and expense of trial). *See also* Jay M. Zitter, Annotation, *Admissibility of Traffic Conviction in Later State Civil Trial*, 73 A.L.R. 4th 691 (1990) (reviewing cases).

355. For differing views on the subject, see 5 Weinstein's Federal Evidence § 803.28[2], at 803–130 (2d ed. Joseph M. McLaughlin ed. 1997) (evidence of guilty pleas in cases punishable by less than a year should not be admissible under other exceptions); Hinshaw v. Keith, 645 F.Supp.

180 (D.Me.1986) (expressly disagreeing with Weinstein, and holding that guilty plea to leaving scene of accident was admissible in subsequent civil case); McCormick v. United States, 539 F.Supp. 1179, 1183 (D.Colo.1982) (guilty plea to traffic light violation admissible in subsequent civil action).

356. *See* advisory committee's notes to Fed. R. Evid. 803(22) and 410. This result is consistent with prior decisions under the Clayton Act, to the effect that guilty pleas are admissible in subsequent litigation, but nolo pleas are not. *See, e.g.,* General Elec. Co. v. San Antonio, 334 F.2d 480, 484–87 (5th Cir.1964).

357. *See* § 7.19.

else not under a "business duty" to the religious organization.[358] The committee's decision to extend the present exception beyond the business records exception was based upon the unlikelihood that false information would be furnished in conjunction with an occasion such as baptism.[359]

Recent federal litigation on the exception has centered on attempts by taxpayers to use church-issued receipts or contribution statements as evidence of charitable contributions. The problem with using the exception for that purpose is that the offered evidence is not a statement of personal or family history similar to the examples listed in the rule. Both the Second Circuit and the Ninth Circuit have held that such evidence is not admissible under the present exception.[360] It is therefore necessary to lay a business record foundation for church records of this nature, showing that it was the regular practice of the church to make such records and that the records were kept in the regular course of the church's activities.

§ 7.42   Marriage, Baptismal, and Similar Certificates [FRE 803(12)]

Federal Rule of Evidence 803(12) provides an exception for marriage, baptismal, or similar certificates. The public records exception, Rule 803(8), covers the same ground when the issuer of the certificate is a public official. However, Rule 803(12) goes further in that it allows records prepared by clergy and other non-public officials who perform marriages and similar ceremonies to be admitted.

Rule 803(9), records of vital statistics, also covers some of the same ground as the present exception. For example, a certification of a marriage made to a public office would be admissible under Rule 803(9) as well as the present exception. However, the present exception covers some matters not covered by Rule 803(9). Records of confirmation in a church, or of baptism, are not required to be reported to a public office, and hence are not admissible under Rule 803(9). They are admissible under the present exception, however.

The present exception differs from Rule 803(11) in that it does not require that the certificate be part of the internal record of the religious organization. It can, for example, be a certificate issued by a member of the clergy to the husband and wife after a marriage ceremony.

The present rule provides a hearsay exception, but does not state how the certificates covered are to be authenticated. The authentication requirements are governed by Rule 902(4).[361]

---

358. *See* Fed. R. Evid. 803(11) advisory committee's note.

359. *Id.*

360. *See* Ruberto v. Commissioner, 774 F.2d 61 (2d Cir.1985); Hall v. Commissioner, 729 F.2d 632 (9th Cir.1984).

361. *See* **Ch. 11**.

§ 7.43 Family Records [FRE 803(13)]

Federal Rule of Evidence 803(13) creates an exception for statements of fact concerning personal or family history contained in family Bibles, genealogies, charts, engravings on rings, inscriptions of family portraits, engravings on urns, crypts, tombstones, or the like. Examples of "statements concerning personal or family history" include statements about marriage, birth, death, ancestry, and the like.

The guarantee of trustworthiness presumed for the exception is the lack of motive to make a false statement and the likelihood that such statements would be screened by the family. It may not be necessary to make a showing of personal knowledge under the current exception, at least not if the family has accepted the record as valid.[362]

The exception is an ancient one that was long recognized at common law.[363] Related exceptions for family history, also of long lineage, are found in Rule 803(19) (reputation concerning personal or family history), Rule 803(23) (judgment as to personal, family, or general history, or boundaries), and Rule 804(b)(4) (statement of personal or family history).

§ 7.44 Records of Documents Affecting an Interest in Property [FRE 803(14)]

A record of a document affecting an interest in property, as proof of the contents of the original document, is excepted from the hearsay rule by Federal Rule of Evidence 803(14). The record must be the record of a public office, and a statute must authorize the recording of documents of that kind in that office. An example of the operation of this exception is the case in which a title record is offered to prove the contents of the record and its execution and delivery. If there is a local statute that authorizes the recording of title records and the recording of data about execution and delivery, then the evidence is admissible. The advisory committee's note indicates that personal knowledge of the recorder is not required:

> Under any theory of the admissibility of public records, the records would be receivable as evidence of the contents of the recorded document, else the recording process would be reduced to a nullity. When, however, the record is offered for the further purpose of proving execution and delivery, a problem of lack of first-hand

362. For an extensive discussion of the exception at common law, see 5 John H. Wigmore, Evidence in Trials at Common Law §§ 1485–1497 (James H. Chadbourn rev. 1974).

363. For an early endorsement of the exception, see Whitelocke v. Baker, 13 Ves. 511, 514 (1804), quoted in 5 Wigmore, *supra* note 362 § 1482, at 373 (noting that statements of family history, including "de-scriptions upon monuments" and "descriptions in Bibles and registry books," are admitted "upon the principle that they are the natural effusions of a party who must know the truth, and who speaks upon an occasion when his mind stands in an even position, without any temptation to exceed or fall short of the truth").

knowledge by the recorder, not present as to contents, is presented.[364]

§ 7.45 Statements in Documents Affecting an Interest in Property [FRE 803(15)]

Federal Rule of Evidence 803(15) provides an exception for statements in documents affecting an interest in property. The statement must have been relevant to the purpose of the document. The exception does not apply if transactions concerning the property, which have occurred since the document was made, are not consistent with the truth of the statement in the document.

The exception covers recitals of fact in documents such as deeds. Examples are a recital that the parties granting title to the property constitute all of the heirs of the last record owner[365] or a recital that parties named in the deed are married to one another.[366]

EXCEPTIONS THAT APPLY ONLY IF THE DECLARANT IS UNAVAILABLE [FRE 804]

§ 7.46 Exceptions That Apply Only if Declarant Is Unavailable; Definition of Unavailability

The exceptions set forth in Rule 804 of the Federal Rules of Evidence apply only if the declarant is unavailable.[367] If the declarant is available, then the law prefers live testimony over hearsay declarations. The proponent must produce the live witness instead of the witness' out-of-court statements.[368]

At first blush, this rule preferring live testimony would seem to be a sensible rule for all instances in which hearsay is offered. Why not have a requirement that the live witness be produced if available? Such a rule would give preference to the best evidence (live testimony), but would not stand in the way of admission of other evidence when the best was not available.

Though superficially attractive, this requirement would be too broad. It would be wasteful to require the testimony of every available declarant—for example, every declarant in the chain of information represented by a business record.[369] Also, sometimes hearsay is fully as reliable as in-court testimony. For example, a present sense impression statement made at the time of the event is probably more reliable than a witness' recollection, recited months afterward and after having been through preparation for litigation, about the same event.[370]

---

364. Fed. R. Evid. 803(14) advisory committee's note.

365. *See* Fed. R. Evid. 803(15) advisory committee's note.

366. *See* Compton v. Davis Oil Co., 607 F.Supp. 1221, 1228 (D.Wyo.1985).

367. Fed. R. Evid. 804(b).

368. Fed. R. Evid. 804(b) advisory committee's note.

369. Fed. R. Evid. 803(6) advisory committee's note.

370. *See* 2 McCormick on Evidence § 271, at 212 (4th ed. John W. Strong ed.

Undoubtedly historical accident has played a role in the assignment of exceptions to one category or the other.[371] Arguably, the statements covered by the exceptions in Rule 804 are more dangerous as substitutes for in-court testimony than are those covered by the Rule 803 exceptions. In addition, the situations represented by Rule 804 are often ones in which it is feasible to produce the witness if the witness is available.[372] It must be conceded, however, that there is a degree of arbitrariness in the division of exceptions between Rule 803 (unavailability immaterial) and Rule 804 (statement admissible only if witness is unavailable). For example, considered as a new matter, it would be hard to justify giving excited utterances (which are likely to be inaccurate because made under stress) preferred treatment over former testimony (which was subject to all of the safeguards of oath and cross-examination).[373] Yet that is what Federal Rules of Evidence 803 and 804 do.[374]

Definition of Unavailability

Death and disability are common causes of unavailability, but they are not the only ones.[375] Anything not the fault of the proponent, that as a practical matter prevents the witness from attending or testifying, constitutes unavailability.[376] If the witness is beyond the subpoena power and there is no other reasonable way to obtain the witness' testimony, the witness is unavailable.[377] If the witness appears and invokes a privilege, the witness is unavailable.[378] If the witness appears, has no privilege, but refuses to testify after being ordered to do so, the witness is unavailable.[379] The witness is also unavailable if the witness appears and testifies to a failure of recollection about the subject matter.[380] Rule 804(a) is broadly designed to accommodate the faultless proponent, and it is only when the proponent has procured the unavailability of the

---

1992) (memory and sincerity dangers not present).

371. *See* Fed. R. Evid. 803, 804 advisory committee's notes.

372. Fed. R. Evid. 804(b) advisory committee's note.

373. *See* Robert M. Hutchins & Donald Slesinger, *Some Observations on the Law of Evidence*, 28 Colum. L. Rev. 432, 437 (1928) (excited utterances unreliable); Fed. R. Evid. 804(b)(1) advisory committee's note ("it may be argued that former testimony is the strongest hearsay and should be included under Rule 803").

374. *See* Fed. R. Evid. 803(2), 804(b)(1).

375. *See* Fed. R. Evid. 804(a)(4).

376. *See* Fed. R. Evid. 804(a); Kirk v. Raymark Indus., 51 F.3d 1206 (3d Cir.1995) (Cowen, J.) (held, expert who testified in prior case not "unavailable" merely because beyond subpoena power; proponent should have tried to contact expert and request his attendance at trial).

377. Fed. R. Evid. 804(a)(5). The mere fact that the witness is beyond the subpoena power is not enough; the Rule states that the proponent must be unable to obtain attendance by process or "other reasonable means." A proponent might have means other than subpoena when, for example, a state could request another state to furnish someone incarcerated in its prison system for testimony. Even if the incarcerated person were technically beyond the subpoena power, the state should make the effort to obtain the testimony by other means. *Cf.* Barber v. Page, 390 U.S. 719, 724–25 (1968) (held, violation of confrontation clause to use declarant's hearsay statement when state failed to make good faith effort to obtain cooperation of federal authorities in delivering declarant for testimony).

378. Fed. R. Evid. 804(a)(1).

379. Fed. R. Evid. 804(a)(2).

380. Fed. R. Evid. 804(a)(3).

witness or has not made proper efforts to subpoena the witness that the proponent will not be allowed to take advantage of the Rule.[381]

Unavailability due to temporary illness poses a special problem. Here the trial judge could allow the witness to be heard in person by granting a continuance. Although trial judges have discretion in this area, a continuance should be granted in criminal cases where the witness is vital and the charge is serious.[382]

Requirement of Deposition

Suppose that a proponent can foresee that the declarant will not be present at trial. Should the proponent be required to depose the declarant, so that the opponent will have a chance for cross-examination during the deposition? The rule makers answered this question in the affirmative. In instances in which the declarant is not present at trial (as opposed to instances in which the declarant is present, but for some reason cannot or will not testify), the proponent of the hearsay testimony must show that reasonable efforts were made to get the declarant's testimony by deposition.[383] However, this requirement does not apply when the hearsay is in the form of former testimony admissible under Rule 804(b)(1).[384] Then, there is no reason to require a deposition because the opportunity for cross-examination was provided at the prior proceeding during which the former testimony was taken.[385]

§ 7.47 The Former Testimony Exception and Related Matters [FRE 804(b)(1)]

A typical instance of the operation of the former testimony exception can arise after a case has been reversed on appeal and remanded for a new trial. If a witness at the first trial is unavailable for the second, then that witness' testimony is admissible under the exception.[386]

When the testimony is offered in the form of a transcript of the prior trial, there are two levels of hearsay. First, the transcript is the statement of the court reporter about what was said on the witness stand at the prior trial. The public records exception creates an exception for this statement.[387] Many jurisdictions have statutes that provide specific ex-

---

381. *See* Fed. R. Evid. 804(a).

382. *See, e.g.,* United States v. Faison, 679 F.2d 292, 297 (3d Cir.1982) (trial court abused discretion in finding that key prosecution witness, who could not testify for at least four to five weeks because of surgery, was unavailable in prosecution for wire fraud and transporting stolen securities in interstate commerce). In *Faison,* the Third Circuit stated that

> In exercising discretion a trial judge must consider all relevant circumstances, including: the importance of the absent witness for the case; the nature and extent of cross-examination in the

earlier testimony; the nature of the illness; the expected time of recovery; the reliability of the evidence of the probable duration of the illness; and any special circumstances counselling against delay.

Id.

383. Fed. R. Evid. 804(a)(5).

384. *Id.*

385. H.R. Rep. No. 650, 93d Cong., 1st Sess. 5 (1973), reprinted in 1974 U.S. Code Cong. & Admin. News 7075, 7088.

386. Fed. R. Evid. 804(b)(1).

387. Fed. R. Evid. 803(8)(B).

ceptions for statements of court reporters.[388] Second, the witness' testimony at the prior trial is also hearsay, at least under the federal definition.[389] The present exception applies to allow it to be received.

Former testimony often comes into evidence through some route other than this exception. For example, former testimony can be used to impeach a witness with a prior inconsistent statement. When the former testimony is used for impeachment of the witness who gave it, the present exception is not needed. Federal Rule of Evidence 801(d)(1)(A) provides the basis for receiving the testimony.[390] Similarly, former testimony of the opposing party is admissible against that party under Rule 801(d)(2) without the need for laying the foundation for the current exception.[391] Also, deposition testimony can be admitted under Rule 32 of the Rules of Civil Procedure without the need for reliance upon this exception.[392] As long as the statements made in the deposition would be

---

388. *See, e.g.,* N.C. Gen. Stat. § 8–85 (1996):

> Testimony taken and transcribed by a court reporter and certified by the reporter or by the judge who presided at the trial at which the testimony was given, may be offered in evidence in any court as the deposition of the witness whose testimony is so taken and transcribed, in the manner, and under the rules governing the introduction of depositions in civil actions.

California's Evidence Code provides for a public records exception in Cal. Evid. Code § 1291 (West 1966). The code also provides an arguably stronger exception for the transcript of a court reporter in Cal. Evid. Code § 273 (West 1966). Transcribed and certified reports as prima facie evidence: "The report of the official reporter, or official reporter pro tempore, of any court, duly appointed and sworn, when transcribed and certified as being a correct transcript of the testimony and proceedings in the case, is prima facie evidence of such testimony and proceedings." *See also* Fed. R. Civ. Proc. 80(c) Stenographic Report or Transcript as Evidence, which provides an exception for the federal courts: "Whenever the testimony of a witness at a trial or hearing which was stenographically reported is admissible in evidence at a later trial, it may be proved by the transcript thereof duly certified by the person who reported the testimony."

389. Under the Federal Rules, hearsay is "a statement, other than one made by the declarant while testifying at the trial or hearing, offered in evidence to prove the truth of the matter asserted." Fed. R. Evid. 801 (c). Excluded from this definition are prior statements by a witness at the same

trial and admissions by party opponents. Fed. R. Evid. 801 (d). Wigmore felt that former testimony should also be excluded from the definition of hearsay. His rational was that since the testimony was subject to cross-examination in the first trial the primary purpose behind the hearsay rule was satisfied. 5 John H. Wigmore, Evidence in Trials at Common Law § 1370 (James H. Chadbourn rev. 1974).

390. *See* § **7.77.**

391. *See* § **7.07**.

392. Fed. R. Civ. Proc. 32(a) provides as follows:

> (a) Use of Depositions. At the trial or upon the hearing of a motion or an interlocutory proceeding, any part or all of a deposition, so far as admissible under the rules of evidence applied as though the witness were then present and testifying, may be used against any party who was present or represented at the taking of the deposition or who had reasonable notice thereof, in accordance with any of the following provisions:
>
> (1) Any deposition may be used by any party for the purpose of contradicting or impeaching the testimony of deponent as a witness, or for any other purpose permitted by the Federal Rules of Evidence.
>
> (2) The deposition of a party or of anyone who at the time of taking the deposition was an officer, director, or managing agent, or a person designated under Rule 30(b)(6) or 31(a) to testify on behalf of a public or private corporation, partnership or association or governmental agency which is a party may be used by an adverse party for any purpose.

admissible under the rules of evidence if they had been made by a live witness at the present trial, and provided that the deposition is being used against a party who was present or represented at the deposition (or at least had adequate notice of the deposition to have been present or represented), then the statements made in the deposition can be offered as evidence under Rule 32. As in Federal Rule of Evidence 801(d)(2) concerning an admission of a party opponent, there is no requirement of witness unavailability when introducing the deposition of a party in the current case. However, there are requirements of witness unavailability similar to those in Federal Rule of Evidence 804(b)(1) when a party offers the deposition of a witness under Federal Rule of Civil Procedure 32(a)(3). Federal Rule of Civil Procedure 32(a)(3)(E) also allows a witness' deposition to be used under "exceptional circumstances" when it is "in the interest of justice." Though this rule potentially could allow in a great deal more evidence, even where the unavailability requirements have not been met, the courts have not read this exception broadly and it has had a rather limited effect in admitting otherwise objectionable evidence.[393]

The former testimony exception is based upon the theory that cross-examination under oath at a prior proceeding is an adequate substitute for cross-examination in the current proceeding.[394] Since the absence of cross-examination is thought to be the principal reason for the exclusion of hearsay, one might expect that former testimony would be freely admissible. However, the exception has been hedged about with restrictions. These restrictions include those discussed in the following sections.

(3) The deposition of a witness, whether or not a party, may be used by any party for any purpose if the court finds: (A) that the witness is dead; or (B) that the witness is at a greater distance than 100 miles from the place of trial or hearing, or is out of the United States, unless it appears that the absence of the witness was procured by the party offering the deposition; or (C) that the witness is unable to attend or testify because of age, illness, infirmity, or imprisonment; or (D) that the party offering the deposition has been unable to procure the attendance of the witness by subpoena; or (E) upon application and notice, that such exceptional circumstances exist as to make it desirable, in the interest of justice and with due regard to the importance of presenting the testimony of witnesses orally in open court, to allow the deposition to be used. (4) If only part of a deposition is offered in evidence by a party, an adverse party may require the offeror to introduce any other part which ought in fairness to be considered with the part introduced, and any party may introduce any other parts.

Substitution of parties pursuant to Rule 25 does not affect the right to use depositions previously taken; and, when an action has been brought in any court of the United States or of any State and another action involving the same subject matter is afterwards brought between the same parties or their representatives or successors in interest, all depositions lawfully taken and duly filed in the former action may be used in the latter as if originally taken therefor. A deposition previously taken may also be used as permitted by the Federal Rules of Evidence.

393. *See* 8A Charles A. Wright & Arthur R. Miller, Federal Practice and Procedure: Civil §§ 2142, 2146, 2150 (2d ed. 1994).

394. *See* Fed. R. Evid. 804(b)(1) advisory committee's note; see also 5 Weinstein's Federal Evidence § 807.04[1][a] (2d ed. Joseph M. McLaughlin ed. 1997); 2 McCormick on Evidence § 301 (4th ed. John W. Strong ed. 1992).

§ 7.48   The Former Testimony Exception and Related Matters [FRE 804(b)(1)]—Unavailability

Like the other Rule 804 exceptions, the former testimony exception does not apply unless the witness is unavailable. (For a discussion of the concept of unavailability, see § 7.46). Common law jurisdictions also required unavailability.[395]

§ 7.49   The Former testimony Exception and Related Matters [FRE 804(b)(1)]—Identity of Parties

Some common law courts required that the party against whom the evidence is offered be the same in both actions.[396] This rule has been criticized on grounds that it results in the exclusion of reliable evidence.[397] For example, in a case in which the issue is whether property was destroyed by arson, the alleged arsonist in a criminal trial who claims the fire was accidentally caused would have every incentive to cross-examine the witness vigorously. Yet if that witness became unavailable in a subsequent civil case involving another party (say, the person who allegedly benefited from the arson), then the testimony would be inadmissible. Yet the testimony has almost all the safeguards of courtroom testimony, and surely the jury could be trusted enough to treat it as being better than nothing.[398]

With this sort of problem in mind, the federal rule makers originally proposed that the exception be liberalized to provide that identity of parties was not necessary so long as the party in the first action had a similar motive to cross-examine as the party in the second action.[399] However, Congress rejected this attempt and the final version of Federal Rule of Evidence 804(b)(1) required that the party against whom the evidence is offered be the same as the party involved in the prior case or, in a civil case, either the same party or a predecessor in interest.[400] Thus, if the current action is a criminal prosecution and the government wishes to offer into evidence the testimony of a witness in a prior proceeding to which the defendant was not a party, that testimony is not admissible under this exception. The same would be true of prior testimony offered by the criminal defendant against the government if the government was not a party to the prior action. To put it more

395. *See, e.g.,* School Dist. of Pontiac v. Sachse, 264 N.W. 396, 397 (Mich.1936).

396. *See* School Dist. of Pontiac v. Sachse, 264 N.W. 396, 397 (Mich.1936) (court required party against whom testimony offered to be the same in prior and current actions). Some courts even required both parties to be the same in both actions; *see, e.g.,* Bulk Trans., Inc. v. Louisiana Pub. Serv. Commn., 209 So.2d 4, 6–7 (La.1968).

397. *See* 2 McCormick on Evidence § 303 (4th ed. John W. Strong ed. 1992).

398. *See* Travelers Fire Ins. Co. v. Wright, 322 P.2d 417, 421–22 (Okla.1958) (allowing admission of former testimony given at criminal arson trial in subsequent civil action).

399. *See* Fed. R. Evid. 804(b) (1) (Supreme Court Proposed Draft 1973), reprinted in 2 James F. Bailey & Oscar M. Trelles, The Federal Rules of Evidence: Legislative Histories and Related Documents, Doc. 7, at 33 (1980).

400. *See* H.R. Rep. No. 650, 93d Cong., 1st Sess., 15 (1973), reprinted in 4 Bailey & Trelles, *supra* note 399, Doc. 13, at 15; *see also* 5 Weinstein's Federal Evidence § 807.04[4][a] (2d ed. Joseph M. McLaughlin ed. 1997).

simply, former testimony is not admissible against the defendant in a criminal case if the defendant was not a party to the prior proceeding.[401] When the prior case was a civil case and the case in which the testimony is offered is a criminal case, some courts take the view that similarity of interest, rather than identity of parties, is the relevant test, at least where the testimony is offered against the government in the criminal case.[402] Given the language of Rule 804(b)(1), this conclusion is difficult to justify.

In a civil case, the question whether prior testimony is admissible against a party not represented in the earlier suit depends upon whether a "predecessor in interest" of that party was represented in the prior action.[403] In its core meaning, the term predecessor in interest describes someone who had a prior interest in property that is now subject to litigation or who was otherwise in privity with a party.[404] However, the term has been given an expansive meaning by some courts so that the exception has potentially much broader application in civil cases, where statements by predecessors in interest can fall under the exception, than in criminal cases. For example, in *Lloyd v. American Export Lines*,[405] the plaintiff, Roland Alvarez, brought a Jones Act claim against American Export Lines, Inc. Plaintiff, a merchant mariner, had been involved in a violent encounter with a fellow crew member on board the freighter on which both worked. Plaintiff's theory of recovery was that American Export had failed to use due care in protecting him against Lloyd. He claimed that he had been harassed by Lloyd and had reported these prior incidents to superiors. Alvarez introduced testimony at trial that Lloyd, while intoxicated, made a vicious unprovoked attack upon him. The jury did not hear Lloyd's side of the story, although the defendant offered it in the form of a transcript of a Coast Guard hearing, as well as the report of the hearing examiner. The trial court excluded the evidence.

401. Fed. R. Evid. 804(b)(1).

402. *See* United States v. McDonald, 837 F.2d 1287, 1291–93 (5th Cir.1988) (dictum), and see cases cited therein. *But see* United States v. Harenberg, 732 F.2d 1507, 1516 (10th Cir.1984) (depositions taken in prior civil action excluded in subsequent criminal case because the United States did not have an opportunity to cross-examine declarants in the civil depositions).

403. Fed. R. Evid. 804(b)(1); see generally 5 Weinstein's Federal Evidence, *supra* note 400 § 807.04[4][a], at 804–35; 2 McCormick on Evidence *supra* note 397 § 303.

404. In Lloyd v. American Export Lines, Inc., 580 F.2d 1179 (3d Cir.1978), Judge Stern, who concurred in the result but disagreed with the majority's interpretation of predecessor in interest in Rule 804(b)(1), noted that the commentators had defined predecessor in interest in terms of a privity relationship, and gave the following definition of privity:

"The term 'privity' denotes mutual or successive relationships to the same rights of property, and privies are distributed into several classes, according to the manner of this relationship. Thus, there are privies in estate, as donor and donee, lessor and lessee, and joint tenants; privies in blood, as heir and ancestor, and co-parceners; privies in representation, as executor and testator, administrator and intestate; privies in law, where the law, without privity of blood or estate casts the land upon another, as by escheat."

The above passage quotes Metropolitan St. Ry. v. Gumby, 99 F. 192, 198 (2d Cir. 1900), which is also quoted in 11 James A. Moore, Moore's Federal Practice § 807.04[02] (2d ed. 1988). For a similar definition, see Black's Law Dictionary 1199 (6th ed. 1990).

405. 580 F.2d 1179, 1181–87 (3d Cir.), *cert. denied*, 439 U.S. 969 (1978).

The Third Circuit held that the hearing examiner's report should have been admitted under the public records exception, see **§ 7.27**, and that the recorded testimony of Lloyd should have been admitted under 804(b)(1). It found that Lloyd's unavailability had been sufficiently established. On what it viewed as the "more difficult" question, the court decided that the Coast Guard, which had been a party in the prior hearing, was a "predecessor in interest" for purposes of Rule 804(b)(1), so the transcript of the hearing was admissible as former testimony. The same alleged misconduct was involved in both the Coast Guard hearing and Alvarez's civil action. The Coast Guard investigating officer at the prior hearing had sought to establish that Lloyd had been intoxicated, that he had started the fight with Alvarez, and that he had harassed Alvarez—all facts that Alvarez sought to establish in the later civil case. The court decided that because the Coast Guard and Alvarez had similar interests in the two cases and a similar motive to cross-examine, the predecessor in interest requirement was satisfied.

The result is a very broad interpretation of that requirement, one that seems to make it essentially the same as the similar motive requirement. For that reason the decision seems contrary to legislative intent. Congress acted affirmatively to supplement the similar motive requirement with a requirement that the parties be either identical or a civil predecessor in interest. To read the predecessor in interest requirement to mean nothing more than that the parties have a similar motive renders this action by Congress meaningless.[406] The House added the requirement either that the parties be identical or, in a civil case, that the party's predecessor in interest have had an opportunity for cross-examination. The House Committee on the Judiciary stated that the reason for the change was that "it is generally unfair to impose upon the party against whom the hearsay evidence is being offered responsibility for the manner in which the witness was previously handled by another party."[407] The Senate Committee on the Judiciary recommended approval of the House change, describing the difference between the original version containing only a similar motive requirement and the amended version as "not great."[408] The *Lloyd* case noted this language and stated, "We, too, fail to see a compelling difference between the two ap-

---

406. *But see* 2 McCormick on Evidence, *supra* note 397 § 303, at 313, where the authors note the changing position of the treatise over time and ultimately opt for an "intermediate" position:

> This state of legislative history has left little concrete guidance in determining congressional intent. Having taken the view in the 1978 Pocket Part that privity was required between the parties to satisfy the "predecessor in interest" requirement and the view in the 1984 Third Edition that the intention was to leave the Supreme Court version intact in civil cases, it is perhaps appropriate that this treatise now take an intermedi-

ate position. That, indeed, appears to be the proper course of action.

(Footnote omitted.) The authors then suggest that the rule be interpreted to "require[] the courts to insure fairness directly by seriously considering whether the prior cross-examination can be fairly held against the later party." *Id*. at 317.

407. H.R. Rep. No. 650, 93d Cong., 1st Sess. 15 (1973), reprinted in 4 Bailey & Trelles, *supra* note 399, Doc. 13, at 15.

408. S. Rep. No. 1277, 93d Cong., 2d Sess. 28 (1974), reprinted in 4 Bailey & Trelles, *supra* note 399, Doc. 15, at 28.

proaches."[409] It specifically rejected the idea that "this change in wording signaled a return to the common law approach to former testimony, requiring privity or a common property interest between the parties."[410] The Sixth Circuit has followed the *Lloyd* test, recognizing that it collapses the two criteria of predecessor in interest and similar motive to cross-examine into the same test, and approving of that result.[411]

§ 7.50 The Former Testimony Exception and Related Matters [FRE 804(b)(1)—Similar Motive To Cross-examine

Federal Rule of Evidence 804(b)(1) requires that the party in the prior action have had an "opportunity and similar motive to develop the testimony by direct, cross, or redirect examination." The similar motive can be lacking, for example, when the party in the first action had less to lose or different goals than in the second action.

The operation of the similar motive requirement is illustrated by the litigation over the deposition of Dr. Kenneth Wallace Smith, the deceased former medical director of Johns–Manville Corporation. The Smith deposition has nourished its own nest of cases on the former testimony exception.[412] Dr. Smith was a former medical director of a manufacturer of asbestos products with 20 years' experience. He was deposed in 1976 in a Pennsylvania state court case, and subsequently died. His deposition was later offered by plaintiffs in various asbestosis cases on issues such as the state of the art during the 1940s and 1950s. The reception it received depended upon the party against whom it was offered and the circumstances of the particular case. For example, in *Murphy v. Owens–Illinois, Inc.*,[413] the court upheld a trial judge's decision to exclude the deposition.[414] The party against whom the deposition was offered at trial had not been a party in the case in which the deposition was taken.[415] This in itself was not enough to support exclu-

409. Lloyd v. American Export Lines, 580 F.2d 1179, 1185 (3d Cir.), *cert. denied*, 439 U.S. 969 (1978).

410. *Id.* at 1185 n.5. *See also* New England Mutual Life Ins. Co. v. Anderson, Nos. 87–2883, 89–3080 (10th Cir.1989) (1989 WL 120406) (court cites *Lloyd* case and apparently accepts its approach to predecessor in interest definition, but holds testimony in prior criminal trial against co-conspirator not admissible against civil party because, under circumstances, co-conspirator had no motive or interest in protecting innocence of party against whom testimony now offered).

411. *See* Murphy v. Owens–Illinois, Inc., 779 F.2d 340, 343 (6th Cir.1985); Dykes v. Ramark Indus., 801 F.2d 810, 815–16 (6th Cir.1986); *see also* Supermarket of Marlinton, Inc. v. Meadow Gold Dairies, Inc., 71 F.3d 119, 127–28 (4th Cir.1995) (in

antitrust action alleging that certain dairies conspired to fix milk prices, trial court improperly excluded testimony of witness who testified against dairies in an earlier criminal trial; testimony should have been admitted because the dominant motive in both trials was to show that a conspiracy never occurred).

412. *See* Dykes v. Raymark Indus., 801 F.2d 810 (6th Cir.1986); Dartez v. Fibreboard Corp, 765 F.2d 456 (5th Cir. 1985); Murphy v. Owens–Illinois, Inc., 779 F.2d 340 (6th Cir.1985); Clay v. Johns–Manville Sales Corp., 722 F.2d 1289 (6th Cir.1983), *cert. denied*, 467 U.S. 1253 (1984); In re Johns–Manville/Asbestosis Cases, 93 F.R.D. 853 (N.D.Ill.1982).

413. 779 F.2d 340 (6th Cir.1985).

414. *Id.* at 347.

415. *Id.* at 343.

sion, in the view of the Sixth Circuit, since it took a generous view of the requirement that the testimony be offered against a party who was represented or had a predecessor in interest in the prior litigation. If the prior litigant had a similar motive, then it qualified as a predecessor in interest. In this case the prior litigant did not have a similar motive.[416] The defendant corporations who were represented at the deposition did not have the same motive to prove a primitive state of the art during the 1940s and 1950s that the defendant against whom it was offered in the Murphy case did.[417] The reason was that the latter defendant, Owens–Illinois, had stopped manufacturing asbestos-containing products in 1958. The parties who took the deposition, Johns–Manville and Raybestos–Manhattan, had continued manufacturing until the 1960s and 1970s. They would possibly have harmed themselves if they had shown a primitive state of the art in the 1940s or 1950s, because that would have highlighted how much had been learned since then.[418] Owens–Illinois, on the other hand, would have wished to prove that the state of the art through 1958 was primitive, and had that company been able to examine Smith at his deposition, it would have sought to establish these facts. Therefore, Owens–Illinois would have conducted its examination of Smith much differently than Johns–Manville and Raybestos–Manhattan. In other cases where the difference in motive was not as pronounced, the Smith deposition has been admitted.[419]

The Supreme Court examined the "similar motive" requirement of the former testimony exception in *United States v. Salerno*.[420] *Salerno* was a case in which two grand jury witnesses had given testimony before the grand jury that was favorable to defendant. At trial, the grand jury witnesses claimed the right against self-incrimination and refused to testify. The defense sought to introduce their grand jury testimony under Rule 804(b)(1). The prosecution objected, arguing that at the grand jury stage its motive to cross-examine the witnesses was not similar to what its motive would have been at trial, and therefore that the "similar motive" requirement of the hearsay exception was not satisfied.

Speaking through Justice Thomas, an 8–1 majority of the Court concluded that the "plain language" of the rule supported the prosecution's contention. The defense had argued that adversarial fairness required that the evidence be admitted, contending that when witnesses testify favorably to the government at the grand jury stage, the government gives them immunity and obtains their trial testimony, but that when the witnesses testify unfavorably the government refuses to give

416. *Id.* at 347.

417. *Id.*

418. *Id.*

419. *See, e.g.,* Clay v. Johns–Manville Sales Corp., 722 F.2d 1289, 1295 (6th Cir. 1983) (where prior and current defendants had similar motive to cross-examine Smith regarding manufacturer's knowledge of hazards of asbestos in products liability cases, deposition was admissible); *see also* Dykes v. Raymark Indus., 801 F.2d 810, 817 (6th Cir.1986) (where objecting party failed to explain why motive and opportunity to cross-examine Smith differed in the first case, deposition was admissible in the second case).

420. 505 U.S. 317 (1992).

immunity and objects to receiving their grand jury testimony. Justice Thomas indicated that the concept of adversarial fairness did not justify carving an exception to the plain requirements of Rule 804(b)(1). The Court remanded the case for a determination as to whether the prosecutor did in fact have a similar motive to develop testimony at the grand jury stage. Justice Kennedy dissented, saying that the record of the particular case did show that the government had the opportunity and similar motive to develop the witness' testimony at the grand jury proceeding.

Whether the "similar motive" requirement of Rule 804(b)(1) has been satisfied is clearly a context-driven issue. Each case must be examined on its own facts, as small changes in legal theory, the line-up of parties, and other factors can affect the outcome. In each case, the parties must be prepared to demonstrate to the court the existence (or nonexistence) of a motive sufficiently similar to satisfy the Rule.[421]

§ 7.51   The Dying Declarations Exception [FRE 804(b)(2)]

The theory behind the dying declarations exception is that one would not want to go to one's Maker with a lie upon one's lips. This has been questioned; some might feel freer to lie, since they could escape earthly retribution. Also, the problems of memory, perception, and narrative mistakes may be amplified when a person is dying.[422] Nonetheless, this time-honored exception—one of the very oldest of hearsay exceptions—shows no signs of mortality itself.

There are several elements to the foundation for the exception, discussed in the ensuing sections.

Knowledge of Imminence of Death

"Over the strong objections of the state prosecutors, Lincoln addressed the preacher: 'State whether you were with Grek Grafton

---

421. *Cf.* Williams v. Commissioner, 999 F.2d 760, 764–66 (4th Cir.), *cert. denied*, 510 U.S. 965 (1993) (in action for tax deficiencies, transcript of testimony by government witness in defendant's prior criminal trial for possession of narcotics admissible where defendant failed to show how motive to cross-examine witness differed from prior trial and where transcript was only used to show commissioner's deficiency calculations were not arbitrary); United States v. Koon, 34 F.3d 1416, 1428 (9th Cir.1994) (federal prosecution in Rodney King case) (held, defendants in federal civil rights/police brutality prosecution case not deprived of 6th amendment right to confrontation by admission of videotaped trial testimony of witness against them in earlier state trial; fact that additional ammunition for cross-examination was developed since first trial did not mean that Rule 804(b)(1)'s requirement

that opponent have "opportunity and similar motive was not satisfied").

422. Roger C. Park, *A Subject Matter Approach to Hearsay Reform*, 86 Mich. L. Rev. 51, 76–77 (1987) (noting these criticisms, but noting also that the circumstances under which these statements are made tends to decrease the dangers of fabrication by the declarant or in-court witness and that dangers of misreporting and improper influence on declarant through police interrogations are lessened); *see also* Fed. R. Evid. 804(b)(2) advisory committee's note; 2 McCormick on Evidence § 310 (4th ed. John W. Strong ed. 1992); 5 Weinstein's Federal Evidence § 807.05[1], at 804–42 to 804–43 (2d ed. Joseph M McLaughlin ed. 1997); Ralph Slovenko, *Deathbed Declarations*, 14 J. Psychiatry & L. 469 (1996).

shortly before he died and at the time he was expecting death, and if so, state what you heard, if you heard anything.' "[423]

Attorney Abe Lincoln may have been jumping ahead a bit in trying to lay the foundation and get in the evidence itself with one triple question, but his question incorporates a version of the most important element of the modern exception. The declarant must have been "expecting death," or, in the words of the Federal Rule, must have made the statement while believing that death was "imminent."[424] The victim's own statement about belief in imminent death may be used in laying the foundation, and it is perhaps the most common method.[425] Evidence that the victim was told of impending death,[426] or occasionally that the injury was so grievous that the imminence of death was obvious,[427] may also be used to lay the foundation.

Concerning the Cause or Circumstances of Death

Suppose that a declarant, knowing that death is imminent, makes the statement "Smith owes me $1000." The exception would not apply. The dying declaration must concern the cause and circumstances of the declarant's expected death.[428] This prevents dying persons from making self-serving statements designed to help their heirs. While the rule does

423. N.Y. Times, Feb. 10, 1989, at 25, col. 4 (excerpt from newly discovered Lincoln transcripts).

424. See Fed. R. Evid. 804(b)(2); see also Pfeil v. Rogers, 757 F.2d 850, 861 (7th Cir.1985) (affidavit containing statements of murder witness who later committed suicide not admissible, since statements were not made immediately before suicide and therefore were not made in contemplation of imminent death); United States v. Layton, 549 F.Supp. 903, 918 (N.D.Cal.1982) (tape-recorded statements of Jim Jones concerning the killing of Congressman Leo Ryan during the mass suicide at Jonestown inadmissible where there was no evidence showing Jones believed his own death was imminent and where statements would have nothing to do with the cause or circumstances of Jones death); State v. Penley, 347 S.E.2d 783, 789 (N.C.1986) (videotape of victim admissible where homicide victim's statements showed belief of imminent death); Boone v. State, 668 S.W.2d 17,20–21 (Ark.1984) (where child had vomited blood after beating and asked whether he was going to die, statements made by the child prior to assurances from his mother that he would live were admissible).

425. See Irving Younger, Hearsay: A Practical Guide Through the Thicket 158–59 (1988); see also Ferdinand S. Tinio, Annotation, Statements of Declarant As Sufficiently Showing Consciousness of Impending Death to justify Admission, 53 A.L.R.3d 785 (1973); Annotation, Opinion of Doctor or Other Attendant As to Declarants Consciousness of Imminent Death So As To Qualify His Statement as Dying Declaration, 48 A.L.R.2d 733 (1956); Commonwealth v. Peyton, 62 A.2d 37, 40 (Pa.1948) (imminence of death established by nature of wound); 5 Weinstein's Federal Evidence, supra note 422 § 805.05[4][b], at 804–44 ("The declarant's belief in the imminence of death may be shown by the declarant's own statements, or through circumstantial evidence such as the nature of the wounds, opinions of declarant's physicians, the fact that declarant received last rites, and statements made in declarant's presence") (footnotes omitted).

426. See Shepard v. United States, 290 U.S. 96, 99–100 (1933) (requiring a positive statement from the declarant as to belief of imminent death); see 5 Weinstein's Federal Evidence, supra note 422 § 805.05[4][b], at 804–44; Annotation, supra note 427.

427. See, e.g., United States v. Mobley, 421 F.2d 345, 347 (5th Cir.1970) (wounds so severe that victim must have known death imminent); see also Commonwealth v. Peyton, 62 A.2d 37, 40 (Pa.1948) (severity of wounds indicated consciousness of imminent death).

428. Fed. R. Evid. 804(b)(2); 5 Weinstein's Federal Evidence, supra note 422 § 805.05[5][b], at 804–45, at 804–130; 2 McCormick on Evidence, supra note 421 § 311.

not bar all such statements (e.g., a person dying from an accident might make a statement about the accident that was later helpful to heirs in a wrongful death action) it does bar statements that are irrelevant to the declarant's current predicament.[429]

In a Civil Case or Homicide Prosecution

At common law, the dying declaration exception was limited to homicide prosecutions.[430] The federal rule makers extended its scope to civil actions. That leaves one area in which the federal exception does not apply—criminal prosecutions for matters other than homicide.[431] It is not clear why the exception was limited in this fashion. The danger of concocting dying declarations about matters other than death would seem to be met by the requirement that the declaration concern the circumstances and cause of death. Apparently the limitation was due to a general distrust of dying declarations, at least where criminal penalties are involved, and the influence of common law precedents.[432]

Unavailability Requirement

As with other Rule 804 exceptions, the declarant must be unavailable.[433] Under the Federal Rule, it is possible for the declarant to be unavailable for some reason other than death.[434] For example, the

429. *See* Fed. R. Evid. 804(b)(2) advisory committee's note ("when the statement deals with matters other than the supposed death, its influence is believed to be sufficiently attenuated to justify the limitation"); United States v. Layton, 549 F.Supp. 903, 918 (N.D.Cal.1982) (statements made by Jim Jones regarding killing of congressman inadmissible because they did not concern the cause or circumstances of Jones's death, and because they were not clearly made with belief of imminent death); United States v. Sacasas, 381 F.2d 451, 454 (2d Cir.1967) (statement that co-indictee had nothing to do with bank robbery held inadmissible); 5 Weinstein's Federal Evidence, *supra* note 422 § 807.05[5][b], at 804–45 (noting that this requirement can result in keeping out some very helpful evidence and arguing for broad treatment of this requirement where "admission of the statement will help the jury in its task, i.e., whether it is sufficiently reliable and relevant to withstand exclusion because its probative value is substantially outweighed by the danger of prejudice to the party against whom it is offered"); Charles W. Quick, *Some Reflections on Dying Declarations*, 6 Howard L.J. 109, 116 (1960).

430. *See* 2 McCormick on Evidence, *supra* note 422 § 311; *see also* Annotation, *Admissibility of Dying Declarations in Civil Case*, 47 A.L.R.2d 526 (1956).

431. Fed. R. Evid. 804(b)(2); 5 Weinstein's Federal Evidence, *supra* note 422 § 807.05[2], at 804–43.

432. *See* H.R. Rep. No. 650, 93d Cong., 1st Sess. 15 (1973), reprinted at 4 James F. Bailey & Oscar M. Trelles, The Federal Rules of Evidence: Legislative Histories and Related Documents, Doc. 13 at 15–16 (1980):

The Committee did not consider dying declarations as among the most reliable forms of hearsay. Consequently, it amended the provision to limit their admissibility in criminal cases to homicide prosecutions, where exceptional need for the evidence is present. This is existing law. At the same time, the Committee approved the expansion to civil actions and proceedings where the stakes do not involve possible imprisonment, although noting that this could lead to forum shopping in some instances.

See also 2 McCormick on Evidence, *supra* note 422 § 283, at 328 ("The subsequent history of the rule is an object lesson in the use of precedents to preserve and fossilize judicial mistake of an earlier generation").

433. *See* Fed. R. Evid. 804(a); 2 McCormick on Evidence, *supra* note 421 § 310.

434. *See* Fed. R. Evid. 804(b)(2) advisory committee's note ("Unavailability is not declarant might have been shot and named the perpetrator while believing that death was imminent, and then have recovered. If the declarant then refuses to testify or is unavailable for any of the other reasons enumerated in Rule 804(a), the requirements of the exception have been met.[435]

Personal Knowledge

As with most other hearsay exceptions, the dying declaration is admissible only to the extent that it would be admissible if the declarant were present and testifying.[436] Thus, the declarant who was shot while sleeping, and who then states a suspicion about who did the shooting, has not made an admissible dying declaration because the declarant lacks personal knowledge.[437]

§ 7.52 The Declarations Against Interest Exception [FRE 804(b)(3)]

The declarations against interest exception[438] is based upon the theory that a person would not make a statement against his or her interest unless the statement was likely to be true.[439]

Admissions Rule Distinguished

The exception must be distinguished from the rule receiving admissions of party opponents:

1. The declaration against interest is admissible only if the person making the statement is unavailable–that is, dead, unable to testify because of mental or physical illness, unwilling to testify

---

limited to death"). Many courts previously only allowed the testimony if the declarant was dead. *See* State v. Carden, 183 S.E. 898, 903 (N.C.1936) (stating rule that declarant must have died before statement admissible).

435. *See* § 7.48. Note, a statement made by a declarant found to be unavailable under 804(a) should be admissible without violating the confrontation clause of the sixth amendment. *See* United States v. King, 552 F.2d 833, 838–40 (9th Cir. 1976).

436. Generally the declarant must have the capacities required of any witness, that is, the declarant must be able to perceive and relate facts, have personal knowledge of the facts testified to, and understand the obligation to tell the truth. *See* Boone v. State, 668 S.W.2d 17, 21 (Ark. 1984) ("In order to qualify as a dying declaration the statement must be made by a witness (1) who was a competent witness"); *see also* Annotation, *Admissibility in Criminal Trial of Dying Declarations Involving an Asserted Opinion or Conclusion*, 86 A.L.R.2d 905 (1962).

437. *See* Fed. R. Evid. 804(b) (2) advisory committee's note ("Continuation of a requirement of first-hand knowledge is assured by Rule 602"); 5 Weinstein's Federal Evidence, *supra* note 422 § 807.05[5][a], at 804–45; Shepard v. United States, 290 U.S. 96, 101 (1933) ("To let the declaration in, the inference must be permissible that there was knowledge or the opportunity for knowledge as to the acts that are declared"). *See also* United States v. Velentzas, No. 91 CR 38415, 1993 WL 37339 (E.D.N.Y. 1993) (denying government's motion in limine to admit murder victim's statements, after being shot repeatedly from car with tinted glass, that "Spiros [defendant] had done this to me" and victim's reply of "Spiros Velentzas" to police questions about who shot him; victim was talking to defendant on phone from defendant's travel agency, where victim had agreed to meet defendant, but victim lacked personal knowledge that defendant had him shot).

438. Fed. R. Evid. 804(b)(3).

439. Fed. R. Evid. 804(b)(3) advisory committee's note.

despite a court order, or not compellable for some other reason.[440]

The admission of a party-opponent, by contrast, is admissible whether or not the declarant is available for testimony. Even if the declarant is sitting in the back of the courtroom when the statement is offered, the opponent can still offer the statement in lieu of live testimony. No one has an obligation to call the party-opponent.[441]

2. The declaration against interest is admissible whether or not the declarant is a party or the agent of a party.[442] The party admission is only admissible when the declarant is a party or the agent of a party, and then only when offered by the opposing party.[443]

3. A declaration against interest must have been against interest when made in order to be admissible.[444] The admission need not have been against interest. If a party made a statement at a time when the statement was self-serving, the opposing party is nonetheless entitled to have that statement received as a party admission at trial should it turn out to be to the advantage of the opposing party to do so.[445]

§ 7.53   The Declarations Against Interest Exception [FRE 804(b)(3)]—Types of Interest That Qualify

The declaration against interest must be against a certain type of interest in order to qualify for the exception and, thus, be admitted into evidence. The common law judges constructed the following hierarchy of interests, with interests nearer the top of the list having a better chance at qualifying for the exception:

1. Pecuniary and proprietary interest (e.g., statements that admit a debt or concede another's property interest).

2. Tort or contract interest (statements that potentially expose the declarant to civil liability).

3. Penal interest (statements that expose the declarant to criminal liability).

4. Self-respect interest (statements that humiliate the declarant, but do not expose the declarant to liability).

Common law jurisdictions tended to admit statements in the first category, and perhaps the second, but not the third or fourth.[446] Thus, "I

---

440. Fed. R. Evid. 804(a), (b)(3); 5 John H. Wigmore, Evidence in Trials at Common Law § 1456 (James H. Chadbourn rev. 1974).

441. Fed. R. Evid. 801(d)(2).

442. Fed. R. Evid. 804(b)(3).

443. Fed. R. Evid. 801(d)(2).

444. Fed. R. Evid. 804(b)(3).

445. Fed. R. Evid. 801(d)(2) advisory committee's note.

446. See, e.g., 5 John H. Wigmore, Evidence in Trials at Common Law § 1477 (3d ed 1940); Donnelly v. United States, 228 U.S. 243, 273 (1913) (declaration against penal interest as opposed to pecuniary interest inadmissible); G.M. McKelvey Co. v.

gave my diamond to my eldest daughter," "I owe Jarvik $100," "He has a right of way across my land," or "I am holding this as agent for Hardwick" would all be admissible as against declarant's interest, whereas the confession "I am Jack the Ripper" would not have been admissible at common law under the present exception.

At first impression this different treatment of statements against pecuniary/proprietary interest and statements against penal interest seems anomalous, even bizarre. Why should a statement that exposes the declarant to a prison term or worse be treated as less reliable than a statement that might only lead to a small money loss? The limitation is not as arbitrary as it appears at first glance, however. If the statement "I am Jack the Ripper" is offered *against the declarant*, then it does not need the help of the present exception to find its way into evidence. The admissions rule is an ample gateway. But when the statement "I am Jack the Ripper" is offered, not to implicate the speaker, but to exonerate another person, the present exception is needed. It is here that the common law judges shut the door.[447]

Why should the statement be accepted with open arms when it incriminates, but turned aside when it exonerates? The common law judges had a skeptical attitude founded on experience. They believed that persons accused of crime would be likely to find friends who would fabricate a confession by a declarant who had conveniently died or disappeared, and that gullible juries would be too ready to treat these concoctions as raising a reasonable doubt.[448] Even before the Federal Rules, there were dissenters from this skeptical attitude. Wigmore condemned it roundly, saying:

> This is the ancient rusty weapon that has always been brandished to oppose any reform in the rules of Evidence, viz., the argument of danger of abuse. This would be a good argument against admitting any witnesses at all, for it is notorious that some witnesses will lie and that it is difficult to avoid being deceived by their lies. The truth is that any rule which hampers an honest man in exonerating himself is a bad rule, even if it also hampers a villain in falsely passing for an innocent.[449]

The limitation has persisted stubbornly, however, though in a diminished form. The current Federal Rules do permit statements against penal interest to be received to exonerate the defendant in a criminal case, but only if they are clearly corroborated.[450] In civil cases, however,

General Cas. Co. of America, 142 N.E.2d 854, 856 (Ohio 1957) (rule limited to declarations against "pecuniary or proprietary interest").

447. For an analysis of the admissibility of statements tending to implicate someone other than the defendant, see David McCord, *"But Perry Mason Made It Look So Easy!" The Admissibility of Evidence Offered By a Criminal Defendant to Suggest*

that Someone Else is Guilty, 63 Tenn. L. Rev. 917 (1996).

448. *See* Fed. R. Evid. 804(b)(3) advisory committee's note.

449. 5 Wigmore, *supra* note 446 § 1477.

450. Fed. R. Evid. 804(b)(3). *See also* United States v. Bahadar, 954 F.2d 821, 828–29 (2d Cir.), *cert. denied*, 506 U.S. 850 (1992) (statement made after arrest by al-

342 THE HEARSAY RULE AND ITS EXCEPTIONS Ch. 7

declarations against penal interest are freely admissible without any requirement of corroboration.[451] The ancient distrust of the scheming prisoner is thus retained, but the criminal defendant has the opportunity to use the third-party confession to escape punishment if it is sufficiently corroborated by other evidence.

There is one type of interest that will not suffice to support admission of a declaration against interest. A declaration that merely humiliates the declarant without exposing the declarant to legal liability will not suffice. For example, a shamefaced confession that the declarant has a secret vice will not suffice, in the absence of potential civil or criminal liability. The advisory committee originally proposed that self-degrading statements of this nature be received as declarations against interest, and the Supreme Court accepted this recommendation when it originally promulgated the Federal Rules of Evidence.[452] The House Committee on the Judiciary, however, eliminated the provision governing self-degrading statements. It stated that the category did not have sufficient guarantees of reliability.[453] Despite the failure of the Federal Rules to embrace declarations against social interest, there is some state authority for including them within the exception,[454] and the commentary contains support for this extension of the traditional declaration against interest exception.[455]

§ 7.54 The Declarations Against Interest Exception [FRE 804(b)(3)]—Statements That Are Only Partly Disserving

Questions sometimes arise about the status of statements that are partly disserving and partly self-serving or neutral. For example, the statement, "I took part in the robbery with X and Y" is both self-inculpatory (the declarant's admission of participating in the crime) and at least facially neutral (the declarant's naming of the others involved). The second part of the statement is self-inculpatory by implication because it demonstrates the declarant's knowledge of details of the crime (the other persons involved), but it is not as clearly inculpatory as the

leged accomplice, admitting accomplice's guilt but attempting to exonerate proponent of statement, inadmissible as lacking in sufficient corroboration; declarant was "all over the place" in his stories exonerating the accused); United States v. Arthur, 949 F.2d 211 (6th Cir.1991) (confession exonerating defendant was adequately against interest and corroborated, despite government argument that declarant had confessed to so many other crimes that the extra liability was insignificant; corroboration included similar confession of another person exonerating the accused, the fact that only two persons were involved in the robbery and the fact that the declarant had been filmed apparently casing the bank hours before the robbery).

451. See id.

452. H.R. Rep. No. 650, 93d Cong., 1st Sess. 16 (1973), reprinted in 1974 U.S. Code Cong. & Admin. News 7075, 7089.

453. Id.

454. See, e.g., Cal. Evid. Code § 1230 (1966) (covering statements that "create[] . . . a risk of making [declarant] an object of hatred, ridicule, or social disgrace in the community").

455. See, e.g., Edward J. Imwinkelried, Declarations Against Social Interest: The (Still) Embarrassingly Neglected Hearsay Exception, 69 S. Cal. L. Rev. 1427 (1996).

admission of participation. Other statements are both self-inculpatory and self-serving. The statement, "I took part in the robbery but X and Y forced me to do it" is both self-inculpatory (declarant's admission of participation) and self-serving (declarant's claim of duress). How should these types of statements be treated under the hearsay exception for declarations against interest?

The Supreme Court provided guidance on this issue in *Williamson v. United States*,[456] a criminal drug possession and distribution case in which the prosecution used the statements of an unavailable declarant against the defendant. In the statements, the declarant admitted some involvement in the drug activity, but he shifted the bulk of the blame to the defendant by implicating him as the owner of the drugs. The defendant was eventually convicted. The Supreme Court vacated and remanded.

The Court held that the most faithful reading of Rule 804(b)(3) renders inadmissible non-self-inculpatory statements, even if they are made within a broader narrative that is generally self-inculpatory. A district court may not assume that a statement is self-inculpatory just because the statement is part of a fuller confession, especially when, as in *Williamson*, the statement implicates someone else.

The Court maintained that this reading will not eviscerate the declaration against interest exception as it still allows admission of those statements which are truly self-inculpatory, rather than those that merely attempt to shift blame or curry favor. The question under the rule is always whether the statement at issue is sufficiently against the declarant's penal interest under the rule's language, and this question can only be answered in light of all the surrounding circumstances.

An interesting case against which to test this standard is *United States v. Barrett*,[457] a pre-*Williamson* case. In *Barrett*, one Tilley had made an out-of-court statement to some card-playing acquaintances that implicated himself in a stamp theft conspiracy. Tilley also said that "Buzzy" was involved. When asked by one of his acquaintances whether he was referring to "Bucky" (the defendant) or "Buzzy," Tilley said "No, Bucky wasn't involved. It was Buzzy." Naturally, the defendant wanted to use this out-of-court statement exonerating him as evidence in his defense. He argued that it was a statement against Tilley's interest because it implicated Tilley in crime.[458] The trial court excluded the statement on grounds that the relevant part—the part exonerating the defendant "Bucky"—was not against the declarant Tilley's interest. The First Circuit reversed, holding that the statement was admissible. It expressed the view that the whole statement was at least "arguably disserving" to Tilley, because knowing exactly who was involved showed an "insider's knowledge" that made Tilley's involvement more likely. It

---

456. 512 U.S. 594 (1994).   **458.** *Id.* at 249.
457. 539 F.2d 244 (1st Cir.1976).

also noted that the case law, "while far from settled," tended to grant a certain latitude to contextual statements.[459]

After *Williamson*, a court could still find that in its specific context, Tilley's statement that Buzzy rather than Bucky took part in the crime might still be found self-inculpatory because it showed specific knowledge of the crime. This would make Tilley's entire statement against interest, and thus admissible upon a showing of Tilley's unavailability.

Before *Williamson*, the treatment of neutral passages in otherwise disserving statements was far from uniform. Many courts, fortified by Wigmore's approval, allowed the entire statement, including the neutral portion, into evidence, as if the utterance of one disserving thought had put the declarant in a truth-telling frame of mind.[460] And there was a contrary view, also amply supported, that would weed the garden, separating the disserving statements from those that are neutral or self-serving.[461] After *Williamson*, it appears that neither extreme position is justified, and that the trial court must examine all parts of a statement to determine whether, in its particular context, each was against the declarant's interest when made. While *Williamson* hardly resolves all cases, and there is plenty of room for differences of opinion as to the admissibility of particular statements, the Supreme Court has at least set forth the principle which is to be followed by the federal courts.[462] Of course, even if a statement qualifies as a declaration against interest, a criminal defendant might sometimes be able to attack its admission successfully on confrontation grounds.[463]

459. *Id.* at 252 (citing McCormick on Evidence § 279(a), at 676 (2d ed. 1972)).

460. *See, e.g.*, United States v. Goodlow, 500 F.2d 954, 956–57 (8th Cir.1974) (declarant's statements that he "was good for the crime" and defendant was not "good for it" must be considered together and are admissible); 5 John H. Wigmore, Evidence in Trials at Common Law § 1465 (James H. Chadbourn rev. 1974).

461. *See, e.g.*, United States v. Seyfried, 435 F.2d 696, 698 (7th Cir. 1970) (where statement is separable and one part is against declarant's interest and one is not, only part against interest is admissible); United States v. Marquez, 462 F.2d 893, 895 (2d Cir.1972) (only proper to admit portion of statement against declarant's interest; portion exculpating another inadmissible).

462. For examples of cases applying *Williamson*, see United States v. Mendoza, 85 F.3d 1347, 1352 (8th Cir.1996) (held, statement by suspect caught with drug money implicating her boyfriend not admissible because she had nothing to lose by making it and may have been trying to curry favor); United States v. Costa, 31 F.3d 1073, 1077 (11th Cir.1994) (*Williamson* requires trial court to make fact-inten-

sive inquiry of statements made during custodial interrogation to determine whether those statements are really against interest). *Compare* First National Bank of Louisville v. Lustig, 96 F.3d 1554, 1574 (5th Cir.1996) (held, no abuse of discretion in civil suit by bank against insurer involving coverage dispute in which key issue was whether loan officer employed by bank had acted with intent to garner person benefit or to harm bank by fraud; not error to admit evidence that loan officer pled guilty to bank fraud indictment that included factual references that would establish coverage under the bond; bank had worked with prosecutor in extraordinary way to add language to indictment that would help bank; *query* whether court sufficiently analyzed case to distinguish between against-interest, neutral, and self-serving aspects of the guilty plea).

463. Because declarations against penal interest were generally not admitted at common law, one might expect courts to find that the hearsay exception is not "firmly rooted" for purposes of the *Roberts* test (described in § 7.66). The majority of federal courts that have considered the issue have, however, deemed the exception firmly rooted. *See* United States v. Jacobs,

When the statement of a declarant implicates both the declarant and the defendant, the declaration against interest exception is frequently not needed, because the statement will often be admissible as the admission of a co-conspirator.[464] Sometimes the co-conspirator route to admission, however, will not be available. For example, it would not be available if the statement was made after the conspiracy ended.[465] Then, the declaration against interest exception would furnish a possible basis for admission under the *Williamson* standard if the court believes that under the circumstances, the part of the statement implicating the defendant was against the declarant's interest. Such a result can find support in the legislative history of Rule 804(b)(3); after considering the issue, the Senate Judiciary Committee rejected a provision that would have prevented the use of confessions by others to implicate the accused.[466] One important limitation must be mentioned, however: Current constitutional doctrine ordinarily prevents use of one defendant's confession against another, on grounds that this use violates the right to confrontation.[467]

Sometimes the very same statement has self-serving and disserving aspects. For example, a statement of income in a tax return is self-serving insofar as it asserts that the declarant's income does not exceed a certain level, but disserving to the extent that it concedes that declarant had income up to a certain level. The sensible way to treat such statements is to receive them when they are offered to show facts that were against the declarant's interest when the statement was made—for example, to show that the income reached up to the level conceded in the return—but judicial treatment has not been uniform.[468]

OTHER HEARSAY ISSUES

§ 7.55   The Residual Exceptions to the Hearsay Rule

Federal Rules of Evidence 803(24) and 804(b)(5) provided identical "residual" or "catchall" exceptions. These exceptions were added in order to "provide for treating new and presently unanticipated situations which demonstrate a trustworthiness within the spirit of the

44 M.J. 301, 306 (Ct. App. Armed Forces 1996) (collecting cases). *But see* United States v. Flores, 985 F.2d 770, 778–80 (5th Cir.1993).

464. *See* § **7.08.**

465. Fed. R. Evid. 801(d)(2)(E).

466. S. Rep. No. 1277, 93d Cong., 2d Sess. 21, reprinted in 1974 U.S. Code Cong. & Admin. News 7051, 7068.

467. *See* § **7.68.**

468. *See, e.g.,* Ghelin v. Johnson, 243 N.W. 443, 446 (Minn. 1932) (declarant's statement on income tax return that he was unmarried was admissible as declaration against interest); Barrera v. Gonzalez, 341 S.W.2d 703, 705–06 (Tex.Civ.App.1960) (declarant's statement that he owed money not admissible because self-serving under circumstances; statement by declarant that he owed money to creditor amounted to assertion that declarant did not transfer real property to creditor in satisfaction of debt as creditor claimed); but see, *e.g.,* Veach's Admr. v. Louisville & I Ry. Co., 228 S.W. 35, 37 (Ky.1921) (declarant's statement of income on tax return self-serving, even to prove income not less than amount stated); 2 McCormick on Evidence § 319, at 343 (4th ed. John W. Strong ed. 1992) (admissibility of statement as declaration against interest turns on perceived harm at time statement made).

specifically stated exceptions," and to leave room "for growth and development of the law of evidence in the hearsay area."[469] In 1997, Rules 803(24) and 804(b)(5) were repealed and replaced with a single exception, now numbered Rule 807. No substantive change was intended.

The main requirements of the residual exceptions can be expressed in three categories:[470]

1. The evidence must have "guarantees of trustworthiness" that are "equivalent" to those of the established exceptions.[471]

2. The evidence must be "more probative" on the point for which it is offered than any other evidence that can reasonably be obtained.[472]

---

469. Fed. R. Evid. 803(24) advisory committee's note. The advisory committee further noted that it would "be presumptuous to assume that all possible desirable exceptions to the hearsay rule have been catalogued and to pass the hearsay rule to oncoming generations as a closed system." This has not been interpreted to mean, however, that these exceptions are to be used to create whole new categories of exceptions. *See generally* 5 Weinstein's Federal Evidence § 803.30[4], at 803–148 (2d ed. Joseph M. McLaughlin ed. 1997). For criticism of the residual exceptions see Jon R. Waltz & James Beckley, *The Exception for Great Hearsay: Some Concerned Comments*, 1 Am. J. Trial Advoc. 123 (1977).

470. *See generally,* 5 Weinstein's Federal Evidence, *supra* note 469 § 803.30[2]; 2 McCormick on Evidence § 324 (4th ed. John W. Strong ed. 1992); United States v. Marchini, 797 F.2d 759, 762–64 (9th Cir. 1986) (discussing each of the requirements for admission under 804(b)(5)); FTC v. Amy Travel Serv., 875 F.2d 564, 576 (7th Cir. 1989) (discussing requirements of residual exception).

471. *See, e.g.,* United States v. Blackburn, 992 F.2d 666, 672 (7th Cir.1993) (held, computer printouts of electronic lensometer readings for lens of eyeglasses left by bank robber in stolen car are admissible under residual exception because test which produces readings used highly reliable method of analysis; further more, at time test was conducted, defendant was not even a suspect in the case); Polansky v. CNA Ins. Co., 852 F.2d 626, 631 (1st Cir. 1988) (proper to exclude letter written by representative of proponent which was self-serving and lacked guarantees of trustworthiness); United States v. Carlson, 547 F.2d 1346, 1354 (8th Cir.1976) (grand jury testimony was sufficiently trustworthy to be admitted where declarant was under oath and never

recanted or expressed reservations about the accuracy of the testimony).

472. *See, e.g.,* United States v. Blackburn, 992 F.2d 666, 672 (7th Cir.1993) (held, computer printouts of electronic lensometer readings for lens of eyeglasses left by bank robber in stolen car are admissible under the residual exception since the machine-created report was at least as probative of the results of the test which produced the readings as any oral statement by someone who observed the process); United States v. Marchini, 797 F.2d 759, 764 (9th Cir.1986) (where unavailable declarant was the only person who could establish the link between drafting of supplier checks and their conversion to cash, thus demonstrating defendant's guilt in action for filing false tax returns, declarant's prior grand jury testimony was admissible under 804(b)(5)); Conoco, Inc. v. Department of Energy, 99 F.3d 387, 392 (Fed.Cir.1996) (purchase summaries prepared, long after the event, by nonparty purchaser of crude oil in response to Conoco's request for information for Department of Energy audit not admissible when offered under residual exception by Department of Energy because not more probative on point than other evidence that could be procured through reasonable efforts); United States v. Trenkler, 61 F.3d 45, 59 (1st Cir.1995) (held, error to admit, under residual exception, testimony that search of ATF database showed that, of bombs on record, only six resembled the one in case at bar and one of those six had been built by the defendant; insufficient showing of trustworthiness); Noble v. Alabama Dept. of Envtl. Management, 872 F.2d 361, 366 (11th Cir.1989) (error to admit letter where proponent made no showing that reasonable efforts would not have brought writer to court to testify). *See, e.g.,* Larez v. City of Los Angeles, 946 F.2d 630, 641–44 (9th Cir.1991)

3. The opponent of the evidence must be given notice of intent to offer it prior to trial.[473] (This requirement of notice *before* trial has been watered down in most—but not all—jurisdictions to allow notice *during* trial if the opponent is not prejudiced and if there is an excuse for not giving earlier notice.[474] This trend does not mean that notice never poses an obstacle, for courts will refuse to apply the exception when there is no excuse for not giving notice. It simply means that the obstacle can be overcome at the trial stage when the proponent has a good excuse. Moreover, it is possible that the trend will be reversed if the Supreme Court applies its evolving "plain meaning" philosophy to the notice provisions of the residual exceptions.[475])

There are also some makeweight provisions, such as the requirements that admitting the evidence be in the interest of justice and in accordance with the purposes of the Rules[476] and that the statement be offered as evidence of a "material" fact.[477]

(newspaper reports describing statements by defendant police chief satisfied trustworthiness requirement of 803(24) where independent reports were consistent with each other, but they did not satisfy the "more probative" requirement where reporters were available for testimony). One questions the continuing validity of the *Larez* dicta about trustworthiness after Idaho v. Wright, 497 U.S. 805 (1990) (*see* § **7.66**), which stated that the trustworthiness required by the confrontation clause must be found in the circumstances under which the statement was made, not in extrinsic corroboration of the statement.

473. *See, e.g.,* United States v. Cowley, 720 F.2d 1037, 1044–45 (9th Cir.1983) (requiring strict compliance with notice provision); United States v. Ruffin, 575 F.2d 346, 357 (2d Cir.1978) (requiring strict compliance with notice provision).

474. *See, e.g.,* United States v. Iaconetti, 540 F.2d 574, 578 (2d Cir.1976), where the court found that defendant was not prejudiced by trial court's decision to allow the government to offer rebuttal testimony under the residual exception even though it did not notify defendant of its intention to offer such testimony until three days before testimony offered. The court noted that the need for the rebuttal testimony did not become apparent until after trial had begun and that defendant did not seek continuance or claim he was unable adequately to prepare to meet rebuttal testimony. The court stressed, however, that "[p]re-trial notice should clearly be given if at all possible, and only in those situations where requiring pre-trial notice is wholly impracticable, as here, should flexibility be accorded." *Id.* at n.6.

See also United States v. Leslie, 542 F.2d 285 (5th Cir.1976) (failure to comply with notice requirement harmless error where defendant had every reason to expect government to call the witnesses). *See* Joseph W. Rand, Note, *The Residual Exceptions to the Federal Hearsay Rule: The Futile and Misguided Attempt to Restrain Judicial Discretion*, 80 Geo. L.J. 873, 885–86 (1992) (collecting cases that have interpreted the notice requirement in a relaxed fashion).

475. *See* Randolph N. Jonakait, *The Supreme Court, Plain Meaning, and the Changed rules of Evidence*, 68 Tex. L. Rev. 745, 762–64 (1990).

476. *See, e.g.,* Marsee v. United States Tobacco Co., 866 F.2d 319, 325 (10th Cir. 1989) (admission of reports establishing link between oral cancer and chewing tobacco not required in the interests of justice where expert testimony had previously established much of the same information); FTC v. Amy Travel Serv., 875 F.2d 564, 576 (7th Cir.1989) (admission of affidavits of injured consumers is in the interests of justice where "it would be cumbersome and unnecessarily expensive" to bring all consumers injured in a nationwide telemarketing scam to court to testify).

477. *Id.* (affidavits probative on issue of whether consumers were injured in telemarketing scam were material); United States v. Carlson, 547 F.2d 1346, 1354 (8th Cir.1976) (grand jury testimony that showed defendant's "intent, knowledge, a common plan or scheme, and the absence of a mistake or accident" was relevant and material in criminal action for conspiracy to distribute cocaine). There is some question as to what "material" means as used in the

Although Congress apparently intended that the residual exceptions be applied only in a limited set of near-unique circumstances, some courts have been willing to apply them to ordinary hearsay that does not fit any other standard exceptions. The consensus of scholarly opinion seems to be that courts construing the residual exceptions have been quite liberal in finding evidence trustworthy enough to be received.[478] Certainly there are some startlingly permissive cases. For example, in some jurisdictions it has become common for federal courts to admit grand jury testimony of absent witnesses, even though they may have a motive to lie, so long as the testimony is corroborated by other evidence.[479] Extension of this line of cases would seem to allow all grand jury testimony to come in as long as the other evidence against the defendant is good. Some courts have been equally permissive in civil cases.[480] If followed to the extent of their logic, the permissive residual exception case could destroy the hearsay rule. Yet often the cases are merely examples of appellate courts upholding district court rulings under an abuse of discretion standard, leaving the district courts free to either admit or exclude, rather than requiring them to admit. In any event, there are decisions of equal status that are less permissive.[481]

In child sex abuse prosecutions, prosecutors have increasingly turned to the residual exceptions, as well as to special state statutes admitting child hearsay. In *United States v. N.B.*,[482] for example, the court found that guarantees of trustworthiness were sufficient to admit under the residual exception a social worker-witness' testimony concerning the child-declarant's statements inculpating defendant in sexual

residual exceptions. Some courts have held that it means the same thing as "relevant" under Rule 401. *See, e.g., United States v. Muscato,* 534 F.Supp. 969, 979 (E.D.N.Y. 1982). Others suggest that it means more than mere relevance and is satisfied only by nontrivial matters. *See United States v. Iaconetti,* 406 F.Supp. 554, 559 (E.D.N.Y.), *aff'd,* 540 F.2d 574 (2d Cir.1976), *cert. denied,* 429 U.S. 1041, *rehg denied,* 430 U.S. 911 (1977).

Some appellate courts have required the district court to make detailed specific findings before admitting a statement under the residual exceptions. *See, e.g.,* Mutuelles Unies v. Kroll & Linstrom, 957 F.2d 707 (9th Cir.1992) (error not to make specific findings, but not unfairly prejudicial).

478. *See* Randolph N. Jonakait, *The Subversion of the Hearsay Rule: The Residual Hearsay Exceptions, Circumstantial Guarantees of Trustworthiness, and Grand Jury Testimony,* 36 Case W. Res. L. Rev. 431 (1986); Myrna S. Raeder, *The Effect of the Catchalls on Criminal Defendants: Little Red Riding Hood Meets the Hearsay Wolf and Is Devoured,* 25 Loy. L.A. L. Rev. 925, 933 (1992); David A. Sonenshein, *The Residual Exceptions to the Federal Hearsay Rule: Two Exceptions in Search of a Rule,* 57 N.Y.U. L. Rev. 867 (1982); Jeffrey Cole, *Residual Exceptions to the Hearsay Rule,* Litig. Mag., Fall 1989, at 26.

479. *See, e.g., United States v. Guinan,* 836 F.2d 350 (7th Cir.), *cert. denied,* 487 U.S. 1218 (1988) (grand jury testimony by estranged wife admissible when corroborated by other evidence); Jonakait, *supra* note 476.

480. *See, e.g.,* Turbyfill v. International Harvester Co., 486 F.Supp. 232 (E.D.Mich.1980) (employee's statement, helpful to employer, admitted against third party under residual exception).

481. *See* United States v. Gomez–Lemos, 939 F.2d 326 (6th Cir.1991) (reversing trial judge who admitted grand jury testimony under residual exception, noting that *Idaho v. Wright,* 497 U.S. 805 (1990) does not allow trustworthiness to be established by extrinsic corroboration); United States v. Fernandez, 892 F.2d 976, 980–84 (11th Cir. 1989), *cert. dismissed,* 495 U.S. 944 (1990) (refusing to admit grand jury testimony under the residual exceptions, and noting that the Eleventh Circuit has never done so).

482. 59 F.3d 771, 776 (8th Cir.1995).

abuse. The court held that in deciding whether statements are sufficiently trustworthy, a court should consider "the training and experience of the social worker; whether the child was interviewed using open-ended questions; the age of the child and whether the child used 'age-appropriate language' in discussing the abuse; the length of time between the incident of abuse and the making of the hearsay statement; and whether the child repeated the same facts consistently to adults."[483] In addition, as the Supreme Court's decision in *Idaho v. Wright*[484] makes clear, the court must also consider whether admission of the child's statements would satisfy the requirements of the confrontation clause. *See* § **7.66**.

§ 7.56   Miscellaneous Hearsay Exceptions

Statements of Recent Perception

The version of the Federal Rules of Evidence that was promulgated by the Supreme Court under its rulemaking power in 1973 had an exception for "statements of recent perception."[485] Congress prevented the Supreme Court's version of the rules from going into effect. By the time the Federal Rules of Evidence had been enacted as a statute by Congress in 1975, the exception had been removed completely.[486] The Supreme Court's version of the statement of recent perception provided an exception for

> A statement, not in response to the instigation of a person engaged in investigating, litigating, or settling a claim, which narrates, describes, or explains an event or condition recently perceived by the declarant, made in good faith, not in contemplation of pending or anticipated litigation in which he was interested, and while his recollection was clear.[487]

The Supreme Court's recent perception exception was one of the Rule 804 exceptions, which meant that the exception did not apply unless the declarant was unavailable.[488] Although Congress rejected the recent perception exception, versions of it have been adopted in some states[489] and as an option in the Uniform Rules.[490] The option provided in

483. *Id. See also* the discussion of *Idaho v. Wright* in § **7.66**.

484. 497 U.S. 805 (1990).

485. *See* Fed. R. Evid. 804(b)(2) (Supreme Court Proposed Draft 1973), reprinted in 2 James F. Bailey & Oscar M. Trelles, The Federal Rules of Evidence: Legislative Histories and Related Documents, Doc. 13, at 33 (1980); see also 5 Weinstein's Federal Evidence § 804App.01[3], at 804App.–12 (2d ed. Joseph M. McLaughlin ed. 1997).

486. *See* H.R. Rep. No. 650, 93d Cong., 1st Sess. 6 (1973), reprinted in 4 Bailey & Trelles, *supra* note 485, at 6; *see also* 5 Weinstein's Federal Evidence, *supra* note 485 § 804App.01[4], at 804App.–15; Kenneth E. Kraus, Comment, *The Recent Perception Exception to the Hearsay Rule-A Justifiable, Record*, 1985 Wis. L. Rev. 1525,

1543–44 (1985) (arguing for reconsideration of the exception).

487. *See* Fed. R. Evid. 804(b)(2) (Supreme Court Proposed Draft 1973), reprinted in 2 Bailey & Trelles, *supra* note 485, Doc. 7, at 33; *see also* 5 Weinstein's Federal Evidence, *supra* note 485 § 804App.01[3], at 804App.–12.

488. *See id.*

489. *See, e.g.,* Haw. R. Evid. 804(b)(5):

Statement of recent perception. A statement, not in response to the instigation of a person engaged in investigating, litigating, or settling a claim, which narrates, describes, or explains an event or condition recently perceived by the

490. See note 490 on page 350.

Uniform Rule 803(b)(5) is like the federal rule rejected by Congress, except that it applies only to civil cases.[491]

Although much of the territory covered by the recent perception exception is also covered by the residual exception and the present sense impression exception, it has a niche of its own. Unlike the residual exceptions, it allows the evidence to be received without notice, and does not require that it be the best evidence on the point.[492] Unlike the present sense impression exception, it does not require that the statement be made during or immediately after the event, though the event must be "recent" at the time of the statement.[493] The exception seems a useful supplement to the other hearsay exceptions. Because the declarant is unavailable, the choice is to hear the declarant's story in hearsay form or not at all. The protections of the recent perception exception, such as recency of perception, clarity of recollection, good faith, and unavailability of the declarant, seem sufficient.[494] Nevertheless, most states have not adopted this exception.

Statements of Deceased Persons

Since 1898, Massachusetts has had a statute making statements of decedents broadly admissible in civil actions. The current version of the statute reads as follows: "In any action or other civil judicial proceeding, a declaration of a deceased person shall not be inadmissible in evidence as hearsay . . . if the court finds that it was made in good faith and upon the personal knowledge of the declarant."[495]

The Massachusetts approach has not spread very widely, though a few states have enacted much more limited statutes for cases involving

---

declarant, made in good faith, not in contemplation of pending or anticipated litigation in which the declarant was interested, and while the declarant's recollection was clear . . . .

    See also Wis. Stat. Ann. § 908.045(2) (West 1993); Kraus Comment, *supra* note 486 at, 1527. For applications of the Wisconsin Rule *see, e.g.,* Kluever by Gonring v. Evangelical Reformed Immanuel's Congregation, 422 N.W.2d 874, 876–78 (Wis.App.1988) (statement of injured worker regarding fall from ladder admissible even though made eight to ten weeks after the accident); State v. Kreuser, 280 N.W.2d 270, 274 (Wis. 1979) (out-of-court declarant's statement made within a day of the event reported admissible as recent perception).

490. *See* Unif. R. Evid. 803(b)(5).

491. Note that the Uniform Rules had previously applied the exception to criminal cases as well. This practice was criticized by commentators. *See, e.g.,* Charles W. Quick, *Hearsay, Excitement, Necessity and the Uni-*

form Rules: A Reappraisal of Rule 63(4), 6 Wayne L. Rev. 204, 219–24 (1960).

492. *Cf.* Fed. R. Evid. 803(24); *see* § 7.55.

493. *Cf.* Fed. R. Evid. 804(b)(3); *see* § 7.11. *See, e.g.,* State v. Kreuser, 280 N.W.2d 270, 274 (Wis.1979) (out-of-court declarant's statement within one day of event described admissible); Kluever by Gonring v. Evangelical Reformed Immanuel's Congregation, 422 N.W.2d 874, 876–78 (Wis.App.1988) (declarant's statement after eight to ten weeks held admissible as recent perception).

494. *See* Kraus Comment, *supra* note 486, at 1537.

495. *See* Mass. Ann. Laws ch. 233, § 65 (Law. Co-op 1986). For cases applying the Massachusetts rule see Cusher v. Turner, 495 N.E.2d 311, 316 (Mass.App.1986) (statements made by decedent in diary and tape recordings admissible); Fire Commr. v. Joseph, 498 N.E.2d 1368, 1370–71 (Mass. App.1986) (no error in not admitting decedent's statement where it was not made in good faith).

suits against the estates of decedents.[496] And in 1996, in the wake of the widely publicized murder trial of O.J. Simpson, California adopted a new hearsay exception covering statements of unavailable declarants that "purport[] to narrate, describe, or explain the infliction or threat of physical injury upon the declarant."[497] Though the rule contains a number of limitations,[498] it is potentially applicable to many types of civil and criminal cases.

Statements by Children Describing Abuse

A number of states have adopted statutory exceptions to the hearsay rule for statements by children about sexual or physical abuse.[499] Many of the statutes apply only when the child is either testifying and subject to cross, or unavailable so that the testimony must be received in hearsay form or not at all.[500] Typical definitions of unavailability include such things as the declarant's incompetence to testify.[501] Of course, many

496. *See* 5 John H. Wigmore, Evidence in Trials at Common Law § 1576 (James H. Chadbourn rev. 1974 & Supp. 1996).

497. Cal. Evid. Code § 1370 (West 1997).

498. The statement must have been made at or near the time of the injury or threat; it must have been made under circumstances indicating its trustworthiness; and it must have been in writing, electronically recorded, or made to a law enforcement official. § 1370(a). In addition, the rule contains a provision requiring the proponent to make known its intention to offer the statement and its particulars "sufficiently in advance of the proceedings to provide the adverse party with a fair opportunity to prepare the meet the statement." § 1370(c).

499. *See generally* Michael H. Graham, *The Confrontation Clause, the Hearsay Rule and Child Sexual Abuse Prosecutions: The State of the Relationship*, 72 Minn. L. Rev. 523, 534–38 (1988); Jean L. Kelly, Comment, *Legislative Responses to Child Sexual Abuse Cases: The Hearsay Exception and the Videotape Deposition*, 34 Cath. U.L. Rev. 1021, 1035–41 (1985); Judy Yun, Note, *A Comprehensive Approach to Child Hearsay Statements in Sex Abuse Cases*, 83 Colum. L. Rev. 1745 (1983).

500. *See, e.g.,* Minn. Stat. Ann. § 595.02(3) (West 1988):

An out-of-court statement made by a child under the age of ten years or a person who is mentally impaired ... alleging, explaining, denying, or describing any act of sexual contact or penetration performed with or on the child ... is admissible as substantive evidence if:

(a) the court or person authorized to receive evidence finds, in a hearing conducted outside of the presence of the jury, that the time, content, and circumstances of the statement and the reliability of the person to whom the statement is made provide sufficient indicia of reliability; and

(b) the child ... either:

(i) testifies at the proceedings; or

(ii) is unavailable as a witness and there is corroborative evidence of the act; and

(c) the proponent of the statement notifies the adverse party of the proponent's intention to offer the statement and the particulars of the statement sufficiently in advance of the proceeding at which the proponent intends to offer the statement into evidence to provide the adverse party with a fair opportunity to prepare to meet the statement....

For applications of this statute see State v. Dana, 422 N.W.2d 246, 248–50 (Minn.1988) (admissibility hearing sufficient; no error in admitting statements of two abused children); State v. Bellotti, 383 N.W.2d 308, 312–13 (Minn.App.1986) (statements of four-year-old sex abuse victim admissible).

501. *See, e.g.,* Fed. R. Evid. 804(a)(4) (defining as unavailable a person who "is unable to be present or to testify at the hearing because of death or then existing physical or mental illness or infirmity"); Cal. Evid. Code § 240(a)(3) (West 1966) (same); Cal. Evid. Code § 240(c) (West 1966) (providing that witness can be found available due to physical or mental illness or infirmity if "[e]xpert testimony ... esstatements of children are admissible under conventional theories, such as the excited utterance,[502] the statement for medical diagnosis or treatment,[503] or one of the residual exceptions.[504]

§ 7.57 Hearsay within Hearsay [FRE 805]

Sometimes the declarant's out-of-court statement will contain another out-of-court statement. For example, a hospital record might contain the patient's story about the cause of the injury. If the entry is offered to prove the cause of injury, the record has hearsay within hearsay. The first level of hearsay is the patient's oral statement to the record-maker about the cause of the injury. The second level is the record-maker's written statement in the hospital record describing what the patient said.

Federal Rule of Evidence 805, in accordance with prior law, provides that hearsay within hearsay is admissible if each level of hearsay falls under an exception to the hearsay rule.[505] In theory, out-of-court statements can be enclosed within each other ten deep if each statement is either not hearsay or falls under an exception.[506] A hearsay scholar who was extremely precise might point out that a nonhearsay statement contained within an admissible hearsay statement does not need Rule 805 to be admitted at all, since it is not hearsay within hearsay.[507] In any event, it is clear that statements within statements are admissible so long as all statements in the chain are either nonhearsay or admissible under an exception.[508] Of course, each statement in the chain must be

tablishes that physical or mental trauma resulting from an alleged crime has caused harm to a witness of sufficient severity that the witness is physically unable to testify or is unable to testify without suffering substantial trauma").

502. *See, e.g.,* United States v. Farley, 992 F.2d 1122, 1125–26 (10th Cir.1993) (trial court properly admitted testimony from child victim's mother as to victim's statements the morning after alleged sexual assault occurred when victim was still "under the stress of the event"); United States v. Nick, 604 F.2d 1199, 1204 (9th Cir.1979) (statements of child admissible as excited utterances in sexual assault case).

503. Goldade v. State, 674 P.2d 721, 722–28 (Wyo.1983) (statements of child sex abuse victim to nurse and physician admissible under the "treatment and diagnosis" exception).

504. *See, e.g.,* Doe v. United States, 976 F.2d 1071, 1074–78 (7th Cir.), *cert. denied,* 510 U.S. 812 (1993) (in Federal Torts Claim Act action alleging sexual abuse at government-owned center, three-year-old children's hearsay statements admissible under residual hearsay exception where essence of their story did not change despite the addition of varying details and where

statements responded to questions by adults); United States v. Dorian, 803 F.2d 1439, 1446 (8th Cir.1986) (statement of child victim of sex abuse admissible under Rule 803(24)). *See generally* Graham, *supra* note 499, at 523.

505. *See* Fed. R. Evid. 805 advisory committee's note; 5 Weinstein's Federal Evidence § 805.02, at 805–4 (2d ed. Joseph M. McLaughlin ed. 1997); 2 McCormick on Evidence § 327.1 (4th ed. John W. Strong. ed. 1992).

506. *See, e.g.,* United States v. Abell, 586 F.Supp. 1414, 1425 (D. Me. 1984) (three levels of statements, all admissible).

507. *See* 2 McCormick on Evidence, *supra* note 505, at §§ 323.1, at 369–709; *see also* United States v. Basey, 613 F.2d 198, 201 n. 1 (9th Cir.1979), *cert. denied,* 446 U.S. 919 (1980) (no double hearsay problem involved where first level statements were admissions or adoptive admissions, and second level fell under Rule 803(6)).

508. *See* Bondie v. Bic Corp., 947 F.2d 1531, 1533–34 (6th Cir.1991) (social worker's written report that child had told her she had started fire with matches, not cigarette lighter as claimed by plaintiff, admisnonhearsay or fall within a hearsay exception for the chain to be admissible; it is not enough for one statement to fit if another does not.[509]

§ 7.58 Hearsay Within Hearsay [FRE 805]—Is Hearsay Within Hearsay Trustworthy?

Federal Rule of Evidence 805's liberal attitude toward hearsay within hearsay is in striking contrast to the requirements of trustworthiness that are set forth in many of the exceptions. Common sense tells us that hearsay within hearsay is likely to pose problems of reliability even if each statement fits an exception, and the Allport and Postman studies confirm what common sense tells us about multiple levels of hearsay.[510]

sible as hearsay within hearsay; social worker's report fit the business records exception and child's statement was the statement of a party-opponent); United States v. Diez, 515 F.2d 892, 895–96 n. 2 (5th Cir. 1975) (out-of-court statement offered to show declarant's state of mind, and falling under the hearsay exception of Fed. R. Evid. 803(3), admissible when contained within co-conspirator's out-of-court statement, which Rule 801(d)(2)(E) classifies as nonhearsay).

509. *See* United States v. Sallins, 993 F.2d 344, 347 (3d Cir.1993) (held, police computer record detailing contents of a 911 call inadmissible; record itself falls within public records exception but government failed to show hearsay exception for statements made by person calling 911); Larez v. City of Los Angeles, 946 F.2d 630, 641–44 (9th Cir.1991) (held, where police chief was defendant, chief's statements to newspaper reporters were inadmissible hearsay where the reporters did not testify; the chief's statement was an admission, but the reporters' statements about what the chief said were inadmissible hearsay); Boren v. Sable, 887 F.2d 1032 (10th Cir.1989) (testimony of wife that her deceased husband told her that he had told his plant manager about a dangerous maintenance procedure was properly excluded since the first level of hearsay, the husband's out-of-court statement to his wife, did not fall under one of the hearsay exceptions); *see also* United States v. Reed, 887 F.2d 1398 (11th Cir. 1989) (multiple hearsay admissible where each level either was nonhearsay or fell under an exception); Cedeck v. Hamiltonian Fed. Sav. & Loan Assn., 551 F.2d 1136, 1138 (8th Cir.1977) (where author of statement to supervisor unknown, the statement did not qualify as admission of party-opponent, thus plaintiff's testimony regarding the supervisor's relating that statement was inadmissible double hearsay). For a

case that could be read as stating broadly that Rule 803(8)(C) cannot be a vehicle for findings based upon hearsay from a declarant who was not under a public duty, see Miller v. Field, 35 F.3d 1088 (6th Cir.1994). Miller was a federal civil rights case arising from an alleged prison rape. The court held that public records must contain either factual findings from firsthand knowledge of the report's preparer or conclusions derived from those facts. Hence, it ruled, state police reports setting forth witness statements and conclusions of investigators were inadmissible. While *Miller* reaches the right result on its facts, it goes too far in its statement of the limits on Rule 803(8)(C). Under Rule 803(8)(C), when a public official actually makes "findings" pursuant to an investigation required by law (as opposed to merely recording information without evaluating it), those findings are admissible unless shown to be trustworthy. Passages of the *Miller* opinion could be read to say that findings based upon statements from declarants who are not under a public duty are simply inadmissible, whether or not they are shown to be untrustworthy. Under that reasoning, findings by hearing officers conducting administrative hearings would be inadmissible whenever based on hearing testimony by person not under a public duty, a result that seems clearly inconsistent with the intent of the rulemakers and the examples given in the Advisory Committee's Note.

510. *See* Gordon W. Allport & Leo Postman, The Psychology of Rumor *75–76 (1947); see also* Comment, Hearsay Under the Proposed Federal Rules: A Discretionary Approach, 15 Wayne L. Rev. 1077, 1231 (1969); *see also* Boren v. Sable, 887 F.2d 1032 (10th Cir.1989) (discussing dangers of multiple hearsay and exclusion of such evidence under Rule 403). United States v. Daniels, 572 F.2d 535, 539 (5th Cir.1978)

Allport and Postman developed a series of experiments in which a subject viewed an illustration, and was asked to describe it to another subject, who described it to another subject, and so forth.[511] Allport and Postman noted that about 70 per cent of the information depicted in the illustration was lost after five or six mouth-to-mouth transmissions, even when the there was virtually no time interval between the statements. The most rapid loss came at the beginning, with the first one or two declarants.[512] The "level"(omission of details) and "sharpening" (selective reporting) effects noted were sometimes startling.[513] As the subjects struggled to assimilate what they had heard from others, they appear also to have added or changed vital details. For example, in more than half of the experiments the subjects erroneously "moved" a weapon (a straight razor blade) from the hand of the white person who held it in the illustration into the hand of a black antagonist during the telling of the story.[514]

Experiments like those performed by Allport and Postman could be used as a basis for arguing that the law should not allow endless levels of hearsay to come in, even if each layer meets an exception. However, one rarely runs into hearsay within hearsay stacked five times deep in litigation, because of the difficulty of fitting each statement into an exception and of showing that each declarant had personal knowledge.[515] Since in practice courts are dealing almost exclusively with one level of hearsay within hearsay, perhaps a rule of thumb that hearsay is admissible if each level fits an exception is the most simple and administrable approach.

In the case of the hospital record containing the account of the patient's injury, discussed in § 7.57, the record-keeper's statement would fall under the business records exception, if it was the regular practice of the hospital to make records of this sort of statement.[516] The patient's statement might be admissible either as an admission (if offered against the patient) or as a statement for purposes of diagnosis or treatment.[517]

§ 7.59 Hearsay Within Hearsay [FRE 805]—Illustrations

The late Irving Younger, whose unmatched talent for vivid illustration provided so many evidence learners with unforgettable memory

(discussing the special problems double hearsay poses in a criminal trial).

511. Allport & Postman, *supra* note 508.

512. *Id.*

513. *Id.* at 75–98.

514. *Id.* at 111.

515. Personal knowledge is required for statements offered under most hearsay exceptions. *See* § **7.63**.

516. *See* § **7.27**.

517. *See* § **7.24** for a discussion of the different situations in which patient's statements in hospital records are admissible. For an example of a hospital record involving hearsay within hearsay, see Felice v. Long Island R.R., 426 F.2d 192, 197 (2d Cir.1970) (where patient's statement to nurse was admissible as a statement for the purpose of a medical diagnosis under 803(4), and nurse's entry of this statement was admissible as a business record under 803(6), entry was admissible as evidence of the cause of patient's injury).

aids, suggested that the hearsay-within-hearsay problem be visualized as follows:[518]

> A trial lawyer who has to deal with this problem every day in the hurly-burly circumstances of the courtroom might want to try the following device, which takes but an instance and is infallible. . . .

> You or your opponent is offering a business record that consists of words. First, be satisfied that the business is a business, within the meaning of the business records statute, and that the record was routinely made in the regular course of business. That makes it a business record, which takes care of the first level of hearsay.

> Next, in your mind's eye, see the record come to life. Imagine it not as a record, but as the person who wrote the record. It takes the witness stand and it talks. It says from the witness stand whatever is written on it. If a real witness would be permitted to say that from the witness stand, then the record is admissible. If a real person on the stand would not be permitted to say it, then the record is not admissible.

Another common example of hearsay within hearsay is the trial or deposition transcript. The first level of hearsay is the witness' statement made at the prior trial or deposition. The second level is the court reporter's statement about what the witness said. The first level may or may not be admissible under the exception for former testimony or for depositions.[519] The second level (the court reporter) would be admissible under the public records exception and, in many jurisdictions, under specially tailored statutes.[520]

Another example of hearsay within hearsay that is nonetheless admissible is the out-of-court statement that shows the declarant's state of mind, contained within an out-of-court statement by a co-conspirator. For example, suppose that the co-conspirator made an out-of-court statement to an undercover agent who was pretending to be part of the conspiracy. In the out-of-court statement, the co-conspirator said that a parking lot attendant told him she was going to close the gates at 10:00. The co-conspirator is now dead. The statement of the dead co-conspirator is offered in evidence through the testimony of the undercover agent. The purpose of the testimony is to prove that the gates were closed at 10:00. Using Professor Younger's method, once the foundation for the co-conspirator exception has been laid, we imagine the co-conspirator has come alive and appeared on the witness stand to testify against the other conspirators. As a live witness, could he testify that the parking lot attendant told him that she was going to close the gates at 10:00? Yes, because under Federal Rule of Evidence 803(3) the statement of intent

518. Irving Younger, Hearsay: A Practical Guide Through the Thicket 127–28 (1988).

519. *See* § **7.47.**

520. *See* § **7.27.** *See also* Ramrattan v. Burger King Corp., 656 F.Supp. 522, 527– 28 (D.Md.1987) (deposition properly excluded where, although deponent's statements in deposition would be admissible as admissions of party, statements included yet a third level of hearsay which did not meet any of the hearsay exceptions).

to do a future act is admissible as evidence that the future act was done. Each statement fits within an exception or exclusion to the hearsay rule and the evidence is admissible.

United States v. Diez provides another illustration.[521] The *Diez* court approved the admission of a statement of intent contained within a co-conspirator statement. The co-conspirator had given the agent an account of something that an IRS agent had told the co-conspirator. The court noted that the co-conspirator's statement was admissible under Rule 801(d)(2), and then noted:

> The fact that (coconspirator] DeGuzman's statement, like numerous others introduced at trial, relied on a statement by another person does not render the testimony inadmissible. [Internal Revenue Service] Agent Hunting's statement, reported to Agent Brock [the witness] by DeGuzman, was a statement of his intention to classify Palori as a dealer in real estate. The statement was received not to prove that Palori was or had been classified as a dealer, but rather to prove that Agent Hunting intended to regard him as one. The statement was thus a "statement of the declarant's then existing state of mind, emotion, sensation, or physical condition (such as intent, plan, motive, design, mental feeling, pain and bodily health)" and falls under the well-established exception to the hearsay rule for such statements. Fed. R. Evid. Rule 803(3).[522]

Statements within statements can also be admissible when an out-of-court statement that is hearsay fitting an exception contains another out-of-court statement that is not hearsay at all. For example, in *Kulick v. Pocono Downs Racing Assn.*,[523] the plaintiff was seeking to prove that state officials were behind his ejection from the racetrack. He offered into evidence a statement by a racetrack employee that a state official had said that he should be ejected. The court noted that the racetrack employee's statement was admissible as the admission of a party-opponent. The statement-within-a-statement of the state official was admissible because it was not offered for the truth of anything asserted, but only to prove that a state official had made a statement that had the effect of contributing to plaintiff's ejection from the racetrack.[524]

§ 7.60 Hearsay Within Hearsay [FRE 805]—Present Sense Impressions as Double Hearsay

Litigators and judges sometimes overlook the possibility of making a Federal Rule of Evidence 805 argument for the admission of a present sense impression contained within a present sense impression. Suppose that Declarant A tells Declarant B the license number of a hit-and-run driver. Declarant B then tells Witness X, a police officer, the license

---

521. 515 F.2d 892 (5th Cir.1975).

522. *Id.* at 895–96 n.2.

523. 816 F.2d 895 (3d Cir.1987).

524. *Id.* at 897 & n.3; *see also* United States v. Basey, 613 F.2d 198, 201 n. 1 (9th

Cir.1979) (no double hearsay problem involved where first level statements were admissions or adoptive statements, and second level fell under Rule 803(6)).

number that the first declarant told him. If both statements were made on personal knowledge and were made at or soon after the event, then the joint operation of Rules 805 and 803(1) (the present sense impression exception) would seem to justify admitting the evidence. What Declarant A said ("The license number was 371 CUB") was Declarant A's statement of her present sense impression of the license number, made immediately after the event. What Declarant B said ("Declarant A told me that the license number was 371 CUB") is declarant B's statement of a present sense impression, from his sense of hearing, made immediately after the relevant event of hearing the other statement.[525]

There are some instances in which the theory outlined would not work because a foundation cannot be laid showing that the hearsay-within-hearsay declarant had personal knowledge. A present sense impression statement must be based upon personal knowledge.[526] Immediacy is also a requirement of the present sense impression hearsay exception.[527] In the car license hypothetical, suppose that Declarant A told Declarant B the license number over a CB radio. Neither Declarant B nor the in-court witness has any way of knowing whether Declarant A was reporting on personal knowledge immediately after the event. So no foundation could be laid showing personal knowledge or immediacy. An example of this problem is shown in *United States v. Cain*,[528] a case in which a "CB'er" reported seeing an event, and the report of the "CB'er" was offered through a witness who heard the broadcast to prove the truth of the event observed by the "CB'er." The court held the evidence inadmissible, noting, "The distances and time lapses involved make it impossible to determine whether the declaration by the "CB'er" was made immediately following the observation or not, but the chances that it was are slim. The exception to the hearsay rule found in Rule 803(1) is, therefore, inapplicable."[529] Suppose, however, that Declarant A said "I just this second saw the car speeding away and its license plate was 371 CUB," and Declarant B reported the statement to the in-court witness in exactly those words. If a specific claim of seeing the other car had been made, then the trial judge has authority to accept it as evidence of the existence of personal knowledge. Under Rule 104(a), which provides that in determining preliminary questions about the admissibility of evidence, the trial judge is not bound by the rules of evidence except those of privilege, the trial judge could consider hearsay in determining whether the personal knowledge requirement was satisfied.[530]

---

525. The courts have recognized a similar possibility where other hearsay exceptions are involved. *See, e.g.,* United States v. Rucker, 586 F.2d 899, 905–06 (2d Cir. 1978) (where both levels of hearsay fell under the exception for admissions of co-conspirators, Rule 801(d)(2)(E), evidence was admissible); *see also* United States v. Christian, 786 F.2d 203, 211–12 (6th Cir. 1986) (same).

526. *See* § 7.11.

527. *See* § 7.11.

528. 587 F.2d 678 (5th Cir.), *cert. denied*, 440 U.S. 975, (1979), *revd on other grounds*, 615 F.Supp. 380 (5th Cir.1980).

529. *Id.; see also* Wolf by Wolf v. Procter & Gamble Co., 555 F.Supp. 613, 620–21 (D.N.J.1982) (hearsay inadmissible under 803(1) and 803(6) where statements not recorded immediately).

530. *See* Bourjaily v. United States, 483 U.S. 171, 176–82 (1987) (held that court could consider the hearsay statements themselves in making Rule 104(a) prelimi-

If the literal language of Rules 805 and 803(1) is followed, there would seem to be no obstacle to accepting the idea that the first level of hearsay, where the declarant reports what another person said immediately after the event, can be a present sense impression. If so, the second level would be admissible if it fit some exception or exclusion. Yet this argument seems to have been overlooked in some hotly contested cases. These cases arise from situations in which undercover agents were dealing with declarants through informer-intermediaries. One of the difficulties of drug investigations is that the targets do not want to meet new people, so it is difficult to get the targets to deal directly with undercover agents instead of dealing through persons whom they already know and perhaps trust. In any event, in each of the cases the informer had conversations over the telephone with the target while the agent was standing at the informer's shoulder. For one reason or another the informer did not testify at trial. The government's case would have benefited had the jury heard what the informer told the agent about what the defendant said over the phone, but the hearsay rule stood as an obstacle. In each case the trial prosecutor sought to solve the problem by putting into evidence the agent's contemporaneous instructions to the informer. The following excerpts from the transcripts illustrate the type of testimony elicited. In *United States v. Check*,[531] the government agent testified, inter alia:

> I instructed William Cali [the informer] that by no means did I intend to front any sum of money to Sandy Check [the defendant].... At that time I told William Cali I didn't particularly care whether or not Check was concerned about rats and not wanting to meet anyone new or about being busted by the man....

In *United States v. Figueroa*,[532] the agent's testimony included the following:

> Mike [the informer] had a conversation [over the telephone after having asked the hotel operator for a co-defendant's room] and Mike asked me, "Would it be all right if we did the two-kilogram deal one pound at a time?" And I told him to tell the people on the other end of the phone that that would be fine, we would deal one pound of cocaine at a time.... After Mike had a conversation with the other people on the phone, I told Mike that it would be all right if Leo [the defendant] sent his man down, Tommie, to count the money.

The trial judge in *Figueroa* made clear that the informer's phone call could be used to incriminate the defendant, stating that the informer had called "someone in the apartment who again gave his name as Leo, and they discussed the distribution of cocaine."[533]

---

nary fact determination); *see also* Fed. R. Evid. 104(a) advisory committee's note (" 'the judge should be empowered to hear any relevant evidence, such as affidavits or other reliable hearsay,' " quoting McCormick on Evidence § 53, at 135 (3d ed. Edward W. Cleary ed. 1984).

531. 582 F.2d 668, 671–73 (2d Cir. 1978).

532. 750 F.2d 232 (2d Cir.1984).

533. *Id.* at 241 (concurring opinion).

In both cases the trial courts admitted the evidence, and in both cases the appellate courts reversed on hearsay grounds. Neither the trial nor appellate courts alluded to the possible theory that the informer's statement reporting what the target said was admissible as a present sense impression. Had that been so, then admissibility would have been no problem, because each level of hearsay would fit an exception. (The target's statements would be admissible as admissions or statements of co-conspirators.) In the Check case, the trial judge seems to have admitted the evidence on the theory that all prior statements of witnesses are admissible. The trial judge apparently accepted the view that if the agent's out-of-court statements were really his own, not merely an artifice to get into evidence another's statements, then they were admissible without limit because the agent was subject to cross-examination.[534] In *Figueroa*, the trial judge admitted the utterances as "verbal acts" through which the agent gave directions to the informer.[535]

The present sense impression theory that we have outlined would seem to be a better way of getting in the evidence, and the witness could have testified directly about what the informer said the target said without attempting the subterfuge of testifying only about the witness' own statements. However, perhaps the courts would be reluctant to do so because the in-court witness had no way to verify what the informer claimed the target said.[536] Although the drafters of Rule 803(1) did not expressly require that a present sense impression be verified by another equally percipient observer (e.g., by having the person who heard the present sense impression also testify that he or she observed the event about which the declarant spoke),[537] the probative value of the statement would certainly be enhanced were the witness reporting the out-of-court declarant's statement in a position to determine whether the declarant was telling the truth.[538]

§ 7.61 Out-of-Court Statements That Are Admissible in Part or for a Limited Purpose

Sometimes an out-of-court statement will be admissible for one purpose but not for another.[539] For example, an out-of-court statement

---

534. *See* the description of the trial court's theory in 582 F.2d at 678–79. Even under the trial judge's own theory, it appears that some of the statements should have been excluded.

535. 750 F.2d at 238–40.

536. *See* Fed. R. Evid. 803(1) advisory committee's note (recognizing similarly that where the declarant is unidentified, cases "indicate hesitancy in upholding the statement alone as sufficient"); see generally 2 McCormick on Evidence § 271, at 214–15 (4th ed. John W. Strong ed. 1992) (discussing fact that 803(1) does not require corroboration).

537. *See* § 7.11.

538. *See generally* Jon R. Waltz, *The Present Sense Impression Exception to the Rule Against Hearsay: Origins and Attributes*, 66 Iowa L. Rev. 869, 898 (1981); *see also* Booth v. State, 508 A.2d 976 (Md.1986) (rejecting a requirement of corroboration, though stating it may be used to determine the weight of the evidence).

539. *See generally* David P. Leonard, The New Wigmore: A Treatise on Evidence: Selected Rules of Limited Admissibility § 1.6.1 (1996); 1 Weinstein's Federal Evidence § 105.04[1] (2d ed. Joseph M. McLaughlin ed. 1997); 1 McCormick on Evidence § 59 (4th ed. John W. Strong ed. 1992). An out-of-court statement may also be admissible against one person but not giving a warning might be admissible to show that the person warned had notice, but not that the condition warned about in fact existed or was dangerous.[540] Or an out-of-court statement offered for impeachment purposes might be admissible to impeach, but not as substantive evidence of the truth of the matter stated.[541] The proponent should be sure to state the admissible purpose for which such evidence is offered unless it is perfectly obvious.[542]

If an out-of-court statement is admissible for one purpose but not for another, under Federal Rule of Evidence 105 the objecting party is entitled to a limiting instruction telling the jury the proper purpose and the forbidden purpose.[543] The request for a limiting instruction must be

another, as in the case of co-defendants. *See generally* Leonard, *supra* this note § 1.6.4; 1 Weinstein's Federal Evidence, *supra* § 105.06 and cases cited therein. Note also that in determining the admissibility of a hearsay statement under Rule 104, the judge may consider any evidence, including the proffered hearsay statement. *See* Fed. R. Evid. 104; Bourjaily v. United States, 483 U.S. 171, 176–80 (1987).

540. *See* § 7.01; *see, e.g.,* Worsham v. A.H. Robins Co., 734 F.2d 676, 686–89 (11th Cir.1984) (hearsay reports of adverse reactions and references to other lawsuits admissible to show defendant had notice of a possible defect in the Dalkon Shield and of possible medical consequences, but not to prove that the reports were true); *see also* 2 McCormick on Evidence § 250 (4th ed. John W. Strong ed. 1992). *But see* United States v. Sallins, 993 F.2d 344, 346 (3d Cir.1993) (in criminal case against African–American defendant, government offered testimony concerning out-of-court statements contained within police radio call, stating there was a black male dressed in black with a gun at a particular location; district court admitted testimony for limited purpose of providing background as to why officers went to location and why they arrested defendant; appellate court reversed defendant's conviction, holding testimony inadmissible as hearsay; prosecution could have explained officers' actions with non-hearsay testimony; furthermore, any inference that radio call's contents were offered at trial for non-hearsay purpose was rebutted by fact that during closing arguments prosecutor used contents for truth asserted). *See also* United States v. Forrester, 60 F.3d 52 (2d Cir.1995). In *Forrester*, the government offered testimony about statements made to an agent identifying the defendant as a drug kingpin on the theory that the evidence explained why the agent had omitted information incriminating the defendant from a report. The inference argued for was that because the agent already

knew from other sources that the defendant was a drug kingpin, information to that effect was not noteworthy enough to go in the report. The court held that though the evidence was not hearsay when offered for that limited purpose, it nonetheless had to be excluded under Rule 403 because of danger that the jury would use out-of-court statements for the truth of matter asserted rather than for a limited nonhearsay purpose. It announced a four-part test for deciding whether to admit an out-of-court statement that is relevant to some other purpose other than its truth but that might be improperly used by the trier to prove the truth of its assertion. The four factors were whether the declaration addressed an important disputed issue in the trial, whether the declarant was knowledgeable and likely to be credited by the jury, whether the declarant is available for testimony, and whether curative or limiting instructions could effectively protect against prejudice. That four-part test is, obviously, a very substantial appellate court elaboration of Rule 403's list of factors to be considered.

541. *See* § 7.74; *see, e.g.,* Kenny v. Southeastern Pa. Transp. Auth., 581 F.2d 351, 356 (3d Cir.1978) (evidence of remedial measure of installing lights in train station after rape of patron inadmissible to prove culpable conduct, but admissible to impeach transit authority's claim that all reasonable care was being exercised at the time of the incident).

542. *See* 1 McCormick on Evidence, *supra* note 539, at n.2 ("It seems, however, that the proponent, to complain of the judge's exclusion of evidence inadmissible in one aspect, must have stated the purpose for which it is competent, unless the admissible purpose is plainly apparent") (citations omitted).

543. *See* Fed. R. Evid. 105; Leonard, *supra* note 539 § 1.11; 1 Weinstein's Federal Evidence, *supra* note 539 § 105.07 and timely and must specifically identify the portions of the testimony to be limited.[544] Failure to request the limiting instruction will result in waiver of the right to assert error in the instructions on appeal.[545] The court may also issue limiting instructions sua sponte when the judge finds them necessary.[546] The most common limiting instruction is the instruction that accompanies the prior inconsistent statement. One version of the instruction runs as follows:

> The testimony of a witness may be discredited or, as we sometimes say, impeached by showing that he or she previously made statements which are different than or inconsistent with his or her testimony here in court. The earlier inconsistent or contradictory statements are admissible only to discredit or impeach the credibility of the witness and not to establish the truth of these earlier statements made somewhere other than here during this trial. It is the province of the jury to determine the credibility, if any, to be given the testimony of a witness who has made prior inconsistent or contradictory statements.

> If a person is shown to have knowingly testified falsely concerning any important or material matter, you obviously have a right to distrust the testimony of such an individual concerning other matters. You may reject all of the testimony of that witness or give it such weight or credibility as you may think it deserves.[547]

cases cited therein; *see, e.g.,* United States v. Barron, 707 F.2d 125, 127–28 (5th Cir. 1983) (court gave limiting instructions to jury that evidence of prior dealings between witness and defendant admitted "for the sole purpose of showing plan, scheme, device on the part of the defendant, if any, toward those matters [at issue], and for that purpose only"). Note that some courts have narrowed this requirement at times by finding that a failure to issue the requested limiting instruction was harmless error. *See, e.g.,* Lubbock Feed Lots, Inc. v. Iowa Beef Processors, 630 F.2d 250, 265–66 (5th Cir.1980) (harmless error for court to have failed to give limiting instruction).

544. *See* Fed. R. Evid. 103(a)(1); United States v. Dozier, 672 F.2d 531, 543 (5th Cir.1982) ("If the defense, having lost the argument on general admissibility, desired a more precise limiting instruction on the extent to which the jury could consider such testimony it could and should have requested one"); United States v. Thirion, 813 F.2d 146, 155–56 (8th Cir.1987) (request denied where defendant did not specifically identify portion of testimony to be limited and where request was not specific or timely); see also 21 Charles A. Wright & Kenneth W. Graham, Jr., Federal Practice and Procedure (Evidence) § 5065, at 327 (1977).

545. Roth v. Black & Decker, United States, Inc., 737 F.2d 779, 782–83 (8th Cir. 1984) ("Black & Decker did not request a limiting instruction which may have been necessary under Rule 105 and 403 of the Federal Rules of Evidence ... not having requested such an instruction, Black & Decker cannot now claim that the district court erred").

546. *See* Leonard, *supra* note 539 § 1.11.1; 1 Weinstein's Federal Evidence, *supra* note 539 § 105.07[3] and cases cited therein.

547. 1 Edward J. Devitt *et al.,* Federal Jury Practice and Instructions § 15.06 (4th ed. 1992). Note that the second paragraph of the instruction concerns a witness who "knowingly testified falsely" about a matter. The theory of impeachment by prior inconsistent statement does not require a showing that the witness made either statement knowing it was false, or which of the two contradictory statements was inaccurate. The theory is simply that a person who makes inconsistent statements is not as credible as one who speaks consistently. A witness' knowing falsehoods can impeach the witness in another way: by character for untruthfulness. *See* § **7.06.**

If the danger that the jury will misuse the statement outweighs the probative value of the statement when used for its limited purpose, then the trial judge may exclude the entire statement under Rule 403.[548] A classic example of a case in which such exclusion would be proper is *Shepard v. United States*.[549] In that case, the defendant was accused of murdering his wife. The trial judge received testimony that shortly before her death, the wife had said, "Dr. Shepard has poisoned me."[550] On appeal, one of the theories of admission advanced by the prosecution was that the statement tended to negate any suicidal intent on the part of the wife. The Supreme Court recognized the theoretical validity of this ground, but held that the evidence should at any rate have been excluded because "the reverberating clang of those accusatory words would drown all weaker sounds."[551]

Sometimes an out-of-court statement can be redacted (edited) to remove inadmissible portions or avoid the danger that the jury will use the statement for an impermissible purpose. For example, the patient's account of who was at fault in an automobile accident can be removed from a hospital record, or references to the guilt of a codefendant might be removed from a confession.[552] The remaining portion of the statement would then be admissible.

§ 7.62 Attacking and Supporting the Credibility of a Hearsay Declarant [FRE 806]

Federal Rule of Evidence 806 provides that the credibility of a hearsay declarant can be attacked or supported as if the declarant were a

---

548. *See* Fed. R. Evid. 105 advisory committee's note ("A close relationship exists between this rule and Rule 403 which ... [provides for] exclusion when 'probative value is substantially outweighed by the danger of unfair prejudice, confusion of the issues, or misleading the jury'"). Some commentators have questioned the effectiveness of limiting instructions in any case since a jury may well ignore the limiting instruction and use the admitted statement for an improper purpose. *See, e.g.*, Note, *The Limiting Instruction—Its Effectiveness and Effect*, 51 Minn. L. Rev. 264 (1966) (the limiting instructions discussed are different, but the argument is still applicable). Other commentators have argued that all relevant evidence should be admitted and limiting instructions should be preferred over exclusion of evidence in all but the most extreme situations. *See* 1 Weinstein's Federal Evidence, *supra* note 539 § 105.03; 1 McCormick on Evidence, *supra* note 539 § 59, at 236; *see also* Petree v. Victor Fluid Power, Inc., 887 F.2d 34, 41–42 (3d Cir.1989) (not harmless error to exclude evidence of placement of safety decal on machine after accident where such evidence was offered to impeach expert testimony and limiting in-

structions could have been issued to assure jury considered evidence for only this purpose).

549. 290 U.S. 96 (1933).

550. *Id.* at 98.

551. *Id.* at 104; *cf.* United States v. Ingraham, 832 F.2d 229, 231–37 (1st Cir. 1987) (evidence of prior threatening letters and phone calls admissible for purpose of establishing identity of perpetrator, but inadmissible to show defendant's proclivities, where probative value outweighed danger of unfair prejudice).

552. *See, e.g.*, Richardson v. Marsh, 481 U.S. 200, 206–208 (1987) (confession of codefendant held admissible where all references to defendant redacted); Ramrattan v. Burger King Corp., 656 F.Supp. 522, 530 (D.Md.1987) (medical records admissible if plaintiff's statements regarding fault in an auto accident contained therein redacted). The court can, as in limiting instructions, order that information be redacted sua sponte. *See, e.g.*, Harris v. Upjohn Co., 115 F.R.D. 191, 192 (S.D.Ill.1987) (court could invoke Illinois physician-patient privilege and order patient names redacted from report offered into evidence at its discretion).

witness.[553] In addition, it dispenses with foundational requirements for impeachment with prior inconsistent statements.[554] Rule 806 also allows a party to call the declarant as a witness, when this is possible, and to question the declarant as if on cross-examination when that declarant's hearsay statements are used against the party.[555]

To illustrate the operation of Rule 806, suppose that Declarant X makes an out-of-court statement that "the light was red." The statement is received at trial as an excited utterance. Obviously, the opponent ought to be able to put in evidence that at some other time declarant X said "the light was green," and the rule so provides. Once Declarant X's credibility has been attacked the proponent may offer any evidence to rehabilitate the declarant that would be admissible if X were a witness.[556]

Now, consider the situation in which Declarant X testified at a deposition that the light was red. The opponent had evidence that the declarant had at some other time stated that the light was green and had an opportunity to confront the declarant with the alleged prior statement and ask the declarant to explain or deny the statement. However, the opponent failed to use this opportunity and did not ask the declarant anything about the prior statement during the deposition. Later the deposition is offered as evidence at trial because the declarant has become unavailable. Should the opponent be precluded from putting in the declarant's inconsistent statement, on grounds that the opponent failed to lay a foundation for it despite the opportunity to do so?[557] The drafters of Rule 806 answered this question in the negative. The rule specifically provides that "evidence of a statement or conduct by the declarant at any time, inconsistent with the declarant's hearsay statement, is not subject to any requirement that the declarant may have been afforded an opportunity to deny or explain."[558]

553. Fed. R. Evid. 806; *see generally* 5 Weinstein's Federal Evidence § 806.02 (2d ed. Joseph M. McLaughlin ed. 1997); 2 McCormick on Evidence § 327.2 (4th ed. John W. Strong ed. 1992). Note that Rule 806 also applies to nonhearsay statements under Rules 801(d)(2)(C), (D) and (E). *See also* Rules 608 and 609.

554. *See* Smith v. Fairman, 862 F.2d 630, 637–38 (7th Cir.1988):

> While the general rule is that a witness may be impeached by his prior inconsistent statements only after a proper foundation has been laid . . . that rule has been dispensed with "where the witness is unavailable and hearsay evidence is offered to impeach the previously admitted hearsay evidence of the statements of the absent witness."

555. Fed. R. Evid. 806; *see also* United States v. Inadi, 475 U.S. 387, 397 (1986) ("if the party against whom a co-conspirator statement has been admitted calls the declarant as a witness, 'the party is entitled

to examine him on the statement as if under cross-examination' ").

556. *See* 5 Weinstein's Federal Evidence, *supra* note 553 § 806.06; United States v. Lechoco, 542 F.2d 84, 88–89 (D.C.Cir.1976) (error to exclude evidence supporting credibility of out-of-court declarant where credibility has been impeached). Note that the inconsistent statement used to impeach the declarant can occur before or after the admitted hearsay statement. *See* Fed. R. Evid. 806 advisory committee's note.

557. For the in-court witness, Rule 612(b) provides that "[e]xtrinsic evidence of a prior inconsistent statement by a witness is not admissible unless the witness is afforded an opportunity to explain or deny the same and the opposite party is afforded an opportunity to interrogate the witness thereon, or the interests of justice otherwise require."

558. Fed. R. Evid. 806; *see also* Smith v. Fairman, 862 F.2d at 637–38. Wigmore

Rule 806 is not limited to impeachment by prior inconsistent statements. The hearsay declarant can be impeached by any method, including impeachment by prior convictions or by a showing of bias.[559]

§ 7.63 Requirement That the Hearsay Declarant Have Personal Knowledge

Suppose that a victim of poisoning tells all to the police just before dying. He says, "I know I am going to die. Dr. Blaeser poisoned me." The foundation for the hearsay exception for dying declarations has been satisfied because the declarant has manifested knowledge of the imminence of death. Yet absent additional facts the statement would not be admissible because the declarant did not have personal knowledge.[560] We do not know whether the declarant is merely speculating or whether, perhaps, the declarant is basing his accusation upon another's hearsay statement. An objection should be sustained.[561] The situation would be different, of course, had the declarant been shot in the chest. Then the trier could infer personal knowledge just from the circumstances. Probably the declarant had a view of the assailant, and the fact that the declarant has accused a particular person makes the likelihood even greater that the declarant had the view.[562]

The personal knowledge requirement applies to most out-of-court statements.[563] However, the requirement is not universal. For example, the admission of a party opponent need not have been made on personal

---

supported a contrary position. He argued that a foundation should be required whenever an opportunity could have been provided to the declarant to explain or deny the inconsistency. Thus, different hearsay statements would be treated differently. For example, in a dying declaration there would very likely not be such an opportunity, but in prior testimony there would. *See* 3 John H. Wigmore, Evidence in Trials at Common Law §§ 1030–1035 (James H. Chadbourn rev. 1970). The Federal Rule treats all hearsay statements in the same way and is based upon the theory that finders of fact will be more likely to reach a just decision if they have all the relevant information. *See* 5 Weinstein's Federal Evidence, *supra* note 553 § 806.04[1].

559. *See* United States v. Becerra, 992 F.2d 960, 965 (9th Cir.1993) (held, in criminal case, district court improperly prevented defendant from attacking out-of-court declarant's credibility with evidence of declarant's prior statements, criminal convictions, and compensation as paid police informant); United States v. Bovain, 708 F.2d 606, 613–14 (11th Cir.1983) (evidence of declarant's prior narcotics and theft convictions held admissible to impeach out-of-court declarant's credibility); United States v. Lawson, 608 F.2d 1129, 1130 (6th Cir.

1979) (court did not err in admitting evidence of out-of-court declarant's felony convictions offered for impeachment purposes).

560. *See* 2 McCormick on Evidence § 313 (4th ed. John W. Strong ed. 1992) (personal knowledge requirement applies to dying declarations); 5 Weinstein's Federal Evidence § 807.05[5][a] (2d ed. Joseph M. McLaughlin ed. 1997); Shepard v. United States, 290 U.S. 96, 101 (1933) ("To let the declaration in, the inference must be permissible that there was knowledge or the opportunity for knowledge as to the acts that are declared").

561. *See e.g.,* Shepard v. United States, 290 U.S. at 101 (statement held inadmissible as a dying declaration on other grounds would almost certainly have failed to meet the personal knowledge requirement as well; the court noted this requirement without deciding whether this statement would meet it).

562. *See, e.g.,* Reese v. Bara, 479 F.Supp. 651, 655–56 (S.D.N.Y.1979) (woman stabbed in the abdomen would have been "a competent witness as to how she came by her stab wounds.").

563. *Cf.* 2 McCormick on Evidence, *supra* note 560 § 255, at 144–45.

knowledge in order to be admissible.[564] If a party says "my wolf bit a little girl" and the statement is offered against the party, then the statement is admissible even if the party can show that she was not present at the time of the alleged biting.[565] In fact, the Advisory Committee specifically noted that the admission rule was free of the personal knowledge requirement.[566] The business records exception is also free of the personal knowledge requirement in the sense that the witness need not have personal knowledge of the transaction recorded, though the information must have been transmitted by a person with knowledge.[567] Some of the other hearsay exceptions also expressly or implicitly dispense with the requirement that the hearsay declarant have personal knowledge. One such exception is Federal Rule of Evidence 803(8)(C), the exception for findings pursuant to investigation, which by its very nature contemplates that sometimes the declarant will make a finding about events that the declarant did not personally observe.[568] For exam-

564. *See id.* at 145.

[A] sufficient basis for generally dispensing with the requirement of firsthand knowledge qualification rests on the argument that admissions that become relevant in litigation usually concern some matter of substantial importance to declarants upon which they would likely have informed themselves. As a result, such admissions possess greater reliability than the general run of hearsay, even when not based on firsthand observation. Moreover, the possibility is substantial that the declarant may have come into possession of significant information not known to the opponent.

But see 5 Weinstein's Federal Evidence, *supra* note 560 § 801.29[3], at 801–57 (arguing that the statement "must be evaluated in light of the requirements that its probative value outweigh any dangers of prejudice or confusion and that its underlying basis has sufficient assurances of accuracy").

565. Mahlandt v. Wild Canid Survival & Research Center, Inc., 588 F.2d 626, 630–31 (8th Cir.1978) (admission by agent that wolf bit child held admissible without requirement of personal knowledge); Union Mutual Life Ins. Co. v. Chrysler Corp., 793 F.2d 1, 8–9 (1st Cir.1986) (letter containing admissions which was written by employee held admissible despite lack of personal knowledge); Freda F. Bein, *Parties' Admissions, Agents' Admissions: Hearsay Wolves in Sheep's Clothing*, 12 Hofstra L. Rev. 393 (1984) (arguing against result in Mahlandt case where agent's admissions are involved).

566. Fed. R. Evid. 801(d)(2) advisory committee's note ("The freedom which ad-

missions have enjoyed from technical demands . . . of the opinion rule and the rule requiring firsthand knowledge . . . calls for generous treatment of this avenue to admissibility").

567. *See* United States v. Norton, 867 F.2d 1354, 136a (11th Cir.1989) (memorandum detailing telephone conversation prepared by one officer was admissible as business record through another officer who had no personal knowledge of its contents); United States v. Iredia, 866 F.2d 114, 119–20 (5th Cir.1989) (business record was admissible where witnesses who testified to the authenticity of the documents had no personal knowledge of "the record keeping practice and of the circumstances under which the objected to records were kept"); 5 Weinstein's Federal Evidence, *supra* note 560 § 803.11[1], at 803–61 to 803–64; 2 McCormick on Evidence, *supra* note 560 § 290. But note that the person initially gathering the information must have personal knowledge. *See* 5 Weinstein's Federal Evidence, *supra* note 560 § 803.11[4]; Meder v. Everest & Jennings, Inc., 637 F.2d 1182, 1186 (8th Cir.1981) (admission of police accident report was in error where officer could not recall where he had obtained the information); Johnson v. Lutz, 170 N.E. 517 (N.Y.1930).

568. *See* 2 McCormick on Evidence, *supra* note 560 § 296, at 291 ("As the name indicates, these reports embody the results of investigations and accordingly are often not the product of firsthand knowledge of the declarant . . ."). Note that investigative reports have been restricted to investigations made pursuant to authority granted by law and to factual findings. *See* 5 Weinstein's Federal Evidence, *supra* note 560 § 803.13[4][a] (arguing for liberally con-ple, in *Beech Aircraft v. Rainey*[569] the Supreme Court held admissible a naval investigator's conclusion about the cause of a fatal air crash. The investigator had not observed the crash nor did the investigator have personal knowledge of the basis for many of the facts and conclusions expressed in his report.[570] Another hearsay exception, the exception for statements of personal and family history in Rule 804(b)(4), expressly eschews any requirement of personal knowledge. It provides that statements concerning the declarant's own birth, adoption, marriage, family relationships, etc. are admissible "even though declarant had no means of acquiring personal knowledge of the matter stated."[571]

Where the hearsay exception requires that the declarant have spoken on personal knowledge, Federal Rule 602 applies. That rule provides that a lay witness "may not testify to a matter unless evidence is introduced sufficient to support a finding that the witness has personal knowledge of the matter." Under this standard, which tracks the standard contained in Rule 104(b) (the conditional relevancy rule), the trial court need not be convinced that the declarant had personal knowledge. The court need only find that there is evidence sufficient to support that conclusion (i.e., that it would not be unreasonable for the jury to conclude that the declarant had personal knowledge). Because this is not a very difficult standard to satisfy, the personal knowledge requirement will not often be a significant obstacle to the admission of hearsay under one of the exceptions.

§ 7.64 Hearsay Through the Mouth of an Expert

In the hands of a skillful trial lawyer, the expert can become a channel through which major fact evidence flows into the ears of jurors. Trial lawyers report that some trial judges allow experts to quote freely the statements of others in support of their opinions. For example, an expert on the causes and origins of fire might testify on the issue of arson. If the expert talked to eyewitnesses in the course of investigation, then the expert might be used as a conduit to put into evidence the narratives of those eyewitnesses without calling them to the stand.[572] Or the expert might be asked to describe the contents of reports of experiments done by others upon which the expert relied.[573] The supposed

---

struing the requirements of investigative reports and the exception for personal knowledge).

569. 488 U.S. 153 (1988).

570. *Id.* at 164–70; *see also* Wolf by Wolf v. Procter & Gamble Co., 555 F.Supp. 613, 625 (D.N.J.1982) (studies conducted by Centers for Disease Control and state health agencies admissible even if the authors did not have firsthand knowledge of the facts upon which findings were made).

571. Fed. R. Evid. 804(b)(4); *see generally* 5 Weinstein's Federal Evidence, *supra* note 560 § 807.07[2]; 2 McCormick on Evidence, *supra* note 560 § 322.

572. *See* Stevens v. Cessna Aircraft, 634 F.Supp. 137, 142–43 (E.D.Pa.), *aff'd*, 806 F.2d 252 (3d Cir.1986) (expert's testimony regarding statements made to him during course of investigation held admissible); State v. Jones, 368 S.E.2d 844 (N.C. 1988) (expert's testimony as to contents of statements relied upon to form opinion held admissible).

573. *See* Roger C. Park, *Confining the Expert: Rule 703(b) of the Rules of Evidence,* in The Bench and Bar of Minnesota 33–35 (March 1990).

justification for this practice is Federal Rule of Evidence 703, which provides:

> The facts or data in the particular case upon which an expert bases an opinion or inference may be those perceived by or made known to the expert at or before the hearing. If of a type reasonably relied upon by experts in the particular field in forming opinions or inferences upon the subject, the facts or data need not be admissible in evidence.[574]

The problem with relying upon this Rule as authority for the proposition that experts can freely give hearsay testimony is that the rule only provides that experts may, within reason, rely upon otherwise inadmissible evidence in forming opinions. The Rule does not state that experts may freely repeat hearsay that they have heard while forming opinions.[575]

Testifying experts are permitted on direct examination to show that they did a careful job of preparing their opinions. To show diligence, it is often reasonable to allow experts to testify to the fact that a conversation took place, without revealing the content of the conversation. An expert might be allowed, for example, to state that the expert had conferred with another expert while forming an opinion, without expressly stating the opinion of the other expert.[576] However, when the expert begins to describe the content of conversations with other persons, the testimony is frequently objectionable.[577]

§ 7.65 Hearsay and the Right to Confrontation

Even if hearsay testimony meets the requirements of a hearsay exception, the criminal defendant still has a last resort. Reception of the testimony would violate the confrontation clause.

---

574. Fed. R. Evid. 703.

575. *See* § **10.08**; *see generally* Ronald L. Carlson, *Collision Course in Expert Testimony: Limitations an Affirmative Introduction of Underlying Data,* 36 Univ. Fla. L. Rev. 234 (1984); *cf.* Stephen A. Saltzburg & Kenneth R. Redden, Federal Rules of Evidence Manual 671 (4th ed. 1986); Henry v. Brenner, 486 N.E.2d 934, 936–37 (Ill.App. 1985) (allowing expert to testify as to content of statements relied upon where jury given limiting instruction as to proper use of these statements). *But see* Paul R. Rice, *Inadmissible Evidence as a Basis For Expert Opinion Testimony: A Response to Professor Carlson,* 40 Vand. L. Rev. 583 (1987) (arguing that admitting the expert's opinion without its basis is illogical because one cannot accept the truth of an opinion without implicitly accepting the facts upon which the opinion is based, and that depriving the jury of the basis of the opinion leads

to undesirable blind deference to the witness; also arguing for adoption of a carefully tailored hearsay exception covering the basis of the expert's opinion).

576. *See* United States v. Rollins, 862 F.2d 1282, 1292–93 (7th Cir.1988), *cert. denied,* 490 U.S. 1074 (1989) (experts testimony that he had conversations with others concerning the meaning of certain codewords used in illegal drug deals admissible where content of these conversations not revealed); Ronald L. Carlson, *Policing the Bases of Modern Expert Testimony,* 39 Vand. L. Rev. 577, 584 & n.23 (1986).

577. See § **10.08** for a discussion of authorities on this point. If the statements of other experts are relevant to some proposition other than the truth of the matters asserted, such statements might be admissible for that purpose.

The confrontation clause of the sixth amendment provides: "In all criminal prosecutions, the accused shall enjoy the right ... to be confronted with the witnesses against him. ..." The language of the amendment does not provide clear guidance about hearsay issues. It is susceptible to a variety of textually plausible interpretations. Under one possible interpretation, all hearsay declarants whose statements are offered by the prosecution would be considered "witnesses against" the defendant, and therefore the Constitution would require that the defendant be confronted with them at trial. This interpretation would lead to the exclusion of all hearsay, even hearsay that fell under an exception established at the time of the adoption of the amendment. Alternatively, one could interpret the amendment to require merely that the defendant be confronted with whatever witnesses the prosecution chose to produce at trial. Under this interpretation, trial witnesses could testify about hearsay declarations, and the confrontation clause would impose no limits upon the creation of new hearsay exceptions. It would merely require the presence of the defendant when evidence was presented to the trier of fact.[578] The amendment could also be construed so that "witnesses against" the defendant referred only to persons who were available to testify. Under this interpretation, the prosecution would be required to produce declarants for cross-examination when possible, but the statements of unavailable declarants could be freely admitted.[579] Over the years, the confrontation clause has been the subject of voluminous scholarly discussion, much of it aimed at analyzing the Supreme Court's jurisprudence on the subject.[580]

§ 7.66 Hearsay and the Right to Confrontation—The *Roberts* Test

The Supreme Court has never adopted either of the extreme interpretations of the confrontation clause. In an early case interpreting the

578. *See* Dutton v. Evans, 400 U.S. 74, 94 (1970) (Harlan, J, concurring); 5 John H. Wigmore, Evidence in Trials at Common Law § 1397, at 131, 134 (3d ed. 1940) (confrontation clause should be construed so that it merely requires cross-examination of witnesses who are required to testify in court by the hearsay rules in effect at the time of trial; nothing in the clause should be construed to inhibit revision and extension of hearsay exceptions).

579. *See* California v. Green, 399 U.S. 149, 174 (1970) (Harlan, J, concurring); Peter Westen, *The Future of Confrontation*, 77 Mich. L. Rev. 1185, 1188–89 (1979), Irving Younger, *Confrontation and Hearsay: A Look Backward, a Peek Forward*, 1 Hofstra L. Rev. 32 (1973).

580. For a small sampling of recent confrontation clause analysis, see Andrew L. T. Choo, Hearsay and Confrontation in Criminal Trials (1996); Robert Bartels, *The Hearsay Rule, The Confrontation Clause, and Reversible Error in Criminal Cases*, 26 Ariz. St. L.J. 967 (1994); Hon. Anthony M. Brannon, *Confrontation and Hearsay: New Wine in an Old Bottle*, 16 Campbell L. Rev. 1 (1994); JoAnne Epps, *Passing the Confrontation Clause Stop Sign: Is All Hearsay Constitutionally Admissible?*, 77 Ky. L.J. 7 (1988); Stanley A. Goldman, *Not So "Firmly Rooted" Exceptions to the Confrontation Clause*, 66 N.C. L. Rev. 1 (1987); Randolph N. Jonakait, *The Origins of the Confrontation Clause: An Alternative History*, 27 Rutgers L.J. 77 (1995); Randolph N. Jonakait, *Restoring the Confrontation Clause to the Sixth Amendment*, 35 UCLA L. Rev. 557 (1988); Charles R. Nesson & Yochai Benkler, *Constitutional Hearsay: Requiring Foundational Testing and Corroboration Under the Confrontation Clause*, , 81 Va. L. Rev. 149 (1995); Eileen A. Scallen, *Constitutional Dimensions of Hearsay Reform: Toward a Three–Dimensional Confrontation Clause*, 76 Minn. L. Rev. 623 (1992).

clause, it rejected the absolute exclusion view by recognizing that dying declarations were admissible, despite the fact that the defendant had never confronted the declarant.[581] Four years later, however, it held that the confrontation clause could prevent legislative creation of a new hearsay exception. The court struck down a federal statute that permitted a third party's theft conviction to be used in a receiving stolen goods prosecution to prove that the goods were in fact stolen.[582] Subsequent cases steered between the two extremes of absolute exclusion of hearsay and absolute deference to hearsay exceptions. It is difficult to generalize about these cases, because they dealt with particular situations without establishing a general principle.[583] In the 1980 case of *Ohio v. Roberts*,[584] however, the Court found majority support for an opinion that outlined a general approach to resolving confrontation issues. The *Roberts* Court established a two-pronged test for determining whether the introduction of hearsay violated the confrontation clause.

The first prong of the *Roberts* test requires that the prosecution produce the hearsay declarant or demonstrate that the declarant is unavailable.[585] This prong has exceptions, however: it only applies in the "usual" case;[586] the prosecution need not demonstrate unavailability in

581. Mattox v. United States, 156 U.S. 237, 243–44 (1895) (dictum). *See also* Kirby v. United States, 174 U.S. 47, 61 (1899) (dictum) ("the admission of dying declarations is an exception which arises from the necessity of the case. This exception was well established before the adoption of the Constitution, and was not intended to be abrogated").

582. Kirby v. United States, 174 U.S. 47 (1899). The actual statute made the conviction conclusive evidence that the goods were stolen, but the Court did not rest its decision on this ground. Instead, it made clear that merely admitting the third party's conviction into evidence was a violation of the confrontation clause. *Id.* at 55–56, 61.

583. *See* Pointer v. Texas, 380 U.S. 400 (1965) (introduction of testimony from preliminary hearing at which defendant was not represented, and at which he did not cross-examine, violates sixth amendment as applied to states); Douglas v. Alabama, 380 U.S. 415 (1965) (allowing prosecutor to, in effect, use accomplice's statement as evidence against defendant is unconstitutional in circumstances of case); Barber v. Page, 390 U.S. 719 (1968) (introducing declarant's former testimony against defendant, without sufficient attempt to produce declarant for trial, violates confrontation clause); Bruton v. United States, 391 U.S. 123 (1968) (admitting co-defendant's confession implicating both defendants violates confrontation clause, despite limiting instruction); California v. Green, 399 U.S. 149 (1970) (re-

ceiving witness' prior inconsistent statement as substantive evidence permissible under circumstances of case); Dutton v. Evans, 400 U.S. 74 (1970) (receiving co-conspirator's prior statement to cellmate permissible under circumstances of case).

In a concurring opinion in California v. Green, 399 U.S. at 172–74 Justice Harlan advocated a general theory-that the confrontation clause required the production of available witnesses, but had no application when the witness was unavailable-but the majority did not adopt it and he soon afterward abandoned it himself. *See* Dutton v. Evans, 400 U.S. 74, 95–100 (1970) (Harlan, J, concurring). Justice Harlan changed his views because he had come to believe that requiring the production of available declarants in every case would be unduly inconvenient and of little utility. *Id.* His later view was that the confrontation clause should be construed only to guarantee the right to be present at trial and cross-examine the witnesses there presented. In flagrant cases, however, the misuse of hearsay might constitute a violation of due process. *Id.* at 98.

584. 448 U.S. 56 (1980).

585. *Id.* at 65.

586. "In the usual case (including cases where prior cross-examination has occurred), the prosecution must either produce, or demonstrate the unavailability of, the declarant whose statement it wishes to use against the defendant." *Id.*

cases in which the utility of confrontation is "remote."[587]

The second prong of the *Roberts* test requires that the hearsay have "adequate 'indicia of reliability.' "[588] In some cases, this prong requires "a showing of particularized guarantees of trustworthiness." However, the court appeared to recognize that the need for certainty in criminal trials required more specific guidance.[589] It indicated that deference should be given to established hearsay exceptions, saying that reliability could be inferred "without more" when evidence fell under a "firmly rooted" hearsay exception.[590]

In its decisions since *Roberts*, the Supreme Court cast doubt on the universal application of its two-pronged test.[591] Nevertheless, the Court has not explicitly abandoned the test, and has in fact taken it seriously in at least one decision, *Idaho v. Wright.*[592] *Wright* was an important case in which the Court addressed the nature of the indicia of trustworthiness required when evidence was admitted under a hearsay exception that was not firmly rooted. Defendant Laura Lee Wright was accused of helping Robert L. Giles in the sexual abuse of her two daughters. The evidentiary issue turned on the admissibility of statements by the younger daughter, who was two-and-one-half years old at the time of the crimes charged. The younger daughter had been questioned by a pediatrician after one of the children told an adult about abuse, and medical examinations revealed physical evidence of abuse. In response to questioning, she told the pediatrician that Giles had had sexual contact with her, and she volunteered that Giles had had sexual contact with the older sister. The trial judge found, and the parties agreed, that the younger daughter was "not capable of communicating to the jury," and hence the younger daughter did not testify. The trial judge admitted the pediatrician's testimony about the child's statements under Idaho Rule of Evidence 803(24), which is identical in relevant respects to Federal rule 803(24).

The issue before the Supreme Court was whether admission of the statements to the pediatrician violated defendant's rights under the confrontation clause. The majority opinion by Justice O'Connor assumed, for purposes of the case, that the child was unavailable for testimony. It held that the child's out-of-court statements were inadmissible under the confrontation clause. No adequate indicia of reliability

---

587. *Id.* at 65, n.7.

588. *Id.* at 65.

589. *See, e.g., id.* at 66 (referring to the "need for certainty in the workaday world of criminal trials" as one reason why, in past cases, the Court had concluded that "certain hearsay exceptions rest upon such solid foundations that admission of virtually any evidence within them comports with the 'substance of the constitutional protection' ").

590. *Id.* at 66. The Court indicated in a footnote that dying declarations fell under a "firmly rooted" hearsay exception, and implied that hearsay falling under the business records and public records exceptions would also pass confrontation clause scrutiny, at least where those exceptions were "properly administered." *Id.* at 66, n.8.

591. *See, e.g.,* White v. Illinois, 502 U.S. 346 (1992); Bourjaily v. United States, 483 U.S. 171 (1987); United States v. Inadi, 475 U.S. 387 (1986), all discussed *infra.*

592. 497 U.S. 805 (1990).

had been shown in the case. The pediatrician had conducted the interview in a suggestive manner. Reliability could not be inferred from corroborating evidence, such as the physical evidence of abuse. In what is perhaps the most significant part of its opinion, the Court's majority ruled that the relevant circumstances that can show particularized guarantees of trustworthiness are only those that surround the making of the statement; evidence corroborating the accuracy of the statement may not be considered.[593]

Wright's prohibition on showing trustworthiness with extrinsic corroboration may not apply to situations in which a declarant testifies at trial, and the proponent offers the declarant's prior inconsistent statements for the truth of what they assert under the residual exception. In *United States v. Valdez–Soto*,[594] the court held that an accomplice's confession implicating the defendant was admissible under the residual exception. Because the declarant testified at trial subject to cross-examination, the court reasoned, there was no problem with the right to

---

593. For an example of a case in which the *Idaho v. Wright* standard was deemed to have been met, see McCafferty v. Leapley, 944 F.2d 445 (8th Cir.1991), *cert. denied*, 503 U.S. 911 (1992) (habeas from state prosecution; held, reception of child declarant's statements accusing defendant of sex abuse not a violation of confrontation clause under the circumstances, which included the following: the statements were explicit and consistent; the initial statement was given spontaneously in response to a nonleading question about how the child got a "hickey" mark on her neck; the child's knowledge of sexual matters was tape recorded; and the child had no motive to testify falsely against the defendant, for whom she still felt affection). *See also* United States v. Ross, 33 F.3d 1507 (11th Cir. 1994), *cert. denied*, 515 U.S. 1132, (1995) (statute providing for admission of certified foreign business records does not violate confrontation clause; while the statutory exception was not "firmly rooted" because the statute did not require the custodian of the records to appear in court as a sponsoring witness, the statute nevertheless required sufficient guarantees of trustworthiness). For an example of a case which failed to meet the *Idaho v. Wright* standard, see Ring v. Erickson, 983 F.2d 818, 819–20 (8th Cir.1992) (admission of videotaped interview between child victim of alleged sexual abuse and social worker violated defendant's rights under the confrontation clause; Minnesota statute which created a special hearsay exception for child victims of sexual abuse was not a firmly rooted hearsay exception, and victim's statements lacked the requisite "particularized guarantees of trustworthiness").

Not surprisingly, some courts have interpreted the "intrinsic trustworthiness" requirement of *Idaho v. Wright* quite liberally. *See* United States v. Ellis, 951 F.2d 580, 582–84 (4th Cir.), *cert. denied*, 505 U.S. 1220 (1992) (no violation of confrontation clause to admit statement of deceased accomplice because of the following guarantees of trustworthiness: (1) the statements were made before his own attorneys as well as government investigators; (2) the statements were made pursuant to a plea agreement that required the accomplice to be truthful; (3) the government agents were taking notes in front of the accomplice while the statements were being made; (4) the accomplice-declarant knew that his statements would be the subject of further investigation; and (5) the accomplice-declarant agreed to secretly record further conversations with the persons he had implicated, thus suggesting that he was willing to have the truthfulness of the statements tested). *See also* United States v. Canan, 48 F.3d 954 (6th Cir.), *cert. denied*, 516 U.S. 1050, (1996) (held, over strong dissent by Judge Martin, that admission of accusatory videotaped statement taken by prosecution from accomplice 15 days before accomplice died of cancer did not violate confrontation clause, even though defendant was not given an opportunity to have attorney present or to cross-examine; fact that the declarant knew he was at death's door noted as factor supporting trustworthiness of his statements).

594. 31 F.3d 1467 (9th Cir.1994) (Kosinski, J.), *cert. denied*, 514 U.S. 1113 (1995).

confrontation. Absent a confrontation problem, other evidence corroborating the trustworthiness of the statement could be admitted to show that it satisfied the statutory trustworthiness requirement of the residual exception. An interesting dissent by Judge Zilly argued that the evidence should be excluded, citing *Wright* and also arguing that Rule 801(d)(1)(A) exemplified Congress's intent not to admit informal prior inconsistent statements for the truth of what they asserted.

In *White v. Illinois*,[595] the Supreme Court seemed to swing toward limiting *Ohio v. Roberts* to former testimony situations. It stated flatly that *Roberts* "stands for the proposition that unavailability analysis is a necessary part of the Confrontation Clause inquiry *only when* the challenged out-of-court statements were made in the course of a prior judicial proceeding."[596]

In *White*, the defendant was convicted of sexually assaulting a four-year-old girl. Although the victim was available to testify, the Court upheld admission of her prior statements under the state law hearsay exceptions for spontaneous declarations and statements made in the course of receiving medical care. The Court took pains to explain how the statements involved in *White* were made in contexts that provided guarantees of trustworthiness that could not be recaptured in the courtroom. Hence, imposing an unavailability requirement that forced in-court testimony would not, in the Court's view, have substantially contributed to accuracy. The *White* case thus may not apply to situations in which there is a strong need to hear the witness in court, even If those situations are not *Roberts*-like former testimony situations.[597]

In a concurring opinion, Justice Thomas, joined by Justice Scalia, argued for a fundamental change in interpretation of the confrontation clause. They argued that the Supreme Court's precedent had been wrong all along in assuming that all hearsay declarants are "witnesses against" a defendant within the meaning of the clause. They suggested a possible reformulation that they considered to be more faithful to the language and history of the clause than the Court's usual approach. Under their formulation, "[t]he federal constitutional right of confrontation extends to any witness who actually testifies at trial, but the Confrontation Clause is implicated by extrajudicial statements only insofar as they are contained in formalized testimonial materials, such as affidavits, depositions, prior testimony, or confessions."[598]

The basic *Roberts* analysis still carries some weight, though shifting majorities and the Court's checkered record on confrontation issues may be reason to doubt the longevity of any theory about the scope of the

595. 502 U.S. 346 (1992).

596. *Id.* at 354 (emphasis added).

597. For commentary on confrontation problems in child sexual abuse prosecutions, see Michael H. Graham, *The Confrontation Clause, the Hearsay Rule, and Child Sexual Abuse Prosecutions: The State of the Relationship*, 72 Minn. L. Rev. 523 (1988);

Robert P. Mosteller, *Remaking Confrontation Clause and Hearsay Doctrine Under the Challenge of Child Sexual Abuse Prosecutions*, 1993 U. Ill. L. Rev. 691.

598. *Id.* at 365 (Thomas, J., dissenting).

clause. Still, it is worthwhile for the advocate, when arguing about confrontation, to argue that *Roberts* is not satisfied because the declarant could be called to testify or because the evidence has not been shown to be reliable.

§ 7.67 Hearsay and the Right to Confrontation—Statements by Co-conspirators

The Court has made clear that one hearsay exception to which it will give deference is the exception for admissions of co-conspirators. In *United States v. Inadi*, it held that, despite language in *Ohio v. Roberts*[599] about the necessity of producing an available declarant in the "usual" case, statements of co-conspirators may be used even when the declarant is available but not produced.[600] The Court reasoned that the purpose of a requirement that available declarants be produced is to get live testimony when possible because live testimony is usually the best evidence. However, in the case of co-conspirator statements, the out-of-court statement was better evidence than the declarant's in-court testimony would be. The statements, according to the Court, provide evidence "of the conspiracy's context" that "cannot be replicated," because "conspirators are likely to speak differently when talking to each other in furtherance of their illegal aims than when testifying on the witness stand."[601] It also suggested that the available witness could be called by the defense, so that "[p]resumably those declarants that neither side believes will be particularly helpful will not have been subpoenaed as witnesses."[602] While there are good answers to both of these arguments— and the dissenting Justices made them convincingly—the current majority of the Supreme Court shows no sign of accepting them.

This reasoning about the unavailability rule is potentially applicable to other hearsay exceptions as well. Many out-of-court statements could be characterized as "better" than in-court testimony because they were made closer to the event and before the witness was influenced by preparation for litigation. So the Supreme Court's stated bases for receiving co-conspirator statements also provide a basis for arguing that other statements by available declarants should be received despite the confrontation clause.

The second prong in *Roberts*, the reliability prong, has also been diluted in cases involving statements by co-conspirators. In the 1987 case of *Bourjaily v. United States*,[603] the majority gave short shrift to the defendant's argument that the prosecution had to make a particularized showing of reliability before a co-conspirator's statement could be received. The Court indicated that so long as the requirements of Federal Rule of Evidence 801(d)(2)(E) were satisfied, nothing further need be shown to surmount a confrontation clause challenge. It pointed out that

---

599. 448 U.S. 56 (1980).

600. United States v. Inadi, 475 U.S. 387 (1986).

601. *Id.* at 395.

602. *Id.* at 397.

603. 483 U.S. 171 (1987).

Roberts had stated that no independent inquiry into reliability would be required so long as the out-of-court statement fell within a "firmly rooted" hearsay exception. Noting that the exception had repeatedly been recognized in its own case law since 1827, the Court described the exception as "firmly rooted." Hence, statements received under the federal exception need not be scrutinized for reliability so long as they meet the statutory requirements of the exception. The Court left open the possibility that such scrutiny might be appropriate when reviewing cases decided under state co-conspirator exceptions that are more permissive than the federal one—for example, under a state co-conspirator exception that applied to receive statements made after the conspirators have been arrested.[604]

By repeating the "firmly rooted" language of *Roberts*, the *Bourjaily* Court also left open the door to confrontation clause attacks on new exceptions that are just beginning to put down roots. The child abuse hearsay exceptions that have been produced by many state legislatures are an example of exceptions that are novel and not "firmly rooted."[605]

Although we have discussed confrontation clause doctrine in terms of the *Roberts* two-pronged test, that test does not, of course, provide answers for every case. In fact, it may make more sense to regard the Supreme Court's confrontation clause jurisprudence more as a set of responses to particular situations than as a product of some over-arching theory.[606]

§ 7.68 Hearsay and the Right to Confrontation—The *Bruton* Case

One well-established subcategory of confrontation doctrine is the rule about co-defendant confessions created by *Bruton v. United States*.[607] *Bruton* was a case in which two co-defendants were tried together. The confession of one, implicating both, was received by the trial judge with instructions not to use it against the nonconfessing co-defendant. The Supreme Court held that this procedure violated the confrontation clause. The limiting instruction was not sufficient to eliminate danger that the jury would use the instruction against both defendants. The danger that the defendant would be convicted by the statement of one he could not cross-examine could have been avoided by severing the trials.

For a time, it appeared that the Supreme Court might be contemplating an exception to the *Bruton* rule for cases in which a co-defen-

---

604. This indicated by the Court's description of Dutton v. Evans, 400 U.S. 74 (1970), as a case where a reliability inquiry was required because the "evidentiary rule deviates from [the] common-law approach [by] admitting coconspirators' hearsay statements made after termination of [the] conspiracy." Bourjaily v. United States, 483 U.S. at 183.

605. *See supra* § 7.66.

606. For a useful and perceptive review, see Roger W. Kirst, *The Procedural Dimension of Confrontation Doctrine*, 66 Neb. L. Rev. 485 (1987).

607. 391 U.S. 123 (1968). Despite *Bruton*, confessions of co-defendants are sometimes admitted as declarations against interest when the statement implicating the defendant was against the declarant's interest. *See* § 7.57.

dant's confession "interlocked" with that of the defendant. However, a majority now appears to have settled upon the position that a co-defendant's interlocking confession is not admissible against the defendant, though the fact that the defendant has also confessed may make the error harmless because of the overpowering impact of the defendant's own confession.[608] On the other hand, a redacted confession of a co-defendant that does not mention the defendant by name and that has only an indirect, inferential incriminating effect may be received in a joint trial without violating the confrontation clause.[609]

§ 7.69   Courtroom Expressions and Their Relationship to Hearsay Doctrine: Catch phrases and Rules of Thumb

When arguing hearsay objections, advocates sometimes use catch phrases and rules of thumb that are hard to track down in works on the rules of evidence.

§ 7.70   Courtroom Expressions and Their Relationship to Hearsay Doctrine: Catch phrases and Rules of Thumb—"It's admissible because it was said in the presence of the defendant"

Advocates often say "it was said in the presence of the defendant" in response to a hearsay objection. Are all statements made in the presence of the defendant admissible? No, they are not. Are most of them admissible? Yes, they are. The response is a good one when the situation is right. Whether a statement was made in the presence of the defendant matters in two situations. First, the statement may be offered to show the effect on the hearer.[610] For example, the statement may be offered to show that the defendant had notice or that the defendant had been warned. Such statements are not hearsay because they are not offered to prove the truth of the matter asserted. They are merely offered to show the impact of the statement on the state of mind of the hearer. Of course, when offered for this purpose it is necessary that the hearer have been present and have heard the statement. Second, the statement may be offered as an adoptive admission. For example, suppose that after an accident a bystander said to the defendant "it was all

---

608. *See* Cruz v. New York, 481 U.S. 186 (1987) (held, reception of confession of codefendant which interlocks with defendant's own confession violates *Bruton*, at least when co-defendant's confession likely to have devastating effect at trial.) *Cf.* Lee v. Illinois, 476 U.S. 530 (1986) (held, confrontation clause bars reception of accomplice's partially interlocking confession implicating both accomplice and defendant).

609. Richardson v. Marsh, 481 U.S. 200 (1987). *See* United States v. Washington, 952 F.2d 1402, 1406–07 (D.C.Cir.1991),

cert. denied, 503 U.S. 1009 (1992) (held, "where—as here—all references to the defendant in a codefendant's statement are replaced with indefinite pronouns or other general terms, the Confrontation Clause is not violated by the redacted statements's admission if, when viewed together with other evidence, the statement does not create an inevitable association with the defendant, and a proper limiting instruction is given").

610. *See* § **7.01**.

your fault." If the defendant said nothing in return, and if the circumstances were such that a person who was not responsible would be expected to deny the accusation, the statement would be admissible as an adoptive admission—the defendant's silence constitutes an adoption of the bystander's accusation.[611]

But the mere fact that a defendant is present does not automatically make the statement admissible. Sometimes the grounds for escaping the hearsay ban that have just been described—effect on hearer and adoptive admission—are not applicable. For example, suppose that the bystander told the defendant, "it's all your fault," and the defendant responded "no, it's not!" The effect on hearer theory does not make the statement admissible because the hearer's state of mind at that time is irrelevant to any of the issues in the personal injury action. The adoptive admission theory does not work because the defendant denied the accusation. In the situation described, the statement is inadmissible despite having been made in the presence of the defendant. If the state of mind is irrelevant and either the defendant denies the statement or the circumstances are such that one would not expect a denial even if the statement was false, then the statement is inadmissible.

§ 7.71 Courtroom Expressions and Their Relationship to Hearsay Doctrine: Catch phrases and Rules of Thumb—"It's part of the res gestae"

"The discredited shibboleth res gestae is no longer uttered in polite legal society, and we hope to lay its ghost to rest," said the Maryland Court of Appeals in 1988.[612] Probably no legal term has been the victim of such an intense eradication campaign. Wigmore long advocated that the phrase be put to death:

> The phrase "res gestae" has long been not only entirely useless, but even positively harmful. It is useless, because every rule of Evidence to which it has ever been applied exists as a part of some other well established principle and can be explained in the terms of that principle. It is harmful, because by its ambiguity it invites the confusion of one rule with another and thus creates uncertainty as to the limitations of both. It ought therefore wholly to be repudiated, as a vicious element in our legal phraseology. No rule of Evidence can be created or applied by the mere muttering of a shibboleth. There are words enough to describe the rules of Evidence. Even if there were no accepted name for one or another doctrine, any name would be preferable to an empty phrase so encouraging to looseness of thinking and uncertainty of decision.[613]

---

611. *See* § **7.07**.

612. Cassidy v. State, 536 A.2d 666 (Md. App. 1988).

613. 6 John H. Wigmore, Evidence in Trials at Common Law § 1767, at 182 (3d ed. 1940).

Morgan, Holmes, and Learned Hand also had unkind things to say about res gestae.[614]

Suppose an advocate makes a hearsay objection. The proponent of the evidence responds that the evidence is part of the res gestae. What answer can the objecting attorney make to this assertion? "There's no such thing as a res gestae exception" or "res gestae doesn't apply under the Federal Rules" are possibilities. If those do not work, then the advocate should attempt to identify the modern equivalent of the argument being made and respond accordingly. For example, "this is not part of the res gestae because too much time had passed between the event and the statement" is appropriate if the phrase is being used as a stand-in for the present sense impression, or "he wasn't still under the stress of excitement" when the phrase seems to have been used to refer to the excited utterance exception.

§ 7.72   Courtroom Expressions and Their Relationship to Hearsay Doctrine: Catch phrases and Rules of Thumb—"It's admissible because it shows state of mind"

The assertion that an out-of-court statement is admissible because it shows state of mind can mean either that the statement is offered to show the declarant's own state of mind, or that it is offered to show something about the state of mind of the hearer or reader of the statement.

A statement offered to show the state of mind of the hearer or reader of the statement is generally admissible on grounds that the statement is not being offered to prove the truth of the matter asserted, and hence is not hearsay.[615] An objection should still be sustained when the state of mind of the hearer or reader is not relevant to the case, or when the probative value of the statement in showing state of mind is outweighed by the danger that the jury will use the statement to prove the truth of what it asserts. For example, if the good faith of a police

---

614. Morgan wrote:

The marvelous capacity of a Latin phrase to serve as a substitute for reasoning, and the confusion of thought inevitably accompanying the use of inaccurate terminology, are nowhere better illustrated than in the decisions dealing with the admissibility of evidence as 'res gestae.' It is probable that this troublesome expression owes its existence and persistence in our law of evidence to an inclination of judges and lawyers to avoid the toilsome exertion of exact analysis and precise thinking. Certain it is that since its introduction at the close of the eighteenth century, on account of its exasperating indefiniteness it has done nothing but bewilder and perplex.

Edmund M. Morgan, *A Suggested Classification of Utterances Admissible as Res Gestae*, 31 Yale L.J. 229 (1922). Holmes wrote that "[t]he man that uses that phrase (res gestae) shows that he has lost temporarily all power of analyzing ideas." Quoted in Cassidy v. State, 536 A.2d 666, 669 (Md. App. 1988). Learned Hand stated: "[A]s for 'res gestae' . . . if it means anything but an unwillingness to think at all, what it covers cannot be put in less intelligible terms." United States v. Matot, 146 F.2d 197, 198 (2d Cir.1944).

615. *See* § 7.01.

officer in making an investigation of a suspect is a bona fide issue, then evidence that the officer had been told by a reliable source that the suspect committed the crime under investigation is admissible. When, however, the only issue is the guilt of the suspect, not the state of mind of the officer, then what the officer was told about the suspect's guilt is inadmissible hearsay.[616]

An utterance offered to show the state of mind of the declarant is generally admissible under the hearsay exception for statements of present state of mind.[617] An objection should still be sustained, however, if the state of mind of the declarant is irrelevant, or though relevant, its probative value is outweighed by the danger that the jury will use the out-of-court statement for some purpose other than showing the declarant's state of mind.

An objection should also be sustained if the purpose of showing the declarant's state of mind is to show something about the past. In that case, the statement does not fit the hearsay exception for statements of present state of mind, because the hearsay exception does not cover statements of memory or belief offered to show the fact remembered or believed.[618]

Occasionally, the proponent will offer a statement to show a fact remembered or believed by the declarant, and assert that the statement is not hearsay at all because it is not offered to prove the truth of the matter asserted, but rather to show state of mind circumstantially.[619] For example, evidence that the declarant told a falsehood might be offered to show the guilty state of mind of the declarant, for purposes of showing that the declarant committed a crime in the past. Often such utterances will be admissible as the admission of a party opponent. When they are not (for example, when they are offered as evidence against someone other than the declarant), then their evidentiary status is problematic. Certainly offering a statement as a falsehood to show guilty state of mind does not seem to be offering it to prove the truth of what it asserts. On the other hand, the statement relies upon the belief of a person not subject to cross-examination, and has most of the infirmities of hearsay. Courts that have considered the admissibility of such statements under the Federal Rules of Evidence have reached divergent results.[620]

---

616. *See, e.g.,* United States v. Dean, 980 F.2d 1286, 1288–89 (9th Cir.1992) (trial judge committed reversible error in admitting out-of-court statement to police officer that defendant possessed weapon in his mobile home; since probable cause for search was not at issue, evidence had no relevance except for hearsay purpose of showing that defendant did in fact possess weapon); United States v. Hernandez, 750 F.2d 1256 (5th Cir.1985) (held, error to admit evidence that special agent had been told by United States Customs that defendant was a drug smuggler; agent's state of mind was not at issue).

617. *See* Fed. R. Evid. 803(3); § **7.13**.

618. *See* Fed. R. Evid. 803(3).

619. *See* § **7.01**.

620. For an extended discussion, see Roger C. Park, *"I Didn't Tell Them Anything About You": Implied Assertions as Hearsay Under the Federal Rules of Evidence,* 74 Minn. L. Rev. 783, 802–10 (1990).

§ 7.73 Courtroom Expressions and Their Relationship to Hearsay Doctrine: Catch phrases and Rules of Thumb—"It's admissible because it's only being offered to impeach"

The assertion "it's admissible because it's only being offered to impeach" is often a valid one. When an out-of-court statement is being offered as a prior inconsistent statement to impeach the person who made the statement, then it escapes the hearsay ban.[621] However, the word "impeach" is not a magic word that destroys the hearsay rule. When the statement of a declarant is used to impeach someone other than the declarant, then it is hearsay because it has no value for impeachment unless the trier first accepts the statement as proof of what it asserts.[622]

Examples

Mr. X testifies in court that "the light was red." Mr. X said to an investigator out of court that "the light was green." The out-of-court statement to the investigator is admissible to impeach. It has impeachment value whether or not one accepts the truth of what it asserts. The mere fact that the witness said different things at different times reflects poorly on the witness' credibility, without regard to the truth of what was said out of court.

Mr. X testifies on the stand "the light was red." Ms. Y said out of court "the light was green." The out-of-court statement of Ms. Y is offered to impeach Mr. X. The statement of Ms. Y is hearsay. It has no value in impeaching Mr. X unless one accepts the truth of the matter asserted in the statement.

§ 7.74 Courtroom Expressions and Their Relationship to Hearsay Doctrine: Catch phrases and Rules of Thumb—"The statement is only offered to show that it was made"

This response to the hearsay objection is an abbreviated way of saying "The statement is only offered to show that it was made, not to prove the truth of any assertion in it." Of course, this is sometimes a valid point, for example, when the statement is legally operative language[623] or when it is offered to show its effect on the hearer or reader.[624] But the words "only offered to show that it was made" are not a magical incantation that allows anything to come into evidence. If the fact that the statement was made is relevant to the case only if one accepts the

---

621. *See* § 7.07.

622. *See* Bemis v. Edwards, 45 F.3d 1369, 1372 (9th Cir.1995) (inconsistent statement by another person not admissible to impeach police report of beating incident: "Whereas an inconsistent statement by a testifying witness can be used to impeach that witness' credibility, an inconsistent account by another source is offered to show an alternative view of the truth").

623. *See* § 7.01.

624. *See* § 7.01.

truth of the matter asserted in the statement, then the statement is hearsay. The statement is being offered to show its truth.

§ 7.75 Courtroom Expressions and Their Relationship to Hearsay Doctrine: Catch phrases and Rules of Thumb—"A question can't possibly be hearsay"

The following excerpt from the transcript of a federal drug case illustrates this response to the hearsay objection. The prosecutor was trying to get the witness, an undercover agent, to describe what happened when the informant, in the presence of the agent, called a target to arrange a drug deal:[625]

Q: After this first telephone conversation about which you've just testified, were there any-further telephone conversations?

A: Yes.

Q. Will you explain how those came about?

A: There was a second telephone conversation. Mike [the informant] went to the phone. He dialed the number and he asked for room 638.

MR. SACHS: I object again to anything that Mike said on the grounds of hearsay. It is being offered for the truth of the things said. There is no way around that, your Honor.

THE COURT: No. Go ahead. What I'm interested in, you had the second phone call. What happened then?

THE WITNESS: Mike had a conversation and Mike asked me, "Would it be all right if we did the two-kilogram deal one pound at a time?" And I told him to tell the people on the other end of the phone that that would be fine, we would deal one pound of cocaine at a time.

THE COURT: This was a two-kilo deal, one kilo at a time?

THE WITNESS: One pound, of about four and a half pounds, at a time. So we deliver one pound at a time. And I told Mike to relay the message that that would be fine, that we could do one pound at a time.

THE COURT: All right.

Q: After these two telephone conversations, did there come a third telephone conversation?

A: Yes. The third telephone conversation—

Q: What room did Mike call?

---

625. United States v. Figueroa, 750 F.2d 232, 233 (2d Cir.1984). The court of appeals reversed on grounds that this line of testimony should have been excluded. However, the particular question that led to the assertion that "a question can't possibly be hearsay" was never answered in the trial court, so the court of appeals did not rule specifically on whether a question could ever be hearsay.

A: He asked for—he called 638.

Q. And did he ask to speak to anybody?

A: Yes. He said "Hello" on the phone again.

Q. And can you describe what you heard-what you instructed him to say on the telephone?

A: I told—after the conversation, I told Mike—Mike asked me—

MR. SACHS: I object to what Mike asked him. That is hearsay once again.

MR. CHERTOFF: A question can't possibly be hearsay.

Mr. Chertoff's contention that "a question can't possibly be hearsay" is probably based upon the definition of hearsay as an assertion offered to prove the truth of the matter asserted. If an utterance is not an "assertion," it is not hearsay. The word "assertion" is not defined in the Federal Rules, and has received virtually no treatment in the case law. However, one usually does not think of a question as being an "assertion." There is some support for the position that only declarative sentences can be hearsay, a position that would exclude questions and imperative sentences from the hearsay definition.[626]

The proposition that "a question can't possibly be hearsay" does not make sense in all situations. A question such as "Why did you go so fast?," offered to show that the addressee was speeding, has no fewer dangers of insincerity than the declaration "you were going very fast." The same can be said of an imperative sentence such as "Throw that thief out of here!" when offered to show that the person referred to was a thief. The sentences just quoted contain implied assertions that the person was speeding or was a thief, and when offered to prove the truth of those implied assertions, they carry just as much of a danger of unreliability as a direct statement. Implied assertions are sometimes treated as hearsay, even under the Federal Rules of Evidence.[627]

626. *See* Edward J. Imwinkelried, Paul C. Giannelli, Francis A. Gilligan & Frederic I. Lederer, Courtroom Criminal Evidence 128 (2d ed. 1993) [UPDATE] ("Because most assertive statements are declarative sentences, many trial judges use a rule of thumb that imperative, interrogative, and exclamatory sentences are not hearsay"; the authors would not follow the "rule of thumb" in all situations); Olin Guy Wellborn III, *The Definition of Hearsay in the Federal Rules of Evidence*, 61 Tex. L. Rev. 49, 72–73 (1982) (suggesting that this is at least a plausible, and perhaps the most plausible, interpretation of the word "assertion" in Rule 801(c)); United States v. Zenni, 492 F.Supp. 464, 466 n. 7 (E.D.Ky.1980) ("the utterance, 'Put $2 to win on Paul Revere in the third at Pimlico,' is a direction and not an assertion of any kind, and therefore can be neither true nor false").

627. *See* United States v. Reynolds, 715 F.2d 99 (3d Cir.1983) ("didn't tell them about you" is inadmissible hearsay when offered to show guilt of person addressed); Lyle v. Koehler, 720 F.2d 426, 431–35 (6th Cir.1983) (Merritt, J) (proof that X wrote letters to X's friends asking friends to set up a false alibi for X and Y is hearsay when offered against Y as evidence of Y's guilt). Though the two cases cited did not deal specifically with the issue whether questions can ever be hearsay, their reasoning would lead to the conclusion that questions are hearsay when the questions contain implied assertions.

§ 7.76 Forfeiture of Hearsay and Confrontation Objections by Wrongdoing

Federal Rule 804(b)(6), promulgated in 1997, provides that the hearsay rule does not bar "a statement offered against a party that has engaged or acquiesced in wrongdoing that was intended to, and did, procure the unavailability of the declarant as a witness." The rule applies, for example, to situations in which the trial judge determines that the defendant murdered a witness to prevent the witness from testifying. The basic principle was widely recognized before the adoption of the new rule.[628]

§ 7.77 Hearsay in Relation to Other Objections

This chapter has dealt with the hearsay rule and its exceptions. Two important reminders are in order at this point.

First, other objections may be made even if the hearsay objection is overruled. The mere fact that an out-of-court statement satisfies the hearsay rule does not mean that it satisfies other exclusionary rules, such as the best evidence rule, the authentication rules, the rule against character evidence, and the rules of privilege.

Correspondingly, the hearsay ban is not satisfied just because some other evidence rule is satisfied. For example, the fact that evidence is admissible under Rule 404(b) as evidence of motive, plan, etc., does not mean that it can be offered in hearsay form without fitting it into some hearsay exception.

---

628. *See, e.g.,* United States v. Houlihan, 92 F.3d 1271, 1278–81 (1st Cir. 1996) (murder of declarant waives confrontation rights; defendant's responsibility for murder need only be shown by preponderance of evidence).

Chapter 8

EVIDENTIARY PRIVILEGES

Analysis

§ 8.01 The Origin and Policy of Privilege

Evidentiary privileges limit a party's ability to ask about certain communications that may be probative and to interrogate certain witnesses who may have important testimony to offer. These restrictions on the reach of the dispute resolution system exist because resolving disputes through discovery of the truth is not the only value cherished by society.

The lawyer-client, doctor-patient, husband-wife privileges and the privilege against self-incrimination are some of the more commonly known and more important evidentiary privileges. Unlike most evidentiary matters, the parties do not control decisions about the exercise of the privilege, the holders of the privilege do. Although the parties may suggest the existence of a privilege to a tribunal, because the values underlying the privilege do not relate to the dispute, only the holder of the privilege may decide to claim or to waive it.[1]

Husband-wife and lawyer-client privileges were the earliest to be recognized by the common law judges in England.[2] The earliest husband-wife privilege was of the kind that prevented a person from testifying at all, while the earliest lawyer-client privilege was of the kind that prevented testimony about communications. Until the early part of the 19th century, all privilege law in the United States was imported from the British common law and was created by the courts. In 1828, the New York legislature passed the first statute creating a privilege between doctor and patient.[3] From that time forward, the law of privilege has been a creature of the legislative process, except in the federal system, where the courts continue to be the creators of privilege.

The initial draft of the Federal Rules of Evidence included an attempt to codify the judicially created privileges applicable in the federal courts, but Congress rejected the proposal, leaving creation or rejection of privilege in the federal system to "reason and experience" as "interpreted by the courts."[4] Rule 501 provides that when a federal court is applying the substantive law of a state, it must apply the state's privilege rules and when applying federal substantive law, it must apply federal privilege law as interpreted in the light of reason and experience.[5] Thus, when the federal district court tries a personal injury diversity case, it applies state law; when it tries a federal antitrust case, it applies general federal common law.[6] Sometimes a case can involve both state and federal privileges, as when a state substantive claim is pendent upon a federal claim.[7]

There were various rationales and procedures for early common law privileges, but most modern privileges relate to professions and are supported by a utilitarian notion that the privilege will facilitate communication between the person in need of help and the professional able to provide it. Even the privileges that do not relate to the professions, such as the marital privileges, are justified by the instrumental concepts of preserving relationships and encouraging communications.

§ 8.02 The Difference Between Privilege and Professional Confidentiality

The professional privileges are often confused with the ethical requirements of the various professions to preserve the confidentiality of the professional relationship. Lawyers, doctors, and many other profes-

---

1. *See, e.g.,* Touma v. Touma, 357 A.2d 25 (N.J. Super. 1976) (marital communications privilege cannot be claimed by marriage counselor.)

2. 1 McCormick on Evidence § 75 (4th ed. John W. Strong ed. 1994).

3. N.Y. Rev. Stats. 1829, Vol. II, Part III, c. 7, tit. 3, art. 8 § 73.

4. Fed. R. Evid. 501.

5. *Id.*

6. H.R. Conf. Rep. No. 93–1597 (1974).

7. *See, e.g.,* FDIC v. Mercantile Nat'l Bank of Chicago, 84 F.R.D. 345, 349 (N.D. Ill. 1979) (state privilege did not bar discovery of information relevant to federal claim, even though also relevant to pendent state claim).

sionals have codes describing aspirations or propounding rules governing their conduct. Most such codes include confidentiality obligations. Even though the breach of those ethical confidentiality obligations might lead to professional discipline or loss of professional license, the professional codes do not provide a legal basis for the exclusion of evidence. Only the existence of a privilege will exclude a confidential communication from evidence.

The ethical obligations of confidentiality are usually broader than the privilege protecting communication between a professional and the client/patient/penitent. They are often designed to further goals other than or in addition to the utilitarian goals of the various privileges. The lawyer-client privilege, for example, only prohibits evidence in a judicial or other proceeding, and only protects communication between lawyer and client. The lawyer's ethical obligation of confidentiality, by contrast, applies in almost any situation and covers all information relating to the representation, whatever the source.[8] While the modern rationale for the privilege is to facilitate communication between client and lawyer, the ethical underpinning of the confidentiality requirement retains overtones of the original justification for the privilege, relating not to the needs of the client, but rather, to the profession's aspirations concerning its own status.

§ 8.03   The Lawyer–Client Privilege

Many states have statutes that deal with the lawyer-client privilege. However, cases interpreting these statutes often do not take a precise or technical view of the language of the statute. State Supreme Courts tend to treat their statutes as if they merely announced "this state has a lawyer-client privilege." They then derive the boundaries of the privilege from case law and treatises, without much attention to the exact language of the statute.[9] Thus, a statute that by its terms applies to all communications is likely to be interpreted to apply only to confidential communications. Common-law exceptions to the privilege, such as the exception for communications made in furtherance of fraud, are likely to be read into the statutes.[10]

Wigmore's definition of the privilege is frequently quoted and cited. He summarized the privilege as follows:

8. ABA Model Rules of Professional Responsibility 1.6, Comment.

9. Note, *Developments in the Law—Privileged Communications*, 98 Harv. L. Rev. 1450, 1458 (1985); Restatement (Third) of the Law Governing Lawyers § 118 (Tent. Draft. No. 2, 1989) ("For the most part, courts do not construe their evidence statutes or codes as technically minute and comprehensive delineations of the privilege").

10. *See, e.g.*, State v. Montgomery, 499 So.2d 709, 711 (La. App. 1986) (court fol-

lowed common law rule that lawyer-client privilege extends to client's communications with lawyer's agents although statute only referred to communications with lawyer); Brown v. St. Paul City Ry. Co., 62 N.W.2d 688, 700–01 (Minn. 1954) (court endorsed Wigmore's definition of the lawyer-client privilege, including requirement that the communication be confidential, despite statute's unqualified language that appeared to apply to all communications).

(1) Where legal advice of any kind is sought (2) from a professional legal adviser in his capacity as such, (3) the communications relating to that purpose, (4) made in confidence (5) by the client, (6) are at his instance permanently protected (7) from disclosure by himself or by the legal adviser, (8) except the protection be waived.[11]

This definition is an accurate summary of the modern privilege, though two matters should perhaps be added. Communications from the lawyer to the client, as well as those by the client[12] to the lawyer are covered. Communications made through a representative of the lawyer or client are usually covered, as well as those involving the lawyer and client directly.[13] In addition, the definition does not describe some of the widely accepted exceptions to the privilege, such as the exception for communications made in furtherance of crime or fraud.

Another frequently quoted formulation of the privilege appears in an opinion by Judge Wyzanski:

> The privilege applies only if (1) the asserted holder of the privilege is or sought to become a client; (2) the person to whom the communication was made (a) is a member of the bar of a court, or his subordinate and (b) in connection with this communication is acting as a lawyer; (3) the communication relates to a fact of which his lawyer was informed (a) by his client (b) without the presence of strangers (c) for the purpose of securing primarily either (i) an opinion on law or (ii) legal services or (iii) assistance in some legal proceeding, and not (d) for the purpose of committing a crime or tort; and (4) the privilege has been (a) claimed and (b) not waived by the client.[14]

A more recent attempt to restate the privilege appears in the tentative draft of an American Law Institute Restatement. Subject to exceptions, the Restatement's drafters provide that [T]he lawyer-client privilege may be invoked . . . with respect to

(1) A communication

(2) Made between privileged persons

(3) In confidence

(4) For the purpose of obtaining or providing legal assistance

---

11. 8 John H. Wigmore, Evidence in Trials at Common Law § 2291 (John T. McNaughton rev. 1961).

12. *See, e.g.,* Natta v. Hogan, 392 F.2d 686, 692–93 (10th Cir. 1968) (lawyer's letters to client privileged); Schwimmer v. United States, 232 F.2d 855, 863 (8th Cir.), *cert. denied,* 352 U.S. 833 (1956) (purpose of lawyer-client privilege to promote communication by preventing disclosure of confidential information, requires protection of lawyer's communications to client); 8 Wigmore, *supra* note 11, § 2320 (seldom questioned that lawyer's communications to client are privileged). *C.f.,* Mead Data Central, Inc. v. United States Dep't. of the Air Force, 566 F.2d 242, 254 (D.C. Cir. 1977) (privilege only extends to lawyer's communications to client if based on confidential information provided by client).

13. *See* § 8.05.

14. United States v. United Shoe Machinery Corp., 89 F. Supp. 357, 358–59 (D. Mass. 1950).

for the client.[15]

"Privileged persons" are elsewhere defined as "the client (including a prospective client), the client's lawyer, communicating agents of either of them, and representing agents of the lawyer.[16]

The lawyer-client privilege seems originally to have been based upon the idea that the barrister was a gentleman of honor, and that a gentleman should not be forced to betray confidences.[17] Under this concept, the privilege was for the benefit of the lawyer and the lawyer had the authority to waive it.[18] This original concept has now generally been replaced by what is sometimes called the "utilitarian" rationale for the privilege. Under the "utilitarian" rationale, the purpose of the privilege is to encourage clients to confide in lawyers, so lawyers can provide full advice.[19]

Bentham made a slashing attack upon the utilitarian theory, saying that its only effect was to help the guilty to receive better advice; the innocent did not need the protection of the privilege, since they had nothing to hide.[20] But Bentham's attack, though powerful, is simplistic. Clients' cases are rarely all good or bad and even people who have a good cause may, also, have something the lawyer should know in order to prepare, but about which they are less than proud. The lawyer can give more realistic advice if the weak points of the client's case are known. Moreover, the more the lawyer knows of both the strengths and the weaknesses of the client's cause, the more likely the matter is to be settled in a way that saves time and expense for both the parties and for society at large.

In any event, abolition of the privilege would encourage misconduct. First, advocates would be more likely to call the opposing counsel to the stand as a litigation tactic, perhaps to sow dissension between lawyer and client or simply to disrupt the other party's case.[21] Second, a rule that allowed the opponent to force testimony would place the lawyer in the trilemma of committing perjury, hurting the client, or committing contempt. Dishonorable lawyers would prefer perjury, to keep the client's loyalty and business, and this would place honorable lawyers at a disadvantage. Despite these grounds for defending the privilege, even its supporters concede that the obstructing influence of the privilege on justice is plain and direct, while its benefits are conjectural and removed.[22]

Only communications, not acts and observations, are protected by the lawyer-client privilege. For example, suppose a client becomes a fugitive, and the lawyer is asked to reveal information about the client's

---

15. Restatement, *supra* note 9, § 118.

16. *Id.* § 120.

17. 8 Wigmore, *supra* note 11, § 2290.

18. *See id.* The privilege was "consideration for the oath and the honor of the lawyer." *Id.*

19. Upjohn v. United States, 449 U.S. 383, 389 (1981); 8 Wigmore, *supra* note 11, § 2291.

20. 5 Jeremy Bentham, Rationale of Judicial Evidence 302–04 (1827).

21. Restatement, *supra* note 9, § 118.

22. 8 Wigmore, *supra* note 11, § 2291.

physical appearance to aid in apprehension. Information about the client's physical appearance is not privileged because it was not acquired through a communication. The lawyer can be forced to testify about the client's physical characteristics, dress, bearing, sobriety, mannerisms, and other matters that are non-communicative.[23]

A controversial application of this concept occurs when the lawyer is required to testify about the mental competency of a client. In *State v. Jensen*,[24] for example, the prosecution called defendant's lawyer in a prior trial to show that the defendant was mentally competent to stand trial. The defendant objected and the prior lawyer stated that he would be unable to divorce confidential information from expressions and other behavioral manifestations of the defendant. The trial court required the lawyer to testify. He testified that the defendant appeared normal during the prior representation and that he had discussed trial tactics with him.[25] The Minnesota Supreme Court ruled that there was no error in admitting the testimony, saying that a lawyer's observations of his client are "simply not communications."[26] Though it would appear that the lawyer's assessment of competency would at least partly be based on what the client communicated to the lawyer, the court ignored this aspect. The result (that lawyers may be required to testify about competency to stand trial) has been very widely accepted.[27] It has been suggested that these cases are really a special exception to the privilege founded on the necessity of getting testimony from the person best able to say whether the client was competent to cooperate in the client's defense.[28]

§ 8.04 The Lawyer-Client Privilege—The Requirement of Confidentiality

The lawyer-client privilege applies only to confidential communications. A communication may be considered non-confidential by reason of the presence of third parties.[29] Obviously, if the client says something to

---

23. *See, e.g.,* United States v. Kendrick, 331 F.2d 110, 113–14 (4th Cir. 1964) (complexion, demeanor, bearing, sobriety, dress, matters "observable by anyone" not privileged); 8 Wigmore, *supra* note 11, § 2306 (facts that another person would observe if present and not intended as a communication not privileged).

24. 174 N.W.2d 226 (Minn. 1970).

25. *See id.* at 228.

26. *See id.* at 230.

27. *See, e.g.,* Darrow v. Gunn, 594 F.2d 767, 774 (9th Cir. 1979) (state privilege protecting only "confidential communications" does not protect lawyer's observation and impressions of client's mental condition); United States v. Kendrick, 331 F.2d 110, 114 (4th Cir. 1964) (lawyer's testimony concerning client's cooperativeness and awareness at trial not privileged); Bishop v.

Superior Court, 724 P.2d 23, 28–29 (Ariz. 1986) (lawyer's observations of defendant's ability to assist in defense not privileged). *But see* Gunther v. United States, 230 F.2d 222, 223–24 (D.C. Cir. 1956) (lawyer's testimony concerning client's competency violates privilege because it would lead to examination of facts underlying opinion, thereby opening door to inquiry of entire lawyer-client relationship).

28. *See* Restatement, *supra* note 9, § 118.

29. *See, e.g.,* United States v. Melvin, 650 F.2d 641, 645–46 (5th Cir. 1981) (third person not part of defense team); United States v. Landof, 591 F.2d 36, 39 (9th Cir. 1978) (second lawyer not representing client or acting as agent of client's lawyer); United States v. Cooper, 1991 WL 60371 (S.D.N.Y. 1991) (defendant waived lawyer-the lawyer at an open meeting of a corporation's shareholders, then the communication is not privileged because not intended to be confidential.

The presence of some third parties may not destroy the privilege. It is universally recognized that the lawyer's secretary or clerk can be present without destroying the privilege.[30] The cases also allow the presence of persons who are necessary for communication, such as translators, without any effect on the privilege.[31] Some cases have extended this principle to include other persons helpful to communication, such as an accountant trusted by the client to interpret financial data, or a close family member who aided the client.[32] The common-law cases are not wholly consistent on this point, but generally it seems that the privilege will be upheld if (1) the client reasonably believed that the discussion was confidential, and (2) the third person's presence was reasonably necessary in the furtherance of the consultation.[33] The unsettled nature of the law and the chance that the third person will be found unnecessary make it dangerous to allow the client to bring third persons to an interview, unless the necessity for having them present is clear.[34] The risk that it will abrogate the privilege is substantial. If the third person also has a privilege with the client and the communication is in furtherance of the service both the lawyer and the third person provide to the client, the circle of privilege is not broken.

Joint consultations present the possibility of unexpected loss of the privilege, if the parties to the joint consultation become adverse.[35]

client privilege by making statement to lawyer in the presence of DEA agent standing five feet away and making no attempt to keep communication confidential); In re Guardianship of Walling, 727 P.2d 586, 592 (Okla. 1986) (grandmother not necessary for transmission of communication); 8 John H. Wigmore, Evidence in Trials at Common Law § 2311 (John T. McNaughton rev. 1961) (presence of third person neither agent of client nor lawyer destroys privilege). *Cf.,* In re Bieter Co. 16 F.3d 929 (8th Cir. 1994) (independent consultant hired by client was functional equivalent of client's employee for purposes of lawyer-client privilege; privilege applies therefore to communications between consultant and client's lawyer); United States v. Bigos, 459 F.2d 639, 643 (1st Cir.), *cert. denied sub nom.,* Raimondi v. United States, 409 U.S. 847 (1972) (presence of client's father did not destroy privilege when circumstances indicated that parties still viewed communications as confidential).

30. *See, e.g.,* Taylor v. Taylor, 177 S.E. 582, 583 (Ga. 1934) (communications to lawyer's confidential secretary privileged); Sibley v. Waffle, 16 N.Y. 180, 183 (1857) (privilege protects communications to lawyer's clerk); 8 Wigmore, *supra* note 29, § 2310.

31. *See, e.g.,* United States v. Kovel, 296 F.2d 918, 921–22 (2d Cir. 1961) (privilege includes translators assisting lawyer to communicate with client).

32. *See, e.g., Kovel,* 296 F.2d at 921–22 (accountant who helped client by interpreting data for lawyer analogized to language translator; privilege upheld); Estate of Weinberg, 509 N.Y.S.2d 240, 242 (N.Y. Sur. Ct. 1986) (privilege covered daughter of client who aided in business).

33. *See, e.g.,* Restatement (Third) of the Law Governing Lawyers § 120, cmt. (Tent. Draft No. 2 1989) ("[W]hether a client's communication in the presence of a third person is protected by the privilege depends upon whether the presence of the third person served to permit client and lawyer to communicate effectively or to permit client to understand or act upon the lawyer's advice").

34. For examples of cases in which the third person was held to have destroyed confidentiality, *see supra* note 29.

35. *See, e.g.,* Grand Trunk W.R. Co. v. H.W. Nelson Co., 116 F.2d 823, 835 (6th Cir. 1941) (communications made to lawyer when representing both parties not privileged in later dispute between parties); Emley v. Selepchak, 63 N.E.2d 919, 922 (Ohio

Suppose that X and Y consult a lawyer for purposes of forming a corporation. Then, as sometimes happens, they have a falling out and end up suing each other. While their original consultation was privileged as against any claim from others to produce its content in a judicial proceeding, neither party's communications with the lawyer are privileged in a dispute between the two clients. This result does not undermine the purpose of the privilege, that of encouraging disclosures to lawyers. The parties would not be inhibited about making disclosures during the joint consultation because neither would know who would profit or lose by later disclosure in a suit between them.[36] At any rate, they did not intend for the matter to be confidential between them and thus on the principle that the communication must be confidential the privilege falls.[37]

Suppose that, without the knowledge of the lawyer or the client, a third person overhears a lawyer-client communication, and that person is called to testify. In general, eavesdroppers are permitted to testify, even if the client and lawyer intended the communication to be confidential.[38] The client and lawyer are responsible for taking precautions. If they don't, or if they try but don't succeed, then the evidence is admissible in many jurisdictions.[39]

Even when third parties are not present at the time the communication is made, a communication may fall outside the lawyer-client privilege because the client intended for the lawyer to make the communication public at some later time. For example, if the client gave the lawyer information to be included in a public document, the information is not privileged.[40]

§ 8.05 The Lawyer-Client Privilege—The Requirement of Communication to a Proper Person

The lawyer-client privilege applies only to communications between the client and the lawyer or the lawyer's representative. A client who seeks legal advice from someone who is not a lawyer is, of course, not entitled to the lawyer-client privilege, unless, perhaps, the client reasonably believed that person to be a lawyer.[41] Confidential communications

App. 1945) (communications made to lawyer by two parties forming contract not privileged in suit for specific performance); 8 Wigmore, *supra* note 29, § 2312 (no privilege between joint clients because no secrecy existed between them at time of communication).

36. *Id.*

37. *Id.*

38. Clark v. State, 261 S.W.2d 339, 342 (Tex. Crim. App. 1953) (telephone operator who eavesdropped on conversation between lawyer and client could testify as to what she heard); 8 Wigmore, *supra* note 29, § 2326 (privilege does not cover third party

overhearing communication with or without client's knowledge).

39. *See, e.g.,* Schwartz v. Wenger, 124 N.W.2d 489, 492 (Minn. 1963) (conversation overheard in the hallway of the courthouse admissible). *But see* discussion at § 8.11.

40. *See* United States v. White, 950 F.2d 426 (7th Cir. 1991) (information given to attorney for inclusion in bankruptcy schedule not confidential and hence not privileged).

41. *See, e.g.,* People v. Velasquez, 237 Cal. Rptr. 366, 371 (App. 1987) (client's communication not privileged because he did not talk to a lawyer or person he rea-with the non-lawyers employed by the lawyer—such as secretaries, investigators, paralegals, and clerks—are usually covered by the privilege, even if the lawyer is not present at the time of the communication.[42]

Experts in various areas, such as doctors, engineers, accountants, and others with specialized knowledge are often employed by a lawyer to assist in preparing particular aspects of the client's case. Whether conversations between the lawyer's client and these experts are covered by the lawyer-client privilege usually depends upon what the expert is being asked to do and by whom the expert is hired. In many jurisdictions, if the lawyer hires the expert and the expert's sole responsibility is to assist the lawyer in preparing the case, the communication between the client and the expert will be covered by the lawyer-client privilege.[43] There are two common circumstances in which the lawyer-client privilege may not cover the communication between the client and an expert assisting a lawyer to prepare the client's case. The first is when the expert is going to be a witness at trial. In that instance, the purpose of the communication between the client and the expert is to prepare the expert to testify, rather than to assist the lawyer in giving legal advice. The communication will not be privileged. The second is when the expert assisting the lawyer also has a separate professional relationship with the client. In that instance, there is some danger that the communication between client and expert will be viewed as one for the purpose of their professional relationship, rather than for the purpose of helping the lawyer to provide legal service. In that event, the communication is unlikely to be privileged, unless the relationship between the expert and the client is one that carries its own privilege. A lawyer is well advised, therefore, not to employ an expert who has either a mixed purpose or a dual relationship, if the lawyer desires to make sure communications between the lawyer's client and the expert are privileged. Doctors

sonably believed to be a lawyer); People v. Barker, 27 N.W. 539, 546 (Mich. 1886) (defendant's confession made to private detective falsely claiming to be a lawyer privileged); 8 John H. Wigmore, Evidence in Trials at Common Law § 2302 (John T. McNaughton rev. 1961) (client entitled to peace of mind, should not bear risk of deception or defective professional title). *Cf.,* Sample v. Frost, 10 Iowa 266, 267 (1859) (statements made to someone not yet admitted to bar not privileged).

42. *See, e.g.,* Hillary v. Minneapolis St. Ry. Co., 116 N.W. 933, 934 (Minn. 1908).

43. *See, e.g.,* United States v. Alvarez, 519 F.2d 1036, 1046 (3d Cir. 1975) (defendant's communications to psychiatrist retained by attorney privileged); City & County of San Francisco v. Superior Court, 231 P.2d 26, 31–32 (Cal. 1951) (client's communications to physician hired by attorney to help prepare for litigation privileged); Re-

statement (Third) of the Law Governing Lawyers § 120 (Tent. Draft No. 2, 1989):

> The privilege ... generally extends to client communications to an expert adviser retained by a lawyer, such as an accountant or a physician, to whom a client makes a communication for the purpose of providing a basis on which the expert adviser may consult with the client's lawyer on a technical or expert matter relevant to the representation. So long as such independent contractors or agents assist the lawyer in a confidential capacity in rendering legal assistance to the client, the privilege applies.

Cf. United States *ex rel* Edney v. Smith, 425 F.Supp. 1038, 1054–55 (E.D.N.Y. 1976), *affd,* 556 F.2d 556 (2d Cir.), *cert. denied,* 431 U.S. 958 (1977) (under state law defendant waived privilege in relation to his communications to psychiatrist by raising insanity as defense).

present a common example. Even in a jurisdiction that does not have a doctor-patient privilege, communications between a client and a doctor, hired by the lawyer for the sole purpose of assisting the lawyer to prepare the case, are covered by the lawyer-client privilege.[44] But even in a jurisdiction that recognizes a doctor-patient privilege, a communication between a doctor and the lawyer's client is not covered by either privilege, if the doctor will be a witness at trial.

The requirement that the client's communication be with the lawyer or lawyer's representative also means that the client's pre-existing documents do not become privileged when the client transfers them to the lawyer.[45] Documents prepared by the client for some business or other purpose, therefore, do not become covered by the lawyer-client privilege when the client transfers them to the lawyer to assist in preparation of the client's case, even if the documents were originally created for a "secret" business or other purpose. The original communication—putting the thoughts or numbers on paper—was not for the purpose of communicating with a lawyer, but rather, for the business or other purpose. On the other hand, a client's recapitulation of business or some other dealings, written out for the lawyer, is covered by the lawyer-client privilege, even if the original dealings were not meant to be "secret."[46]

§ 8.06   The Lawyer-Client Privilege—The Requirement That the Purpose Be to Obtain Legal Advice or Service

The lawyer-client privilege applies only when the client seeks legal advice from the lawyer. But neither the formality of a lawyer-client retainer nor the condition of a professional environment is necessary for the communication to be covered by the privilege.[47] The communications

44. *In re* Grand Jury Proceedings (Nos. 9 1–50 1 2, 9 1–50 1 3, 9 1–50 1 6), 947 F.2d 1 1 88, 1 190–9 1 (4th Cir. 1991) (when client consults accountant without consulting lawyer, no privilege attaches to matters discussed with accountant even if lawyer is later consulted; but when accountant is used as client's agent in communicating with lawyer, lawyer-client privilege attaches as to matters that client discussed with accountant).

45. *See, e.g.,* Colton v. United States, 306 F.2d 633, 639 (2d Cir. 1962), *cert. denied*, 371 U.S. 951 (1963) (pre-existing documents related to preparation and filing of tax returns, not prepared by client for purpose of communicating with lawyer not privileged); City of Philadelphia v. Westinghouse Elec. Corp., 205 F. Supp. 830, 831 (E.D. Pa. 1962) (client may not refuse to disclose relevant information merely because she incorporated it into communication to lawyer); State ex rel Dudek v. Circuit Court, 150 N.W.2d 387, 389 (Wis. 1967) (client cannot hide a pre-existing document be merely giving it to lawyer).

46. *See, e.g.,* Upjohn v. United States, 449 U.S. 383, 395 (1981) (responses to lawyers' questionnaires used for providing legal advice to corporation privileged); *City of Philadelphia*, 205 F. Supp. at 831 (client cannot be compelled to testify as to what she said or wrote to lawyer).

47. *See, e.g.,* In re Dupont's Estate, 140 P.2d 866, 871–72 (Cal. App. 1943) (preliminary communications made by client seeking to contest will privileged, although lawyer refused employment; otherwise no person could safely consult lawyer for first time); Taylor v. Sheldon, 173 N.E.2d 892, 895 (Ohio 1961) (communications made to lawyer by client seeking preparation of will privileged, even though lawyer chose not to prepare will); 8 John H. Wigmore, Evidence in Trials at Common Law § 2304 (John T. McNaughton rev. 1961) (preliminary com-of a person who comes for a preliminary discussion and decides not to hire the lawyer is as covered as the communication between the lawyer and a client paying a million-dollar fee. Similarly, a communication about legal advice is covered when conducted during a cocktail party as when conducted in the lawyer's office, so long as the person seeking the advice and the lawyer take measures to keep the communication confidential.

Communications made to a lawyer as a friend are not covered by the lawyer-client privilege, even if the friend is also a client.[48] If, for example, a friend's business lawyer receives a call in which the despondent friend discusses committing suicide and an issue arises in later litigation concerning whether the friend died a natural death, the conversation between friends is not privileged.[49]

A business in which the lawyer is, also, an executive or is regularly consulted for business as well as legal advice often presents the issue of the communication's purpose. Consider, for example, when a corporate vice president says in confidence to another corporate vice president who is, also, a lawyer: "We're thinking about acquiring IBM. What do you think?" If the question is asked to gain only business advice, it is not privileged.[50] If it is asked to gain legal advice, it is privileged, even if there is a secondary purpose to receive business advice.[51]

The context of a communication that might be business or legal or both almost always will determine whether the communication will be covered by the lawyer-client privilege. If the question following the statement about acquiring IBM had been, "Will this give us a great

munications made by person seeking legal counsel privileged whether person does not hire lawyer or lawyer declines employment). *Cf.*, McGrede v. Rembert Nat'l. Bank, 147 S.W.2d 580, 584 (Tex. Civ. App. 1941) (communications made after lawyer declines employment not privileged).

48. *See, e.g.*, Modern Woodmen of America v. Watkins, 132 F.2d 352, 354 (5th Cir. 1942) (communication of suicidal intent made to lawyer as friend not privileged); G & S Investments v. Belman, 700 P.2d 1358, 1364–65 (Ariz. App. 1984) (speaker's conversation with lawyer-friend about nature of speaker's interest in business partnership not privileged where speaker's purpose was to inform lawyer-friend that he was going to receive a bequest, rather than to get legal advice); 1 McCormick on Evidence § 88 (4th ed. John W. Strong ed. 1994) (communications made to lawyer as friend not privileged).

49. *See e.g.*, *Modern Woodmen*, 132 F.2d at 354.

50. *See, e.g.*, In re Grand Jury Investigation, 842 F.2d 1223, 1224–25 (11th Cir. 1987) (communications about income to lawyer acting as tax return preparer not

privileged because lawyer not giving legal advice; extensive citation of authority); United States v. Huberts, 637 F.2d 630, 640 (9th Cir. 1980) (lawyer who represented client in consignment sale of printing press, served as business agent and may not assert privilege); 1 McCormick, *supra* note 48, § 88, at 209–210 (consultations with lawyer as business advisor not privileged). *See generally*, Scott N. Stone & Ronald S. Liebman, Testimonial Privileges § 1.38 (1983) (scope of lawyer-client privilege in relation to communications involving business advice).

51. *See, e.g.*, United States v. United Shoe Machinery Corp., 89 F. Supp. 357, 359 (D. Mass. 1950) (presence of relevant nonlegal considerations in communications primarily related to legal advice did not destroy privilege; "modern lawyer almost invariably advises his client upon not only what is permissible but also what is desirable"). *See also* Linde, PC v. Resolution Trust Co., 5 F.3d 1508, 1514–15 (D.C. Cir. 1993) (attorney client privilege does not apply to communications between law firm and its insurer); Burroughs Wellcome Co. v. Barr Labs, Inc., 143 F.R.D. 611 (E.D.N.C. 1992) (attorney-client privilege does not protect nonlegal business advice).

market share, or what?" the conversation is probably to seek business not legal advice and, therefore, should not be privileged. If, on the other hand, the question had been, "Do we have an antitrust concern here?" there would be little doubt that the conversation was for the purpose of gaining legal advice and should be privileged. Notice, however, even if the question is about antitrust problems, if the communication is in the presence of others in the company, the privilege might not apply because the confidentiality requirement of the privilege might not have been met.[52]

§ 8.07 The Lawyer-Client Privilege—Failure of the Privilege to Cover Fact of Employment, Identity of Client, and Payment of Fees

Information about the fact of employment and the identity of the client is generally not covered by the privilege.[53] No special principle is needed, usually, to reach this result. The client's name is likely to appear in correspondence to third parties from the lawyer, on bills from the lawyer that are sent through the mail, and perhaps on pleadings in litigation in which adversaries are entitled to know against whom they are contending.[54] Because clients rarely expect their name and the fact that they have retained a lawyer to be confidential, the general principle of the lawyer-client privilege, protecting only material intended to be confidential, does not apply.[55]

There are a number of circumstances, however, in which a client might expect and even expressly ask for confidentiality. A whistle-blower with information about official corruption may want to hire a lawyer to convey the information to the proper authorities while keeping the whistle-blower's identity confidential to reduce the likelihood of retaliation or legal consequence.[56] A client may wish to use a lawyer to

52. *See, e.g.,* Simon v. G D Searle & Co., 816 F.2d 397, 402–04 (8th Cir.), *cert. denied,* 484 U.S. 917 (1987) (communication of data to lawyer not privileged partly because data was business data, partly because it was shared with nonlawyer officers).

53. *See, e.g.,* Alexiou v. United States, 39 F.3d 973, 976 (9th Cir. 1994), *cert. denied,* 514 U.S. 1097 (1995) (attorney client privilege does not protect client from revelation of name, address, date, and amount of money paid to attorney in case in which client paid attorney with counterfeit $100 bill; information would not constitute "last link" in chain of testimony necessary to convict client, and was therefore unprotected by the privilege); In re Grand Jury Investigation, 723 F.2d 447, 451 (6th Cir. 1983), *cert. denied sub nom.,* Durant v. United States, 467 U.S. 1246 (1984) (identity of client, with limited exceptions, not privileged); Colton v. United States, 306 F.2d 633, 637 (2d Cir. 1962), *cert. denied,* 371 U.S. 951 (1963) (identity of client and years of employment not privileged); People v. Adam, 280 N.E.2d 205, 207–08 (Ill.), *cert. denied,* 409 U.S. 948 (1972) (client's arrangement to meet and retention of lawyer not privileged).

54. *See* 1 Mccormick on Evidence § 90 (4th ed. John W. Strong ed. 1994).

55. *See* 8 John H. Wigmore, Evidence in Trials at Common Law § 2313 (John T. McNaughton rev. 1961).

56. *See* In re Kozlov., 398 A.2d 882, 883 (N.J. 1979) (juror falsely testified that he neither knew nor was prejudiced against defendant). *See also* Stephan A. Saltzburg, *Communications Falling Within the Lawyer-client Privilege,* 66 Iowa L Rev. 811, 822–23 (1981) for a persuasive argument that if the privilege does not protect the client's identity in this situation, the authorities may be denied the information.

accomplish some personal mission, such as the anonymous payment of taxes, hoping that this will provide a basis for arguing against penalties, if the IRS ever discovers that the client has failed to pay taxes.[57] A client who has committed a crime, but who has not yet been identified by the authorities, may seek to have a lawyer engage in plea bargaining without revealing the client's identity.[58] Although courts have commonly recognized a limited exception to the general rule that client identity is not privileged, they have been divided over the exact nature of the exception.[59] The draft of the Restatement of the Law Governing Lawyers adopts the view that a client's identity is privileged whenever revealing the client's identity would necessarily reveal a confidential communication.[60]

The same general rule and exception that applies to the name of a client applies generally to information about a lawyer's fee. It is not privileged unless providing the fee information would divulge a confidential communication,[61] or providing the name of a third party who paid

57. *See,* Baird v. Koerner, 279 F.2d 623, 626–27 (9th Cir. 1960). The lower federal courts have divided over the question of whether the attorney-client privilege and the attorney's ethical duty of confidentiality permit the attorney to refuse to disclose the client's identity when required by IRS regulations. *Id. Compare* United States v. Monnat, 853 F. Supp. 1301, 1302–04 (D. Kan. 1994) (privilege applicable) *with* United States v. Leventhal, 961 F.2d 936, 941 (11th Cir. 1992) (no privilege in such circumstances).

58. *See* Scott N. Stone & Ronald S. Liebman, Testimonial Privileges § 127 (1983); *Lawyer Refuses to Identify Hit–Run Driver*, 133 Chicago Daily L. Bull., Nov. 11, 1987, at 1, col. 5.

59. *See, e.g.,* In re Grand Jury Subpoenas Duces Tecum, 695 F.2d 363, 365 (9th Cir. 1982) (identity of client privileged where it would implicate client in very matter for which client sought legal advice); In re Grand Jury Proceedings, 680 F.2d 1026 (5th Cir. 1982) (identity of client privileged when "last link" of evidence necessary to incriminate client); NLRB v. Harvey, 349 F.2d 900, 905 (4th Cir. 1965) (identity of client privileged where it amounts to disclosure of otherwise confidential information). *See also* In re Grand Jury Subpoena Issued to Cerson S. Horn, 976 F.2d 1314, 1315–18 (9th Cir. 1992) (identity of clients ordinarily not protected, but letters of consultation and retainer agreements protected); In re Grand Jury Proceedings, 946 F.2d 746 (11th Cir. 1991) (attorney was not required to disclose client's identity, even though government already knew client's reason for seeking legal advice). In re Grace D'Alessio, 617 N.Y.S.2d 484 (App.Div.1994) (name of hit-and-run driver represented by

attorney in plea negotiations need not be revealed to civil litigant). *But see* United States v. Leventhal, 961 F.2d 936, 940–41 l (5th Cir. 1992) (in suit to compel attorney to reveal client's identity on IRS Form 8300, held, identity of client and fact of payment were not protected by attorney client privilege; court noted that these facts ordinarily have nothing to do with legal advice, and information was not protected by the "last link" doctrine, which was said to apply to cases in which "disclosure of nonprivileged attorney-client communication also would reveal privileged information" (*id.*); thereby, court held that the cash-reporting statute itself created an exception to the attorney-client privilege (*id.*); United States v. Monnat, 853 F. Supp. 1301, 1305 (D. Kan. 1994) (an attorney is bound to disclose client's identity in Form 8300 and may not advise client on how to avoid requirement, but should inform client regarding the statutory disclosure requirement); *See generally* In re Grand Jury Investigation, 723 F.2d 447, 451–54 (6th Cir. 1983), *cert. denied sub nom.*, Durant v. United States, 467 U.S. 1246 (1984) (discussing various limited exceptions to general rule that identity of client not privileged).

60. Restatement (Third) of the Law Governing Lawyers § 119, at 91–94, cmt. & illus. 7 (Tent. Draft No. 2, 1989) (identity of client who anonymously paid back taxes through lawyer privileged because it would reveal confidential communication).

61. *See, e.g.,* In re Shargel, 742 F.2d 61, 62 (2d Cir. 1984) (fee information that government sought as evidence of unexplained wealth potentially derived from criminal activity not privileged); In re Osthe fee would incriminate the client.[62]

§ 8.08 The Lawyer-Client Privilege—Duration of the Privilege Beyond the Life of the Client

The lawyer-client privilege has been held, generally, to survive the death of the client.[63] In the absence of implied or express consent from the client to reveal confidences after death, the lawyer should claim the privilege on behalf of the client. The principle of privilege survival does not apply in disputes over the disposition of a client's estate. Those claiming under the client's will and other claimants to an estate are entitled to have access to the confidential material, the privilege being impliedly waived in order to fulfill the client's testamentary intent.[64]

The long-standing principle of privilege survival came under attack in 1997, when an independent counsel appointed to investigate the President of the United States subpoenaed a lawyer's notes of a privileged communication between the lawyer and a former White House aide who had committed suicide shortly after the conversation. The trial court quashed the subpoena, but the appellate court reversed in a two to one panel decision, the majority stating that the principle of privilege survival was more presumed than decided in the common law.[65] Confronted with the United States Supreme Court's 1996 decision in *Jaffee v. Redmond*[66] explicitly rejecting a balancing test for the newly recognized federal therapist-patient, the majority tried to carve out a "discrete zone"[67] in which it thought a balancing test might be appropriate. The "discrete zone" it chose was all of criminal litigation. In *Swidler & Berlin v. United States*,[68] the Supreme Court acknowledged that the

---

terhoudt, 722 F.2d 591, 594 (9th Cir. 1983) (fee information not privileged unless it would reveal substance of confidential communication); In re Slaughter, 694 F.2d 1258, 1260 (11th Cir. 1982) (fee information not privileged unless it would reveal identity of previously undisclosed client/suspect).

62. *See, e.g.,* In re Grand Jury Subpoenas, 803 F.2d 493, 498, *modified,* 817 F.2d 64 (9th Cir. 1987) (identity of third party who paid lawyer's fees for defendants in narcotics prosecution not privileged); Priest v. Hennessy, 409 N.E.2d 983, 987 (N.Y. 1980) (identity of third party who paid lawyer's fees for defendant's charged with prostitution not privileged). *But see* In re Grand Jury Proceedings, 517 F.2d 666, 671–73 (5th Cir. 1975) (identity of third party paying lawyer's fees for defendants in narcotics prosecution privileged because it would incriminate client under circumstances).

63. *See, e.g.,* United States v. Osborn, 561 F.2d 1334, 1340 (9th Cir. 1977) (privilege continues after client's death; case remanded for determination of whether communications privileged before death);

Wigmore, *supra* note 11, § 2323 (privilege continues even after death of client); McCormick, *supra* note 2, § 94 (privilege generally survives death of client).

64. Glover v. Patton, 165 U.S. 394, 406 (1897) (deceased's communications with lawyer concerning will not privileged in dispute between her daughters over construction of will). *See also* United States v. Osborn, 561 F.2d 1334, 1340 (9th Cir. 1977) (communications concerning will not privileged in dispute between testator's heirs, legatees, devisees, or other parties, all claiming under the will); McCormick, *supra* note 2, § 94 (privilege does not apply in dispute between parties claiming under will); Wilcox v. Coons, 220 S.W.2d 15, 19 (Mo.1949) (deceased client's privilege may be waived by either grantees under deed or devisees under will).

65. In re Sealed Case, 124 F.3d 230 (D.C. Cir. 1997).

66. 116 S.Ct. 1923 (1996).

67. 124 F.3d 230 (D.C. Cir. 1997).

68. 66 USLW 4538 (1998).

principle of survival had as often been presumed as decided, but rejected the appellate court's attempt to narrow the lawyer-client privilege by establishing a balancing test in criminal cases where the client was no longer alive. Proclaiming that "[k]nowing that communications will remain confidential even after death encourages the client to communicate full and frankly with counsel," the Court refused to introduce "substantial uncertainty into the privilege's application."

§ 8.09　The Lawyer-Client Privilege—Application of the Privilege to the Corporate Client

A corporation consults with a lawyer through human agents, who are not usually the lawyer's clients in their individual capacities. Any number of corporate employees, from the CEO to the newest hire in the stockroom might have occasion to communicate with the corporation's lawyer, but they are not entitled, in their individual capacities, to claim the protection of the lawyer-client privilege. The courts have held that a corporation may claim protection of the lawyer-client privilege for communications between its human agents and its lawyers, but they have not agreed as to which communications from which human agents are covered.

The "control group" test, first enunciated in *City of Philadelphia v. Westinghouse Electric Corp.*,[69] was at one time the majority rule in the federal courts.[70] It provided a privilege for communications from officers or employees in the upper echelon of the corporation—those employees in a position to control, or at least take a substantial part in, the decisions that the corporation might take upon the advice of the lawyer.

The "control group" test was criticized as being too narrow, and as failing to protect communications from lower-level employees who might possess information vital to the lawyer. Consequently, some courts accepted a broader view of the privilege under what became known as the "subject matter" test. The subject matter test protected communications to a corporation's lawyers by persons who were not part of the "control group" if (1) the employee made the communication at the direction of superiors, and (2) the subject of the communication concerned a matter within the scope of the employee's duties.[71]

In *Diversified Indus., Inc. v. Meredith*[72] the Eighth Circuit added another requirement to the "subject matter" test, placing the burden on the corporation to show that the communication was made for the purpose of securing legal advice.[73] This was an attempt to narrow the

---

69. 210 F. Supp. 483, 485 (E.D. Pa.1962), *cert. denied*, 372 U.S. 943 (1963).

70. *See* John E. Sexton, *A Post–Upjohn Consideration of the Corporate Lawyer-client Privilege*, 57 N.Y.U. L. Rev. 443, 451 (1982).

71. *See, e.g.*, Harper & Row Publishers, Inc. v. Decker, 423 F.2d 487, 491–92 (7th Cir. 1970).

72. 572 F.2d 596 (8th Cir.1977) (en banc).

73. The Diversified Industries court defined the test as follows:

[T]he lawyer-client privilege is applicable to an employee's communication if (1) the communication was made for the purpose of securing legal advice; (2) the employee making the communication "subject matter" test, so that it did not become a routine mechanism by which corporations could place a protective shield over all employee communications, irrespective of the need for legal advice, by funneling them through the corporate lawyer to create the lawyer-client privilege.

When the United States Supreme Court granted certiorari in *Upjohn Co. v. United States*,[74] many observers expected it to establish a comprehensive approach to the lawyer-client privilege for corporate cases. The *Upjohn* Court rejected the "control group" test, but it is difficult to say exactly what else it did.

In *Upjohn*, the Internal Revenue Service attempted to subpoena the results of an investigation that had been conducted by the Upjohn Company's General Counsel following an independent audit that discovered suspicious payments by one of Upjohn's foreign subsidiaries. The internal investigation, aimed at discovering whether the payments were illegal bribes to foreign officials, included a questionnaire to corporate managers. The questionnaire, which went out over the signature of the Chairman of the corporation, stated that the General Counsel was conducting an investigation of questionable payments, and sought detailed information about such payments. The recipients of the questionnaire were told to treat the investigation as "highly confidential" and not to discuss it other than with employees who might be able to provide useful information. Responses were sent directly to the General Counsel. The General Counsel and outside counsel also interviewed the managers who received the questionnaire and thirty-three other officers and employees of Upjohn.[75]

In March 1976, the company voluntarily submitted a report to the SEC and the IRS that disclosed certain questionable payments. The IRS began an investigation to determine the tax consequences of the payments and subpoenaed the questionnaire answers and the interview notes.[76] The company refused to provide the material, citing the lawyer-client privilege and the work product doctrine.

The Court of Appeals, applying the "control group" test, ruled in favor of the government, saying that, "only the senior management, guiding and integrating the several operations, . . . can be said to possess an identity analogous to the corporation as a whole."[77]

The Supreme Court disagreed. It rejected the "control group" test, stating that a broader privilege was needed to encourage communications to corporate lawyers. The narrow "control group" approach would "limit the valuable efforts of corporate counsel to ensure their clients'

did so at the direction of his corporate superior; (3) the superior made the request so that the corporation could secure legal advice; (4) the subject matter of the communication is within the scope of the employee's corporate duties; and (5) the communication is not disseminated beyond those persons who, because of the corporate structure, need to know its contents.

Id.

74. 449 U.S. 383 (1981).

75. *Id.*

76. *See id.* at 387–88.

77. United States v. Upjohn Co., 600 F.2d 1223, 1226 (6th Cir. 1979), *rev'd*, 449 U.S. 383 (1981).

compliance with the law.[78] The Court, however, declined to lay down a specific alternative rule.[79] Instead, it simply held that under the circumstances of the case, the communications to the corporate lawyer were privileged, enumerating some circumstances that influenced its judgment:

1. "The communications at issue were made by Upjohn employees to counsel for Upjohn acting as such, at the direction of corporate superiors in order to secure legal advice from counsel."[80]

2. "The communications concerned matters within the scope of the employees' corporate duties, and the employees themselves were sufficiently aware that they were being questioned in order that the corporation could obtain legal advice."[81]

3. "Pursuant to explicit instruction from the Chairman of the Board, the communications were considered 'highly confidential' when made and have been kept confidential by the company."[82]

In addition, the court may have been influenced by the fact that the information sought by the general counsel was not available from upper-level management.[83]

While *Upjohn* left open several issues (e.g., whether the privilege covers ex-employees whose information is sought by the lawyer), it suggests some guidelines that lawyers representing corporations should follow to ensure that information will be protected:

1. Make sure the corporation directs the employees to provide the information.

2. Ensure the employees know that the purpose of the inquiry is to obtain legal advice for the corporation.

3. Instruct the employees to keep the information strictly confidential.

4. Ask only for information that relates to matters within the scope of the employee's duties, as opposed to collecting information about unrelated matters.

The scope of the employee's duties appears to be the lynchpin for the expansion of the group whose communication the Court is willing to protect by the corporate lawyer-client privilege. A clerical employee who witnessed an accident involving a company vehicle would apparently not be covered under *Upjohn*, while the driver of the vehicle might be.

Upjohn might cause unintended mischief, if other courts follow the decision in *Baxter Travenol Laboratories, Inc. v. Lemay*.[84] In a remarkable extension of the *Upjohn* rationale, *Baxter* suggests that an outside witness' statement to corporate counsel may become privileged, simply

---

78. *Upjohn*, 449 U.S. at 392.
79. *See id.* at 386.
80. *Id.* at 394.
81. *Id.*

82. *Id.* at 395 (citation omitted).
83. *See id.* at 394.
84. 89 F.R.D. 410 (S.D. Ohio 1981).

by putting the witness on the payroll. Baxter hired, as a litigation consultant, a person who had previously worked for Lemay. The litigation consultant's job was to provide Baxter's lawyer with information about Lemay's alleged misuse of Baxter's proprietary information.[85] The court upheld Baxter's assertion that the confidential communications of the "litigation consultant" were protected by the privilege, finding that nearly all of the features of Upjohn were present.[86] The effect of Baxter is to allow a corporation to hire an informant from the other side and then blanket the "espionage" with the lawyer-client privilege.

Upjohn does not demand the *Baxter* result. It could have been distinguished easily on grounds that the employees in *Upjohn* were communicating about matters within the scope of the duties they performed for the corporation claiming the privilege. Baxter's "litigation consultant" communicated about matters concerning employment for Lemay, another corporation, and one that had no interest in Baxter's privilege.

It is worth noting that, although *Upjohn* and its progeny create a broad corporate lawyer-client privilege, they do not prevent the opposing party from seeking the same information from other sources. The lawyer-client privilege covers only confidential communications between lawyer and client, and not the underlying data upon which those communications were based.[87] The IRS in *Upjohn*, for example, was free to depose Upjohn's employees to ask them what they knew about illegal payments; it was only precluded from gathering what they had told corporate counsel about illegal payments.[88]

The *Upjohn* case is not, of course, binding on state courts, and a few have refused to follow it. They are free to follow the control group test or some other test for application of the privilege in the corporate context.[89]

The Limited Protection for a Lawyer's Work Product

When material in the hands of corporate counsel is sought during discovery, the claim of lawyer-client privilege is likely to be accompanied by a claim that the material is protected under the Federal Rules of Civil Procedure as the lawyer's "work product." Under Rule 26(b)(3) a party may obtain discovery of documents and tangible things prepared "in anticipation of litigation" by a lawyer or other agent of the opposing party only by showing "substantial need" and that it is unable, without undue hardship, to obtain the substantial equivalent from other sources.

---

85. *See id.* at 412.

86. *See id.* at 413–14.

87. Upjohn Co. v. United States, 449 U.S. 383, 395–96 (1981).

88. *See id.* at 396.

89. *See, e.g.*, Alaska R. Evid. 503 (a)(2) ("A representative of the client is one having authority to obtain professional legal services and to act on advice rendered pursuant thereto, on behalf of the client");

Nalian Truck Lines v. Nakano Warehouse & Transp. Corp., 8 Cal. Rptr.2d 467 (1992) (control group test maintained); Day v. Illinois Power Co., 199 N.E.2d 802, 806 (Ill. App. 1964) (employees' written reports to corporation's lawyer concerning investigation, repair or replacement of ruptured gas line not privileged because employees had no authority to determine corporate action based on lawyer's advice).

Moreover, even if the requisite showing of need is made, the court must protect against disclosure of "the mental impressions, conclusions, opinions, or legal theories of a lawyer or other representative of a party concerning the litigation."[90] However, under the Federal Rules of Civil Procedure, a party or a witness is entitled to obtain a copy of the party's own statement as a matter of course.[91]

On discovery, both the "work product" and the lawyer-client privilege rules protect material gathered for purposes of litigation. The two protections are distinct and there are several differences between them:

1. Material that is covered by the lawyer-client privilege cannot be discovered even upon a showing of special need.[92] Material that is covered by work product protection can be discovered with such a showing, except for material that would reveal the mental impressions, etc., of the party's lawyer or other representative.[93]

2. Only confidential communications between lawyer and client (or between the client and a representative of the lawyer) are covered by the lawyer-client privilege.[94] A much larger category of material is covered by the work product protection. A lawyer's memorandum about a statement to the lawyer from someone who is not a client, for example, falls within the work product privilege.[95] For that matter, a lawyer need not be involved at all for the work product protection to take effect. Information gathered by the party or the party's agent (such as a claim adjuster) are covered by the work product doctrine so long as the information is gathered in anticipation of litigation.[96]

90. Rule 26(b)(3), in relevant part, reads as follows:

> Subject to the provisions of subdivision (b)(4) of this rule [concerning trial preparation by experts], a party may obtain discovery of documents and tangible things otherwise discoverable under subdivision (b)(1) of this rule and prepared in anticipation of litigation or for trial by or for another party or by or for that other party's representative (including the other party's lawyer, consultant, surety, indemnitor, insurer, or agent) only upon a showing that the party seeking discovery has substantial need of the materials in the preparation of the party's case and that the party is unable without undue hardship to obtain the substantial equivalent of the materials by other means. In ordering discovery of such materials when the required showing has been made, the court shall protect against disclosure of the mental impressions, conclusions, opinions or legal theories of a lawyer or other representative of a party concerning the litigation.

91. Rule 26 (b)(3) provides that "A party may obtain without the required showing a statement concerning the action or its subject matter previously made by that party. Upon request, a person not a party may obtain without the required showing a statement concerning the action or its subject matter previously made by that person."

92. *See, e.g.,* Diversified Indus., Inc. v. Meredith, 572 F.2d 596, 602 (8th Cir. 1977) (privilege is absolute where it exists).

93. Fed. R. Civ. P. 26(b)(3).

94. *See* § 8.05.

95. *See, e.g.,* Upjohn Co. v. United States, 449 U.S. 383, 400 (1981) (purposes of Rule 26 included protection of memoranda based on oral statements of witnesses); Hickman v. Taylor, 329 U.S. 495, 507–14 (1947) (lawyer could not be forced to disclose memoranda on statements of witnesses).

96. *See,* Fed. R. Civ. P. 26(b)(3). Those protected materials include those produced by "party's lawyer, consultant, surety, indemnitor, insurer, or agent." *Id.*

3. The work product protection applies only to information gathered in "anticipation of litigation."[97] The lawyer-client privilege covers confidential communications to the lawyer seeking legal advice or services, whether or not litigation is expected.[98]

§ 8.10 The Lawyer-Client Privilege—The Crime–Fraud Exception to the Privilege

The crime-fraud exception removes the mantle of the privilege from communications between lawyer and client. If a client seeks advice or aid from a lawyer to facilitate a crime or fraud, the communications are not protected.[99] This exception to the lawyer-client privilege only applies to communications made in furtherance of a future or ongoing crime or fraud.[100] While the confidentiality of lawyer-client communications is important enough to our system of justice to protect a revelation to a lawyer of a past crime or fraud, there is no rationale for protecting communication to facilitate crime or fraud in the future.[101]

The crime-fraud exception, while easy to state, presents a ticklish problem of enforcement. A client seeking advice in aid of submitting a false insurance claim, laundering money, committing mail fraud, and the like is not entitled to the privilege. But how does a court determine whether the exception applies? Whether the communication was made in furtherance of crime or fraud cannot be known without knowing what was stated in the communication. Yet the communication may be privi-

---

97. *Id.*

98. *See* § 8.06.

99. *See, e.g.,* Clark v. United States, 289 U.S. 1, 15 (1933) (privilege does not protect communications in furtherance of crime or fraud regardless of lawyer's guilt); In re Grand Jury Proceedings, 87 F.3d 377 (9th Cir. 1996)(client's intent to procure aid in crime or fraud is all that is needed to establish exception to privilege); In re Grand Jury Proceedings, 680 F.2d 1026, 1028–29 (5th Cir. 1982) (privilege does not protect identity of third party who hired lawyer in course of drug smuggling conspiracy to defend clients charged with transporting narcotics even though lawyer did not know of illegal purpose); In re Doe, 51 F.2d 899, 900–01 (2d Cir. 1977) (client's revelation to lawyer that he planned to bribe juror not privileged); 1 McCormick on Evidence § 95 (4th ed. John W. Strong ed. 1994) (privilege does not apply where client seeks advice to further illegal or fraudulent scheme); 8 John H. Wigmore, Evidence in Trials at Common Law § 2298 (John T. McNaughton rev. 1961) (advice concerning criminal or fraudulent transaction is not privileged).

100. *See, e.g.,* In re John Doe Corp., 675 F.2d 482, 491 (2d Cir. 1982) (communication in furtherance of ongoing crime not

privileged). *Cf.,* In re Grand Jury subpoena, 926 F.2d 847 (9th Cir. 1991). The government alleged that counsel aided in illegal export of goods to Iran, and the district court should not have examined in camera documents generated after the completion of the alleged crime. The court held that the crime-fraud exception does not cover communications about past or completed crimes where the government had not alleged an ongoing cover-up. *Id.* In the authors' opinion, the court's holding is dubious, because communications made after the completion of a crime might throw light upon whether earlier consultations with counsel were made for purposes of obtaining aid in planning the crime. *See also* Charles Wolfram, Modern Legal Ethics § 6.4 at 281 (1986) (exception applies to crimes ongoing at time of consultation).

101. *See, e.g.,* In re Grand Jury Proceedings (Appeal of FMC Corp.), 604 F.2d 798, 803–04 (3d Cir. 1979) (communications privileged if crime completed before retention of counsel; 1 McCormick, *supra* note 99, § 95 (advice concerning past crimes or misconduct privileged as opposed to advice in furtherance of a crime or fraud which is not).

leged. Hence the apparent paradox: to determine whether the privilege applies, one must breach the privilege.

The United States Supreme Court reached a typical solution to this problem in *United States v. Zolin*.[102] Briefly put, the solution was to have the district court review the allegedly privileged materials in camera to determine whether the exception applied, but only after some kind of a preliminary showing of crime or fraud.[103]

In *Zolin*, the Church of Scientology sought to prevent the IRS from obtaining access to tape recordings of meetings between Church representatives and legal counsel. The IRS argued that the tapes fell within the crime-fraud exception to the lawyer-client privilege. It urged the District Court to listen to the tapes in camera to determine whether the exception applied. In support of its position, it submitted affidavits from an undercover agent who gave reasons for believing that the tapes were relevant, and who provided a partial transcript of the contents of the tapes.[104]

The Court held that while fishing expeditions were not to be permitted, a judge could, upon a proper showing, examine allegedly privileged materials alone in chambers and determine whether the crime-fraud exception applied. The requisite showing was that of "a factual basis adequate to support a good faith belief by a reasonable person."[105] Such a showing permits, but does not require a judge to review the materials in camera. Additional factors, such as the burden of reviewing voluminous materials, and the degree of need for the evidence in the litigation, should also be considered.[106] Further, the mere making of the showing does not mean that the privilege evaporates. It only means that the judge examines the materials alone, for the purpose of making a determination whether the protection of the privilege should be stripped away.

Zolin also raised the issue of what materials could be used in making the preliminary showing. If an employee of the privileged party leaked privileged material to the opponent, or if an undercover agent acquired the material by participating in lawyer-client conferences, could that pilfered knowledge be used in making the preliminary showing? While purporting to recognize the dangers of abuse, the *Zolin* Court allowed that the showing could be made with knowledge acquired in an underhanded fashion, so long as the information had not previously been adjudged to be privileged and so long as the leaking or undercover work was not otherwise illegal.[107]

---

102. 491 U.S. 554 (1989).

103. *See id.* at 571–2.

104. *See id.* at 559.

105. *Id.* at 572 (quoting Caldwell v. District Court, 644 P.2d 26, 33 (Colo. 1982)).

106. *See id.*

107. *See id.* at 574. In United States v. Chen 99 F.3d 1495 (9th Cir. 1996), the Ninth Circuit Court of Appeals, interpreting *Zolin*, held that a past corporate employee's affidavit disclosing privileged material could not be considered in conjunction with a motion invoking the crime-fraud exception, until after the court had determined that there was a good faith basis to

§ 8.11 The Lawyer-Client Privilege—Waiver of Privilege

Like other objections, the privilege can be waived at trial simply by failure to object. There are a number of other acts that can result in waiver of the privilege:

1. Putting privileged material in issue. The privilege can be waived by putting privileged material in issue.[108] A client who claims to have believed a course of conduct to be legal, because of a lawyer's advice, waives the right to claim the privilege as to that advice.[109] This does not mean that merely because the subject matter of communications between the lawyer and client is the same as the subject matter of litigation the privilege is waived. The fact that lawyer and client discussed a contract, for example, does not mean the privilege is waived for those communications about the contract when the client later sues for its enforcement. Rather, the client must do something to put the lawyer-client confidential communications in issue in order to be deemed to have waived the privilege.[110]

2. Intentional disclosure. Testimony about, or other disclosure of privileged material, can constitute waiver. The party cannot be allowed to selectively disclose, that is, to reveal in a self-serving way part of the privileged communications, while withholding the rest. Intentional partial disclosure of a communication will result, at least, in loss of the privilege with regard to the remainder of that communication.[111] The better rule goes further: intentional partial disclosure results in loss of the privilege with regard to all communications on the same subject matter.[112]

---

believe that an in camera review would show a crime or fraud.

108. *Zolin*, 491 U.S. at 574.

109. *Miller*, 600 F.2d at 501–02.

110. *See, e.g.*, Pitney–Bowes, Inc. v. Mestre, 86 F.R.D. 444, 447 (S.D. Fla. 1980) (although party did not waive privilege by seeking arbitration in contract dispute, it did by placing intent of the parties in issue during subsequent litigation); Hearn v. Rhay, 68 F.R.D. 574, 581 (E.D. Wash. 1975) (a party waives privilege where: (1) assertion of privilege resulted from party's affirmative act; (2) party placed information in issue; and (3) application of privilege would deny opposing party information required to respond effectively).

111. *See, e.g.*, Handgards, Inc. v. Johnson & Johnson, 413 F. Supp. 926, 929 (N.D. Cal. 1976) (voluntary partial disclosure of communication waives privilege as to remainder of communication concerning same subject matter); 8 John H. Wigmore, Evidence in Trials at Common Law § 2327 (John T. McNaughton rev. 1961) (offer of testimony as to any part of communication

waives privilege as to whole communication).

112. *See, e.g.*, In re Sealed Case No 81–1717, 676 F.2d 793, 824 (D.C. Cir. 1982) (company's submission of report to the Securities and Exchange Commission concerning bribes of foreign officials, waived privilege as to any document necessary to evaluate report); Chinnici v. Central Dupage Hosp. Ass'n., 136 F.R.D. 464, 465 (N.D. Ill. 1991) (condominium association's voluntary disclosure of meeting minutes summarizing attorney's advice waived attorney-client privilege with respect to all communications on the same subject); Haymes v. Smith, 73 F.R.D. 572, 576–77 (W.D.N.Y. 1976) (client's disclosure of letter waived privilege as to all communication involving same subject matter); Scott N. Stone & Ronald S. Liebman, Testimonial Privileges § 1.57 (1983) (where client reveals privileged communication concerning an issue or raises issue, privilege waived as to communications related to that issue). *See also* United States v. Thomas, 953 F.2d 107 (4th Cir. 1991) (trial judge violated confrontation clause by excluding client and client's present attorney from in camera hearing in which former attorney

3. Disclosure by mistake. Inadvertent revelation of privileged material, such as mistakenly turning over a privileged document during discovery, can result in waiver of the privilege.[113] If, however, the privileged party has taken reasonable precautions to protect the material, in fairness the waiver should not extend beyond the particular document. This result is suggested by the growing application of the privilege to conversations overheard by an eavesdropper. At common law, when an eavesdropper overhears an otherwise privileged conversation, the eavesdropper can testify about the contents of the conversation.[114] Recent authority suggests that the privilege is not waived and the testimony will not be allowed, if the client and lawyer have taken reasonable precautions to keep the conversation confidential.[115] This is particularly true when the eavesdropper's conduct involves some degree of invasion of privacy, or is actually illegal, as in the case of an illegal wiretap. The notion that the reasonable precautions taken by the lawyer and the client should limit the waiver of the privilege when material is disclosed by mistake has not had universal acceptance. There is authority that extends the waiver of the privilege not only to the mistakenly disclosed document or conversation, but also to the general subject matter covered by the mistaken disclosure.[116]

4. Refreshing memory with a privileged document. Showing a privileged document to a witness on the witness stand, even if the witness is a client or lawyer, will waive the privilege.[117] There is some authority for finding waiver when documents have been used before trial

was examined to determine whether privilege had been waived).

113. See, e.g., 8 Wigmore, supra note 111, § 2325, at 633 (privilege waived as to any information attorney reveals in litigation because attorney acts on implied authority of client). But see Hydraflow, Inc. v. Enidine, Inc., 145 F.R.D. 626, 639 (W.D.N.Y. 1993) (inadvertent facsimile transmittal of documents for patent application did not waive privilege for documents to which the privilege applied); Resolution Trust v. Dean, 813 F. Supp. 1426 (D. Ariz. 1993) (privilege not waived by publication of internal memo in unauthorized newspaper article); Martin v. Valley Nat'l. Bank, 1992 WL 196798 (S.D.N.Y. 1992) (plaintiff did not waive attorney-client privilege with respect to five inadvertently disclosed documents, where plaintiff took reasonable measures to avoid disclosure; plaintiff's attorneys screened the 50,-000 pages of documents produced, and plaintiff requested return of inadvertently disclosed documents in timely manner); SCM Corp. v. Xerox Corp., 70 F.R.D. 508, 519 (D. Conn.1976) (client did not waive privilege by inadvertently disclosing privileged information in transfer of voluminous unscreened documents; client would have

waived privilege, however, if it had individually screened documents).

114. See, e.g., Schwartz v. Wenger, 124 N.W.2d 489, 493 (Minn. 1963) (conversation between lawyer and client overheard in the hallway of the courthouse admissible).

115. See, e.g., In re Grand Jury Proceedings Involving Berkley & Co., 466 F. Supp. 863, 869 (D. Minn. 1979) (where employee retained documents without employer's consent and disclosed them, court held in camera hearing to determine if documents were privileged; modern trend preserves privilege when lawyer and client take reasonable precautions); Stone & Liebman, supra note 112, § 1.54, (privilege applies as long as reasonable precautions taken).

116. Id. § 1.43 (unreasonable searches or seizures may warrant exclusion on Fourth Amendment grounds).

117. See, e.g., Bailey v. Meister Brau, Inc., 57 F.R.D. 11, 13 (N.D. Ill. 1972) (client waived privilege by viewing documents to refresh memory; application of privilege would place unfair burden on cross-examiner). See also Fed. R. Evid. 612 (disclosure of document used to refresh memory while testifying required).

to refresh memory,[118] though the better view is that the privilege should ordinarily prevail.[119]

5. Disclosure during negotiations. Disclosure of privileged facts during negotiations ordinarily does not waive the privilege as to related matters not disclosed. The policy of promoting settlement militates in favor of the privilege and against treating this conduct as waiver.[120] There is authority, however, to the contrary.[121] If it is necessary to reveal privileged matter during settlement negotiations, precautions, such as obtaining a confidentiality agreement from the opponent, should be taken.[122] Reliance on Rule 408, which excludes statements by a lawyer during settlement negotiations, may not be sufficient to protect all privileged material. Rule 408 does not require the exclusion of evidence otherwise discoverable, merely because the existence or nature of the evidence is revealed during compromise negotiations.[123] Pre-existing documents containing privileged information disclosed during a settlement conference, therefore, may not be protected, because the statements in them were made before, not during, the negotiations.

§ 8.12 The Lawyer-Client Privilege—Disputes Between Client and Lawyer

When a lawyer and client become involved in litigation against each other, the privilege disappears. The lawyer may reveal confidential information necessary to establish a claim or defense.[124] The lawyer may

---

118. *See, e.g.*, People v. Scott, 193 N.E.2d 814, 821–22 (Ill. 1963) (prosecution must produce documents that police officer testified he used to refresh memory before trial); 1 McCormick on Evidence § 9 (4th ed. John W. Strong ed. 1994) (witness's consultation of document before testifying should constitute waiver of privilege). *See also* Fed. R. Evid. 612 (court has discretion to require disclosure of document used to refresh memory before testifying).

119. *See, e.g.*, Jos. Schlitz Brewing Co. v. Muller & Phipps (Hawaii) Ltd., 85 F.R.D. 118, 120 (W.D. Mo. 1980) (court should give privileged documents special discretionary safeguard against disclosure under Rule 612); Stone & Liebman, *supra* note 112, § 1.49 (although court has discretion under Rule 612 to compel disclosure of privileged information, Congress intended that doubts be resolved against disclosure).

120. *See, e.g.*, Sylgab Steel & Wire Corp. v. Imoco–Gateway, 62 F.R.D. 454, 458 (N.D. Ill. 1974), *aff'd*, 534 F.2d 330 (7th Cir. 1976) (lawyer did not waive privilege by incorporating certain legal conclusions from an opinion letter to a client into letter sent to opposing party); International Business Mach. Corp. v. Sperry Rand Corp., 44 F.R.D. 10, 13 (D. Del. 1968) (disclosure during negotiations of privileged informa-

tion concerning a specific subject did not waive privilege as to all related information); Stone & Liebman, *supra* note 112, § 1.51.

121. R. J. Hereley & Son Co. v. Stotler & Co., 87 F.R.D. 358, 359 (N.D. Ill. 1980) (partial disclosure of privileged memorandum from client to lawyer at settlement meeting waived privilege as to remainder of memorandum, and opponent is entitled to discovery of remainder of memorandum).

122. Stone & Liebman, *supra* note 112, § 1.51 (lawyer should avoid reference to confidential information in negotiations and when necessary, consider requesting opposing party to sign confidentiality agreement or moving for protective order).

123. See §§ 5.45–5.51.

124. *See, e.g.*, United States v. Ballard, 779 F.2d 287, 292 (5th Cir.), *cert. denied*, 475 U.S. 1109 (1986) (lawyer-client privilege does not apply in dispute between client and lawyer over fees or improper conduct); 8 John H. Wigmore, Evidence in Trials at Common Law §§ 2312(2), 2327(6) (John T. McNaughton rev. 1961) (privilege does not apply in dispute over fees or claim of negligence; client waives privilege by claiming breach of duty by lawyer); 1 McCormick on Evidence § 91 (4th ed. John reveal client confidences, for example, when sued for malpractice,[125] or when necessary to establish the lawyer's right to be paid a fee by a recalcitrant client.[126]

This exception to the privilege, according to many courts, is not limited merely to litigation between the lawyer and client. It extends to certain other disputes involving third persons. There is authority, for example, for the position that when the client casts aspersions upon the lawyer's competence, even in a suit in which the lawyer is not a party, the lawyer may reveal confidences to defend the lawyer's reputation.[127]

§ 8.13 The Physician–Patient Privilege

The Federal Rules of Evidence do not create privileges, but rather, provide that privileges are governed by federal common law when a federal substantive rule provides the rule of decision and by state law when state substantive law provides the rule of decision.[128]

The doctor-patient privilege was not recognized at common law.[129] A doctor was considered to be under a professional obligation to be discreet, but when called as a witness could be compelled to tell all that the doctor knew. Federal courts have generally declined to recognize the doctor-patient privilege as a matter of federal common law.[130]

Most state legislatures have sought to remedy this perceived defect in the common law and have passed privilege statutes,[131] usually at the behest of interest groups representing the medical profession.[132] The

W. Strong ed. 1994) (privilege does not apply in dispute between lawyer and client or when client attacks lawyer indirectly in litigation between third persons); Scott N. Stone & Ronald S. Liebman, Testimonial Privileges § 1.66 (1983) (privilege does not apply in dispute between client and lawyer or when client attacks lawyer in separate litigation).

125. *See, e.g.*, Kracht v. Perrin, Gartland & Doyle, 268 Cal. Rptr. 637, 641 n. 6 (App. 1990) (client may not sue former lawyer for malpractice and simultaneously claim privilege to obstruct lawyer's defense); Nave v. Baird, 12 Ind. 318, 320 (Ind. 1859) (lawyer present at confidential conference could testify as to communications between client and another lawyer when client sued the other lawyer for disobeying instructions and negligence).

126. *See, e.g.*, Sokol v. Mortimer, 225 N.E.2d 496, 501 (Ill. App. 1967) (lawyer could testify as to privileged and confidential communications with the client in suit against client for fees).

127. *See, e.g.*, United States v. Weger, 709 F.2d 1151, 1156–57 (7th Cir. 1983) (in criminal prosecution against former client for making false statements to secure a loan, law firm could rebut client's implica-

tion that it was involved in producing fraudulent title opinion by giving prosecutor confidential letter from former client written on her typewriter to demonstrate that client forged title opinion on firm's letterhead); Tasby v. United States, 504 F.2d 332, 336 (8th Cir. 1974), *cert. denied*, 419 U.S. 1125 (1975) (lawyer permitted to testify when former client claimed ineffective assistance of counsel in habeas corpus proceeding, asserting that lawyer forced client to testify at trial).

128. Fed. R. Evid. 501.

129. *See* Crow v. State, 230 S.W. 148 (Tex. Crim.App. 1921); 8 John H. Wigmore, Evidence in Trials at Common Law § 2380 (John T. McNaughton rev. 1961).

130. Scott N. Stone & Ronald S. Liebman, Testimonial Privileges § 7.01 (1983). *But see* Mann v. University of Cincinnati, 824 F. Supp. 1190, 1196–98 (S.D. Ohio 1993) (recognizing existence of general physician-patient privilege under federal common law).

131. 8 Wigmore, *supra* note 129, § 2380; Stone & Liebman, *supra* note 130, § 7.01.

132. 8 Wigmore, *supra* note 129, § 2380.

statutes, however, are diverse. Some states recognize a general physician-patient privilege.[133] Others restrict the privilege to therapists.[134] Some recognize other health professionals.[135]

The strongest argument for the privilege is simply that the patient has a privacy interest that outweighs the contribution that the medical information would make to the judicial process. Sometimes a utilitarian rationale similar to that advanced for the lawyer-client privilege is advanced for the doctor-patient privilege. The theory is that potential patients would be deterred from seeking medical advice if the privilege did not exist. The self-interest in getting sound medical advice and treatment, however, would seem to outweigh the danger that the information would at some later time be used detrimentally in court.[136]

Because of the great diversity among state statutes, it is difficult to generalize about medical privileges. The following features, however, are generally present:

1. A patient is the holder of a privilege if there is a professional relationship between physician and patient, if the patient is consulting the doctor for medical treatment. Thus, when a court-appointed psychiatrist examines a patient for purposes of determining the patient's mental condition, there is no privilege because no professional relationship exists.[137] The same holds true when the opposing side has a doctor examine an adverse party.[138] When a lawyer for the patient has a doctor examine the patient, not for treatment but for an expert opinion, the better view is that the doctor-patient privilege does not apply, but that the lawyer-client privilege applies because the doctor is acting as the lawyer's representative.[139] Note, however, that in most of these circum-

133. *See, e.g.*, Mich. Comp. Laws Ann. § 600.2157 (West 1980) (physicians); *Id.* at § 333.18237 (psychologists); Tex. Civ. Code Ann. art. 4459b § 508 (Vernon Supp. 1990) (physicians); *id.* at art. 5561h (professionals involved in treatment of "any mental or emotional condition or disorder").

134. *See, e.g.*, Fla. Stat. Ann. § 90.503 (West 1979) (psychotherapists); Md. Code Ann. [Cts. & Jud. Proc.] § 9–109 (West 1989) (psychiatrists and psychologists).

135. *See, e.g.*, Minn. Stat. § 595.02 (West 1988) (physicians, psychologists, chiropractors, dentists, registered nurses, and sexual assault counselors); 42 Pa. Cons. Stat. Ann. § 5929 (1982) (physicians); *id.* at § 5944 (psychologists); *id.* at § 5945 (school personnel); *id.* at § 5945.1 (sexual assault counselors).

136. 8 Wigmore, *supra* note 129, § 2380a; Zechariah Chafee, *Privileged Communications: Is Justice Served or Obstructed by Closing the Doctor's Mouth on the Witness Stand?*, 52 Yale L.J. 607, 609–10 (1943).

137. People v. Primmer, 444 N.E.2d 829, 834 (Ill. App. 1983) (state appointed

psychiatrist's testimony is admissible over defendant's objection since state had defendant examined to prepare for defendant's possible insanity defense); State v. Jensen, 174 N.W.2d 226, 230 (Minn. 1970) (defendant could not assert privilege to block psychiatrist's testimony about defendant's mental state because psychiatrist was appointed by court to judge defendant's competency to stand trial, not to offer diagnosis and treatment).

138. Van Sickle v. McHugh, 430 N.W.2d 799, 801–2 (Mich. App. 1988) (in action for injuries in auto accident, plaintiff could not block testimony of physician employed by his no-fault insurance carrier since he lacked "reasonable expectation that the consultation [would be] cloaked with a veil of confidentiality" and examination was conducted by the insurance company which could be an adversary if plaintiff disputed his insurance award).

139. United States v. Alvarez, 519 F.2d 1036, 1046 (3d Cir. 1975) (in case where defense counsel retained psychiatrist to help prepare insanity defense, defendant's stances the privilege will be waived either by putting the patient's condition in issue or by offering the doctor's testimony.[140]

2. The privilege is not restricted to confidential communications, but covers other information acquired by the physician that is necessary to diagnosis or treatment. Even if the patient is in a coma when observed by the doctor, the facts learned by the doctor are covered by the privilege. In this respect, the doctor-patient privilege is broader than the lawyer-client privilege. In the latter case, observations of physical condition are not usually an integral part of the professional relationship, and so the latter privilege covers only confidential communications.[141] In the case of the doctor-patient relationship, the patient is entitled to have protection for information learned from examination and testing as well as information learned from patient communications.[142]

3. Statements to a physician that are not pertinent to diagnosis or treatment are not covered by the privilege. Thus, a patient's statement that the patient was wounded while trying to escape from police, or that the patient was hit by a car going through a red light, would not be covered.[143]

4. The privilege is riddled with exceptions. Some jurisdictions do not recognize it in criminal cases.[144] Others provide a more limited exception for treatment that is sought in furtherance of criminal activity, such as patching a wound incurred in escape from prison, or plastic surgery designed to change a fugitive's appearance.[145] Many states impose reporting requirements when necessary for the public health or safety. Examples include mandatory reporting of sexually transmitted disease and child abuse.[146]

The privilege is waived easily. Most jurisdictions provide that once the party voluntarily places the party's mental or physical condition in

statements to psychiatrist are privileged because doctor was an agent offering expert assistance to counsel).

140. *See* § **8.19**.

141. In situations in which something about the client's appearance, not obvious to the casual observer, is shown to the lawyer, the lawyer-client privilege probably would cover what the lawyer observes.

142. *See, e.g.,* State v. Santeyan, 664 P.2d 652, 654 (Ariz. 1983) (results of defendant's urinalysis privileged when test was made in the course of his treatment for injuries sustained in a car accident and request for treatment was made by defendant, not by a law enforcement officer).

143. State v. Sweet, 453 A.2d 1131, 1133 (Vt. 1982) (where defendant told nurse he was too drunk to sign a consent-to-treatment form, that statement was not privileged because the nurse did not need defendant's statement in order to render

treatment). *See* Stone & Liebman, *supra* note 130, § 7.12 (citations omitted).

144. *See, e.g.,* Cal. Evid. Code § 998 (West 1966) (physician-patient privilege does not apply in criminal trials); 42 Pa. Cons. Stat. § 5929 (1982) (privilege exists only in civil cases).

145. People v. Traylor, 377 N.W.2d 371, 373 (Mich. App. 1985) (physician-patient privilege does not apply in case where physician testified in defendant's armed robbery trial about defendant's gunshot wound because Mich. Comp. Law § 750.411 requires that any wound inflicted by a deadly weapon be reported to the local authorities).

146. *See, e.g.,* Cal. Penal Code § 11171(b) (West 1982) (imposes affirmative duty to report all suspected cases of child abuse on both physicians and psychotherapists; statute explicitly provides exception to physician-patient and psychotherapist-patient privileges).

controversy, the privilege is waived.[147] A party who brings a personal injury action, for example, has waived the privilege with regard to information relevant to evaluating the injury.[148] The privilege may also be waived in the same fashion as the lawyer-client privilege—for example, by selective disclosure,[149] or by calling the doctor to testify.[150]

§ 8.14   The Psychotherapist–Patient Privilege

The therapist-patient privilege is supported by stronger policy justifications than the doctor-patient privilege, which explains why some states and the federal courts have accepted only the former. The therapist is more likely to be the recipient of damaging, embarrassing and personal information than is the ordinary physician. Also, the deterrence hypothesis is stronger; some patients might not go to the therapist at all if there was a danger that their communications would become public.[151]

The Supreme Court of the United States, settling a split in the circuits, interpreted the principles of the common law "in the light of reason and experience"[152] in *Jaffee v. Redmond*[153] and established the federal therapist-patient privilege. The "reason" was the need for the privilege to encourage effective therapy. The "experience" was that of the fifty states, each of which have a therapist-patient privilege of some kind.

The Court determined that the therapist-patient privilege would serve a "public good transcending the normally predominant principle of utilizing all rational means for ascertaining truth."[154] It followed the lead of many states in expanding the privilege to cover licensed social workers, observing that "drawing a distinction between the counseling provided by costly psychotherapists and the counseling provided by more readily accessible social workers serves no discernible public purpose."[155] Though it accepted most of the lower court's decision, the Court disagreed with the judgment that a balancing test to nullify the privilege in certain circumstances would be appropriate. In deciding not to allow a trial judge to determine that the need for testimony might be greater in a particular case than a patient's interest in privacy, the Court observed

---

147. Leslie v. Brames, 682 F. Supp. 608 (D. Me. 1988) (where plaintiff claimed he suffered head and back injuries in accident with defendant; that plaintiff put his physical condition in issue, thus waiving the physician-patient privilege).

148. *See, e.g.*, Minn. R. Civ. P. 35.03.

149. *See, e.g.*, Jones v. Superior Court for County of Alameda, 174 Cal. Rptr. 148, 155 (App. 1981) (because plaintiff's mother testified she ingested DES, plaintiff's mother waived physician-patient privilege regarding that subject).

150. People v. Newbury, 290 N.E.2d 592, 596 (Ill. 1972) (defendant who voluntarily consults psychiatrist and offers psychiatrist's testimony waives the psy-

chiatrist-patient privilege); Matthews v. Commonwealth, 709 S.W.2d 414 (Ky. 1985) (psychiatrist-patient privilege was not violated in case where defendant had psychiatrist testify he acted under extreme emotional disturbance and prosecution cross-examined psychiatrist on same subject but asked more detailed questions about defendant's communications with him).

151. Scott N. Stone & Ronald S. Liebman, Testimonial Privileges § 7.02 (1983).

152. Fed. R. Evid. 501.

153. 518 U.S. 1 (1996).

154. *Id.* at 1931.

155. *Id.* at 1932.

that such a balancing test would "eviscerate the effectiveness of the privilege."[156]

The Court did not detail the scope and operation of the privilege. It cited the Supreme Court Standard that had been originally submitted to Congress as Rule 504,[157] suggesting that the privilege as there detailed might be influential in determining the nature of the privilege as it is drawn by future decision. The standard applied to psychotherapists engaged in diagnosis or therapy,[158] took account of the need for confidentiality in situations where third parties, such as family members or group therapy members, are present,[159] and was expanded to include treating a drug addiction.[160] It contained an exception for court ordered examinations, limited to the purpose of the examination,[161] and did not apply when the patient relied upon the condition as part of a claim or defense.[162] The Standard did not address issues of confidentiality for the name of the patient and permissible disclosure in the event of a dispute between therapist and patient. Although courts may be tempted to look at the lawyer-client privilege for guidance on these issues, disclosure of the identity of a person in therapy and the nature of communications during therapy may have more important privacy implications for the therapist's patients than for the lawyer's clients.

§ 8.15 The Marital Privileges

There are two spousal privileges. The first is the privilege against adverse spousal testimony. Designed to protect the peace and harmony of an existing marriage,[163] when successfully claimed, it prevents the spouse from taking the witness stand. Because exercise of the adverse spousal privilege renders the spouse incompetent to be a witness, it applies to all subject matter, not merely confidences and communications.[164] A wife, for example, could invoke the privilege to avoid testifying about her husband's reckless driving while she was a passenger. This would be so even though the driving is done for anyone to see and even if the marital partners said nothing to each other while the husband was driving. The second is the privilege for marital confidences. It applies only to confidences shared by marital partners.[165] It is often described as

---

156. *Id.*

157. *Id.* at 1927.

158. Fed. R. Evid. 504(a)(2) (Proposed draft 1972).

159. Fed. R. Evid. 504(a)(3) (Proposed draft 1972).

160. *See* 42 U.S.C. § 290ee–3 (confidentiality of drug abuse program patient records).

161. Fed. R. Evid. 504(d)(2) (Proposed draft 1972).

162. Fed. R. Evid. 504(d)(3) (Proposed draft 1972).

163. United States v. Byrd, 750 F.2d 585, 590 (7th Cir. 1984) (privilege against adverse spousal testimony protects the marriage from the impact of negative testimony); In re Grand Jury Subpoena Koecher, 601 F. Supp. 385, 391 (S.D.N.Y. 1984) (the goal of privilege is "prevention of dissension between spouses which might result from testimony of one against the other").

164. *See* § 8.16.

165. United States v. Hamilton, 19 F.3d 350, 354 (7th Cir. 1994) (defendant's wife had not been divorced from previous husband, therefore no valid marriage and no privilege for marital confidences).

a privilege for confidential communications,[166] though some jurisdictions have extended it to acts that are performed in confidence before the spouse.[167]

Although the spousal privileges are not codified in the Federal Rules of Evidence, they have been recognized in the federal system.[168] Many states have passed statutes governing spousal privilege,[169] though some have created the privilege through case law.

§ 8.16 The Marital Privileges—The Privilege Against Adverse Spousal Testimony

The marriage that ends in divorce or death needs no further protection. Similarly, when one spouse is ready and willing to testify against the other, the marriage is already in ruins and the adverse testimony will do little to damage it more. For that reason, the Supreme Court held in *Trammel v. United States*[170] that it is the witness spouse, not the party spouse, who holds the privilege. If the witness spouse chooses not to testify, the opponent cannot force the testimony. But if the witness spouse wishes to testify against the party spouse, then the party spouse cannot prevent it. Of course, it is possible that the witness spouse is willing to testify, not because the "peace and harmony" of the marriage has been destroyed, but because the government has threatened to prosecute the witness spouse on the underlying crime if the privilege is claimed. Government pressure, not the deterioration of the marriage, may well have been the situation in *Trammel*, but the possibility did not seem to bother the Supreme Court. Evidently the court valued the testimony higher than what might be left of the marriage.

Not all states have followed the *Trammel* doctrine. Some make the party spouse the holder of the privilege.[171] Although some states allow the privilege in both civil and criminal cases,[172] in many jurisdictions it is limited to criminal cases.[173]

The adverse spousal testimony privilege protects the marriage against outsiders who seek to force testimony, but does not apply when the spouses are adversaries, such as a divorce action or an action in which one spouse is accused of a crime against the other.[174] It also does

---

166. *See, e.g.,* 8 John H. Wigmore, Evidence in Trials at Common Law §§ 2332–2341 (John T. McNaughton rev. 1961); 1 McCormick on Evidence §§ 78–86 (4th ed. John W. Strong ed. 1994).

167. *See* § 8.17.

168. *See* §§ 8.16, 8.17.

169. *See, e.g.,* Conn. Gen. Stat. § 4–84a (West 1985); Minn. Stat. § 595.02(1)(a) (1985); N.C. Gen. Stat. § 8–57 (1986).

170. 445 U.S. 40 (1980).

171. *See, e.g.,* Ariz. Rev. Stat. Ann. § 13–4062(1) (1989) (criminal); *id.* § 12–2231 (1982) (civil); Minn. Stat.

§ 595.02(1)(a) (1988); Mont. Code Ann. § 26–1–802 (1989).

172. *See, e.g.,* Alaska R. Evid. (505)(a)(1) (1989); Minn. Stat. § 595.02(1)(a) (1988); Mont. Code Ann. § 26–1–802 (1989).

173. *See, e.g.,* Conn. Gen. Stat. §§ 54–84a (West 1985); N.C. Gen. Stat. §§ 8–57 (1986); Or. Rev. Stat. § 40–255(3) (1988).

174. Brown v. Commonwealth, 292 S.E.2d 319, 323 (Va. 1982) (husband shot his wife and her grandmother and trial court severed cases for trial; wife may testify against defendant-husband in both trials); Hudson v. Commonwealth, 292 S.E.2d not apply in cases involving an alleged crime by one spouse against the children.[175] At least one state has created an exception for homicide cases in which the marriage occurs after the crime. When the crime is homicide the societal interest in hearing the testimony outweighs the benefits of preserving the harmony of a new marriage that may have been consummated just to establish the privilege.[176]

As with other privileges, the adverse spousal testimony privilege can be waived. If a spouse testifies in favor of the other, or if the party spouse uses an out-of-court statement of the other as affirmative evidence, the privilege is waived, at least as to adverse testimony on the same subject matter.[177]

The adverse spousal privilege, though it is broader in subject matter coverage than the privilege for marital confidences, does not have the staying power of the marital communications privilege. Because the adverse spousal testimony privilege is based on the notion that the "peace and harmony" of the marriage should not be endangered by forcing one spouse to testify against another, the privilege does not survive the marriage.[178]

§ 8.17   The Marital Privileges—The Privilege for Marital Confidences

The privilege for marital confidences is rooted in the natural repugnance against the state's invasion of marital privacy. Although some jurists have suggested that the marital confidences privilege exists to encourage spouses to share confidences in the fashion of the lawyer-

317, 319 (Va. 1982) (spouse may testify against defendant husband regardless of whether the offense is committed against the spouse's person or her property).

175. United States v. Allery, 526 F.2d 1362, 1367 (8th Cir. 1975) (privilege does not apply when spouse commits crime against child of either spouse, in case where wife testified against husband accused of attempting to rape their daughter).

176. Minn. Stat. § 595.02(a) (1988). For a similar result in a case not involving homicide, see United States v. Blair; 54 F.3d 639, 644–45 (10th Cir.), cert. denied, 516 U.S. 883 (1995) (not only did "sham" marriage not immunize defendant's wife from testifying against defendant regarding his involvement in illegal wagering, but it also resulted in a two-point sentence enhancement for obstruction of justice).

177. Donovan v. State 584 P.2d 708, 710 (Nev. 1978) (prosecution's use of wife's prior statement to impeach her testimony not improper since defendant-husband waived right to assert privilege by calling wife as witness). Cf., State v. Walker, 403 A.2d 1, 4 (N.J. 1979) (defendant who testi-

fied he was with his wife at the time of the victim's rape, and wife was present during his testimony, "conveyed the impression" she supported the truth of his testimony; defendant thus made wife a "crucial" witness, and proper for prosecution to comment on defendant's failure to have his wife testify).

178. United States v. Bolzer, 556 F.2d 948, 951 (9th Cir. 1977) (testimony of defendant's ex-wife admissible because the privilege does not continue after marriage is legally ended). See also In re Witness Before Grand Jury, 791 F.2d 234, 238 (2d Cir. 1986) (woman unable to assert privilege because she had not lived with husband for eleven years and her husband lived with another woman); United States v. Snyder, 707 F.2d 139, 147 (5th Cir. 1983) (privilege can not be asserted when woman lived with defendant, but was not married to him); United States v. Cameron, 556 F.2d 752 (5th Cir. 1977) (policy reasons for privilege are "non-existent" when the couple's marriage is "moribund" with no chance for a possible reconciliation despite the fact the couple was still legally married; therefore, the privilege can not be asserted).

client privilege,[179] it seems doubtful that the existence of the privilege has much effect on marital intimacy, even in today's climate of ubiquitous law. Because it is limited in scope to communications during the marriage, but not limited in time to the existence of the marriage, the privilege for marital confidences is more complex than the privilege against adverse spousal testimony.

The privilege for marital confidences differs from jurisdiction to jurisdiction, but generally has the following features:

(1) The privilege is applicable only to confidences that were shared during the marriage. Confidential communications made after divorce are not covered. If the husband and wife are married but living separately, the applicability of the privilege is in doubt.[180] There is at least one case, however, extending the privilege to communications between separated spouses during an attempted reconciliation.[181]

(2) The privilege for confidences shared during the course of the marriage continues after the termination of the marriage.[182] This result may be based on the notion that the policy of the privilege is to encourage confidential communications during the marriage relationship, and allowing divorce to pierce the veil might conceivably discourage spouses from reposing confidences.[183] The former spouse has no legal obligation, however, to refrain from broadcasting marital confidences, so it is doubtful that the ordinary person takes the remote possibility of potential courtroom testimony into account in deciding whether to repose confidences in a spouse. The idea that the privilege survives marriage for pre-dissolution statements seems, nonetheless, to be well established.[184]

(3) In many jurisdictions, the privilege protects only confidences.[185] Express requests for secrecy, however, are uncommon in most marriages

179. *See, e.g.,* 8 John H. Wigmore, Evidence in Trials at Common Law § 2332 (John T. McNaughton rev. 1961); Scott N. Stone & Ronald S. Liebman, Testimonial Privileges § 5.09 (1983).

180. United States v. Porter, 986 F.2d 1014 (6th Cir. 1993) (privilege does not apply to statements made by one spouse to the other after the spouses have permanently separated; whether permanent separation had occurred prior to statement is to be determined by district court); United States v. Jackson, 939 F.2d 625, 627 (8th Cir. 1991) (not error to admit defendant's statement to wife made while the couple was permanently separated without any semblance of a marital relationship, even though the couple was not divorced; not protected by marital communication privilege); United States v. Fulk, 816 F.2d 1202 (7th Cir. 1987) (defendant could not assert communication privilege when communication was made at time when defendant-husband and wife were permanently separated); In re Witness Before Grand Jury,

791 F.2d 234, 239 (2d Cir. 1986) (spouse could not claim marital communication privilege because she had lived apart from defendant-husband for four years when alleged communication occurred); Hazelwood v. State, 609 N.E.2d 10, 14–16 (Ind. App. 1993) (privilege does not extend to engaged couple weeks before their marriage). *See also* 8 Wigmore, *supra* note 179, § 2335.

181. People v. Oyola, 160 N.E.2d 494, 498, (N.Y. App. Div. 1959).

182. *See* 8 Wigmore, *supra* note 179, § 2341 (citations omitted).

183. *See id.* at § 2341.

184. *See, e.g.,* Cal. Evid. Code § 980 (West 1966); Mich. Comp. Laws Ann. § 600.2162 (West 1986); Minn. Stat. § 595.02(a) (1988); N.J. Stat. §§ Ann. § 2A:84A–22 (West 1976).

185. Cal. Evid. Code § 980 (West 1966); Fla. Stat. Ann. § 90.504 (West 1979). *See also* 8 Wigmore, *supra* note 179, § 2336.

and in many jurisdictions, marital communications are presumed to be confidential until the contrary appears.[186] The confidentiality requirement means that the presence of a third person during a communication between marital partners will destroy the privilege, as will the intention of the marital partner making the communication that it be relayed to a third person.[187] In jurisdictions that do not recognize a parent-child privilege, the presence of a child during the communication destroys confidentiality.[188]

(4) Although the privilege in most jurisdictions is limited to communications, some jurisdictions have extended it to testimony about conduct performed under circumstances suggesting reliance on the confidential nature of the marital relationship.[189] The act of hiding something in the presence of one's spouse, therefore, might be covered by the privilege for marital confidences in some jurisdictions.[190] One can argue in favor of this extension, on grounds that the security that the privilege is supposed to foster applies to conduct as well as words. The extension does not, however, cover all acts observed by the spouse. If a spouse sees the other start a fight on the subway, the privilege does not apply because there is nothing confidential about the fighter's public conduct.

(5) The spouse reposing the confidence is the holder of the privilege in many jurisdictions, on the theory that it is that spouse's communication or act that the privilege is designed to encourage.[191] The witness spouse, therefore, cannot testify to confidences reposed during the marriage, even if the witness spouse is eager to testify.[192] The wife who confides in her husband that she has committed a crime, therefore, is able to invoke the privilege successfully, even if her husband wants to testify against her. Some jurisdictions require the consent of both spouses to waive the marital communications privilege.[193]

---

186. *See, e.g.,* Cal. Evid. Code § 917 (West 1966); 8 Wigmore, *supra* note 179, § 2336.

187. United States v. Pensinger, 549 F.2d 1150, 1152 (8th Cir. 1977) (communication privilege did not apply because husband's conversation with wife about details of his bank robbery in the presence of two other people destroyed the confidential nature of the communication); Resnover v. State, 372 N.E.2d 457, 459 (Ind. 1978) (information in husband's letter to wife was intended to be given to third parties and thus could not be protected by communication privilege).

188. People v. Sanders, 457 N.E.2d 1241, 1244 (Ill.1983) ("presence of children of spouses destroys confidentiality unless they are too young to understand what is being said").

189. Arnold v. State, 353 So.2d 524, 527 (Ala. 1977)(defendant-husband's act of driving by burned building with his wife is privileged communication because it was

"performed with the confidence of the marriage in mind"); Commonwealth v. Byrd, 689 S.W.2d 618, 621 (Ky. App. 1985) (witness-spouse may not testify she saw her defendant-husband examine the contents of a stolen purse because husband did so in the marital home and would not have done so if they had not been married); Commonwealth v. Clark, 500 A.2d 440, 443 (Pa. Super. 1985) (defendant-husband could claim communication privilege in second degree murder case where wife witnessed husband washing and disposing the murder weapon).

190. 8 Wigmore, *supra* note 179, § 2337.

191. *See, e.g.,* Kan. Stat. Ann. § 60–428 (1983); 8 Wigmore, *supra* note 179, § 2340.

192. United States v. Neal, 532 F.Supp. 942, 947 (D. Colo. 1982), 8 Wigmore, *supra* note 179 § 2340.

193. *See e.g.,* Neb. Rev. Stat. § 27–505 (1984)

(6) If the holder of the privilege calls his or her spouse to testify about marital confidences, the privilege has been waived as to the subject matter.[194] In this respect, the privilege for marital confidences resembles the broader privilege against adverse spousal testimony. The privilege also can be waived by voluntary disclosure to a third person, as for example in a letter.[195] In this respect, the privilege for marital confidences is different than the privilege against adverse spousal testimony. The marital confidences privilege is based upon the confidentiality of the communication, so once the confidence is breached, there is no purpose to the marital confidences privilege.[196] The adverse spousal testimony privilege, however, is based upon the peace and harmony of the marriage, so even if the communication has been disclosed to another, there is reason to maintain the adverse spousal testimony privilege to avoid causing a rift in the marriage by the spouse's testimony.

(7) Accidental disclosure to persons outside the marriage can result in a waiver of the privilege. As in the case of the lawyer-client privilege, eavesdroppers, so long as they overhear legally, can testify to matters covered by the marital confidences privilege.[197] The same result occurs when a holder spouse accidentally discloses a writing, such as by losing a

194. However, the fact that a party calls the party's spouse to the witness stand does not mean that the opponent can cross-examine the spouse about prior invocations of the privilege. *See* United States v. Morris, 988 F.2d 1335, 1339–40 (4th Cir. 1993) (reversible error for prosecutor to cross-examine defendant's wife and secretary of more than 20 years about her prior invocation of marital privilege during the grand jury investigation preceding trial). *See also* United States v. Hall, 989 F.2d 711, 715–16 (4th Cir. 1993) (reversible error for prosecutor during cross-examination of defendant to read from text of inculpatory statements made by defendant's wife when wife had invoked privilege after having made statements); Stone & Liebman, *supra* note 179, § 5.14.

195. *See, e.g.,* State v. Johnson, 643 P.2d 146, 152 (Kan. 1982) (common-law wife's daughter could testify about conversation she had with her mother that defendant-husband had shown his wife over $900 in cash because husband had shown both the testifying daughter and another daughter the money as well, in case where defendant-husband was on trial for first degree murder and aggravated robbery). *See also* Kan. Stat. Ann. § 60–437 (1983).

196. For a case that stretches the concept of waiver to the breaking point, see United States v. Smith, 33 M.J. 114, 117–18 (C.M.A. 1991). The majority of the court held that a wife waived the privilege for

marital confidences with regard to a letter she wrote to her husband. In the letter, she urged him to testify that he had forced her to commit the crime with which she was currently charged, and to give other exculpatory testimony. *Id.* The court held that she waived the privilege by testifying at trial to conversations with the husband in which he placed her in fear. *Id.* She did not testify about the letter, but the court said that all the communications could properly be considered as one. *Id.* Hence the holding suggests that revealing one communication with a spouse waives any objection to other communications at different times that touch on the same general subject matter. The court avoided basing its decision on the theory that the letter was an invitation to commit perjury, apparently on grounds that it was doubtful that the Military Rules of Evidence contained a crime-fraud exception to the marital confidences privilege. *See also* 8 Wigmore, *supra* note 179, § 2340 .

197. *See* State v. Summerlin, 675 P.2d 686, 695 (Ariz. 1983) (defendant-husband was told he could not have a private meeting with his wife, that defendant-husband could not claim communication privilege because prison guard in room could possibly overhear the conversation); Sumlin v. State, 617 S.W.2d 372, 376 (Ark. 1981)(defendant-husband could not claim communication privilege because inmate overheard husband's conversation with his wife).

letter.[198] Bad faith disclosure by a turncoat spouse, however, does not destroy the privilege. If a husband gossips about his wife's secrets, for example, the privilege stops the recipient of the gossip from testifying against the wife, even if the court can find a way around the hearsay problem.[199] Of course, if it had been the wife, herself, who had disclosed her secret conversations with her husband, she would be precluded from objecting to the testimony.[200]

(8) The exceptions to the privilege for marital confidences are similar to the exceptions that apply to the privilege against adverse spousal testimony. The privilege, generally, does not apply in suits between husband and wife, including marriage dissolution, custody battles,[201] criminal charges of assault on the spouse,[202] crimes against a child of either spouse, or other matters involving the child, as where the state seeks to terminate parental rights.[203] In addition, a fraud exception to the application of the privilege has been recognized.[204]

§ 8.18　The Privilege Against Self-incrimination

The source of the privilege is the Fifth Amendment to the United States Constitution. It provides, in part, that "No person shall be ... compelled in any criminal case to be a witness against himself...." In 1964, the Supreme Court held that the Fifth Amendment was incorporated by the due process clause of the Fourteenth Amendment and therefore was applicable to states.[205] The protection of the Fifth Amendment is supplemented by various state constitutional provisions that are sometimes interpreted more broadly than the Fifth Amendment.[206]

It is impossible to state a simple and satisfying rationale for the privilege. The privilege seems to have evolved as a reaction to the religious and political persecutions in England prior to the Restoration,[207] particularly the practice of examining suspects under oath to determine whether they held forbidden beliefs. When applied to crimes other than crimes of conscience, Bentham's charge that the privilege benefits only

---

198. 8 Wigmore, *supra* note 179, § 2339.

199. United States v. Neal, 532 F. Supp. 942, 947 (D. Colo. 1982) (neither FBI agent or defendant's wife could testify about content of phone conversation between defendant and his wife because wife allowed FBI agent to monitored the call and defendant did not know call was monitored and expected his call to be confidential) *See also* 8 Wigmore, *supra* note 179, § 2339.

200. *See* State v. Johnson, 643 P.2d 146 (Kan. 1982).

201. Ariz. Rev. Stat. Ann. § 12–2232 (1982); Cal. Evid. Code § 984 (West 1966); Minn. Stat. § 595.02(a) (1988).

202. Cal. Evid. Code § 985 (West 1966); Minn. Stat. § 595.02 (1988).

203. *Id.*

204. *See* In re Donald Sheldon & Co, 191 B.R. 39, 48 (Bankr. S.D.N.Y. 1996) (privilege will not immunize spouse from disclosing marital communications where there was an effort to conceal assets from creditors; New York courts do not recognize the marital privilege when asserted to protect efforts to perpetrate fraud on third-party victims).

205. Malloy v. Hogan, 378 U.S. 1, 11 (1964).

206. *See, e.g.,* People v. Disbrow, 545 P.2d 272 (Cal. 1976); State v. Santiago, 492 P.2d 657 (Haw. 1971); Hansen v. Owens, 619 P.2d 315 (Utah 1980).

207. 8 John H. Wigmore, Evidence in Trials at Common Law § 2250 (John T. McNaughton rev. 1961).

the guilty because the innocent will be eager to explain is hard to meet,[208] at least as it relates to gaining the "right" result in an individual case. The values it may have for the definition of a society and the importance of the individual may be a different matter.

Wigmore lists no fewer than a dozen policies that have been advanced in support of the privilege.[209] Perhaps the strongest are that the privilege serves as a prophylaxis against unreasonable interrogation methods, and that it is inherently inhumane to confront an individual with the trilemma of committing perjury, being held in contempt, or serving as the prosecution's witness.[210]

The privilege against self-incrimination is a personal privilege. It cannot be claimed on behalf of or used to protect another person, however unselfish one's motives may be.[211]

The privilege can be claimed only when there is a danger of incrimination, not merely of humiliation or degradation. It is not necessary, however, to show that prosecution is probable so long as some danger of incrimination exists.[212]

The privilege allows the witness to refuse to answer questions, if the answers would directly incriminate the witness. But it goes much further. It covers questions, the answers to which might provide an investigative lead for prosecution of the witness. For example, a witness is entitled to refuse to say whether the witness is acquainted with a certain person, if the information might provide the government with a lead.[213]

The privilege applies only to "testimonial" incrimination. So long as the government does not require a suspect to engage in communicative conduct that conveys factual assertions or information,[214] it can compel the suspect to commit acts that aid an investigation, even if those acts help incriminate the suspect. An investigative target may be compelled, for example, to sign a form permitting the government to examine foreign bank records,[215] to furnish handwriting and voice

---

208. Jeremy Bentham, Rationale of Judicial Evidence (1827), (cited in 8 Wigmore, *supra* note 207, § 2251).

209. 8 Wigmore, *supra* note 207, § 2251.

210. *Id.* at § 2251. *See also* Murphy v. Waterfront Comm., 378 U.S. 52, 54 (1964):

> [The privilege] reflects many of our fundamental values and most noble aspirations: our unwillingness to subject those suspected of crime to the cruel trilemma of self-accusation, perjury or contempt; our preference for an accusatorial rather than an inquisitorial system of criminal justice; our fear that self-incriminating statements will be elicited by inhumane treatment and abuses; our sense of fair play which dictates a fair state-individual balance by requiring the government to leave the individual alone until good

cause is shown for disturbing him and by requiring the government in its contest with the individual to shoulder the entire load.

211. Rogers v. United States, 340 U.S. 367 (1951).

212. Hoffman v. United States, 341 U.S. 479 (1951).

213. *See id.* at 486 (witness may refuse to state whether he knows an alleged criminal and where the alleged criminal is located if answers to those questions would "furnish a link in the chain of evidence needed to prosecute the claimant for a federal crime").

214. *See* Doe v. United States, 487 U.S. 201, 212 (1988).

215. *Id.* at 218.

exemplars,[216] to appear in a lineup,[217] or to give a blood sample.[218]

The privilege belongs only to human beings. A corporation or other organization cannot claim the benefit of the privilege.[219]

Although the Court, not the witness, decides whether the privilege applies,[220] a witness' assertion that an answer raises a danger of incrimination will usually stand up. The Supreme Court has indicated that the claim of privilege should be sustained unless it is "perfectly clear, from a careful consideration of all the circumstances in the case, that the witness is mistaken, and that the answer cannot possibly have [a] tendency to incriminate."[221] This statement appears to place the burden on the government to show that the answers could not possibly incriminate.

The privilege protects against incrimination, so a grant of immunity will abrogate the privilege, even if the answers may cause the witness embarrassment or disgrace. Early precedent suggested that the immunity had to be transactional, that is, the immunity had to protect the witness against prosecution for the entire transaction about which testimony was being compelled. It is now clear, however, that use immunity, prohibiting the compelled testimony to be used against the witness, is constitutionally sufficient.[222] If the government decides to prosecute the witness, the government has the burden of showing that the compelled testimony did not provide an investigatory lead helpful to the prosecution.[223]

The witness may also lose the right to invoke the privilege because the danger of incrimination has been removed through acquittal or conviction of the underlying charge. The constitutional prohibition against double jeopardy prevents a subsequent prosecution, so there is no longer any danger of incrimination. If, however, the questioning about the adjudicated crime could lead to prosecution for other crimes, the privilege may still be invoked.[224]

The accused in a criminal case has a right not only to refuse to answer self-incriminating questions, but also to refuse to take the witness stand at all. Moreover, the prosecution may not allude to the defendant's failure to testify,[225] nor may it suggest in closing argument

---

216. United States v. Dionisio, 410 U.S. 1, 7 (1973); Gilbert v. California, 388 U.S. 263, 266–7 (1967).

217. United States v. Wade, 388 U.S. 218, 221–2 (1967).

218. Schmerber v. California, 384 U.S. 757, 765 (1966).

219. Bellis v. United States, 417 U.S. 85, 101 (1974); Hale v. Henkel, 201 U.S. 43, 75 (1906).

220. Rogers v. United States, 340 U.S. 367 (1951).

221. Hoffman v. United States, 341 U.S. 479, 488 (1951).

222. Kastigar v. United States, 406 U.S. 441 (1972).

223. *Id.* at 460 ("This burden of proof ... imposes on the prosecution the affirmative duty to prove that the evidence it proposes to use is derived from a legitimate source wholly independent of the compelled testimony").

224. Malloy v. Hogan, 378 U.S. 1, 13 (1964).

225. Griffin v. California, 380 U.S. 609 (1965).

that the prosecution's evidence was uncontradicted, if the argument provides any implication that the defendant could have been the witness to provide the contradiction.[226] When a witness in a criminal case, other than the defendant, is likely to claim the privilege, especially if that witness is identified with the defendant, it is appropriate to make a motion in limine to prohibit the government from calling the witness. The jury may be confused or prejudiced against the defense by the spectacle of the witness who claims the privilege, and may not know how to interpret this conduct.[227]

Even though the privilege is against self-incrimination that could lead to criminal liability, witnesses in civil cases may exercise the privilege to refuse to answer on grounds of self-incrimination. They must, however, take the stand and claim the privilege. In civil cases, it is proper for the opposing party to ask the jury to draw an adverse inference from the witness' claim of the privilege.[228] If the person claiming the privilege is a litigant and not merely a witness, other adverse consequences may occur, including in some jurisdictions the dismissal of a plaintiff's case for withholding information.[229]

A witness may waive the right against self-incrimination. A witness who has testified about part of a transaction cannot claim the right to self-incrimination when cross-examined about the remainder.[230] Testimony on a question of preliminary fact, however, such as testimony on a motion to suppress evidence resulting from an allegedly illegal search, does not waive a criminal defendant's right to assert the privilege.[231]

The right against self-incrimination applies to certain interrogations conducted by law enforcement officers before trial. In the celebrated case

226. *Compare* Lent v. Wells, 861 F.2d 972 (6th Cir. 1988) (where defendant was the only one who could contradict), *with* Lindgren v. Lane, 925 F.2d 198 (7th Cir. 1991) (prosecutor argued that government witness was not contradicted because defense witness testifying on the same point was not believable).

227. *See, e.g.,* Namet v. United States, 373 U.S. 179 (1963) ("Error may be based upon a concept of prosecutorial misconduct, when the Government makes a conscious and flagrant attempt to build its case out of inferences arising from [the witness'] use of the testimonial privilege"); Foster v. State, 687 S.W.2d 829, 832 (Ark. 1985) (reversible error for prosecution to call wife of the deceased—whom the prosecution knew would invoke her privilege against self-incrimination—in defendant's murder trial because "there was an attempt by the prosecutor to build the state's case out of inferences arising from [the witness'] assertion of her fifth amendment privilege"). *See also* Commonwealth v. Brown, 619 S.W.2d 699, 703 (Ky. 1981) (prosecution could not call witnesses to stand because prosecution

knew the witnesses would claim the fifth amendment privilege).

228. Brinks Inc. v. City of New York, 717 F.2d 700, 710 (2d Cir. 1983). *See also* Robert Heidt, *The Conjurer's Circle—The Fifth Amendment Privilege in Civil Cases,* 91 Yale L. J. 1062, 1107–8 (1982).

229. Lyons v. Johnson, 415 F.2d 540, 542 (9th Cir. 1969), *cert. denied,* 397 U.S. 1027 (1970) (plaintiff's suit was properly dismissed because plaintiff refused to answer interrogatories, despite fact plaintiff refused on fifth amendment grounds); Penn Communications Specialties, Inc. v. Hess, 65 F.R.D. 510, 512 (E.D. Pa. 1975) (plaintiff's suit can be dismissed unless plaintiff answers defendant's interrogatories, despite fact plaintiff refused on fifth amendment grounds); Master v. Savannah Surety Associates, Inc., 252 S.E.2d 186, 187 (Ga. App. 1979) (dismissing suit).

230. Rogers v. United States, 340 U.S. 367, 372 (1951); United States v. Hearst, 563 F.2d 1331, 1341 (9th Cir. 1977).

231. Simmons v. United States, 390 U.S. 377, 394 (1968).

of *Miranda v. Arizona*, the Supreme Court ruled that statements made during custodial interrogation could not be used at trial, unless the person in custody had been given what have become known as the "Miranda warnings." The interrogation must be preceded by a warning that the suspect had a right to remain silent, that any statement made could be used in evidence, and that the suspect had a right to counsel, either retained or appointed.[232] If the warnings are not given of if the suspect does not waive the rights, any statement obtained through custodial interrogation is inadmissible. Such a statement may, however, be used to impeach a defendant who testifies.[233]

Silence, too, may be used to impeach a criminal defendant, even though the Constitution seems to guarantee the right of silence to a criminal defendant. A defendant who remains silent after receiving "Miranda warnings" and then testifies to an alibi or some other explanation may not be impeached with the previous silence in response to police interrogation. In *Doyle v. Ohio*, the Supreme Court recognized that the silence was likely to be in response to the *Miranda* warning's reminder of the right to remain silent.[234] A defendant who testifies during trial and who did not tell law enforcement about the gist of the testimony before trial may, however, be impeached by the silence, under certain circumstances. In *Jenkins v. Anderson*,[235] the government was allowed to impeach the defendant's testimony in pursuit of his self-defense claim by asking the defendant why he had initially remained silent about the homicide, not reporting it for two weeks. The defendant in *Fletcher v. Weir*,[236] who was arrested, not given the proper *Miranda* warnings, exercised his right to remain silent while in police custody, and exercised his right to testify at trial that the killing was in self-defense was impeached by his silence after arrest. The impeachment, which after *Doyle* would not have been allowed had the police officers followed the proper procedure and given the defendant *Miranda* warnings, was allowed precisely because the officers had not followed the proper procedure. The Court's reasoning–that the lack of a warning avoided the risk that the silence might be a response to the warning's caution–might have been better logic than law. Ignoring the purpose and the spirit of *Miranda,* the *Weir* decision provides an incentive for police officers to forgo *Miranda* warnings after arrest as a way to ensure that a confused defendant cannot offer exculpatory testimony at trial.

§ 8.19   The Government's Privileges

Military and state secrets are protected from compelled disclosure.[237] The privilege covers information that might harm the national defense

---

232.   384 U.S. 436, 467–73 (1966).

233.   Harris v. New York, 401 U.S. 222, 226 (1971) (defendant's statement to authorities that was given without defendant having received a proper Miranda warning was admissible to impeach defendant's testimony even though the statement was inadmissible in prosecution's case in chief).

234.   426 U.S. 610 (1976).

235.   447 U.S. 231 (1980).

236.   455 U.S. 603 (1982).

237.   *See, e.g.,* United States v. Reynolds, 345 U.S. 1, 6–7 (1953) (Air Force accident report containing secret information or international relations of the United States if disclosed. The trial judge may make a limited in camera review to determine whether the privilege applies.[238] If the privilege applies, it is absolute and cannot be overcome by a showing of necessity.[239]

In *United States v. Nixon*[240] the Supreme Court recognized an "executive privilege" for presidential communications made in confidence.[241] Unless military or state secrets are involved, however, the privilege is not absolute. It may be overcome by a showing of specific need for information that will be key evidence in a criminal trial.[242]

There are a variety of other privileges for governmental information. Often the privileges are governed by statute and protect information that individuals or corporations are required to provide to the government.[243] They cover matters ranging from grand jury proceedings[244] to census information.[245]

The informer's privilege is often asserted in criminal cases. It allows the government not to disclose the identities of informers, who for obvious reasons would rather not be known to those whom they have incriminated.[246] Where the identity of the informer is helpful to the defendant's case or is essential to a fair trial, the informer's identity must be revealed, or the case dismissed.[247] If, however, the informer was merely a supplier of probable cause to arrest or search, then the informer's identity need not be revealed.[248]

§ 8.20 Other Privileges

Priest-penitent. A privilege for confidential communications between parishioners and clergy is widely recognized.[249] Though early versions of the privilege applied only to communications required by the discipline for the religion[250]–confessions made by Roman Catholics, for

---

that could not be disclosed without harming national security, privileged).

238. *Id.* at 9–10.

239. *Id.* at 10–11.

240. 418 U.S. 683 (1974).

241. *Id.* at 705–06.

242. *Id.* at 706–07.

243. *See* Scott N. Stone & Ronald S. Liebman, Testimonial Privileges § 9.23 (1983) (such privileges are collectively known as required reports or official information privileges).

244. *See, e.g.,* Fed. R. Crim. P. 6(e) (general rule imposing secrecy of grand jury proceedings).

245. *See, e.g.,* 13 U.S.C. §§ 8(b), 9(a) (1988) (access to and disclosure of census information limited to insure confidentiality).

246. *See, e.g.,* Roviaro v. United States, 353 U.S. 53, 59 (1957) (government not

required to disclose communication that would reveal identity of person providing information concerning violation of law).

247. *See, e.g., id.* at 60–61 (identity of informer who witnessed crime not privileged because testimony might have been crucial to defense).

248. *See, e.g.,* McCray v. Illinois, 386 U.S. 300, 312 (1967) (identity of informant who told police defendant was dealing drugs, pointed defendant out to police, and then left, privileged).

249. Scott N. Stone & Ronald S. Liebman, Testimonial Privileges §§ 6.02, 6.04, (1983) (privilege recognized by statute in nearly every state and recognized in federal courts as application of Fed. R. Evid. 501).

250. *See, e.g.,* People v. Gates, 13 Wend. 311, 323 (N.Y. Sup. Ct. 1835) (admission not pursuant to church discipline not privileged); 8 John H. Wigmore, Evidence in Trials at Common Law § 2395 (John T.

example–modern versions tend to include other communications made for spiritual guidance, comfort, or advice.[251]

Journalists. A privilege for journalists and other news gatherers has achieved recognition in several jurisdictions.[252] The United States Supreme Court has considered and rejected the argument that the First Amendment requires acceptance of a general privilege for journalists.[253] Some federal courts, nevertheless, recognize a qualified First Amendment journalists' privilege.[254]

The journalist's privilege is quite different from all of the other privileges insofar as it is not aimed at keeping communications confidential. On the contrary, the whole idea is that it will facilitate communication of information that might not otherwise be available. The privilege generally protects a reporter from being required to reveal the identity of a confidential source of information.[255] In some jurisdictions, it covers unpublished notes and materials prepared by the news gatherer. The statutory privileges are not absolute, and generally yield by application of some sort of balancing test. A statute might provide, for example, that the privilege must yield when there is a compelling reason for disclosure and no alternative means of getting the information.[256] Even where a statutory privilege purports to be absolute, an accused person's constitutional right to obtain witnesses may require that the privilege be pierced when the reporter seeks to conceal information crucial to the defense.[257] *In re Farber* grew out of a homicide prosecution of a physician for a death in a New Jersey hospital. Farber, a reporter for the New York Times, had been deeply involved in investigative reporting about the case, and may have been the driving force behind the prosecution. The trial judge held a hearing on the application of the privilege. At the hearing, the defendant showed that the main accuser had talked to Farber five times; that there was evidence suggesting that Farber might be in possession of a prior inconsistent statement of a witness; that another important witness, interviewed by Farber, would not talk to the defense; and that another witness interviewed by Farber had died.[258] The

McNaughton rev. 1961) (privilege applies to communications made in pursuance to church discipline).

251. *See,* *e.g.,* Minn. Stat. § 595.02(1)(c) (1988) (privilege includes clergy's communications to "any person seeking religious or spiritual advice, aid, or comfort").

252. Stone & Liebman, *supra* note 249, § 8.08 (privilege recognized by statute in 26 states as of 1983).

253. Branzburg v. Hayes, 408 U.S. 665, 690 (1972).

254. *Id.*

255. *See, e.g.,* Ill. Comp. Stat. Ann. ch. 110 para. 8–901–09 (West 1990) (reporter generally cannot be compelled to disclose source of any information); Minn. Stat. §§ 595.021–595.024 (1988) (forced disclo-

sure of confidential sources generally prohibited); N.J. Stat. Ann. §§ 2A:84A–21 (West Supp. 1990) (reporter has privilege to refuse to disclose source of information).

256. *See, e.g.,* Ill. Stat. Comp. Ann. ch. 110 para. 8–907 (West Supp. 1990) (exception to basic privilege); Minn. Stat. § 595.024(2) (1988).

257. *See* In re Farber v. Jascalevich, 394 A.2d 330, 337 (N.J.), *cert. denied sub nom,* New York Times Co. v. New Jersey, 439 U.S. 997 (1978) (criminal defendant's right under New Jersey constitutional to compel attendance of witness and production of documents prevails over facially absolute language of statute).

258. *Id.* at 340.

New Jersey Supreme Court upheld a criminal contempt conviction imposed upon Farber for refusing to turn over his materials for in camera inspection by the trial court.[259]

Parent-child. A few jurisdictions recognize a parent-child privilege.[260] This privilege allows a parent to refuse to reveal confidential communications from a child. It is subject to exceptions analogous to those applicable to the marital privileges. Communications involving crimes against the family, for example, are not covered.[261]

Accountant-client. A few states recognize an accountant-client privilege,[262] but there is no such privilege under Federal law.[263] In *United States v. Arthur Young & Co.*[264] the Supreme Court faced the issue whether an IRS subpoena for tax accrual work papers prepared by the corporation's independent CPA could be discovered pursuant to an IRS summons. The papers, prepared for a mandatory SEC filing, contained an evaluation of possible tax liability of the corporation, based on information including "opinions, speculations, and projections of management with regard to unclear, aggressive, or questionable tax positions that may have been taken on prior tax returns."[265] Despite the sensitive nature of the information, the Supreme Court held that it was not protected either by privilege or by the work product doctrine.[266]

---

259. *Id.* at 341.

260. *See, e.g.,* Minn. Stat. § 595.02(1)(i) (1988) (communications made in confidence by minor to minor's parent privileged); People v. Fitzgerald, 422 N.Y.S.2d 309, 312, 317 (N.Y. 1979) (parent-child privilege flows directly from United States and New York Constitutions; adult child's confidential communication with parent concerning hit and run accident privileged in criminal prosecution);.

261. *See, e.g.,* Minn. Stat. § 595.02(1)(i) (1988) (communications involving crimes against family members not privileged).

262. *See, e.g.,* Ill. Comp. Stat. Ann. ch. 111 para. 5533 (West 1990) (confidential communications with accountant privileged); Tex. Rev. Civ. Stat. Ann. art. 41a–1 (West 1982–83) (confidential communications with licensed accountant privileged).

263. *See, e.g.,* Couch v. United States, 409 U.S. 322, 335 (1973) (tax records in possession of her accountant not privileged).

264. 465 U.S. 805 (1984).

265. *Id.* at 812.

266. *Id.* at 817–18.

Chapter 9

IMPEACHMENT AND
REHABILITATION
OF WITNESSES

Analysis

---

§ 9.01 Impeaching One's Own Witness; Objection to Calling Witness Solely to Impeach with Prior Inconsistent Statement [FRE 607]

A scholar or jurist who refers to the "common law rule" on a given subject is always engaging in a degree of simplification, even fictionalization. The common law of evidence was a growing, changing, fractious, and often contradictory body of precedents. Yet it is often useful to try to extract the common law attitude toward a topic even at the risk of oversimplification. If nothing else, it provides a useful background that helps explain the motives and goals of later codifiers who decided to depart from what they saw as the common law position. With those caveats, we will briefly sketch the broad outlines of the common law position on impeaching one's own witness, and then describe the Federal Rules position.

425

The common law rule prohibited impeaching one's own witness.[1] The prohibition applied whatever the method of impeachment—whether by character attack, showing of bias, impeachment by prior inconsistent statements, or by any other method.[2] In the case of impeachment by prior inconsistent statement, however, the common law developed a dispensing exception to aid the attorney whose witness has suddenly turned unfavorable. The exception had two requirements. First, the turncoat witness' testimony had to be actually harmful and not merely neutral.[3] In other words, it was not enough for the turncoat merely to testify "I don't know" or "I don't recall"; the witness' testimony had to be affirmatively harmful to allow impeachment. Second, the attorney had to be surprised by the witness' harmful testimony.[4] When the attorney knew beforehand that the witness was going to testify detrimentally, the attorney was supposed simply not to call the witness, rather than putting the witness on the stand and then impeaching the witness.

The historical roots and policy basis for the common law rule forbidding impeachment of one's own witness are unclear.[5] Wigmore thought the rule probably arose from an ancient form of trial known as "compurgation" in which a party's "witnesses" were called not for their personal knowledge of the facts of the case (in fact, they likely had no such knowledge), but rather for their belief in the party's truthfulness and general good character. Under such a system, it would be illogical to impeach one's own "oath-helper." Instead, the party was thought to "vouch" for the credibility of the witnesses the party called.[6] Another

1. In re San Miguel Gold Mining Co, 197 F. 126, 127 (W.D.Pa.1912) (party who called witness to institute bankruptcy proceeding vouched for the witness' credibility by putting him on the stand; therefore, he may not impeach his testimony); In re Calvi, 185 F. 642, 652 (N.D.N.Y.1911) ("when a party calls a witness, he represents him as worthy of credit, and cannot impeach him in any way"); 3A John H. Wigmore, Evidence in Trials at Common Law § 896 (James H. Chadbourn rev. 1970).

2. See 3A Wigmore, supra note 1 §§ 896–99.

3. Mitchell v. Swift & Co., 151 F.2d 770, 772 (5th Cir.1945) (plaintiff may not introduce ex parte statement of witness called by him solely because witness' testimony was not favorable to plaintiff's case); Arine v. United States, 10 F.2d 778, 780 (9th Cir.1926) (impeachment attempts by prosecutor improper in case where testimony is not harmful, but immaterial). See, e.g., State v. Perez, 594 N.E.2d 1041, 1045–46 (Ohio App. 1991) (trial court committed reversible error by declaring state's witness hostile and allowing impeachment by leading questions about prior inconsistent statement; Ohio R. Evid. R 607 allows impeach-

ment of own witness only on showing of "surprise and affirmative damage"; these elements are not shown in case at bar).

4. Bedell v. United States, 68 F.2d 776, 777 (D.C.Cir.1934) (prosecutor may impeach witness with prior written statement because he was genuinely surprised by witness' testimony, but prior statement may only be used for impeachment, not substantive purposes); Sullivan v. United States, 28 F.2d 147, 149 (9th Cir.1928) (held, in case where three convicts had signed a Joint statement implicating defendant, that failure of first witness to testify he saw defendant at robbery gave "fair warning" to government that other two convicts would very likely not testify against defendant; therefore government could not impeach latter two witnesses because it could not claim it was surprised by their statements).

5. See 27 Charles A. Wright & Victor J. Gold, Federal Practice and Procedure (Evidence) § 6092, at 489 (1990) ("The origins of the voucher rule are obscure").

6. Wigmore wrote that the voucher rule may have been based on "[t]he primitive notion, that a party is morally bound by the statements of his witnesses." 3A Wigmore, supra note 1 § 899.

prominent commentator believed this "voucher" rule probably did not arise from trial by compurgation, but rather was a consequence of the transition from inquisitorial to adversary systems of trial. Because under the inquisitorial system jurors decided the case based on their personal knowledge of the facts, there was simply no opportunity to call witnesses on one's own behalf. The author wrote, "Until there were witnesses in the modern sense, there could be no reason for the idea that a party was bound by his witness or that he could not impeach him."[7] The rationale that one vouches for one's witnesses ceased to have a sensible basis centuries ago, at least for occurrence witnesses as opposed to character and expert witnesses.[8] The common law litigant of modern times has had to take occurrence witnesses where they could be found, and had no control over the character and credibility of those who happened to have personal knowledge.

Another justification sometimes offered for the anti-impeachment rule is that allowing impeachment of one's own witness gave the proponent an opportunity for blackmail, because the proponent could put the witness on the stand under the threat of revealing dark secrets about the witness' past if the witness did not testify favorably to the proponent.[9] That might in a few cases be true, but it would pose an actual danger only in cases in which the proponent had character-smearing evidence that was not available to the opponent, because otherwise the witness would be subject to attack from either side. In any event, the theory does not explain why the anti-impeachment rule applied across the board, and not merely to prevent impeachment of a witness with evidence of the witness' bad character. Finally, the anti-impeachment rule may have served to prevent a proponent from calling an unfavorable witness solely for purposes of putting into evidence a prior inconsistent statement, in hopes that the jury would disregard instructions not to use the statement for the truth of what it asserts. This danger is real and worthy of consideration,[10] but it does not justify a broad rule prohibiting any impeachment of one's own witness.

Rule 607 of the Federal Rules of Evidence provides, "The credibility of a witness may be attacked by any party, including the party calling the witness." These seventeen words abolish the hoary and troublesome common law rule. Primarily, abolition of the rule helps to secure the important goal of accurate factfinding by increasing the admissibility of

---

7. Mason Ladd, *Impeachment of One's Own Witness—New Developments*, 4 U. Chi. L. Rev. 69, 72 (1936). For discussion of the Wigmore and Ladd views, see Don Johnsen, Note, *Impeachment With an Unsworn Prior Inconsistent Statement as Subterfuge*, 28 Wm. & Mary L. Rev. 295, 296 n.1 (1987).

8. Wigmore wrote that the "traditional notion of a witness, that of a person 'ex officio' a partisan pure and simple, persisted as a tradition long past the time when their function had ceased to be that of a

mere oath-taker and had become that of a testifier to facts." 3A Wigmore, *supra* note 1 § 896.

9. *See, e.g., id.* § 899.

10. *See, e.g.,* 1 Michael H. Graham, Handbook of Federal Evidence § 609.3, at 680–81 (4th ed. 1996); Randolph N. Jonakait, *The Supreme Court, Plain Meaning and the Changed Rules of Evidence*, 68 Tex. L. Rev. 745 (1990).

relevant evidence, in this case, evidence concerning a witness' credibility.[11]

The new rule has caused little difficulty except in cases involving allegations that the proponent has called a witness *solely* to impeach the witness with evidence that is admissible only to impeach. The problem that sometimes arises may be illustrated by the following hypothetical. Suppose a prosecutor wishes to put witness W on the stand to testify that he had been at D's house on January 19 and that D had shown W $100,000 in currency. W gave a police investigator a written statement about seeing the $100,000. Subsequently W recanted and now maintains that although present at D's house on the day in question, D did not show any currency. Suppose the prosecutor knows to a certainty that the witness will testify that nothing happened at D's house—even that the defense counsel conducted a voir dire of the witness at this very trial and the witness testified that nothing happened at D's house. Nevertheless, the prosecutor seeks to put W on the stand before the jury. The prosecutor's aim is to have W testify that he saw no currency at D's house and to impeach W with W's prior statement to the investigator.

The prior statement to the investigator is not admissible for the truth of the matter asserted.[12] However, under a literal reading of Rule 607, one could argue that the prosecutor is permitted to impeach the prosecutor's own witness and that, when used only to impeach, the statement is not being offered to prove the truth of what it asserts.

What the prosecutor hopes, of course, is that the jury will disregard the instruction not to use the statement to prove the truth of what it asserts and that the jury will use the statement for exactly that purpose. Otherwise, there would be no reason to call the witness. The witness has no testimony that helps the prosecution, and merely showing an unhelpful witness to be a liar proves nothing.

Although most cases involving the improper calling of a witness solely to impeach with otherwise inadmissible evidence involve prior inconsistent statements, not all arise in that context. In *United States v. Gomez–Gallardo*,[13] for example, defendant was charged with conspiracy to distribute cocaine. The government called as a witness one Gutierrez, who had previously pleaded guilty to participation in the conspiracy. Gutierrez testified that he had participated in one cocaine deal with another individual and that he knew defendant but had never participated in any drug transactions with him. He also testified that defendant was at the home of another alleged drug dealer, but only for innocent purposes. The government then called three witnesses to impeach Gutierrez by contradiction and by showing that he had a bad character. These witnesses contradicted Gutierrez by, among other things, describ-

---

11. *See* 27 Wright & Gold, *supra* note 5 § 6092.

12. Had the statement been made under oath in a grand jury or other proceeding, it would have been admissible for the truth of what it asserts under Fed. R. Evid. 801(d)(2)(A). This statement, however, is admissible, if at all, only because it is not offered for the truth of what it asserts within the meaning of Fed. R. Evid. 801(c).

13. 915 F.2d 553 (9th Cir.1990).

ing other drug and illegal weapons transactions in which Gutierrez had participated, none of which involved defendant. In its closing argument, the government argued that there was no doubt of Gutierrez's guilt, and urged the jury to reject his testimony. The jury then found defendant guilty. On appeal, the court reversed. None of the contradiction evidence was properly admissible as substantive evidence of defendant's guilt, and the evidence suggesting Gutierrez's bad character was only admissible to impeach Gutierrez. Thus, the court held that "the government called Gutierrez for the primary purpose of impeaching Gutierrez's credibility to prove the substance of the charges against Gallardo."[14] This was impermissible.

In these types of situations, a number of courts have prevented the prosecutor from impeaching the prosecutor's own witness.[15] To hold otherwise is to invite parties to call witnesses and offer evidence solely in hopes that the witnesses will disregard limiting instructions and use the evidence for an improper purpose.[16]

§ 9.02   Methods of Impeachment—In General

A witness may be impeached in many different ways.[17] Among them are by a showing of bias or interest, by an attack on character for truthfulness, by contradiction through another witness, by a showing that the witness made a prior inconsistent statement, by showing defects in the witness' perception or ability to observe, or by showing a mental disease or defect of the witness.[18] Trial judges have leeway to regulate

14. *Id.* at 556.

15. United States v. Hogan, 763 F.2d 697, 702 (5th Cir.1985) ("prosecution . . . may not call a witness it knows to be hostile for the primary purpose of eliciting otherwise inadmissible impeachment testimony, for such a scheme merely serves as a subterfuge to avoid the hearsay rule"); United States v. Crouch, 731 F.2d 621, 624 (9th Cir.1984) (improper for prosecution to call witness to testify in order to get her previous statement into evidence under the guise of impeachment, but not reversible error because defendant's guilt clearly demonstrated by admissible evidence). *Compare* United States v. Johnson, 977 F.2d 1360, 1381–82 (10th Cir.1992), *cert. denied*, 506 U.S. 1070 (1993) (trial court may allow prosecutor to question federal marshal about prior, inconsistent statements made by government witness when prosecutor expected witness to testify that defendant fired on law enforcement officials with an automatic weapon, but witness testified he saw and recalled no weapons).

16. United States v. Pollard, 38 M.J. 41, 50 (C.M.A. 1993) (held, trial court committed reversible error by allowing trial counsel to read, under guise of impeach-

ment, the pretrial statements of 13–year-old alleged, sexual assault victim despite her subsequent recantation of those statements); Whitehurst v. Wright, 592 F.2d 834, 840 (5th Cir.1979) (proper for court to exclude use of witness' prior inconsistent statement for impeachment purposes when plaintiff knew witness would deny the facts asserted in previous statement during his testimony, because use of impeachment merely a ploy to "use hearsay evidence for substantive purposes").

17. The authors of one treatise suggest five principal bases for attacking a witness' credibility: showing that the witness has made prior inconsistent statements, demonstrating the witness' bad character for truthfulness, showing that the witness is biased, contradicting the witness' testimony concerning a fact, and demonstrating the witness' impaired capacity to perceive, recall, or narrate facts. 27 Charles A. Wright & Victor J. Gold, Federal Practice and Procedure (Evidence) § 6094 (1990).

18. The credibility of a witness may also be attacked in other ways, such as by demonstrating the implausibility of the witness' story and by observing the demeanor of the witness while testifying. For a useful cross-examination on these subjects, and many allow fairly free-ranging cross-examination.[19] But when the impeacher is not satisfied with cross-examination of the witness being impeached, but wants also to bring in extrinsic evidence—evidence from a source other than the witness under attack—then the common law barred "collateral" evidence for certain categories of impeachment. It is to this set of rules about collateral evidence that we now turn.

In determining the propriety of offering any evidence to impeach a witness, it is crucial to identify not only that the evidence tends to impeach, but the precise *way or ways* by which it does so—the impeaching tools. This is because rules limiting certain forms of impeachment do not apply to all other forms. Thus, evidence that might be inadmissible if offered to impeach by one means might be admissible if offered to impeach on a different basis.

§ 9.03   Good Faith Cross–Examination of Witnesses

Trial courts have authority to prevent or curtail any impeachment or cross-examination that risks exposing the jury to potentially prejudicial innuendo. In particular, counsel conducting cross-examination is not permitted to conduct any inquiry in the absence of a good faith basis for the factual validity of any matters raised by the questions.[20] Though the application of this rule is highly situation-dependent, there are some guidelines. Counsel need not know the answer to every question before it is asked, nor need counsel demonstrate to the court a factual basis for every question asked of a witness. Courts have suggested that it is sufficient for counsel to possess a "well reasoned suspicion that a circumstance is true,"[21] that "although counsel may explore certain areas of inquiry in a criminal trial without full knowledge of the answer to anticipated questions, [counsel] must, when confronted with a demand for an offer of proof, provide some good faith basis for questioning

list of factors affecting the credibility of a witness, see Cal. Evid. Code § 780 (West 1966). These additional ways of attacking credibility are typically not subject to special evidentiary rules.

19. United States v. Phelps, 733 F.2d 1464, 1472 (11th Cir.1984) (trial court has discretion about scope and extent of cross-examination, and "presumption favors free ranging cross-examination on possible bias, motive, ability to perceive and remember, and general character for truthfulness").

20. *See* United States v. Sampol, 636 F.2d 621, 658 (D.C.Cir.1980) ("It is true, of course, that defense counsel need not proffer a factual foundation for all questions asked on cross-examination. A well reasoned suspicion that a circumstance is true is sufficient.... On the other hand, counsel must have a reasonable basis for asking questions on cross-examination which tend to incriminate or degrade the witness and thereby create an unfounded bias which subsequent testimony cannot fully dispel.... The general rule in such situations is that" the questioner must be in possession of some facts which support a genuine belief that the witness committed the offense or the degrading act to which the questioning relates." Citing United States v. Fowler, 465 F.2d 664, 666 (D.C.Cir. 1972).) *See also* United States v. Katsougrakis, 715 F.2d 769, 778–79 (2d Cir.1983) ("Although counsel may explore certain areas of inquiry in a criminal trial without full knowledge of the answer to anticipated questions, he must, when confronted with a demand for an offer of proof, provide some good faith basis for questioning that alleges adverse facts").

21. United States v. Sampol, 636 F.2d 621, 658 (D.C.Cir.1980).

that alleges adverse facts,"[22] and that when counsel will inquire about the witness' criminal or otherwise bad conduct, " 'the questioner must be in possession of some facts which support a genuine belief that the witness committed the offense or the degrading act to which the questioning relates.' "[23] Although these standards have special application in criminal cases (particularly in the government's cross-examination of defendant or defendant's witnesses), they also apply in civil cases. If it would be improper for the government to ask a criminal defendant's witness whether the witness was having an affair with the defendant in the absence of a good faith belief that the fact is true, it would be equally improper to ask the question of a party's witness in a civil case.

While the court must exercise control over improper cross-examination, the Supreme Court has made clear that trial courts must permit the parties to conduct probing cross-examination:

> Cross-examination is the principal means by which the believability of a witness and the truth of his testimony are tested. Subject always to the broad discretion of a trial judge to preclude repetitive and unduly harassing interrogation, the cross-examiner is not only permitted to delve into the witness' story to test the witness' perceptions and memory, but the cross-examiner has traditionally been allowed to impeach, i.e., discredit, the witness.[24]

The balance is therefore a delicate one. While courts may and indeed should curtail fishing expeditions that consume too much time and raise too great a danger of unfair prejudice, courts must also allow sufficient leeway for probing cross-examination of adverse or reluctant witnesses. The balance must be struck on a case-by-case basis, with the general standards as a guide.

§ 9.04   Impeachment by Contradiction

Impeachment by contradiction simply refers to impeachment by means of introducing contradictory testimony.[25] If witness X testifies that the light was red, and witness Y testifies that it was green, then witness X has been impeached by contradiction. This type of impeachment is to be distinguished from impeachment by prior inconsistent statement (self-contradiction). In one the witness is being attacked by contrary evidence about the underlying facts, in another by the witness' own prior inconsistent statement.

It has often been stated that a witness may not be impeached with collateral evidence that contradicts the witness through "extrinsic" evidence. An example of this type of forbidden impeachment is the

---

22. United States v. Katsougrakis, 715 F.2d 769, 779 (2d Cir.1983).

23. United States v. Lin, 101 F.3d 760, 768 (D.C.Cir.1996).

24. Davis v. Alaska, 415 U.S. 308, 315 (1974).

25. See 27 Charles A. Wright & Victor J. Gold, Federal Practice and Procedure (Evidence) § 6096, at 537 (1990) ("The credibility of a witness is attacked by contradiction when evidence is introduced suggesting that a fact to which the witness testified is not true").

evidence offered in *State v Oswalt*.[26] In *Oswalt*, the defendant was accused of robbing a house in Seattle. An alibi witness for the defendant testified that the defendant had been at the witness' restaurant in Portland on the day in question. On cross-examination, the witness also ventured that the defendant had been in the restaurant in Portland every day for a period of two months before the robbery. The prosecution then offered in evidence the testimony of a police officer that he had seen the defendant in Seattle on a date about a month before the robbery. One theory of admissibility was that this testimony impeached the alibi witness by contradiction. The alibi witness had testified that the defendant had been in a restaurant in Portland on that day; the police witness indirectly contradicted this testimony because it was unlikely that the defendant would be in the restaurant in Portland and also be in Seattle on the same day. The court held that the evidence should have been excluded at trial. In doing so, it endorsed an often-stated test: the contradicting evidence is inadmissible if it is "collateral." The court stated that the test for determining whether evidence is collateral is, "Could the fact, as to which error is predicated, have been shown in evidence for any purpose independently of the contradiction?"[27] Because the officer's testimony was only relevant to impeach the alibi witness by contradicting the witness' testimony about the defendant's whereabouts a month before the robbery, the evidence was collateral. And because the evidence was offered other than during cross-examination of the defendant's alibi witness, it was "extrinsic" evidence and thus inadmissible.[28]

Examples

A witness shown by other evidence to have observed the accident in question testifies to seeing the accident while on the way home. Actually, the witness was on the way to a poker game. Extrinsic evidence that the witness lied when testifying to being on the way home is not admissible. The evidence has no relevance to the case except that of impeaching the witness by contradiction.

A witness for the plaintiff testifies to not having met the plaintiff before the litigation. Actually, the witness was involved in a business deal with the plaintiff. Extrinsic evidence of the prior relationship is admissible, because it not only impeaches the witness by contradiction; it also is relevant to the bias or interest of the witness. The

---

26. 381 P.2d 617 (Wash.1963).

27. *Id.* at 619, quoting 3A John H. Wigmore, Evidence in Trials at Common Law § 1003 (James H. Chadbourn rev. 1970). This standard suggests a relevancy basis for determining whether evidence is "collateral." The principal is probably more complicated, however. *See* 27 Wright & Gold, *supra* note 25 § 6096, at 541–45 (suggesting that the Wigmore test is underinclusive, encompassing only two of three types of non-collateral evidence that commentators have identified).

28. Of course, the trial judge retains the power to exclude the impeaching evidence even if offered during cross-examination. If, for example, the judge finds that the evidence is of infinitesimal probative value for impeachment purposes, and the time required to offer the evidence (even on cross-examination) would not justify its presentation, the judge may exclude it on Rule 403 grounds.

business relationship between the plaintiff and the witness may bias the witness in the plaintiff's favor.

A witness for the plaintiff testifies to having been on the way home from a school meeting at the time of the accident. In fact, the witness had been drinking in a bar all night long. Extrinsic evidence of the drinking is admissible because it is relevant to the witness' perception, not merely to contradiction of the witness' testimony.

The second and third illustrations demonstrate why it is important to identify not only whether evidence is offered to impeach the witness, but the precise *means* by which it does so. In the second example, the testimony tends to impeach both by contradiction and by showing bias. Because bias impeachment is not limited in the same way as impeachment by contradiction,[29] the party is permitted to call the witness to offer the impeaching evidence. The same is true in the third illustration. While the evidence does tend to impeach by contradiction, it also impeaches by showing the possibility of impaired perception, a form of impeachment that is not limited by the collateral issue-extrinsic evidence rule.

The principal purpose of the rule prohibiting extrinsic evidence to impeach when the evidence concerns a collateral matter is to prevent confusion and waste of time.[30] It is wasteful to receive testimony on both sides about the collateral issue of whether the witness was going home or to a poker game, when the only relevance of the evidence would be on the question whether the witness gave inaccurate testimony about a matter irrelevant to the lawsuit. Showing an instance of an irrelevant matter has some probative value in demonstrating that a person is wrong about one fact and thus might be wrong about other, relevant facts, but it is not probative enough to justify the consumption of time with proof and counter-proof. The rule prohibiting extrinsic evidence of collateral matter is also supported by the danger that the jury may misuse the evidence when it involves information prejudicial to the witness or the party who called the witness.[31] This danger is particularly great when the witness is a party.

There is a question whether the rule against collateral impeachment has survived the adoption of the Federal Rules of Evidence, which make no explicit mention of the rule. The only provision of the Federal Rules that appears in any way related is Rule 608, but that rule on its face governs only impeachment of a witness by "character and conduct," not by contradicting the witness' testimony. Therefore, although Rule 608 does resemble the common law contradiction rules in that it contains limitations on the use of extrinsic evidence, it would be a mistake to

---

29. *See* § **9.10.**

30. *See* 27 Wright & Gold, *supra* note 25 § 6096, at 539 ("When the fact contradicted is not material, the trier of fact may become confused by the attention directed at an unimportant fact. As a result, the trier of fact may attach undue importance to extraneous matters").

31. *See id.*

assume without careful analysis that the subject of impeachment by contradiction is governed by that rule.

Some courts in Federal Rules jurisdictions have continued to follow the common-law collateral impeachment rule.[32] However, most other courts have held that the common-law rule is not embodied in Rule 608.[33] In addition, influential commentators[34] have maintained that a more flexible test should be used and that Federal Rule of Evidence 403 replaces the old rule.[35] The balancing test of Rule 403 makes no mention of any rule against collateral impeachment, nor do any of the other rules in the Federal Rules of Evidence. However, the traditional exclusion of collateral impeachment can be reconciled with the Federal Rules. The traditional rule can be regarded as just a rule of thumb that carries out the purposes of Rule 403 and is consistent with it. In other words, for ease of administration, one can argue that collateral evidence ought to be considered a waste of time, rather than inquiring in each case whether it is a waste of time. Exclusionary rules need not always be specifically stated in the Rules of Evidence so long as they are consistent with the general rules.[36]

32. *See, e.g.*, United States v. Payne, 102 F.3d 289, 294 (7th Cir.1996) (evidence relevant only to impeach a witness' statement on cross-examination that his girlfriend did not know of his criminal activity inadmissible; collateral issue rule invoked); United States v. Edwards, 696 F.2d 1277, 1281 (11th Cir.), *cert. denied*, 461 U.S. 909 (1983) (extrinsic evidence that government witness was a drug dealer inadmissible to impeach by contradiction); United States v. Terebecki, 692 F.2d 1345, 1351 (11th Cir. 1982) ("Since the statement did not concern a major issue in the case, impeachment would have been on a collateral issue and was properly excluded").

33. *See, e.g.*, United States v. Whiting, 28 F.3d 1296, 1301 (1st Cir.), *cert. denied*, 513 U.S. 956 (1994) (Rule 608(b) does not exclude evidence offered for non-character purpose); United States v. Fleming, 19 F.3d 1325, 1331 (10th Cir.), *cert. denied*, 513 U.S. 826 (1994) (Rule 608(b) inapplicable when extrinsic evidence offered to show statement made by defendant on direct examination is untrue, even if statement concerns collateral issue); United States v. Chu, 5 F.3d 1244, 1249 (9th Cir.), *cert. denied*, 511 U.S. 1035 (1994) (Rule 608(b) does not address whether extrinsic evidence is admissible to impeach by contradiction); Boutros v. Canton Regional Transit Authority, 997 F.2d 198, 205 (6th Cir.1993) (Rule 608(b) ban on extrinsic evidence not applicable to use of such evidence to contradict witness as to a material issue); Bufford v. Rowan Companies, Inc., 994 F.2d 155, 159–60 (5th Cir.1993) (Rule 608(b) does not bar extrinsic evidence offered to contradict wit-

ness' testimony concerning material issue); United States v. Tarantino, 846 F.2d 1384, 1409 (D.C.Cir.), *cert. denied*, 488 U.S. 840 (1988) (Rule 608(b) inapplicable to impeachment by contradiction).

34. *See* 4 Weinstein's Federal Evidence § 609.06[3] (2d ed. Joseph L. McLaughlin ed. 1997).

35. *But see* 28 Charles A. Wright & Victor J. Gold, Federal Practice & Procedure (Evidence) § 6119 (1993). The authors recognize that the great weight of authority suggests that Rule 608 applies only to character impeachment evidence, and that this result is supported by the language of the rule, the Advisory Committee's Note, and United States v. Abel, 469 U.S. 45, 55–56 (1984), which held that the Rule 608(b) prohibition on extrinsic evidence does not apply to extrinsic evidence of bias. However, they note that impeachment by character and impeachment by contradiction are often "logically entwined," and that if a witness questioned about alleged misconduct probative of untruthfulness denies the misconduct, extrinsic evidence of the misconduct should not be admitted. The authors' reasoning is that if extrinsic evidence were admitted in this situation, Rule 608(b) would never keep the extrinsic evidence from the jury unless the witness admits the misconduct on cross-examination. This would defeat the purpose of Rule 608(b). *Id.* at 114.

36. *See* § 6.07. For example, rules against using hypnotically refreshed testimony have been endorsed in several juris-

§ 9.05 Impeachment by Prior Inconsistent Statement [FRE 613]

Witnesses are often impeached by showing that they made statements out of court that are inconsistent with their trial testimony. Showing that the witness said different things at different times throws doubt on credibility, whether the prior statements are believed or not.[37] Inconsistency as to one fact casts a shadow over the witness' reliability as to other facts.[38] Perhaps because of the popularity of this method of impeachment, a collage of rules have grown up around it. This section will deal with some of the common objections to attempts to impeach witnesses with prior inconsistent statements.

Objection—Prior Statement Is Consistent With Trial Testimony

Sometimes an objection to impeachment is based on the idea that what the witness said out of court is consistent with what the witness has asserted in the courtroom testimony. Suppose, for example, that the witness testifies in court that the witness has forgotten an event. A prior statement by the witness describes the event. Arguably, the two statements are consistent with each other. It is possible that the witness remembered the event soon after it occurred, but has now forgotten it.

In dealing with this sort of objection, the purpose of impeachment must be kept in mind. The cross-examiner is trying to throw doubt on credibility. The ultimate question is whether the prior statement actually throws light on the witness' believability. In this instance, it throws enough light to justify receiving it. It is true that the witness might have remembered before and forgotten now. It is also possible that the witness now remembers, and is not telling the truth. Which of these inferences is the correct one is a question for the jury to resolve. The test

dictions, despite the lack of any specific provision against it. *See, e.g.*, State ex rel Collins v. Superior Court, County of Maricopa, 644 P.2d 1266, 1294 (Ariz.1982) (hypnotically refreshed testimony is inadmissible, but witness may testify about facts recalled before hypnosis); People v. Gonzales, 329 N.W.2d 743, 748 (Mich.1982) (hypnotically refreshed testimony is "tainted" and must be excluded, but witness' prehypnotic statement may be retained with a deposition). The hypnotically refreshed testimony cases can be regarded as an elaboration either of Rule 403 or of the helpfulness requirement of Rule 702. Similarly, the collateral impeachment rule could be regarded as a useful elaboration of Rule 403. For a contrary view, see Edward J. Imwinkelreid, *Federal Rule of Evidence 402: The Second Revolution*, 6 Rev. of Litig. 129 (1987), arguing that "Rule 402 permits trial judges to exclude relevant evidence only on grounds recognized in the Constitu-

tion, by statute, or by court rule ...Rule 402 impliedly abolishes all common-law evidentiary rules that have not been codified").

37. *See* 28 Charles A. Wright & Victor J. Gold, Federal Practice and Procedure (Evidence) § 6206, at 534 (1993) ("Evidence that a witness has told one story on the stand and a conflicting story at an earlier time suggests that the witness has lied or was mistaken when he made the prior statement or when he testified or both").

38. The validity of this assumption has been challenged. *See id.* at 536 (challenging the assumption that evidence of a prior inconsistent statement carries much value for impeachment purposes, stating that "[i]t is simply not true to human nature to conclude that, because a person errs or even lies as to one matter, he is more likely to err or lie as to all other matters").

of admissibility is whether the statement really throws light on the witness' credibility, not whether it is inconsistent in some technical sense.[39]

A similar question arises when the witness testifies in detail about an event and adds in testimony a fact that the witness did not mention in the prior statement or report about the event. If the fact was one that would naturally have been mentioned in the report, then courts generally allow the report to be treated as a prior inconsistent statement.[40]

Objection—No Foundation for Extrinsic Evidence

Under the traditional common law rule, a foundation had to be laid with the witness being impeached before extrinsic evidence of the witness' prior inconsistent statement could be introduced. The impeaching attorney could freely ask the witness who made the statement about it without any foundation. But if the attorney wanted to bring in another witness to describe the statement—i.e., to use extrinsic evi-

---

39. United States v. Malik, 928 F.2d 17, 22–23 (1st Cir.1991) (not error to admit evidence of defendant's prior statements about heroin-smuggling after defendant's testimony, "We don't believe in heroin because we don't like it. And we don't do it"; contradiction need not be in "plain terms"); United States v. Stock, 948 F.2d 1299, 1300–01, (D.C.Cir.1991) (error, though harmless, to exclude evidence that officer's police, report omitted a statement allegedly made by defendant; police officer testified that defendant said "I don't have anything" as defendant pulled his hand out of dumpster in which drugs were later found); United States v. Causey, 834 F.2d 1277, 1283 (6th Cir.), cert. denied, 486 U.S. 1034 (1988) (trial court did not abuse discretion in allowing prosecution to impeach witness with prior statement in case where witness testified she did not remember a conversation with her husband but had in fact called an FBI agent about the conversation previously); United States v. Jackson, 748 F.2d 1535 (11th Cir.1984) (defendant may be impeached with prior statement because testimony that he was supposed to receive football tickets and video game passes was inconsistent with earlier statement that he did not know what was in the envelope he received, in case where defendant was charged with extortion involving approval of bank loans); United States v. Rogers, 549 F.2d 490, 496 (8th Cir.1976), cert. denied, 431 U.S. 918 (1977) ("A statement's inconsistency may be determined from the circumstances and is not limited to cases in which diametrically opposite assertions have been made. Thus inconsistencies may be found in changes in position; they may be implied through silence; and they may also be found in denial of recollection"). Compare United States v. Devine, 934 F.2d 1325, 1344–45 (5th Cir.), cert. denied, 502 U.S. 929 (1991) (witness' prior conversation about defendant's role in conspiracy was not inconsistent with trial testimony that he could not remember conversation; not error to exclude prior statements); United States v. Poindexter, 942 F.2d 354, 361 (6th Cir.), cert. denied, 502 U.S. 994 (1991) (testimony, in response to cross-examination questions, denying that drug use caused her to have memory loss, was now inconsistent with trial testimony that she was not using drugs; not error to exclude prior testimony).

40. See, e.g., United States v. Misher, 99 F.3d 664, 669–70 (5th Cir.1996) (held, no abuse of discretion in excluding detective-witness' prior search warrant affidavit which did not list defendant as one of the conspirators; trial testimony implicating defendant was not inconsistent; court noted that the detective "had one and one-half years to change his opinion regarding the scope of the conspiracy"; query validity of decision, which seems contrary to general rule that a significant omission from a prior statement is admissible to impeach even if there is no direct contradiction); State v. Irving, 555 A.2d 575, 581 (N.J.1989) (held, in case where defendant testified his roommate was with him at the time of the alleged crime but did not name his roommate as a possible witness when he filed his original notice-of-alibi statement with the court, that the omission of his roommate's name was inconsistent with defendant's testimony).

dence—then a foundation had to be laid by giving the witness who made the statement the opportunity to explain or deny the statement on the witness stand. This was done by calling the witness' attention to the statement and the surrounding circumstance. A typical formulation of the requirement provided that "the [impeaching] statements must be related to him, with the circumstances of times, places, and persons present; and he shall be asked whether he has made such statements, and if so, allowed to explain them."[41]

The foundation requirement was designed to give the witness a fair chance to explain any circumstances, such as duress or influence, that might excuse the inconsistency; to reconcile the statements by explaining why they were not really inconsistent; or to deny having made the statement at all. The foundation requirement was also intended to require that the impeacher seek first to authenticate the inconsistent statement through the witness who made it. In many cases, this would obviate the need to call another witness to authenticate the statement.

The federal foundation requirement is more relaxed than its common law counterpart. Federal Rule of Evidence 613(b) provides that extrinsic evidence of a prior inconsistent statement is not admissible "unless the witness is afforded an opportunity to explain or deny the same and the opposite party is afforded an opportunity to interrogate the witness thereon, or the interests of justice otherwise require." This rule might at first glance seem to be the same as the common law requirement, but it is not. The advisory committee's note points out that the rule does not specify any particular time at which the witness must be given the opportunity to explain or deny. With this in mind, some courts have held that the rule is satisfied even if the witness is not asked about the prior statement on the stand, so long as the witness is still available.[42] The reasoning in support of this position is that the witness has the opportunity to explain or deny so long as the witness could be recalled for additional testimony. The federal liberalization has not been universally accepted, even by states that use the Federal Rules as a model.[43]

The foundation requirement (whether under federal or common law) does not apply to statements of a party-opponent. These statements are

---

41. Coles v. Harsch, 276 P. 248, 250 (Or.1929) (quoting 1920 Or. Laws § 864).

42. Wammock v. Celotex Corp., 793 F.2d 1518, 1521–22 (11th Cir.1986) (Rule 613(b) does not require that witness be confronted with the inconsistent statement before extrinsic evidence is introduced, but the traditional method is still preferred especially if witness might be unavailable later); Theriot v. Bay Drilling Corp., 783 F.2d 527, 533 (5th Cir.1986) (Rule 613 only requires that a witness have the chance to deny or explain the inconsistent statement at some point in the proceedings, it does not require that the witness have that chance prior to the introduction of extrinsic evidence).

43. *See, e.g.,* Alaska R. Evid. 613(b) ("before extrinsic evidence of a prior contradictory statement . . . may be admitted, the examiner shall lay a foundation for impeachment by affording the witness an opportunity, while testifying, to explain or deny any prior statement"); Minn. R. Evid. 613(b) ("Extrinsic evidence of a prior inconsistent statement by a witness is not admissible unless the witness is afforded a prior opportunity to explain or deny the same").

admissible whether or not a foundation has been laid by asking the party-opponent about them.[44]

Objection—Document Should Be Shown to Witness Before Using It to Impeach

It is the fate of proceduralists to remember great cases for trivial rules. *Queen Caroline's Case* was known in its day as a spectacular contested divorce action in which George IV, King of England, accused his wife, Caroline, of adultery. The Queen resisted, and the case was dropped after a hearing in the House of Lords.[45]

The case is remembered today among evidence lecturers for the *Rule in the Queen's Case*, a rule about the foundation for prior inconsistent statements. Under that rule, announced by the Law Lords in response to a question from the House, a witness could not be cross-examined about a document written by the witness unless the document was first shown to the witness.[46]

The requirement that a document be shown to the witness first can sometimes be an impediment to cross-examination, especially when the cross-examiner is trying to destroy the witness rather than to get the witness to qualify unhelpful testimony. To illustrate how cross-examination could be hampered, suppose the theory of the cross-examiner is that the witness has taken an illicit payment. Cross-examination will be more effective if the cross-examiner conceals from the witness the fact that the cross-examiner has in hand a letter by the witness in which the witness describes receiving money from the person supposed to have given the illicit payment. If the witness denies ever having received money from that person, then the letter can be a bombshell. If the witness is allowed to view the letter first before being asked about transactions with the person, then the witness might come up with some relatively innocuous explanation, such as the explanation that the money was payment for legal services.[47] To prevent this blunting of cross-examination, the Federal Rules of Evidence abolish the Rule in the Queen's Case.[48] Rule 613(a)

---

44. *See* Fed. R. Evid. 613(b); 4 John H. Wigmore, Evidence in Trials at Common Law § 1051 (James H. Chadbourn rev. 1972).

45. Caroline had gone abroad after being excluded from court by her husband during his regency. When her husband ascended to the throne in 1820, she returned and claimed her rights as Queen. Her husband claimed that she had had an Italian lover while abroad. A bill was brought in the House of Lords seeking to deny the Queen all rights associated with her title and to grant the King a divorce, based on alleged adultery. After a hearing, the bill was abandoned for lack of support even though it had passed by a slim margin on the third reading. Caroline lived out her few remaining days as titular Queen of England with an annuity of 50,000 pounds,

though she never regained admission to court. For a vivid account of the facts of the case, see Richard H. Underwood, *Perjury: An Anthology*, 13 Ariz. J. Int'l & Comp. L. 307, 323–28 (1996). *See also* Encyclopedia Britannica 887 (1989).

46. The Queen's Case, 2 Br. & B. 284, 286–90, 129 Eng. Rep. 976, 11 Eng. R.C. 183 (1820); 4 Wigmore, *supra* note 44, at §§ 1259–60.

47. Examples of crushing cross-examination in which the cross-examiner's knowledge was concealed from the witness are collected in 4 Wigmore, *supra* note 44 § 1260.

48. *See* 28 Wright & Gold, *supra* note 37 § 6202, at 506 (Federal Rule 613 "appears to abolish the requirement that the now provides that "when examining a witness concerning a prior statement made by the witness, whether written or not, the statement need not be shown nor its contents disclosed to the witness at that time, but on request the same shall be shown or disclosed to opposing counsel."

While the opportunity for devastating confrontation with a document that the witness has forgotten has been somewhat diminished in the modern era of discovery, the rule makers contemplated that it would sometimes arise, and that when it did, the witness' normal right under the rules of discovery to see the witness' own statement would be suspended temporarily until the end of cross-examination.[49]

Two things should be noted about Rule 613(a). First, when the cross-examiner is using a document that has not been placed in evidence, the rule expressly provides that the opposing counsel has the right to see the document. This rule is designed to prevent misquoting or misuse of the document. Second, if the cross-examiner purports to read from the document, some judges will require that it be shown to the witness despite the express language of Rule 613(a). This is arguably in the interest of fairness, since the cross-examiner may be distorting the document or reading it out of context. The witness might be able to prevent counsel from using the document in a misleading fashion. Were it not for Rule 613(a), there would be ample authority for this exercise of authority by the trial judge under the general power of Rule 611(a) to control the mode of interrogation of witnesses. Yet the plain language of 613(a) seems contrary to this exercise of authority.[50]

Objection—Collateral Impeachment

A prior inconsistent statement may not be proven with extrinsic evidence when the statement is being offered solely for collateral impeachment.[51] The impeachment is collateral when the statement is not independently relevant to some issue other than impeachment.[52]

impeaching party reveal an inconsistent statement to the witness before proceeding with impeachment").

49. *See* Fed. R. Evid. 613(a) advisory committee's note.

50. The authors of one treatise argue that the policy justification for abandoning the common law rule is weak, and that in situations in which the justifications for the old rule are particularly strong, courts should have the power under Rule 611(a) to require the impeaching party to adhere to the common law rule by showing the statement to the witness before cross-examining the witness concerning it. 28 Wright & Gold, *supra* note 37 § 6203, at 510–11.

51. *Id*. § 6206, at 537 (noting a common law rule, generally followed by the federal courts, recognizing that when an inconsistency relates to a collateral matter, the inconsistency cannot be proven by extrinsic evidence. For a discussion of collat-

eral impeachment in the context of impeachment by contradiction, see § **9.04.**

52. United States v. Roulette, 75 F.3d 418, 423 (8th Cir.), *cert. denied*, ___ U.S. ___, 117 S.Ct. 147 (1996) (endorsing independent relevance test and finding it satisfied under facts of case); United States v. Laughlin, 772 F.2d 1382, 1393–94 (7th Cir. 1985) (held, when witness testified her defendant-husband only used drugs if his friends brought drugs to his house, that extrinsic evidence that she previously told an FBI agent that her husband had a "source" for drugs was independently relevant, in case where defendant was charged with possession of cocaine with intent to distribute); United States v. Nace, 561 F.2d 763, 771 (9th Cir.1977) (held, in case where witness testified that he did not owe defendant any money but had listed the loan as a liability in his bankruptcy petition, that defendant could not impeach witness with his

There is a distinction between collateral impeachment out of the witness' own mouth and collateral impeachment with extrinsic evidence. Trial judges have discretion to allow collateral impeachment by questioning of the witness being impeached. A collateral impeachment objection can still be made, but the trial judge has great leeway in deciding whether to sustain or overrule it. When collateral questioning is allowed, then the questioner is bound by the witness' answer. The questioner may not bring in another witness to prove the making of the out-of-court statement. To do so would violate the rule against using extrinsic evidence for collateral impeachment.[53]

For example, suppose that in a sexual harassment case the witness denies that anything improper happened at the office picnic. On cross-examination the witness is questioned about the witness' prior inconsistent statements about (a) what food was served at the picnic and (b) whether the defendant tried to kiss the plaintiff. The trial judge would have discretion to allow cross-examination about both issues. The question about what food was served deals with a collateral matter of no importance, but so long as the cross-examiner is content merely to ask questions of the witness being impeached, not much time is wasted. The answers may reveal a confused or forgetful witness. However, if the witness denies making an inconsistent statement about what food was served, then the cross-examiner cannot bring in another witness (extrinsic evidence) to prove the making of the statement. That would be a waste of time. In contrast, if the prior inconsistent statement concerned something independently relevant—such as whether the defendant tried to kiss the plaintiff—then the extrinsic evidence would be admissible.

A prior inconsistent statement can be independently relevant because it goes to one of the substantive issues of the lawsuit, as in the example of the kiss at the picnic.[54] Or it can be independently relevant because it goes to bias (e.g., the witness denies making a prior statement that the witness was paid for testimony) or perception (the witness denies having made a prior statement saying that the witness was drunk at the picnic).[55]

bankruptcy petition statement because the issue was whether defendant used extortion to get repayment of the alleged loan, not whether the witness had in fact borrowed money from the defendant); *cf.* United States v. Nazarenus, 983 F.2d 1480, 1485 (8th Cir.1993) (improper to impeach defendant, who told police officer who stopped him on night of alleged sex crime that he had sped only to test car's alignment, with evidence that he frequently drove fast); *see also* 3A John H. Wigmore, Evidence in Trials at Common Law § 1020 (James H. Chadbourn rev. 1970).

53. *See, e.g.,* State v. Mangrum, 403 P.2d 925, 929 (Ariz.1965) (opponent could inquire on cross-examination about witness' alleged statement that witness had testified falsely in an unconnected case, but could not bring in extrinsic evidence about the alleged statement); 3A Wigmore, *supra* note 52 §§ 1020–23. *See also* United States v. Grooms, 978 F.2d 425, 428–29 (8th Cir. 1992) (in prosecution for child sex abuse, victims' mother denied stating that the victims' father coached their testimony; held, defendant may not call witness to testify that mother made the statement because issue was collateral; in authors' opinion, court's conclusion is questionable because the prior statement was relevant not only to the mother's credibility but also to bias of the child, witness).

54. 3A Wigmore, *supra* note 52 § 1021.

55. *Id.* § 1022.

The requirement of independent relevance flirts with forbidden use of the inconsistent statement. The inconsistent statement is not admissible for the truth of the matter asserted.[56] To allow extrinsic evidence of a statement only when it is independently relevant is to say that such statements are more valuable than statements that go only to impeachment. The proposition that the statement is more valuable when relevant to something other than impeachment seems to rest on the assumption that the jury will in fact use it for something other than impeachment, i.e., for the truth of what it asserts—a forbidden use. On the other hand, perhaps the honest witness will be more careful to be truthful and accurate about an issue the witness knows to be important. If so, impeachment on a peripheral issue, such as whether steak or chicken was served at lunch, does not reveal as much about the witness' veracity as impeachment about an issue known to the witness to be central to the truth-finding process. By this reasoning one can observe the ban on using the statement for its truth while still retaining the independent relevance requirement.

The rule requiring independent relevance was arguably abolished by the Federal Rules of Evidence, which do not expressly require that inconsistent statements be independently relevant before they can be proven with extrinsic evidence. However, the requirement can be viewed as a useful rule of thumb that implements the general injunction in Rule 403 against wasting time. In any event, whether the rule is accepted in its particularized common law form or whether the exclusion of extrinsic evidence is viewed as a matter for the discretion of the trial judge, the result from fair-minded judges is likely to be the same: collateral impeachment by extrinsic proof of a prior inconsistent statement is not permissible.

§ 9.06 Showing Untruthful Character of Witness [FRE 608]

A witness may be impeached by showing that the witness has a bad character for truthfulness. This evidence comes in under an exception to the general rule prohibiting the use of character evidence to prove conduct.[57]

The impeachment may take one of three forms. First, the impeaching party can attack by offering generalities about character. It can do so by presenting testimony that the target witness has a bad reputation for truth or veracity. Under the Federal Rules of Evidence, it is also permissible to show that in the opinion of the impeaching witness the target witness has a bad character for truthfulness. Second, subject to the court's approval, the impeaching party may cross-examine the witness regarding specific misconduct of the witness that did not result in

56. This example assumes that the statement is admissible only to impeach. If the statement was made under oath at a proceeding, then the statement would be admissible without limit under Rule 801(d)(1)(A).

57. *See* § 5.05.

conviction and that reflects on truthfulness. Finally, the impeaching party may offer evidence of a prior criminal conviction of the witness, to show that the witness is untruthful.

Each of these methods of character attack is subject to fairly strict limits. It is worth noting at the outset, then, that the limits are only applicable when the attack is on the witness' character. If the witness is being impeached by some other method, such as a showing of bias or defects in perception or of mental health, then the attack is not an attack on character and the limits do not apply.[58] This is true even if the other evidence may reflect poorly on character, as would be the case if the evidence consisted of testimony that the witness took a bribe to testify falsely in the case. So long as the trier is being asked to follow a narrower inferential path than the path from testimony to general disposition to acts, the evidence is not character evidence and the restrictions on character evidence do not apply.

§ 9.07 Showing Untruthful Character of Witness [FRE 608]—Impeachment of Truthfulness of the Witness by Reputation and Opinion Testimony as to Character [FRE 608(a)]

The opponent of a witness may impeach the witness by calling another witness who testifies to reputation or, in jurisdictions following the Federal Rules of Evidence, opinion as to character.[59] The testimony must be restricted to the character trait of truthfulness. As with other reputation and opinion testimony, the testimony is supposed to be extremely general in form. An example of a minimalist examination of such a witness follows:

Q. Do you know Mr. X, the witness?

A. Yes.

Q. Do you know other persons in the community who know Mr. X?

A. Yes.

Q. Have you had occasion to hear Mr. X's reputation for truth and veracity discussed among those persons?

A. Yes, many times.

Q. Do you know Mr. X's reputation for truth and veracity?

A. Yes.

Q. What is that reputation?

58. United States v. Abel, 469 U.S. 45, 49 (1984) (held, in case where witness and defendant were in a prison gang that required its members to commit perjury to help another gang member, that witness' membership in defendant's gang was probative of bias and admissible despite tendency of evidence to also show witness was a liar.

59. *See* Fed. R. Evid. 608(a). *See also* State v. Lewis, 847 P.2d 690, 690–94 (Kan. 1993) (in prosecution for attempted rape, reversible error for trial court to exclude four witnesses' testimony about victim's reputation for lack of veracity).

A.   It is very bad. He has the reputation of being a terrible liar.

Tradition allows the direct-examiner to add the following question:

Q.   Based on that reputation, would you believe Mr. X when he testified under oath?[60]

A.   No.

Note that although the reputation could come in, the specific acts of lying upon which it was based could not.

The Federal Rules go further, and permit the witness to be questioned about opinion, as well as about reputation. The stated reason for this addition is that much reputation testimony is actually opinion testimony in disguise, and that at any rate in a modern atomistic society a person who knows character may not know reputation for character.

The reception of opinion testimony leads to a danger of attempting to put testimony of specific acts in through the back door, by putting in facts about the witness' connection with the subject of the impeachment that will allow the jury to infer specific acts of dishonesty. Consider the following hypothetical examination:

Q.   Do you know Mr. X?

A.   Yes.

Q.   How do you know him?

A.   We work for the same company.

Q.   What is your position with that company?

A.   I am the comptroller.

Q.   Do your duties as comptroller include the review of expense accounts?

A.   Yes.

Q.   Have you reviewed Mr. X's expense account?

A.   Yes.

Q.   Do you have an opinion about Mr. X's character for truthfulness?

A.   Yes.

Q.   What is that opinion?

A.   He is extremely untruthful.

The examination just described is a borderline case of putting in specific instances of conduct by extrinsic evidence, a form of impeach-

---

60. This is technically opinion and not reputation evidence. In theory, it would not be admissible at common law, where only reputation testimony was permitted. But custom sanctioned its reception even at common law. *See* 7 John H. Wigmore, Evidence in Trials at Common Law § 1982 (James H. Chadbourn rev. 1978). The Federal Rules do permit opinion testimony, though a technical objection could be made to the question in text on grounds that there is insufficient foundation to show a basis for a personal opinion of character. It is not clear how long or how well the testifying witness has known the witness whose character is being attacked.

ment prohibited by the Federal Rules and common law.[61] The examination carries with it the strong implication that the testifying witness examined Mr. X's expense account and found that it contained falsehoods. The examiner's conduct warrants an objection or, if foreseeable, a motion in limine.[62]

Another possible danger of abuse is testimony by police agents about the character of investigative targets. For example, in *United States v Dotson*[63] the government called an FBI agent to the stand and elicited the following testimony:

Q. Have you had occasion to conduct an investigation into the activities of the defendant, Fred Dotson, and his associates?

A. Yes, sir, I have.

Q. As a result of this investigation and what you have learned and all that you have seen in this case, have you formed an opinion as to the truthfulness of the defendant, Frederick Leon Dotson?

A. Yes, sir, I have.

Q. Is that opinion of his truthfulness good or bad.

A. Bad.

Q. Would you believe Frederick Leon Dotson under oath?

A. No, sir, I would not.

The court held that the evidence should have been excluded. Its decision, however, was a limited one. It did not hold that government agents could not testify to an opinion about the character of defendant-witnesses that was formed during an investigation. It merely held that the foundation was insufficient in the case before it, because the agent had not described anything more than minimal contact with the defendants.[64]

61. Fed. R. Evid. 608(b); United States v. Perez–Perez, 72 F.3d 224, 227 (1st Cir., 1995) (held, complaints by other police officers about the witness' misconduct were properly excluded under rule 608(b); while certain prior good or bad acts of a witness may constitute character evidence bearing on veracity, they are not evidence of enough force to justify the detour of extrinsic proof. For the common law rule, see 3A John H. Wigmore, Evidence in Trials at Common Law § 979 (James H. Chadbourn rev. 1970), on how one cannot put in extrinsic evidence of bad acts not resulting in conviction.

62. For a case in which such testimony was approved, see United States v. Dotson, 799 F.2d 189, 193 (5th Cir.1986) (IRS agent's opinion about lack of financial truthfulness of witness, based on interviews, examination of tax returns, and study of witness' testimony before grand jury, noted approvingly in dictum as example of character opinion based on proper

and sufficient foundation); see also People v. Bieri, 396 N.W.2d 506, 513 (Mich.App. 1986) (prison guard may testify about witness' reputation for untruthfulness because he had known the witness for five months and had discussed witness' reputation with other correctional officers).

63. 799 F.2d 189, 191 (5th Cir.1986).

64. *See also* United States v. Cortez, 935 F.2d 135, 139–40 (8th Cir.1991), *cert. denied*, 502 U.S. 1062 (1992) (error, though harmless, to admit testimony of two law enforcement officers who spent less than one day each interviewing defendant about his conversations with a third person and who spoke only of their belief in a particular story rather than of defendant's general character for truthfulness); United States v. Williams, 822 F.2d 512, 516 (5th Cir.1987) (prosecution laid adequate foundation for opinion testimony by government agents about witness' character for truthfulness by showing both had learned about the witness

Because of the potential dangers of character-based impeachment, the trial court has discretion to forbid or limit such impeachment.[65] The trial court may exclude such evidence when it finds that its value for impeachment purposes is substantially outweighed by any of the dangers listed in Rule 403, and the court may also place limits on the number of witnesses who may be called to attack the character of a witness. Where their testimony would all be the same, even a limit to one attacking witness has been upheld as a reasonable exercise of discretion to limit, pursuant to the authority granted by Rule 403, the introduction of cumulative evidence.[66]

§ 9.08 Showing Untruthful Character of Witness [FRE 608]—Impeachment of Truthfulness of the Witness with Evidence of Conduct That Did Not Lead to Conviction [FRE 608(b)]

The trial judge has discretion to permit a witness to be questioned about conduct that has not resulted in conviction, for purposes of supporting or attacking the truthfulness of the witness. The conduct must relate to truthfulness, not to some other character trait.[67] Thus, a witness could be questioned about the witness' dishonesty in falsifying an academic record on an employment application, but not about sexual misconduct.[68]

through surveillance and by interviewing his acquaintances [note: court used the plain error standard to review the issue because defendant did not make proper objection during his trial]).

65. Rule 608 itself states only that such evidence "may" be admitted. *See* 27 Charles A. Wright & Victor J. Gold, Federal Practice and Procedure (Evidence) § 6114, at 51–52 (1990).

66. *See* United States v. Haynes, 554 F.2d 231 (5th Cir.1977).

67. *See* 28 Charles A. Wright & Victor J. Gold, Federal Practice and Procedure (Evidence) § 6115 (1993) (discussing the meaning of the phrase "character for truthfulness or untruthfulness" in Rule 608(a)); *id.* § 6118, at 102–09 (discussing meaning of phrase "if probative of truthfulness or untruthfulness" in Rule 608(b)).

68. United States v. McMillon, 14 F.3d 948, 955–56 (4th Cir.1994) (held, in conspiracy prosecution, defendant not entitled to cross-examine government's witness regarding witness' prior homosexual activities); Ad–Vantage Tel. Directory Consultants, Inc. v. GTE Directories Corp., 37 F.3d 1460, 1464 (11th Cir.1994) (held, error to allow party's expert witness, a CPA and former lawyer, to be impeached. by cross-examination about his bankruptcy and his failure to pay debts; "seeking discharge in bankruptcy does not show a disregard for truth that would cast doubt on a witness' veracity"; remarkably, the court held it was also error to allow same witness to be cross-examined about forgery accusation that led to witness' resignation from the bar); Wood v. Alaska, 957 F.2d 1544 1550–51 (9th Cir.1992) (evidence that alleged victim had modeled for pornographic magazines and movies was not admissible to impeach credibility in rape case); United States v. Blake, 941 F.2d 334, 339–41 (5th Cir.1991), *cert. denied*, 506 U.S. 998 (1992) (error, though harmless, to impeach narcotics defendant with questions about whether he had ever killed anyone and whether he had told police officer that he had killed 10 people); Wanke v. Lynn's Transp. Co., 836 F.Supp. 587, 597 (N.D.Ind.1993) (in wrong full death action against trucking company, evidence of truck driver's prior arrests for disorderly conduct held, on motion in limine, not admissible under Rule 608(b) because not probative of veracity; evidence of alleged theft by truck driver also not admissible to impeach his testimony as witness, subject to reconsideration at trial should proponent be able to demonstrate that the conduct involved deception or "otherwise demonstrates lack of veracity"; fact that truck driver gave testimony at deposition, later corrected in deposition errata sheet, that he had no other arrests did not render

If the witness denies the misconduct, then the cross-examiner must "take the answer."[69] This does not mean that the cross-examiner is prohibited from further efforts to get the witness to admit the misconduct,[70] but it does mean that extrinsic evidence of the misconduct is not admissible.[71] The main purpose of this ban on extrinsic evidence is to prevent the waste of time and confusion that would occur if mini-trials were held about blemishes in each witness' past.[72] Confusion of issues and unfair surprise also underlie the rule.[73]

What constitutes extrinsic evidence? As the language of the rule itself makes clear, testimony from the mouth of the witness during cross-examination is not "extrinsic."[74] Just as clearly, testimony of another witness would be extrinsic.[75] Also, the rule would forbid the use of

evidence of arrest on theft charge admissible). *See, e.g.,* People v. Chaplin, 313 N.W.2d 899, 902 (Mich.1981) (reversible error to permit cross-examination suggesting witness was prostitute and defendant may have been her pimp); Heshelman v. Lombardi, 454 N.W.2d 603 (Mich.App.1990) (error to allow cross-examination of doctor about prior malpractice action).

See also Mason v. Texaco, Inc., 948 F.2d 1546, 1555–56 (10th Cir.1991), *cert. denied,* 504 U.S. 910 (1992) (held, district court was within discretion in ruling that plaintiff's expert witnesses could not be cross-examined about allegedly biased study they prepared on subject unrelated to the instant suit; court states that such impeachment is barred on ground, among others, that the cross-examination would not have challenged character for truthfulness but merely objectivity on a particular study; in authors' opinion, court is in error in stating that evidence did not reflect on character, though its overall ruling that exclusion was within the district court's discretion is supportable. For an example of cross-examination that was permissible because it did go to character for truthfulness, see United States v. Waldrip, 981 F.2d 799, 802–03 (5th Cir.1993) (under Rule 608(a), permissible for government to cross-exam defendant about incident in which defendant signed another's name to document without authorization, even though incident resembled crime charged).

69. *See, e.g.,* Lambert v. Commonwealth, 383 S.E.2d 752, 754 (Va.App.1989).

70. As one treatise states:

Courts often summarize the no-extrinsic-evidence rule by stating that "the examiner must take his or her answer." This phrase ... is misleading if it is taken to suggest that the cross-examiner cannot continue pressing for an admission—a procedure authorized by the second sentence of Rule 608(b).

4 Weinstein's Federal Evidence § 608.12[3], at 608–28 to 608–30 (2d ed. Joseph M. McLaughlin ed. 1997) (footnotes omitted).

71. Fed. R. Evid. 608(b) (forbidding use of extrinsic evidence).

72. *See* United States v. Martz, 964 F.2d 787, 789 (8th Cir.), *cert. denied,* 506 U.S. 1038 (1992) (the reason for barring extrinsic evidence "is to avoid holding mini-trials on peripherally related or irrelevant matters").

73. *See* Frederick C. Moss, *The Sweeping–Claims Exception and the Federal Rules of Evidence,* 1982 Duke L.J. 61, 70 ("The policy reasons for excluding extrinsic evidence are the avoidance of undue prolongation of the trial, confusion of the issues, and unfair surprise to the witness").

74. "Specific instances of the conduct of a witness, for the purpose of attacking or supporting the witness' credibility, ... may, ... in the discretion of the court, if probative of truthfulness or untruthfulness, be inquired into on cross-examination...."

75. *See* United States v. McNeill, 887 F.2d 448, 453 (3d Cir.1989), *cert. denied,* 493 U.S. 1087 (1990) ("Extrinsic evidence is evidence offered through other witnesses, rather than through cross-examination of the witness himself or herself"); Russess J. Davis, Annotation, *Construction and Application of Rule 608(b) of Federal Rules of Evidence, dealing With Use of Specific Instances of Conduct to Attack or Support Credibility,* 36 A.L.R. Fed. 564, at §§ 3–6 (1978) (reviewing cases); 28 Wright & Gold, *supra* note 67 § 6117, at 88 (language of Rule 608(b) "invites the inference that the testimony of any other witness does constitute extrinsic evidence"). Wigmore found this limitation to be entirely consistent with the underlying purposes of the rule forbidding extrinsic evidence. 3A John H. Wigmore, Evidence in Trials at Common Law documents to impeach when it is necessary to call another witness to authenticate those documents.[76] Therefore, if on cross-examination, counsel asks the witness to admit that she once lied about her age in an effort to enter an adults-only bar. In its discretion, the court could allow this question because it concerns conduct reflecting on the witness' truthfulness. If the witness refuses to admit that the event occurred, the opponent would not be permitted to call a friend to testify that she was with the witness when this event occurred, nor would the opponent be permitted to call an employee of the bar to authenticate a document reporting on the incident.

Suppose, however, that during cross-examination, the witness admits engaging in the conduct also evidenced by the document, or simply admits the authenticity of the document reporting the conduct? Would introduction of the document still violate the extrinsic evidence rule? The courts are divided on this question. Some courts hold that the document still constitutes extrinsic evidence.[77] Others, however, hold that the extrinsic evidence rule would not be violated by its admission.[78] These latter courts appear to have the better argument. As one court stated, "[w]hen . . . the extrinsic evidence is obtained from and through examination of the very witness whose credibility is under attack, . . . [Rule 608(b)'s] core concerns are not implicated."[79] Because no other witness is involved, no extra time is spent inquiring into the credibility of yet another person.[80] The jury is less likely to be confused, and the witness is unlikely to be surprised by the document.[81]

§ 979, at 826 (James H. Chadbourn rev. 1970).

76. *See* United States v. Lashmett, 965 F.2d 179, 181–82 (7th Cir.1992) (court filings in related civil action inadmissible under Rule 613, which contains same extrinsic evidence limitation); United States v. Peterson, 808 F.2d 969, 972–74 (2d Cir.1987) (where witness denied forging endorsement on check, party could not introduce check); Davis Annotation, *supra* note 77 §§ 7–10 (reviewing cases). *Cf.* United States v. Elliott, 89 F.3d 1360 (8th Cir.1996) (trial court did not err when it refused to allow defendant to use documentary exhibits during cross-examination of government witness in an effort to impeach witness by showing that she misrepresented her educational and work experience on her resume; though court based decision on Rule 608(b), defendant also appeared to have offered evidence substantively to prove a defense, for which purpose Rule 608(b) would not have applied).

77. *See, e.g.*, United States v. Whitehead, 618 F.2d 523, 529 (4th Cir.1980) (refusing to admit document even if the witness admits engaging in the conduct).

78. *See, e.g.*, Carter v. Hewitt, 617 F.2d 961, 969–70 (3d Cir.1980) (extrinsic evidence rule not violated when, during cross-examination of a witness, a letter that the witness admittedly had written and which evidenced his character for truthfulness was admitted into evidence).

79. *Id.* at 970.

80. Of course, even asking additional questions of a witness consumes a small amount of time, and where the witness has actually admitted the conduct, the court may well exclude the document as cumulative and a waste of time. 28 Wright & Gold, *supra* note 67 § 6117, at 90. *See also* Carter v. Hewitt, 617 F.2d 961, 970–71 (3d Cir. 1980) (noting that where witness admits conduct, court may exclude evidence under Rule 403 as cumulative).

81. Most commentators have approved of the practice of allowing the use of a document on cross-examination where the witness admits the conduct or the authenticity of the document. As the authors of one treatise state:

> Where a witness admits to specific instances of conduct, admission of documentary evidence of the same instances cannot be unfair harassment in the sense described by Wigmore. The witness cannot complain of the unfairness

Even if the witness denies the conduct or the authenticity of the document, the extrinsic evidence rule does not bar the attorney from using the document solely to attempt to refresh the witness' recollection.[82] Under those circumstances, any testimony still comes from the mouth of the witness; the document is not offered as evidence.[83]

Where the situation involves impeachment of a hearsay declarant under Rule 806,[84] it is not practicable to apply the precise limitations of Rule 608(b). If the declarant does not testify, there is no opportunity to cross-examine and it is necessary to call another witness or use other means to offer the impeaching evidence. If the declarant is available, the opponent presumably can call the defendant to the stand. The impeachment would then occur on direct examination rather than cross-examination, though without extrinsic evidence.[85]

One approach to avoiding the impact of the extrinsic evidence rule as applied to documents is to send the inculpating documentation to the witness and counsel before trial. While this will tip off the witness about the nature of the expected cross-examination, it will put the witness on notice before trial, so that the witness may feel obliged to tell the truth.[86]

of having to disprove conduct to which he admits. Similarly, because the witness so admits, there will be no confusion or delay generated by a protracted exchange of conflicting evidence pertinent to that conduct.

28 Wright & Gold, *supra* note 67 § 6117, at 90. *See also* Moss, *supra* note 77, at 70 (noting that in the context of the common-law rule governing impeachment by contradiction, which also contains an extrinsic evidence limitation, "[n]one of [the] policies [underlying the extrinsic evidence rule] is necessarily violated when a witness is confronted with nontestimonial evidence on cross-examination. If he is confronted with a document and admits its authenticity, the contradiction is completed, swiftly and clearly"). *But see* 3 Christopher B. Mueller and Laird C. Kirkpatrick, Federal Evidence § 267, at 183 (2d ed. 1994). The authors state that allowing the use of documents relating to or describing the conduct of witness violates the extrinsic evidence rule and can constitute reversible error in some cases. "Letting the attacking party offer documents is likely to sidetrack proceedings and invite further examination and explanation." However, where the witness has made a dishonest oral or written statement, the authors would approve the use of the document while questioning the witness. "Referring to the substance of the statement during questioning, and even making it obvious that the questioner has a writing that embodies the statement (or could pro-

duce a witness who heard it) should not run afoul of the restriction." *Id.* at 183–84.

Whether the reasoning described above approving the use of documents during cross-examination would support the use of self-authenticating documents in the face of the witness' refusal to admit the conduct or authenticate the document is not clear. Time is not of particular concern, as no additional witnesses need be called. However, issues of harassment and surprise might be implicated in some circumstances, counseling against admission.

82. *See* United States v. Chevalier, 1 F.3d 581, 584 n. 1 (7th Cir.1993) (in effort to convince defendant-witness to admit bank fraud, court properly allowed prosecution to use loan document to refresh recollection concerning statement defendant had made).

83. *See* § 7.15.

84. *See* § 7.62.

85. Rule 806 appears to accommodate this reasoning. *See* Fed. R. Evid. 806 advisory committee's note; United States v. Friedman, 854 F.2d 535, 570 n. 8 (2d Cir.1988).

86. *See* B. House, Great Trials of Famous Lawyers 180–81 (1962) (describing counsel's preparation for cross-examination of witness who was a member of Congress; counsel sent witness letter asking witness to refresh memory on subjects so that witness would not claim to have forgotten facts surrounding prior falsifications).

The prohibition of extrinsic evidence applies only to extrinsic evidence that relates to the character of a witness. Extrinsic evidence that impeaches the witness by showing bias is admissible.[87] Similarly, evidence that a witness engaged in a distinctively similar type of lying on different occasions may be received. It is admissible not as character evidence to impeach the witness, but as non-character evidence of a common scheme or plan. Thus, the fact that a witness has made prior false accusations of the same crime in the same circumstances is admissible.[88] Of course, if the evidence of a witness' bad acts tends independently to support a claim or defense regardless of whether it impeaches the witness, then the evidence is admissible.[89] This would be the case, for example, when the witness' prior acts included concealing from the defendant criminal activity of the type that the defendant is now alleged to have committed in concert with the witness. In these cases, even if the evidence is independently admissible for a non-impeachment purpose, the court should examine carefully whether the evidence should be excluded as unfairly prejudicial under Rule 403.[90]

87. *See* United States v. Abel, 469 U.S. 45 (1984) (extrinsic evidence that witness belonged to secret prison organization whose tenets required members to commit perjury, theft, and murder on each other's behalf admissible to show that witness was biased in favor of another member of the organization). This result is consistent with the common law, though one must place a gloss on Rule 608(a) in order to reach it. The Rule provides that "specific instances of the conduct of a witness, for the purpose of attacking or supporting the witness' credibility, other than conviction of crime as provided in rule 609, may not be proven by extrinsic evidence." The rule should be read, after *Abel*, to refer only to attacking or supporting the witness' credibility with character evidence, not with other evidence. The Uniform Rules, see Unif. R. Evid. 616 (1986), were amended in 1986 to make explicit that extrinsic evidence attacking credibility with evidence of bias, prejudice, or interest is admissible. For an example of state adoption of this rule, see Minn. R. Evid. 616 (as amended Jan. 1, 1990).

88. *See* Fed. R. Evid. 404(b); United States v. Stamper, 766 F.Supp. 1396 (W.D.N.C.1991), *aff'd, In re* One Female Juvenile Victim, 959 F.2d 231 (4th Cir. 1992) (complainant's previous allegedly allegations of sexual abuse by, three other men admissible to motive of manipulating complainant's custodians) (table); People v. Mikula, 269 N.W.2d 195, 199 (Mich.App. 1978) defendant can prove by extrinsic evidence that complainant-witness made a previous allegation that a fourteen-year-old boy raped her, in case where complainant accused defendant of rape several months later). *See also* People v. Evans, 40 N.W. 473, 478 (Mich.1888) (defendant can show complainant had made several false accusations about sexual assault prior to her complaint against him, in case where defendant's daughter had previously accused her two brothers, among others, of raping her).

89. See United States v. Costa, 947 F.2d 919, 925–26 (11th Cir.1991), *cert. denied*, 504 U.S. 946 (1992) (while Rule 608(b) prohibits use of, extrinsic evidence of bad acts solely to impeach character, it does not prohibit extrinsic evidence that is independently relevant to defendant's defense that he was not involved in the drug ring which was the subject of the testimony of government witnesses).

90. *Cf.* United States v. Smith, 80 F.3d 1188, 1193 (7th Cir.1996), where the court held, in a case in which defendant was charged with cargo theft, that it was not plain error to allow him to be cross-examined about uncharged cargo thefts for purposes of impeachment under Fed. R. Evid. 608(b), remarking that "Prior acts of theft or receipt of stolen property are, like acts of fraud or deceit, probative of a witness' truthfulness or untruthfulness under Rule 608(b)." *Query* whether any jury could be expected to use the fruits of such a cross-examination solely for the permitted purpose of impeaching credibility while ignoring its natural probative force in showing propensity to commit cargo theft.

The prohibition against use of extrinsic evidence to impeach the witness by showing bad character for truthfulness applies also to ban extrinsic evidence to support the witness by showing good character for truthfulness. For example, the government may not, in a criminal trial on the merits, support the credibility of its informer-witness by adducing testimony that the witness had previously given information that proved accurate and that resulted in arrests and convictions.[91]

Sometimes a witness, by voluntarily injecting an assertion about specific instances into testimony, will open the door to counter-attack that otherwise would not be permissible. For example, a witness who proclaims never to have been suspected of involvement with drugs opens the door to counter-evidence showing a prior drug arrest.[92] Of course, the information must be elicited on direct or volunteered in a non-responsive answer; the cross-examiner cannot force the witness into making the avowal for purposes of contradicting it.[93]

§ 9.09 Impeachment of Witness With Evidence of Prior Convictions [FRE 609]

The ground rules for admitting prior convictions have been a source of continuous controversy. Some jurists have argued that only crimes of falsehood should be admitted to impeach, on grounds that crimes of violence are likely to prejudice the jury without throwing much light on credibility.[94] Others have argued that one who will maim or kill is enough of an outlaw to lie under oath, and that the jury should be trusted to handle the evidence.[95]

These viewpoints have led to a variety of approaches to prior convictions. Some states follow the *crimen falsi* approach, admitting only

---

91. *See* United States v. Taylor, 900 F.2d 779 (4th Cir.1990) and cases cited therein.

92. *See* United States v. Garcia, Camacho, 900 F.2d 571 (2d Cir.), *cert. denied,* 498 U.S. 862 (1990). *See also* State v. Syriani, 428 S.E.2d 118, 135 (N.C.1993) (in prosecution for first-degree murder of defendant's wife, when defendant testified he was a "loving and supportive husband and father," trial court admitted evidence of prior threats and specific acts of violence by defendant against his wife and children).

93. *See* § 1.10.

94. *See, e.g.,* United States v. Fountain, 768 F.2d 790 (7th Cir.1985) (Posner, J.) ("Violent men are not necessarily liars, and indeed one class of violent men consists of those with an exaggerated sense of honor"); Mason Ladd, *Credibility Tests–Current Trends,* 89 U. Pa. L. Rev. 180–82 (1940) (quoting 7 Jeremy Bentham, Rationale of Judicial Evidence 407 (Bowrings ed. 1827)):

"Take homicide in the way of duelling. Two men quarrel; one of them calls the other a liar. So highly does he prize

the reputation of veracity, that, rather than suffer a stain to remain upon it, he determines to risk his life, challenges his adversary to fight, and kills him. Jurisprudence, in its sapience, knowing no difference between homicide by consent, by which no other human being is put in fear-and homicide in pursuit of a scheme of highway robbery, of nocturnal housebreaking, by which every man who has a life is put in fear of it,—has made the one and the other murder, and consequently felony. The man prefers death to the imputation of a lie,—and the inference of the law is, that he cannot open his mouth but lies will issue from it. Such are the inconsistencies which are unavoidable in the application of any rule which takes improbity for a ground of exclusion."

95. *See* 3A John H. Wigmore, Evidence in Trials at Common Law § 982 (James H. Chadbourn rev. 1970) and cases cited therein.

crimes of dishonesty or false statements.[96] Others have a more wide-open approach, either mandating or allowing judges to receive evidence of other crimes.[97]

After a checkered path through the legislative and rulemaking process, the federal rule makers arrived at a compromise position.[98] Convictions for crimes of dishonesty and false statement, regardless of the punishment, are admissible to impeach any witness without limit (except as set forth in subparts (b), (c), and (d) of the Rule). The trial judge has no authority to exclude.[99] Federal Rule of Evidence 403 does not apply and there is no weighing of probative value against prejudicial effect.[100] Crimes for which the sentence is one year or less (typically misdemeanors) and that do not involve dishonesty or false statement are never admissible to impeach any witness. The admissibility of evidence of conviction for crimes punishable by death or imprisonment in excess of a year and which do not involve dishonesty or false statement depends on the witness being impeached, but in all cases, the court must consider the probative value of the evidence for impeachment purposes and the unfair prejudice the evidence might cause.[101]

Rule 609(a)(1) Crimes

Rule 609(a)(1) establishes two balancing tests; which one applies to a given situation depends on the witness being impeached. The Rule reads:

> [E]vidence that a witness other than an accused has been convicted of a crime shall be admitted, subject to Rule 403, if the crime was punishable by death or imprisonment in excess of one year under the law under which the witness was convicted, and evidence that an accused has been convicted of such a crime shall be admitted if the court determines that the probative value of admitting this evidence outweighs its prejudicial effect to the accused....

Thus, if any witness other than a criminal accused has been convicted of a serious crime that is not one of dishonesty or false statement, the court may only exclude evidence of the conviction if Rule 403 so requires. This places the burden on the objecting party to demonstrate that the probative value of the evidence for impeachment purposes is substantial-

---

96. Commonwealth v. Randall, 528 A.2d 1326, 1329 (Pa.1987); Alaska R. Evid. 609(a); Iowa R. Evid. 609(a).

97. *See* Cal. Evid. Code § 788 (West 1966); Idaho R. Evid. 609(a).

98. For a detailed examination of the legislative history of Rule 609, and of the compromise represented by the rule that emerged from the debates, see 28 Charles A. Wright & Victor J. Gold, Federal Practice and Procedure (Evidence) §§ 6131–6132 (1993). *See also* Victor J. Gold, *Impeachment by Conviction Evidence: Judicial Discretion and the Politics of Rule 609*, 15 Cardozo L. Rev. 2295 (1994).

99. *See* 28 Wright & Gold, *supra* note 98 § 6134, at 216 (if the crime involves dishonesty or false statement, "analysis under subdivision (a)(1) [of Rule 609] stops; the conviction will be admitted under subdivision (a)(2) and no weighing of probative value and prejudice need take place").

100. Fed. R. Evid. 609(a)(2); United States v. Wong, 703 F.2d 65, 68 (3d Cir. 1983). This absolute approach was not affected by the 1990 amendments to Rule 609.

101. Fed. R. Evid. 609(a)(1).

ly outweighed by the unfairly prejudicial effect (or other dangers listed in Rule 403), a showing that will be very difficult to make in most cases. If, on the other hand, the witness is the accused in a criminal case, then the court must affirmatively determine that the probative value of the evidence outweighs its prejudicial effect to the accused. This test provides greater protection for the accused than the normal Rule 403 balancing test, because it places the burden on the proponent to show probative value and because it does not require that prejudice "substantially outweigh" probative value.[102]

Neither the language of Rule 609 nor the commentary provide meaningful assistance in understanding the nature of the probative value/prejudicial impact balance the court must undertake.[103] In deciding whether a conviction is unduly prejudicial to the accused, a variety of factors should be taken into account. These include:

1. The degree to which the crime reflects on credibility. For example, a sex crime may not reflect on credibility as much as a robbery conviction.[104]

2. The nearness or remoteness of the prior conviction. A person who has led a blameless life for years after a conviction is entitled to more consideration than one who was recently convicted. If the conviction is more than 10 years old, the Rule requires a strong showing of probative value after advance written notice, regardless of the nature of the crime.[105] Even for

---

102. Rule 403 provides that "evidence may be excluded if its probative value is substantially outweighed by the danger of unfair prejudice, confusion of the issues, or misleading the jury, or by considerations of undue delay, waste of time, or needless presentation of cumulative evidence." Rule 609(a)(1) provides that "evidence that an accused has been convicted of such a crime shall be admitted if the court determines that the probative value of admitting this evidence outweighs its prejudicial effect to the accused."

103. *See* 28 Wright & Gold, *supra* note 98 § 6134, at 230–45 (noting the lack of clarity in the rule and suggesting factors the courts should consider when conducting the balancing test).

104. United States v. Larsen, 596 F.2d 347, 348 (9th Cir.1979) (error for trial court to admit defendant's two prior felony convictions for child molestation since crime "bears only nominally on credibility," but not reversible error because court "relied exclusively" on prosecution's case-in-chief in defendant's trial for uttering counterfeit government obligations); *see* United States v. Walker, 613 F.2d 1349, 1354 (5th Cir. 1980) (misdemeanor prostitution conviction

is not admissible under Rule 609(a) because it does not involve dishonesty or false statement); *compare* United States v. Lipscomb, 702 F.2d 1049, 1072 (D.C.Cir.1983) (court did not abuse discretion in admitting witness' one-year-old robbery conviction into evidence, since crime was recent and witness' credibility was central to the case because he corroborated defendant's testimony); United States v. Cordoba, 104 F.3d 225, 229 (9th Cir.1997) (held, in drug case in which defendant denied awareness of cocaine in Plymouth van he was driving, defendant's prior 1985 cocaine conviction admissible to impeach under Rule 609; no need to consider admissibility under Rule 404(b)).

105. Fed. R. Evid. 609(b). If confinement is imposed, the ten-year period does not start running until release. *Id.* If a mistrial is offered and refused by the opponent, that refusal may be deemed a waiver of the objection to lack of notice. *See* Zinman v. Black & Decker (U.S.), Inc., 983 F.2d 431, 434–35 (2d Cir.1993) (in 1992 civil trial where 1975 conviction for Medicaid fraud admitted, plaintiff waived objection to sufficiency of notice by twice declining mistrial).

shorter periods, though, the time span is a significant factor.[106]

3. The similarity of the prior offense to the offense charged. This is a factor that weighs against admissibility when the only theory of admission is impeachment of the accused as a witness. The reason is that the jury may use the evidence not for its bearing upon the credibility of the witness, but for the inference that "because she did it before she probably did it again"—or, even worse, decide to re-punish the accused for the prior crime whether or not the current one was committed. Thus, a stronger case can be made for receiving a prior auto theft conviction in a bank robbery case than in an auto theft case.[107] Of course, if the two auto thefts were so similar that the first one was admissible under Rule 404(b) to show plan, intent, modus operandi, or the like, then the evidence should not be excluded on this ground.[108] But when the only basis for receiving it is to impeach credibility, similarity between the two crimes is a factor disfavoring admission.

4. The extent to which defendant's testimony is needed for fair adjudication of the trial. If defendant's testimony is crucial for his defense, this fact weighs against the admissibility of the prior convictions,[109] because if the evidence will be admissible, it is less likely the defendant will testify.

5. Whether the defendant's credibility is central to the case.[110]

Some courts will also consider whether the witness' credibility can be explored adequately without using evidence of the witness' prior

106. United States v. Rein, 848 F.2d 777, 782 (7th Cir.1988) (time of witness' prior conviction and her post-conviction behavior is factor to consider when evaluating probative value of conviction). *See also* People v. Allen, 420 N.W.2d 499, 522, *rehg denied*, 423 N.W.2d 215 (Mich.1988) (when determining probative value of conviction, trial court must consider the recency of the conviction).

107. *See, e.g.*, People v. Barrick, 187 Cal.Rptr. 716, 722, 654 P.2d 1243, 1250 (Cal. 1982) (en banc) (error, under circumstances, to impeach defendant with prior conviction for an offense identical to the one charged). Though *Barrick* was not a Federal Rules case, it illustrates a principle that is equally applicable under the Federal Rules. For federal case examples, see United States v. Wallace, 848 F.2d 1464, 1473 (9th Cir.1988) (error for trial court to admit defendant's prior conviction for heroin trafficking in defendant's trial for possession with intent to distribute heroin, especially since prosecution could also use his prior conviction for perjury for impeachment purposes); United States v. Field, 625 F.2d 862, 872 (9th Cir.1980) (defendant's prior con-

viction for receiving stolen property was sufficiently different from his alleged armed bank robbery that it was admissible for impeachment purposes).

108. *See* **Ch. 5**.

109. *See* United States v. Rein, 848 F.2d 777, 782 (7th Cir.1988).

110. United States v. Wesley, 990 F.2d 360, 366 (8th Cir.1993) (evidence of defendant's prior convictions for possession of firearm and possession of crack cocaine was properly admitted where, in subsequent case, he denied possessing both seized revolver and seized cocaine base); United States v. DeVore, 839 F.2d 1330, 1333 (8th Cir.1988) (evidence of defendant's prior weapons conviction was properly admitted because his credibility was central to the jury's decision of his guilt/innocence, in case where defendant offered an alibi to his alleged robbery that was contradicted by other witnesses); United States v. Johnson, 720 F.2d 519, 522 (8th Cir.1983) (defendant's prior felony convictions were properly admitted in case where he testified he lacked intent to sell cocaine in his trial for cocaine distribution).

conviction. If the witness can be impeached convincingly using other means (e.g., bias, prior inconsistent statement), the existence of such alternative impeachment methods is a factor weighing against allowing use of the prior conviction.[111]

Rule 609(a)(2) Crimes

Under Federal Rule 609(a)(2), crimes of dishonesty or false statement must be received. The judge has no discretion under this part of the Rule, and cannot balance probative value against prejudice or even exclude on grounds that the crime was a minor one. Only if the court makes the necessary findings under subparts (b), (c), and (d) of the Rule may the court exclude the evidence.[112]

Some crimes clearly fall in the category of crimes of dishonesty or false statement. The paradigm example is perjury. Other core examples include fraud and forgery.

In common usage, stealing is also a crime of dishonesty. However, there are good reasons to doubt that ordinary stealing should be considered "dishonest" within the meaning of Rule 609(a)(2). As the advisory committee's note to the 1990 Amendment states,

> Congress extensively debated the rule, and the Report of the House and Senate Conference Committee states that "[b]y the phrase 'dishonesty and false statement,' the Conference means crimes such as perjury, subornation of perjury, false statement, criminal fraud, embezzlement, or false pretense, or any other offense in the nature of *crimen falsi*, commission of which involves some element of deceit, untruthfulness, or falsification bearing on the accused's propensity to testify truthfully."

The 1990 advisory committee expressed disapproval of "some decisions that take an unduly broad view of 'dishonesty,' admitting convictions such as bank robbery or bank larceny." However, it did not recommend a clarification of the rule, stating that the legislative history gave sufficient guidance.[113]

Clarification would have been useful, since there are decisions under Rule 609(a) that use the ordinary meaning of "dishonesty" and not the special gloss offered by the Conference Committee and the Advisory Committee. For example, a panel of the First Circuit has held that armed robbery is a crime of dishonesty within the meaning of the Rule.[114]

111. United States v. Reeves, 730 F.2d 1189, 1196 (8th Cir.1984) (evidence of witness' prior conviction for breaking and entering properly excluded since defendant offered several character witnesses and proof of witness' more recent conviction for selling controlled substances).

112. These subparts deal, respectively, with older convictions; the effect of pardon, annulment, or certificate of rehabilitation; and juvenile convictions.

113. For discussion of the lack of clarity in the phrase "crimes involving dishonesty or false statement," and a discussion of approaches to interpreting the phrase, see 28 Wright & Gold, *supra* note 98 § 6135.

114. United States v. Del Toro Soto, 676 F.2d 13, 18 (1st Cir.1982) (grand larceny is a crime of dishonesty under Fed. R. Evid. 609(a)(2)). *But see* United States v. Brackeen, 969 F.2d 827, 827–31 (9th Cir. 1992) (en banc) (bank robbery is not neces-

But there are also many cases that use "dishonesty" in the special sense intended by the Committee, holding that theft crimes are not crimes of dishonesty.[115] Others courts have looked beyond the definition of the crime to see whether under the particular facts the crime was carried out in a deceitful way,[116] an approach that raises dangers of collateral disputes and waste of time.

Summary of Admissibility of Convictions Under Rule 609(a)

The operation of Rule 609(a) can be presented in graph form. The horizontal axis represents the type of crime, and the vertical axis represents the type of witness being impeached. In all cases, the indicated result will occur unless other parts of Rule 609 require otherwise.

	CRIMINAL ACCUSED	**ANY OTHER WITNESS**
DISHONESTY/ FALSE STATEMENT	always admissible[117]	always admissible
SERIOUS NON–DIS- HONESTY/FALSE STATEMENT	only admissible if probative value exceeds unfair prejudice	admissible unless probative value substantially outweighs by a 403 danger
MINOR NON–DISHONESTY/ FALSE STATEMENT	never admissible[118]	never admissible

Extrinsic Evidence of Prior Convictions

When prior convictions qualify for admission under Rule 609, the proponent of the evidence may prove them with extrinsic evidence. The

sarily a crime of dishonesty under Rule 609(a)(2)); State v. Eugene, 536 N.W.2d 692, 694 (N.D.1995) (possession of an imitation controlled substance with intent to deliver is not a crime of dishonesty, and therefore automatically admissible, since crime does not necessarily involve dishonest conduct or false statement; defendant's belief that the substance being delivered was actually a controlled substance, not an imitation, is no defense to the charge). Relying on legislative history, the court interpreted Rule 609 narrowly as applicable only to perjury, false statement, criminal fraud, embezzlement, false pretense, and the like. The court cited cases in accord from the Second, Fourth, Sixth, Seventh, Eighth, Tenth, and D.C. Circuits and a case in contradiction from the First Circuit.

115. *See, e.g.,* United States v. Yeo, 739 F.2d 385, 388 (8th Cir.1984) (theft is not a crime of dishonesty or false statement within the meaning of Fed. R. Evid. 609(a)(2)); United States v. Entrekin, 624 F.2d 597, 599 (5th Cir.1980) (shoplifting is not a crime of dishonesty or false statement under Fed. R. Evid. 609(a)(2)). *Cf.* United States v. Estes, 994 F.2d 147, 148–49 (5th

Cir.1993) (misdemeanor conviction for impersonating a public official not admissible as a Rule 609(a)(2) conviction).

116. *See* Altobello v. Borden Confectionary Prods., Inc., 872 F.2d 215, 217 (7th Cir.1989) (held, in case where plaintiff had previously been convicted for the misdemeanor offense of tampering with electric meters, that if the prior offense could possibly involve the use of deceit the trial court must discover if the method used to commit the crime was deceitful; if so, the prior conviction is admissible under Fed. R. Evid. 609(a)(2); government may impeach with prior conviction under Fed. R. Evid. 609(a)(2) if it can prove that the crime was committed using deceitful means, even if deceit is not an element of the crime).

117. This assumes the crime is not excludable under another part of Rule 609, such as Rule 609(b), involving convictions over ten years old.

118. This chart concerns only admissibility of other convictions to impeach the credibility of a witness, not any other use of conviction evidence, such as under Rule 404(b).

cross-examiner is not bound by the witness' denial of the prior conviction, but may prove its existence by public record. Often, the party supporting the witness, knowing that it will be admissible, will bring out the prior conviction on direct examination to blunt its impact.[119]

Eliciting the Details of Prior Convictions

Sometimes a party will want to go into the details of the prior conviction or present facts that are not on the face of the document constituting the certified conviction. The impeached witness may want to say that the guilty plea was entered to protect a loved one, or claim intoxication at the time of the crime. The impeacher may want to show that the crime was committed in a cruel and barbarous fashion or parade before the jury other details that show how deep and dirty is the gutter from which the witness has crawled. The courts have not settled on a single approach to the degree of detail that may be elicited.[120]

Turning first to the impeacher, one finds cases which purport to set forth fairly strict limits. One formulation of these limits would restrict the impeacher to asking about (1) the existence of prior conviction(s); (2) the name of the crime(s); and (3) when the conviction(s) occurred.[121] Another common formulation would also allow inquiry into the length of the punishment imposed.[122] However, the impeaching party may go into details of the witness' conviction if the witness attempts to "explain away" the convictions.[123]

Certain tactics are also available to the party calling the witness who has been or will be impeached with prior convictions. For one thing, the

---

119. Former Fed. R. Evid. 609 spoke in terms only of bringing in the evidence during cross-examination. Fed. R. Evid. 609 (as amended effective Dec. 1, 1990) simply provides that qualifying convictions are admissible; it does not limit admission to situations in which the information is elicited on cross-examination.

120. *See* 28 Wright & Gold, *supra* note 98 § 6134, at 221–28.

121. *See, e.g.*, United States v. Sampol, 636 F.2d 621, 670 (D.C.Cir.1980) (court properly prevented defendants from cross-examining witness about the length of his confinement in prison when the prosecution had already established his criminal record and the dates of his convictions); United States v. Tumblin, 551 F.2d 1001, 1004 (5th Cir.1977) (held, improper to inquire about matters such as length of time spent in prison and length of time between release from prison and arrest for current offense); *see also* dicta in Shows v. M/V Red Eagle, 695 F.2d 114 (5th Cir.1983) (inquiry into witness' length of confinement for robbery conviction is impermissible even when impeachment is permissible under Fed. R. Evid. 609).

122. State v. Amburgey, 515 N.E.2d 925, 927 (Ohio1987) ("a trial court has broad discretion to limit any questioning of a witness on cross-examination which asks more than the name of the crime, the time and place of conviction and the punishment imposed, when the conviction is admissible solely to impeach general credibility"); 1 McCormick on Evidence § 42, at 151–52 (4th ed. John W. Strong ed. 1992).

123. *See* United States v. Amahia, 825 F.2d 177, 181 (8th Cir.1987) (prosecution may cross-examine witness about details of prior conviction in case where defendant testified he only pleaded guilty to four felony counts because he was assured he would only receive probation and because of the strain of working and going to school); United States v. Wolf, 561 F.2d 1376, 1381 (10th Cir.1977) (defendant may be cross-examined about facts underlying his conviction for making false claims to the federal government in case where defendant claimed he agreed to plead guilty because he did not have the money to defend the charges).

party anticipating impeachment often will elicit the fact of the conviction during direct examination to blunt its effect on cross-examination.[124] Also, counsel expecting the opponent to impeach the witness with prior convictions may wish to elicit sufficient detail during direct examination to demonstrate that the convictions were minor, that the punishment was slight, or that other details of the convictions show that the convictions do not affect the witness' credibility.

If the party calling a witness chooses to elicit testimony concerning prior convictions of a witness, the cross-examiner still has the right to fill in details to the extent allowed by the governing law of the jurisdiction. For example, the cross-examiner could ask about when the conviction occurred and what the punishment was.[125] The fact that it is easy to step over the line, even in jurisdictions that give latitude to ask about punishment, is illustrated by *United States v. Harding*.[126] There, the appellate court considered it proper to impeach a defendant charged with a cocaine sale with evidence of a conviction for possession of marijuana with intent to sell. However, the prosecutor went beyond asking about the name of the crime, when it occurred, and the punishment. The prosecutor also asked questions that revealed that the crime involved 80 pounds of marijuana and that the marijuana was found in defendant's home, and another question that suggested that it might have been there at the time of the cocaine sale charged in the instant case.[127] The court reversed the conviction. It conceded that it was proper for the prosecutor to elicit information about the existence of the prior conviction and even about the fact that it involved 80 pounds of marijuana. These were facts that appeared on the written record of the conviction, and the court regarded the written record as an appropriate guideline in the case concerning what could be inquired about on cross-examination. However, the court thought that the prosecutor went too far in asking a question revealing that the marijuana was found at the defendant's home, and in suggesting that it might have been there at the time of the alleged cocaine transaction. The court regarded this as an emphasis on the similarity of the two offenses that "was plainly intended to convince the jury of appellant's guilt as opposed to his lack of veracity."[128] It would have been proper to use a marijuana conviction purely for the

124. *See, e.g.*, Michelson v. United States, 335 U.S. 469, 471 (1948) (in prosecution for bribing a federal revenue agent, defendant testified on direct examination concerning an old misdemeanor conviction dealing with trading in counterfeit watch dials); Gill v. Thomas, 83 F.3d 537 (1st Cir.1996) (in federal civil rights action, plaintiff, anticipating impeachment with several crimes, introduced them "preemptively to 'remove the sting' from [the] anticipated impeachment). *See* United States v. Berry, 661 F.2d 618, 621 (7th Cir.1981) (noting that "defense counsel often uses this trial tactic to preclude the Government from first bringing out a defendant's prior criminal record").

125. This, of course, assumes that, as seems to be commonly the case, the jurisdiction allows questions about punishment. *See Amburgey*, 515 N.E.2d at 119.

126. 525 F.2d 84 (7th Cir.1975).

127. The discovery of the marijuana occurred after the alleged cocaine sale, but the marijuana conviction was obtained before the cocaine trial.

128. 525 F.2d at 90.

purpose of showing that the witness is a liar, but not to show that the witness has the character of being a drug dealer.[129]

Though limits on eliciting the details of prior convictions are sensible when the prior conviction goes only to impeachment, the impeacher may be able to find another theory under which the details of a crime can be ushered into evidence. That would be so if the witness being impeached were the criminal defendant, and the details revealed that the defendant had used the same modus operandi in the prior crime as in the current one. Then, the prior crime is not being used only to impeach, but to show, under Rule 404(b), a common pattern.[130] Yet the similarity of the prior crime can cut both ways. When the prior crime is not quite similar enough to qualify under Rule 404(b), then one sometimes finds judges saying that similarity increases the prejudice of going into the details, because the jury is more likely to use the prior crime as evidence of propensity to commit the type of offense, rather than limiting its use purely to assessing credibility.[131]

Sometimes the details of a crime shed special light on credibility. For example, when the crime charged is larceny, the fact that the larceny was accomplished by a false statement bears on truthfulness. At least where the defendant is not the witness being impeached, this sort of limited inquiry might be helpful in assessing the witness. Yet there is authority upholding exclusion even in this situation.[132] Perhaps there is some justification for exclusion, since this type of inquiry could lead to a "mini-trial" of the witness, wasting time and distracting the jury.

Stale Convictions

The Federal Rules contain an express provision limiting the use of convictions when more than 10 years has elapsed since conviction or

---

129. In the authors' opinion, the conviction should have been excluded completely. Its probative value on the issue of truthtelling ability is far overshadowed by the danger that the jury will use it to show that the defendant had the character of being a drug dealer.

130. *See* United States v. Fountain, 768 F.2d 790, 796 (7th Cir.1985) (Posner, J.) (murder of prison guard; defendant's prior use of knife in stabbing other inmate 57 times admissible on grounds that it would illuminate intent and modus operandi under Rule 404(b); strong dissent by Swygert, J.).

131. *Cf.* United States v. Harding, 525 F.2d 84, 91 (7th Cir.1975) (described in text; held, improper to go into details of marijuana conviction in cocaine prosecution; similarity of crimes considered a factor weighing against going into details). Although it does not deal with receiving the details of the conviction, compare United States v. Wallace, 848 F.2d 1464, 1473 (9th Cir.1988), which suggests the duality of

courts' attitudes toward similarity of crimes. There, the court said that an old conviction for heroin distribution should have been barred in a prosecution for the same crime, saying that similarity weighs against receiving the evidence, not in favor of receiving it. Had the crime been more similar—say, heroin distribution using the same highly unusual method then the prior conviction would have been admissible under 404(b).

132. *See* State v. Amburgey, 515 N.E.2d 925, 927 (Ohio1987). The *Amburgey* court upheld, as not an abuse of discretion, a trial judge's refusal to allow the complaining witness in an attempted rape case to be questioned about the basis for a grand theft conviction. The question would apparently have revealed that the basis was welfare fraud, which would have made the crime one that more directly reflected on the witness' truthfulness than the general offense of grand theft.

release from confinement, whichever is later. The trial judge has authority to admit the conviction, but only upon a special showing and after notice and an opportunity to contest the use of the evidence.[133] The showing should not be confused with that required for exclusion under Rule 403. In fact, it is the opposite. The court must exclude evidence of the old conviction unless the *proponent* demonstrates that its "probative value ... supported by specific facts and circumstances substantially outweighs its prejudicial effect." In addition, the party wishing to offer the conviction must give "sufficient advance written notice of intent to use such evidence to provide the adverse party with a fair opportunity to contest the use of such evidence."

Pardons; Juvenile Adjudications

Crimes that have been pardoned and juvenile adjudications are generally not admissible. However, evidence of pardoned offenses may be received if the person was convicted of a subsequent crime and the pardon was grounded upon a basis other than a finding of innocence.[134] Juvenile convictions may be received if the convicted witness is someone other than the accused and the judge decides that justice requires the impeachment.[135]

§ 9.10   Impeachment With Evidence of Bias

Opponents may freely attack the credibility of a witness with evidence of bias or interest. For example, the following types of evidence are admissible:

1. That a witness is a friend or relative of a party

2. That a witness bears a grudge against a party

3. That a witness has a business relationship with a party

4. That a witness testifying for the government has hopes of leniency in a criminal case pending against the witness

5. That a witness' expenses (or expert fee) are being paid by a party

6. That a witness has been coached by a party or the party's lawyer[136]

---

133.   *See* Fed. R. Evid. 609(b).

134.   *See* Fed. R. Evid. 609(c).

135.   *See* Fed. R. Evid. 609(d). *Cf.* Davis v. Alaska, 415 U.S. 308 (1974) (unconstitutional to exclude juvenile record of witness under circumstances).

136.   *See generally* 3A John H. Wigmore, Evidence in Trials at Common Law § 948–969. (James H. Chadbourn rev. 1970); *see also* State v. Sweeney, 443 So.2d 522, 529–30 (La.1983) (held, in case where government's two key witnesses had arrested one of defendant's proffered witnesses,

that prosecution may cross-examine defense witness about his previous arrest by those officers to explore defendant's witness' bias towards the two officers). *But cf.* Malek v. Federal Ins. Co., 994 F.2d 49, 54 (2d Cir. 1993) (held, in property owners' suit to recover proceeds from fire insurance policy, it was improper for district court to permit defendants to impeach plaintiffs' expert witness on cross-examination with evidence that plaintiffs were members of Hasidic Jewish community, that the witness was also Jewish, and that witness had other Hasidic clients; such impeachment violates

Evidence of bias and interest has never been subject to the rule against collateral proof. The cross-examiner is not obliged to "take the answer" of the witness. For example, if the witness is asked about fighting with the defendant, and the witness answers "no," the opponent is entitled to call another witness to introduce evidence that the fight took place.[137] The Supreme Court endorsed the view that extrinsic evidence of bias is admissible the case of *United States v. Abel*.[138] In that case, the government offered a witness who would testify that a defense witness belonged to the same prison gang as the defendant, and that the gang required its members to commit perjury, theft, and murder for each other. The Court upheld the admission of this evidence, noting that the common law of evidence permitted extrinsic evidence of bias while requiring the cross-examiner to "take the witness' answer" with regard to less favored forms of evidence. The Federal Rules of Evidence did not change this common law rule.

The Federal Rules of Evidence do not treat bias impeachment directly, though the Rules contain some language that could have been read to restrict the use of extrinsic evidence of bias. Rule 608(b) prohibits the use of extrinsic evidence about specific acts, except for evidence of prior convictions, for purposes of "attacking or supporting the witness' credibility." The quoted language was apparently intended to apply only to character attack, not to attack for bias, but read literally it could apply to both forms of attack. However, the *Abel* case settled the issue for the federal courts firmly in favor of admissibility of this type of evidence to demonstrate bias. An amendment that adopted the *Abel* rule would help clarify the codified rules of evidence. The Commissioners of the Uniform Rules of Evidence have promulgated just such a rule. Uniform Rule 616 provides that "for the purpose of attacking the credibility of a witness, evidence of bias, prejudice, or interest of the witness for or against any party to the case is admissible."[139]

Extrinsic evidence of specific conduct is admissible to show bias, but not to attack character. When attacking a witness' character for truthfulness, the cross-examiner can ask about pertinent bad acts, but must "take the witness' answer" if the witness denies them. Extrinsic evidence is not admissible, unless it is evidence of an actual conviction.

Rule 610, which provides that "evidence of the beliefs or opinions of a witness on matters of religion is not admissible for the purpose of showing that by reason of their nature the witness credibility is impaired or enhanced"; dissent argued that evidence. was properly admitted as evidence of bias since it demonstrated that witness depended in part on Hasidic community for his livelihood).

137. " 'Bias is never classified as a collateral matter which lies beyond the scope of inquiry, nor as a matter on which an examiner is required to take a witness' answer. Bias may be proved by extrinsic evidence even after a witness' disavowal of partiality' " United States v. Keys, 899 F.2d 983, 986 n. 2 (10th Cir.), *cert. denied*, 498 U.S. 858 (1990); United States v. Anderson, 881 F.2d 1128, 1139 (D.C.Cir.1989); United States v. Robinson, 530 F.2d 1076, 1079 (D.C.Cir.1976). *See also* United States v. Harvey, 547 F.2d 720, 723 (2d Cir.1976) (reversible error to exclude extrinsic evidence that witness had bias against defendant, consisting of witness' accusation charging defendant with fathering her child and refusing to take responsibility for it).

138.   469 U.S. 45, 52 (1984).

139.   Unif. R. Evid. 616 (1986); *see also* Minn. R. Evid. 616.

Sometimes the border between bad acts that show character and bad acts that show bias is indistinct. For example, in a criminal case the defense might claim that uncharged misconduct by a prosecution witness automatically goes to bias, because the witness is motivated by a desire not to be prosecuted by the government. However, the existence of this conceivable motive does not give defense counsel license to bring in evidence of every bad act of the witness. A foundation must be laid showing that there is a basis for believing that the witness is influenced by fear of prosecution. Some cases have required a showing of a deal between the government and the witness before the extrinsic evidence comes in.[140] For example, in *United States v. West*,[141] the Seventh Circuit described a fairly elaborate foundation requirement, stating that before the defense could question a prosecution witness about prior misconduct in order to establish bias and motive, a foundation had to be laid establishing (1) the bad act; (2) the government's knowledge of the act; (3) the lack of any prosecution; and (4) the existence of a promise not to prosecute.[142] These requirements ask too much, in view of the fact that the witness might well be influenced by fear of the government even in the absence of any explicit threat or promise. On the other hand, some foundation requirement is needed to keep the defense from bringing in witnesses to testify about collateral bad acts that would not be admissible against any nongovernment witness, and that serve only to destroy the character of a witness who may not be prepared to defend an entire lifetime of activity. A showing that the bad acts were known to the government under circumstances that would give rise to a reasonable fear of prosecution should be considered a sufficient foundation.

Even when the evidence goes to bias, and not to character, the fact that extrinsic evidence is admissible does not give the impeaching party unlimited license. The trial judge has leeway under Rule 403 to exclude details that are cumulative, a waste of time, or prejudicial.[143]

140. United States v. Capozzi, 883 F.2d 608, 616 (8th Cir.1989), *cert. denied*, 495 U.S. 918 (1990) (defendant claimed that government witness testified for the government to avoid prosecution for misconduct, and sought to put in extrinsic evidence of misconduct; court recognized that extrinsic evidence showing bias was admissible but upheld exclusion in this case because '[t]he record ... reveals no evidence of any arrangement or deal between the government and [the witness]'). *But see* United States v. Lankford, 955 F.2d 1545, 1548–49 (11th Cir.1992) (trial court violated defendant's Sixth Amendment right to cross-examine witnesses for possible bias by excluding evidence that two sons of prosecution's key witness were on probation for state court drug distribution convictions, even though witness had made no deal precluding federal investigation of his sons in exchange for the witness' testimony).

141. 670 F.2d 675, 683 (7th Cir.), *cert. denied*, 457 U.S. 1124 (1982).

142. *Cf.* United States v. Rovetuso, 768 F.2d 809, 817 (7th Cir.1985) (defendant-appellant may not offer evidence about witness' activities in Panama, based on theory that witness was afraid of being deported to Panama, on grounds that defendant had neither argued bias at trial nor laid a factual foundation).

143. United States v. Phillips, 888 F.2d 38, 42 (6th Cir.1989) (defendant, in trial for unlawful cocaine distribution, cannot offer extrinsic evidence about government witnesses using drugs at a party, after witnesses denied the accusation because the only bias that could possibly exist were government witnesses lying about a "remote matter" in order to save their jobs; trial court acted within its discretion because the information "might be more damaging than probative"); United States v.

One form of bias evidence consists of prior statements by the witness. For example, a witness might have made a statement about hating the defendant, or about intending to hurt the defendant. A plausible objection can be made if the cross-examiner fails to lay a foundation with the witness before extrinsic evidence of these statements becomes admissible. In addition, if (as in the example) the statement constitutes hearsay, the court must exclude it unless it is covered by an exception.

Must the witness being impeached be asked about the statement before extrinsic evidence becomes admissible? The point of such a requirement would be to give the witness being impeached a fair chance to explain or deny the bias-exhibiting statement. The Federal Rules of Evidence expressly impose a foundation requirement for prior inconsistent statements, but are silent about prior statements that exhibit bias. Nonetheless, authority for requiring a foundation could be grounded on the trial judge's general authority to control the "mode and order of interrogating witnesses and presenting evidence" under Rule 611(a). There is a division of authority on the question whether a foundation is required.[144]

Ferrell, 625 F.Supp. 41, 46–47 (E.D.Pa. 1985), *aff'd*, 815 F.2d 694 (3d Cir.1987) (held, in case where government witness testified he had not sold drugs in the past, that defendant could not offer extrinsic evidence that witness had sold drugs in the past because defendant could offer no theory on why evidence was probative of bias). *See also* Cummings v. Malone, 995 F.2d 817, 827 (8th Cir.1993) (in inmate's Eighth Amendment action for excessive force by prison officers, trial court property excluded testimony that two of the defendants testified in inmate's attempted rape prosecution, resulting in an additional 15 years of imprisonment, when record already contained indications of inmate's bias against defendants). *Compare* State v. McCall, 549 N.W.2d 418, 422 (Wis.1996) (held, not error to exclude evidence that the prosecutor had dismissed two pending charges against the alleged victim and sole prosecution witness in a prosecution growing out of a shooting in which the victim was rendered a quadriplegic; Justices Abramson and Bablitch dissented); United States v. Triplett, 104 F.3d 1074, 1079 (8th Cir.1997) (held, no error to exclude testimony that police search found a possible controlled substance in home of prosecution witness, despite possible bias due to witness' hope of leniency; court notes that "the confiscated substance was never tested or positively identified as a controlled substance" and that the witness was never charged); United States v. Morrison, 98 F.3d 619, 627–28 (D.C.Cir.1996), *cert. denied*, ___ U.S. ___, 117 S.Ct. 1279 (1997) (held, no abuse of discretion for trial judge to cut off questioning of witness about whether she was testifying against defendant to get lower sentence and thus avoid losing children; question called for "speculative answer" by witness; *query* correctness of rationale since even a speculative belief of witness that cooperation would help her keep children would be probative of her motive to testify falsely); United States v. DiMarzo, 80 F.3d 656, 660 (1st Cir. 1996) (held, no error to refuse to allow drug defendant to put in evidence of harsh sentence that he faced in order to show motive of others to put the blame on him in order to escape prosecution themselves; "providing jurors sentencing information invites them to ponder matters that are not within their province, distracts them from their factfinding responsibilities, and creates a strong possibility of confusion").

144. *Compare* United States v. DiNapoli, 557 F.2d 962, 965 (2d Cir.), *cert. denied*, 434 U.S. 858 (1977) (extrinsic evidence of prior statement showing bias is inadmissible unless witness is allowed to explain or deny statement); United States v. Marzano, 537 F.2d 257, 265 (7th Cir. 1976), *cert. denied*, 429 U.S. 1038 (1977) (foundation is required when witness' prior statement is offered to prove bias) *with* State v. Kehn, 361 N.E.2d 1330, 1335 (Ohio1977), *cert. denied*, 434 U.S. 858 (1977) (no foundation required before offering extrinsic evidence showing bias); State v. Carlson, 508 N.E.2d 999, 1002 (Ohio App. 1986) (held, in case where victim of assault had a civil suit filed against defendant, that

Even if the foundation is required, the requirement should not be treated as a rigid technical one. It is worth noting that even as to prior inconsistent statements, where the common law courts were fairly uniform in requiring a foundation, the Federal Rules of Evidence have liberalized foundational requirements. The relevant part of Federal Rule of Evidence 613(b) provides that "[e]xtrinsic evidence of a prior inconsistent statement by a witness is not admissible unless the witness is afforded an opportunity to explain or deny the same." Some courts have held that this provision means only that the witness must have an opportunity to come back and explain or deny the statement, not that the witness must be asked about it while originally on the witness stand.[145] In jurisdictions accepting this interpretation of Rule 613(b), it would be anomalous to impose a stricter foundation requirement on prior statements showing bias. Also, Rule 613(b) gives the trial judge authority to depart from the foundation requirement when the interests of justice require, and it would be doubly anomalous to say that this discretion did not exist when the ground for impeachment was bias, not inconsistency.

§ 9.11   Impeachment With Evidence of Defects in Perception, Memory, or Mental Health

One potentially powerful form of impeachment is to attack the witness' capacity to perceive, recollect, or narrate.[146] Defects in the witness' capacity may generally be shown on cross-examination or by the production of extrinsic testimony.[147] Much, however, depends on the nature of the particular defect and the attendant likelihood of prejudice.

Defects in the Five Senses

Such defects may freely be shown to cast doubt upon the witness' ability to perceive the events that were the subject of the witness' testimony.[148] Most commonly, the evidence concerns the witness' eye-

evidence of victim/witness' suit was admissible to show bias even though witness was not given an opportunity to explain or deny the alleged bias). *See also* United States v. Hudson, 970 F.2d 948 (1st Cir.1992) (foundation for admission of prior inconsistent statement to show witness' bias requires only that witness be available to be recalled to explain or deny the prior inconsistent statement; note that the trial court's exclusion of evidence of prior statement was reversed on other grounds; concurring opinion urged court to reconsider rule en banc at earliest opportunity and to join the majority of the circuits in requiring that witness first be given opportunity to explain or deny prior inconsistent statement).

145. *See* § 9.05.

146. *See* 27 Charles A. Wright & Victor J. Gold, Federal Practice and Procedure (Evidence) § 6097 (1990) (an attack on ca-

pacity "undermines credibility by showing that the witness lacks the perceptual, recall, or narrative abilities presupposed by his testimony").

147. *See, e.g.,* 1 McCormick on Evidence § 44 at 160 (4th ed. John W. Strong ed. 1992) (witness may be impeached by eliciting facts discrediting witness through cross-examination, or by proving facts discrediting witness through extrinsic evidence); 3A John H Wigmore, Evidence in Trials at Common Law § 931 at 758–59 (James H Chadbourn rev. 1970) (extrinsic evidence admissible to prove defective power of observation, recollection, or communication.)

148. *See, e.g.,* 1 McCormick on Evidence, supra note 147 § 45 at 160 (any deficiency of senses lessening the witness' ability to perceive facts, to which witness sight or hearing, although questioning about the sense of touch, smell, or taste would be permitted when relevant. Impeaching counsel may cross-examine on these subjects, but is not bound by the witness' answer; extrinsic evidence is freely admissible.[149]

Alcohol Intoxication and Alcoholism

Whether evidence of a witness' alcohol intoxication or alcoholism is admissible to impeach the witness is a complicated question. There is no doubt that counsel can show by evidence of drinking on the occasion in question that the witness' capacity to observe was impaired.[150] The difficult issues arise when the attempt is to attack credibility by showing chronic alcoholism or when evidence of chronic alcoholism is offered for the purpose of inviting the inference that the witness was intoxicated on the occasion in question. The traditional approach has been to exclude evidence of alcoholism as overly prejudicial.[151] If counsel is able to lay the foundation for a more specific showing that the witness habitually became intoxicated on a certain occasion or at a certain place, however, then the evidence may be admissible.[152] Thus, if the witness invariably joined drinking buddies after work in a certain bar and drank excessively, the proponent of the impeachment evidence has a better chance of getting it admitted than if the evidence took the form of testimony that the witness had been drunk several times at different places and times.

testified is provable to attack that witness' credibility)

149. *See id,* (may prove defects in witness' sense by producing other witnesses); 3A Wigmore, supra note 147 § 931 at 758 (extrinsic evidence demonstrating defective power of observation of the events to which witness testifies admissible)

150. *See, e.g.,* United States v. Infelise, No.90 Cr. 87, 1992 WL 7837 (N.D.Ill.1992) (prohibiting, inquiry into, witness' pattern of drinking during any particular period, but, allowing inquiry into whether he had had a drink on the particular day about which he testified); Rheaume v. Patterson, 289 F.2d 611, 614 (2d Cir.1961) (testimony that driver had been drinking before accident admissible to impeach credibility of driver's version of how accident happened); People v. McGuire, 163 N.E.2d 832, 833 (Ill.1960) (evidence indicating intoxication of witness at time of event to which witness testifies admissible); 4 Weinstein's Federal Evidence § 609.05[3], at 607–53 (2d ed. Joseph M. McLaughlin ed. 1997) (general rule in most jurisdictions is that extrinsic evidence admissible to show witness intoxicated at time of events to which witness testifies or intoxicated when testifying). *See generally* C.C. Marvel, Annotation, *Impeachment of Witness with Respect to Intox-*

ication, 8 A.L.R.3d 749, 758 (1966) (widely recognized rule that intoxication of witness at time of the matter about which witness testifies is relevant to witness' credibility).

151. *See, e.g.,* United States v. DiPaolo, 804 F.2d 225, 229–30 (2d Cir.1986) (trial court properly refused to permit defendant to impeach prosecution witness on basis of drinking problem); Springer v. Reimers, 84 Cal.Rptr. 486, 494–95 (Cal. App.1970) (trial court erred in admitting evidence that witness had drinking problem where impeaching party did not show witness intoxicated when observing events about which he testified or when testifying); Smith v. State, 644 S.W.2d 500, 502 (Tex.App.1982) (trial court properly excluded evidence of general habit of intoxication to prove witnesses were drunk at time they observed events about which they testified); 4 Weinstein's Federal Evidence, *supra* note 150, § 609.05[3], at 607–53 to 607–54 (evidence of chronic alcoholism inadmissible to challenge general credibility); 3A Wigmore, *supra* note 147, § 933, at 767 (general habit of intemperance usually inadmissible because it reveals nothing about witness' testimonial capacity unless it indicates intoxication at time event observed or when testifying).

152. *See* § 5.30.

Drug Use and Drug Addiction

Drug use and addiction often have been treated differently than alcohol intoxication and alcoholism. The witness who is a heavy drinker traditionally has been treated with more delicacy and regard than the witness who is a heavy, or even occasional, user of other drugs. Of course, evidence of drug use on the day that the witness made the observations reported in the witness' testimony is freely admitted[153]—just as in the case of alcohol use. Some courts have gone much further, and have been receptive to the idea that drug abuse on other occasions is admissible for impeachment purposes.[154] A broad-gauge acceptance of this approach is unjustified, in view of the different effects of different drugs and the prejudicial impact of evidence of use of forbidden psychoactive drugs. Accordingly, there appears to be a trend toward excluding evidence that the witness used drugs on occasions other than the one that was the subject of witness' testimony, unless there is evidence that habitual drug use has impaired the witness' ability remember and communicate observations.[155] One prominent treatise suggests that impeachment by evidence of drug abuse be allowed only if accompanied by expert testimony or proof from reliable scientific literature about the effects of the particular drug.[156]

Mental Defect, Abnormality, or Disease

In considering evidence of mental defects and diseases, first note that many states have competency rules that prohibit testimony by witnesses whose mental state prevents them from accurately relating facts.[157] The present section deals with use of the evidence for impeach-

---

153. *See, e.g.*, United States v. Fowler, 465 F.2d 664, 665–66 (D.C.Cir.1972) (trial court erred in not allowing defendant to cross-examine prosecution witness as to whether he was using narcotics at the time he observed the defendant commit alleged offense).

154. *See, e.g.*, People v. Strother, 290 N.E.2d 201 (Ill.1972) (evidence of narcotics addiction admissible to impeach witness' general credibility because addicts are notorious liars); 3A Wigmore, *supra* note 147, § 934, at 763 (evidence of drug habit should be admissible).

155. *See, e.g.*, Gonzalez v. Van Zandt, No. 90 Civ. 4273 (S.D.N.Y. Feb. 5, 1992) (trial court did not violate defendant's Sixth Amendment confrontation right by limiting cross-examination of state's key witness about drug use history, where witness testified that he "felt all right" on the day in question and that his heroin habit hadn't "interfere[d] with anything" even though he had been without heroin for a few days); United States v. Cameron, 814 F.2d 403, 405 (7th Cir.1987) (trial court properly excluded evidence of witness' drug use to attack general character; evidence of drug use admissible only when probative to witness'

inability to recollect and relate); Lusher v. State, 390 N.E.2d 702, 704 (Ind.App.1979) (trial court erred in refusing to permit cross-examination of witness' use of different drugs causing problems with hallucinations; evidence of drug use admissible where it may have substantially affected witness' ability to perceive, remember, and testify).

156. 4 Weinstein's Federal Evidence, *supra* note 150 § 609.05[4][a] (counsel should furnish court with specific information about drugs, dosage, its probable effect on witness, when witness took drugs, and how frequently he used them on other occasions; counsel should also be prepared to substantiate claim by expert testimony or recognized literature). *Accord* People v. Balderas, 711 P.2d 480, 507 (Cal.1985) (trial court properly refused to permit inquiry into prosecution witness' use of narcotics on days other than the day to which he testified where defendant failed to offer expert testimony on probable effect of such use on general recall and perceptive abilities).

157. *See* § 6.02. The Federal Rules of Evidence, however, have no such competency requirement. Fed. R. Evid. 601.

ment of a witness, not its attempted use to prevent the witness from testifying altogether under the rules of competency.[158]

When offered for impeachment, evidence of low intelligence or mental retardation is admissible unless its value is substantially outweighed by considerations such as waste of time. Thus, evidence about how the witness did in school would ordinarily be excluded, while evidence of severe retardation would be admissible. [159]

Evidence of mental disease is admissible if relevant to the witness' ability to accurately perceive, recollect, or communicate information.[160] Its admissibility, however, is subject to standard Rule 403 considerations, such as prejudice or confusion of the issues.[161] Considerations of embarrassing the witness are not often mentioned, but undoubtedly are also taken into consideration, as they should be.[162] Some conditions, such as schizophrenia, clearly have more probative value in showing that the witness' testimony may have been deluded than do others, such as depression in reaction to an exogenous event.[163]

158. Although an attack on competency will not usually result in keeping the witness off the stand, it may provide a chance to acquire information about the witness' mental condition or get a mental exam, which, of course, can be used for impeachment purposes if the incompetency attack fails.

159. *Compare* Polson v. State, 207 N.E.2d 638 (Ind.1965) (trial court did abuse discretion in sustaining objection to defendant's question as to whether witness was "a little behind in school") *with* State v. Armstrong, 62 S.E.2d 50, 51 (N.C.1950) (trial court erred in refusing to permit physician and another witness to testify that prosecution witness was retarded, having the mind of a child 9 to 12 years old).

160. *See, e.g.*, United States v. Diecidue, 603 F.2d 535, 551 (5th Cir.1979), *cert. denied*, 445 U.S. 946 (1980) (trial court did not err in refusing to admit witness' psychiatric records where witness' treatment had occurred 12 years before event to which he testified and were not probative of his ability to testify accurately); United States v. Partin, 493 F.2d 750, 763 (5th Cir.1974) (reversible error to refuse to admit evidence concerning witness' mental condition and treatment where witness entered hospital five months before events to which he testified occurred, complaining of auditory hallucinations and belief that he was some other person); People v. Cooks, 190 Cal.Rptr. 211, 268 (Cal.App.1983), *cert. denied*, 464 U.S. 1046 (1984) (trial court did not abuse discretion in refusing to allow defendant to cross-examine witness as to psychiatric treatment, where no evidence demonstrated that witness' mental condition impaired his ability to accurately

perceive, recollect, or communicate); 3A Wigmore, *supra* note 147 § 932, at 759 (evidence of insanity admissible to discredit the witness, if the mental condition affected the witness at the time the event to which the witness testifies occurred, while the witness testifies, or in the meantime so as to impair the witness' ability to recollect). *Compare* United States v. Pryce, 938 F.2d 1343, 1345–50 (D.C.Cir.1991), *cert. denied*, 503 U.S. 941 (1992) (trial court committed reversible error in refusing to allow cross-examination about witness' hallucinations, which occurred four months before events to which witness testified).

161. *See, e.g.*, United States v. Rivera–Santiago, 872 F.2d 1073, 1084–85 (1st Cir.), *cert. denied*, 492 U.S. 910 (1989) (trial court properly refused to permit counsel to question witness as to court-ordered referral for psychiatric evaluation, because jury could improperly infer that witness needed psychiatric treatment; no other evidence supported such inference); United States v. Lopez, 611 F.2d 44, 45–46 (4th Cir.1979) (cross-examination concerning witness' mental condition subject to Rule 403 limitations; must not introduce collateral issue which would confuse jury).

162. *Lopez*, 611 F.2d at 45 (trial court did not err in refusing to permit defendant to cross-examine prosecution witness as to psychiatric examination where examination had no relevance to witness' qualification and was merely an attempt to stigmatize witness).

163. *Compare* United States v. Lindstrom, 698 F.2d 1154, 1163 (11th Cir.1983) (trial court erred in refusing to permit de-

If expert testimony is offered, an objection can sometimes be based on the expert's lack of opportunity to acquire information necessary for the diagnosis. If the expert did not do a clinical examination of the witness, some courts will exclude, or use the absence of the clinical examination as a factor in excluding.[164]

Expert testimony that the witness has an emotional condition that makes the witness a liar is often objectionable. Such evidence may be unhelpful to the jury in its special province of determining truthfulness; its scientific basis is often questionable; and it can amount to making a character attack under the guise of medical testimony.[165]

§ 9.12 Improper Rehabilitation of Witness

The general principle governing limits on rehabilitation of witnesses is simple. It is that there can be no support in absence of attack.[166] The

fendant to cross-examine prosecution witness as to her mental condition, to support theory of vendetta against defendant, where witness' medical records suggested history of psychiatric disorders, including schizophrenia, manifesting themselves in violent threats and manipulative and destructive conduct) *with* United States v. Brumbaugh, 471 F.2d 1128, 1129 (6th Cir.), *cert. denied*, 412 U.S. 918 (1973) (trial court did not err in refusing to permit defendant to introduce hospital report concerning witness' treatment for depression into evidence to impeach witness).

164. *See, e.g.*, United States v. Riley, 657 F.2d 1377, 1387 (8th Cir. 1981) (trial court did not err in excluding expert testimony as to witness' mental condition and her capacity for telling the truth where expert's opinion was based only on court observations of witness); United States v. Daileda, 229 F.Supp. 148, 153–54 (M.D.Pa. 1964) (trial court properly excluded expert testimony concerning witness' capacity to tell the truth where expert did not treat or examine witness, but only observed witness testify), *aff'd*, 342 F.2d 218, *cert. denied*, 382 U.S. 815 (1965).

165. *See, e.g.*, People v. Ainsworth, 755 P.2d 1017, 1033–34, 248 Cal.Rptr. 568, 583–85 (Cal. 1988) (dictum) (psychiatrist may not testify as to whether witness is telling truth on particular occasion where only purpose of testimony is to impeach witness' credibility); State v. Munro, 680 P.2d 708, 710 (Or.App.), *review denied*, 683 P.2d 1372 (1984) (trial court properly excluded expert testimony concerning victim's emotional disturbance and effect on her perceptions and veracity; experts cannot testify as to veracity of particular witness). *Cf.* Westcott v. Crinklaw, 68 F.3d 1073, 1076–77 (8th

Cir.1995) (in civil action alleging excessive force by a police officer, trial court erroneously admitted testimony of expert that police officer suffered from post-traumatic stress disorder to explain officer's incomplete and inaccurate statements after the shooting; expert testimony usurped the jury's role to determine credibility); United States v. Shay, 57 F.3d 126, 129–34 (1st Cir.1995) (held, abuse of discretion for trial judge to prevent defense from explaining defendant's self-incriminating statements with expert testimony by psychiatrist that defendant suffered from "pseudologia fantastica").

166. United States v. Binker, 795 F.2d 1218, 1223 (5th Cir.1986), *cert. denied*, 479 U.S. 1085 (1987) (government on redirect may ask witness to testify that his plea agreement makes the promise that the witness will testify truthfully *after* defendant cross-examined witness for bias due to the plea agreement) United States v. Jackson, 588 F.2d 1046, 1055 (5th Cir.1979), *rehg denied*, 591 F.2d 1343, *cert. denied*, 442 U.S. 941 (1979) (defendant who takes the stand to testify does not, as a matter of course, have the right to support his testimony; however, if his credibility is attacked defendant may introduce evidence of good character for truthfulness; *see also* 27 Charles A. Wright & Victor J. Gold, Federal Practice and Procedure (Evidence) § 6098 (1990) (describing the common law principle "that evidence supporting credibility is admissible only if credibility has been or certainly will be attacked") (footnotes omitted); 4 John H. Wigmore, Evidence in Trials at Common Law § 1104 (James H. Chadbourn rev. 1972) ("every witness may be assumed to be of normal moral character for veracity).

witness who has not been attacked cannot be bolstered, whether by character evidence, prior consistent statements, or other support.

One specific instance of this rule is that rehabilitation with evidence of good character for truthfulness is not permitted unless the witness' character for truthfulness has been attacked.[167] When character for truthfulness has been attacked, in any fashion, the witness can be rehabilitated with reputation or opinion testimony about character for truthfulness.[168] Because impeachment by showing bias is not normally a character attack, the witness attacked with evidence of bias cannot be rehabilitated with testimony about character for truthfulness.[169] Other types of impeachment may be considered attacks on character. If the facts of the case show the impeachment to involve an attack on character for truthfulness (as may be the case when the witness is impeached by contradiction or with a prior inconsistent statement), evidence showing good character for truthfulness should be admissible.[170]

Rehabilitation with evidence of prior consistent statements is permitted in response to attack for fabrication or other improper influence.[171] Under the prevailing view, the consistent statement, to be

---

167. Fed. R. Evid. 608(a)(2); *see also* United States v. Dring, 930 F.2d 687, 690–95 (9th Cir.), *cert. denied*, 506 U.S. 836 (1992) (not error to exclude rehabilitative evidence of defendant's truthful character, where prosecution merely emphasized inconsistency between defendant's testimony and that of other witnesses and noted defendant's interest in outcome of case but did not offer evidence of defendant's general character for truthfulness); United States v. Jackson, 588 F.2d 1046, 1055 (5th Cir.), *cert. denied*, 442 U.S. 941 (1979) (mere fact prosecution pointed out defendant's version of facts was different than other witnesses was not an attack on defendant's credibility and defendant could not bolster his credibility by offering evidence of defendant's character for veracity).

Even where the defendant testifies, issues can arise about whether it is proper to admit consistent statements in anticipation of impeachment. *See* Ross v. Saint Augustine's College, 103 F.3d 338, 342 (4th Cir. 1996) (no error to allow plaintiff to put in her consistent statements prior to her testimony; evidence was linked up to later impeachment efforts by defendant when she did testify; court distinguished United States v. Bolick, 917 F.2d 135, 138–39 (4th Cir.1990), a case where the government pursued a deliberate strategy of attempting to minimize the unpalatability of its witnesses by putting in their statements through a federal agent first).

168. Beard v. Mitchell, 604 F.2d 485, 503 (7th Cir.1979) (defendant may offer proof of reputation for truthfulness after

plaintiff introduced prior inconsistent statement by defendant in order to attack defendant's credibility); *see also* Fed. R. Evid. 608 (a)(2); 4 Wigmore, *supra* note 166, at § 1105.

169. Fed. R. Evid. 608 advisory committee's note.

170. *Id.* (recognizing that whether impeachment by contradiction constitutes a character attack must depend on circumstances); 1 McCormick on Evidence § 47, at 175–76 (4th ed. John W. Strong ed. 1992) (cautioning against categorical rules and stating that "the judge should consider in each case whether a particular impeachment for inconsistency or a conflict in testimony, or either of them, amounts in net effect to an attack on character for truth and should exercise his discretion accordingly to admit or exclude the character-support") (footnotes omitted).

171. United States v. Montague, 958 F.2d 1094, 1096 (D.C.Cir.1992) (trial court did not abuse discretion in allowing government to rehabilitate witness by introducing prior consistent statement, where defense's cross-examination of witness about terms of plea agreement was at least an "implied charge of improper motive"); United States v. Duncan, 693 F.2d 971, 980 (9th Cir.1982) (held, in case where customs agent testified that defendant made admission to him but did not include the admission in his notes from the interview, that government could introduce three prior consistent statements by agent to rebut defendant's claim that the agent fabricated the admission); United admissible, must have been made prior to the time alleged motive for fabrication or improper influence arose.[172] Thus, if a prosecution witness is attacked for bias arising from a deal with the prosecution after the witness' arrest on a criminal charge, consistent statements by the witness made before the arrest would be admissible (the motive not having yet arisen), but statements made after the motive to cooperate with the prosecution arose would not. They simply do not bolster the witness. In *Tome v. United States*,[173] the Supreme Court approved this approach, holding that when a statement is offered under Rule 801(d)(1)(B) to rebut a charge of recent fabrication or improper influence or motive, the statement is admissible only when made before the charged recent fabrication or improper influence or motive.[174]

For the federal courts, the *Tome* case settled the question whether, when a statement is offered under Rule 801(d)(1)(B), the trial judge has discretion to admit pre-motive evidence to bolster the witness. The majority endorsed a per se rule that the statements must be excluded unless they were made before the motive to fabricate or improper influence arose.

Note, however, that *Tome* involved statements offered under Rule 801(d)(1)(B), which allows prior consistent statements to be used not only to bolster credibility, but also as substantive evidence to show the truth of the matter asserted. The Court did not directly address the question whether prior consistent statements might sometimes be admissible on the theory that they fall outside the hearsay ban because they are offered to show something other than the truth of the matter asserted. For example, suppose that an elderly witness testifies about the details of a transaction, and is impeached by cross-examination that

States v. Allen, 579 F.2d 531 (9th Cir.1978) (government may offer witness' prior consistent statement after defendant argued that witness' testimony was based on fear of being prosecuted herself); see also Fed. R. Evid. 801 (d)(1)(B); *compare to* Minn. R. Evid. 801 (d)(1)(B) (consistent statement may be admitted if it is helpful to the trier of fact in evaluating the witness' credibility; consistent statement admissible even if the witness is not charged with a recent fabrication).

In some jurisdictions; the statement in text would need to be qualified to be completely accurate. There is a division of authority about whether prior consistent statements (1) may be used only to rebut a charge of recent fabrication, undue influence, or improper motive, or (2) may in special situations also be used to bolster credibility in other ways, for example by rebutting a charge that the witness' memory is faulty. *See* Norman M. Garland & Romy Schneider, *Prior Consistent Statements As Evidence in the United States and Canada*, 2 S.W.U. J.L. & Trade in the

Americas 451 (1995). Though Tome v. United States, 513 U.S. 150, 115 S.Ct. 696 (1995), does not directly address this issue, some of the language in the case suggests that the Court assumed that Rule 801(d)(1)(B) was the only route through which evidence of a prior consistent statement could be received to counter impeachment of a witness.

172. 4 Wigmore, *supra* note 166 § 1128.

173. 513 U.S. 150, 115 S.Ct. 696 (1995).

174. *See also* United States v. Forrester, 60 F.3d 52 (2d Cir.1995) (government precluded from admitting prior consistent statement of witness, defendant's co-conspirator, including post-arrest interview notes, because motive to fabricate arose as soon as witness was arrested; government's purpose was to "bolster the credibility of a discredited witness whose motive to shade the truth existed before she drafted the contested statement" and statement is inadmissible under *Tome*).

touches on problems of forgetting as well as on the witness' motive to help the proponent. The elderly witness' prior statements made soon after the transaction would arguably be admissible to show that the witness' memory was accurate. Just as a prior inconsistent statement might be admitted for a purpose other than showing its truth, so might a prior consistent statement. If so, then the Tome pre-motive requirement might not apply to those consistent statements. In Tome, the Court expressly states that "Our holding is confined to the requirements for admission under Rule 801(d)(1)(B),"[175] so one might infer that the ruling does not cover the use of prior consistent statements to rehabilitate a witness when the proponent does not rely upon Rule 801(d)(1)(B) but instead offers the statement on the theory that it is not being offered to prove its truth. However, there is language elsewhere in Tome that suggests that the Court may have believed that Rule 801(d)(1)(B) was the only route through which prior consistent statements could be received to combat impeachment. For example, the Court states that "Prior consistent statements may not be admitted to counter all forms of impeachment or to bolster the witness merely because she has been discredited."[176]

Rehabilitation of a witness solely with character evidence is subject to the Rule 608(b) prohibition against extrinsic evidence of specific acts. This prohibition does not apply if the rehabilitation addresses a charge of bias, as opposed to character attack.[177]

---

175. *Tome*, 513 U.S. at 169.

176. *Id.* at 159. For a full analysis, see Garland & Schneider, *supra* note 171.

177. *See* United States v. Lindemann, 85 F.3d 1232, 1243 (7th Cir.), *cert. denied,* ___ U.S. ___, 117 S.Ct. 392 (1996) (Rule 608 does not limit rehabilitation of witness attacked for bias and hence extrinsic evidence is admissible for that purpose; government could show that prosecution witness had incriminated other persons who had pled guilty in order to meet defense contention that witness was fabricating case against defendant to save his own hide, the evidence showed that witness had many "bargaining chips," hence reducing his need to fabricate a case against the defendant).

Chapter 10

OPINION EVIDENCE & EXPERT TESTIMONY

Analysis

§ 10.01 The Common Law Rule Against Opinion Testimony

Concern for trustworthiness of the evidentiary database has been the hallmark of the common law system of proof. Witnesses who have observed events are supposed to relate the observations to the jurors, whose task it is to interpret those observations, reach conclusions about what happened, and come to a decision between the contending presenters, in light of the law.

The common law's insistence on personal knowledge as the bedrock for testimony is codified in the Rule 602 admonition that "[a] witness may not testify to a matter unless evidence is introduced sufficient to support a finding that the witness has personal knowledge of the matter."

Rule 602 captures the essence of what Wigmore described as the British rule against opinion evidence. For centuries, the British courts have prohibited witnesses from speculating about subjects for which they had no personal knowledge base.[1] A witness' opinion, for example, that

---

1. John H. Wigmore, Evidence in Trials at Common Law § 1917 (James H. Chadbourn rev. 1976) [hereinafter, Wigmore]. McCormick on Evidence § 11, (4th ed. John W. Strong ed. 1994) (quoting Coke's 1622 admonition from *Adams v. Canon,* Dyer 53b, "It is no satisfaction for a the queen dressed in purple on her birthday was not admissible if the witness had not seen the queen on her birthday.

Nineteenth century American courts did more than enforce the British rule against opinion testimony. They expanded upon it. Wigmore complained that in addition to prohibiting speculation about matters for which the witness had no personal knowledge, courts prohibited any inference or conclusion about matters for which the witness did have personal knowledge.[2]

The American opinion rule assumed a division between "fact" and "opinion." The orthodox American opinion rule was that witnesses testified to "facts," but the "opinion" about what those facts meant was for the jurors to decide. The witness, therefore, who did see the queen on her birthday could say that she wore purple, but only the jury could decide that she did not look good in purple. Under this approach, one could argue that a witness could testify that a person had bloodshot eyes, slurred speech, poor motor control, and breath that smelled of alcohol, but that it was for the jurors, not the witness, to conclude that the person was drunk.[3]

The rule prohibiting a witness from testifying to inferences based upon perception, except in cases of "necessity," was the orthodox view in almost every American common law jurisdiction, though it may never have been enforced as often or as vigorously as it was articulated. The dividing line between the "facts" of what a witness observes and the witness' "opinion" about those facts is rarely so clear as theory and the obvious examples suggest. More often than not—as in the case of the person who was red-eyed, foul smelling, word slurring, and could not crawl in a straight line—the "opinion," "conclusion," or "inference" that the person was drunk is only a more general articulation of the "facts" observed by the witness. Notice, for example, that the "fact" of "poor motor control" is really a "conclusion" about the comparative motor ability between the person observed and other persons the witness has observed. Similarly, "breath that smelled of alcohol" is not a "fact" about an odor, but rather is an "inference" about where on the person the smell came from and what it was that created the odor. Even in the halcyon days of the American opinion rule, courts were often better at articulating the distinction between "fact" and "opinion" than they were at identifying it and excluding "opinion."

Opinions from expert witnesses were not much more welcome in nineteenth and early twentieth century American courts than inferences from lay witnesses. Until adoption of the Federal Rules, experts were relatively rare and their testimony comparatively limited. The distaste for expert opinion testimony led to rules that sharply curtailed the

witness to say that he 'thinketh' or 'persuadeth himself.'")

2. Wigmore, *supra* note 1, § 1917.

3. Even during the heyday of the orthodox rule, however, courts found it hard to resist common sense, and often admitted lay opinion about drunkenness. *See* Wigmore, *supra* note 1, § 1974 n. 1 (collecting authorities).

influence that an expert might have on the trial. The expert witness could testify only if necessary to provide information that was beyond the ken of the average juror, could testify only in response to a hypothetical question, could not assume anything that was not already in evidence, and could not offer an opinion on the ultimate issue before the jury.[4]

Article VII of the Federal Rules, Opinions and Expert Testimony, codified a sea change in the American courts' approach to opinion evidence. Rule 701 explicitly allows inference testimony from lay witnesses, if the inference is rationally based upon perception. The overall liberalizing influence of the Federal Rules has been nowhere more apparent than in its expansion of expert witness testimony in Rules 702 through 706. Testimony of once rare experts has become commonplace, if not overbearing,[5] in courts of every jurisdiction and the limitations on their testimony have been relaxed substantially. Expert testimony need no longer be necessary to provide information beyond the ken of the jurors to be admissible. It is enough if the testimony will "assist" the jurors. Experts now may be asked their opinions about the specific case, without resort to a hypothetical question. They may offer opinions about the ultimate issue for the jurors' consideration. They need not offer the bases for their opinions before offering their opinions. Their opinions may be based on material that is not and could never be admitted into evidence.[6]

§ 10.02 Opinion Testimony From Lay Witnesses [FRE 701]

Wigmore's view that American courts should abolish their inference rule, because they had misapplied and unwisely added to the British opinion rule,[7] did not prevail entirely. The rule against a lay (non-expert) witness testifying to an inference has evolved into Rule 701 — a rule that prefers more specific testimony to more general testimony, but allows inferential testimony under certain circumstances.

Rule 701 allows a lay witness to offer "opinions or inferences" if they are "rationally based on the perception of the witness" and "helpful to a clear understanding of the witness' testimony or the determination of a fact in issue."

The requirement that the inference be "based on the perception of the witness" is a restatement of the Rule 602 insistence on personal knowledge. Rule 701 prohibits lay opinion if it is speculation about events for which the witness has no personal knowledge. But the Rule permits the witness to testify to inferences from matters about which the

---

4. *See* §§ **10.06, 10.08, 10.09.**

5. *See e.g., Barry J. Brett, Expanded Use of Expert Witnesses Poses New Problems for Counsel*, Nat'l L.J., Dec. 31, 1979, p. 22; Walter Olson, *The Case Against Ex-*

pert Witnesses, Fortune, Sept. 15, 1989 at 133.

6. *See infra* §§ 10.07–10.09.

7. Wigmore, *supra* note 1, § 1929.

witness has personal knowledge, if the inference will be "helpful" to the jurors.

The "helpful" test fits no formula. It signals that the trial judge will exercise discretion that is unlikely to be reversed on appeal. The judge's prior predilection about opinion evidence and the lawyer's ability to persuade the judge that a particular opinion is either not "rationally based" or will not be "helpful" to the jurors almost always will be determinative.

Inferences that are not logically connected to the underlying facts do not meet the Rule 701 requirement that the inference be "rationally based." A witness' opinion, for example, that a person walking unsteadily was drunk is arguably inadmissible, even though the inference is "based on the perception of the witness." The argument is that the inference of "drunk" is not "rationally based" on the perception of "walking unsteadily," because unsteady walking can be caused by too many phenomena. To allow the witness to speculate that drunkenness was the cause of the perceived unsteadiness ignores illness, concussion, ingestion of drugs, weariness, vertigo, or lameness, any of which is an equally likely cause.

"Drunk," however, is a conclusion that courts routinely allow lay witnesses to express when there are sufficient perceptions to make the inference "rationally based." The conclusion of drunkenness that is, arguably, not rational when based on a single ambiguous perception, may be "rationally based," if the witness smelled the odor of whiskey, or saw empty whiskey bottles, or heard slurred speech, or made some other observation consistent with drunkenness.

The idea that multiple perceptions will make a conclusion "rationally based" is sometimes called the collective facts doctrine. Even though the "rationally based" opinion the witness will give may be very general, the judge may consider it "helpful" to the jurors, because the underlying bundle of perceptions is universally understood. When the witness says "drunk," the jurors have no difficulty in picturing the collected facts the witness perceived. (If the judge is in doubt about whether the witness perceived the underlying bundle, Rule 104(a) allows the judge to require the proponent to demonstrate the witness' perception to the court before allowing the opinion.)

The collective facts doctrine is particularly helpful when a witness offers opinion testimony for which the collective facts are not as easily articulated as in the case of drunkenness. "I felt fine" or "he had an ominous look about him" are very general opinions that almost everyone would recognize and understand, but might be hard pressed to articulate specifically. "I was not coughing, not feverish, not debilitated, not crying, not sneezing, not taking medicine, and the like might begin to convey "fine", but it is hardly complete and does not convey the same idea as the opinion "I felt fine." "He had an ominous look about him" defies even an attempt at specification.

Whether a particular opinion is "helpful" to jurors is often contested from two diametrically opposing positions. The first is that the opinion is too general to be helpful to the jurors in understanding the underlying perceptions.[8] The second is that because of extensive testimony about the underlying perceptions the opinion is too obvious to be helpful to the jurors.[9]

A witness who perceives an accident and whose only testimony is that one of the drivers was "careless" arguably has said something too general to be helpful to the jurors. The problem is not that the witness has stated an inference or that the inference is not "rationally based on the perception of the witness." The problem is that the inference is not "helpful." The jurors have no idea whether the driver who was "careless" was not looking, was speeding, was swerving in and out of traffic, was talking on a cellular phone, or any number of other possibilities. Moreover, "careless" is an opinion capable of more specific description.

If, on the other hand, the witness describes in detail what happened at the intersection, any additional testimony that the driver was "careless" may, also, not be "helpful" to the jurors. The witness testifying that a driver was talking on a cellular phone, weaving in and out of traffic, traveling faster than other cars, and looking at the front seat passenger instead of the road, arguably adds nothing "helpful" to the jurors by testifying that the driver was being "careless."

The two reasons for not allowing a witness to testify that a driver was "careless" are examples of the law's preference for the more specific, rather than the more general. In the first instance, the testimony is too general to be helpful. In the second, it is superfluous. Superfluity, however, is not the whole story. There is another concern lingering behind the easy ruling that the inference of "careless" adds nothing.

Although the common law rule prohibiting witnesses from giving opinions on the ultimate question for the jury is specifically rejected in Rule 704,[10] some concern about the proposition seems to remain with those who speak the language of the courtroom. A judge is more likely to prohibit a witness from offering an opinion close to the question for the jury than to prohibit an opinion about something more remote. If the issue for the jury is whether the driver was careless, the witness' opinion that the driver was careless is unlikely to be received. If, on the other hand, the question is whether someone arrived at a particular destination at a particular time, a witness' testimony about seeing that someone driving carelessly on the way to the time and place in question is likely to be admitted. In each case, the opinion of carelessness is of such a general nature that a judge might, but need not, exclude the testimony,

8. United States v. Rea, 958 F.2d 1206 (2d Cir. 1992)(court found a witnesses testimony too general to be helpful to the jurors, who needed to know what words were used and the context in which they were said).

9. *See United States v. Skeet*, 665 F.2d 983(9th Cir.1982) the court held, "If it is impossible or difficult to reproduce the data

observed ... the witness may state ... opinions.... If the jury can be put into a position of equal vantage with the witness for drawing the opinion, then the witness may not give an opinion." *Id.* at 985.

10. *See infra* § **10.09**.

as not "helpful" to the jurors. The likely different results suggest that the less important the opinion, the more likely the judge will be tolerant of the opinion that is too general to be "helpful;" the more important the opinion, the more scrutiny the judge will give to whether the general opinion is "helpful."

The judge's discretion to allow or disallow lay opinion testimony will not be overturned on appeal absent a clear abuse of discretion.[11] Because the trial judge is effectively the court of last resort, the lawyer trying to exclude lay opinion testimony must be prepared to persuade the judge of the prejudice that will result if the inference rather than the underlying perceptions is communicated to the jury.

The lawyer contemplating an objection that the witness is about to offer an opinion should remember the admonition to "be careful what you ask for; you might get it." The witness who tells the jurors only that the person was "drunk" asks the jurors to accept the witness' opinion on faith. Nothing could be worse than the judge sustaining an objection that "drunk" is too general to be "helpful," followed by the witness explaining in detail that the person was stumbling, had red eyes and slurred speech, was disheveled, stunk of whiskey, and could not crawl in a straight line.

§ 10.03 Testimony by Experts [FRE 702]—In General

Rule 702 allows "a witness qualified as an expert by knowledge, skill, experience, training, or education" to testify by opinion or otherwise to "scientific, technical, or other specialized knowledge" if it will "assist the trier of fact."

Jurors in all jurisdictions regularly hear dissertations and opinions from "experts" about everything from how drug deals work to how brakes work, to why airplanes crash, to what a dead person is worth. Some subjects, such as the permanence of injury, the value of lost opportunity, the operation of various criminal enterprises, and the results of various kinds of laboratory analysis have become staples of the system. The list of the possible areas for expert testimony is endless.

The influence of the adversary system of justice on expert testimony—each side hiring its own expert to fortify its own position—has long been compared unfavorably to other systems in which "neutral" experts present opinions untainted by the interest of one of the parties.[12] The description of the expert in an American courtroom as "the best expert that money can buy" has never been meant to be flattering, but the paid expert did not become an epidemic until enactment of the Federal Rules.[13]

11. United States v. Hoffner, 777 F.2d 1423 (10th Cir.1985).

12. Learned Hand, *Historical and Practical Considerations Regarding Expert Testimony*, 15 Harv. L. Rev. 40 (1901).

13. David Faigman et al., *Check Your Crystal Ball at the Courthouse Door, Please: Exploring the Past, Understanding the Present, and Worrying about the Future of Scientific Evidence*, 15 Cardozo L. Rev. 1799, 1808 (1994).

The "liberal thrust" of the Federal Rules combined with the "general approach of relaxing the traditional barriers to 'opinion' testimony"[14] has changed the face of American litigation. Testimony of experts, be it generally descriptive or an opinion central to the resolution of the particular case, has become a staple of the common law trial.

Whether expert testimony ought to be admitted pursuant to Rule 702 is a "preliminary question" for the judge to decide under Rule 104(a). The question has four, sometimes overlapping, parts:

1) Does the testimony involve knowledge that is "scientific, technical, or . . . specialized?"

2) Is the witness an expert by virtue of "knowledge, skill, experience, training, or education?"

3) Will the expert's testimony "assist the trier of fact?"

4) If the first three questions are answered in the affirmative, is the probative value of the testimony such that it is not "substantially" outweighed by its prejudicial effect?

Many of the cases excluding testimony—discussed or noted in the next three sections—may not articulate the various parts of the analysis or may assign more than one of the four reasons for the exclusion. While the judge's rationale may not always be explicit when excluding expert testimony, the judge's ruling on the admissibility of expert testimony will survive appeal in the absence of a clear abuse of discretion.[15]

§ 10.04 Testimony by Experts [FRE 702]—The *Daubert* Test

Rule 702 describes knowledge that might be the subject matter of expert testimony, as if there were three separate and readily identifiable

---

14. Beech Aircraft Corp. v. Rainey, 488 U.S. 153, 169 (1988).

15. Federal Trade Commission v. Amy Travel Serv., Inc., 875 F.2d 564, 572–73 (7th Cir.1989)(magistrate did not abuse her discretion in determining that witness did not possess necessary expertise to testify about how consumers would react to sales pitch); United States v. Davis, 772 F.2d 1339, 1343 (7th Cir.1985), *cert. denied sub nom,* Davis v. United States, 474 U.S. 1036 (1985)(trial judge did not abuse discretion in excluding evidence about compulsive gambling by psychiatrist lacking experience in field); United States v. Lopez, 543 F.2d 1156 (5th Cir.1976), *cert. denied sub nom.,* Lopez v. United States, 429 U.S. 1111 (1977) (psychologist without clinical experience could be barred from testifying on insanity defense; trial judge has "broad discretion" that is not to be disturbed unless decision "manifestly erroneous"); Floyd v. Worobec, 537 N.W.2d 512, 517 (Neb. 1995)(court did not abuse its discretion by excluding testimony of chiropractor who lacked state license but had finished a premedical course at the University of Kansas, graduated from the National College of Chiropractic at Lombard, Illinois, and pursued several postgraduate specialties); Swanson v. Chatterton, 160 N.W.2d 662 (Minn.1968)(trial court's decision to excluded internal medicine expert from testifying about orthopedic issue upheld; expert was relying upon knowledge derived from medical school training fifteen years earlier and had not kept up with literature relevant to orthopedic issues raised by case). *But c.f.,* Salem v. United States Lines Co., 370 U.S. 31, 35 (1962)(court upheld trial courts excluding experts testimony after concluding that the jury was competent to determine the issue); In re Paoli R.R. Yard PCB Litigation, 35 F.3d 717 at 750 (3d Cir. 1994)(trial court exclusion of scientific opinion testimony that results in summary judgment that extinguishes a claim may not receive the same appellate deference).

categories: "scientific, technical, and other specialized." Although examples of knowledge in each category are easy to identify–the existence and structure of the atom is "scientific," the diagram for putting together a computer is "technical," and the best shape for a perfect apple might be considered "other specialized"–not every example is as easy to categorize. Is how a cyclotron smashes atoms scientific or technical? Is how a computer processes information technical or scientific? What is psychology? Is it different from psychiatry? What do you call it when someone knows enough about racehorses to make a living handicapping races? What do you call it when someone knows enough about economics to predict how much someone might have earned had the person lived for twenty-five years?

Before enactment of the Federal Rules, the beginning inquiry for the judge in deciding whether expert testimony was appropriate was whether the testimony provided information beyond the ken of the average juror. There was little need to categorize expert testimony. Indeed, in the nineteenth and early twentieth centuries, courts did not look to the nature of the expertise, but rather, to whether the proposed witness qualified as an expert. If the witness was an expert, there must be an expertise around somewhere.[16] Medical testimony by doctors was among the earliest forms of expert testimony.[17] Doctors were respected and well educated about the magic of medicine, a subject about which jurors knew almost nothing.

In 1923, William Marston, an attorney and research psychologist, had conducted extensive psychological research and would have been, under normal circumstances, one of those experts who could bring to the trial something beyond the ken of the average juror. But Marston was called to testify to something that was not only beyond the ken of the jurors, but beyond the ken of almost everyone else in the world. He was proffered to testify that James Frye, a criminal defendant claiming innocence, had passed the "systolic blood pressure deception test," an early form of the lie detector. The trial judge would not permit Marston to testify, nor to conduct a test in the presence of the jury, because the subject matter was not proper.

> Just when a scientific principle or discovery crosses the line between the experimental and demonstrable stages is difficult to define. Somewhere in this twilight zone the evidential force of the principle must be recognized, and while courts will go a long way in admitting expert testimony deduced from a well-recognized scientific principle or discovery, the thing from which the deduction is made must be sufficiently established to have gained general acceptance in the particular field in which it belongs.[18]

16. David Faigman, et al., Modern Scientific Evidence § 1–2.1 [hereinafter Scientific Evidence].

17. Stephan Landsman, *Of Witches, Madmen, and Products Liability: An Histor-* *ical Survey of the Use of Expert Testimony,* 13 Behav. Sci. & L. 131(1995).

18. Frye v. United States, 293 F. 1013, 1014 (D.C.Cir.1923).

The Frye "general acceptance" test, devised by Associate Justice Van Orsdel to determine the admissibility of testimony about what he considered to be a "novel" scientific principle, became the dominant standard by which scientific expert testimony would be measured for more than half a century.

Scientific testimony is different in one sense from most other expert testimony, because it is more than merely an addition to the knowledge of the average juror. Science is way over the head of the average juror, not to mention the average judge, who "went to law school to avoid science or, for that matter, anything else that uses numbers other than to reference volumes and page numbers."[19] While ballistics, fingerprint analysis, various chemical tests for the presence of controlled substance, radar speed-readings and the like are now so familiar in our courts that their foundations are a matter of judicial notice, it was not always so. Imagine a trial judge's reaction the first time a lawyer claimed to have a witness who would testify that some numbers appearing on the back of a black box held by a police officer constituted the exact speed of an approaching automobile. That judge, who probably never heard of the top secret World War II invention of radar, had to decide whether the numbers on the back of the box were science or hokum. It is not surprising that a standard that left the admissibility of new and mysterious material to the "general acceptance" of those educated people familiar with the scientific field at issue seemed reasonable to judges.

Although the Frye test dominated admission of and discussion about expert scientific testimony, not all jurisdictions followed Frye and not all judges and commentators supported it. Those who opposed the "general acceptance" test argued that Frye created a lag period during which reliable evidence was excluded while the scientific community evaluated the novel technique.[20] The Frye objectors gained some allies following enactment of the Federal Rules, as the federal courts divided over the question of whether the "general acceptance" test survived enactment of Rule 702.[21]

The 1993 Supreme Court case of *Daubert v. Merrell Dow Pharmaceuticals*[22] resolved the matter for the federal system, holding that the "austere standard" of Frye, that "made 'general acceptance' the exclusive test for admitting expert scientific testimony," was "incompatible with the Federal Rules and should not be applied in federal trials."[23]

---

19. G. Michael Fenner, *The Daubert Handbook*, 29 Creighton L. Rev. 939 (1996) [hereinafter *Daubert Handbook*]. Professor Fenner's observation is not limited to judges. While it may not be true for all of us who went to law school, there are not enough objectors to fill a telephone booth.

20. *See, e.g.,* Paul C. Giannelli, *The Admissibility of Novel Scientific Evidence: Frye v. United States, a Half–Century Later*, 80 Colum. L. Rev. 1197 (1980).

21. *Compare, e.g.,* United States v. Shorter, 809 F.2d 54 (D.C.Cir.1987)(applying the "general acceptance" standard), *with,* DeLuca v. Merrell Dow Pharmaceuticals, Inc., 911 F.2d 941 (3d Cir. 1990)(rejecting the "general acceptance" standard).

22. 509 U.S. 579 (1993).

23. *Id.* at 589.

Just as *Frye* dominated the discussion about the admissibility of scientific evidence for half a century,[24] *Daubert* seems destined to be the starting point for the discussion of expert testimony over the next half-century. While there is disagreement about *Daubert's* reach to non-scientific expert testimony,[25] there is no room for disagreement about the impact of the case on the general subject of expert testimony. *Daubert* has become the label for an industry, spawning endless discussion about the general subject of expert testimony, well beyond the bounds of science or the issues before the *Daubert* court.[26] Pre-trial hearings about expert testimony, now more common than in the *Frye* era, are called "Daubert hearings," when they involve a challenge to the validity of the expert's field.[27]

Daubert was one of a number of cases in the federal system claiming that the drug Bendectin caused birth defects. The literature on Bendectin was substantial and consistent. It had been the subject of more than thirty published epidemiological studies, covering over a hundred thousand patients. None of the studies concluded that Bendectin was the cause of birth defects. Nevertheless, plaintiff's eight experts were prepared to testify–based on test tube and animal studies and on recalculation of some of the prior epidemiological studies–that Bendectin was a teratogen (a substance that causes birth defects) and that when ingested by the mothers during pregnancy caused the limb reduction defects suffered by the infant plaintiffs.[28]

The trial court ruled the plaintiffs' expert testimony was not "scientific knowledge" and, because that left plaintiffs with no causation evidence, granted defendant's motion for summary judgment:

> The federal courts have held that epidemiological studies are the most reliable evidence of causation in this area. Accordingly, expert opinion which is not based on epidemiological evidence is not admissible to establish causation because it lacks the sufficient foundation necessary under FRE 703.[29]

The Ninth Circuit Court of Appeals affirmed, citing *Frye,* and the importance of the "general acceptance" standard:

> We impose this requirement because such evidence 'create[s] a substantial danger of undue prejudice or of confusing the issues or of misleading the jury ... because of its aura of special reliability and trustworthiness.'[30]

24. "Indeed the debates over Frye are such a well-established part of the academic landscape that a distinct term—'Frye-olo-gist'—has been advanced to describe those who take part. *Id.* at 587, fn.4.

25. *Daubert Handbook, supra* note 19, at 954.

26. In the four years since it was decided, Daubert has been cited in 911 articles in legal periodicals and in more than 1000 cases—about once every day by some com-

mentator and some judge, excluding, of course, the Sabbath and holidays.

27. *See, e.g.,* United States v. Starzec-pyzel, 880 F.Supp. 1027 (S.D.N.Y.1995).

28. See the opinion below, Daubert v. Merrell Dow Pharmaceuticals, Inc.,727 F.Supp. 570 (S.D.Cal.1989).

29. *Id.* at 575.

30. 951 F.2d 1128, 1129–30 (9th Cir. 1991) (citations omitted).

In reversing the Ninth Circuit, the Supreme Court did not discuss the wisdom of the *Frye* standard, but made it clear that the *Frye* standard had not survived enactment of Rule 702:

> "General acceptance" is not a necessary precondition to the admissibility of scientific evidence under the Federal Rules of Evidence, but the Rules of Evidence—especially Rule 702—do assign to the trial judge the task of ensuring that an expert's testimony both rests on a reliable foundation and is relevant to the task at hand.[31]

The Court found in Rule 702 a requirement that the judge admit expert testimony only if it "rests on a reliable foundation and is relevant," but the Court provided little help for a scientifically challenged judiciary, suddenly denied the ability to rely entirely upon the scientific community to validate scientific knowledge. The Court admonished judges to focus "solely on principles and methodology, not on the conclusions that they generate."[32] It provided a non-exclusive list of factors that might, but would not necessarily, be helpful in determining whether knowledge was "scientific." The judge might consider whether a particular theory or technique can be and has been tested, has been subject to peer review and publication, has a known error rate, and whether it has acceptance within the scientific community.

Even these sparse suggestions drew criticism. Chief Justice Rehnquist, joined in partial dissent by Justice Stevens, warned that " '[g]eneral observations' by this Court customarily carry great weight with lower federal courts," complained that the majority's list was "vague and abstract," and urged that "unusual subject matter should cause us to proceed with great caution in deciding more than we have to, because our reach can so easily exceed our grasp."[33] Commentators observed that the majority's distinction between methodology and conclusion is often illusory, because "scientific conclusions are inextricably connected to the methodologies used to reach them."[34]

Whether *Daubert* is the standard for all expert testimony is among the more important questions awaiting further word from the Supreme Court. "Does all of this *dicta* apply to an expert seeking to testify on the basis of 'technical or other specialized knowledge'. . . or are the 'general observations' limited only to 'scientific knowledge'?"[35] Lower federal courts disagree on whether *Daubert* speaks only to scientific evidence,[36] but the difficulty in identifying the boundary between "scientific" knowledge and "technical or other specialized" knowledge suggests that, at a minimum, *Daubert* will be influential in reconstructing the method by which all judges consider all expert testimony.

---

31. 509 U.S. 579, 597 (1993).

32. *Id.* at 595.

33. *Id.* at 599.

34. Scientific Evidence, *supra* note 16, § 1–3.3.1[2].

35. Daubert, 509 U.S. at 600.

36. *Compare* Berry v. City of Detroit, 25 F.3d 1342 (6th Cir.1994)(*Daubert* applied to non-scientific expert testimony) *with* United States v. Sinclair, 74 F.3d 753 (7th Cir.1996)(*Daubert* applies only to scientific expert testimony).

United States v. Starzecpyzel[37] presents a startling example of the influence of *Daubert* in a case in which the Court determined that the *Daubert* validity standard had no applicability. Faced with the prosecution's proffer of a forensic document examiner prepared to testify that critical signatures in a conspiracy to steal artwork and jewelry were forgeries, the judge held an extended pre-trial "Daubert hearing." The judge determined that handwriting analysis is "technical," not "scientific," and that *Daubert* did not provide a new standard for non-scientific expert testimony. The judge found, nevertheless, that Rule 702 imposed a significant gatekeeper responsibility on the trial judge for all expert testimony, scientific or not.

The *Starzecpyszel* court's extended discussion of the admissibility of expert testimony concerning handwriting demonstrates the current influence of the *Daubert* decision and its potential for changing the face of expert testimony, even when the court determines the *Daubert* validity standard is not applicable to the testimony in question.

There has been disagreement about whether *Daubert* would increase or decrease the amount of expert scientific testimony in the courts, but it is not yet clear whether *Daubert's* articulation of how the law approaches scientific testimony has resulted in more, less, or different expert testimony than *Frye's* articulation. Time has not validated the predictions that abandoning the "general acceptance" standard would lead to a " 'free for all' in which befuddled juries are confounded by absurd and irrational pseudoscientific assertions."[38] Nor has it shown that *Daubert's* judicial gatekeeper will reduce expert testimony by rejecting scientific evidence that *Frye's* scientific community gatekeeper would allow.[39]

Some of the more intense speculation about the influence of *Daubert* has centered on two familiar areas of expert testimony: forensic science and social science.

Forensic science–the application of the natural and physical sciences to the resolution of conflict in a legal setting–has been so familiar in courts (particularly the criminal courts) that the validity of the particular expertise is rarely contested. Handwriting analysis, hair and fiber analysis, fingerprints, and ballistics are just a few of the identification subjects traveling under the label, forensic science.

The social sciences—the study of human behavior—have not had the same long acceptance in the courts enjoyed by the forensic sciences. Although expert testimony about insanity, diminished capacity, and potential for violence have long histories in the courts, rape trauma, battered women, battered child, and other syndromes have only more recently become regular areas for expert testimony. Expert testimony

37. 880 F.Supp. 1027 (S.D.N.Y.1995).

38. 509 U.S. 579, 595 (1993).

39. *See* Reforming the Civil Justice System (NYU Press Larry Kramer, Editor)(Samuel R. Gross, *Substance & Form in Scientific Evidence: What Daubert Didn't Do* p. 234 at 246).

about the unreliability of eyewitness identification, the accuracy of repressed memory, or the suggestiveness of interview techniques are among those mysteries that continue to be treated skeptically in many courts, but admitted in others.[40]

The more the courts treat forensic science and social science as "scientific" knowledge, the more the *Daubert* hurdles of testability and error rate may diminish expert forensic and social science testimony. The more the courts follow the lead of *Starzecpyzel*, identify these "sciences" as "technical or other specialized" knowledge, and do not require some kind of validation, the more likely it is that expert testimony about subjects like handwriting and abuse syndromes will survive unabated.

Daubert represents the beginning of an answer to the debate that raged over "junk science" in the courtroom.[41] Commentators have suggested and courts have held that the main lesson of *Daubert*—that the theoretical underpinnings of scientific expert testimony must be reliable and relevant—should apply to all forms of expert testimony.[42]

Irrespective of how future cases resolve the issue of *Daubert's* reach, the case represents a warning for lawyers offering expert testimony and an opportunity for lawyers opposing it. After *Daubert*, trial judges are likely to take more notice of the issue of whether particular knowledge qualifies as "scientific, technical or other specialized," mindful of the concern voiced by the Ninth Circuit that "such evidence 'create[s] a substantial danger of undue prejudice ... because of its aura of special reliability.' "[43] The decision of the trial judge will stand, absent a clear abuse of discretion. Even rulings that exclude expert testimony, resulting in summary judgment, once thought to justify a "hard look" by the appellate courts,[44] will be overturned only if the trial court engages in an abuse of discretion.[45]

40. *See, e.g.* United States v. Kime, 99 F.3d 870, 885 (8th Cir. 1996) (held, not abuse of discretion to determine defendant's proffer of testimony about fallibility of eyewitness identification did not satisfy *Daubert*); United States v. Norwood, 939 F. Supp. 1132, 1133, 1141 (D. N.J. 1996) (held, expert testimony on reliability of eyewitness identification admissible; case contains useful description of what this type of expertise could contribute); United States v. Rouse, 111 F.3d 561, 572 (8th Cir. 1997) (on rehearing) (divided panel indicates that expert testimony about suggestiveness of pretrial treatment of child witnesses should have been admitted).

41. *See e.g.,* Peter Huber, Galileo's Revenge: Junk Science in the Courtroom (1991); Kenneth J. Chesebro, *Galileo's Re-*

tort: Peter Huber's Junk Scholarship, 42 Am. U. L. Rev. 1637 (1993).

42. Edward J. Imwinkelried, *The Next Step After Daubert: Developing a Similarly Epistemological Approach to Ensuring the Reliability of Non-scientific Expert Testimony*, 15 Cardozo L. Rev. 2271 (1994).

43. 951 F.2d 1128, 1129–30 (9th Cir.1991)(citations omitted), *vac'd*, 509 U.S. 579 (1993).

44. In re Paoli R.R. Yard PCB Litig., 35 F.3d 717, 750 (3d Cir. 1994). "[W]hen the district court's exclusionary evidentiary rulings with respect to scientific opinion testimony will result in summary or directed judgment, we will give them a 'hard look.' "

45. General Electric Co. v. Joiner, 118 S.Ct. 512 (1997).

§ 10.05 Testimony by Experts [FRE 702]—Determining Whether the Witness Qualifies as an Expert

Rule 702 provides that anyone qualified by "knowledge, skill, experience, training, or education" might provide expert testimony. Though witnesses with extensive education and many degrees are common as expert witnesses, an expert need not have acquired expert knowledge through formal education. A carpenter or other skilled worker without a day of formal education might qualify as an expert, if the person's experience provides specialized knowledge.[46]

Before a witness is permitted to give an expert opinion, the party offering the testimony must show that the expert is qualified to testify to the particular knowledge to be offered. This showing is normally made by direct examination of the proffered expert. After the witness' qualifications have been presented on direct examination and before the witness gives an opinion on the substantive issues of the case, a party who objects to admitting the testimony of the expert may cross-examine the witness to expose defects in training and experience. The trial judge has discretion to require that the parties conduct this portion of the witness examination beyond the hearing of the jury.[47] If the trial judge determines that the witness is qualified, the party offering the testimony then continues the examination of the witness to elicit the witness's expert testimony. Afterward, the opposing party has another opportunity to cross-examine for purposes of exposing defects in the opinion, obtaining concessions, or impeaching the witness.

In cases involving medical experts, controversies often arise about whether the testimony of a specialist is required. The general tendency

---

46. See, e.g., Fed. R.Evid. 702 advisory committee's note. *Compare,* Scott v. Yates, 643 N.E.2d 105 (Ohio 1994)(abuse of discretion to allow officer with no accident reconstruction training to testify about cause of accident); Peavey Co. v. M/V ANPA, 971 F.2d 1168, 1174 (5th Cir.1992) (affirming trial court's determination that insurer-defendant's claims manager was unqualified to testify as to whether insured-plaintiff's failure to retain a "qualified" electrical engineering expert to inspect damages prejudiced defendant),*with,* Sullivan v. Rowan Co., 952 F.2d 141 (5th Cir.1992) (trial judge did not abuse discretion by ruling that expert who had PhD in geology, but who was not an engineer and whose only formal study in metallurgy was a three-day seminar, was not qualified to testify about metal failure despite fact that expert had been employed for more than 10 years in private laboratories performing metal failure analyses using scanning electron microscopes; query whether district judge might have given too much weight to lack of formal education in particular field); United States v. Welch, 945 F.2d 1378 (7th Cir.1991) (court held that there was error in holding

that defense witness, a chief production engineer and professor, was not qualified as expert, where witness lacked sufficient training or experience in forensic tape analysis and where witness was unfamiliar with the use of technological instruments used to detect alterations in taped conversations;), *cert. denied,* 502 U.S. 1118 (1992); *c.f.,* Asplundh Mfg. Div. v. Benton Harbor Eng'g, 57 F.3d 1190, 1192 (3d Cir. 1995)(lay witness could not testify about metal fatigue in absence of showing of sufficient special knowledge or experience).

47. *See,* United States v. Bartley, 855 F.2d 547, 552 (8th Cir.1988) (no requirement that court determine in presence of the jury that witness is qualified to testify as expert); Hall v. General Motors Corp., 647 F.2d 175, 182–183 (D.C.Cir.1980) (trial judge did not abuse her discretion when refusing to permit cross-examination as substitute for voir dire inquiry concerning witness' expertise). Weinstein's Federal Evidence, § 702.02[1] (2nd ed. Joseph M. McLaughlin 1997).

of courts has been to admit the testimony of general practitioners, even where a specialist might be more knowledgeable. Even if the general practitioner has no special training, medical school training and general experience qualify the general practitioner to testify about a variety of matters that are often referred to specialists. For example, a general practitioner may testify to the psychological damage caused by an injury.[48]

In the case of a highly qualified expert, the party opposing the expert may offer to stipulate that the witness is qualified as an expert, hoping thereby to avoid having the expert's impressive credentials paraded before the jury. That party may then make an objection to testimony about the witness' background, education, and achievements on grounds that it is irrelevant or immaterial, since the witness' competence to testify as an expert is not in dispute. The objection should be overruled.[49] The testimony is relevant and material because the jurors must still assess the credibility of the expert. The jurors are entitled to know the witness' background and achievements in order to assess credibility. Nonetheless, the lawyer making this objection may succeed in limiting the duration of the direct examination, since extended and detailed review of qualifications may be a waste of time when the witness' competence to testify as an expert is not in dispute.

It should be noted that the stipulation that the expert is competent to testify is only a stipulation that the expert's testimony is admissible; not that it is accurate or correct.

§ 10.06   Testimony by Experts [FRE 702]—Determining Whether the Testimony Will Assist the Trier of Fact

The liberalizing influence of the Federal Rules of Evidence is nowhere more evident than in the standard for the admissibility of expert testimony. Much of the expert testimony that would not have been admissible under the common law is admissible under the Federal Rules. Under the common law, the burden was on the proponent to demonstrate that the testimony of the expert was "necessary" because it was about matters beyond the ken of the average juror.[50] Under the Federal

---

48. *See, e.g.,* Holbrook v. Lykes Bros. S.S. Co., 80 F.3d 777, 782 (3d Cir. 1996) (trial court committed reversible error in excluding testimony by nonspecialist treating physician diagnosing patient's cancer as mesothelioma); Nunley v. Kloehn, 888 F.Supp. 1483,1487–88 (E.D.Wis.1995) (dermatologist who had performed lip augmentations could testify about standard of care of plastic surgeons performing the same procedure with different substances). *But c.f.,* Fortney v. Al–Hajj, 425 S.E.2d 264, 269–71 (W.Va.1992) (though West Virginia Code requires that malpractice expert be engaged or qualified in a substantially similar field as the defendant health care provider, this requirement does not mean that witness's board certification must be in the same field).

49. Murphy v. Nat'l. R.R. Passenger Corp., 547 F.2d 816, 817 (4th Cir.1977). Despite stipulation of the witness' expertise, "a jury can better assess the weight to be accorded an expert's opinion if the witness is permitted to explain his qualifications." *Id.*

50. Bridger v. Union Ry., 355 F.2d 382, 387 (6th Cir. 1966).

Rules of Evidence, the proponent's burden is so easily met that the onus is effectively on the opponent to show that the testimony will not "assist the trier of fact."

The relative ease of demonstrating that something will "assist the trier of fact" does not guarantee that all expert testimony about any area of knowledge will be admitted. Courts have differed markedly on whether a particular "expertise" will "assist the trier of fact." The cases are more important for their demonstration of the breadth of the trial court's discretion and the deference given to that discretion by the appellate courts than they are as precedent regarding any particular expertise. Some of the most interesting divisions of opinion regarding the "helpfulness" of a particular kind of knowledge are over the reliability of eyewitness testimony,[51] the modus operandi of drug dealers,[52] the identification of the individual depicted in a photograph or videotape,[53] the future earnings of a deceased individual,[54] and the cause of an automobile accident.[55]

Court language that a particular expertise will not "assist the trier of fact" sometimes masks a decision that the expertise in question is not reliable in the *Daubert* sense. Although the requirement that expert testimony "assist the trier of fact" is primarily a relevance judgment,[56] the "helpfulness" that makes expert testimony admissible has occasional overtones of a validity judgment about whether the testimony qualifies as "scientific, technical, or other specialized" knowledge under Rule 702.[57] This phenomenon is particularly apparent for some of the "soft" sciences, such as forensic or social science. When a particular expertise is rejected, this expanded notion of relevance or "fit"[58] is sometimes articulated as a Rule 702 problem of not "assisting the trier of fact" and

51. *Compare* United States v. Moore, 786 F.2d 1308 (5th Cir. 1986)(approving expert testimony on the reliability of eyewitness identification) *with* United States v. Fosher, 590 F.2d 381 (1st Cir.1979)(approving exclusion of expert testimony on the reliability of eyewitness identification).

52. *Compare* United States v. Chin, 981 F.2d 1275 (D.C.Cir.1992) *cert. denied*, 508 U.S. 923 (1993)(expert testimony on the modus operandi of drug dealers admissible under Rule 702) *with* United States v. Cruz, 981 F.2d 659 (2d Cir.1992)(expert testimony on the role of the broker in a a drug operation not admissible under Rule 702).

53. *Compare* United States v. Snow, 552 F.2d 165 (6th Cir. 1977)(admitting expert testimony comparing photographs)*with* United States v. Brown, 501 F.2d 146 (9th Cir.1974)(expert testimony comparing photographs not admissible).

54. *Compare* Hooks v. Washington Sheraton Corp., 578 F.2d 313 (D.C.Cir.1977)(economist testimony about

the future earnings of an eighteen year old admissible) *with* Barnes v. Smith, 305 F.2d 226 (10th Cir. 1962)(economist testimony about the future earnings of a seventeen year old not admissible).

55. *Compare* Seese v. Volkswagenwerk A.G., 648 F.2d 833, 844 (3d Cir.), *cert. denied* 454 U.S. 867 (1981)(admitting accident reconstructionist's testimony) *with* Dallas & Mavis Forwarding Co. v. Stegall, 659 F.2d 721, 722 (6th Cir.1981)(excluding accident reconstructionist's testimony

56. 509 U.S. 579, 591 (1993).

57. "Rule 702's 'helpfulness' standard requires a valid scientific connection to the pertinent inquiry as a precondition to admissibility." *See id.,*at 591.

58. Coined by Judge Becker in United States v. Downing, 753 F.2d 1224, 1242 (3d Cir. 1985) and adopted by the Supreme Court in *Daubert*, "fit" may be another way to describe a failure to meet the reliability requirement of Rule 702, at least as related to the issues in the particular case.

sometimes as a Rule 403 problem of being "confusing, misleading or prejudicial."[59]

Whether compelled, because *Daubert* ultimately applies to non-scientific expert testimony, or inclined, because they interpret Rules 702 and 403 in light of the wisdom of *Daubert*, courts are likely to begin to ask forensic and social scientists "where are the data?"[60] This is particularly significant because many forensic techniques, along with areas of scientific testimony, have been the subject of judicial notice in many jurisdictions. Along with scientific theories such as radar and various chemical reactions, courts have long dispensed with the need to prove the underlying validity of fingerprint analysis, ballistics tests, handwriting analysis, and other forensic techniques.[61] Some of those subjects may now require a second look. The *Starzecepel* court, for example, took a fresh look at the reliability of handwriting analysis. Although the judge allowed the testimony from the forensic document examiner, it was under very different conditions from the past. The witness was not allowed to refer to laboratories or to adopt any of the other "trappings of science" and the jury was instructed about the non-scientific nature of the testimony.[62] Other courts might not be as confident that shaping the testimony and instructing the jurors about the potential flaws of the expertise will overcome the Rule 403 problem of testimony substantially more prejudicial than probative. They might begin to exclude expert testimony that cannot demonstrate a reliability base sufficient to make the Court comfortable that the testimony will "assist" rather than "mislead" the jurors.

§ 10.07 Examining the Expert Witness [FRE 705]; Hypothetical Questions

The manner of examination of an expert witness was of critical importance under the common law. It was formalistic. Failure to follow the formula with precision could result in exclusion of the expert's opinion.

An expert was not allowed to offer an opinion unless it was based upon personal knowledge of the underlying information (a relatively rare occurrence) or upon facts that had already been admitted into evidence.[63]

---

59. *See, e.g.,* United States v. Curry, 977 F.2d 1042 (7th Cir.1992) (trial court non-specific exclusion of expert testimony regarding the reliability of eyewitness identification either because the testimony was something about which the jurors were "generally aware" or because it would be "confusing"). The court's ambivalence leaves room for the view that, despite a footnoted bow to the growing acceptability of the area, the court does not think much of the underlying "expertise."

60. Faigman, *supra* note 16, at § 1–3.41[1].

61. McCormick, *supra* note 2, § 206 (examples include radar tests for speed, tests for intoxication, fingerprints, and handwriting comparisons). *See* Giannelli, *supra* note 20.

62. 880 F.Supp. at 1049.

63. *See, e.g.,* Stanley Co. of Am. v. Hercules Powder Co.,108 A.2d 616, 621 (N.J. 1954). "The opinions of experts must be based either upon facts within their own knowledge which they detail to the jury or upon hypothetical questions embracing facts supported by the evidence upon which the expert opinion is sought." *Id.* at 621.

Moreover, the nature of the facts relied upon had to be made specific, so that the trier of fact could reject the opinion if it rejected its factual basis. The rule of examination, therefore, was that no opinion could be elicited from an expert without first identifying the underlying facts or data the expert relied upon in forming the opinion.

The following example, though maybe not wise, is allowable under Rule 705, "unless the court requires otherwise."

Lawyer:	[After first qualifying the witness.] Do you have an opinion, to a reasonable medical certainty, about the cause of Billy Johnson's death?
Witness:	Yes.
Lawyer:	What is your opinion?
Witness:	The removal of his spleen during surgery caused him to lose his resistance to infection, and as a result he contracted an overwhelming infection that led to his death.
Lawyer:	In your opinion, was it sound medical practice to remove Billy's spleen?
Witness:	No.
Lawyer:	In making his decision to remove Billy's spleen, did Dr. Smith exercise the professional care and skill ordinarily possessed by others in his profession in this community?
Witness:	No, he did not.

The common law would not tolerate the foregoing examination. To make sure the underlying facts and data were before the witness and the jury, the common law developed the hypothetical question as the universally accepted device for eliciting expert testimony. The examining lawyer would ask the expert to assume the existence of certain specified facts and then to give an opinion based upon those facts—hence the term "hypothetical." If the expert had been in the courtroom and heard previous testimony, the examining lawyer could ask the expert to assume the truthfulness of specified testimony and to give an opinion based upon the facts from the testimony. Often the examining lawyer would ask a hypothetical that combined the two approaches.[64]

If, in the above splenectomy example, the treating doctor (defendant) had testified as an adverse witness and Billy's hospital records had been admitted, Billy's lawyer might next call a non-treating expert to offer the opinion that Billy's treatment had not been proper. If the

---

64. Wigmore, *supra* note 1, §§ 672–84 .

expert had not heard the testimony, the hypothetical would recount the information:

> "Doctor, suppose that a twelve year old boy suffered a fall that resulted in a two-centimeter laceration of the spleen, [and every other fact in evidence the lawyer wants the jury to remember], would it be sound medical practice to remove the spleen?"

If the expert had been in the courtroom, heard the testimony, and seen the exhibits, the hypothetical might avoid recitation of the facts:

> "Doctor, you heard the testimony of Dr. Smith. Assume it to be true. You have seen the hospital records admitted into evidence. Assume them to be correct. Based on the facts stated by Dr. Smith and the information in the hospital records, do you have an opinion about whether it was sound medical practice to remove Billy's spleen?"[65]

The hypothetical question form, though a logical outgrowth of the desire to show the trier of fact the basis for the expert's opinion, was repeatedly criticized by scholars and reformers who objected to lawyers using extended hypothetical questions as vehicles for arguing their cases to juries.[66]

The Federal Rules of Evidence take a more liberal and flexible approach to expert testimony than did the common law. One of the consequences was to diminish the importance of the manner of examination. The Federal Rules do not require the use of hypothetical questions, nor do they prohibit them. Some lawyers in Federal Rules jurisdictions continue to use the hypothetical, believing that the form provides an opportunity to control and focus the expert and to sum up damaging testimony in the middle of trial.

Hypothetical questions present a particular challenge to the examiner and the opponent because they usually involve an extended recitation of facts upon which the expert is expected to base an opinion. If the hypothetical omits material undisputed facts, misstates facts, or includes prejudicial facts it may be misleading, confusing, or prejudicial and, thereby, improper under Rule 403. In order to preserve rights on appeal, the objecting party should be careful to specify omitted, misstated, or prejudicial facts that make the hypothetical objectionable.[67]

Although a hypothetical question may be deemed misleading for a mishandling of the facts, it is not misleading if it merely fails to include the opponent's version of disputed facts. When material facts are in

65. *See,* Treffinger v. Sterling, 305 A.2d 829, 831(Md.1973) (question asking witness to assume truth of testimony a proper substitute for hypothetical question setting forth specific facts); Annotations, *Modern Status of Rules Regarding Use of Hypothetical Questions in Eliciting Opinion of Expert Witness,* 56 A.L.R.3d 300, 312–315 (1974).

66. "Its abuses have become so obstructive and nauseous that no remedy short of extirpation will suffice. Wigmore, *supra* note 1, § 686." [A] failure in practice and an obstruction to the administration of justice." McCormick, *supra* note 2, § 16.

67. First Nat'l Bank of Dunmore v. WCAB, 532 A.2d 526, 528 (Pa. Commw.1987); Serafin v. Workmen's Compensation Appeal Bd., 436 A.2d 1239, 1241–42 (Pa.Commw.1981).

dispute, the examiner may include the client's version of the dispute and exclude the opponent's without running the risk of having an objection sustained on grounds that the question is misleading. If, for example, one witness testifies that plaintiff was exposed to a toxic chemical and others testify that plaintiff was not exposed, it is permissible to ask the expert to assume the plaintiff was exposed to the chemical, and to base an opinion on that assumption.[68] This slanting of the hypothetical is not objectionable, because the opponent is free, on cross-examination, to ask the expert what the opinion would be if the cross-examiner's version of the disputed fact were true.[69]

Three common ways in which facts are mishandled in a hypothetical will make the question objectionable: omission of a material undisputed fact, addition of a fact either by misstatement or invention, or inclusion of a prejudicial fact.

Stumpf v. State Farm Mutual,[70] is an example of omitted material facts that were not in dispute. The issue in the case was whether the insured had made an intentionally false statement on an automobile insurance application when he stated that he did not have a mental or physical disability. The insured had been suffering from epilepsy for several years, but contended that it did not constitute a disability. His lawyer asked the following question to a specialist in internal medicine who had been called as an expert witness:

> Doctor, assuming that you have a patient who is gainfully employed and has a history of infrequent epileptic seizures of the grand mal type over a period of years, takes regular oral medication for his epileptic condition three times daily, assume further that the patient, before suffering an epileptic seizure gets warning of the impending seizure sufficient to allow him to sit down and make adjustments, do you have an opinion, based on reasonable medical probability, whether that patient has a mental or physical disability?"[71]

State Farm's objection that the question omitted several material facts was sustained by the trial court and affirmed on appeal. The question omitted that the insured had also suffered petit mal seizures (which, unlike grand mal seizures, came upon him without warning) and that he had been discharged from the Marine Corps with a 30% disability because of epilepsy.[72] The Court of Appeals said that the omissions caused the question to fall short of the standard that a hypothetical question "should contain a fair summary of the material facts in evi-

---

68. *See, e.g.,* Taylor v. Reo Motors, 275 F.2d 699 (10th Cir.1960).

69. Johns–Manville Products Corp. v. Indus. Comm., 399 N.E.2d 606, 611 (Ill. 1979). On the other hand, if certain facts are not in dispute, they must be incorporated in the hypothetical question if the ques-

tion would be misleading without them. *See, e.g.,* De Donato v. Wells, 41 S.W.2d 184, (Mo.1931).

70. 251 A.2d 362 (1969).

71. 251 A.2d at 372 (1969).

72. *Id.* at 372–73.

dence essential to the formulation of a rational opinion concerning the matter to which it relates."[73]

Courts have displayed various degrees of liberality in allowing the omission of undisputed facts from hypothetical questions, depending mostly upon the importance of the fact. A certain amount of leeway is given when the omission is not materially misleading and may be subject to correction by an alert cross-examiner.[74] When, however, the omission of undisputed fact reduces the value of the resulting opinion to a point where its probative value is outweighed by dangers of prejudice or of misleading the trier of fact, the question will not be allowed.[75]

Stanley Co of America v. Hercules Powder Co.[76], is an example of adding a fact either by misstatement or invention.[77] Plaintiff claimed that an explosion in defendant's plant caused structural damage to plaintiff's theater. Plaintiff's expert on the cause of damage was asked to assume that there had been one explosion of 30,000 tons of nitroglycerin. The only evidence on the point indicated that there had been three separate smaller explosions adding up to 30,000 tons. The court reversed on grounds that the hypothetical question was improper because it misstated a material fact.

The line between a misstated fact and a fact that is slanted toward the proponent's perspective can be sufficiently indistinct so that it is unlikely the trial court's view will be reversed on appeal. In *Cortrim Mfg. Co. v. Smith*,[78] for example, an expert was asked whether an employee's exertion while "setting up"[79] a large machine could have contributed to the employee's fatal heart attack. "Setting up" was characterized by the question as requiring a "tremendous amount[80]" of stretching, bending and reaching down. The evidence showed that the employee had been engaged in adjusting the machine, not setting it up. "Tremendous amount" exaggerated the exertion involved.[81] The trial court permitted the question and the appellate court affirmed, noting that the record indicated that the work did require somewhat strenuous

---

73. *Id.* at 372, (quoting Wolfinger v. Frey, 162 A.2d 745, 749 (Md.1960).

74. *See* Wigmore, *supra* note 1, § 682.

75. *See, e.g.,* Podedworny v. Harris, 745 F.2d 210, 218–19 (3d Cir. 1984) (hypothetical question about whether claimant's disability was defective because it failed to mention claimant's dizziness and blurred vision); Baugus v. Secretary of Health & Human Services, 717 F.2d 443, 447 (8th Cir.1983)(similar).

76. 108 A.2d 616 (N.J.1954).

77. *See also,* Raugust v. Diamond Int'l Corp., 692 P.2d 368, 369–70 (Idaho 1984) (hypothetical question assuming that victim had suffered neck injury in accident improper when evidence showed no injury to neck); Rosenberg v. Pritchard Serv., Inc., 774 F.2d 293, 295–97 (8th Cir.1985) (hypothetical question and answer properly

stricken when question assumed that defendant's servant always emptied ashtrays directly into trashbags, when evidence, construed most favorably to plaintiff, showed only that she sometimes did so); Johnson v. Toscano, 136 A.2d 341 (Conn. 1957) (hypothetical question properly excluded, both because it omitted material facts and because it referred to inadmissible facts); *Modern Status, supra* note 67, at 319–23; Wigmore, *supra* note 1, § 672.

78. 570 S.W.2d 854 (Tenn.1978); *see also,* Coleman v. De Minico, 730 F.2d 42, 46 (1st Cir.1984).

79. 570 S.W.2d at 855.

80. *Id.*

81. *See id.*

effort and that the defendant had the opportunity to restate the question on cross-examination.

A constant pre-rules criticism of the hypothetical was centered around the use lawyers made of the question to inject or unduly emphasize case facts unrelated to anything the expert needed as a basis for an opinion. In the hands of a skilled practitioner, the hypothetical question was transformed into a final argument. *Ingram v McCuiston*[82] is an example—and not as atypical as the length of the hypothetical might suggest. The plaintiff's lawyer asked the expert a twenty-three-para-graph question, purportedly to elicit the expert's opinion as to whether the plaintiff had been disabled by her injury. The question was replete with facts relevant to liability, but not to damages. The lawyer included in the question, for example, that the plaintiff had been hit from behind while stopped "in obedience to a traffic control device."[83] The lawyer included in the question the assertion that the plaintiff had slowed down because "she saw, and anyone who was properly observant could and should have seen"[84] that the traffic ahead was slowing down. In holding that the hypothetical question was improperly prejudicial because it was "slanted and argumentative," the court said: "it was no part of the legitimate purpose of the hypothetical question under consideration to establish defendants' negligence."[85]

§ 10.08 Examining Expert Witness—The Bases for the Expert Witness' Opinion [FRE 703]

The Federal Rules changed much more than the form of the question posed to an expert. They changed the permissible base upon which the opinion might rest. The combination of Rule 705–permitting an expert to give an opinion without prior disclosure of the underlying facts (unless the court directs otherwise)–and Rule 703–allowing the expert to base the opinion on information (even inadmissible information) provided before or during the hearing–was a revolution. It not only unseated the hypothetical as the dominant form for questioning an expert, it overthrew the notion that the expert's opinion must be based on facts available to the jurors.

Rule 703 reverses the common law rule that the expert must base an opinion upon facts already presented to the jurors. It not only permits the expert to base the opinion upon matters not presented to the jury, it allows the expert to base the opinion upon matters that would not be admissible in evidence in the normal course. So long as the information is "of a type reasonably relied upon by experts in the particular field in forming opinions or inferences upon the subject,"[86] the expert may use it to form an opinion.

---

82. 134 S.E.2d 705 (1964).

83. *Id*. at 708

84. *Id*.

85. *Id*. at 712.

86. Fed. R. Evid. 703.

The combination of Rule 705 and 703 would, therefore, allow the cursory examination in the splenectomy example set out at the beginning of § 8.07, irrespective of the basis for the doctor's opinion. The effect of Rule 703 is to allow the medical expert to examine hospital records, talk to the patient and family members, review reports by other doctors, and to use their hearsay statements and their opinions as the basis for the doctor's opinion. Though the rules of persuasion might suggest an examination in which the expert first describes the facts upon which the opinion is based, Rule 705 does not require it.

Rule 703's limitation on the use of inadmissible evidence to those facts and data upon which experts "reasonably" rely, when combined with Rule 705's discretion for the judge to require testimony about the opinion basis before allowing the opinion, provides an opportunity to protect against improper opinion. The lawyer who believes that the expert opinion will be based upon material not "reasonably relied upon" by experts in the field, should ask for a sidebar and signal to the judge that a procedure is needed to safeguard the jurors from hearing what may be an improper opinion. While Rule 705 suggests that the normal procedure for handling the problem is to require testimony about the underlying facts or data before hearing the expert's opinion, that procedure may not always solve the problem. If the opinion is improperly based upon an inadmissible opinion or upon inadmissible hearsay, there might be as much damage from testimony about the basis for the opinion as from testimony about the opinion, itself. Whether an expert opinion is based upon the kind of information "reasonably relied upon" is a "preliminary question" that Rule 104 requires the trial judge to decide[87] in a manner that will "prevent inadmissible evidence from being suggested to the jury."[88]

Opinions Based Upon the Opinions of Others

The Advisory Committee Note to Rule 703 explains the rationale for allowing an expert witness to base an opinion upon the opinion of others. Using, as an example, "reports and opinions" from nurses, technicians, and other doctors that a physician relies upon to make "life-and-death decisions" the Committee opines that those opinions "ought to suffice for judicial purposes" as well. The Rule is not restricted, however, to life-and-death situations. Experts testifying about everything from product liability[89] to land value[90] to chemical composition[91] have relied upon the opinions of others in presenting their testimony.

It does not follow, however, that all opinions based on other opinions are admissible. An opinion that merely parrots the opinion of another without adding any independent consideration by the testifying expert is

---

87. *See, e.g.,* Head v. Lithonia Corp., Inc., 881 F.2d 941, 944 (10th Cir.1989) (failure to make preliminary determination about whether data of the kind "reasonably relied upon" is reversible error).

88. Fed. R. Evid. 103(c).

89. *See, e.g.,* Lewis v. Rego Co., 757 F.2d 66 (3d Cir. 1985).

90. *See, e.g.,* United States v. 1,014.16 Acres, 558 F.Supp. 1238(W.D.Mo.1983).

91. *See e.g.,* United States v. Smith, 964 F.2d 885 (D.C. Cir. 1992).

not admissible under Rule 703.[92] An opinion prepared for litigation, even if it is of the kind upon which a testifying expert might have "reasonably relied" had it been available at the time the expert would have exercised professional judgment, cannot provide the basis for the expert testimony.[93]

Opinions Based Upon Inadmissible Hearsay Statements

No aspect of Rule 703 has caused more consternation than the use of hearsay statements to support expert opinion testimony. The same rationale that allowed expert testimony to be based upon opinion not before the jury suggested that expert testimony based upon statements not before the jury should be admissible, if the statements fit the requirement of being the kind of information upon which experts in the field "reasonably relied." Anticipating the objection to expert testimony based upon hearsay, the Advisory Committee said:

> If it be feared that enlargement of permissible data may tend to break down the rules of exclusion unduly, notice should be taken that the rule requires that the facts or data "be of a type reasonably relied upon by experts in the particular field." The language would not warrant admitting in evidence the opinion of an 'accidentologist' as to the point of impact in an automobile collision based on statements of bystanders, since this requirement is not satisfied.[94]

In contrast to the Committee's view of the limited potential for hearsay coming in through the testimony of an expert, at least one Court has assumed that "expert witness testimony is a well recognized exception to the rule against hearsay testimony."[95]

Stevens v. Cessna Aircraft Co.[96] seems to present precisely the situation about which there were fears—fears the Advisory Committee attempted to assuage with its reference to "accidentologists."[97] The accident was with an airplane, rather than an automobile, and the expert testimony was about the cause of the accident, rather than the point of impact, but the basis for the testimony was the same—hearsay from occurrence witnesses. Recognizing that "Cessna's explanation for what it termed Mr. Stevens' inexplicable misuse of the plane came from Dr.

---

92. TK–7 Corp. v. Estate of Barbouti, 993 F.2d 722 (10th Cir.1993) (no demonstration of any basis for expert's opinion other than opinion of other experts); State v. Towne, 453 A.2d 1133, 1135 (Vt.1982) (expert may not put into evidence the opinion of a nontestifying expert); Bunyak v. Clyde J. Yancey & Sons Dairy, Inc., 438 So.2d 891, 893 (Fla.Dist.Ct.App.1983) (expert witness may not testify to an expert opinion given to him by another expert).

93. United States v. Tran Trong Cuong, 18 F.3d 1132 (4th Cir.1994). *See also,* Borden v. Brady, 92 A.D.2d 983 (N.Y. App. Div. 1983) (the court adopted the essence of Federal Rule of Evidence 703 by case law, held that an opinion prepared for litigation is not the kind of opinion upon which a professional reasonably relies upon in conducting the professional activity).

94. Fed. R. Evid. 703 advisory committee note.

95. United States v. Williams, 447 F.2d 1285, 1290 (5th Cir.1971).

96. 634 F.Supp. 137 (E.D.Pa.1986).

97. *See also,* Cravens v. County of Wood, 856 F.2d 753 (6th Cir.1988)(state police officer allowed to give expert opinion that motorcycle traveling at 83 m.p.h, based on reading accident report and viewing pictures).

Charles Berry, a physician trained in aeronautical psychology,"[98] the Court, nevertheless, refused motions for a new trial, specifically rejecting the complaint that Dr. Berry's testimony was based almost entirely upon hearsay:

> Hearsay Statements. Dr. Berry, an expert with many years of experience in aeronautical medicine, undertook an investigation of Mr. Stevens' background. As part of this investigation, he interviewed many of Mr. Stevens' associates, such as his friends, co-workers, and professors. In his presentation to the jury, Dr. Berry explained that he believed that Mr. Stevens was under a great deal of stress—stress that might well have hampered his performance as a pilot. In fact, Dr. Berry concluded that Mr. Stevens was so preoccupied with personal problems—such as his relationship with Ms. Graham, financial troubles, and difficulties at school—that he was not in top shape to fly an airplane.
>
> During his testimony, Dr. Berry made reference to what he had learned from those whom he had interviewed. Mrs. Stevens correctly points out that such testimony would normally be excludable hearsay. In this case, however, I allowed the testimony to proceed on the grounds that such statements were routinely relied upon by experts such as Dr. Berry. Rule 703 authorizes the introduction of otherwise inadmissible evidence if it is "of a type reasonably relied upon by experts in the particular field in forming opinions or inferences upon the subject." Based on his many years of experience, Dr. Berry said that interviews such as those he conducted would normally be relied upon by those evaluating the fitness of pilots.... I find that this evidence was properly admitted in accordance with Rule 703.[99]

Although hearsay is a common base for expert opinion, it does not follow that hearsay information is always "reasonably relied upon by experts in the particular field." In contrast to the *Stevens* court, the testimony of "accidentologists" based largely upon hearsay from bystanders has been excluded, because the information was not of the kind that experts "reasonably relied upon."[100]

In *Lilley v. Dow Chemical Co.*[101] the trial judge rejected the testimony of a qualified medical expert who concluded decedent's death and illness were the result of exposure to Agent Orange. The expert's opinion was based upon conversations with family members who received much of their information from the decedent. The Judge acknowledged that in some cases statements by a spouse might be reasonably relied upon by medical experts, but this spouse's statements were not sufficiently reliable.[102]

98. Stevens v. Cessna Aircraft Co., 634 F.Supp. 137, 140 (E.D.Pa.1986).

99. *Id.* at 142–143.

100. *See, e.g.,* Dallas & Mavis Forwarding Co. v. Stegall, 659 F.2d 721 (6th Cir. 1981).

101. 611 F.Supp. 1267 (E.D.N.Y.1985).

102. *See also,* In re Agent Orange Product Liability Litig., 611 F.Supp. 1223, 1246–47 (E.D.N.Y.1985) (exclusion of expert testimony because hearsay checklists concerning health conditions completed for

There is disagreement among the courts about how the trial judge should decide whether the particular inadmissible evidence is "of a type reasonably relied upon by experts in the particular field in forming opinions or inference upon the subject." Judge Weinstein justifies his *Agent Orange* approach by assigning a judicial gatekeeping role for the court in determining whether Rule 703 "facts and data" are the kind "reasonably relied upon by experts" similar to the gatekeeping role the *Daubert* Court assigned for deciding what constitutes Rule 702 "knowledge": "[T]he court may not abdicate its independent responsibilities to decide if the bases meet minimum standards of reliability."[103] The Third Circuit Court of Appeals took an opposite approach in *In re Japanese Electronic Products Litigation.*[104] "The proper inquiry is not what the court deems reliable, but what experts in the relevant discipline deem it to be."[105]

The language of Rule 703 and the notion that experts should be able to rely on the same material in the courtroom as they rely upon when acting professionally favors the Third Circuit approach when the facts and data are of the kind used in the expert's professional non-courtroom activities. In cases where the expert would never use the underlying facts and data in a professional capacity, but only as a witness, there should be no difference between the court's Rule 702 gatekeeping responsibility and the Rule 703 inquiry.

Presenting the "Inadmissible" Opinion Base to the Jurors

Even if inadmissible facts and data provide a sufficiently reliable base to allow the jurors to hear the expert's opinion, it does not follow, necessarily, that the jurors should hear the inadmissible facts and data. The expert could give an opinion without quoting hearsay statements on which it is based. Neither the rule makers nor the courts have yet decided that the theoretical justifications for various rules of exclusion are mooted when the information is deemed an appropriate base for an expert's opinion. Nothing in Rule 703 makes admissible the otherwise inadmissible base of an expert's opinion and it is generally agreed that an underlying hearsay base is not admissible to prove the truth of the matter asserted in the hearsay statement.[106] On the other hand, offering expert testimony without providing the underlying basis is often unpersuasive and more often than not the underlying material will be available to the jurors in one form or another.[107]

---

litigation by litigants is not the type of information relied upon by reputable physicians).

103.   611 F.Supp. 1223, 1246 (E.D.N.Y. 1985).

104.   723 F.2d 238 (3d Cir. 1983),*rev'd on other grounds sub nom.*, Matsushita Elec. Indus. Co. v. Zenith Radio Corp., 475 U.S. 574 (1986)

105.   *Id.* at 276.

106.   Weinstein,   *supra*   note   47, § 703.04.

107.   *See, e.g.*, Paddack v. Dave Christensen, Inc., 745 F.2d 1254, 1261–62 (9th Cir.1984) (stating that Rule 703 permits such hearsay, or other inadmissible evidence, upon which an expert properly relies, to be admitted to explain the basis of the expert's opinion). *See also*, Lewis v. Rego Co., 757 F.2d 66, 73–74 (3d Cir. 1985); S. Saltzburg & K. Redden, Federal Rules of Evidence Manual, 671 (4th ed. 1986).

The courts have responded to the inevitable by trying to control the method by which the otherwise inadmissible evidence is presented to the jurors. In *United States v. McCollum*,[108] for example, the defense presented expert testimony that the defendant acted under hypnosis—an opinion based in part on inadmissible hearsay. The court did not exclude the underlying hearsay, but limited the method by which it was presented. The testimony of the expert, Dr. Jorgensen, was based upon interviews with the defendant while the defendant was under hypnosis. The trial judge ruled that the defense could introduce an edited segment of the videotape of the interviews and of Jorgensen purporting to hypnotize the defendant for the purpose of demonstrating the basis for Jorgensen's opinion. It would not admit the part of the videotape in which the defendant recited his "enhanced memory" version of events on the day in question, but did allow Jorgensen to present the information concerning the basis for his opinion through his own testimony.

In addition to limiting the means by which the otherwise inadmissible underlying data is presented to the jurors, the courts have tried to cure the problem of admitting inadmissible evidence by instructing the jurors about the limited use of the information. When the inadmissible information is communicated to the jurors for explanatory purposes, the opposing party is entitled to a limiting instruction to the jury that the evidence may be considered "solely as a basis for the expert opinion and not as substantive evidence."[109]

Some courts have recognized the difficulty in persuading jurors that they might accept the opinion of an expert, accept that the expert reasonably relied upon certain facts, but not, themselves, accept those facts as proof of what they assert. In situations where the underlying inadmissible facts are critical and the courts are persuaded that no limiting instruction will work, those courts have not allowed the underlying data to be presented to the jurors, usually relying on Rule 403 for the exclusion.[110]

The admissibility of hearsay through the conduit of an expert remains a significant area of controversy. In addition to the suggestion of an ABA committee to amend the rule to limit the freedom of experts to repeat hearsay,[111] the problem has attracted substantial comment from scholars.[112]

108. 732 F.2d 1419, 1422–23 (9th Cir. 1984), *cert. denied,* 469 U.S. 920 (1984).

109. 745 F.2d at 1262.

110. *See, e.g.,* Nachtsheim v. Beech Aircraft Corp., 847 F.2d 1261, 1270–71 (7th Cir.1988).

111. ABA Criminal Justice Section, Committee on Rules of Criminal Procedure and Evidence, *Federal Rules of Evidence: A Fresh Review and Evaluation,* 120 F.R.D. 299, 369–74 (1987).

112. Ronald L.Carlson, *Policing the Bases of Modern Expert Testimony,* 39 Vand. L. Rev. 577 (1986); Paul Rice, *Expert Testimony: A Debate Between Logic or Tradition Rather than Between Deference or Education,* 87 Nw. U.L. Rev. 1166(1993); Richard Lempert, *Experts, Stories, and Information,* 87 Nw. U.L. Rev. 1169 (1993); Edward J. Imwinkelried, *The Educational Significance of the Syllogistic Structure of Expert Testimony,* 87 Nw. U.L. Rev. 1148 (1993); Ronald L. Carlson, *In Defense of a Constitutional Theory of Experts,* 87 Nw. U. L. Rev. 1182 (1993).

§ 10.09 Examining the Expert Witness [FRE 705]—Opinions About the Ultimate Issue and Opinions About the Law [FRE 704]

Until about the middle of the century, many jurisdictions had prohibitions against asking experts to express an opinion about the ultimate issue[113]. A psychiatrist testifying in an insanity defense case, for example, might be precluded from testifying that the defendant could not distinguish right from wrong, on grounds that it is the ultimate issue to be decided by the jurors. Exclusion of such testimony was justified on grounds that the testimony concerned the "very issue before the jury"[114] and that by giving it the expert would be "usurping the function of the jury."[115] Critics of the rule argued that it placed an undue restriction on expert testimony and created unnecessary litigation about whether questions concerned ultimate facts or not—an illusory dichotomy. The charge that the expert would be "usurping the function of the jury" was rebutted with the observation that the jury could always reject the expert's testimony.[116]

When the Federal Rules of Evidence were originally enacted in 1975, Rule 704 abolished the ultimate issue objection completely. In the wake of controversy over expert testimony in insanity defense cases that followed the shooting of a President, however, Congress partially resurrected the prohibition. It carved out an exception to the rule allowing expert testimony on the ultimate issue, prohibiting expert testimony about whether a criminal defendant possessed a mental state or condition at issue in the case.

Rule 704 Opinion on Ultimate Issue

(a) Except as provided in subdivision (b), testimony in the form of an opinion or inference otherwise admissible is not objectionable because it embraces an ultimate issue to be decided by the trier of fact.

(b) No expert witness testifying with respect to the mental state or condition of a defendant in a criminal case may state an opinion or inference as to whether the defendant did or did not have the mental state or condition constituting an element of the crime charged or of a defense thereto. Such ultimate issues are matters for the trier of fact alone.

Although Rule 704 no longer prohibits expert opinion on the ground that it is about the ultimate issue—except in certain criminal cases—the Advisory Committee Note explains that some of the testimony previously objectionable as going to the ultimate issue is still objectionable on other grounds:

113. McCormick , *supra*, note 2, § 12.

114. Wigmore, *supra* note 1, § 1921.

115. Wigmore, *supra* note 1, § 1920.

116. Wigmore, *supra* note 1, § 1920–1921. *See* Stoebuck, *Opinions on Ultimate Facts: Status, Trends, and a Note of Caution*, 41 Den. L. C. J. 226 (1964).

The abolition of the ultimate issue rule does not lower the bars so as to admit all opinions. Under Rules 701 and 702, opinions must be helpful to the trier of fact. Rule 403 provides for exclusion of evidence that wastes time. These provisions afford ample assurances against the admission of opinion that would merely tell the jury what result to reach somewhat in the manner of the oath-helpers of an earlier day. They also stand ready to exclude opinions phrased in terms of inadequately explored legal criteria.

The traditional rule that experts may not give opinions about domestic law[117] has survived enactment of Rule 704, either by force of its common law rationale, that it would trench on the area reserved to the judge,[118] or because it would not "assist the trier of fact" under Rule 702.[119] Whatever the reason, the rule that an expert ordinarily may not express an opinion about law is often articulated when an opinion about the ultimate issue is excluded.

In an important sense, the "legal opinion/ultimate issue" problem is more a problem of artful examination for the lawyer than it is a problem about the exclusion of ideas. The Advisory Committee Note provides an example. "Did the testator have the capacity to make a will?" is about the ultimate issue, but it is excludable because it asks for an opinion about "inadequately explored legal criteria." "Did the testator have sufficient mental capacity to know the nature and extent of his property and the natural objects of his bounty and to formulate a rational scheme of distribution?" is about the same ultimate issue, but it would be allowed because the legal criteria are spelled out.

Whether a lawyer is trying to put before the jury expert testimony about the ultimate issue of mental state in a criminal case or about an opinion on the law, the goals are likely to be achieved, despite the rules prohibiting them, if the lawyer and the witness avoid legal terms. The discussion by the court in *United States v. Kristiansen*[120] is instructive.

> We have interpreted rule 704(b) to exclude testimony that "specifically comments on the presence or absence of an element of the crime charged, . . . too conclusory to be helpful to the jury." We concluded that the trial court in Gipson properly excluded the

117. *See,* Adalman v. Baker, Watts & Co., 807 F.2d 359, 366 (4th Cir.1986), *rev'd in part on other grounds,* Baker, Watts & Co. v. Miles & Stockbridge, 876 F.2d 1101 (4th Cir.1989); Specht v. Jensen, 853 F.2d 805, 808 (10th Cir.1988), *cert. denied,* 488 U.S. 1008 (1989) (expert testimony of lawyer in § 1983 case as to whether search occurred and whether plaintiffs consented was improperly admitted. Testimony concerned broad array of legal conclusions, not ultimate issue of fact.); Wigmore, *supra* note 1, § 1952; McCormick, *supra* note 2, § 12.

118. McCormick, *supra* note 2, § 12, (relying upon Marx & Co. v. Diners' Club,

Inc., 550 F.2d 505, 510 (2d Cir. 1977), *cert. denied,* 434 U.S. 861 states flatly that the exclusion of opinion about law was not affected by the adoption of Rule 704. The rule applies when there is a risk that the jurors might accept the expert's view of the law rather than the law as given to them by the judge. The rule does not apply in a bench trial, where the judge is as free to take the law through the testimony of a witness as through the briefs of the parties. *See, e.g.,* Knisley v. United States, 817 F.Supp. 680, 690 (S.D.Ohio 1993).

119. *See,* Note, *Expert Legal Testimony,* 97 Harv. L. Rev. 797 (1984).

120. 901 F.2d 1463 (8th Cir.1990).

question, " 'did [Gipson] have the requisite mental state to have willfully or intentionally attempted to escape,' " because it asked "for a mere legal conclusion." We approved asking the expert whether the defendant was suffering from a mental disease or defect at the time the crime was committed. Similarly, in United States v. Dubray, 854 F.2d 1099 (8th Cir.1988), we permitted a doctor to testify that the defendant was not suffering from psychosis at the time of the offense. We reasoned that this testimony related to the defendant's mental state which "has definite implications for the determination of Dubray's legal sanity," but that it did not state a legal conclusion "and did not state an opinion whether Dubray was able to appreciate the wrongfulness of his actions."

Under Gipson and Dubray, the defense clearly could ask whether Kristiansen was suffering from a mental disease or defect at the time of the offense. Just as clearly, the defense could not ask whether Kristiansen was unable to appreciate the nature and quality of his actions.... The more difficult question is whether the court erred in not permitting the defense to ask whether the mental disease or defect of the type that Kristiansen allegedly had *would* affect a person's ability to appreciate their actions.

We conclude that the defense should have been permitted to ask this question because it relates to the symptoms and qualities of the disease itself and does not call for an answer that describes Kristiansen's culpability at the time of the crime. Rule 704(b) was not meant to prohibit testimony that describes the qualities of a mental disease. "Under this proposal, expert psychiatric testimony would be limited to presenting and explaining their diagnoses, such as whether the defendant had a severe mental disease or defect and what the characteristics of such a disease or defect, if any, may have been."[121]

The choice of the language used to communicate the expert opinion has been determinative as to the admissibility of legal opinion in a variety of circumstances, from an attorney's fraudulent intent,[122] to whether lease unitholders must "sign off" of purchase agreements to transfer their interests,[123] to whether facts suggested that a criminal defendant had the requisite "intent" to distribute drugs.[124]

---

121. 901 F.2d 1463, 1465–1466 (citations omitted)(emphasis added).

122. United States v. Cavin, 39 F.3d 1299(5th Cir.1994).

123. Allison v. Ticor Title Ins. Co., 979 F.2d 1187 (7th Cir.1992).

124. United States v. Mitchell, 996 F.2d 419 (D.C.Cir.1993). *See generally,* Deon J. Nossel, *The Admissibility of Ultimate Issue Expert Testimony by law Enforcement Officers in Criminal Trials,* 93 Colum. L. Rev. 231 (1993).

Chapter 11

AUTHENTICATION, IDENTIFICATION, AND EXHIBITS

Analysis

§ 11.01 Authentication and Identification Under the Rules [FRE 901, 902]

Any tangible item that a lawyer intends to offer into evidence must first be authenticated. Rule 901(a) requires the lawyer to present evidence "sufficient to support a finding that the matter in question is what its proponent claims." Is the computer offered into evidence the very computer that was stolen from the victim? Is the white powder being offered into evidence the same powder that was found when the police searched the defendant? Is the letter containing an offer to sell corn one that was sent by the person alleged to be the offeror? Each of the foregoing is a question of authentication. Rule 901 applies, also, to some *viva voce* evidence. A party to a telephone conversation, for example, may not testify to the contents of that conversation or even establish the existence of the call without sufficient identification of the party on the other end of the line.[1]

Some items are self-authenticating. Rule 902 lists ten items that will be admitted into evidence without any extrinsic evidence of authenticity,

---

1. Fed. R. Evid. 901(b)(5) & (6).

including various official, public, or acknowledged documents,[2] newspapers,[3] trade inscriptions,[4] and commercial paper.[5]

Most items require extrinsic evidence of authenticity. Rule 901(b) contains ten illustrations (the list is not exclusive) of the kind of extrinsic evidence that meets the rule's authentication and identification requirements. Opinion about the similarity of handwriting or other specimens,[6] distinctive characteristics of items,[7] and demonstration that various processes produce accurate results[8] are exemplary.

The authentication required before an item may be admitted into evidence is not the same as a determination that the item is authentic. The difference between the process of "authentication" for an item to be admitted into evidence and a finding that the item is "authentic" has to do with who decides and how much proof is needed.

The division of labor contemplated by Rule 104(a) and (b) applies to authentication. The judge decides whether the "authentication" is sufficient for an item to be admitted into evidence.[9] The jury decides whether the evidence is sufficient to decide that the item is, in fact, "authentic."[10]

"Authentication"–the judge's call–requires only enough extrinsic evidence to establish a *prima facie* case that the item is what it purports to be.[11] If the evidence persuades the judge that a reasonable jury could find the item to be what the proponent claims it to be, that is enough, even if the judge personally believes that, on balance, the item is not what it purports to be.[12] As a practical matter, the judge looks only to the proponent's evidence. Assume that a witness testifies to familiarity with the defendant's handwriting and that the handwriting on a letter being offered into evidence is the defendant's. The judge must find the letter

---

2. Fed. R. Evid. 902(1),(2)(3),(4),(5),(8), & (10).

3. Fed. R. Evid. 902(6).

4. Fed. R. Evid. 902(7)

5. Fed. R. Evid. 902(9).

6. Fed. R. Evid. 901(b)(2) & (3).

7. Fed. R. Evid. 901(b)(4).

8. Fed. R. Evid. 901(b)(9).

9. *See* Fed. R. Evid. 901 advisory committee's note. This requirement of showing authenticity or identity falls in the category of relevancy dependent upon fulfillment of a condition of fact and is governed by the procedure set forth in Rule 104(b). *Id. See also* 2 McCormick on Evidence § 227 (4th ed. John W. Strong ed. 1994). The judge's ruling on an authentication question can only be reversed on the basis of an abuse of discretion. *See* United States v. Feldman, 788 F.2d 544, 556 (9th Cir. 1986), *cert. denied*, 479 U.S. 1067 (1987).

10. United States v. Thompson, 615 F.2d 329, 333 (5th Cir. 1980) (the jury, not the judge, is responsible for determining

the credibility of the evidence); United States v. Henderson, 588 F.2d 157, 160 (5th Cir. 1979), *cert. denied*, 440 U.S. 975 (1979) (the jury is responsible for determining the weight of the evidence).

11. *See* Fed. R. Evid. 901(a); United States v. Caldwell, 776 F.2d 989, 1001–02 (11th Cir. 1985) ("Authentication or identification under Rule 901 merely involves the process of presenting sufficient evidence to make out a prima facie case that the proffered evidence is what it purports to be"). *See also* 5 Weinstein's Federal Evidence, § 901.02[2] (2d ed. Joseph McLaughlin ed. 1997).

12. *See* United States v. Sutton, 426 F.2d 1202, 1207 (D.C. Cir. 1969) (test for authentication is whether a reasonable mind might, though not necessarily would, conclude that the evidence is what it purports to be); 5 Weinstein, *supra* note 11, § 901.02[2] ("The rule requires only that the court admit evidence if sufficient proof has been introduced so that a reasonable juror could find in favor of authentication or identification").

has been authenticated, even though the defendant has an expert to testify the handwriting is not the defendant's, the defendant will testify that the letter is a forgery, and the judge believes the defendant's evidence is more persuasive.[13]

"Authentic"–the jury's call–is about the comparative persuasive power of defendant's expert handwriting testimony and the defendant's testimony that the letter is a forgery as opposed to the plaintiff's opinion that the handwriting is the defendant's.[14]

§ 11.02   Handling Exhibits in the Courtroom

Exhibits present unique visual opportunities in an otherwise heavily oral environment, so most lawyers work very hard to achieve maximum persuasive advantage from the process of authenticating and offering an exhibit. But no matter the nature of the exhibit–document, photograph, diagram, model, etc. or the particular persuasive approach employed, a lawyer offering an exhibit follows a basic procedural pattern.[15] The pattern may vary a bit from courtroom to courtroom, but the basic requirements remain. Pre-trial marking of exhibits or informality of practice will sometimes allow exhibits to be offered and received into evidence, without going through each of the steps of proper exhibit handling. A lawyer must understand the process, nevertheless, for those times when an exhibit must be marked and offered in a courtroom in which the judge expects exhibits to be handled in the formal fashion.

1. *Ask the court's permission to have the clerk, the court reporter, or the bailiff (whoever marks exhibits in the particular courtroom) mark the exhibit for identification.*

Exhibits are numbered or lettered in sequence. In many jurisdictions the plaintiff's or prosecution's exhibits are numbered and the defendant's exhibits are lettered.

2. *Show the exhibit to the opposing lawyer.*

More often than not, the lawyer will have seen the item during discovery, but it is important to show the exhibit, nevertheless. The lawyer who is being shown the prospective exhibit and has seen it during discovery is well advised to make sure that the exhibit is in the same shape and represents the same information at trial that it did during discovery.

---

13. 5 Weinstein, *supra* note 11, § 901.02[2]:

   Thus, if the question is whether one of the parties signed the contract being offered, it will be admitted if a witness testifies that he is familiar with the signature and identifies it, regardless of what other evidence may subsequently be introduced to rebut that testimony. *Id.*

14. *See* United States v. Caldwell, 776 F.2d 989, 1002 (11th Cir. 1985) ("Once that prima facie showing has been made, the evidence should be admitted, although it remains for the trier of fact to appraise whether the proffered evidence is in fact what it purports to be"); 5 Weinstein, *supra* note 11, § 901.02[2].

15. *See* Steven H. Goldberg, The First Trial (Where Do I Sit? What Do I Say?) 26 (Presenting Exhibits "By the Numbers") (1982).

While walking around the courtroom with an exhibit that can be identified easily upon sight, such as a photograph or a gun, it is important to ensure that jurors do not see the exhibit before it is admitted into evidence. If the exhibit is one that ultimately will not be received, exhibition of it to the jurors could result in sanctions against the lawyer and, if the prejudice is sufficiently serious, a mistrial.

Some items may be difficult to handle without exposing them to the jurors during the authentication process. If the exhibit is not seriously contested, or if the item is one that will not cause much prejudice if the jurors see it during the process, opposing counsel may agree or the court may allow it to be within the jurors' view before it has been received in evidence.

3. *Ask the court's permission to approach the witness. Hand the exhibit to the witness and ask whether the witness can identify the exhibit.*

It is important for the lawyer to refer to the item by its identification number so that the record is clear, in the event an appellate court is asked to review it.

Proponent:	I hand you what has been marked Plaintiff's Exhibit No. 1 for identification. Do you recognize it?
Witness:	Yes.
Proponent:	What is it?

The same care must be taken with the question to the witness about the nature of the exhibit as must be taken in concealing certain exhibits from the jurors before they are received in evidence. The lawyer must ensure that neither the question nor the answer tells the jurors about the contents or the nature of the exhibit—information that is appropriate only after the exhibit has been received. A questions such as, "Mr. Smith, would you examine the shrunken head that has been marked as State's Exhibit No. 1 for identification?" is likely to provoke an objection and could provide the basis for a mistrial.[16]

4. *Ask the witness the questions needed to lay the foundation for the admission of the exhibit into evidence.*

The particular authenticating questions will vary from exhibit to exhibit, but all authentication testimony involves the witness explaining to the jury why the exhibit is what it purports to be. In preparing a witness to lay the foundation for an exhibit, the lawyer should remember that the testimony serves two purposes. It provides the authentication so

---

16. *See* United States v. Bayer, 331 U.S. 532, 537–39 (1947) (unauthenticated record of long distance phone call properly excluded since allowing the jury to view it would have been prejudicial and would have necessitated a mistrial); Mayer v. Angelica, 790 F.2d 1315, 1338–41 (7th Cir. 1986), *cert. denied,* 479 U.S. 1037 (1987) (admission of unauthenticated letters was prejudicial, thus requiring new trial). An objection to the unauthenticated evidence must be made at trial in order to preserve the error for appeal. *See* Falcon v. General Tel. Co., 626 F.2d 369 (5th Cir. 1980).

the judge will admit the evidence, but more importantly, it provides the information that will persuade the jurors that the exhibit is authentic, or that it is one from which they should draw inferences important to the lawyer offering the exhibit.

5. *Offer the exhibit into evidence: "Your honor, I offer (whatever the item is) that has been marked as Plaintiff's exhibit number one for identification into evidence as plaintiff's exhibit number one."*

In some jurisdictions, an item is marked originally with a number or letter, without the "for identification" limitation. In such a jurisdiction, the lawyer need not refer to the marked item as an exhibit "for identification" and might offer the exhibit by saying, "Your honor, I offer plaintiff's exhibit number one (whatever the item is) into evidence."

In jurisdictions in which the original marking is "for identification," the judge will have the court personnel who marked the exhibit strike the "for identification" limitation when the exhibit is received in evidence.

6. *Make sure that the contents or the nature of the exhibit is apparent to the jurors.*

The most important part of having an exhibit admitted into evidence is its influence on the jurors in deciding the case. The lawyer should make sure that the full force of the exhibit is brought to bear when it is accepted into evidence. If it is a document, the lawyer should ask the court's permission to have the witness read the contents to the jurors. Providing copies of a document for distribution to each juror is another way to bring the contents of the document to the jurors' attention. Copies of a diagram might be distributed, as well, but more often displaying a blown up version of the diagram on an easel is more effective, and allows the witness to use the exhibit to make the testimony memorable. Photographs, as well, might be blown up and displayed to the jurors or passed among the jurors. Objects are often passed among the jurors for closer inspection.

Whatever method the lawyer chooses for bringing the exhibit to the attention of the jurors, the lawyer should be sure to receive the court's permission. "Your honor, may I distribute copies of plaintiff's exhibit number one to the jurors?" "Your honor, may the witness read plaintiff's exhibit number one to the jurors?" "Your honor, I have a blow up of the photograph that has been received as plaintiff's exhibit number one. May it be displayed to the jurors?"

§ 11.03   "Laying a foundation" for a Variety of Exhibits

The presentation of the extrinsic evidence to authenticate an exhibit is usually called "laying the foundation." The foundation can be laid either by direct evidence or by circumstantial evidence. Sometimes one witness is sufficient; in other cases, more than one is necessary.

In determining what evidence must be offered to lay the foundation for a particular exhibit, the lawyer must determine what it is the exhibit is offered to prove. A diagram of an intersection, for example, may be used to assist a witness in describing what the witness saw, but it might prove, also, exactly where items of importance were located. For the first purpose, the witness can lay the foundation merely by testifying to three simple matters. 1) The witness is familiar with the intersection. 2) The diagram is a fair and accurate representation of the way the intersection looked on the day of the collision. 3) The diagram would be helpful to the witness in explaining to the jurors what happened. For the second purpose, to show the exact position of cars, skid-marks, glass fragments, etc., a more detailed foundation is required from one or more witnesses. 1) How the diagram was drawn to scale and the scale used. 2) How the measurements of the location of items shown on the diagram were taken at the scene. 3) The measurements taken at the scene were converted in accord with the scale to which the diagram was drawn.

All foundations for exhibits fall into one of three general categories: foundations for real evidence, demonstrative evidence that is illustrative of other evidence, and demonstrative evidence that carries its own substantive value.

§ 11.04   "Real" Evidence—"The Chain of Custody"

Items that were actually involved in the transaction or occurrence that gave rise to the litigation are called "real evidence."[17] The stolen goods in a burglary case, the signed agreement in a contract case, and headlight glass fragments found on the road in a personal injury case are common examples. Real evidence is authenticated by showing that the exhibit in court is the actual item from the transaction or event and that it has not undergone any significant change.[18] The requirement that the exhibit be in the same condition as it was at the time of the transaction or event applies only if the condition that has been changed matters in the litigation. If the changes can be explained or understood by the jurors, the change is not a bar to admission. In a counterfeiting trial, therefore, the seized counterfeit money could be authenticated as the "real" counterfeit despite a change in the color of the money to blue during government fingerprint analysis of the bills. The identification of the counterfeit money and its relevance to the litigation did not depend upon the color.[19]

17.   4 John H. Wigmore, Evidence in Trials at Common Law § 1150 (James H. Chadbourn rev. 1972).

18.   Robinson v. F.W. Woolworth & Co., 420 So.2d 737, 741 (La. App. 1982) (plaintiff fell because spilled paint was on defendant-store's floor; the defendant could not offer can of paint into evidence because paint can was not the one that had spilled and defendant did not testify that the paint can was the same type as the can which caused the problem); Victory Park Apartments, Inc. v. Axelson, 367 N.W.2d 155, 163 (N.D. 1985) (blanket that was allegedly on couch during a fire was properly excluded from evidence because blanket was washed and thus not in same condition as it was immediately after the fire occurred).

19.   United States v. Skelley, 501 F.2d 447, 451 (7th Cir. 1974) (counterfeit bills were admissible to prove defendant's knowledge that they were counterfeit be-

"Real evidence" is frequently authenticated in the manner of 901(b)(4) by reference to its distinctive characteristics. If the condition of the item is not important or if the item is distinctive, real evidence often can be authenticated by simple identification. Documents, for example, are probably the most common "real evidence" and they are usually authenticated in the fashion of 901(b)(2) or (3), by identification of the handwriting.[20] Real evidence that is non-documentary is often authenticated in the fashion of 901(b)(4), by distinctive characteristics or circumstances. A police officer, who initialed a weapon upon seizing it from a suspect, might authenticate the weapon by recognizing the initials and testifying about circumstances of the seizure and marking. Money, televisions sets, automobiles, etc. may be authenticated by showing that the witness recorded the item's serial number at the time of the seizure and that the serial number of the proposed exhibit matches.

When the item of real evidence is not distinctive, or when its condition at the time of testing or trial is critical, a chain of custody is the most effective way to authenticate the exhibit. A perfect demonstration of the chain of custody would include testimony about every link in the chain, from the moment the item was picked up at the scene of the event to the time it is offered into evidence. Each person who touched the exhibit would describe how and from whom it was received, where it was and what happened to it while in the witness' possession, the condition in which it was received and the condition in which it was delivered to the next link in the chain. The witnesses would describe the precautions taken to ensure there was no change in the condition of the exhibit and no opportunity for someone not in the chain to have possession of the item.

Testimony about the perfect chain is almost impossible and has never been the standard. Before adoption of the Federal Rules, a chain of custody could be established only if there was reasonable certainty that all the links in the chain were firmly connected. The Rules may have made the required showing less onerous. The authentication standard in Rule 901(a) requires only enough evidence to support a finding that the item is what it purports to be. Some courts in Federal Rules jurisdictions have take the new standard literally and have allowed greater gaps between the links in a chain of custody.[21] Other courts have remained

cause they had identical serial numbers and were found on defendant).

20. *See* § 11.10 for examples of document foundations.

21. *See, e.g.,* United States v. Correa-Tobon, 748 F.2d 1509, 1511 (11th Cir. 1984) (court deferred to jury in deciding whether defendant occupied the master bedroom where incriminating evidence was found); United States v. Johnson, 637 F.2d 1224, 1247 (9th Cir. 1980) ("The proffered evidence should be admitted once a prima facie case has been made on the issue … the matter is [then] committed to the trier of fact to determine the evidence's credibility and probative force"). *See also* United States v. Goichman, 547 F.2d 778, 784 (3d Cir. 1976) ("[T]here need only be a prima facie showing, to the court, of authenticity … once a prima facie case is made, the evidence goes to the jury and it is the jury who will ultimately determine the authenticity of the evidence, not the court").

strict and have repeated the reasonable certainty standard of the pre-Rules era.[22]

Custody chains are commonly used to demonstrate that a substance seized in one place is the same substance and in the same condition as the substance tested in another place and then returned for use in court. The exhibit will have passed through many hands from its point of origin to the laboratory to the courtroom, and it also will have been processed or analyzed. The exhibit and the laboratory analysis will not be admissible unless the proponent can show the chain of custody of the exhibit from the time it was seized to the time it arrives in court.[23] Urine samples, bloody gloves, trace elements of hair, are exemplary of the myriad of objects that might require the showing of a custody chain, but drugs seized in a drug bust are the most common example.

In the typical drug case, someone associated with the government secures the drugs. Often it is an undercover officer or an informer who made the buy. The drugs are often transferred to at least one other law enforcement officer. The drugs are then stored in an evidence locker; sent via some delivery service to a laboratory for testing; stored, handled, and tested in the laboratory by at least one technician; and sent via some delivery service back to the law enforcement officer. If at any of these links there is tampering, inadvertent alteration, or substitution of white powder from some other case in which similar evidence was seized, the test results may be wrong and the exhibit offered in court may not be that originally seized or procured by the first law enforcement personnel to handle the drugs.

The chain of custody can be established without testimony from everyone who handled the drugs. The habit rule, the business record exception and the public record exception to the hearsay rule make it possible for documentary evidence to be used to establish some of the links in the chain.[24] Moreover, imperfect chains and minor gaps are often accepted for purpose of authentication, the issue of the weight to be given to the testimony left to the jury.[25] Despite the flexibility shown

---

22. *See, e.g.,* United States v. Jones, 687 F.2d 1265, 1267 (8th Cir. 1982) (reasonable certainty standard used by the trial court to assess the adequacy of the chain of custody).

23. Paul C. Gianelli, *Chain of Custody and the Handling of Real Evidence*, 20 Am. Crim. L. Rev. 527, 538 (1983).

24. *See* United States v. Harrington, 923 F.2d 1371, 1373–74 (9th Cir. 1991), *cert. denied,* 502 U.S. 854 (1991); United States v. Coleman, 631 F.2d 908, 912 (D.C. Cir. 1980).

25. *See, e.g.,* United States v. Pressley, 978 F.2d 1026, 1028–29 (8th Cir. 1992) (trial court properly admitted substance in package marked by an officer at the scene of the crime, when chemist testified she tested substance in same package; held, "[t]he government is not required to maintain an eternal vigilance over all evidence in its custody"); United States v. Shaw, 920 F.2d 1225, 1229–30 (5th Cir.), *cert. denied,* 500 U.S. 926 (1991) (break in the chain of custody of physical evidence does not render the evidence inadmissible but instead goes to the weight that the jury should give it; methamphetamine properly admitted although custodian of search team could not recall whether he or another officer delivered the drug to lab and whether drug was hand-delivered or placed in night deposit box, and although many lab chemists had access to the drug); Bell v. State, 610 N.E.2d 229, 233 (Ind. 1993) (in robbery and battery prosecution, sufficient chain-of-command shown when backlog at one laboratowhen there are minor gaps in the chain, courts will not admit exhibits if the defect in the chain might reasonably affect the authenticity of the exhibit.

In *Graham v. State*,[26] an informer made a supervised purchase of a substance that was later analyzed as heroin. The break in the chain of custody occurred after the exhibit was deposited in the police property room. The property room records showed that before the exhibit was analyzed, one officer removed the exhibit from the property room and six days later, another officer returned the exhibit to the property room. Neither officer testified at trial. There was no evidence of where the exhibit was, or in whose possession, during the six days that it was not in the police property room. The trial judge admitted the evidence. In holding that it was error to admit the exhibit with the break in the chain of custody, the appellate court emphasized the special nature of substances such as narcotics. It said that "the danger of tampering, loss, or mistake with respect to an exhibit is greatest where the exhibit is small and is one which has physical characteristics fungible in nature and similar in form to substances familiar to people in their daily lives."[27] It noted the white powder seized could have been heroin, or it could have been sugar or baking powder. It stated the chain of custody rule for substances such as narcotics as follows:

> Unless the state can show by producing records or testimony, the continuous whereabouts of the exhibit at least between the time it came into their possession until it was laboratory tested to determine its composition, testimony of the state as to the laboratory's findings is inadmissible.[28]

Robinson v. Commonwealth,[29] is a case in which the authentication did not match the purpose for which the exhibit was offered. The victim of a rape identified her panties and blouse in court, which had been handed over to the investigating officer shortly after the incident. The evidence would have been sufficient to authenticate the clothing as that she was wearing when she was attacked. The clothing items were offered, however, as the base for the opinion of an FBI expert. The expert testified about the semen stains, blood stains, and wool fibers

---

ry required sending evidence to another laboratory to be tested).

26. 255 N.E.2d 652, 655 (Ind. 1970). For more recent cases in which evidence was excluded for defects in the chain of custody, see Laws v. State, 562 So.2d 305 (Ala. Crim. App. 1990) (cocaine exhibit inadmissible because prosecution offered no evidence of where the cocaine was stored for the twenty days that passed between the time the cocaine was taken from defendant and examined by the Department of Forensic Sciences); State v. Weber, 768 S.W.2d 645, 648 (Mo. App. 1989) (state exhibits of controlled substances are inadmissible because prosecution failed to ask when the exhibits were labeled, who labeled the

exhibits, and whether they were in the same condition at trial as when they were seized); People v. Steiner, 539 N.Y.S.2d 217, 219 (App. Div. 1989) (where cocaine allegedly seized from defendant changed in color and consistency and the chemist who analyzed cocaine neither testified at trial or initialed the container after examining it as per proper procedure, that cocaine exhibit is inadmissible because government could not show exhibit was in unchanged condition).

27. *Graham*, 255 N.E.2d at 655.

28. *Id.*

29. 183 S.E.2d 179 (Va. 1971).

found on the clothing–evidence that linked the defendant to the crime. The prosecution did not offer any evidence as to who had handled or what happened to the items of clothing from the time they were taken from the victim to the time they were given to the local police for storage–the time during which the FBI analysis took place. In reversing the conviction because the chain of custody was inadequate to authenticate the items, the court said:

> It is true that the blouse and panties were identified at the trial by the victim as a part of the clothes she was wearing when attacked. The Commonwealth contends that they were properly admitted because the victim identified them. If they had been admitted only to establish what the victim was wearing when attacked, then we would agree with the Commonwealth's position. But the blouse and the panties were also admitted to supply a basis for the opinion testimony of the FBI agents. The mere fact the blouse and the panties were identified did not prove the chain of possession necessary to validate the FBI analysis of them.[30]

§ 11.05 Demonstrative Exhibits That Are Illustrative of Other Testimony

Demonstrative evidence that illustrates, clarifies, and amplifies *viva voce* testimony brings life to a lawsuit. Trial lawyers are constantly in search of visual aids that will assist them in persuading jurors. They use diagrams, models, similar objects, photographs, and drawings to illustrate the ideas to which witnesses testify. The simplest and most common example is the intersection diagram on which a witness illustrates the many simultaneous movements that make up the average intersection collision.

The foundation for demonstrative evidence that is offered only to illustrate other testimony is deceptively simple. The witness must demonstrate familiarity with whatever it is that is depicted, must testify that the exhibit fairly and accurately represents what is depicted, and, in some courts, that the exhibit will assist the witness in explaining the testimony to the jurors. It does not matter whether it is a photograph or a diagram, or a duplicate object, for that matter. The foundation that the exhibit is a fair and accurate representation can be laid by anyone who knows what the thing depicted looks like. So the testimony of the photographer or the diagram maker, for example, is not required.

The foundation for most demonstrative evidence offered for illustrative purposes, fits the pattern that follows for a diagram.

Example

Direct examiner: Are you familiar with the intersection of First Avenue and Maple?

30. *Id.* at 181.

Witness:	Yes.
Direct examiner:	How are you familiar with that intersection?
Witness:	I drive through it regularly—at least three times a week.
Direct examiner:	I show you what has been marked Plaintiff's exhibit number one for identification. Do you recognize it?
Witness:	Yes, I do.
Direct examiner:	What is it?
Witness:	Looks like the intersection of First Avenue and Maple.
Direct examiner:	Does Plaintiff's exhibit number one for identification fairly and accurately represent the way the intersection of First Avenue and Maple appeared on (the date of incident?)
Witness:	Yes, it does.
Direct examiner:	Would the diagram assist you in explaining to the jurors what you saw?
Witness:	Yes.
Direct examiner:	Your honor, I offer the diagram of First Avenue and Maple into evidence as Plaintiff's exhibit number one.
Opposing attorney:	Your honor, I request a limiting instruction be given informing the jurors that the diagram is not drawn to scale.
Judge:	Members of the jury. The diagram that has just been received in evidence as Plaintiff's exhibit number one is not drawn to scale. While it is basically accurate as to the intersection of First Avenue and Maple, the distances shown are approximate, and should not be taken by you to necessarily represent the distance relationships on the intersection.

The foundation–that the exhibit fairly and accurately represents whatever it is it represents and that it would assist the witness in testifying–is as sufficient for a complex model or for a hologram as it is for a simple diagram.

Demonstrative evidence used for illustrative purposes is handled differently from jurisdiction to jurisdiction and sometimes from courtroom to courtroom. Trial courts have great discretion in the handling of demonstrative evidence offered for illustrative purposes.[31] Demonstrative exhibits that are used for illustrative purposes are not even marked in some courtrooms, though a lawyer who insists upon having such an exhibit marked to make the record understandable for an appellate court should prevail. Some courts allow the use of demonstrative evidence for illustrative purposes, but do not allow the exhibits to be admitted into evidence.[32] In other courts, demonstrative evidence used for illustrative purposes is received in evidence, but the jurors are given an instruction that the exhibit is for illustrative purposes only. In some instances, such as when a replica of a gun used in a robbery is admitted for illustrative purposes, it may be error not to give an instruction reminding the jury that the gun is not the actual gun.[33] At one time demonstrative exhibits were routinely excluded from the jury room during deliberations. The modern tendency is to allow most exhibits to be taken into the jury room,[34] unless it is impractical (bulky items or contraband) or, in some cases, when the evidence is merely testimonial evidence in written form.[35]

The most common objection to demonstrative evidence used for an illustrative purpose is that it is misleading. Diagrams that appear to be to scale but are not can mislead the jurors into forgetting that the distances shown are approximate. A photograph taken under different lighting conditions can mislead the jurors into thinking that the lighting shown in the photograph reflects what someone on the scene could see at the time. Sometimes the problem is handled by an instruction, but if the evidence is sufficiently misleading, the judge may exclude it under Rule 403.

§ 11.06 Demonstrative Exhibits That Are Illustrative of Other Testimony—Diagrams and Models

Diagrams and models used to illustrate testimony are used in many cases and are a staple in tort cases. Many diagrams are offered with the first occurrence witness and remain in front of the jury throughout the trial, often referred to or marked on by more than one witness. Courts have different preferences about how diagrams are handled. If the diagram is one that a witness or a number of witnesses will mark on, some judges will not admit the diagram until all of the marking has been completed. Others will allow the diagram to be admitted and then amended as others mark on it. In some courts, diagrams are considered

---

31. Carson v. Polley, 689 F.2d 562 (5th Cir. 1982).

32. *See, e.g.,* United States v. Walt, 117 F.3d 1427 (9th Cir. 1997).

33. United States v. Cox, 633 F.2d 871, 874 (9th Cir. 1980).

34. 2 McCormick on Evidence § 217 (4th ed. John W. Strong ed. 1994). *See also*

McCaffrey v. Glendale Acres, Inc., 440 P.2d 219 (Or. 1968) (exhibits are part of the evidence and should go to the jury room).

35. United States v. DeCoito, 764 F.2d 690, 695 (9th Cir. 1985) (jurors are generally entitled to see exhibits received in evidence).

entirely illustrative and are neither admitted in evidence nor allowed in the jury room during deliberations.

Marking on diagrams is one way to make sure that the jurors understand what happened and that the appellate court can figure it out as well. While the jurors know what a witness means by pointing to a spot on a diagram and saying, "I was standing right here," they may not remember it when they arrive in the jury room. The appellate court will never know what "here" meant. If the witness marks clearly on the diagram, the jurors will remember when they take the diagram into the jury room and the appellate court will be able to understand by looking at the diagram.

While the foundation for most diagrams is the one set out in § 11.05, if the diagram is drawn to scale and is offered to illustrate testimony about precise measurements the witness must lay a much more complete foundation. Moreover, the witness must be one who can testify from first hand knowledge about the creation of the diagram. The witness must be able to explain how the measurements were obtained, how they were converted to the diagram, and the scale used.

Example

Direct examiner:	Are you familiar with the intersection of First Avenue and Maple?
Witness:	Yes.
Direct examiner:	How are you familiar with that intersection?
Witness:	I have driven through it, have gone over the construction plans for the intersection in the city engineer's office, and have taken measurements on the intersection itself.
Direct examiner:	I show you what has been marked Plaintiff's exhibit number one for identification. Do you recognize it?
Witness:	Yes, I do.
Direct examiner:	What is it?
Witness:	It is a diagram of the intersection of First Avenue and Maple.
Direct examiner:	Do you know how it was constructed?
Witness:	Yes, I do.
Direct examiner:	How was it constructed?

Witness:	I drew it to scale, based on information about its dimensions gained from the current plans in the city engineer's office and from measurements made on (the date of the incident) by the investigating police officer as to the position of various objects and marks.
Direct examiner:	How did you draw it to scale?
Witness:	I used a scale of five feet—sixty inches—to one inch. By using a standard ruler, I re-created the intersection and the objects on the diagram from the measurements I had. Every five feet or sixty inches of distance on the intersection is represented by one inch on the diagram.
Direct examiner:	How were you able to locate the various objects in the intersection?
Witness:	I had the measurements for every object that the investigating officer identified in his report and four measurements—one from each direction, N, S, E & W—from identified landmarks or points on the intersection to each object.
Direct examiner:	Your honor, I offer the scale diagram of First Avenue and Maple—drawn to a scale of 60 to 1 into evidence as Plaintiff's exhibit number one.

Once a diagram is accepted into evidence as a scale diagram, non-scale marks added to the diagram may destroy the foundation and the exhibit. Markings that show directions, etc. might be added, because they do not purport to represent distances, but any other marking that reflects a distance must be made to scale with a ruler or placed on an overlay that can be separated from the scale diagram.

When more than one witness will mark on a diagram, a number of different methods might be employed to ensure that the diagram is an aid to testimony, rather than something that makes matters more confusing. Using a different colored pen for each witness, and creating a legend on the bottom of the diagram, so the jurors can remember which witness used which colored pen is one method. Using a different clear acetate overlay for each witness—making sure that the acetates are individually marked—is another method that provides the lawyer with flexibility.

Models used for illustrative purposes are merely three-dimensional diagrams. Courts are occasionally less careful about the marking and offering of models used to illustrate testimony than they are about diagrams. A skeleton used by an orthopedic surgeon, for example, to show the jurors where the various bones the doctor is talking about are located may often be used without being either marked or admitted. The better practice, however, is to have the model marked and offered. Among other things, it is more likely to be allowed into the jury room if admitted.

A model with working parts requires greater foundational detail to ensure that the working parts on the model do not work in a different fashion than the parts represented. "Misleading" remains the condition that will persuade the court to exclude demonstrative evidence used for illustrative purposes.

§ 11.07   Demonstrative Exhibits That Are Substantive

Demonstrative evidence that is not real evidence can, nevertheless, often have substantive value, independent of any testimony to which it might relate. Photography, sound recordings, and documents are the three major areas in which demonstrative evidence might have independent substantive value. A photograph, properly authenticated, may be received as independent evidence of what it shows. A tape recording might be admitted as independent evidence of the conversation. While a written contract constitutes real evidence, if the contract is ambiguous, one party's memorandum about the contract may be admissible as independent substantive evidence of whether there was a meeting of the minds. If these pieces of demonstrative evidence are to have independent evidentiary value, the foundation requires something more than a witness who will testify that the exhibit is a "fair and accurate representation" of what it depicts. The foundation must demonstrate the reason that the exhibit should be considered authentic. A determination that the photograph, document, or recording is authentic does not, however, end the question of admissibility. The exhibit must still pass the hearsay and best evidence hurdles.[36] Authentication is a cumulative requirement.

§ 11.08   Demonstrative Exhibits That are Substantive— Photography

Photography, whether it is in the form of a still photo, film, or videotape has a history of being viewed first with suspicion by the courts and then being viewed as common. Each succeeding technology has had to travel the authentication trail from a detailed explanation of the entire technology to acceptance by the court based upon the affirmation from any witness with knowledge that the picture is a fair and accurate representation of what it shows. In discussing the journey for still photographs, the Court in *United States v. Hobbs*[37] described the journey that each of the photographic technologies has taken:

---

36. *See* Fed. R. Evid. 901(b) advisory committee's note ("It should be observed that compliance with requirements of authentication or identification by no means assures admission of an item into evidence, as other bars, hearsay for example, may remain"). *See also* United States v. Carroll, 860 F.2d 500, 507–08 (1st Cir. 1988) (microfilm prints of checks held properly authenticated and admissible under best evidence rule); United States v. Mouzin, 785 F.2d 682, 692–93 (9th Cir. 1986) (ledger entries held inadmissible hearsay under Rule 801(d)(2)(E) despite having been properly authenticated); Comment, *Limits of Admissibility: Authentication, Identification, and the Best Evidence Rule*, 36 La. L. Rev. 59 (1975).

37.   403 F.2d 977 (6th Cir. 1968).

When photographs first began finding their way into judicial trials they were viewed with suspicion and received with caution. It was not uncommon to place upon the offering party the burden of producing the negative as well as the photograph itself, and of proving that neither retouching or other manual or chemical intervention was reflected in the proffered print. That burden has now shifted, and the proponent of a proffered photograph has established a prima facie case for its admissibility when he has shown it to be an accurate representation of the scene in question. The opposing party should then be afforded an opportunity for voir dire to show that the picture is not in fact an accurate representation.[38]

Today, most courts will accept pictures—stills, film, videotapes—into evidence upon a showing that in accord with 901(b)(1) a witness with knowledge has testified that the picture "fairly and accurately" represents what the witness saw.

Example

[Witness has been identified and the photograph has been marked and shown to opposing counsel.]

Direct examiner:	Where were you at 3:00 p.m. on November 1, 1997?
Witness:	On the southeast corner of First Avenue and Maple.
Direct examiner:	What happened while you were on the corner?
Witness:	There was a collision between a Ford and a Chevrolet.
Direct examiner:	I show you what has been marked Plaintiff's exhibit number one for identification. Do you recognize it?
Witness:	Yes.
Direct examiner:	What is it?
Witness:	It is a picture of the intersection of First Avenue and Maple shortly after the collision.
Direct examiner:	Does Plaintiff's exhibit number one fairly and accurately represent the scene at the intersection of First Avenue and Maple on November 1, 1997 as you saw it shortly following the collision between the Ford and the Chevrolet?
Witness:	Yes it does.

38. *Id.* at 978.

Direct examiner:	Are there any differences between plaintiff's exhibit number one for identification and the scene at the intersection of First Avenue and Maple as you saw it immediately following the collision?
Witness:	Only one that I can see.
Direct examiner:	What is that difference?
Witness:	The photograph includes a police car parked off to the side that was not there right after the collision. The police officer arrived about five minutes later.
Direct examiner:	Other than the police car, is there anything different?
Witness:	No.
Direct examiner:	Your honor, I offer the picture of the intersection of First Avenue and Maple following the collision into evidence as Plaintiff's exhibit number one.

As a persuasive matter, the lawyer might expand the examination about what the witness saw. If the witness saw the photographer take the picture, that, too, might be the subject of examination. But neither is necessary to lay the foundation for the photograph.[39]

Although earlier twentieth century courts treated photographs of the kind now authenticated under 901(b)(1) as "pictorial testimony," merely illustrative of other testimony,[40] the modern trend is to accept that photographs inevitably carry their own independent evidentiary value.[41] Many of the details in the photograph will not have been the subjects of the witness' testimony, but the photograph constitutes evidence of everything that it shows, based on judicial notice of the general reliability of the photographic process.[42] Photographs and the purposes for which they are admitted are uniquely within the trial court's discretion, which will not be overturned unless there is an apparent abuse of

---

39. Kleveland v. United States, 345 F.2d 134, 137 (2d Cir. 1965) (witness qualifying a photograph need not be the photographer or see the picture taken).

40. *See generally*, Annotation, *Authentication or Verification of Photograph as Basis for Introduction in Evidence*, 9 A.L.R.2d 899 (1949); (§ 10 superceded by Diane M. Allen, Annotation, *Admissibility of Visual Recording of Event or Matter Giving Rise to Litigation or Prosecution*, 41 A.L.R.4th 812 (1986)); Annotation, *Admis-*

sibility of Posed Photograph Based on Recollection of Position of Persons or Movable Objects, 19 A.L.R.2d 877 (1951) (admissibility of photographs of reenactment of crime or accident scenes).

41. *See* People v. Bowley, 382 P.2d 591, 594–95 (Cal. 1963) (once identified, a photograph has a probative force of its own).

42. 1 Charles Calvin Scott, Photographic Evidence 351–52 (1969).

discretion.[43]

While the trend is to allow photographs into evidence for whatever they show, so long as there is sufficient foundation,[44] the sufficient foundation varies with the purpose. When something more, or instead of, a witness' affirmation that the picture "fairly and accurately represents" what the witness saw is needed, authentication is often demonstrated by showing a Rule 901(b)(9) process that produces accurate results.

"Silent Witness" Photographs

The idea of the "silent witness" first appeared in the discussion of whether a photograph was merely illustrative or had independent evidentiary value.[45] Today, however, when most jurisdictions consider all photographs to have some independent evidentiary value,[46] the term is used for those photographs for which there is no witness and no photographer. The picture with no witness and no photographer has become common with the proliferation of security cameras in apartment buildings, banks, and many other places. Despite the lack of a witness to or a photographer of the scene, pictures of intruders and robbers taken by these silent sentinels have been received in evidence, under the "silent witness" theory of authentication, when the proper foundation has been laid.[47] While there are a myriad of circumstances that might in a particular case authenticate a picture when there is no witness or photographer, a common approach is for the proponent to show the process by which the camera is activated, the scene is recorded, and the film is processed.

The courts' relatively recent comfort with the "silent witness" theory, upon which pictures are accepted as evidence of what they show, even though no live witness is available, may be short lived. The risk of alteration of a picture has been considered reasonable because, among other things, alterations were detectable. Detection is no longer possible if the alteration is done through the now widespread use of digital technology. Whether the new world of digital creation and re-creation will also provide a kind of electronic fail-safe remains to be seen. In considering the possibility of federal guidelines related to various criminal law issues raised by the burgeoning computer technology, The Computer Search and Seizure Working Group, made up of members of various federal agencies, hypothesized the following evidentiary horror story:

> Agents and prosecutors were shown a photograph of a body—twisted on the floor, a gaping wound in the chest. Across the room on the

---

43. McCrary–El v. Shaw, 992 F.2d 809, 811, 813 (8th Cir. 1993).

44. *See, e.g.,* United States v. Stearns, 550 F.2d 1167, 1171 (9th Cir. 1977).

45. *See* United States v. Bynum, 567 F.2d 1167 (1st Cir. 1978); Fisher v. State, 643 S.W.2d 571 (Ark. App. 1982) (citing all the cases).

46. 3 John H. Wigmore, Evidence in Trials at Common Law § 792 (James H. Chadbourn rev. 1970).

47. *See, e.g.,* United States v. Taylor, 530 F.2d 639 (5th Cir. 1976).

floor was a large pistol. On the white wall above the victim's body, scrawled in the victim's own blood, were the words, "I'll kill again. You'll never catch me."

... [T]his picture was not created with film, but with a digital camera ... law enforcement agents, using commercially available software, started rearranging the digits. They "cleaned" the wall ...closed the chest wound, choosing instead to have blood trickling from the victim's temple ...moved the gun into the victim's hand. The case was now solved: the report would claim, and the photograph would "prove," the victim committed suicide.[48]

Various Medical Imaging Machines

The authentication of x-rays, MRIs and CAT scans is similar to that developed in the "silent witness" approach to the authentication of photographs and videotapes, in that authentication depends upon proof that the process produces an accurate result. This Rule 901(b)(9) method of authentication is in many respects similar to the showing that is a pre-condition to admission of expert scientific opinion testimony.

X-rays have been around for sufficient time to realize the Advisory Committee's assumption that courts may well take judicial notice of the accuracy of the x-ray process.[49] The MRI and CAT scan may well be sufficiently familiar to have courts take judicial notice of the accuracy of their processes. In a court taking judicial notice of the validity of the scientific process by which the device produces a picture of internal portions of the human body not visible to any witness, the foundation focuses on the normal operation of the process and of the proper matching of picture to person.

Some courts admit x-rays and other medical imaging pictures as the hospital business records, accepting the x-ray custodian's testimony that the proper x-ray record was located and brought to court. Many hospitals avoid even this authentication by using a lead identification number with each x-ray assembly, making each x-ray picture a separately identifiable item. The normal foundation, absent stipulation or statutory shortcut involves the testimony of a qualified x-ray technician who can testify:

1.   that particular parts of a particular person's body were x-rayed at a particular time,

2.   that well maintained and working x-ray equipment was used, and

3.   that the operator used the proper procedures in identifying and taking the x-ray.

---

48.   56 Cr. L. 2023, 2053 (December 21,1994).

49.   The advisory committee's note to Rule 901(b)(9) lists the x-ray as a "familiar instance" and states specifically that example 9 "does not foreclose taking judicial notice of the accuracy of the process or system." In addition, some states have passed statutes and rules providing for the easy admission of properly identified x-rays, for example, N.Y. C.P.L.R. 4532–a.

In addition, the witness should testify to the process for handling and storing the x-ray in the hospital.

Motion Pictures and Videotape

There is nothing about authentication of film or videotape that is analytically any different from still photographs. Because the technology was not as familiar, courts treated film and videotape differently for many years, requiring more elaborate foundations that described in detail the qualifications of the camera operator and the detail of the film process.[50] Most modern courts accept motion pictures and videotape on a lesser showing.[51]

The authentication problems that arise from the introduction of film or videotape are related more to the subject matter than to the technical process. When a tape or film purports to show conditions as they existed at the time of an accident or crime, then of course an objection can be interposed on grounds that conditions may have changed between the event and the recording.[52] When the tape or film reenacts a crime or accident, questions about whether the reenactment is slanted, misleading, or prejudicial are often raised.[53] Hearsay objections may also be interposed, on grounds that the reenactment is an assertion by an out-of-court declarant about how something happened, offered to show the truth of the assertion.[54] A voice narration accompanying the reenactment may also be the legitimate target of a hearsay objection, and the objecting party may succeed at least in having the tape or film played without its narrative. The tape or film of an experiment, if the condi-

50. *See, e.g.,* State v. Hewett, 545 P.2d 1201, 1204–05 & n. 4 (Wash. 1976). To lay the technical foundation for videotape, the proponent must demonstrate

> (1) that the video and audio portions of the video tape are functioning properly; (2) the operator is trained and experienced in the use of video taping equipment; (3) the audio and visual portions of the recording are authentic and accurate; (4) no changes, additions, or deletions have been made; (5) the video tape has been properly preserved; (6) the video portion is clearly visible and the audio portion sufficiently understandable; and (7) the speakers must be identified.

51. *See, e.g.,* Hendricks v. Swenson, 456 F.2d 503, 506 (8th Cir. 1972) (authentication standard applicable to photographs also applicable to motion pictures, film or videotape).

52. *See, e.g.,* James v. Carnation Co., 562 P.2d 1192, 1203 (Or. 1977) (trial court did not erroneously exclude motion picture of highway during heavy traffic when accident occurred during period of relatively light traffic); Rollie Johnson Plumbing & Heating Serv., Inc. v. Dept. of Transp., 235 N.W.2d 528, 533 (Wis. 1975) (trial court's

exclusion of photographs and movie of condemned property and surrounding parcels offered to prove relatively low value of property not erroneous where pictures taken nearly two years after defendant's acquisition of property and considerable development had occurred on other parcels).

53. *See, e.g.,* Randall v. Warnaco, Inc., Hirsch–Weis Div., 677 F.2d 1226, 1234 (8th Cir. 1982) (video reenactment using actors to demonstrate defendant's theory of accidental spill of fuel viewed as potentially prejudicial); Pittman v. Mississippi Power & Light Co., 368 So.2d 238, 240 (Miss. 1979) (reenactment of accident involving tractor and utility pole misleading because materially different from conditions of actual accident); Gregory P. Joseph, *Videotape Evidence in the Courts,* 1985 A.B.A. Sec. Subcomm. Evid. (courts carefully scrutinize reenactments, because they afford opportunity for confusion, misconception, and manipulation).

54. *See* Grimes v. Employers Mut. Liab. Ins. Co., 73 F.R.D. 607, 611 (D. Alaska 1977) (film showing plaintiff performing tasks to exhibit disability comparable to witness testifying about assertive conduct).

tions of the experiment are not similar to those pertaining at the time of the event, can cause a film or tape to be excluded on the basis that the experiment is unfair or misleading.[55]

One of the common uses of videotape is the video diary of the "day in the life" of a personal injury plaintiff. It is used to show the pain and difficulties the plaintiff suffers as a result of the injury by focusing on the difficulty of things as mundane as moving around the home, performing daily tasks, and interacting with other members of the household. Authentication should not be particularly difficult in theory. The plaintiff, the plaintiff's family, or the filmmaker are all potential witnesses to testify that the film "fairly and accurately represents" an average day in the plaintiff's life. Some courts, however, have taken a very restrictive approach to admission of "day in the life" films.

In *Bolstridge v. Central Maine Power Co.*,[56] the defendant made various claims that the film was unrealistic or slanted. According to defendant, the film was unfair in depicting experiences that plaintiff would only perform very rarely, such as ordering a wheelchair, and in emphasizing difficulties instead of giving a true slice of a day's activities.[57] Without making a specific finding that the film was slanted in this fashion, the court excluded the film. It said the plaintiff could depict the same difficulties in the courtroom, and that physicians and relatives could testify about her handicap. It expressed concern about the dangers of slanted presentation and the impossibility of cross-examining a videotape. A "day in the life" film, in the court's view, should be admissible only when the plaintiff could give a specific reason why in-court testimony would not be sufficient to convey the information, and that such a showing had not been made in the case before it.[58]

Bannister v. Town of Noble,[59] is representative of those courts that have admitted "day in the life" films.[60] In an opinion that recognized the benefits as well as the dangers of such evidence, the court noted that the tape could illustrate, better than words, the impact of the injury.[61] The trial judge had viewed the film before it was shown to the jury and was persuaded the film fairly represented the impact of the injury on the plaintiff's day-to-day activities. It was not full of exaggerated difficulties or heart-wrenching staged episodes. Moreover, the participants in the

---

55. *See, e.g.,* Hale v. Firestone Tire & Rubber Co., 756 F.2d 1322 (8th Cir. 1985) (abuse of discretion to admit film of experiment not similar to event).

56. 621 F. Supp. 1202 (D. Me. 1985).

57. *Id.* at 1203 & n 1.

58. *Id.* at 1204.

59. 812 F.2d 1265 (10th Cir. 1987).

60. *See, e.g.,* Grimes v. Employers Mut. Liab. Ins. Co., 73 F.R.D. 607, 610 (D. Alaska 1977) ("day in the life" film illustrates injury better than words); Burke v. 12 Rothschild's Liquor Mart, Inc. 568 N.E.2d 80,84 (Ill. App. 1991) (not error to admit day-in-the-life film, despite opposing counsel's lack of advance notice and opportunity to be present at filming, as long as probative value of film outweighs potential prejudice and there are no demonstrated improprieties in content or production); Wagner v. York Hosp., 608 A.2d 496, 499–501 (Pa. Super. 1992) (day-in-the-life film properly admitted over objection that it inaccurately depicted reflexive sounds and movements as voluntary and conscious; not misleading because victim's consciousness of surroundings was disputed).

61. *Bannister*, 812 F.2d 1265, 1269.

film were present and available for cross-examination about the accuracy of the film.

In jurisdictions that recognize the "day in the life" film, the objecting party cannot merely rest upon an assertion that in-court testimony would be adequate to depict injuries. Counsel should be prepared to show, with as much specificity as possible, what is wrong with the film. Perhaps the film does not show a typical slice of a day, exaggerates difficulties, or depicts rarely encountered obstacles. Perhaps the film makes an undue appeal to sympathy, for example by showing tearful scenes or the emotional reaction of the family to the plaintiff's injuries. Perhaps it has been edited in a misleading way, for example by including "reaction shots" that were not filmed at the same time as the rest of the film. Defects of this nature can support a Rule 403 objection that the film is prejudicial, misleading, or a waste of time.[62] As a matter of tactics, defense counsel may ask to be present at plaintiff's filming of a "day in the life" film. If the court grants a formal request, counsel will be in a position to know if something was left out of the final edited film, redone, or was in some other way at variance with the experience of the day. Even if the court does not grant a formal request to observe,[63] counsel may be able to argue the unfairness of the process to the jury. Correspondingly, if plaintiff has a strong case on damages, plaintiff may want to invite defense counsel to be present at the filming, either to promote settlement or to demonstrate fairness to the tribunal. Any "day in the life" film that has a voiceover narration or other verbal component is also potentially subject to a hearsay objection, on grounds that the film contains statements by an out-of-court declarant offered to prove the truth of what they assert. Moreover, if the film depicts assertive conduct that is the equivalent of a statement by the plaintiff about the nature of a disability, then a hearsay objection can also be interposed.[64]

Photographs Used to Prove "Actual" Conditions

What if a witness' ability to see under the existing lighting at the scene is at issue? Can a lawyer prove what the witness could (or could not) see by showing the witness a picture taken at the same place and

---

62. *See generally,* Joseph M. Herlihy, Note, *Beyond Words: The Evidentiary Status of "Day in the Life" Films,* 66 B.U. L. Rev. 133, 136–41 (1986) (common objections to "day in the life" films based on unfair prejudice and cumulative evidence). *See also* Hahn v. Tri–Line Farmers Co-op, 478 N.W.2d 515, 524–25 (Minn. App. 1991) (under Minn. R. Evid. 403, not error to admit film segments in which paraplegic withdraws small amount of money from bank and bends over to pick up newspaper from floor, over objection that segment prejudicially suggested financial hardship and was cumulative and inflammatory; even though injured party, his family, doc-tors, and vocational experts testified about his rehabilitation).

63. Cisarik v. Palos Community Hosp., 579 N.E.2d 873, 874–75 (Ill. 1991) (reversing protective order that would have allowed opposing counsel to be present during day-in-the-life film, to have edited-out footage, and to have copy of completed film).

64. *See* Grimes v. Employer's Mut. Liab. Ins. Co., 73 F.R.D. 607, 610–11 (D. Alaska 1977) (noting hearsay dangers, but receiving film under residual exception to hearsay rule).

hour and asking whether it "fairly and accurately" represents the light level at the time of the incident and the objects the witness could see? Such an offer should provoke a Rule 403 objection that the photograph is misleading as to the purpose for which it is offered. While the judge might admit such a photograph without hesitation, if it were offered to show merely what was at the scene, the greater purpose should require a more precise authentication. Just as the 901((b)(1) showing that something is "what it is claimed to be" requires a scale diagram to be authenticated as an "exact" rather than a "fair and accurate" representation, so too with a photograph or videotape that purports to be exact in some respect.[65] The misleading issue is based upon the potential for distortion. The more the authentication can demonstrate that conditions are similar, the more likely the picture will be admissible. A picture taken simultaneously with the time the witness is observing is superior to one taken on a different day at a time calculated to show the same light level. Similarly, the camera settings, lenses, filters, etc. used when the picture was made will be important. Whether the problem is that the picture shows a re-creation of events or circumstances, or is that the picture shows the actual events under technical circumstances that might be distorting, the lawyer's task is to lay a foundation that demonstrates a lack of disparity. The judge's decision under Rule 403 will be based upon how serious the judge views the disparity between the authentication and the reality of the event.

Authentication as something more than "fair and accurate," be it termed "exact" or "actual," does not guarantee that a picture will be admitted. No matter how strong the authentication or how close to reality the picture may be, Rule 403 may provide a further basis for objection. Courts have been quite liberal in admitting revolting or repulsive pictures even when their probative value on disputed issues is meager,[66] but the Rule remains a vehicle by which the judge may exclude such evidence, irrespective of its authenticity.[67]

65. *See, e.g.,* Powell v. Indus. Comm'n., 418 P.2d 602, 610 (Ariz. App. 1966) (excluding motion picture of personal injury plaintiff working at another job after injury; speed at which plaintiff worked was faster in film than actual speed); Utley v. Heckinger, 362 S.W.2d 13, 17 (Ark. 1962) (trial court admitted defendant's film showing personal injury plaintiff walking on crutches faster than actual speed; held, exclusion of misleading motion picture preferred to limiting instruction).

66. *See, e.g.,* Olympia Spa v. Johnson, 547 So.2d 80, 83 (Ala. 1989) (photographs of woman burned to death in steam room, held admissible; depicted location and severity of death-causing injuries); Light v. State, 547 N.E.2d 1073, 1080–81 (Ind. 1989) (not an error to admit three photos of badly decomposed, charred body for purposes of

"revealing the reality of the offense"). *See generally,* Andre A. Moenssens, et al., Scientific Evidence in Criminal Cases § 2.14 (4th ed. 1995).

67. *See, e.g.,* McNeal v. State, 551 So.2d 151, 159 (Miss. 1989) (error to receive repulsive photographs of murder victim; "we believe that the state could have shown the angle and entry of the bullet wound without the full-color, close-up view of the decomposed, maggot-infested skull"); People v. Burns, 241 P.2d 308, 318–19 (Cal. App.1952) (trial court erred in receiving post-autopsy photographs, showing surgical cuts, shaved head, and other gruesome effects of autopsy; photos would not help jury decide whether relatively faint bruises existing before autopsy were caused by defendant or by fall).

§ 11.09 Demonstrative Exhibits That are Substantive— Sound Recordings and Other Conversations

Authentication of sound recordings, like that of "silent witness" photographs and videotapes, is in significant part about proof of process in the fashion of 901(b)(9), as discussed above in § 11.08. Authentication of sound recordings, like that of documents, is often as much about the "best evidence" rule as discussed in § 11.11, as it is about identification.

Authentication of sound recordings and other conversations, be they telephonic or in person, always begins with identifying the participants by identifying the voices in the fashion of 901(b)(5) & (6). Motivated perhaps by the imperative of criminal law, courts have been less than rigorous in the familiarity required for a witness to identify a voice as belonging to a particular individual. A witness' testimony that a voice heard on the phone is the same as one heard a month later in person has been deemed sufficient for identification, even when there were no other instances of hearing or identifying the voice.[68] Although experts differ on the validity of voiceprints, some courts have ruled that sound spectrography may be used to identify unidentified voices in conversations.[69]

Someone who has not previously heard a person's voice may, nevertheless, authenticate a telephone conversation with a person. Rule 901(b)(6) provides for authentication of a telephone call by evidence that "a call was made to the number assigned . . . to a particular person" and "circumstances, including self-identification, show the person answering to be the one called." In the case of a business, a call placed to a number assigned to the business can be authenticated, if "the conversation related to business reasonably transacted over the telephone." Although there is no similar authentication illustration for incoming calls, because of the ease of fabrication on the part of the caller,[70] the advent of the technology by which the receiving telephone instrument records the number from which a call is placed may provide a different result.

Reference to other events or conversations that identify the speaker are common circumstantial methods of identifying a voice sufficiently to authenticate a conversation.

Sound recordings are commonly used in the prosecution of organized crime cases in which wiretaps and bugs are *de rigueur*. A tape recording may occasionally be authenticated by someone hearing the conversation and testifying that the recording is an accurate rendition,[71] but often the recording is the result of surreptitious recording to which there is no

---

68. United States v. Axselle, 604 F.2d 1330, 1338 (10th Cir. 1979).

69. *See*, Edward J. Imwinkelried, Evidentiary Foundations 56 (3d ed. 1995) and cases cited therein.

70. *See, e.g.*, United States v. Pool, 660 F.2d 547, 560 (5th Cir. 1981) (call from one who self-identifies cannot be authenticated by the self-identification, without more).

71. *See, e.g.*, United States v. Carrasco, 887 F.2d 794, 803 (7th Cir. 1989) (tape recordings of conversations authenticated where eyewitness to conversations testified that tape recordings accurately depicted conversations); United States v. Lance, 853 F.2d 1177, 1181–82 (5th Cir. 1988) (tape recording of conversation authenticated where witnesses testified that tape was accurate recording of conversation).

willing witness. When the "silent witness" approach is required, someone must provide the 901(b)(9) testimony about the process that produces an accurate result, in the same fashion as is required for videotape from a surveillance camera.[72]

§ 11.10 Demonstrative Exhibits That Are Substantive— Documents

Documents are the most common of trial exhibits. There are three hurdles to admission of a document: hearsay, best evidence, and authentication.

The authentication of a document depends upon the purpose for which it is offered. A document's appearance, contents, substance, internal patterns, or other distinctive characteristics, taken in conjunction with circumstances can provide sufficient indicia of reliability to permit a finding that it is authentic.[73] Direct testimony, however, of a person with first hand knowledge that the document is what it purports to be (901(b)(1)) or of someone who can identify handwriting (901(b)(2) & (3)) is the common method for authenticating documents.

901(b)(1) Example

[Witness has been identified and the document has been marked and shown to opposing counsel.]

Direct examiner: I hand you what has been marked as Plaintiff's exhibit number two. Do you recognize it?

Witness: Yes.

Direct examiner: What is it?

Witness: A letter.

Direct examiner: Have you seen plaintiff's exhibit number two before?

Witness: Yes.

Direct examiner: Please describe the circumstances?

Witness: I was at Mr. Writer's office about a week ago when he was sending out a series of letters to potential investors. He handed me the pile so

---

72. *See, e.g.,* United States v. McMillan, 508 F.2d 101, 104 (8th Cir. 1974), *cert. denied,* 421 U.S. 916 (1975); Solomon, Jr., Inc. v. Edgar, 88 S.E.2d 167, 171 (Ga. App. 1955). For a full and helpful example of the "strict, traditional foundation," see Imwinkelried, *supra* note 69, at 58–62. *See also* State v. Smith, 540 P.2d 424, 429 (Wash. 1975) (tape recording of shooting found on victim's body admissible where shown that device capable of recording, microphone and recorder in operating condition, accuracy of tape corroborated, preservation of tape documented, chain of custody proven, speakers identified, and statements not made under duress).

73. United States v. Paulino, 13 F.3d 20, 23 (1st Cir. 1994).

that I could see who it was that he hoped would invest in the enterprise.

Direct examiner: Do you recognize plaintiff's exhibit number two?

Witness: Yes.

Direct examiner: How do you recognize it?

Witness: Well, I went through the letters to check the list and the amounts that the various potential investors were asked for. I remember this letter by the name of the person to whom it was sent and the suggested investment amount.

Direct examiner: Your honor, I offer plaintiff's exhibit number two for identification into evidence as plaintiff's exhibit number two.

901 (b)(20) Example

[Witness has been identified and the document has been marked and shown to opposing counsel.]

Direct examiner: I hand you what has been marked as Plaintiff's exhibit number two. Do you recognize it?

Witness: Yes.

Direct examiner: What is it?

Witness: A letter I received on November 5th of this year.

Direct examiner: Is it signed?

Witness: Yes.

Direct examiner: Do you recognize the signature?

Witness: Yes, I do.

Direct examiner: How do you recognize it?

Witness: It is a signature that I have seen many times on letters and occasionally on a check.

Direct examiner: Who signed plaintiff's exhibit number two for identification?

Witness: Walter Writer.

Direct examiner: Your honor, I offer the letter from Walter Writer to Willie Witness into evidence as plaintiff's exhibit number two.

Rule 901(b)(3) contemplates authentication of a writing by either expert or juror handwriting comparison of the document in question to a known, authenticated exemplar. Courts have allowed this kind of expert authentication, despite the growing concern that forensic document examination may not be scientifically valid.[74]

Indeed, if the trial judge believes that the handwriting on a document in question is sufficiently similar to the handwriting on a known exemplar so that a reasonable jury could find them to be written by the same person, the judge may admit the document and leave it to the jurors to decide its authenticity.[75]

Documents can be authenticated by circumstantial evidence. The content of a reply letter is an example of the kind of circumstantial evidence that can, on its own, authenticate a letter. The Advisory Committee note to 901(b)(4) incorporates the common law reply letter doctrine. If one party sends a letter to another, and then receives a letter purporting to be from that person with contents suggesting it is in reply to the first letter, that is sufficient to authenticate the second letter.[76]

Rules 901 and 902 (self-authentication) provide relatively simple and straightforward methods for authenticating ancient documents, business documents, and public documents.

§ 11.11   The Special Problems of Computer Generated Exhibits

The computer, which has had a major influence on society, has also had an enormous influence on the courtroom. Some of that influence has been on the generation of evidence. Computers generate demonstrative evidence that is illustrative of other testimony as well as demonstrative evidence that carries its own independent evidentiary value.

Business records are the most common example. The computer is on its way to becoming the universal record keeper in businesses. The use of a computer to generate business records does not change the necessary foundation under Rule 803(6), but it can require additional proof of the underlying operating theory and reliability of the computer. To the extent that computer output is a product of a process that relies upon certain assumptions that are not immediately apparent to those outside the field, it may be seen as a type of scientific evidence. Some courts require almost nothing in addition to the normal business record foundation other than an affirmation that the business has successfully used the computer. They take judicial notice of the operating theory and reliability of computer generated information in the same fashion as they

---

74. *See, e.g.,* United States v. Blackwood, 878 F.2d 1200, 1202 (9th Cir. 1989) (approving expert testimony authentication). *Cf.,* § **10.04** (discussion of the growing controversy over forensic document examination).

75. United States v. Wylie, 919 F.2d 969, 978 (5th Cir. 1990).

76. United States v. Weinstein, 762 F.2d 1522, 1533 (11th Cir. 1985).

take judicial notice of the validity of radar.[77] Some courts have required an affirmation or demonstration that the particular computer or software is reliable,[78] but the affirmation could be made without the witness having any particular knowledge of the workings of the hardware or software.[79]

There have been some calls by commentators for a more rigorous foundation for computer generated business records,[80] but few courts have responded. When computer generated business records have not been received in evidence, the failure has almost always been related to the failure of the normal business record foundation as it relates to computers.[81]

A person who can identify the computer system used, testify to the method by which information is gathered and put into the computer, and can relate the procedures by which the particular record offered in court is produced will almost always be a "qualified person" as required by Rule 803(6).[82]

Computer simulations and animations may create both easier and more difficult authentication issues than those presented by computer generated business records. As a matter of consistent theory regarding demonstrative evidence offered for illustrative purposes, computer animation is no different from any other diagram or picture offered for the same purpose—it must be a "fair and accurate" representation of what someone saw or of the oral testimony that it illustrates.[83] But the fact is that a computer animation or simulation is not just another diagram. The impact on a jury of a filmed re-creation generated by data in a computer is tremendous and there is a suspicion in the courts that no instruction minimizing the evidentiary status of the computer simulation can be effective. As a result, many courts require a more complex foundation for computer animations and simulations.[84]

77. *See, e.g.,* United States v. Moore, 923 F.2d 910, 915 (1st Cir. 1991) (nothing special needed for computer generated business record, citing cases).

78. *See, e.g.,* Burleson v. State, 802 S.W.2d 429, 441 (Tex. App. 1991).

79. *See, e.g.,* United States v. Linn, 880 F.2d 209, 216 (9th Cir. 1989)

80. *See, e.g.,* Rudolph J. Peritz, *Computer Data Reliability: A Call for Authentication of Business Records Under the Federal Rules of Evidence,* 80 Nw. U.L. Rev. 956 (1986).

81. *See, e.g.,* People v. Bovio, 455 N.E.2d 829, 833 (Ill. App. 1983) (no testimony about computer equipment); People v. Boyd, 384 N.E.2d 414, 420 (Ill. App. 1978) ("(I)t must be shown that the electronic computing equipment is recognized as standard, that the entries are made in the regular course of business at or reasonably near the time of the happening of the event recorded, and that the testimony sat-

isfies the court that the sources of information, method and time of preparation were such as to indicate its trustworthiness and justify its admission."); O'Shea v. IBM, 578 S.W.2d 844, 848 (Tex. Civ. App. 1979) (no testimony that computer standard or concerning the method of input).

82. *See, e.g.,* United States v. Miller, 771 F.2d 1219, 1237 (9th Cir. 1985) (billing supervisor); Rosenberg v. Collins, 624 F.2d 659, 665 (5th Cir. 1980) (comptroller).

83. *See, e.g.,* Pierce v. State, 671 So. 2d 186, 190 (Fla. App. 1996) (computer animation must be a fair and accurate depiction of that which it purports to be, the same foundation that must be established to admit any pictorial representation); People v. McHugh, 476 N.Y.S.2d 721, 722, 723 (1984) ("fairly and accurately" reflect the oral testimony).

84. *See, e.g.,* Bray v. Bi–State Development Corp. 949 S.W.2d 93(E.D. Mo. 1997) (collecting and discussing the cases from

Computer simulations are most common in airline disaster cases[85] and in automobile accident re-constructions.[86] They usually reflect or are the basis for expert testimony. To lay the foundation for the simulation, the expert must lay the same foundation as would be necessary for the expert's testimony,[87] plus an explanation of how the computer either contributed to or reflects the opinion. Although there is little case law in a rapidly developing area, the foundation described in *Commercial Union v. Boston Edison*,[88] decided in a *Frye* jurisdiction, has been quoted with approval in many jurisdictions. The *Commonwealth Union* court required a showing that (1) the computer was functioning properly, (2) the input and underlying equations were sufficiently complete and accurate (and disclosed to the opposing party so they might be challenged), and (3) the software used is generally accepted in the appropriate community of scientists.[89]

Unlike the expert testimony that a computer simulation may illustrate, the computer cannot be cross-examined. Some of the expert's assumptions are built into the computer software. This requires the cross-examiner to cross-examine the expert on how the computer is programmed to "decide" what happened as well as to conduct the normal cross-examination concerning the bases and scientific assumptions that may be involved in the expert's testimony.

The use of computer animations, simulations, and conclusions will continue to grow. The more the computer generates the information or conclusion, the more rigorous the courts will be in requiring a complete scientific evidence foundation.

§ 11.12   The "Best Evidence" of the Contents of Writings, Recordings and Photographs [FRE 1001–1006]

Every time a lawyer wants to prove the contents of a document, photograph, or recording, the lawyer must take account of the "best evidence" rule–more commonly referred to under the Federal Rules as the "original documents" rule–though it applies to recordings and photographs as well as to writings. As a general matter, the rule requires use of the original or a mechanically reproduced duplicate to prove the contents of a photograph, recording or writing, unless the proponent can show that the original is unavailable.[90] Proof of compliance with the original documents rule usually comes from the same source as, and is

---

various jurisdictions); *see also* Note, Carole E. Powell, *Computer Generated Visual Evidence: Does Daubert Make a Difference?* 12 Ga. St. U.L. Rev. 577 (1996).

85.   *See* Paul Marcotte, *Animated Evidence: Delta 191 Crash Re-Created Through Computer Simulations at Trial*, A.B.A. J., Dec. 1989 at p. 52 for a description of competing uses of computer simulations accepted by court as substantive evidence in In re Air Crash at Dallas/Fort

Worth Airport on August 2, 1985; Kathleen Connors, et al. v. United States, 720 F. Supp. 1258 (N.D. Tex. 1989).

86.   *See, e.g.,* Kudlacek v. Fiat S.p.A., 509 N.W.2d 603 (Neb. 1994).

87.   *See* **Ch. 10.**

88.   591 N.E.2d 165 (Mass. 1992).

89.   *Id.*

90.   Fed. R. Evid. 1002.

usually presented as an integral part of, the foundation testimony for the exhibit. The common law "best evidence" rule applied only to documents,[91] but the Federal Evidence Rule applies to writings, recordings, and photographs.[92]

Example

Direct examiner:	Did your wife communicate with you after that?
Witness:	Yes.
Direct examiner:	In what way?
Witness:	I got a letter from her in the mail.
Direct examiner:	When did you receive the letter?
Witness:	On July 13, 1998.
Direct examiner:	What did the letter say?
Opponent:	Objection!

There are three bases upon which to object to "What did the letter say?"

1. Hearsay. A document is an out-of-court statement, and if offered to prove the truth of the matter asserted, is hearsay, unless it falls within one of the Rule 801(d) categories. If the lawsuit is between the husband and wife, the letter is an admission of a party opponent.[93]

2. Authentication. The witness has not laid the foundation for authentication or identification of the letter. Even though the letter itself is not being offered, no evidence of its contents can be admitted until the letter is authenticated. The husband can satisfy the authentication objection by testifying that he recognized his wife's handwriting.[94]

3. Best evidence. If the hearsay and authentication objections are satisfied, the question "What did the letter say?" is still objectionable. The question asks about the contents of the letter, which is not admissible unless the proponent of the testimony can (a) produce the original of the letter, (b) produce a mechanically created "duplicate," or (c) demonstrate that the letter was lost, destroyed, otherwise unavailable, or concerned with a collateral matter.[95]

---

91. *Cf.,* Burdine v. State, 719 S.W.2d 309, 318 (Tex. Crim. App. 1986) (stating that prior to September 1, 1986, best evidence rule was common law rule and did not apply to electronic recordings); In re Reed, 672 P.2d 829, 834 (Wyo. 1983) (quoting 5 David W. Louisell & Christopher B. Mueller, Federal Evidence § 549 (1981) as stating that best evidence rule "expand[s] to some extent the common law tradition, which had sometimes insisted that the doctrine applied only to writings").

92. Fed. R. Evid. 1002.

93. Fed. R. Evid. 801(d)(2)(A).

94. Fed. R. Evid. 901(a)(2).

95. *See* Fed. R. Evid. 1002 (general rule that evidence of contents not admissible unless original produced); Fed. R. Evid.

The drafters of the Federal Rules avoided applying the term "best evidence" to Article X (Contents of Writings, Recordings, and Photographs) because "best evidence" is a misnomer at best, and a vestige of a different and inapplicable principle at worst. The heart of the Federal Rule is that "to prove the content of a writing recording, or photograph, the original writing, recording, or photograph is required."[96]

At least some common law courts were confused about whether there was a general rule that an advocate must use the best evidence in presenting a case. Most courts held there was no such rule,[97] although every once in a while a case such as *State v. Price*,[98] would occur in which the court would get it wrong. The *Price* court allowed the use of the branded hide of a dead calf instead of the deteriorating carcass to prove the loss of the heifer only because the hide was the best available evidence. The court stated that the best evidence rule, as it understood it, "requires that the highest degree of proof of which a case is susceptible must be produced, if such proof is accessible."[99]

The *Price* court was almost assuredly wrong under the common law, but whatever the circumstance, the Federal Rules contain no "best evidence" requirement. A lawyer might try to offer the most persuasive evidence possible as a matter of strategy, but not because evidence law has any general hierarchy of evidence. Live testimony, for example, need not be presented in lieu of hearsay that is admissible because it fits one of the many exceptions to the rule excluding hearsay. Similarly oral testimony about an object central to the event in question is admissible even if the item is not offered, in spite of it being available, and capable of authentication.[100] So, if Carrie Nation–the famous late 19th century temperance agitator who prayed in saloons before busting them up–is charged with breaking a saloonkeeper's mirror, there is no "best evidence" rule that requires production of the mirror shards in court or an explanation of why they are not produced. The saloonkeeper's oral testimony about breaking the mirror is fully admissible and legally sufficient to prove the mirror was broken.[101]

There was, for a brief time, concern about what a lawyer was to do when attempting to prove the "content" of an inscribed item. Commentators were concerned about whether a tombstone, a branded cow, an automobile with a VIN number, and the like constituted very big writings to which the original documents rule might apply. The commentators favored a balancing approach toward inscribed chattels, taking into account the need for the evidence and the ease or difficulty of

---

1004 (excuses for not producing the original).

96.   Fed. R. Evid. 1002.

97.   2 McCormick on Evidence § 229 4th ed. John W. Strong ed. 1994).

98.   265 P.2d 444 (Ariz. 1954).

99.   *Id.* at 446.

100.   *See* Weinstein's Federal Evidence § 1001.03[2] (2d ed. Joseph M. McLaughlin ed. 1997); *cf.,* United States v. Yamin, 868 F.2d 130, 134 (5th Cir. 1989) (best evidence rule does not apply to chattels).

101.   *Cf.,* People v. Ojeda, 758 F.2d 403, 407 (9th Cir. 1985) (in burglary case, it is not necessary to produce stolen jewelry or excuse for non-production).

production.[102] The problem with the approach, of course, is that there is no express basis in the rules for balancing the difficulty of obtaining the original against the need for it.[103] Courts that have been forced to deal with this weighty problem have taken slightly different approaches. The Alabama court, in *Drummond v. State*,[104] avoided the potential danger of cow dung in the courtroom (at least on the floor) by fiat: "We conclude it was competent for the witness to testify as to the markings he saw on the cow without producing her in court." The federal courts have engaged in a more sophisticated analysis, interpreting Rule 1002 not to apply to chattels.[105] The result has been the same. There is little need for wranglers in federal courtrooms.

The only hierarchy of evidence in the Federal Rules applies to writings, recordings, and photographs, and only if their contents are to be proved. In a prosecution for exhibition of an obscene movie, therefore, where the contents of the film must be proved to make the case, the prosecutor must produce the original film or an acceptable excuse for not having it.[106] Similarly, a plaintiff seeking to enforce a written contract with a defendant must produce the contract or an acceptable excuse for not having it.

It is important to remember that the rule does not require producing the writing, recording, or photograph, merely because it exists. If a witness is giving testimony about the underlying event based on knowledge from a source other than the writing, recording, or photograph, there is no requirement that the writing, recording, or photograph be produced. Consider the following examples.

If the court reporter who transcribed an earlier hearing at which Walter testified is asked, "What did Walter say at the hearing you transcribed?" the witness may answer. The testimony is about what the witness heard, not what is in the transcript.[107] If the witness is asked, "What does your transcript say Walter said at the hearing you transcribed?" the witness may not answer. That testimony would be about

---

102. *See* 2 McCormick, *supra* note 97, § 232; 4 John H. Wigmore, Evidence in Trials at Common Law § 1182 (James H. Chadbourn rev. 1972).

103. Rule 1004 lists various excuses for not producing the original of a writing, but the physical difficulty of producing an inscribed chattel is not one of the listed excuses.

104. 67 So.2d 280, 282 (Ala. App. 1953).

105. *See* United States v. Yamin, 868 F.2d 130, 134 (5th Cir. 1989) (in case involving counterfeiting of watches, court notes that, at least in part, the writing (trademark) on the watch makes it counterfeit; however court states that "an object bearing a mark is both a chattel and a writing, and the trial judge has discretion to treat it as a chattel, to which the best evidence rule does not apply") (*citing* United States v. Duffy, 454 F.2d 809, 812 (5th Cir. 1972)).

106. *See* People v. Enskat, 98 Cal. Rptr. 646 (Cal. App. Dept. Super. Ct. 1971).

107. *See* Meyers v. United States, 171 F.2d 800, 812 (D.C. Cir. 1948), *cert. denied*, 336 U.S. 912 (1949); *cf.,* United States v. Fagan, 821 F.2d 1002, 1008–09 n. 1 (5th Cir. 1987), *cert. denied*, 484 U.S. 1005 (1988) (testimony about conversation admissible even though conversation had been tape recorded and tape not offered); Herzig v. Swift & Co., 146 F.2d 444, 446 (2d Cir. 1945) (oral testimony by witness with knowledge about earnings of partnership admissible, even if facts about partnership earnings are also recorded in books of account).

the contents of the transcript and is inadmissible, unless the original is produced.

If a witness to an accident that was videotaped is asked, "Which car entered the intersection first?" the witness may answer. The testimony is about what the witness saw, not what is on the videotape. If the witness is asked, "Which car does the videotape show entering the intersection first?" the witness may not answer. The testimony would be about the contents of the videotape and is inadmissible, unless the original is produced.[108]

In a child custody proceeding, one spouse seeks to show that the other is unfit by producing evidence that the other spouse engaged in group sex, which was captured in a photograph. If the witness is one of the participants and is asked, "Did the spouse engage in group sex?" the witness may answer. But if the witness is someone who was not present, but to whom the photograph was shown, the witness may not answer the question, "Did the spouse engage in group sex?" The witness has no first hand knowledge, so must be reciting the contents of the photograph the witness saw. The proponent must produce the photograph or an excuse for not having it.[109]

The principal concern of the best evidence rule is the danger of mistakes in the oral reporting (or human copying) of the contents of documents, photographs, and recordings. Mechanically produced copies are considered accurate and are admissible, therefore, in lieu of originals, without any need to explain the absence of the original. The duplication can take the form of a copy machine or photographic copy of a document,[110] a re-recording of a tape recording,[111] or equivalent techniques that accurately reproduce the original.[112] These "duplicates" are admissible "to the same extent as an original" under Rule 1003, "unless (1) a genuine question is raised as to the authenticity of the original or (2) in the circumstances it would be unfair to admit the duplicate in lieu of the original." The mere assertion, without supporting evidence, that a duplicate is an inaccurate reproduction is not enough to raise a genuine question.[113]

Non-Production Allowed

The prohibition against proving the contents of a writing, recording, or photograph without the original does not apply when the "the writing, recording, or photograph is not closely related to a controlling issue."

108. *See* Weinstein's Federal Evidence, *supra* note 100, § 1001.04[1].

109. *See* Heinz v. Heinz, 165 P.2d 967, 971 (Cal. App. 1946) (court recognizes applicability of best evidence rule to testimony about contents of nude photos, but admits testimony because original photos beyond reach of subpoena power).

110. *See* United States v. Morgan, 555 F.2d 238 (9th Cir. 1977) (photostatic copy); United States v. Rodriguez, 524 F.2d 485 (5th Cir. 1975) (photocopy).

111. United States v. DiMatteo, 716 F.2d 1361 (11th Cir. 1983).

112. Fed. R. Evid. 1001(4).

113. Fed. R. Evid. 1001(4).

Example

Direct examiner:	Where were you going?
Witness:	I continued down Kirby Avenue.
Direct examiner:	You didn't stop?
Witness:	No. I was late for an appointment.
Direct examiner:	Did you later report that you had seen the accident?
Witness:	Yes.
Direct examiner:	When?
Witness:	The next day.
Direct examiner:	Why did you report it the next day?
Witness:	I read in the newspaper someone had been killed in the accident and I did not agree with the description of how it all took place.

If the testimony is offered solely for the purpose of explaining why the witness called the police the next day, the contents of the newspaper are collateral and the newspaper itself need not be produced.[114]

Even when the matter is not collateral, the best evidence rule should rarely prevent a diligent lawyer from introducing testimony about the contents of a writing. If neither an original nor a duplicate is available, the lawyer should be able to have a witness lay the foundation for oral testimony about the contents of a document by establishing the writing was

1. lost or stolen; or

2. destroyed (in good faith); or

3. in someone else's hands, and not obtainable by judicial process; or

4. in the possession of the opponent, and the opponent had notice to produce it, by the pleadings or otherwise.[115]

If the lawyers properly prepare their cases, the only circumstance in which the best evidence rule should actually exclude evidence is when the client has destroyed it in bad faith.

---

114. *See, e.g.,* Farr v. Zoning Board of Appeals of Town of Manchester, 95 A.2d 792, 794 (Conn. 1953)(issue of land ownership relates only to standing to appeal, not to substance of the dispute, and is, therefore, collateral, allowing oral testimony.)

115. *See* Fed. R. Evid. 1004.

Any Secondary Evidence Will Do

There are no degrees of secondary evidence under Rules 1001–1006. If the proponent satisfies the judge that the original is missing or that there is some other valid excuse for not producing the original, the proponent can prove the contents of the original either by oral testimony or by producing a copy. There is no "second best evidence" rule requiring the proponent to produce the best that is available.[116] If, for example, the original of a hospital record is not available because it is not subject to subpoena, oral testimony about its contents is permitted, even though a machine copy might be obtained easily and offered.

Strict logic might call for extending the principle of preference beyond simply preferring the original, but the drafters believed that creating a hierarchy of preferences and a procedure for making it effective involved unwarranted complexities.[117] Most, if not all, that would be accomplished by an extended scheme of preferences will be achieved through the normal motivation of a party to present the most convincing evidence possible and the arguments and procedures available to the opponent in the absence of the more persuasive evidence.

Official records are the single exception to the rule that there is no hierarchy of secondary evidence. Rule 1005 states a clear preference for copies that are certified or that are presented through the testimony of a witness who has compared the copy with the original. Other evidence of the contents of an official record is admissible only if the certified or compared copy cannot be obtained by the exercise of due diligence.[118]

Summaries

Rule 1006 allows into evidence charts, summaries, or calculations to prove the content of voluminous writings, recordings, or photographs. This exception to the requirement of the original to prove the contents of a document, recording or photograph is intended to make it more convenient for the trier of fact to assimilate the information.[119] The Rule requires the originals to be so "voluminous" that they "cannot conveniently be examined in court" and requires that the originals be made available for other parties to examine at a "reasonable time and place."

Charts have been admitted under the Rule to summarize as few as 20 drug transactions when inspection of various underlying hotel receipts and phone bills would be inconvenient.[120] The need for a summary of voluminous material increases when the material involves hard-to-

---

116. Advisory committee's note to Rule 1004 ("The rule recognizes no 'degrees' of secondary evidence").

117. *Id.*

118. Compliance with Rule 1005 will satisfy both the authentication requirement—showing the copy to be what it purports to be—and the best evidence rule. In order for the record to be admissible under the public records exception to the rule

against hearsay, it must also satisfy the requirements of Rule 803(8). A public record that does not describe any of the matters set forth in rule 803(8) is not admissible merely because it satisfies Rule 1005.

119. Fed. R. Evid. 1006 advisory committee's note.

120. United States v. Possick, 849 F.2d 332, 339 (8th Cir. 1988).

understand technical data,[121] or when it clarifies a confusing sequence of events.[122]

The chart or summary that is admitted under Rule 1006 is evidence and not merely an illustration to aid the trier in understanding other admitted evidence.[123]

Admission of summaries under Rule 1006 is committed to the discretion of the courts.[124] Discretion should be guided by whether the summary will be helpful under the circumstances. In the circumstances of a given case the court may feel that the jury ought to consider the source documents in resolving a fact issue and that, on balance, a summarization of such evidence would detract from the proper weight or emphasis to be given it.[125]

The proponent of a Rule 1006 chart or summary must show that the materials on which it is based are admissible in evidence.[126] Any part of a Rule 1006 summary that is based on inadmissible evidence is itself inadmissible,[127] and the entire chart or summary is inadmissible, unless the admissible portion can be segregated and identified.[128]

The source documents must be available to the opposing party prior to introduction of the summary,[129] although the summary, itself, need not be.[130] This requirement is met when the trial judge determines that the underlying documents were made available at a reasonable time and place[131] even if opposing counsel fails to make use of the opportunity to review the documents.[132]

Although Rule 1006 is designed to provide an alternative to admitting voluminous records, admission of the underlying records does not prohibit the use of a Rule 1006 chart or summary. If despite their

121. *See* United States v. Campbell, 845 F.2d 1374, 1381 (6th Cir. 1988) (summary chart admitted in evidence when " ...without the chart, the jury would have been forced to review hundreds of pages of technical information which may not have been readily understandable to the lay reader").

122. *See* United States v. Meyers, 847 F.2d 1408, 1412 (9th Cir. 1988) (summary chart admitted where underlying FBI surveillance logs for the day in question were admissible and available, but the sequence of events was confusing).

123. United States v. Smyth, 556 F.2d 1179 (5th Cir.), *cert. denied,* 434 U.S. 862 (1997).

124. *See, e.g.,* James v. Nico Energy Corp., 838 F.2d 1365, 1373 (5th Cir. 1988); Gomez v. Great Lakes Steel Div., 803 F.2d 250, 257 (6th Cir. 1986).

125. *Smyth,* 556 F.2d at 1184 n. 11.

126. See, e.g., State Office Systems v. Olivetti Corp., 762 F.2d 843, 845 (10th Cir. 1985); Paddack v. Christensen, Inc., 745 F.2d 1254, 1260 (9th Cir. 1984); United

States v. Johnson, 594 F.2d 1253, 1255–57 (9th Cir.), *cert. denied,* 444 U.S. 964 (1979).

127. *See* Hackett v. Housing Authority of the City of San Antonio, 750 F.2d 1308, 1312 (5th Cir. 1985).

128. Paddack v. Dave Christensen, Inc., 745 F.2d 1254, 1260–61 (9th Cir. 1984) (audit report based in part on inadmissible hearsay excluded).

129. *Hackett,* 750 F.2d at 1312 (summary inadmissible under Rule 1006 because proponent party failed to produce underlying documents). *Cf.,* United States v. Miller, 771 F.2d 1219, 1238 (9th Cir. 1985).

130. Coates v. Johnson & Johnson, 756 F.2d 524, 550 (7th Cir. 1985).

131. *See* Davis & Cox v. Summa Corp., 751 F.2d 1507, 1516 (9th Cir. 1985) (summaries inadmissible where underlying documents not made available to party opponent until just before trial).

132. Frank Music Corp. v. Metro–Goldwyn–Mayer, 772 F.2d 505, 515 n. 9 (9th Cir. 1985).

admission into evidence, the records are too voluminous to "conveniently be examined in court," a Rule 1006 chart or summary is admissible.[133]

The question that has caused confusion in the courts is whether a judge has the discretion to allow the use of a chart or summary when the underlying material is admitted into evidence and has been examined in court. The courts have universally agreed that the judge has authority to allow the use of the summary, but have disagreed about the status and use of the summary. Although some courts talk about Rule 1006 in this circumstance, the language of the rule says that a Rule 1006 summary is conditioned upon the notion that the underlying information "cannot conveniently be examined in court." The better analysis is that admission of the summary is within the court's discretion under Rule 611(a)— Mode and Order of Interrogation and Presentation.[134]

The difference between admission under Rule 1006 and Rule 611 is the difference between demonstrative evidence that has its own independent value and demonstrative evidence that is merely illustrative. The courts have called the summaries of the second kind, "pedagogic." One court has suggested that the difference is important in determining whether the summary or chart should go back to the jury room during deliberations—allowing the Rule 1006 summary into the jury room, but not the pedagogic summary.[135] Another court has not seemed so concerned about whether the summary goes to the jury room as that the court gives the jury the proper instructions about the lack of evidentiary value in the summary.[136]

There is a growing danger in the courts' willingness to admit summaries of already examined evidence under Rule 611(a) that the summary will become a vehicle for prematurely and unfairly arguing the case to the jury. It happens mostly in criminal cases and almost always to the advantage of the government. In *United States v. Scales*,[137] the court found that a chart was admissible under Rule 1006, because the underlying material, though admitted, could not "conveniently be examined in court." The court allowed, also, that if the summary had not been admissible under Rule 1006, it would have been under Rule 611(a).

133. United States v. Stephens, 779 F.2d 232, 239 (5th Cir. 1985).

134. *See, e.g., United States v. Baker,* 10 F.3d 1374, 1412 (9th Cir. 1993); United States v. Pinto, 850 F.2d 927, 935–36 (2d Cir.), *cert. denied,* 488 U.S. 867 (1988); United States v. Scales, 594 F.2d 558, 563–64 (6th Cir.), *cert. denied,* 441 U.S. 946 (1979) (alternative holding). *See also* Weinstein's Federal Evidence, *supra* note 100, § 1006.08[4] (a summary chart "prepared by a witness from his own knowledge to assist the jury in understanding or remembering a mass of details . . . is admissible, not under an exception to the best evidence rule, but under such general principles of good sense embodied in a court's duty to control the presentation of evidence"). The decision whether to admit such summary evidence pursuant to Rule 611(a) is left to the sound discretion of the district court. *Pinto,* 850 F.2d 927, 935–36; *see also Bailey,* 990 F.2d at 122 (district court's admission of evidence "will not be overturned on appeal unless its decision is shown to be arbitrary or irrational").

135. Pierce v. Ramsey Winch Co., 753 F.2d 416, 431 (5th Cir. 1985); United States v. Gardner, 611 F.2d 770, 776 n. 3 (9th Cir. 1980).

136. United States v. Johnson, 54 F.3d 1150 (4th Cir.), *cert. denied,* 516 U.S. 903 (1995).

137. 594 F.2d 558(6th Cir.), *cert. denied,* 441 U.S. 946 (1979).

It warned, however, that conclusory summaries, or those that presented the evidence from the government's perspective, ought not be allowed.[138] In *United States v. Johnson*,[139] the Fourth Circuit refused to reverse a conviction where the government offered a summary that not only reiterated objective information that was before the jury, but that commented on the credibility of witnesses and summarized the evidence in a manner most favorable to the government. The summary was not only admitted into evidence, but was allowed into the jury room. The appellate court held that the procedure was within the discretion of the court, since it instructed the jury that the summary was not evidence.[140]

138. *Id.* at 564.

139. 54 F.3d 1150 (4th Cir.), *cert. denied*, 516 U.S. 903 (1995).

140. *Id.* at 1159. For sharp criticism of the result as giving the government an extra final argument, *See* Emilia A. Quesada, *Summarizing Prior Witness Testimony: Admissible Evidence, Pedagogical Device, or Violation of the Federal Rules of Evidence?* 24 Fla. St. U. L. Rev. 151(1996).

Chapter 12

APPELLATE REVIEW OF RULINGS ON OBJECTIONS

Analysis

---

§ 12.01 Meaning of Error in Evidentiary Context

A trial is much like a living organism. It is dynamic, changing from moment to moment; its appearance and character are affected not only by the entities that brought it about, but its own history since its creation. Though all are governed by a set of general rules and principles, those rules and principles must be adapted to each case. Like living things, no two are truly identical in both heredity and environment.

As a result, trial judges must be granted a good deal of leeway in applying evidentiary rules if they are to help maximize the chances that the trial will achieve its principal goal of truth-determination.[1] It is primarily for this reason that the Federal Rules of Evidence contain a good deal of flexibility.[2] Most of its provisions are not categorical in nature, but instead grant the trial court the authority—guided by the terms of the rules themselves—to reach a result appropriate to the particular trial. The most obvious example is Rule 403, which allows the

---

1. For discussion of the many goals of the trial, see 1A John H. Wigmore, Evidence in Trials at Common Law § 37.1, at 1018 (Peter Tillers rev. 1983); Milner S. Ball, *The Play's the Thing: An Unscientific Reflection on Courts Under the Rubric of Theater*, 28 Stan. L. Rev. 81, 83 (1975); David P. Leonard, *The Use of Character to Prove Conduct: Rationality and Catharsis in the Law of Evidence*, 58 U. Colo. L. Rev. 1 (1987); Charles R. Nesson, *The Evidence or the Event? On Judicial Proof and the Acceptability of Verdicts*, 98 Harv. L. Rev. 1357, 1360 (1985); Laurence H. Tribe, *Trial by Mathematics: Precision and Ritual in the Legal Process*, 84 Harv. L. Rev. 1329, 1376 (1971).

2. For discussion of the flexibility of the Federal Rules and the authority this gives to trial judges, see David P. Leonard, *Power and Responsibility in Evidence Law*, 63 S. Cal. L. Rev. 937 (1990); Thomas R. Mengler, *The Theory of Discretion in the Federal Rules of Evidence*, 74 Iowa L. Rev. 413 (1989); Jon R. Waltz, *Judicial Discretion in the Admission of Evidence Under the Federal Rules of Evidence*, 79 Nw. U.L. Rev. 1097 (1984).

trial court to exclude otherwise admissible evidence when the court finds that its probative value is substantially outweighed by certain specified dangers.[3] Guided by the terms of the Rule itself, as well as certain general provisions of the Federal Rules,[4] the court must make its 403 rulings in the specific context of the trial. Many other provisions of the Federal Rules are similar; in whole or in part, they contain standards rather than categorical admission or exclusion rules.[5]

When an evidence rule provides "discretion" to the trial court, the appellate court is rarely in as good a position as the trial court to determine the most appropriate ruling. The appellate court, after all, is faced with the cold, written record, and cannot observe the demeanor of witnesses, the effect certain evidence appears to have on the jury, other factors one would have to "be there" to observe. Thus, it is said that the appellate court should only reverse the trial court's application of such rules if the trial court "abused its discretion," a standard rarely satisfied in actual practice.[6] Whether this is justified can be debated, but the fact remains that trial courts are granted a virtual shield from reversal based on error in applying discretionary rules.

Nevertheless, not all evidentiary rules are alike in terms of the authority granted to trial judges. As already pointed out, some rules are categorical. The court has no authority, for example, to allow the prosecution to offer evidence of the defendant's character to prove circumstantially that the defendant committed the crime, unless the defendant has opened the door to such evidence by offering character to prove innocence.[7] Conversely, most courts hold that the trial court has no discretion to *exclude* evidence that a witness committed a crime involving dishonesty or false statement, when that evidence is offered to impeach the witness's credibility.[8] If the rule applied by the trial court

3. *See* § 5.04.

4. *See, e.g.,* Fed. R. Evid. 102 (requiring the court to construe the rules in such a way as "to secure fairness in administration, elimination of unjustifiable expense and delay, and promotion of the growth and development of the law of evidence to the end that the truth may be ascertained and proceedings justly determined"); Fed. R. Evid. 611(a) (requiring the court to "exercise reasonable control over the mode and order of interrogating witnesses and presenting evidence so as to (1) make the interrogation and presentation effective for the ascertainment of the truth, (2) avoid needless consumption of time, and (3) protect witnesses from harassment or undue embarrassment").

5. A key example of a hybrid rule is Fed. R. Evid. 608(b), which absolutely forbids the use of extrinsic evidence of other misconduct of a witness to impeach the witness's credibility, but allows inquiry into such misconduct on cross-examination "in the discretion of the court, if probative of

truthfulness or untruthfulness." The Rule thus has both categorical and "discretionary" aspects.

6. *See* Margaret A. Berger, *When, If Ever, Does Evidentiary Error Constitute Reversible Error?*, 25 Loy. L.A. L. Rev. 893, 894 (1992) (finding only 30 officially reported decisions out of over 20,000 tried federal cases during 1990 in which a federal appellate court reversed a trial court for evidentiary error); David P. Leonard, *Appellate Review of Evidentiary Rulings*, 70 N. Caro. L. Rev. 1155, 1212–29 (1992) (finding virtually no reversals for error in applying Rules 608(b) and 611 for a ten-year period). While the measure of actual reversals does not correlate perfectly with the number of instances of "harmless" error, courts rarely even find harmless error in reviewing trial court discretionary rulings.

7. *See* Fed. R. Evid. 404(a). *See* §§ **5.07–5.08.**

8. *See* Fed. R. Evid. 609(a)(2). *See* § **9.09.**

did not confer discretion on the judge, the appellate court's standard of review should not be abuse of discretion," but a more searching standard such as "error of law."[9] For example, if in a murder prosecution, the trial court allowed the government to call a witness during its case in chief to testify to defendant's prior acts of murder, for the purpose of showing a character-based propensity to commit such crimes,[10] the appellate court should not review the trial court's ruling for "abuse of discretion," for the trial court had no discretion to allow the government to offer such evidence. Rather, the appellate court should simply find that the trial court erred as a matter of law.[11]

Unfortunately, appellate courts all too often do not recognize that trial courts do not always have discretion in applying evidence rules. It is not uncommon for courts to state simply, and generally, that they review evidentiary rulings for abuse of discretion.[12] Once such a statement is made, the result is virtually preordained.[13]

9. *Cf.* United States v. McConney, 728 F.2d 1195 (9th Cir.1984) (en banc) (reviewing possible standards of review of trial court's ruling on constitutionality of federal agents' entry into defendant's home with a search warrant, and distinguishing situations in which review should be based on "clearly erroneous" standard and those in which appellate court should review for "error of law").

10. We are assuming, for purposes of this example, that the prosecution does not argue that the prior murders are admissible for some other purpose, such as to show motive for the charged offense. *See* Fed. R. Evid. 404(b), discussed in **Ch. 5**.

11. The trial court's ruling would have constituted error for two reasons. First, the government would not be entitled to offer character evidence under these circumstances. *See* Fed. R. Evid. 404(a). Second, even were character evidence admissible, it could not be offered in the form of specific instances of conduct during direct examination. *See* Fed. R. Evid. 405(a).

12. *See, e.g.,* Holmes v. Elgin, Joliet & E. Ry., 18 F.3d 1393, 1397 (7th Cir.1994) ("We review the trial court's admission of evidence under the abuse of discretion standard, inquiring not whether we would have ruled the same way but rather whether any reasonable person would have agreed with the trial court"); United States v. Kristiansen, 901 F.2d 1463, 1465 (8th Cir.1990) ("We review evidentiary rulings under the abuse of discretion standard").

13. Some federal courts have acknowledged that even in situations in which the trial court has discretion in evidentiary rulings, a more searching review is sometimes called for. In In re Paoli Railroad Yard PCB Litigation, 35 F.3d 717 (3d Cir.1994), *cert. denied*, 513 U.S. 1190 (1995), the question concerned the admissibility of expert scientific testimony. While recognizing that the *Daubert* standard confers discretion on the trial court in assessing the reliability of scientific methodologies and data, the court was nevertheless concerned that the trial court might set the admissibility threshold too high and effectively force plaintiffs to prove their case twice (once to the court, and once to the jury). *Id.* at 749–50. To avoid this problem, the court wrote:

> We acknowledge that there is arguably a tension between the substantial deference normally accorded to rulings where the trial court has a superior vantage point and the preference for admissibility of the Federal Rules of Evidence. We resolve any such tension by holding that when the district court's exclusionary evidentiary rulings with respect to scientific opinion testimony will result in a summary or directed judgment, we will give them a "hard look" (more stringent review, . . .) to determine if a district court has abused its discretion in excluding evidence as unreliable.

Id. at 750 (Becker, J.). *See also* United States v. Criden, 648 F.2d 814, 817 (3d Cir.1981) ("the justifications for committing decisions to the discretion of the court are not uniform, and may vary with the specific type of decisions. Although the standards of review in such instances is generally framed as 'abuse of discretion,' in fact the scope of review will be directly related to the reason why that category or type of decision is committed to the trial court's discretion in the first instance");

When arguing evidentiary issues on appeal, counsel should review carefully the nature of the rule in dispute and be prepared to argue for the appropriate standard of review. Though a finding that the trial court erred is only the first hurdle in winning reversal (such error must also be found prejudicial[14]), the first hurdle must be overcome to have even a chance of reversal.

§ 12.02   Preserving Error for Appeal—In General

To preserve an error for appeal, counsel generally must make a timely and specific objection, obtain a ruling from the court, and make certain that the objection and ruling appear in the record.[15] The path to a properly preserved error, however, is fraught with dangers of forfeiture at many points in the lower court proceeding. Failure to make motions, to strike or move for a mistrial,[16] or to request a limiting instruction[17] may result in forfeiture of the right to pursue an otherwise properly made objection. When an objection which is sustained results in the exclusion of evidence, opposing counsel's failure to make an offer of proof may also forfeit the right to claim error.[18]

Counsel, in addition, must navigate successfully the narrows of posttrial procedure in order to have an error reviewed. Failure to make posttrial motions for a new trial or for judgment n.o.v. may lead to forfeiture of claims of error otherwise properly preserved.[19] Error properly preserved at trial but not raised on appeal is generally considered forfeited,[20] as is error from which appeal is not timely filed.[21] The right to raise constitutional errors in a collateral proceeding such as habeas corpus may be forfeited by "procedural default," thus preventing the review of a federal constitutional claim by a federal court.[22]

§ 12.03   Prejudicial Error and Harmless Error

Introduction

Generally speaking, an appellate court will reverse because of an erroneous ruling on an objection if the error was serious and prejudiced one of the parties. If, however, the reviewing court finds that the error

Brody v. Spang, 957 F.2d 1108, 1115 (3d Cir.1992) (We review a denial of a motion to intervene as of right for abuse of discretion, although this review is 'more stringent' than the abuse of discretion review we apply to a denial of a motion for permissive intervention").

14. See § **12.03.**

15. See **Ch. 2.**

16. See id.

17. See id.

18. See id; Wright v. Hartford Accident & Indemnity Co., 580 F.2d 809, 810 (5th Cir.1978); Yost v. A.O. Smith Corp., 562 F.2d 592, 595 (8th Cir.1977).

19. Barry Sullivan, Barry Levenstam & David von Ebers, Preserving Error in Civil Cases: Some Fundamental Principles, 32 Trial Law. Guide 1, 13–15 (1988).

20. See, e.g., McClure v. State, 648 S.W.2d 667, 677 (Tex.Crim.App.1982), cert. denied, 464 U.S. 841 (1983); see also 5 Am. Jur. 2d Appeal & Error §§ 654–55 (1962).

21. See 5 Am. Jur. 2d Appeal & Error § 665 (1962).

22. Procedural default occurs when a defendant waives the right to state court review by procedural error. See United States v. Frady, 456 U.S. 152, 167–69 (1982) (collateral attacks are reviewed unwas "harmless"—that is, the error did not affect substantial rights of a party or did not significantly affect the outcome of the case—the error will not justify a reversal. Most types of errors are subject to this harmless error analysis, including most constitutional errors.[23] The harmless error doctrine is codified in federal and state rules.[24]

Although errors which were not properly preserved below are generally deemed waived, federal and many state courts also have discretion to find "plain error" if failure to address an unpreserved error would result in a miscarriage of justice. The plain error doctrine[25] is applied most often in criminal cases, but some jurisdictions also find plain error in civil cases.

Judicial Standards for Prejudicial and Harmless Error

The Federal Rules of Evidence,[26] Federal Rules of Civil Procedure,[27] and Federal Rules of Criminal Procedure[28] all mandate that courts disregard errors that do not "affect the substantial rights of the parties."[29] Thus, reversible or prejudicial errors are those which affect the substantial rights of parties. The party challenging a nonconstitutional error has the burden of proving that the error was substantial.[30] The definition of substantial rights is vague and courts review the entire record in making the determination of prejudice.[31] Therefore, prejudice is determined on a case-by-case basis. Some generalizations emerge, however, from the case law, rules, and commentators. On the one hand, purely technical errors that do not go to the merits of the case are never prejudicial.[32] On the other hand, "[i]f the evidence is insufficient to support the verdict without the erroneously admitted evidence, the error must be held prejudicial."[33] In between these two extremes, courts look at the entire case to determine prejudice. No presumptions guide the court in this determination of whether the trial was unfairly tainted by an error.[34]

The Supreme Court has held that substantial rights are affected if

der cause-and-prejudice test of Wainwright v. Sykes, 433 U.S. 72, 87 (1977); **§ 12.04.**

23. Some constitutional errors are always grounds for reversal. *See* **§ 12.05.**

24. *See, e.g.,* Fed. R. Evid. 103(a); Fed. R. Civ. Proc. 61; Fed. R. Crim. Proc. 52(a).

25. The doctrine is called fundamental error in some states. *See, e.g.,* State v. Flores, 682 P.2d 1136, 1141 (Ariz.App. 1984); State v. Rutherford, 693 P.2d 1112, 1117 (Idaho App.1985).

26. *See* Fed. R. Evid. 103(a).

27. *See* Fed. R. Civ. Proc. 61.

28. *See* Fed. R. Crim. Proc. 52(a).

29. *See id.*

30. United States v. Montoya, 827 F.2d 143, 154 (7th Cir.1987).

31. *See* United States v. Young, 470 U.S. 1, 12 (1985).

32. *See* Kotteakos v. United States, 328 U.S. 750, 760 (1946); 1 Weinstein's Federal Evidence § 103.41, at 103–48 (2d ed. Joseph M. McLaughlin ed. 1997) ("Determining whether a substantial right has been affected is not susceptible to a mechanical analysis. the facts of each case are crucial. . . .").

33. 11 Charles A. Wright, Arthur R. Miller & Mary Kay Kane, Federal Practice and Procedure § 2885, at 466 (2d ed. 1995); *see also* United States v. Silverman, 861 F.2d 571, 580 (9th Cir.1988) (finding error prejudicial because it was "undoubtedly the bas[i]s for the jury's conclusion").

34. *See* 5 Am. Jur. 2d *Appeal & Error* § 780 (1962).

the error "substantially swayed" the jury's verdict[35] or "materially affected the deliberations of the jury."[36] Thus, if the error did not affect the jury deliberations or the outcome of the case, it will be harmless error, not prejudicial error. Courts differ on what degree of certainty that the error did not affect the outcome is required to find an error harmless. The standard employed by courts ranges from "beyond a reasonable doubt"[37] to "more probable than not."[38]

The purposes of the prejudicial error/harmless error doctrine are to avoid clogging the appellate courts with appeals from technical violations and to avoid unnecessary reversals where no real injustice was done.[39] The leading Supreme Court case articulating the harmless error doctrine is *Kotteakos v. United States*.[40] In *Kotteakos*, the Court was interpreting § 269 of the Judicial Code of 1911, an early formulation of the harmless error rule, but the Court has cited the holding in recent harmless error cases,[41] as have the lower courts.[42]

In *Kotteakos* the Court stated:

It comes down ... to a very plain admonition: "Do not be technical, where technicality does not really hurt the party whose rights in the trial and in its outcome the technicality affects." ...

If, when all is said and done, the conviction is sure that the error did not influence the jury, or had but very slight effect, the verdict and the judgment should stand, except perhaps where the departure is from a constitutional norm or a specific command of Congress.... *But if one cannot say, with fair assurance, after pondering all that happened without stripping the erroneous action from the whole, that the judgment was not substantially swayed by the error, it is impossible to conclude that substantial rights were not affected.* The inquiry cannot be merely whether there was enough to support the result, apart from the phase affected by the error. If is rather, even so,

---

35. *See* Kotteakos v. United States, 328 U.S. 750, 765 (1946); *see also* United States v. Lane, 474 U.S. 438, 449 (1986); United States v. Donahue, 948 F.2d 438, 442 (8th Cir.1991), *cert. denied*, 503 U.S. 976, (1992) (error based on constitutional hearsay grounds is not harmful unless it may have "substantially swayed" the jury).

36. *See* Holloway v. Arkansas, 435 U.S. 475, 490 (1978).

37. *See* Chapman v. California, 386 U.S. 18, 24 (1967) (the standard for evaluating whether an error is harmless is whether it was "harmless beyond a reasonable doubt"); State v. VanWagner, 504 N.W.2d 746, 750 (Minn.1993) (prosecutor's pointed and persistent references to police interview with witness which led them to charge defendant with drunk driving improperly alluded to excluded hearsay statements, and, although misconduct was probably harmless beyond a reasonable doubt,

court reversed for "prophylactic reasons" and to protect the "integrity of the factfinding process").

38. *See* United States v. Valle–Valdez, 554 F.2d 911, 914–15 (9th Cir.1977).

39. Historically, any error was ground for reversal and, as a result, counsel began sowing error in the record to create an escape hatch from an unfavorable verdict. To stem this tide, the courts developed the harmless error doctrine. *See* 11 Wright, Miller & Kane, *supra* note 33 § 2881.

40. 328 U.S. 750 (1946).

41. *See* United States v. Lane, 474 U.S. 438, 446 (1986); Brecht v. Abrahamson, 507 U.S. 619 (1993). *See also* 11 Wright, Miller & Kane, *supra* note 33 § 2881, at 272 n.4.

42. *See, e.g.*, United States v. Pirovolos, 844 F.2d 415, 425 (7th Cir.), *cert. denied*, 488 U.S. 857 (1988).

whether the error itself had substantial influence. If so, or if one is left in grave doubt, the conviction cannot stand.[43]

A finding of harmlessness should be based on the probable effect of the error on the jury's deliberation.[44] When the evidence of guilt is overwhelming, however, some courts disregard the effect of the error on the jury and find the error harmless, because the court below reached the "right" result.[45] While the *Kotteakos* Court noted that the quantity of evidence cannot be ignored in evaluating whether the jury's determination was affected by an error, it placed primary emphasis on the effect of the error on the jury's determination, not on the correctness of the result.[46] Despite the continuing vitality of *Kotteakos*, in several recent cases, the Supreme Court has emphasized the existence of overwhelming guilt in its findings of harmless error.[47]

In reviewing the entire record to determine whether an error is harmless or prejudicial, courts consider several factors,[48] including: the number of errors in relation to the length of the trial, the closeness of factual disputes, whether the evidence related to a material consequential fact, the prejudicial effect of the evidence, the instructions given, whether the evidence was important corroboration of other testimony, whether the evidence was cumulative,[49] and the amount of reliance counsel placed on the tainted evidence in their arguments.[50]

43. *Kotteakos*, 328 U.S. at 760–65 (citations omitted; emphasis added).

44. *See* 1 John H. Wigmore, Evidence in Trials at Common Law § 21, at 933 (Peter Tillers rev. 1983).

45. *Id.* at 930–31. *See* United States v. Fortna, 796 F.2d 724, 735 (5th Cir.), *cert. denied*, 479 U.S. 950 (1986) (finding error in admitting testimony was harmless because the witness was not a significant one and the evidence of guilt was overwhelming).

46. *Kotteakos*, 328 U.S. at 761, 764–65).

47. *See* Darden v. Wainwright, 477 U.S. 168, 182 (1986); United States v. Young, 470 U.S. 1, 19 (1985). *See also See also* United States v. Simon, 995 F.2d 1236 (3d Cir.1993) (held, trial court's "otherwise reversible error" in failing to give burden of proof jury instruction was harmless where government presented overwhelming evidence of defendant's guilt); United States v. Pirovolos, 844 F.2d 415, 427 (7th Cir.), *cert. denied*, 488 U.S. 857 (1988) (noting that "evidence of Pirovolos's guilt was truly overwhelming" and finding the error harmless); United States v. Montoya, 827 F.2d 143, 152 (7th Cir.1987) (citing overwhelming evidence of guilt); United States v. Fortna, 796 F.2d 724, 735 (5th Cir.), *cert.*

denied, 479 U.S. 950 (1986) (noting that evidence of guilt was overwhelming).

In objecting to this use of overwhelming evidence as the test for harmless error, Judge Clark of the Fifth Circuit wrote: "Unnecessary language seems to invite review of the sufficiency of the non-objectionable evidence *alone*, even though our attention over and over again is *properly* called to the prejudicial impact of the objectionable evidence." Harryman v. Estelle, 616 F.2d 870, 885 (5th Cir.) (Clark, J., concurring in part and dissenting in part), *cert. denied*, 449 U.S. 860 (1980); *see also* Fahy v. Connecticut, 375 U.S. 85, 86–87 (1963) ("The question is whether there is a reasonable possibility that the evidence complained of might have contributed to the conviction"); United States v. Ruffin, 575 F.2d 346, 359–60 (2d Cir.1978) (noting that error may be prejudicial even though "there was sufficient other evidence to sustain the conviction. The crucial question is whether the error influenced the jury's verdict").

48. *See* 1 Weinstein's Federal Evidence, *supra* note 32 § 103.41[5].

49. *See* United States v. Austin, 823 F.2d 257, 260 (8th Cir.1987), *cert. denied*, 484 U.S. 1044 (1988).

50. *See* 1 Weinstein's Federal Evidence, *supra* note 32 § 103.41[5][f].

Courts using the effect-on-the-jury analysis for harmlessness differ on how small the likelihood of the error affecting the jury deliberation must be to justify a finding of harmlessness.[51] For example, the Ninth Circuit uses a "more probably harmless than not" test for nonconstitutional errors.[52] The Third Circuit standard is more onerous, requiring reversal unless it is "highly probable" that the verdict would have been the same if the error had not occurred.[53] In the Fifth Circuit, reversal is required unless the court is "sure that the error did not influence the jury, or had but slight effect."[54] In the case of constitutional errors, the Supreme Court has held that the prosecution has the burden of proving that the error was harmless beyond a reasonable doubt.[55]

Courts generally apply the same standard for harmless error in civil cases as in criminal cases,[56] although some cases argue that the standards should differ in accordance with the differing standards of proof applicable to civil and criminal cases.[57] State courts standards for determining harmless error are similar to federal court standards.[58] In diversi-

---

51. *See* United States v. Valle–Valdez, 554 F.2d 911, 914–15 (9th Cir.1977) (noting that "standards guiding appellate determination of harmless error are variable, often confusing and frequently left unarticulated ..., however, those standards are statements of the degree of certainty an appellate court must achieve regarding the effect of error on the verdict").

52. *See* United States v. Gwaltney, 790 F.2d 1378, 1383 (9th Cir.1986), *cert. denied,* 479 U.S. 1104 (1987); *see also* U.S. Indus., Inc. v. Touche Ross & Co., 854 F.2d 1223, 1252–53 (10th Cir.1988) (applying the more probably harmless than not standard in civil case).

53. *See* United States v. Grayson, 795 F.2d 278, 290 (3d Cir. 1986), *cert. denied,* 481 U.S. 1018 (1987) (court must have " 'sure conviction that the error did not prejudice the defendant,' but need not disprove every 'reasonable possibility' of prejudice"); McQueeney v. Wilmington Trust Co., 779 F.2d 916, 924 (3d Cir.1985); *see also* United States v. Thompson, 716 F.2d 248, 251 (4th Cir.1983), *vacated by* 728 F.2d 654 (4th Cir.1984) (stating that a "fair assurance" that verdict was not affected by error is the standard).

54. United States v. Arias–Diaz, 497 F.2d 165, 171, 172 (5th Cir.1974), *cert. denied,* 420 U.S. 1003 (1975) (citing *Kotteakos*); *see also* McKinnon v. Skil Corp., 638 F.2d 270, 276 (1st Cir.1981) (finding error harmless because it did not affect substantial rights). This standard is similar to the requirement that constitutional errors are prejudicial unless proven harmless "beyond

a reasonable doubt." *See* Chapman v. California, 386 U.S. 18, 23 (1967).

For a discussion of the possible standards for determining whether an error is prejudicial, see Roger Traynor, The Riddle of Harmless Error 35 (1970).

55. *See* Chapman v. California, 386 U.S. 18, 23 (1967); *see* § **12.05.**

56. *Cf.* McDonough Power Equip., Inc. v. Greenwood, 464 U.S. 548, 553–54 (1984).

57. *See* U.S. Indus., Inc. v. Touche Ross & Co., 854 F.2d 1223, 1252 n. 39 (10th Cir.1988) (noting that "it seems reasonable, absent some countervailing policy, that the harmless error standard should mirror the standard applied at trial"); *see also* Stephen A. Saltzburg, *The Harm of Harmless Error,* 59 Va. L. Rev. 988, 988 (1973).

58. *See, e.g.,* State v. Naoum, 548 A.2d 120, 124 (Me.1988) (using "highly probable" standard); People v. Stubl, 385 N.W.2d 719, 721 (Mich.App.1986) (holding erroneous admission of hearsay was harmless based on "beyond a reasonable doubt" standard); State v. Davis, 401 N.W.2d 721, 725 (S.D.1987) (holding errors are prejudicial when "jury might and probably would have returned a different verdict if the alleged error hadn't occurred") (emphasis omitted)); State v. Dyess, 370 N.W.2d 222, 231– 32 (Wis.1985) (stating that "no reasonable possibility" standard applies to nonconstitutional and constitutional errors). *But cf.* State v. VanWagner, 504 N.W.2d 746, 750 (Minn.1993) (harmless error rising from deliberate prosecutorial misconduct is still grounds for reversal as a prophylactic meaty cases, however, a federal court applies its own harmless error standard, rather than the state court standard.[59]

§ 12.04   Plain Error

When no objection was made at trial, the appellate court will reverse only if it finds "plain error."

Courts enforce the procedural requirements for preserving error for three reasons: (1) judicial economy, (2) to encourage lower courts to correct errors at the time they occur, and (3) to avoid unfairness to a prevailing party.[60] At the same time, federal courts and many state courts recognize that enforcing the rights of the parties should be of greater concern than enforcing legal technicalities.[61] Because trials are stressful and often fast-paced, even the most competent attorney[62] may fail to object to improper evidence, comment, or argument, or may omit one technical step in the procedure for properly preserving error. The plain error doctrine embodies this overriding concern for preserving important rights.[63] The rule is set out in the Federal Rules of Evidence,[64] the Federal rules of Criminal Procedure,[65] and analogous state court rules.[66]

Plain error is found most often in criminal cases, where the defendant appeals from a conviction that takes away some form of liberty. Under Rule 52(b) of the Federal Rules of Criminal Procedure, plain error

sure against future prosecutorial misconduct).

59. *See* 11 Wright & Miller, *supra* note 33 § 2883, at 450.

60. Barry Sullivan, Barry Levenstam & David von Ebers, *Preserving Error in Civil Cases: Some Fundamental Principles*, 32 Trial Law. Guide 1, 2 (1988).

61. *See* Hormel v. Helvering, 312 U.S. 552, 557 (1941); *see generally* 1 Weinstein's Federal Evidence § 103.42[3], at 103–67 to 103–68 (2d ed. Joseph M. McLaughlin ed. 1997) ("the doctrine should be applied only when the error is so obvious that a failure to notice it would seriously affect the fairness, integrity, and public reputation of the judicial proceeding"); John E. Theuman, Annotation, *Supreme Court's views as to what constitute harmless errors or plain errors, under Rule 52 of Federal Rules of Criminal Procedure*, 84 L.Ed.2d 876, 878 (1987).

62. It has been pointed out that the need for the plain error doctrine is especially great in the cases of children and of criminal defendants who have court-appointed counsel. *See* Government of the Canal Zone v. P (Pinto), 590 F.2d 1344, 1353 (5th Cir.1979) (defendant had a series of court-appointed attorneys).

63. *See* United States v. Atkinson, 297 U.S. 157, 160 (1936) (describing plain error).

64. Fed. R. Evid. 103(d) states: "Nothing in this rule precludes taking notice of plain error affecting substantial rights although they were not brought to the attention of the court."

65. Fed. R. Crim. Proc. 52(b) states: "Plain errors or defects affecting substantial rights may be noticed although they were not brought to the attention of the court." The notes of the advisory committee on rules state that this rule is a restatement of existing case law.

See also Sup. Ct. R. 34.1(a) ("At its option, however, the Court may consider a plain error not among the questions presented, but evident from the record and otherwise within its jurisdiction"). For a discussion of Supreme Court review of errors not raised in briefs, see Girardeau A. Spann, *Functional Analysis of the Plain Error Rule*, 71 Geo. L.J. 945, 946–47 (1983).

66. *See, e.g.*, Minn. R. Crim. Proc. 31.02: "Plain errors or defects affecting substantial rights may be considered by the court upon motions for new trial, post-trial motions, and on appeal although they were not brought to the attention of the trial court."

applies to direct appeals and petitions for certiorari of criminal cases. It does not apply, however, to habeas petitions by federal or state prisoners; those prisoners are required to meet the cause-and-prejudice test of *Wainwright v. Sykes*[67] before a waived or "defaulted" error will be reviewed by the federal courts.[68]

Federal courts and some state courts also apply the plain error doctrine in civil cases.[69] While there is no plain error rule in the Federal Rules of Civil Procedure, the rule is embodied in Federal Rule of Evidence 103(d),[70] and the circuit courts have recognized the doctrine as necessary for fairness and justice in some cases.[71]

Plain error is not easily defined and allows for substantial judicial discretion. Courts employing the doctrine have found plain error when "substantial rights" are involved, the error was "particularly egregious,"[72] a "miscarriage of justice"[73] resulted from the error, or the error deprived the defendant of a fair trial.[74] The facts of the case, the gravity of the offense, and the probable effect of the error are factors considered by the court in determining whether substantial rights have been violated.[75] Some courts require that the error be obvious in the record.[76]

---

67. 433 U.S. 72, 84–86 (1977). The test, based on Fed. R. Crim. Proc. 12(b)(2), requires the petitioner to demonstrate both cause for noncompliance and actual prejudice resulting from the alleged violation.

68. 8 Moore's Federal Practice § 52 (2d ed. 1988); *see also* United States v. Frady, 456 U.S. 152, 167–69 (1982).

69. *See* 1 Weinstein's Federal Evidence, *supra* note 61 § 103.42[3]; *see, e.g.,* Bannister v. Town of Noble, 812 F.2d 1265, 1271 (10th Cir.1987); Jackson v. Firestone Tire & Rubber Co., 788 F.2d 1070, 1075 (5th Cir.1986); Teen–Ed, Inc. v. Kimball Intl., Inc., 620 F.2d 399, 401–02 (3d Cir. 1980); Liner v. J.B. Talley & Co., 618 F.2d 327, 329 (5th Cir.1980); Edwards v. Sears, Roebuck 7 Co., 512 F.2d 276, 286 (5th Cir. 1975); Alger v. Hayes, 452 F.2d 841, 845 (8th Cir.1972).

70. Rule 103(d) provides: "Nothing in this rule precludes taking notice of plain errors affecting substantial rights although they were not brought to the attention of the court."

71. *See Teen–Ed, Inc.,* 620 F.2d at 401–02. The rationale underlying the plain error doctrine in criminal cases—protecting those whose liberty is at risk from the inadequacies of counsel—does not apply in civil cases.

In addition to finding plain error in civil trial court rulings on evidentiary matters and arguments of counsel, appellate courts occasionally find plain error in trial court decisions on matters of law, such as rulings on motions for directed verdict or summary judgment. In this regard one state court has explained that plain error "is reserved for situations where it is necessary to preserve confidence in the fairness and integrity of the adjudicative process, or where the issue is important to the development of the law." Daley v. Gaitor, 547 A.2d 1375, 1378 (Conn.App.), *cert. denied,* 552 A.2d 430 (1988) (finding plain error in trial court's granting of directed verdict); *see also* Harper v. Landers, 348 S.E.2d 698, 701 (Ga. App.1986) (finding plain error in grant of motion to dismiss in custody action).

72. *See* United States v. Gwaltney, 790 F.2d 1378, 1383–84 (9th Cir.1986), *cert. denied,* 479 U.S. 1104 (1987).

73. *See* United States v. Frady, 456 U.S. 152, 163 (1982); United States v. Griffin, 818 F.2d 97, 99 (1st Cir.), *cert. denied,* 484 U.S. 844 (1987).

74. *See* State v. Smith, 561 P.2d 739, 744 (Ariz.1977). *See also* State v. Salitros, 499 N.W.2d 815, 819–20 (Minn.1993) (ordering new trial "in the interests of justice" when defense counsel failed to object to prosecutor's improper statements in closing arguments that constitutional guarantees "are designed to protect the innocent ... [t]hey have never been designed to serve as a shield for the guilty to hide behind" and his urging the jury to "pull this defendant out from behind that shield and hold him accountable for the crimes that he was involved in committing").

75. *See* 1 Weinstein's Federal Evidence, *supra* note 61 § 103.42[a]; *see also*

---

76. See note 76 on page 549.

Subsumed in the plain error determination is consideration of whether the alleged error was prejudicial to the rights of the appealing party.[77] Thus a finding of plain error has the identical effect on a proceeding as a finding of prejudicial error—the lower court's decision will be reversed, and, in most cases, remanded.

In an interpretation of language in the Federal Rules of Criminal Procedure that is similar to language in Federal Rule of Evidence 103, the Supreme Court clarified the scope of review for plain error. In *United States v. Olano*,[78] the Court first held that the doctrine applies only to "forfeited" rights (rights lost by failure to assert them in a timely fashion), and not to "waived" rights (rights intentionally relinquished).[79] Second, the error must be "plain" in that it was clear under current law.[80] Third, the error must affect substantial rights.[81] The defendant bears the burden of persuasion that the error was prejudicial and must demonstrate that the error affected the outcome of the trial proceedings; normally, the defendant must make a specific showing of prejudice.[82] If the forfeited error is plain and affects substantial rights, the appellate court may but is not required to exercise its discretion to remedy the error.[83] The appellate court should exercise discretion when the error " 'seriously affect[s] the fairness, integrity or public reputation of judicial proceedings.' "[84]

The Ninth Circuit has employed this analysis to hold that it was not plain error to admit a witness's prior inconsistent out-of-court statement, which was not made under oath, without an instruction limiting the jury's use of the statement for purposes of impeachment only.[85]

Reversal for plain error is relatively rare.[86] Therefore counsel should never rely on the discretion of appellate courts to find plain error. It is counsel's duty to effectively present the client's case and protect the client's rights by avoiding error and preserving error made by opposing counsel or the court.[87] This principle applies both to the erroneous

United States v. Young, 470 U.S. 1, 12 (1985); United States v. Santana–Camacho, 833 F.2d 371, 374 (1st Cir.1987) (plain error in mischaracterizing defendant as "illegal" alien); United States v. Roenigk, 810 F.2d 809, 816 (8th Cir.1987); Rojas v. Richardson, 703 F.2d 186, 190–92 (5th Cir.), *rehg denied*, 718 F.2d 1096 (5th Cir.1983); United States v. Grunberger, 431 F.2d 1062, 1069 (2d Cir.1970); United States v. Segna, 555 F.2d 226, 231 (9th Cir.1977).

76. *See* Lowery v. State, 762 P.2d 457, 459 n. 1 (Alaska App.1988).

77. *See* § 12.03 (discussing prejudicial error).

78. 507 U.S. 725 (1993).

79. *Id.* at 731–34.

80. *Id.* at 734.

81. *Id.* at 734–35.

82. *Id.* at 735.

83. *Id.*

84. *Id.* at 736 (quoting United States v. Atkinson, 297 U.S. 157, 160 (1936)).

85. *See* United States v. Armijo, 5 F.3d 1229, 1233–34 (9th Cir.1993).

86. *See* United States v. Robinson, 485 U.S. 25, 35 (1988) (Blackmun, J., concurring in part and dissenting in part); United States v. Young, 470 U.S. 1, 15 (1985) (noting that plain error exception to the contemporaneous objection rule is to be "used sparingly" (quoting United States v. Frady, 456 U.S. 152, 163 n. 14 (1982)).

87. *See* § 2.10; Sykes v. United States, 373 F.2d 607, 613 (5th Cir.1966), *cert. denied*, 386 U.S. 977 (1967) ("Whether or not there was error was not visible because all of the circumstances of the arrest were not before the court. That which is not visible cannot be 'plain.' We are not equipped for divination").

admission and erroneous exclusion of evidence. Thus, if counsel believes the court has improperly admitted evidence, it is counsel's responsibility to place on the record the reasons for the claimed error. If counsel believes the court has erroneously excluded evidence, counsel must make a record of precisely what the excluded evidence was in order to provide the appellate court with a basis both for holding both that the trial court erred and that the error was prejudicial. Without a complete record, it is often very difficult for the appellate court to make the desired findings.

Note that error in rulings on evidence can be prejudicial but not plain. Suppose, for example, that in response to an objection wrongly based on relevancy grounds, the trial judge admits devastating evidence that should have been excluded on hearsay grounds. This error would be prejudicial (because the jury heard very damaging evidence it should not have heard), but if the hearsay question was actually close, it would not likely be "plain." Reversal in such a case is highly unlikely.

Similarly, it is also possible to have plain error that is not prejudicial. For example, if the trial judge erroneously excluded a lay opinion that the plaintiff was intoxicated, but admitted evidence of the person's specific behavior and symptoms of intoxication, the error might be "plain" (because the opinion should have been permitted), but harmless (because the testimony admitted by the court was most likely a reasonable substitute for the evidence wrongly excluded). In such a case, the appellate court will not reverse.

When litigating under state law, counsel must research the case law and statutes to determine whether plain error will be applied in the courts of the state. Some states do not accept the plain error doctrine, holding instead that failure to object is an absolute forfeiture of the right to appeal.[88] Some states will find plain error when the court errs on issues of law such as instructions to the jury or rulings on motions to dismiss or for summary judgment, but may not find plain error in relation to unpreserved errors in evidentiary rulings.[89]

§ 12.05 Constitutional Error

Issues of constitutional error arise most frequently in criminal cases. These errors include violations of the fourth amendment, the fifth amendment, self-incrimination clause, due process rights under the fifth and fourteenth amendments, sixth amendment rights to counsel, to an impartial tribunal and to confrontation, and eighth amendment protections against excessive punishment. Counsel should be aware that in

88. *See, e.g.,* Calhoun v. State, 530 So.2d 259, 262 (Ala.Crim.App.1988) ("plain error doctrine applies only to death cases"); Barker v. State, 453 S.W.2d 413, 416–17 (Ark.1970); Jones v. State, 453 S.W.2d 403, 404 (Ark.1970); State v. Miles, 344 N.W.2d 231, 233 (Iowa 1984).

89. *Compare* State v. Patterson, 755 P.2d 551, 556 (Kan.1988) (reviewing jury instruction for plain error) *with* State v.

Bird, 708 P.2d 946, 961–62 (Kan.1985) (stating that "failure to comply with the contemporaneous objection rule bars a challenge to the [prosecutor's argument] in a state court"). For further discussion of plain error in the context of jury instructions, see 9A Charles A. Wright, Arthur R. Miller & Mary Kay Kane, Federal Practice and Procedure § 2558 (2d ed. 1995).

criminal cases, constitutional error is not limited to cases in which the trial court erroneously admits evidence offered by the prosecution. Trial courts may also commit constitutional err by excluding evidence offered by the defense. Potential constitutional issues arise in a variety of situations in which the trial court employs evidence rules to exclude crucial exculpatory evidence offered by the defendant.[90] These types of cases have spawned a body of law setting forth parameters for those situations in which exclusionary rules of evidence must give way to the defendant's constitutional rights, primarily under the due process clauses of the sixth and fourteenth amendments and the right to present a defense created by the sixth amendment.[91]

Prior to the Supreme Court's decision in *Chapman v. California*,[92] it was thought that constitutional errors were always grounds for reversal.[93] *Chapman* held, however, that the harmless error doctrine applies to most[94] constitutional errors.[95] Thus a constitutional error that did not contribute to a criminal conviction may be deemed harmless. However, "before a federal constitutional error can be held harmless, the court must be able to declare a belief that it was harmless *beyond a reasonable doubt.*"[96] This is a higher standard than the one applied to nonconstitutional errors.[97] A court, for example, will reverse for improperly obtained evidence if the jury's decision was influenced beyond a reasonable doubt by the improper evidence.[98] If, however, the improper evidence is merely cumulative of other, properly admitted evidence, the error may be found harmless because the jury's judgment was not affected.[99]

The burden of proving that a constitutional error was harmless is on the prosecution.[100] Courts consider the entire record in deciding whether a constitutional error was harmless[101] and the factors considered are the same as in nonconstitutional errors.[102] The plain error doctrine also applies to constitutional errors.[103]

Although *Chapman* required "courts to focus on the possible impact

---

90. *See, e.g.*, Chambers v. Mississippi, 410 U.S. 284 (1973), in which the Supreme Court held that the state court's application of hearsay doctrine and the "voucher rule" to exclude evidence strongly suggesting defendant's innocence violated defendant's due process rights.

91. For a detailed examination of the right to present exculpatory evidence, see Edward J. Imwinkelried, Exculpatory Evidence (1990).

92. 386 U.S. 18 (1967).

93. *See* 1 John H. Wigmore, Evidence in Trials at Common Law § 21, at 937 (Peter Tillers rev. 1983).

94. A few constitutional errors are not subject to harmless error analysis. *See infra* notes 111–116 and accompanying text.

95. *Chapman*, 386 U.S. at 23.

96. *Id.*

97. *See* § 12.02.

98. *See, e.g.*, Holland v. Attorney General, 777 F.2d 150, 159 (3d Cir.1985) (reversing for *Bruton* error); United States v. McKinney, 707 F.2d 381, 385 (9th Cir.1983) (reversing for confrontation clause error).

99. *See, e.g.*, Brown v. United States, 411 U.S. 223, 231 (1973) (Burns v. Clusen, 798 F.2d 931, 943–44 (7th Cir.1986).

100. Schneble v. Florida, 405 U.S. 427, 428 (1972).

101. *See* United States v. Hasting, 461 U.S. 499, 509 (1983).

102. *See* § 12.03.

103. *See, e.g.*, United States v. Mouzin, 785 F.2d 682, 693 (9th Cir.), *cert. denied*, 479 U.S. 985 (1986).

of the erroneously admitted or excluded evidence on the jurors' minds,[104] subsequent Supreme Court decisions have found constitutional errors harmless because the evidence of guilt was "overwhelming."[105] Commentators have criticized the *Chapman* harmless error rule as having no substantive doctrinal base,[106] and as outcome-oriented.[107] They note that the current Supreme Court is most concerned about the accuracy of the guilt/innocence determination[108]—"reaching the right result"—rather than the protection of an individual's constitutional rights.[109]

Some constitutional errors continue to be prejudicial per se because the rights affected are "so basic to a fair trial that their infraction can never be treated as harmless error."[110] These errors include right to counsel violations,[111] absence of an impartial tribunal,[112] and complete denial of the opportunity to cross-examine.[113] At one time, the Court considered the use of coerced confessions never to be harmless,[114] but in 1991, the Court reversed course on its treatment of coerced confessions, holding that harmless error analysis applies even to cases involving illegally coerced confessions.[115] Some constitutional errors, while not prejudicial per se, mandate reversal unless the defendant can make a relatively low threshold showing. For example, the prosecution's failure to disclose material exculpatory evidence requires reversal if the defendant can demonstrate a "reasonable probability that, had the evidence

104. 1 Weinstein's Federal Evidence § 103.43[3][b] (2d ed. Joseph M. McLaughlin ed. 1997); United States v. Berkery, 865 F.2d 587, 590, *vacated on other grounds and reh'g.*, 889 F.2d 1281 (3d Cir.1989) (citing *Chapman*, 386 U.S. at 24).

105. *See* Milton v. Wainwright, 407 U.S. 371, 377 (1972); *cf.* United States v. Pirovolos, 844 F.2d 415, 427 (7th Cir.), *cert. denied*, 488 U.S. 857 (1988).

106. *See* Steven H. Goldberg, *Harmless Error: Constitutional Sneak Thief*, 71 J. Crim. L. & Criminology 421, 427 (1980).

107. *See* Tom Stacy & Kim Dayton, *Rethinking Harmless Constitutional Error*, 88 Colum. L. Rev. 79, 84 (1988).

108. Delaware v. Van Arsdall, 475 U.S. 673, 677–78 (1986) (stating that "the central purpose of a criminal trial is to decide the factual question of the defendant's guilt or innocence").

109. Stacy & Dayton, *supra* note 107, at 143.

110. *Chapman*, 386 U.S. at 23; *see also* Sullivan v. Louisiana, 508 U.S. 275 (1993) (reversing conviction because trial court's incorrect definition of reasonable doubt in jury instructions deprived defendant of right to trial by jury; due to trial court's error, jury could not render a verdict of guilty beyond a reasonable doubt); Stacy & Dayton, *supra* note 107, at 80 (quoting Rose

v. Clark, 478 U.S. 570, 577–78 (1986), in which the Court stated these rights are so fundamental that in their absence "a criminal trial cannot reliably serve its function as a vehicle for determination of guilt or innocence ... and no criminal punishment may be regarded as fundamentally fair").

111. Gideon v. Wainwright, 372 U.S. 335, 343 (1963).

112. Tumey v. Ohio, 273 U.S. 510, 535 (1927).

113. Davis v. Alaska, 415 U.S. 308, 318 (1974) (complete denial of cross-examination held constitutional error); *cf.* United States v. Owens, 484 U.S. 554, 560 (1988) (finding no confrontation clause violation where witness could not be thoroughly cross-examined about a prior statement of which he had no memory due to brain damage); Delaware v. Van Arsdall, 475 U.S. 673, 684 (1986) (unconstitutional restriction on defendant's right to cross-examine a witness subject to harmless error analysis).

114. *See* Payne v. Arkansas, 356 U.S. 560, 568 (1958).

115. Arizona v. Fulminante, 499 U.S. 279 (1991) (a 5–4 decision). For criticism of that decision, see Charles J. Ogletree, *Arizona v. Fulminate: The Harm of Applying Harmless Error to Coerced Confessions*, 105 Harv. L. Rev. 152 (1991).

been disclosed to the defense, the result of the proceeding would have been different."[116]

The *Chapman* standard does not apply to collateral attacks on constitutional error. In *Brecht v. Abrahamson*,[117] the Supreme Court reviewed a habeas case arising from a trial in which the prosecutor was erroneously allowed to refer to the defendant's post-*Miranda* silence. The Court rejected the argument that the *Chapman* "harmless-beyond-reasonable-doubt standard" had to be satisfied in order to uphold the conviction. Instead, it held that when a conviction is collaterally attacked for constitutional error, the more lenient *Kotteakos* standard applies, so that the judgment will be upheld unless it is shown that the error "had substantial and injurious effect or influence in determining the jury's verdict."[118] However, the Supreme Court has cautioned that a constitutional error cannot be considered harmless where the trial judge has a "grave doubt" or is uncertain about the injurious effect of the error.[119]

In response to *Brecht*, the Eighth Circuit has held that *Chapman* is the proper standard for collateral review of constitutional error when the state courts did not already apply the *Chapman* test to the contested error.[120]

Whether an error in a criminal trial rises to the level of constitutional error depends on the rights allegedly violated. If the error involves violation of a specific provision of the Bill of Rights (e.g., the right to counsel or the fifth amendment privilege against self-incrimination), it will be deemed a constitutional error.[121] Because of the liberty interests at stake in a criminal trial, however, many errors that would affect the outcome of the case, and therefore are prejudicial, but are not violations of a specific provision of the Bill of Rights, may be raised on appeal as due process violations under the fifth or fourteenth amendments. Errors in the prosecutor's closing argument often fall into this category. In these due process cases, the Supreme Court evaluates whether the error "so infected the trial with unfairness as to make the resulting conviction a denial of due process."[122] Because the entire proceeding is examined for unfairness, error that does not implicate a specific right will rarely be found to be constitutional error.[123] Even if a specific right is implicated,

---

116. Kyles v. Whitley, 514 U.S. 419, 433 (1995), quoting United States v. Bagley, 473 U.S. 667, 682 (1985).

117. 507 U.S. 619 (1993).

118. *Accord*, California v. Roy, 519 U.S. 2 (1996) (*Kotteakos* "harmless error" standard applies where trial court failed to instruct jury that in order to find defendant guilty of murder committed by a confederate, it must find that defendant had knowledge and intent or purpose of committing, encouraging, or facilitating the killing; error was "trial error" rather than "structural error").

119. O'Neal v. McAninch, 513 U.S. 432, 436–43 (1995).

120. Orndorff v. Lockhart, 998 F.2d 1426, 1429 (8th Cir.1993), *cert. denied*, 511 U.S. 1060 (1994).

121. *See* Donnelly v. DeChristoforo, 416 U.S. 637, 643 (1974).

122. *Id.*

123. *See, e.g.*, Darden v. Wainwright, 477 U.S. 168, 182 (1986). *But see* Wainwright v. Greenfield, 474 U.S. 284, 295 (1986) (holding that use of *Miranda* silence as evidence of sanity rendered trial fundamentally unfair).

Despite constitutional guarantees of due process, errors in criminal trial that do not involve violations of specific provisions of for instance, the right against self-incrimination, the Court may find that no constitutional error occurred based on the whole record.[124] In the case of closing arguments, the Court often invokes the invited response doctrine[125] in concluding that no constitutional violation occurred.[126] Counsel appealing due process errors, therefore should also challenge the error on non-constitutional grounds.

the Bill of Rights generally are not considered constitutional, because the "interests involved are not sufficiently important to merit explicit constitutional protection." United States v. Valle–Valdez, 554 F.2d 911, 916 (9th Cir.1977).

124. *See* United States v. Robinson, 485 U.S. 25, 32–33 (1988).

125. *See* § 1.10.

126. *See Robinson* at 33–34; Darden v. Wainwright, 477 U.S. 168, 182 (1986).

Appendix

RESEARCHING THE LAW OF EVIDENCE ON WESTLAW®

Analysis

Section 1. Introduction

Evidence Law, A Student's Guide to the Law of Evidence as Applied in American Trials provides a strong base for analyzing even the most complex problem involving the law of evidence. Whether your research requires examination of rules, statutes, case law, expert commentary or other materials, West books and Westlaw are excellent sources of information.

To help keep you up-to-date with current developments, Westlaw provides frequently updated databases. With Westlaw, you have unparalleled legal research resources at your fingertips.

Additional Resources

If you have not previously used Westlaw or have questions not covered in this appendix, see the *Westlaw Reference Manual* or call the West Group Reference Attorneys at 1–800–850–WEST (1–800–850–9378). The West Group Reference Attorneys are trained, licensed attorneys, available 24 hours a day to assist you with your Westlaw search questions.

Section 2. Westlaw Databases

Each database on Westlaw is assigned an abbreviation called an *identifier*, which you use to access the database. You can find identifiers for all databases in the online Westlaw Directory and in the printed *Westlaw Database Directory*. When you need to know more detailed information about a database, use Scope. Scope contains coverage information, lists of related databases and valuable search tips. To access Scope, click the **Scope** button while in the database.

The following chart lists Westlaw databases that contain information pertaining to evidence law. For a complete list of evidence law databases, see the online Westlaw Directory or the printed *Westlaw Database Directory*. Because new information is continually being added to Westlaw, you should also check the Welcome to Westlaw window and the Westlaw Directory for new database information.

Selected Westlaw Databases

Database	Identifier	Coverage
Federal Rules, Orders and Statutes		
Federal Rules	US–RULES	Current data
Federal Orders	US–ORDERS	Current data
Federal Rules of Practice & Procedure Advisory Committee Minutes	US–RULESCOMM	Varies by committee
United States Code Annotated®	USCA	Current data
United States Public Laws	US–PL	Current data
Congressional Bills	CONG–BILLTXT	Current Congress
Federal and State Case Law Combined		
Federal & State Case Law	ALLCASES	Begins with 1945
Federal & State Case Law–Before 1945	ALLCASES–OLD	1789–1944
Federal Case Law		
Federal Case Law	ALLFEDS	Begins with 1945
Federal Case Law–Before 1945	ALLFEDS–OLD	1789–1944
U.S. Supreme Court Cases	SCT	Begins with 1945
U.S. Supreme Court Cases–Before 1945	SCT–OLD	1790–1944
U.S. Courts of Appeals Cases	CTA	Begins with 1945
U.S. Courts of Appeals Cases–Before 1945	CTA–OLD	1891–1944
U.S. District Courts Cases	DCT	Begins with 1945
U.S. District Courts Cases–Before 1945	DCT–OLD	1789–1944
State Rules, Orders and Statutes		
Individual State Court Rules	XX–RULES (where XX is a state's two-letter postal abbreviation)	Varies by state
State Court Rules	RULES–ALL	Varies by state

Database	Identifier	Coverage
Individual State Court Orders	XX–ORDERS (where XX is a state's two-letter postal abbreviation)	Varies by state
State Court Orders	ORDERS–ALL	Varies by state
Individual State Statutes–Annotated	XX–ST–ANN (where XX is a state's two-letter postal abbreviation)	Varies by state
State Statutes–Annotated	ST–ANN–ALL	Varies by state
State Case Law		
State Case Law	ALLSTATES	Begins with 1945
State Case Law Before 1945	ALLSTATES–OLD	1821–1944
Individual State Case Law	XX–CS (where XX is a state's two-letter postal abbreviation)	Varies by state
Texts, Periodicals and Research Tools		
Texts & Periodicals–All Law Reviews, Texts & Bar Journals	TP–ALL	Varies by publication
Bankruptcy Evidence Manual	BKRMANUAL	1997 edition
California Evidence	WITEVID	Third edition
Daubert Citator	DAUBERT	Begins with January 1994
Federal Rules Decisions (Articles from West Reporter)	FEDRDTP	Begins with 1986 (vol. 186)
Handbook of Federal Evidence	FEDEVID	Fourth edition and 1998 pocket parts
Reference Manual on Scientific Evidence	RMSCIEVID	Published in 1994
The Rutter Group™–California Practice Guide: Civil Trials and Evidence	TRG–CACIVEV	1997 edition
The Rutter Group–Practice Guide: Texas Civil Evidence	TRG–TXEV	1996 edition
News and Current Events		
All News	ALLNEWS	Varies by source
American Journal of Trial Advocacy	AMJTA	Selected coverage begins with 1982 (vol 6); full coverage begins with 1993 (vol 17)
Legal Newspapers	LEGALNP	Varies by publication
National Law Journal, The	NLJ	Begins with October 1989
United States Law Week	BNA–USLW	Begins with January 1986
Westlaw Topical Highlights–Litigation	WTH–LTG	Current data

Section 3.   Retrieving a Document with a Citation: Find and Jump

3.1   Find

Find is a Westlaw service that allows you to retrieve a document by entering its citation. Find allows you to retrieve documents from anywhere in Westlaw without accessing or changing databases. Find is available for many documents, including rules (state and federal), the *United States Code Annotated*, state statutes, case law (state and federal), administrative materials, and texts and periodicals.

To use Find, simply access the Find service and type the citation. The following list provides some examples:

To Find This Document	Access Find and Type
Fed. R. Evid. 612	fre 612
Colorado R. Evid. 612	co st rev 612
Frye v. United States, 293 F. 1013 (App.D.C. 1923)	293 f 1013
State v. Cary, 264 A.2d 209 (N.J. 1970)	264 a2d 209

For a complete list of publications that can be retrieved with Find and their abbreviations, consult the Find Publications List. Click the **Pubs List** button after accessing Find.

3.2 Jump

Use Jump markers (> or f) to move from one location to another on Westlaw. For example, use Jump markers to go directly from the rule, statute, case or law review article you are viewing to a cited rule, statute, case or article; from a headnote to the corresponding text in the opinion; or from an entry in a statutes index database to the full text of the statute.

Section 4. Natural Language Searching: WIN—Westlaw is Natural

Overview: With WIN, you can retrieve documents by simply describing your issue in plain English. If you are a relatively new Westlaw user, Natural Language searching can make it easier for you to retrieve cases that are on point. If you are an experienced Westlaw user, Natural Language gives you a valuable alternative search method.

When you enter a Natural Language description, Westlaw automatically identifies legal phrases, removes common words and generates variations of terms in your description. Westlaw then searches for the concepts in your description. Concepts may include significant terms, phrases, legal citations or topic and key numbers. Westlaw retrieves the 20 documents that most closely match your description, beginning with the document most likely to match.

4.1 Natural Language Searching

Access a database, such as Federal Case Law (ALLFEDS). If the Terms and Connectors Query Editor is displayed, click the **Search Type** button and choose **Natural Language**. At the Natural Language Description Editor, type a Natural Language description such as the following:

is testimony of a witness after hypnosis admissible

4.2 Next Command

Westlaw displays the 20 documents that most closely match your description, beginning with the document most likely to match. If you want to view additional documents, click your right mouse button and choose **Next 10 Documents** from the pop-up menu or choose **Next 10 Documents** from the Browse menu.

4.3 Browsing a Natural Language Search Result

Best Mode: To display the best portion (the portion that most closely matches your description) of each document in your search result, click your right mouse button and choose **Next Best** from the pop-up menu or click **Best** f.

Standard Browsing Commands: You can also browse your Natural Language search result using standard Westlaw browsing commands, such as citations list, Locate, page mode and term mode. When you browse your Natural Language search result in term mode, the five portions of each document that are most likely to match your description are displayed.

Section 5.   Terms and Connectors Searching

Overview: With Terms and Connectors searching, you enter a query, which consists of key terms from your issue and connectors specifying the relationship between these terms.

Terms and Connectors searching is useful when you want to retrieve a document for which you know specific details, such as the title or the fact situation. Terms and Connectors searching is also useful when you want to retrieve documents relating to a specific issue. If the Natural Language Description Editor is displayed when you access a database, click the **Search Type** button and choose **Term Search**.

5.1 Terms

Plurals and Possessives: Plurals are automatically retrieved when you enter the singular form of a term. This is true for both regular and irregular plurals (e.g., **child** retrieves *children*). If you enter the plural form of a term, you will not retrieve the singular form.

If you enter the nonpossessive form of a term, Westlaw automatically retrieves the possessive form as well. However, if you enter the possessive form, only the possessive form is retrieved.

Automatic Equivalencies: Some terms have alternative forms or equivalencies; for example, *5* and *five* are equivalent terms. Westlaw automatically retrieves equivalent terms. The *Westlaw Reference Manual* contains a list of equivalent terms.

Compound Words, Abbreviations and Acronyms: When a compound word is one of your search terms, use a hyphen to retrieve all forms of the word. For example, the term **along-side** retrieves *along-side, alongside* and *along side*.

When using an abbreviation or acronym as a search term, place a period after each of the letters to retrieve any of its forms. For example, the term **f.r.e.** retrieves *fre, f.r.e., f r e* and *f. r. e.* Note: The abbreviation does *not* retrieve *federal rule of evidence*, so remember to add additional alternative terms to your query such as **"federal rule of evidence"**.

Root Expander and Universal Character: When you use the Terms and Connectors search method, placing a root expander (!) at the end of a root term generates all other terms with that root. For example, adding the ! symbol to the root *admiss!* in the query

admiss! /5 evidence

instructs Westlaw to retrieve such terms as *admission, admissive, admissible* and *admissibility.*

The universal character (*) stands for one character and can be inserted in the middle or at the end of a term. For example, the term

withdr*w

will retrieve *withdraw* and *withdrew.* Adding three asterisks to the root *elect*

elect* * *

instructs Westlaw to retrieve all forms of the root with up to three additional characters. Terms like *elected* or *election* are retrieved by this query. However, terms with more than three letters following the root, such as *electronic,* are not retrieved. Plurals are always retrieved, even if more than three letters follow the root.

Phrase Searching: To search for a phrase, place it within quotation marks. For example, to search for references to *judicial notice,* type **"judicial notice".** When you are using the Terms and Connectors search method, you should use phrase searching only if you are certain that the phrase will not appear in any other form.

5.2 Alternative Terms

After selecting the terms for your query, consider which alternative terms are necessary. For example, if you are searching for the term *admissible,* you might also want to search for the term *inadmissible.* You should consider both synonyms and antonyms as alternative terms. You can also use the Westlaw thesaurus to add alternative terms to your query.

5.3 Connectors

After selecting terms and alternative terms for your query, use connectors to specify the relationship that should exist between search terms in your retrieved documents. The connectors you can use are described below:

Use:	To retrieve documents with:	Example:
& (and)	both terms	expert & opinion
or (space)	either term or both terms	relevan! irrelevan!
/p	search terms in the same paragraph	hearsay /p exception
/s	search terms in the same sentence	character /s witness
+s	the first search term preceding the second within the same sentence	burden +s prov! proof
/n	search terms within "n" terms of each other (where "n" is a number)	refresh! /3 memory
+n	the first search term preceding the second by "n" terms (where "n" is a number)	excited +3 utterance
" "	search terms appearing in the same order as in the quotation marks	"past recollection recorded"

Use:	To exclude documents with:	Example:
% (but not)	search terms following the % symbol	d.n.a. "deoxyribonucleic acid" % criminal

5.4 Restricting Your Search by Field

Overview: Documents in each Westlaw database consist of several segments, or fields. One field may contain the citation, another the title, another the synopsis and so forth. Not all databases contain the same fields. Also, depending on the database, fields with the same name may contain different types of information.

To view a list of fields for a specific database and their contents, see Scope for that database. Note that in some databases not every field is available for every document.

To retrieve only those documents containing your search terms in a specific field, restrict your search to that field. To restrict your search to a specific field, type the field name or abbreviation followed by your search terms enclosed in parentheses. For example, to retrieve a case in the Federal & State Case Law database (ALLCASES) entitled *Daubert v. Merrell Dow Pharmaceuticals,* search for your terms in the title field (ti):

ti(daubert & "merrell dow")

The fields discussed below are available in Westlaw databases you might use for researching evidence issues.

Digest and Synopsis Fields: The digest (di) and synopsis (sy) fields, added to case law databases by West's attorney-editors, summarize the main points of a case. The synopsis field contains a brief description of a case. The digest field contains the topic and headnote fields and includes the complete hierarchy of concepts used by West's editors to classify the headnotes to specific West digest topics and key numbers. Restricting your search to the synopsis and digest fields limits your result to cases in which your terms are related to a major issue in the case.

Consider restricting your search to one or both of these fields if

- you are searching for common terms or terms with more than one meaning, and you need to narrow your search; or

- you cannot narrow your search by using a smaller database.

For example, to retrieve cases that discuss nonverbal conduct as hearsay, access the State Case Law database (ALLSTATES) and type

sy,di(non-verbal /s conduct /p hearsay)

Headnote Field: The headnote field (he) is a part of the digest field, but does not contain topic numbers, hierarchical classification information or key numbers. The headnote field contains only a one-sentence summary for each point of law in a case and any supporting citations given by the author of the opinion. A headnote field restriction is useful when you are searching for specific statutory sections or rule numbers. For example, to retrieve headnotes from federal cases that cite Fed. R.

Evid. 803(1), access the Federal Case Law database (ALLFEDS) and type the following query:

he(803(1))

Topic Field: The topic field (to) is also a part of the digest field. It contains hierarchical classification information, including the West digest topic names and numbers and the key numbers. You should restrict search terms to the topic field in a case law database if

- a digest field search retrieves too many documents; or
- you want to retrieve cases with digest paragraphs classified under more than one topic.

For example, the topic Evidence has the topic number 157. To retrieve United States district court cases that discuss the admissibility of hearsay evidence based on the excited utterance exception, access the U.S. District Courts Cases database (DCT) and type a query like the following:

to(157) /p "excited utterance"

To retrieve cases classified under more than one topic and key number, search for your terms in the topic field. For example, to search for cases discussing evidence in criminal proceedings, which may be classified to Criminal Law (110), Double Jeopardy (1354), Evidence (157), Grand Jury (193) or Witnesses (410), among other topics, type a query like the following:

to(eviden! & crim!)

For a complete list of West digest topics and their corresponding topic numbers, access the Key Number service; click the **Key Number Service** button or choose **Key Number Service** from the Services menu.

Prelim and Caption Fields: When searching in a database containing rules, statutes or regulations, restrict your search to the prelim (pr) and caption (ca) fields to retrieve documents in which your terms are important enough to appear in a section name or heading. For example, to retrieve federal rules regarding hearsay, access the Federal Rules database (US–RULES) and type the following:

pr,ca(hearsay)

5.5   Restricting Your Search by Date

You can use Westlaw to retrieve documents *decided* or *issued* before, after, or on a specified date, as well as within a range of dates. The following sample queries contain date restrictions:

da(1998) & "dying declaration"

da(aft 1996) & sy,di("prior inconsistent statement")
da(5/14/1998) & "present sense" /5 impression

You can also search for documents *added to a database* on or after a specified date, as well as within a range of dates. The following sample queries contain added-date restrictions:

ad(aft 1995) & declaration /s against /5 interest

ad(aft 2–1–1998 & bef 2–17–1998) & custodian /s record

Section 6. Topic and Key Number Searching

To retrieve cases that address a specific point of law, use topic and key numbers as your search terms. If you have an on-point case and want to find additional cases, run a search using the topic and key number from the relevant headnote in an appropriate database to find other cases containing headnotes classified to that topic and key number. For example, to search for federal cases containing headnotes classified under topic 157 (Evidence) and key number 551 (Hypothetical Questions and Answers), access the Federal Case Law database (ALLFEDS) and enter the following query:

157k551

For a complete list of West digest topic and key numbers, access the Key Number service: click the **Key Number Service** button or choose **Key Number Service** from the Services menu.

Section 7. Verifying Your Research with Citators

Overview: A citator service is a tool that helps you ensure that your cases are good law; retrieve cases, legislation or articles that cite a case, rule or statute; and verify that the spelling and format of your citations are correct.

For citations not covered by the citator services, including persuasive secondary authority such as restatements and treatises, use a technique called Westlaw as a citator to retrieve cases that cite your authority (see Section 7.3).

7.1 KeyCite

KeyCite is the citation research service from West Group that integrates all the case law on Westlaw. KeyCite helps you trace the history of a case, retrieve a list of all cases and selected secondary sources that cite a case, and track legal issues decided in a case.

KeyCite provides both direct and negative indirect history for any case within the scope of its coverage. The History of the Case window displays a case's direct appellate history and its negative indirect history, which consists of cases outside the direct appellate line that may have a negative impact on its precedential value. The display also includes related references, which are opinions involving the same parties and facts but resolving different issues.

In addition to case history, the Citations to the Case window in KeyCite lists all cases on Westlaw and secondary sources, such as law review articles and ALR® annotations, that cite the decision. These citing references are added to KeyCite as soon as they are added to Westlaw.

All citing cases on Westlaw are included in KeyCite—even unpublished opinions.

For citation verification, the KeyCite display provides the case title; parallel citations, including many looseleaf citations; court of decision; docket number; and filing date.

7.2 Shepard's Citations

For case law, Shepard's provides a comprehensive list of cases and other documents that have cited a particular case. Shepard's also includes explanatory analyses to indicate how the citing cases have treated the case, e.g., "followed" or "explained."

For rules and statutes, Shepard's Citations provides a comprehensive list of cases citing a particular rule or statute, as well as information on subsequent legislative action.

7.3 Using Westlaw As a Citator

Using Westlaw as a citator, you can search for documents citing a specific rule, statute, regulation, agency decision or other authority. For example, to retrieve federal cases citing Fed. R. Evid. 801, access the Federal Case Law database (ALLFEDS) and type a query like the following:

f.r.e. fed.r.e! evid.r! f.r.ev! fed.ev! evid! /5 801

Section 8. Research Examples

8.1 Retrieving Law Review Articles

Recent law review articles are often a good place to begin researching a legal issue because law review articles serve 1) as an excellent introduction to a new topic or review for a stale one, providing terminology to help you formulate a query; 2) as a finding tool for pertinent primary authority, such as rules, statutes and cases; and 3) in some instances, as persuasive secondary authority. For example, suppose you need to gain more background information on the factors that courts have considered in determining whether it is appropriate for lay witnesses to give opinion testimony.

Solution

- To retrieve recent law review articles relevant to your issue, access the Texts & Periodicals–All Law Reviews, Texts & Bar Journals database (TP–ALL). Using the Natural Language search method, enter a description like the following:

opinion testimony by lay witnesses

- If you have a citation to an article in a specific publication, use Find to retrieve it. For more information on Find, see Section 3.1 of this appendix. For example, to retrieve the article found at 12 Touro Law Review 513, access Find and type

12 touro l rev 513

- If you know the title of an article but not which journal it appeared in, access the Texts & Periodicals–All Law Reviews, Texts & Bar Journals database (TP–ALL) and search for key terms from the title in the title field. For example, to retrieve the article "The Movement from Frye to Daubert: Where Do the States Stand?" type the following Terms and Connectors query:

ti(movement & frye & daubert & states)

8.2   Retrieving Rules

Suppose you need to retrieve federal rules dealing with relevancy of character evidence.

Solution

- Access the Federal Rules database (US–RULES). Search for your terms in the prelim and caption fields using the Terms and Connectors search method:

pr,ca(relevan! & character)

- When you know the citation for a specific rule, use Find to retrieve the rule. For example, to retrieve Fed. R. Evid. 410, access Find and type

fre 410

- To look at surrounding rules, use the Table of Contents service. Select a Jump marker in the prelim or caption field. You can also use Documents in Sequence to retrieve the rules following Fed. R. Evid. 410. Click the **Docs in Seq** button.

- When you retrieve a rule on Westlaw, it will contain an Update message if a court order amending or repealing it is available online. To display such an order, select the Jump marker in the Update message.

8.3   Retrieving Case Law

Suppose you need to retrieve New York case law dealing with the priest-penitent privilege.

Solution

- Access the New York Cases database (NY–CS). Type a Natural Language description such as the following:

waiver of the priest-penitent privilege

- When you know the citation for a specific case, use Find to retrieve it. (For more information on Find, see § 3.1 of this appendix.) For example, to retrieve *Darrow v. Gunn*, 594 F.2d 767 (9th Cir. 1979), access Find and type

594 f2d 767

- If you find a topic and key number that is on point, run a search using that topic and key number to retrieve additional cases discussing that point of law. For example, to retrieve cases containing headnotes classified under topic 410 (Witnesses) and key number 215 (Confessions or other communications to clergyman or minister of religion), type the following query:

410k215

- To retrieve cases written by a particular judge, add a judge field (ju) restriction to your query. For example, to retrieve cases written by Judge White that contain headnotes classified under topic 157 (Evidence), type the following query:

ju(white) & to(157)

8.4 Using the Citator Services

Suppose one of the cases you retrieve in your case law research is *Frye v. United States*, 293 F. 1013 (App.D.C. 1923). You want to determine whether this case is good law and to find other cases that have cited this case.

Solution

Use KeyCite to retrieve direct history and negative indirect history for *Frye v. United States*. While viewing the case, click the **KeyCite** button.

To Shepardize® *Frye v. United States*, click the **Shepard's** button.

8.5 Following Recent Developments

As the evidence law specialist in your firm, you are expected to keep up with and summarize recent legal developments in this area of the law. How can you do this efficiently?

Solution

One of the easiest ways to stay abreast of recent developments in the area of evidence and litigation is by accessing the Westlaw Topical Highlights–Litigation database (WTH–LTG). The WTH–LTG database contains summaries of recent legal developments, including court decisions, legislation and changes in the area of litigation. Some summaries also contain suggested queries that combine the proven power of West's topic and key numbers and West's case headnotes to retrieve additional pertinent cases.

- When you access WTH–LTG you will automatically retrieve a list of documents added to the database in the last two weeks.

- To read a summary of a document, double-click its entry in the list.

- To view the full text of a document, access Find while viewing its summary.

- To search this database, choose **New Search** from the Search menu. At the Terms and Connectors Query Editor, type your query. For example, to retrieve references discussing a patient's treating physician testifying as an expert, type a query like the following:

    treat! /5 doctor physician /p expert

*

Table of Cases

*

Table of Statutes and Rules

UNITED STATES

UNITED STATES CONSTITUTION

	This Work	
Amend.	Sec.	Note
1	8.20	
4	12.05	
5	8.18	
5	8.18	227
5	8.18	229
5	12.05	
6	7.15	162
6	7.51	435
6	7.66	583
6	9.11	155
6	12.05	
8	9.10	143
8	12.05	
14	8.18	
14	12.05	

UNITED STATES CODE ANNOTATED

13 U.S.C.A.—Census

	This Work	
Sec.	Sec.	Note
8(b)	8.19	245
9(a)	8.19	245

28 U.S.C.A.—Judiciary and Judicial Procedure

	This Work	
Sec.	Sec.	Note
2671	5.55	361

42 U.S.C.A.—The Public Health and Welfare

	This Work	
Sec.	Sec.	Note
290ee–3	8.14	160
1983	7.27	225
1983	10.09	117

STATUTES AT LARGE

	This Work	
Year	Sec.	Note
1994, Sept. 13, P.L. 103–322, § 1, 108 Stat. 1796	5.09	78

STATUTES AT LARGE

	This Work	
Year	Sec.	Note
1994, Sept. 13, P.L. 103–322, § 1, 108 Stat. 1796	5.24	194

POPULAR NAME ACTS

CIVIL RIGHTS ACT OF 1964

	This Work	
Sec.	Sec.	Note
Tit. VII	4.08	59
Tit. VII	5.10	92

STATE STATUTES

ALABAMA CODE

	This Work	
Sec.	Sec.	Note
12–21–45	5.55	360

ALASKA RULES OF EVIDENCE

	This Work	
Rule	Sec.	Note
404	5.32	234
503(a)(2)	8.09	89
505(a)(1)	8.16	172
609(a)	9.09	96
613(b)	9.05	43

ARIZONA REVISED STATUTES

	This Work	
Sec.	Sec.	Note
12–2232	8.17	201
13–4062(1)	8.16	171

WEST'S ANNOTATED CALIFORNIA CIVIL CODE

	This Work	
Sec.	Sec.	Note
3294	4.04	16

WEST'S ANNOTATED CALIFORNIA EVIDENCE CODE

	This Work	
Sec.	Sec.	Note
110	4.06	27

KANSAS STATUTES ANNOTATED

Sec.	This Work Sec.	Note
60–437	8.17	195

MAINE RULES OF EVIDENCE

Rule	This Work Sec.	Note
403	5.56	370
403	5.56	371

MARYLAND ANNOTATED CODE

Art.	This Work Sec.	Note
27, § 461A	5.09	80

MARYLAND CODE, COURTS AND JUDICIAL PROCEEDINGS

Sec.	This Work Sec.	Note
9–109	8.13	134

MASSACHUSETTS GENERAL LAWS ANNOTATED

Ch.	This Work Sec.	Note
233, § 21B	5.09	79
233, § 65	7.56	495

MICHIGAN COMPILED LAWS ANNOTATED

Sec.	This Work Sec.	Note
600.2157	8.13	133
600.2162	8.17	184
750.411	8.13	145
750.520j	5.09	79

MICHIGAN RULES OF EVIDENCE

Rule	This Work Sec.	Note
601	6.02	14
601	6.02	15

MINNESOTA STATUTES ANNOTATED

Sec.	This Work Sec.	Note
595.02	8.13	135
595.02	8.17	202
595.02	8.17	203
595.02(a)	8.16	176
595.02(a)	8.17	184
595.02(a)	8.17	201
595.02(1)(a)	8.15	169
595.02(1)(a)	8.16	171

MINNESOTA STATUTES ANNOTATED

Sec.	This Work Sec.	Note
595.02(1)(a)	8.16	172
595.02(1)(c)	8.20	251
595.02(1)(f)	6.02	15
595.02(1)(i)	8.20	260
595.02(1)(i)	8.20	261
595.02(1)(l)	6.03	20
595.02(3)	7.56	500
595.021—595.024	8.20	255
595.024(2)	8.20	256

MINNESOTA RULES OF CIVIL PROCEDURE

Rule	This Work Sec.	Note
35.03	8.13	148

MINNESOTA RULES OF CRIMINAL PROCEDURE

Rule	This Work Sec.	Note
7.05	5.32	233
31.02	12.04	66

MINNESOTA RULES OF EVIDENCE

Rule	This Work Sec.	Note
403	5.04	34
403	11.08	62
404(c)	5.09	79
404(c)	5.09	81
613(b)	9.05	43
616	9.08	87
616	9.10	139
801(d)(1)(B)	7.05	45
801(d)(1)(B)	9.12	171

REVISED STATUTES OF MISSOURI

Sec.	This Work Sec.	Note
566.025	5.10	95

MONTANA CODE ANNOTATED

Sec.	This Work Sec.	Note
26–1–802	8.16	171
26–1–802	8.16	172

NEBRASKA REVISED STATUTES

Sec.	This Work Sec.	Note
27–505	8.17	193

Index

References are to sections

References are to sections

†